THE RELIGIOUS

FRINGE

A HISTORY OF ALTERNATIVE RELIGIONS IN AMERICA

RICHARD KYLE

INTERVARSITY PRESS
DOWNERS GROVE, ILLINOIS 60515

InterVarsity Press® is the book-publishing division of InterVarsity Christian Fellowship®, a student
movement active on campus at hundreds of universities, colleges and schools of nursing in the United
States of America, and a member movement of the International Fellowship of Evangelical Students. For
information about local and regional activities, write Public Relations Dept., InterVarsity Christian
Fellowship, 6400 Schroeder Rd., P.O. Box 7895, Madison, WI 53707-7895.

All Scripture quotations, unless otherwise indicated, are from the HOLY BIBLE, NEW
INTERNATIONAL VERSION®. NIV®. Copyright© 1973, 1978, 1984 by International Bible Society.
Used by permission of Zondervan Publishing House. All rights reserved.

Cover illustration: Roberta Polfus

ISBN 0-8308-1766-2

Printed in the United States of America ∞

Library of Congress Cataloging-in-Publication Data

Kyle, Richard G.
  The religious fringe: a history of alternative religions in
  America/Richard Kyle.
      p.   cm.
  Includes bibliographical references and index.
  ISBN 0-8308-1766-2 (alk. paper)·
  1. United States—Religion—History.   2. Cults—United States—
History.   3. Sects—United States—History.   I. Title.
  BL2525.K85   1993
  200'.973—dc20   93-7443
                                                          CIP

17   16   15   14   13   12   11   10   9   8   7   6   5   4   3   2   1
06   05   04   03   02   01   00   99   98   97   96   95   94   93

To my sons, Bryan and Brent

Preface _____ 9

Part I Backgrounds in the West _____ 15
1 Introduction _____ 17
   Religion/Withdrawal and World-Affirming Movements/
   Cult/Related Terms/The Occult/Categories of Cults
2 Fringe Groups in the West _____ 31
   Hellenistic Age/The Middle Ages/Renaissance and Reformation
   Europe/The Early Modern World

Part II Religious Innovations in Early National America _____ 51
3 Early National America: Social and Religious Movements ____ 53
   Millennialism/Intellectual Currents/Revivalism/
   Religious Pluralism
4 Early Metaphysical and Occult Movements _____ 62
   Transcendentalism/Spiritualism
5 Religious Communalism _____ 72
   The Shakers/Oneida Perfectionists/Universal Friend
6 Mormonism and the Christadelphians _____ 82
   Mormonism/Strangites/Reorganized Church of Latter-day
   Saints/Christadelphians

Part III Cracks in the Protestant Empire: The Civil War to World War II _____ 93
7 American Culture in the Late Nineteenth Century _____ 95
   The Religious Setting/Social and Economic Conditions/
   The Intellectual Climate
8 Nineteenth-Century Occult and Metaphysical Movements ____ 107
   Theosophy/Theosophical-Related Bodies/New Thought/
   New Thought Groups/Christian Science
9 Early Eastern Groups _____ 127
   Eastern Contacts/Hinduism as a World Religion/Hindu Groups
   in America/Buddhism as a World Religion/Buddhist Groups
   in America/Islam as a World Religion/Islamic Groups in America
10 Christian-Related Bodies _____ 148
   Adventism/The Holiness Movement/Pentecostalism/
   Fundamentalism/Jehovah's Witnesses/The Worldwide Church of God/
   The Jesus Only or Oneness Movement
11 Black Religious Groups _____ 167
   Black Sects and Cults/The Universal Peace Mission
   of Father Divine/United House of Prayer for All People

Part IV Eastern Groups in Post-Christian America ———— *179*
12 Religious Innovations in Post-Christian America ———— *181*
   Society in Change/Major Developments in the Religious
   Setting/The Watershed of the 1960s
13 The Turn East: Why Now? ———— *197*
   Social and Religious Factors/Personal Factors
14 Hindu, Sikh and Jain-Related Bodies ———— *203*
   Transcendental Meditation/Hare Krishna/The Divine Light
   Mission/The Rajneesh Foundation International
15 Buddhist Groups ———— *227*
   Zen Buddhism/Nichiren Shoshu (Soka Gakkai) of America
16 Islam-Related Groups ———— *238*
   Black Muslims (The American Muslim Mission)/Meher Baba/
   Gurdjieff-Ouspensky Groups (G-O)

Part V The Occult, Psychic Groups and the New Age Movement
   in Post-Christian America ———— *255*
17 Twentieth-Century Occult and Metaphysical Movements ———— *257*
   The Occult Explosion/Astrology/Divination/Witchcraft/
   Satanism/Psychic and Spiritualistic Phenomena/UFO Cults
18 The New Age Movement ———— *285*
   Description and Definition/Historical Development/Vision and Beliefs
19 Psychospiritual or Self-Improvement Groups ———— *299*
   Consciousness Revolution/The Church of Scientology/
   Est (the Forum)/Silva Mind Control/Synanon

Part VI Christian Bodies in Post-Christian America ———— *323*
20 The Christian Background ———— *325*
   Dualistic Groups/Evangelical Origins/Current Status
21 The Unification Church ———— *331*
   A Brief History/Beliefs/Recruiting/Response to American Culture/
   Future Direction
22 The People's Temple ———— *344*
   Characteristics/A Brief History/Ideology
23 Aberrational Groups in the Jesus Movement ———— *355*
   The Jesus People/The Children of God (Family of Love)/
   The Way International
24 Epilogue ———— *374*
Notes ———— *379*
Selected Bibliography ———— *453*
Index ———— *461*

Preface

The outburst of new religions in post-World War II America has prompted an avalanche of publications on the occult, cults and related movements. These books and articles range over a wide spectrum. Some appeal to a popular audience, while others are quite scholarly. The scholarly publications touch on a large number of religious groups and approach the subject from the perspective of several academic disciplines, especially sociology, theology and religious studies.

These many publications notwithstanding, several gaps still exist in respect to the coverage of new religions. The study of the occult and cults has been largely the domain of the social sciences and theology. While many authors have given the historical background to a particular alternative religion, the history of the occult and cults in America has been a neglected subject. The most ambitious projects to date by an historian have been the various works of Gordon Melton, and these have been largely in an encyclopedia format.

With the present volume I hope to partially alleviate such neglect. I make no claims to comprehensiveness. Fringe religions in America are too numerous for any one-volume work to cover. So I have selected a few of the better-known groups in several chronological periods and have attempted to relate them to their historical context. While ten chapters address alternative religions before World War II, the emphasis is on contemporary America; I have devoted twelve chapters to this period.

A historical approach to alternative religions must wrestle with several problems. A work on the occult and cults often involves a study of phenomena—that is, exceptional and unusual persons, things or occurrences. History measures and evaluates events in the human or natural dimension, not the supernatural. Thus, any historical study of such phenomena must answer the questions of cause and effect in human or natural terms. Even the Christian historian does not have license to attribute cause and effect to supernatural forces, whether divine or demonic. While the Christian historian may allow for the possibility of such supernatural forces, he or she must focus on what can be measured in the human or natural dimension. For the most part, then, this study will consider the occult and cults as products of their historical and cultural contexts.

Another problem has to do with value judgments. While no historian is free of personal biases, all of us must resist the temptation to preach or to polemicize a work of history. This problem arises in any serious endeavor to write history. But the difficulty is compounded in any attempt to write a history of the occult and cults. In recent years these subjects have evoked much emotion and controversy. Some evangelicals have vigorously attacked the cults, and some cults have countered with lawsuits.

While I am an evangelical Christian, I have attempted to write a descriptive history. Certainly, my evangelical background has prompted me to regard religious beliefs as an important factor in evaluating the cults. Yet this book is neither a devotional nor an attack on alternative religions. Some readers might be disappointed in not finding a chapter on how to combat the occult and cults. But such a task is not the job of the historian. By its very nature, the discipline of history leads to a critical analysis. Nevertheless, such an examination should not turn into a polemic. *po-le-mic*

Still, I hope that a better understanding of where alternative religions have come from, what they believe and practice and the conditions that enable them to flourish will be of value to the larger Christian community. And in the epilogue I have shed my historian's garb and have attempted to tell the reader something about the future direction of fringe religions.

Another problem is terminology, especially the word *cult*. As will be noted in chapter one, a cult is very difficult to define. In fact, the word *cult* is not a satisfactory term to the historian; the designations *fringe religions, alternative religions* and *new religions* are more useful. Nevertheless, the word *cult* is widely used, and I have attempted to define it, adopting ideas from both the social sciences and theology.

I hope this study demonstrates that the occult and cultic movements found in modern America have their roots in the past and are a product of the culture that has spawned them. While certain occult and cultic groups appear to be new, they usually have precursors that bear close resemblance. There may not always be a direct connection between past and current movements. But resemblances and parallels exist between the occult and cults of the past and present. In fact, some alternative religions in contemporary America are simply old movements in new clothes. Also, in one way or another, alternative religions reflect their culture—at times by exaggerating current trends, at times by rejecting society and taking an opposite path. Either way, fringe religions provide insights into the culture in which they reside.

This story of the occult and cultic movements in America follows a pattern. There are six sections and twenty-four chapters in this volume. Part one, "Backgrounds in the West," begins with an introduction that defines some terms; the following chapter briefly describes fringe religions from the Hellenistic era to early national America. Part two, "Religious Innovations in Early National America," describes American society at that time and then focuses on such movements as Transcendentalism, Spiritualism, the Shakers, Oneida Perfectionists, the Universal Friend, Mormonism and the Christadelphians. Part three looks at religious innovations from the Civil War to World War II. With an eye to late-nineteenth-century American culture, the following alternative religions are covered: Theosophy, New Thought, Christian Science, several Eastern religious groups, the Jehovah's Witnesses, the Worldwide Church of God, the Jesus Only movement and several African-American cults.

The rest of the volume focuses on fringe religions in post-World War II America. Part four tells the story of Eastern cults in America. I take a look at the social conditions that foster fringe religions, and then several Eastern groups are surveyed: Transcendental Meditation, Hare Krishna, the Divine Light Mission, the Rajneesh Foundation, Zen Buddhism, Nichiren Shoshu, the Black Muslims, Meher Baba and Gurdjieff. Part five looks at the occult, psychospiritual groups and the New Age movement. The specific occult practices include astrology, divination, witchcraft, Satanism, psychic and spiritualistic phenomena and UFO cults. The vision and development of the New Age movement are described. Then certain psychospiritual groups are noted—Scientology, est, Silva Mind Control and Synanon. Section six focuses on groups that are loosely connected with the Christian tradition. Included are the Unification Church, the People's Temple, the Children of God and The Way.

In the formal sense, this book began as a research project during my 1987 sabbatical from Tabor College. Informally, however, this book began several years earlier. I developed an interest in this subject during the occult explosion of the early 1970s, and subsequently taught several courses on the occult and cults at Tabor College. One of my earlier books, *From Sect to Denomination,* pushed me in a related direction. While that book did not deal with the occult or cults, it employed the disciplines of history, sociology and theology.

No one writes a book alone. In the time that this book has been in gestation, I have accumulated debts to several individuals and institutions. I hope that my memory is not short in this regard and that I do not inadvertently omit any thanks that are due. Appreciation must go to the library staffs of Princeton Theological Seminary and Tabor College. Particular thanks must go to Bruce Entz and his staff at Tabor for arranging for the acquisition of many books and articles through interlibrary loan. Without these sources, my work would not have been possible. Thanks must also go to Gordon Lewis of Denver Seminary for reading an earlier version of this manuscript. Although he would not agree with all of my interpretations of the occult and cults, his comments on my manuscript have been appreciated, and many of them have been incorporated in the final version. Some material in this book has been previously published in a different form in articles. While these articles are my own work, thanks must go to the editors and publishers of *Encyclopedia USA* and *The Christian Leader* for permission to use the material in modified forms here.

Many debts also have been incurred in the production of this book. I especially thank Marcella Mohn for typing the various drafts. Without her efforts, this book would have been difficult to produce. Appreciation must be offered to Tabor College for my 1987 sabbatical, the time when this book was begun. Academic publishing entails many problems. Therefore, much appreciation must go to the staff of InterVarsity Press for publishing this book—especially to its academic editor, James Hoover.

My gratitude goes also to some who were involved only indirectly with the writing and publishing process. In particular, I am grateful to my wife, Joyce, and two sons, Bryan and Brent, for sharing me with this project. Without their support and patience, this book would not have been possible.

PART I

Backgrounds
in the West

O ccult and cultic groups have a long history in Western culture. After defining some basic but controversial terms, this section briefly sketches the occult and cultic tradition in Western society prior to the nineteenth century. Like the late twentieth century in America, the Hellenistic world was marked by cultural and religious pluralism, with a proliferation of many occult and cultic groups and philosophies. The Middle Ages, of course, had much less religious diversity. Nevertheless, fringe groups existed and were associated with Christian heresies, witchcraft, Cabala, astrology and alchemy. Being a time of change and turmoil, the Renaissance-Reformation era saw a surge of fringe religions, some linked to the Christian tradition, others related to an explosion of the occult. While early modern Europe and colonial America witnessed something of a lull in respect to the growth of new religions, as the modern worldview developed there was a corresponding transition in the occult and cultic traditions.

1

Introduction

T he hallmark of American religion is diversity. As a consequence, swarms of fringe religions have abounded throughout American history. The term *alternative religions* could include just about anything but Catholicism, mainstream Protestantism, Eastern Orthodoxy and evangelical Protestantism. In fact, in earlier times Catholics could have been regarded as a marginal group. Individuals and groups have been on the fringes of American religion because of their gender, race, ethnicity, beliefs and practices. The range of selection is quite wide. I have therefore arbitrarily narrowed the scope of this study to the occult and cults in America, and to some difficult-to-classify alternative religions that incorporate occult and cultic elements.

The line between sectarian and cultic groups is rather murky. Sectarian movements are outside the religious mainstream and could thus be included in this study. Nevertheless, certain criteria which I will use to define a cult set such sect groups outside the purview of this study. The occult and cults were included because they overlap considerably, often holding to similar worldviews. Moreover, the occult and cults are more deviant, more shadowy, more transient than are sect groups, and consequently less prone to be assimilated into the religious mainstream.

Occult and cult groups are numerous, and only selected movements can be examined here. The scope of this book is limited by yet another factor—methodology. The study of the occult and cults has been largely the domain of sociological and religious studies. Few historians have ventured down this path. Though information derived from sociology, psychology, theology, philosophy and anthropology will be used extensively in my study, my approach is historical. The focus of this book is the *history* of occult and cultic movements in the United States after World War II. Yet considerable attention will be given to the development of such fringe religions in earlier periods of Western and American history.

Behind the details of various occult and cultic movements, two themes should arise within this study. First, the so-called new religions of the modern world are not so new. The cults and occult have a long history. While specific new religious groups rise and fall throughout history, there exists considerable continuity in the types and patterns of fringe religions. Second, occult and cultic movements address certain trends in the larger culture. Sometimes they exaggerate these trends. On other occasions, they resist them, creating something of a subculture. But at all times they provide a window by which to look at society.

Historical reality is seldom a neat and tidy affair. Thus historians hesitate to utilize restrictive definitions and typologies. Generalizations are always dangerous, and typologies represent ideal models. Still, a judicious use of these tools can enhance a better understanding of fringe religions. The first word is *religion:* What is it? What is a quasi-religion? In particular, the terms *sect, cult* and *occult* require explanation: What are they? How do they differ, and in what ways are they "fringe religions"? Scholars differ radically in their answers to some of these questions. So I will move to establish some working definitions.

Religion
Religion is an elusive concept—one that is difficult, if not impossible, to define. Any definition entails problems. Various academic disciplines—psychology, sociology, philosophy and theology—have drawn up definitions to serve their ends, but these definitions are seldom useful for general purposes. Any definition of religion must be broad but not too broad. On one hand, it must easily encompass the vast array of faiths normally regarded as religions. On the other hand, it cannot be so vague as to be applicable to all phenomena, whether religious or nonreligious.[1] A third problem relates to the issue of the supernatural. Some approaches limit religion to systems that presuppose the existence of the supernatural. Conversely, other ap-

proaches avoid this issue by defining religion as broad enough to include scientific humanism, Marxism, and other nonsupernatural philosophies.[2]

According to Martin Marty, historians seem to utilize a middle-range approach to defining religion, one that is neither restrictive nor so inclusive as to leave nothing out. They are inclined to consider an entity or event as religious if it evinces a combination of three or four of several elements. Religion would have to address *issues of ultimate concern.* But ultimate concern may be represented in private, agnostic or philosophic viewpoints that fall short of most historical definitions of religion. To qualify as religious, this concern normally must be expressed in the context of other elements, linked to creeds, codes, ritual and community.[3] Creeds, which are descriptive of a belief system or explain the meaning of life, vary greatly, ranging from oral traditions to highly developed theologies and sacred myths. Codes establishing the rules that govern everyday life range from customs to great moral and ethical systems. Rituals give the understandings found in creeds and codes a concrete expression. Lastly, religion is usually expressed in communities. Creed, code and ritual bind people together, sometimes in structured organizations, sometimes in only an informal manner.[4] Of course, religion can be a private affair, as when Thomas Luckmann speaks of "invisible religion," but it is of particular interest when sustained in the context of community.[5]

Though most religions contain some concept of the supernatural, this issue presents a vexing problem. Secularization may be defined briefly as the erosion of belief in the supernatural.[6] In the face of such a process, it may be helpful to note Catherine Albanese's approach: namely, to speak of "ordinary" and "extraordinary" religion. Ordinary religion is more or less synonymous with culture. It functions as the religion of the community and stays within the boundaries established by a specific culture. Extraordinary religion helps people to transcend, or move beyond, their everyday culture and concerns. This type of religion involves an encounter with some form of "otherness," whether natural or supernatural. It is specific and particular, containing strongly identifiable religious forms, and is easily recognized as religion.[7]

The forces of secularization and modernization, with their many meanings, have helped to blur the distinctions between religion and nonreligion. Americans certainly do not draw rigid lines between these two entities, for we tend to live simultaneously in the overlapping spheres of the religious and secular orders. Many contemporary movements also fall between the cracks. While they do not meet all the criteria used to describe religion, particularly supernatural postulations, they do have spiritual dimensions. Where does one place private religion, the occult, the "psychoreligious" movements or civil religion? I will designate them as *quasi-religions,* indicating that such movements in one way or another put their adherents in touch with ultimate meaning or some aspect of the sacred. Some quasi-religious groups borrow from religious traditions, but for others the main sources have been the modern social sciences, particularly psychology and sociology.[8]

Magic, though practiced by many religions, is not itself synonymous with religion. Magic is more elementary than religion, seeking technical and utilitarian ends without wasting its time on speculation. Magic deals with relatively specific compensators, while religion seeks more general rewards. A *compensator* may be defined as a promise of future reward based on hope and faith rather than on knowledge. Because magic deals in specific compensators, such as curing warts or bringing rain, it often becomes subject to empirical verification, making it vulnerable to disproof. Conversely, the general compensators, such as eternal life, offered by religion are not readily subject to disconfirmation.[9]

Withdrawal and World-Affirming Movements
In the tradition of the sociology of religion descended from Max Weber and Ernst Troeltsch through Milton Yinger, two major tendencies are evident in the relationship between Christianity (and religion by extension) and the world. The first inclination is to come to terms with secular society and culture and generally to compromise with the world. The second tendency, a minority opinion, rejects the spirit of compromise and opposes important aspects of secular culture and its institutions.[10] Both of these inclinations are found in the alternative religious movements, though the second one predominates.

Many people erroneously place all alternative and fringe religions in the withdrawal category, labeling them as either sects or cults. Actually, the new religious movements in America since the 1960s display a wide range of diversity, incorporating both accommodation and culture-rejecting tendencies. Though the majority of the new religions display tensions with their social environment, not all fit the model.

Roy Wallis places all new religions on a continuum marked by two poles: world-rejecting and world-affirming movements. The world-affirming religions, often associated with the New Age and human potential movements, view the social order "less contemptuously" than do the world-rejecting groups, "seeing it as possessing many highly desirable characteristics." Humanity contains within itself "enormous potential power" that has not been effectively utilized. These world-affirming movements claim to possess "the means to enable people to unlock their physical, mental and spiritual potential, without the need to withdraw from the world."[11] Given any definition of religion that rests on supernatural assumptions, many of these world-affirming movements must be classified as quasi-religions.

The withdrawal or culture-rejecting groups, usually called sects and cults, clearly state that the majority religion is inadequate, corrupt, hopelessly lukewarm or downright heretical, and that a true believer must "come out from among them" to the extent of making a clean break and aligning with a purer, more faithful assembly. The sect is an established religious type that has received considerable scholarly attention since Ernst Troeltsch's pioneering work on church-sect types. Consequently, among the academics there exists considerable consensus regarding the nature of the sect. The sect and the cult share many characteristics. Only in respect to the blurring of distinctions between these two religious groups has disagreement arisen, with some scholars regarding them as one type.[12]

The most prevalent and consistent of the withdrawal groups are sectarian bodies. According to Bryan Wilson, sects are decentralized religious organizations that maintain separation from the world. Consequently, hierarchy rarely exists, and where it does it is virtually never that of a professional clergy. Sectarian groups are voluntary societies with high entrance standards. Consequently, they tend to be exclusive. Scholars generally agree that sect groups arise as protest movements. The protest can be ideological, but it usually focuses on ethics. Sectarian groups tend to take a narrow and often unrealistic attitude toward purity, believing secular society and its institutional churches have compromised and confused right with wrong, the sacred with the profane. Hence, the sect is convinced that it must separate from the world and establish its own uncompromised group of believers. At its very core, the sect is schismatic. It breaks off from another group, believing that it is restoring the true faith.[13]

A sect is usually orthodox, maintaining and even preserving the beliefs of the parent religion. A sect, therefore, focuses on the past and does not regard itself as a new religious group. Some examples of groups that historically have been regarded as Christian sects are the Quakers, Mennonites, Plymouth Brethren and Pentecostals. Other world religions such as Hinduism, Buddhism, and Islam also have their sectarian spinoffs.

Cult

The cult can be regarded as a world-rejecting or a world-affirming religious body, depending on the specific group. Whereas a large measure of agreement exists regarding the sect, the cult remains a much more vague and unsatisfactory concept, despite being the object of considerable scholarly attention in recent years. In fact, because a religious cult virtually defies definition and because of its close affinity to a sect, more inclusive terms such as *new religion, alternative religion* and *fringe religion* might be more appropriate, though they are rather cumbersome and vague. Nevertheless, the term *cult* is widely used and deserves an attempt at definition and description.

Generally speaking, at least six problems can be detected in the various attempts to define *cult*. One, in common parlance the word is a pejorative term, evoking negative stereotypes. People do not call their own religious body a cult. Rather, this label is given to a group by an outsider.[14] Two, there exists considerable disagreement regarding what is acceptable religious belief and practice. Consequently, one religious group can regard another as cultic because of serious differences over faith and practice. For example, many evangelical Christians support the activities of Jews for Jesus and see this organization as a legitimate missionary group. But members of the Jewish community regard Jews for Jesus as an evil and deceptive cult. Quite often it boils down to one criterion: the dominant religious group regards serious deviation from its norms as cultic.

A third factor is the difficulty of applying the conceptual models of church, denomination, sect and cult to *any* religious group. In historical reality, few religious groups have ever manifested completely the characteristics of any one of these types. Thus these models best serve to point out general characteristics rather than to identify specific bodies. So instead of labeling a group as a cult, it is more appropriate to say that a particular religious body demonstrates cultic characteristics.

A fourth problem arises because scholars have focused on the particular perspective of their respective disciplines while minimizing the vantage points of other areas of academic studies. For instance, social scientists view cults primarily as social movements and tend to ignore what these groups believe, regarding such matters as inconsequential.[15] Conversely, theologians, especially those of an evangelical persuasion, focus on doctrinal matters, while largely ignoring the important social aspects of cultic groups.[16] Any proper definition, if one exists, must take into account the perspectives of *both* the social sciences and theology. Five, if one is to define a cult, generalizations regarding so-called cultic characteristics must be made. Alternative religions are so numerous and diverse, however, that they defy any easy general descriptions. Last, as indicated earlier, the cult and sect share many characteristics, making it difficult to distinguish between the two. Consequently, the term *alternative religion* or *nontraditional religion* are often applied to both groups.

What, then, is a religious cult? In attempting to answer this question, I will utilize the approaches of both sociology and theology. A cult is a social movement with many unusual social characteristics. But it is more than this. I regard religious beliefs as an important aspect of any definition of a cult. This study will consider a significant departure from orthodox beliefs, especially in the case of Christian groups, as a cultic characteristic. At the onset it must be stated that there is no "right" or "wrong" definition per se for the word *cult*. Rather, as Robert Ellwood notes, the "heuristic value" of a definition—that is, its value in describing a set of religious phenomena—must rank high.[17] Consequently, I will not utilize the word *cult* in a pejorative sense, but in an effort to describe a religious type that has evoked considerable interest, emotion, debate and controversy since 1960.

A cult, as defined by this study, manifests deviant or unusual social practices and beliefs. It is an alternative religion. As Gordon Melton and Robert Moore indicate, a cult is "a religious group that presents a distinctly alternative pattern for doing religion and adhering to a faith perspective than that dominant in the culture." A cult, in other words, is relative to the culture and religious context in which it resides.[18] For example, Hindu or Buddhist subgroups may be regarded as cultic in the United States, but not so in their native environment. Moreover, cults and even sect groups should not be confused with world religions. In one way or another, they are subgroups that have not attained a global status as bearers of a particular sacred tradition. The nature of these alternative religions, called cults, can best be understood, however, not by an abstract definition, but by focusing on some characteristics that many of these groups have in common.

Sociologically, cults have much in common with sect groups. Most cults also live in tension with their social environment, although sometimes not as overtly or as consistently as sects. Cults tend to regard the society and its dominant values as evil or at least incorrect.[19] Consequently, the cults take two approaches to this problem. Like sects, a cult may separate from society, striving to maintain distinct boundaries between itself and the "outside." Unlike sects, other cults attempt to transform the world, or perhaps even promise to help their followers acquire what the world values—health, wealth and happiness. But even these so-called world-affirming cults regard society's values or perceptions of reality as incorrect and in need of change. The cult, then, advocates an alternate view of reality and a different lifestyle, one that it says is the true path to the desired goal. Because some cults do promote a success orientation, they may draw most of their members from the middle and upper social classes. Sect groups, on the other hand, are often made up of people at the lower end of the socioeconomic scale.[20]

Organizationally and structurally, cult and sect groups display both similarities and differences. Both types of groups usually have strong leadership, but such a characteristic is more pronounced in the cults. In most cases, cults are begun by a charismatic leader, one who has inherent leadership qualities and who proclaims that he or she has new religious truth or a new way of understanding the traditional ideas.[21] Whereas sects are always schismatic, cults usually are not. According to Stark and Bainbridge, sect groups are breakoffs, having previous ties to another religious organization, even if that body happens to be another sect. Cults, with some exceptions, usually do not have prior ties with another religious body, but instead regard themselves as a new religious group with new perceptions of truth. "The cult may represent an alien (external) religion, or it may have originated in the host society—but through innovation, not fission."[22]

Herein lies not only a major structural difference between sects and cults but also a point that has major theological ramifications. Stark and Bainbridge tell us that sects "present themselves to the world as something old." Consequently, they are schismatic. They leave the parent body not to devise a new faith, but "to reestablish the old one, from which the parent group had drifted" (usually because of a compromise with society). "Sect groups claim to be the authentic, purged, rehabilitated version of the faith from

24

which they split."[23] Therefore, a sect usually does not offer a major doctrinal deviation from the faith perspective of the dominant culture in which it resides. Because there are often no insurmountable ideological barriers separating sects from the mainstream religion, they are prone to make lifestyle compromises and become denominations.

Whether imported or domestic, when compared with other religious bodies of a particular society, a cult is something new. If domestic—even if it is breaking from another group in the same culture—the cult adds to that culture a new insight or revelation to justify the claim that it is new, different and more advanced. In the United States, domestic cults usually depart from the major tenets of the Christian faith and thus maintain an unorthodox belief system. Therefore, a primary characteristic of cults is that they claim to have new truths or insights that are unique to them. Consequently, though a domestic cult may share some theological ideas with the mainstream religion, it is made distinctive by adding new truth or, at least, a new interpretation of old theological ideas.[24]

Imported cults share few characteristics with the religions currently existing in a society. These cults may be old in some other society, but they are new and different in the importing society, and thus represent a significant alternative to the beliefs of the dominant religion. Hare Krishna, for example, would not be regarded as cultic in its native environment, but in the United States it is an alternative religion, usually designated as a cult. Cults, whether domestic or imported, represent an independent religious tradition in a society.[25] As a consequence, cults seldom join the religious mainstream. Even when they become large and institutionalized, as have the Mormons, or make a conscious effort to be accepted by society, as has the Unification Church, serious differences in respect to belief prevent them from joining the mainstream.

The cult focuses on meeting personal needs and inducing powerful subjective experiences. Strong experiences brought about by chanting, meditation, initiations, magical rites and the presence of a charismatic leader are at the very core of cultic activity. Such experiences give the participant a sense of inner identity and significance of character. Reality now becomes something that is sustained by the cultic group.[26] Drug trips were replaced by spiritual states of rapture induced by forms of spiritual technology. Consciousness exploration and experimentation remain as central features of the new cultic groups. Indeed, as Ronald Enroth notes, "the thrust of the new religious groups—whether Eastern mystical, occult, or aberrational Christian—is experience over doctrine, feeling rather than rationality." Religious truth, for many people, is not attained by traditional modes of learning, but by mystical insight. In fact, many people join new religious groups in pursuit of "peak experiences" and "moments of bliss."[27] Theodore Roszak regards this emphasis on experience as the greatest discovery of the religious awakening of the 1960s and 1970s.[28]

Related Terms

The approach to the cults that I have outlined is not without its problems. Several difficulties arise, but three stand out. First, how does one categorize the classic cults—e.g., Christian Science, Mormons, Jehovah's Witnesses, Theosophy—that have existed for a lengthy period and have to some extent become institutionalized? If a group ensures its existence by becoming organized and shedding some of its cultic characteristics, but maintains a belief system at variance with the "mainstream" tradition, such a religious body might be called an *established cult*.[29]

Two, there is the matter of heresy. *Orthodox* means conforming to established doctrine. Any religion can have constituted beliefs and standards of orthodoxy. Christian orthodoxy means an acceptance of the major doctrines of the three main branches of the Christian faith (Catholic, Protestant and Orthodox). These doctrines usually concern such issues as the Trinity, the person of Christ, the authority of Scripture, salvation and the atonement. Heresy can be defined as a heterodox form of Christianity—that is, deviating from the Catholic, Protestant and Orthodox traditions on a major point of doctrine. Thus, Buddhists or Hindus cannot be called heretics. Some of their offshoots in America, such as Hare Krishna, might be described as cultic because they deviate from the "mainstream" religious tradition, but the term *heretical* is inappropriate.[30]

What about the Christian groups that deviate from a major doctrine of orthodox Christianity? Are they sectarian, cultic or heretical? They can legitimately be called heretical, and if they have many of the social characteristics of a cult, the label *cult* is appropriate. Groups that deviate at a major point of doctrine but lack cultic social characteristics might best be considered as heretical or even an entirely new religion. The Unitarians would be such an example.

A third problem relates to the use of the terms *new religion, aberrational*

Christian and *Christian fringe group*. The term *new religion* is used frequently, at times referring to a cultic body. I will use the term in a generic sense, defining a new religion as a religion that is new to a particular culture. New religions are often cults, but not always. They may be new but not necessarily unorthodox or so deviant as to merit the label *cult*.

This study will also use the terms *aberrational Christian* and *Christian fringe group* in a very broad sense. Many Christian groups are deviant, perhaps even bizarre, but not heretical at a major point of doctrine. Sociologically these bodies fit closely the cult category, but doctrinally they are essentially orthodox. They share some characteristics with sect groups, but while sectarian bodies are separationist, they usually are not extremely deviant. The labels *aberrational Christian* and *Christian fringe group* might be more appropriate for such deviant bodies. *Aberration* is applied to something that departs substantially from the normal or natural way. In religion, such deviance may come in either belief or practice. Cults certainly depart from the norms of Christian belief and practice. But so do some other bodies that do not qualify as cults. Thus, I will use the terms *aberrational Christian* and *Christian fringe group* generically. They will be applied to any marginal Christian body, including cults, some unusual sect groups and other deviant bodies that are difficult to classify.

The Occult
The term *occult,* though not as controversial as the word *cult,* does present some difficulties. According to the *Oxford English Dictionary,* the term *occult* was first used in 1545, meaning that which is "not apprehended, or not apprehensible, by the mind; beyond the range of understanding or of ordinary knowledge." In 1633, the word received an additional meaning, denoting the subject of "those ancient and medieval reputed sciences, held to involve the knowledge or use of agencies of a secret and mysterious nature (as magic, alchemy, astrology, and theology.)"[31]

Modern definitions contain similar ideas. One, the occult is mysterious, beyond the range of ordinary knowledge. Two, it is secret and disclosed or communicated only to the initiated. Three, the occult pertains to magic, astrology and other alleged sciences claiming use or knowledge of the secret, mysterious or supernatural. But in any modern definition, further delineation is necessary. From its Latin root *occulere* (to cover over, hide, conceal), the basic meaning of *occult* is "hidden," "concealed" and "secret." But the word no longer applies in a general sense to anything hidden from sight. Robert Galbreath points out that modern occultism pertains to matters that are "hidden" or "secret" in one of three ways: extraordinary matters (e.g., omens, portents, apparitions, prophetic dreams) that intrude into the mundane world; the teachings of the so-called mystery schools, which are kept hidden from the uninitiated and unworthy; and matters that are intrinsically hidden from ordinary understanding but are nonetheless knowable through the awakening of hidden, latent faculties of appropriate sensitivity.[32]

A problem with defining *occult* is that the word has a variety of common designations, and individuals tend to emphasize one property or another. Some authorities stress the occult's antiscientific and mystical aspects, while others emphasize its magical qualities. Still other individuals focus on the occult's religious aspects. Others, however, regard secrecy as the chief characteristic of the occult. The occult is seen as akin to superstition and the unreal. On the other hand, the word may be used objectively merely to suggest that which is not entirely known.

Occultism is multidimensional. As Marcello Truzzi notes, the occult is "a wastebasket" for many deviant beliefs and practices. Thus, in any definition of the occult certain questions need to be asked: "Who is labeling the belief as occult, where the labeling is being done (the social context), and at what time is the designation made (the historical period)."[33]

The occult also encounters problems in its relationship to science and religion. Prior to the seventeenth century, science and the occult maintained a close relationship. With the rise of modern science, however, the occult was perceived as having more magical and supernatural qualities. In the last half of the twentieth century another change is detectable. While scientists still view the occult negatively, occultists have tended to secularize the term. Increasingly, the occult has concerned itself with things paranormal or supernormal rather than supernatural. Claims are made of techniques and knowledge that science has yet to investigate or validate. In fact, some aspects of the occult, such as hypnosis and parapsychology, have achieved a degree of scientific legitimacy. But once an occult viewpoint attains some scientific validity, it usually rejects any description of itself as occultic.[34]

How does the occult relate to religion? It is best seen as a quasi-religious development. The occult comes in two related forms. It includes certain occult practices—that is, the occult arts such as divination, fortune-telling, spiritism, magic and so forth. There is also an occult/mystical worldview.

Though the practice of the occult arts presuppose an occult/mystical world-view, this aspect of the occult tends to be more magical. It is a more mechanical expression of the occult. Yet even the occult arts have religious aspects—that is, they attempt to provide meaning, contacts with the "sacred" and at times a basis for community.[35] However, the occult's clearest religious expression is in its worldview. An occult/mystical worldview undergirds many cults that are presently active in America, especially those associated with Eastern religions, the New Age and human potential movements and the many psychospiritual groups. Such expressions of the occult have taken the strongest hold during the last quarter of the twentieth century.

What is the relationship of the occult to the cults? Though many so-called cultic groups are occultic, the two expressions are not synonymous. While the cults usually presuppose a group or a community, the occult arts may be practiced individually and privately. Also, some cults with Christian roots do not maintain an occult/mystical worldview. Their worldview still derives from the Judeo-Christian tradition, but they have twisted major Christian beliefs or practices to the extent that they can be described as cultic. On the other hand, the practice of certain occult arts is an essential ingredient of many cults, even with some of the so-called Christian cults. More important, the occult/mystical/Eastern worldview is basic to the great majority of the new religions that are designated as cults, the New Age and human potential movements and psychospiritual groups.

Categories of Cults

Cults are as difficult to classify as they are to define. This is especially true for historians, who feel less comfortable with types and categories than do sociologists and theologians. There are so many variations of cults as to nearly defy classification. Moreover, many cults could fit into more than one category. Yet for the sake of organization and for a better understanding of such bodies, some attempt at classifying cultic groups is desirable.

The approaches to classifying cults and alternative religions that I have found most helpful are those used by Ronald Enroth and Gordon Melton. Taking a sociological and theological focus, Enroth offers six basic categories: Eastern-mystical, aberrational Christian, psychospiritual or self-improvement, eclectic-syncretistic, psychic-occult-astral, and institutionalized or established.[36] Employing a more historical approach, Melton places alternative religions in North America in eight families: the Latter-day Saints or Mormons, communalists, the metaphysicians, the psychic-spiritualist groups, ancient wisdom schools, magical groups, Eastern religions and the Middle Eastern faiths.[37]

In discussing one historical period or another I have used the following classifications: metaphysical and occult movements, religious communalism, Mormonism, Eastern religious groups, Christian groups, black religious groups, the New Age movement and psychospiritual or self-improvement groups. In drawing from the disciplines of sociology, theology and history, I have employed these classifications in only a loose way. The various religious groups in this study have been placed in the categories that seem most appropriate. Placement of a religious body in a particular classification does not mean that the group originated in this category or that it could not be housed elsewhere. Rather, it means that a particular cult is most closely related to a specific category. For example, the Unification Church and Mormonism have never been orthodox Christian bodies. Yet they relate more closely to Christianity than they do to other groups.

2

Fringe Groups
in the West

A t the risk of oversimplification, it can be argued that despite much religious diversity, Western spiritual life can be divided into three camps. These traditions sprang from the world of antiquity and represent three views of reality. First, there existed among both the ancient Hebrews and the Homeric Greeks an assumption that human beings are separate entities, living in the stream of world history above nature, over which they are dominant. Though Christianity contains elements of several worldviews, it built on this Hebrew and Greek view of reality. Christian theism, which has dominated in the West from the early Middle Ages, accentuates that God is infinite, personal and transcendent—that is, beyond people and creation. Theism also argues that humanity was created in God's image and is thus over nature. Science also borrows from this Hebrew and Greek view of reality. Rather than only attaining a mystical unity with nature, humans are to analyze and exploit it.[1]

The West has also known two other views of reality, which are prominent in many cult and occult groups. The most notable of these two views is usually called monism. It can be traced to early contacts with India and developed in Platonism and Neoplatonism. This view, based in the Platonic wonder at being itself, sees one all-inclusive reality out of which every particular emanates. Human beings are part of nature. A person's task is thus to attain an expansion of consciousness until he or she becomes mentally one with the whole cosmos. A smaller minority stream is ethical or religious dualism. Dualism envisions two eternal realities, spirit and matter—the one good, the other evil. The universe becomes a battleground for these forces of good and evil. Dualism can be traced to the ancient Persian religion, Zoroastrianism, through Gnosticism, Manichaeanism and Catharism. Christianity accepts a modified dualism by recognizing a powerful and evil Satan. But this is not the usual dualism, for Satan has only limited authority.[2]

In *Religious and Spiritual Groups in Modern America,* Robert Ellwood speaks frequently of what he calls "the alternative reality tradition." He is referring primarily to groups that maintain a monistic view of reality. I will also employ the terms *alternative reality* and *alternative reality tradition,* but in a slightly different way. By *alternative reality tradition* I mean any group or practice that upholds either a monistic or dualistic worldview.

The roots of fringe religions can be traced to all three views of reality. While some cultic groups maintain a theistic worldview, most do not. From the dominant Western worldview have come many of the Christian sectaries that separate from the mainstream not because they hold to a different view of reality, but because they differ on a point of doctrine or demand a more rigorous form of ethics. Some of these groups have pushed their doctrinal differences to the degree that they might be labeled as cultic. The worldview of Islam is also theistic. Like Christianity, Islam has experienced a number of sectarian and cultic spinoffs. However, the worldviews of many modern cult and occult groups have come out of the two minority streams of monism and dualism. These options have never been absent in Western history and represent alternative reality traditions. While dualism is not dead in the modern world, the merger of Western occult monism with that of the Eastern religions has produced a more powerful minority force in modern America.[3]

Our story begins in early-nineteenth-century America. A full account of fringe religions in the West, however, would go back to the early centuries of the Christian era and run the course of Western history. Such a story, of course, is not uniform. At times these religions blossomed forth; on other occasions they were largely hidden from view. Most of the early fringe religions were related to the occult tradition or were Christian heresies.

Hellenistic Age
According to Robert Ellwood, the exuberant activity of the new religious

groups in modern America "has a precedent," one that has significantly influenced the shape of the recent religious consciousness. The last half of the twentieth century has not been the only period in which a struggle with the hectic pace of life has thrown up a radical reaction in the form of new religious movements. During the Hellenistic Age, fringe movements also sprang from the world of Eastern religions.[4]

Culturally, the Hellenistic period can be dated from about 300 B.C. to A.D. 200. Hellenistic culture grew out of the confrontation of Greek philosophy with Egyptian and Near Eastern life and represented a new culture, one that was mystical, syncretistic and cosmopolitan. The culture of the Hellenistic period bore much resemblance to that of modern Western civilization. Like the twentieth century, the Hellenistic era witnessed several forms of government and the expansion of big business, the growth of trade, a devotion to material prosperity, an interest in technology, the growth of cities with crowded slums, and a widening gap between rich and poor. In the areas of art and the intellect, Hellenistic civilization also displayed modern characteristics: a narrow specialization of learning, an emphasis upon science, an inclination toward realism and materialism, an enormous production of mediocre literature and an interest in mysticism side by side with dogmatic unbelief and extreme skepticism.[5]

Even the methods used for the transmission of ideas, especially religious thought, have some parallels with the modern era. The international atmosphere was conducive to the exchange of information. The empires of Alexander, the Hellenistic rulers and Rome sent out soldiers, merchants and administrators. These individuals returned bringing back new cultures and new religions. Jews, wandering philosophers, slaves, Greek traders and missionaries swarmed toward the various cultural centers, as the teachers of Hinduism and Buddhism do today. The mention of these similarities, however, should not cloud the fact that there were great differences between the Hellenistic civilization and the modern world.[6]

The Hellenistic period evidenced a growing interest in religion. The central and eastern Mediterranean in the first and second centuries after Christ teemed with a multitude of religious ideas, all struggling to propagate themselves. Nearly every religious group was unstable and fissiparous, splitting up and reassembling in new forms. As Paul Johnson notes, Rome was "in some respects a liberal empire." In particular, Rome displayed tolerance "towards the two great philosophical and religious cultures which it con-

fronted in the central and eastern Mediterranean: Hellenism and Judaism."
Rome insisted on adherence to a minimal civic creed, but Roman subjects
could practice a second religion if they chose. This freedom plus the fer-
menting of ideas produced an atmosphere of religious pluralism, something
that was not duplicated in the West until the twentieth century. By the time
of Christ there existed hundreds of cults, perhaps even thousands of sub-
cults. The array of choices was tremendous.[7]

Within all this diversity there existed four major religious groupings during the Hellenistic Age: the Hellenistic cults, Judaism and Christianity, the
older Greek and Roman deities, and the civic and state religions. In addition, belief in astrology and magic flourished. Except for the older deities
and the civil religions, these religious groups have been prominent in par-
enting fringe religions at one time or another in subsequent Western history.

Several of these entities have had either a direct or an indirect relationship
with fringe religions in America. Neoplatonism has influenced occult and
cultic bodies throughout history. Plotinus (A.D. 204-70) and his followers
presented a new construction of Platonic philosophy. According to Plotinus, the cosmos consists of emanations from the One, and humanity's objective is to return to the One by a mystical experience. In such an experience the individual is to transcend the boundaries established by matter
and the intervening mental emanations—that is, the archetypes and the
world soul.[8]

Shamanism is another important religious phenomenon quite relevant to
understanding the dynamic of new religious movements through history.
Shamans are mediumistic persons, often of an unstable type, who are chosen as religious leaders solely because of their peculiar gifts, especially for
curing or causing disease and communicating with the spirit world. In several ways the brilliance of the primitive shaman is revived in the individuals
called masters, magi, adepts, magicians or mediums, who have been so
important to cults and new religions.[9]

A related subject is Hermeticism, the name for much of the "ancient
wisdom" type of teaching and magic. The name comes from the *Book of
Hermes Trismegistus,* written in Alexandria in the third or fourth century
after Christ. *Hermeticism* has often been used both in the ancient world and
in the present day to denote an ill-defined mass of Gnostic and Neoplatonic
philosophy, magic and astrology derived from the Hellenistic and Judaic
milieu of Alexandria. Many contemporary cultists regard Hermeticism as

the oldest accessible human wisdom.[10]

Astrology, one of the oldest occult activities, was prominent in the ancient Near East. It began in the dim recesses of history, by at least 3000 B.C. Astronomy is the study of the heavenly bodies, while astrology is the study of their influence on earth and on human beings.[11]

The astrological system available in the modern world came from about 150 B.C. From his base in Mesopotamia, Hipparchus provided a strange mix of astronomy and astrology that would characterize the pseudoscience for 1,600 years. The learned Alexandrian scholar Claudius Ptolemy (second century A.D.) incorporated much of Hipparchus's work and developed his own system, one that provided the fundamental theoretical scheme for astrology. First, this system regarded the earth as the center of the universe. Such a perspective more readily supports the claims that the total forces of the universe focus exclusively on human destiny. Next, the Ptolemaic system places the earth at the center of the solar and planetary motions, suggesting that these movements can influence life on earth in a meaningful way.[12]

Christianity not only thrived in the pluralism of the Hellenistic world but also contributed to the diversity. As in the modern world, where a measure of tolerance exists, Christianity not only expanded but also experienced splits and divisions.[13]

Consequently, ceaseless controversies arose, reflecting the basic instability of Christian belief during the early centuries, before creedal statements had been written, the canon established and an ecclesiastical structure built up to propagate and protect orthodox beliefs. Before the last half of the third century, a dominant strain of orthodox Christianity barely existed. In fact, during the first two centuries A.D. many Christians espoused varieties of Christian Gnosticism or belonged to sects grouped around charismatic leaders.[14]

Though these specific Christian split-offs do not exist today, some of the same factors that prompted them to deviate from the early church still foster divisions, thus creating sects, cults and occultic groups. Some examples of these factors include the following: emphasis on a particular doctrine to the exclusion of others; divisions regarding the nature of the Godhead and the status of Christ; a focus on a particular part of Scripture or a truncated canon; the development of a pronounced dualism; and strenuous demands for asceticism and a holy, pure church.

35

Gnosticism must be regarded as important in both the ancient and modern worlds: it posed a threat to the early church, and its alternate view of reality has parented several modern cults.[15] Though superficially Christian and often identified as a Christian heresy, Gnosticism has origins independent of Christianity and at heart combines elements of Judaism and Platonism.[16] Edwin Yamauchi speaks of Gnosticism as a version of dualism, setting "a transcendent God over against an ignorant creator (who is often a caricature of the God of the Old Testament)." All Gnostics regarded the material world as evil; however, encapsuled in the bodies of certain "spiritual" individuals destined for salvation are sparks of divinity. God therefore would send a "redeemer who brings them salvation in the form of secret knowledge *(gnosis)* of themselves, their origin and their destiny." After being awakened, "the 'spirituals' escape from the person of their bodies at death" and are united with God. Many Gnostic ideas, especially Gnosticism's alternative view of reality, have lived on in modified forms, influencing important aspects of the occult and cultic worlds through history.[17]

A vexing problem, one that goes right to the very heart of Christianity, namely the nature of the Christian deity, has produced a number of cults and sects in Christian history. This problem persisted throughout the early years of the church's history, but came to a head during the fourth and fifth centuries, after the Hellenistic Age had passed. Paul Johnson says that the "divinity of Christ gave Christianity its tremendous initial impact and assisted in its universality. But it left Christian theologians with a dilemma: how to explain the divinity of Christ while maintaining the singularity of God." Was there one God or two? Or, to complicate matters more, if the Holy Spirit was presented as a separate manifestation of divinity, were there not three gods?[18]

This issue became an irritant at a very early stage of Christian history. One possible solution was to regard Christ as a manifestation of the monolithic God and therefore not a man at all. In one way or another, several groups followed this line. A partial list would include the Gnostics, Docetists, Monarchianists and Sabellianists.[19] A second solution to the deity problem was to stress the humanity of Christ. This option, of course, had been preferred all along by the Judaizing elements and was the essence of the heresy maintained by the Ebionites.[20] The midpoint on this continuum was to deny Christ's preexistence as God, a position more or less taken by Arius, the most important of the Christological-trinitarian heretics. While

Arius acknowledged Christ's divinity, he insisted that the Son emanated from the Father and is thus subordinate to God the Father.[21]

The issue of Christ's deity, if not the same religious heretical bodies, has persisted to the present day, fostering deviant Christian groups that have been labeled as both sects and cults, depending on how far they have moved from the center of orthodoxy and on one's definition of a cult. Some modern groups in America associated with the Christian tradition, but deviating from the trinitarian doctrine as formulated by the early church councils, include Mormonism, the Jehovah's Witnesses, The Way, the Children of God, Unity and the Worldwide Church of God.

The Middle Ages

The Hellenistic era witnessed such religious diversity that no one religion prevailed. During the Middle Ages, the opposite was true. The Catholic Church dominated. Jesus Christ said that his Father's house has many mansions, but his followers have persisted in the conviction that everyone should live in the same one.[22] Such a statement fits the Middle Ages well. Still, the Catholic Church did not dominate the religious landscape to the extent that is commonly assumed. Stark and Bainbridge say that "the Catholic Church may well have been the noblest attempt ever made to serve the whole range of the religious market . . . but it never quite succeeded."[23] Dissenters, heretics and sect and cult groups always existed, even flourishing at times, and occasionally threatening to infest the church.

Breaks in religious uniformity occurred throughout the entire Middle Ages, but for different reasons and in varying numbers. During the early Middle Ages (c. 400-1050), the church did not have a firm grip on society. Divisions existed within the church, and paganism and Arianism persisted.[24] During the high Middle Ages (c. 1050-1350) the church attained its greatest strength, establishing something of a total Christian society in which most people acquiesced to the beliefs of the church. From this point on dissent became vocal, developing in part as a protest against ecclesiastical power and its accompanying corruptions. Sect and cult groups often arise during periods of intense religious consciousness. The high Middle Ages was such a time: it experienced an outburst of religious vitality.[25] The late Middle Ages (c. 1350-1500) witnessed great religious dissatisfaction, prompting many to seek alternatives outside the church. The church, having been humiliated by secular powers and racked by schism, was in decline. The upheavals and horrors of the age—famines, plagues and a pronounced economic decline—created support for new and strange religious movements.[26]

The various religious groups living on the margins of Catholic society during the Middle Ages can be placed in four broad categories: Hellenistic survivals, pre-Christian or pagan elements, Jewish mysticism and Christian deviations. The lines between these four groups are by no means rigid; at times the overlap is considerable. For example, the Hellenistic alternative-reality tradition influenced aspects of Christian dissent during the Middle Ages. Also, Christianity and paganism interacted considerably, even borrowing from each other.

Many of the Christian dissent groups contained elements that would emerge later in Protestantism, and thus have little connection with modern fringe religions. But a more radical dissent movement developed in the mid-twelfth century. For the first time a large-scale popular heresy movement swept over western Europe. The arrival and rapid spread of dualism into Italy and southern France, in particular, threatened to infest the church. Catharism, called Albigensianism in southern France, was a form of Eastern dualism. Like the Zoroastrians, Gnostics and Manichaeans before them, the Catharists believed that all matter was created by an evil principle and therefore the flesh should be thoroughly mortified. While Catharism is not directly connected with fringe groups in modern America, such dualism between spirit and matter bears resemblance to the thinking of several contemporary bodies.[27]

During the Middle Ages there appeared a number of dissenters who taught partly intellectual and partly mystical doctrines. Best known was Joachim of Flora (d. 1201), a millenarian whom some modern-day New Age adherents regard as one of their forerunners. His complicated metaphysics included the belief that there were three ages of the world: the age of God the Father, the age of the Son, in which Joachim lived, and the age of the Holy Spirit, which was shortly to begin. In the third age, humanity, filled with the Spirit, would create a kingdom of God on earth.[28] A prominent mystical theorist whose views bore some resemblance with those of contemporary Eastern religious leaders was the German Dominican Meister Eckhart (c. 1260-1327). He taught that a power or "spark" deep within every human soul was really the dwelling place of God. By renouncing all sense of selfhood one could retreat into one's innermost recesses and then find divinity.[29]

A major fringe religion in the Middle Ages, one that still exists today, was witchcraft. The European witchcraft phenomenon related to pagan survivals and Christian heresy, though the latter was most prominent. Moreover, no clear lines existed between late medieval witchcraft and that of the Renaissance-Reformation period. Jeffrey Russell points out that historically there are three types of witch: "the sorcerer who practices the simple magic found worldwide; the heretic who allegedly practiced diabolism and was prosecuted during the witch-craze; and the modern neopagan." Significant differences exist between these types, but they have "in common the name of witch and the practice of magic."[30]

Western or European witchcraft can be placed in three historical periods. During the early Middle Ages witchcraft existed as pagan religion, sorcery and folklore. In the late Middle Ages, about 1300, there occurred a temporary marriage between diabolical witchcraft, or Christian heresy, and sorcery. Simple sorcery has existed through Western history to the present day. Diabolical witchcraft developed in the late Middle Ages, flourished between 1450 and 1650 during the witch-craze, and then declined and fell. The collapse of the witch-craze between 1650 and 1750 was brought about by a combination of intellectual, pragmatic and social changes. The religion of modern Western witchcraft is a revival of paganism. Modern witches are individuals who worship pre-Christian gods and practice magic.[31]

The alternative-reality tradition, namely monism and dualism, though placed on the back burner, survived during the Middle Ages and has lingered as an underground alternative to Christianity to the present day. This tradition touched both Christian heresies and pre-Christian witchcraft. The dualistic heresies, especially the Catharists, had their ultimate inspiration in the Gnostic Manichaean religion. Like the earlier Manichaeans, the Cathars believed in two gods: a good god who created the invisible world and the evil god who created the visible material world. Furthermore, the alternative-reality tradition and ceremonial magic inspired aspects of pre-Christian witchcraft in the early Middle Ages.[32]

The strongest impact of the Hellenistic tradition, however, came in groups often associated with occultism: the Cabala, alchemy, magic and astrology. As Robert Ellwood indicates, "Witchcraft was not the only medieval counter-culture." The Jews who produced a unique expression of the occult were another. "Judaism's most profound mystical statement of the period, and its major contribution to later occultism, was the Kabbalah."

The Cabala is a complicated "symbol for expressing spiritual knowledge." Cabala's distinctive is the hermeneutical principle of finding hidden or spiritual meanings in the Hebrew Bible. Human language in Scripture is examined not only allegorically and analogically but also through the interpretation of words and letters according to numerical equivalents. Such a method allows for new interpretations, many with occult meanings.[33]

Cabalism has maintained a presence in the occult tradition since the Middle Ages. It pictures God as being above all existence. The world was created through a series of ten emanations. Good deeds by pious Jews supposedly affect the emanations, ultimately influencing God in behalf of humanity. Cabala includes a version of reincarnation. The pure soul, once the body dies, will be present among the emanations that control the world. An impure soul must be reborn in another body, and the process continues until it has been made pure. Evil is only the negation of good, and in the Jewish setting evil is overcome through the three great emphases of repentance, prayer and good deeds, along with strict adherence to the law.[34]

Alchemy must be mentioned, because it is part of the alternative-reality tradition and many of its adherents were deeply involved in magic and Cabala. Alchemy's primary importance rests in its mixing of the occult with science, a method that is still prevalent on the contemporary scene. Alchemy was a medieval occult science and speculative philosophy aiming to achieve the transmutation of base metals into gold, the discovery of a universal cure for disease and the discovery of a means of indefinitely prolonging life. Alchemy is not a religion by itself. But as Ellwood demonstrates, "alchemy is by no means merely a practical science of metallurgy. The serious alchemist regarded his or her craft as a spiritual venture," a quest for wholeness, a mystical path.[35]

Renaissance and Reformation Europe
Together the Renaissance and Reformation movements (c. 1400-1650) represent a period of transition from the Middle Ages to the modern world. In respect to religious toleration and diversity, these years were paradoxical. Extreme bigotry and intolerance existed well into the seventeenth century, and minority religions were often repressed. Yet the fragmentation of Christendom by the Reformation, the bitter wars over religion, new intellectual developments and a changing worldview all worked together to further the development of religious toleration and the growth of fringe religions.[36]

During the span from 1400 to 1650, Catholicism and the Protestant state churches dominated the religious scene. But the fringe religions were numerous, and they took a more visible stance than they had during the Middle Ages. By the end of the seventeenth century, there were many more religious groups than there had been at the beginning of the Reformation. Yet the prevailing church-state pattern, that of one religion for one area, remained largely intact until after 1650. Even after this date the dominant religions, the Catholic and Protestant state churches, continued to be established by law with dissenters legally permitted to practice their faith only in a restricted fashion. The American experiment in the late 1700s was the first break from such a pattern.[37] During the Renaissance-Reformation period, the fringe religions included a bewildering assortment of Christian sect groups, religious bodies outside the norm of orthodoxy though marginally related to Christianity, a resurgence of the occult and the peak of the witchcraft craze.

Robert Wuthnow contends that "religious movements have been distributed neither evenly nor at random in space and time." They seem to occur during times of rapid social change and in periods of crisis and transition in the world order.[38] The century and a half from 1500 to 1650 witnessed both. There occurred an upheaval in nearly every sphere of thought and action—much of it imparting religious developments. Though religion did not develop uniformly during this era, in general it was a time of great religious experimentation. Religious activity was intense, and many new movements were spawned.[39]

The explosion of religious activity from 1500 to 1650, including the growth of fringe religions, must be seen in the context of the major events of these years. The revival of knowledge during the Renaissance, the overseas expansion, the Protestant Reformation, economic growth and stagnation, the incessant wars and the changing world order worked in various ways to provide a climate suitable for the growth of nontraditional religion.

The Renaissance represents a rebirth of the culture and learning of antiquity, including many aspects of the occult. As the Renaissance dawned, several expressions of the alternative-reality tradition associated with Hellenism rose to the surface as a reaction against the medieval system. Neoplatonism, occultism, alchemy, astrology and the like flourished in Europe as never before or since. The individuals who took up these things were among the most independent and intelligent of the age. Ellwood tells us that occult activities were by "no means a reaction into mindless superstition." Rather, they represented "a plunge into the depths of the unconscious and its symbols, and into the past, in order to integrate all of humanity and its story in preparation for the imminent leap into the modern world." For many, Neoplatonism seemed to contain eternal laws upon which science was based. Astrology became astronomy, chemistry can be traced to alchemy, and there is a possible connection between Cabala and psychoanalysis. But teachers of the occult tradition have valued the occultism and Neoplatonism of the Renaissance for their own sake. They maintain that such ideas, "far from being outdated, are a deeper seed of wisdom which the world is privileged to experience only once in many centuries."[40] Some occultists would claim that the late twentieth century is one of these times.

While few new movements were introduced during the Renaissance, some new wrinkles were introduced in these Hellenistic holdovers. From the time of Petrarch (1304-74) until the end of the Renaissance, Neoplatonism occupied a large place in Western thought, captivating some of the major thinkers of the time and incorporating Christian elements. Marsilo Ficino (1433-99) introduced specifically Christian theology into his Neoplatonic system. He identified Christ with the Neoplatonic intermediary between the pure One and the subdivided spiritual and material world.[41] With the expulsion of the Jews from Spain in 1492, the Cabala underwent some significant changes, a dispersion through Europe and a Christianization.[42] Alchemy also experienced changes during the Renaissance and Reformation. On one hand, Paracelsus (1492-1541) began a new era in alchemy. He insisted that all things in the universe consist of sulphur, salt and philosophical mercury or azoth. On the other, alchemy began to decline with the humanistic and rationalistic development of Western thought.[43]

Astrology, another Hellenistic holdover, was also in transition. While astrology was commonplace during the Renaissance-Reformation period, forces were at work that ultimately produced its decline. Astrology was part of the intellectual framework of late medieval and Renaissance Europe. Scores of people perceived that astrology discharged many useful functions. Nevertheless, astrology rapidly declined in status largely for practical and intellectual reasons. The intellectual pretensions of astrological theory were irreparably shattered by the astronomical revolution initiated by Copernicus and consummated by Newton. Also, improved living conditions took much of the anxiety out of life and thus reduced the need for predicting the future.[44]

A similar trend can be seen in witchcraft. According to Jeffrey Russell, by 1300 the various components of European witchcraft had been assembled. As a concept, witchcraft underwent little development. "For the next century and one-half, fear of witches spread gradually throughout Europe. Then, about 1450, at the end of the Middle Ages, the fear became a craze which lasted more than two hundred years," peaking from 1550 to 1650. The notion that the craze was medieval is largely due to the negative stereotypes associated with the so-called Dark Ages. Instead, "the witch-craze was a product of the Renaissance and Reformation." In fact, a number of Renaissance intellectuals and Reformation leaders staunchly advocated a belief in diabolical witchcraft.[45]

There have been many attempts from the perspective of several academic disciplines to explain the rise of the witch-craze in Europe. However, none are entirely satisfactory. Thus it is more profitable to examine some probable factors involved in such a development. In part, witchcraft may be a product of the general anxiety linked to the social unrest, plagues, famines and wars of the period from 1300 to 1700. The tremendous series of changes affecting many areas of life during these years completely altered the dominant European outlook.[46]

Psychology is a useful supplement to these social explanations. As Russell notes, "people projected evil desires and passions most easily upon isolated and lonely outsiders such as old widows and crones." Some of the accused, propelled by guilt and fear, came to believe in their own culpability. "The witch-craze is an important study in collective evil," says Russell, perhaps "comparable to the Nazism and Stalinism in the present century."[47]

Legal developments also pushed the witch-craze into more excesses. Each new conviction justified harsher measures, including torture. In turn, torture produced more confessions, confessions produced more convictions, and belief and repressions fed one another. The intensification of theology helped to promote the witch-craze. Theologians and jurists regarded witchcraft as the worst of heresies.[48]

One new occult movement did emerge on the scene. The shadowy roots of Rosicrucianism go back to at least the seventeenth century. Rosicrucianism is active in the twentieth century and by most standards can be regarded as cultic. It has much in common with Unity, Christian Science, Theosophy and the Mighty I AM. Secret societies have existed in many ages and countries. But in Western culture, the modern idea of the secret society can be traced to late-sixteenth- and early-seventeenth-century Rosicrucianism, which had a definite relationship with esoteric Gnostic alchemy. Moreover, Rosicrucianism has close ties to Freemasonry, whose French and Scottish rites both incorporate the Rose-Cross.[49]

The earliest Rosicrucian writings are *The Confession of the Rosicrucian Fraternity* and the *Fama Fraternities*. These two documents, both published anonymously in 1614-15, present the myth of "Christian Rosencreutz" (Rosy Cross), the society's alleged founder, who supposedly lived from 1378 to 1484. While traveling in the Near East, he acquired the ability to communicate with elementary spirits and learned many occult secrets, some medical, magical and cabalistic. Upon returning to Europe, Rosencreutz began to show people their mistakes and the true path to follow. When they scorned him, he founded his secret society. According to John Warwick Montgomery, "Rosicrucianism was (and is, in its current American form) a corporate technique for self salvation, which differs little from the individualistic works-righteousness carried out by Paracelsus and other esoteric alchemists."[50]

Europe witnessed the birth of many new religious groups from the start of the sixteenth century to the end of the seventeenth. Most of these new bodies stood outside the religious mainstream, namely Catholicism and the Protestant state churches, but still within the Christian tradition. Also, most of these groups were schismatic, breaking from another religious body, quite often a larger, older one, in order to establish a purer form of the Christian faith. Such bodies, which are usually labeled sectarian, fall outside the scope of this study.

There were, however, several mystical and rational religious bodies that departed significantly from Christianity. In fact, they repudiated many of the basic tenets of the Christian faith and by some modern criteria might be regarded as cultic. Nevertheless, these new religious groups are now largely extinct. Thus, this study will only note the two major trends of this development—namely, the groups related to the Radical Reformation and the turbulence of seventeenth-century England.

The Protestant Reformation spawned many radical groups. Their radicalism was confined for the most part to social teachings, and most remained within the limits of orthodoxy. There were, however, some antitrinitarians who carried their dissent much further.[51] The turmoil of the Puritan revolution and English Civil War produced an outburst of new religions, some pantheistic, some antitrinitarian and some apocalyptic, that waited for the imminent end of the world.[52]

The Early Modern World

The years from the end of the Thirty Years' War to the constitutional settlement in America and the French Revolution in Europe represented a lull in respect to the birth of new religions. The Renaissance and Reformation era witnessed a proliferation of new religious groups. Such an unfolding would not occur again until the first half of the nineteenth century in America. However, the 150 years in between were by no means devoid of significant religious activity. In fact, these important years saw several landmark developments that would change forever the face of religion in the West. These unfoldings would provide a backdrop for the religious outburst that occurred in the early nineteenth century in America.

The decades of the 1640s and 1650s were pivotal in the history of Christianity. Until this time, the ideal of the total Christian society still seemed attainable, if only within territorial limits. The many religious conflicts that culminated in the Thirty Years' War helped to end the idea of religious unity in a geographical area. To some extent, both the secularization and the religious pluralism of the modern world owe a debt to the destruction of such a concept.[53]

In respect to intellectual developments, by the middle of the seventeenth century Europe stood on the threshold of the modern world. The years from 1650 to 1800 would witness increased scientific developments, an intellectual revolution and a gradual change in worldview from one that was predominantly medieval to one which is essentially modern. The supernatural, especially its magical components—astrology, healing, prophecies, alchemy, witchcraft, ghosts, omens and aspects of church ritual—were regarded as practical. They met specific human needs. But various developments robbed the old magical systems of their capacity to satisfy the educated elite. As a consequence, the importance of the supernatural was greatly reduced. The adjustment of religion to this unfolding helped to produce new religious movements.[54] Of less immediate importance, the hardening of orthodoxy in the late sixteenth and early seventeenth centuries provided a catalyst for new religious activities. People reacted to this dry dogma by emphasizing a religion of the heart, which in turn fostered further religious fragmentation.[55]

During the seventeenth and eighteenth centuries in Europe and America,

45

the dominant religions were Catholicism and the major Protestant denominations, e.g., the Anglicans, Lutherans, Presbyterians, Congregationalists, and Baptists. The religious outsiders or fringe religions came in four categories—the sects, cults, the occult, and liberal religions. Most fringe religions of this period must be regarded as sectarian bodies. Though there existed few groups that could be labeled as cultic, the occult maintained a substantial presence. Also, the nontrinitarian or liberal religions, which are difficult to classify, were clearly outside the religious mainstream during the early modern period.

Most sectarian groups were related to Anabaptism, Pietism or radical Puritanism. While these movements were not heretical, they spawned bodies that at times transcended the bounds of orthodoxy. In particular, Pietism's emphasis on experience and the feeling of the heart, when pushed to extremes, fostered many fringe groups.[56]

The seventeenth and eighteenth centuries witnessed the development of two liberal and antitrinitarian religions. Deism and Unitarianism have much in common, but they are not the same and have developed more or less independently along different lines. While both these groups were clearly heretical, they are not viewed as cultic. Deism does not exist in the modern world, while Unitarianism is often the religion of the educated upper classes and does not have the social characteristics of some other nontrinitarian groups that are designated as cults. Moreover, both Deism and Unitarianism were rational religions, products of the Enlightenment. As such they are often seen as new and even non-Christian religions.[57]

A common view, widely propagated by Keith Thomas's work *Religion and the Decline of Magic,* is that the occult went into a decline around the end of the seventeenth century.[58] Such a view can be sustained with a major qualification: the decline of the occult during the eighteenth century was a variable process, taking place at different rates in elite and popular cultures, in different locations and in different areas of the occult. The occult certainly did not disappear. In part, it withdrew from the educated elite while remaining strong in the popular culture; in part, it went underground and survived in secret societies. Also, certain aspects of occultism remained strong while other areas experienced a decline.[59]

Another possible explanation is that the early modern period represented a time of transition for the occult. Three radically different worldviews— those of hermetic magic, material science and traditional Christianity—

began to separate in the seventeenth century. During much of Western history, the occult was in touch with the major strands of European culture. But as Catherine Albanese notes, after the Enlightenment the new science radically revised "the way educated people viewed the world." As science grew in status it challenged the traditional worldview, while occultism became more and more "a secret knowledge" and even "a rejected knowledge." Traditionally, the occult had been "an assorted mixture of elements" taken from paganism and blended with "insights from Judaism and Christianity." Such a mixture now was regarded as superstition. Therefore, by the nineteenth century to maintain such beliefs was to "run counter" to the main trend of Western culture. Occultists were often estranged people, alienated from the ordinary religion of the culture by their beliefs and practices.[60]

In yet another way, the eighteenth century may be regarded as a period of transition for occultism. Albanese also points out two types of the occult, though the lines between them are not set in concrete. First is the "natural and traditional occultism," the simple folk beliefs that supported individuals as they tried to cope with everyday tasks. A partial list would include planting crops by the zodiac, using anatomical charts and observing the rules about breaking mirrors and avoiding black cats. This type of occultism remained strong in the seventeenth and eighteenth centuries and then gradually declined. However, it still exists today in rural areas. Second is the learned and scholarly aspects of occultism, often associated with serious astrology, alchemy, high magic, numerology and even some witchcraft beliefs. These elements of the occult declined more rapidly and thoroughly than did the simple folk beliefs. But a new occultism with scholarly and educated elements developed in the nineteenth century. This occultism was metaphysical and concerned more with spiritual than material things as sources of reality. The metaphysical occult had its roots in the eighteenth century and began to develop as the older intellectual occult went into decline.[61]

In Europe during the eighteenth century, there appeared entities connected with the alternative-reality tradition that have clear continuity with American occultism today. Some examples of these groups or movements include Freemasonry, Swedenborgianism, mesmerism and Rosicrucianism. The eighteenth century was a time of increasing polarization between belief and feeling, reason and fascination. There was, therefore, great interest in secret societies.[62]

The earliest of these societies was the Rosicrucian Brotherhood, which first announced itself in a manifesto published in 1614. There is great dispute over whether the society existed in the seventeenth century. Nevertheless, people believed that it existed and that it was in possession of secret knowledge. By the eighteenth century, English occultists had become interested in a secret society that had a definite existence, one with which the Rose-Cross came to be associated. This fraternity, Freemasonry, was the most important of the eighteenth-century phenomena for the dissemination of alternative-reality ideas. Freemasonry developed from the combination of two earlier strands: the ancient guild of working masons, who were secretive about their craft, and the Rosicrucianism of the seventeenth century.[63]

The modern history of Freemasonry began in 1717, with the inauguration of the Grand Lodge of England. This new endeavor bore the stamp of a combination of rational science, Rosicrucian occultism and biblical literalism. The association of Masonry with occult knowledge grew and was reinforced in its early years when its lodges were penetrated by occultists, who instituted ceremonies based on occult symbolism, particularly that of alchemy and the Cabala, and attempted to duplicate the effects of the mystery religions by a series of initiations. English Masonry featured grades or levels. Eventually there arose the legend of the Secret Chiefs. This story, which always lives behind occult Masonry, says that there were "Hidden Chiefs" or "Unknown Superiors" who held themselves aloof from the daily affairs of the fraternity but were themselves in possession of the ultimate secrets. Such a notion was to become a common occult doctrine. For example, the Theosophical Masters were derived from the same theory.[64]

The narrow dogmatism of the post-Reformation theologies spawned several reactions, one being a spiritual option. Spiritualism can fall into a Christian framework, but it can also be related to occultism. Of the main leaders of seventeenth- and eighteenth-century spiritualism, Emanuel Swedenborg is more closely related to the occult. In fact, Swedenborg (1688-1772) has been regarded as perhaps the most influential eighteenth-century individual in respect to the occult. He is regarded as the major link between the old medieval alchemist or Rosicrucian secretive activity and the Spiritualist séance in America or the modern Theosophical lecture. After his death, his teachings produced the Church of the New Jerusalem, which has survived into the twentieth century, and a Swedenborgian Society. Both of these organizations have disseminated Swedenborg's ideas, which are regarded as occultic.[65]

Swedenborg, the son of a Lutheran bishop in Sweden, was a man of superb intellectual gifts and the recipient of the best education available. More than anyone else during this time, he successfully popularized ideas emanating from the alternative-reality tradition. Except for direct Eastern imports, modern occult and metaphysical movements owe a great debt to him. He had success because he did not deal directly with concealed cabalistic puzzles, but from his concrete visions which addressed the questions asked by ordinary Christians: How do spirits live? Can they help or harm people? What is heaven really like? What goes on in hell?[66]

Swedenborg had a vision which he said had carried him into the spiritual world, where he had been able to see eternal truths. He began to write voluminously, believing that his writings were the dawn of a new age in the history of the world and of religion. In fact, he asserted that what had occurred when he received his revelations was actually what the Bible meant in its references to the Second Coming of Christ. Not surprisingly, his ideas were not well received by most of his contemporaries. Yet as a precursor of modern occult thought, he contributed much to following generations. He taught the Spiritualist notion of communication with persons on the other side, the cabalist and gnostic belief in a pre- and postexistence in a spiritual state, a gnostic idea of important events that occur in an invisible world known only to those being inducted into an occult society, and a monistic concept of God. Most important, Swedenborg declared that the Second Coming of Christ happened spiritually in 1757. His focus on this invisible end of an age can be seen as a forerunner of modern "Aquarian Age" and "New Age" ideas.[67]

Several other eighteenth-century figures pointed toward the modern occult. One of the better known was the Austrian doctor Franz Antoine Mesmer (1733-1815). He engaged in what scientists label pseudoscience. While the word *mesmerism* is derived from his name, Mesmer did not personally practice the induced trance. Rather, he claimed to have discovered a universal fluid which he called animal magnetism, supposedly a health-giving matter transported by iron rods from a tank to patients seated nearby. What modern people call the power of suggestion was in operation. Background music created an atmosphere. Patients often went into strange convulsions and finally lethargy. From the further developments of such a process by his followers, modern hypnotism was born.[68]

PART II

Religious
Innovations in Early
National America

Early national America witnessed the greatest surge of new religious activities since the Reformation era. America in the early nineteenth century was going through rapid social change. Economic, political and cultural forces including urbanization, the growth of democracy, millennial fever, Romanticism, perfectionism and evangelical revivalism combined to produce an atmosphere conducive to the growth of fringe religions. Most of these new groups were Protestant sectarian bodies, usually evangelical splitoffs. Nevertheless, religious groups did arise outside the boundaries of orthodox Christianity. Some have been linked with the occult and cultic traditions. They would include Transcendentalism, Swedenborgianism, Spiritualism, some food and health cults, the Shakers and other communal groups, Mormonism and the Christadelphians.

3

Early National America:
Social &
Religious Movements

Early-nineteenth-century America, particularly during the decades of the 1830s and 1840s, witnessed an explosion of new religious movements such as had not been seen since the sixteenth century. The nineteenth century was one of extraordinary religious diversity that continued into the twentieth. Such diversity had started in the colonial period; it surged in the first half of the nineteenth century and increased during the last half of that century and the first half of the twentieth. Though several factors allowed this diversity to continue and even accelerated it, comparatively speaking the period from about 1860 to 1960 did not witness the same intensity of religious activity, nor did it produce as many new religious movements condensed into several decades, as had the antebellum period—that is, the years prior to the Civil War. Another such dramatic increase in new religions had to await the decades of the 1960s and 1970s.[1]

The relationship between social change and fringe religions, whether they be sectarian developments or new religions, is not entirely clear. This difficulty is illustrated by the comparative difference in the levels of religious activity between the ante-and postbellum periods, despite the fact that both halves of the nineteenth century experienced rapid social, economic and intellectual changes. One must bear in mind, however, that both periods gave rise to significant religious innovations and schisms. Only when the postbellum period is compared to the period before the Civil War is it correct to depict it as a time of declining religious enthusiasm.[2]

Nevertheless, the religious upheavals prior to 1860 did occur in a context of rapid social and economic change. As major demographic shifts, rapid urbanization, westward expansion, unprecedented advances in transportation and communication, and industrial development transformed American society between 1820 and 1860, the fabric of most people's lives—workplace, residence, family life and religion—changed dramatically. Political developments, especially increased democratization, an accentuated nationalism and "manifest destiny" (the belief that America's expansion into the adjacent western areas had a divine mandate) influenced many individuals. A dramatic increase in immigration and the church-state separation complicated the already diverse social and religious picture. Ideas drawn from sources as eclectic as the Enlightenment, Romanticism, science and millennialism influenced different aspects of American life, and often worked in diverse directions, but their total impact must be regarded as significant.

These social and economic changes helped facilitate significant religious developments.[3] According to William McLoughlin, the cultural consensus and the dominant religious trend emerging from the First Great Awakening was a Calvinism that stressed conversion and God's favor on America. This consensus provided the authority for most of the major denominations: the Presbyterians, Congregationalists, Reformed and Baptists. Yet Calvinism as the dominant religious and cultural consensus could not effectively cope with the vast number of social and economic changes, and it faded fast after 1800. In its place arose a new consensus, an evangelical Arminianism, which could cope better with a reordered society.[4]

Several related political and philosophical concepts influenced the general thrust of religion in early national America. The long process of democratization begun during the colonial period, facilitated by the Revolution and accelerated by the influence of the frontier made American society by the 1830s, according to the words of the French traveler Michael Chevalier, "essentially and radically a democracy, not in name merely but in deed."[5] The presence of the frontier, with its individualism, came into conflict with the authoritarianism of not only the colonial governments but also the established churches and Calvinist theology. This democratic impulse fostered the growth of evangelical Arminianism and produced revivals, schisms and new religious bodies.

Even groups with a communal and authoritarian character were propelled west by the lure of the frontier. In particular, the Methodists with their message of free will and the Baptists with their congregational polity benefited from the democracy of the frontier. The voluntary support of a church by committed laity, called voluntarism, was closely related to the separation of church and state, but it was also propelled by the democratic principle.

The notion of manifest destiny played a greater role in religious developments after the Civil War and in relationship with the religious mainstream, especially civil religion. This concept was already active, however, during the first half of the century, though at times implicitly. Though the phrase *manifest destiny* was not coined until 1845, the concept had emerged in the late eighteenth century. In its broad sense, it proposed that Americans are a peculiar race, chosen by God to perfect the world. Such an outlook had a diverse effect on religion. It fueled the religious optimism of the Second Great Awakening, Arminianism and perfectionism, and provided a backbone for civil religion. Manifest destiny also promoted the racism, religious bigotry and hypernationalism that emerged at times during the nineteenth century.[6]

Millennialism

The millennial idea powerfully affected both mainstream and fringe religions throughout the course of the nineteenth century. This millennial appeal continued during the twentieth century, exploding in the post-World War II era, at a time when its impact has been registered primarily on groups with a sectarian and cultic outlook. Millennialism, in its generic usage, is concerned with the future of the human community on earth and with the chronology of coming events, just as history is involved with the study of the record of the past. In particular, the American millennial look into the future relates to the Second Coming of Christ and a period of earthly bliss or progress.[7]

Individuals and groups who believed in a millennium were deeply divided in early national America, as they have been throughout much of history. The various millennial types are difficult to categorize. Perhaps the simplest way to classify millennialists is to place them in two categories whose names vary.

The progressives, also called millennialists or postmillennialists, assumed that the kingdoms of this world will eventually become those of Christ, and that through the endeavors of Christians the world will get better and better until it is finally worthy to receive Christ at his Second Coming. This view projected an optimistic view of the future and increasingly came to be equated with the idea of progress.[8]

The progressive millennial doctrine was dominant in America during the eighteenth century, and it remained strong in the nineteenth, receiving reinforcement from the growth of industry and technology and a general improvement in the standard of living. During the nineteenth century, liberal Protestants, such as the Unitarians, and also moderate evangelicals, like Lyman Beecher, held postmillennialist views. The Methodist teaching of perfection as a second work of grace after conversion was postmillennial in its thrust, and perfectionism was spread by revivals until it became a widespread belief. Charles G. Finney preached perfectionism, and some diverse communal groups adopted versions of it.[9]

The second group also has several names: pessimists, millenarians or, most commonly, premillennialists. Adherents of this view expected a divine intervention to establish a divinely ruled state, after evil had reached its fullest extent in the world at large. Somewhat like the Jehovah's Witnesses of today, these premillennialists believed the faithful should separate from the world. Since trials and tribulations would increase before the return of Christ, premillennialists tended to see any negative event as a sign that the world was growing worse and thus evidence that the end was near.[10]

Though premillennialism had its proponents throughout the eighteenth and first half of the nineteenth centuries, postmillennialism overshadowed it and held the day. Nevertheless, events such as the Lisbon earthquake of 1755 and the French Revolution excited a flood of biblical interpretations on both sides of the Atlantic designed to show that the world was entering its last days. After the Civil War, however, came a resurgence of premillennialism, carrying down to the present day. The Millerites were the clearest expression of this view in America prior to the Civil War. Though they did not clearly fit the premillennial pattern, the Shakers and, to a degree, the Mormons were not progressives. Both groups held little hope for the world and separated themselves from it.[11]

Intellectual Currents

In the early national period, several intellectual currents had a significant bearing on religion, with Romanticism making perhaps the greatest inroad.

Romanticism was a movement in art, literature, philosophy and religion in the latter eighteenth and early nineteenth centuries, but as a movement it nearly defies definition. Romanticism arose in Europe largely as a reaction to the rigidity and cold rationalism of the Enlightenment. In America, however, Romanticism was less a reaction than the beginning of something new. From the onset it became closely related to the developing sense of nationalism. Whereas European Romanticism was in large part a revolt against previously established traditions, in America it provided a new way for writers to articulate their feelings about their land.[12]

Romanticism can be regarded as a parallel movement to revivalism, and indeed it powerfully reinforced the Second Great Awakening. Both movements stressed the individual's role in finding truth and the validity of his or her inner, intuitive convictions. Both Romanticism and revivalism placed emphasis on the emotions. Certain that the impulses of the heart were more convincing than those of the head, the Romantics placed great faith in that "moment of intense feeling" instead of the calculations of logic. Furthermore, Romanticism expressed, as did many manifestations of religion, an optimism that was hopeful of human progress and an acceptance of irrationality in the world. Romanticism energized many areas of religion and quasi-religion. It interacted with philosophy and religion (idealism, evangelicalism, Transcendentalism, Unitarianism), with social change (Prohibition, women's rights, abolition) and with social systems (Brook Farm, Oneida, New Harmony).[13]

The idea of progress—that humanity is advancing toward a better world—is at least as old as the Greeks. This belief received its contemporary expression in the seventeenth and eighteenth centuries, growing out of the Enlightenment's emphasis on rationalism and its faith in humankind's perfectibility. According to Russel Nye, this concept of progress, as it took shape in the eighteenth century, found ardent "supporters in America. The Revolution and the Constitution, in American opinion, marked a new phase in the inexorable march of events toward a better world." The eighteenth-century American's belief in progress presupposed a world improved by reason, moving forward toward an inevitable, divinely ordained perfection.[14]

After the turn of the nineteenth century, the American idea of progress became much more positive and related to material betterment. Standards of living had improved markedly over the preceding century: scientific discoveries increased, technological advances became noticeable, and economic conditions rose visibly. Consequently, in the early nineteenth century Americans firmly believed in a kind of progress that could be advanced by education, government, technology and science, and by the efforts of individual and community action.[15]

The doctrine of perfectionism can be regarded as a religious affirmation of several secular trends in early nineteenth-century America: the contemporary beliefs in optimism, progress and democratic individualism. Perfectionism places a strong emphasis on Christian holiness, contending that the believer through God's grace can achieve and maintain a moral perfection in this life. In its modern manifestation, perfectionism nearly always lays stress on a postconversion experience of God. The quest for religious perfection has been an important goal throughout Judeo-Christian history. With variations in regard to the degree and chronology of the perfection of the Christian life, many individuals and groups normally regarded as within the context of orthodoxy have embraced this doctrine. In addition, perfectionism has been expressed in many forms by bodies on the fringes of Christianity. Some of these groups include Gnostic dualists, Montanists, Albigensians, Brethren of the Free Spirit and the English Ranters.[16]

Perfectionism in nineteenth-century America also found a home with groups and individuals considered to be both inside and outside the Christian mainstream. Movements and individuals more or less within the mainstream included the Methodist Church, revivalism—especially Charles G. Finney and what became known as Oberlin Theology—and several humanitarian movements containing religious overtones (e.g., abolitionism, temperance, the peace movement). In various degrees, perfectionism also influenced some fringe religions: Spiritualism, the Shakers, the Oneida Perfectionists and other communal and utopian groups.

In fact, the reform impulse in the United States received its strongest support from the religious evangelism that swept the country in the 1920s and 1930s. Nye says that evangelical revivalism spawned two beliefs: perfectionism, the belief "that American life could be reformed and rearranged" to meet the moral standards that "God had set down for the perfect society"; and that "saved or perfected Christians" must make their salvation complete, apply their religion to life and make their piety practical. Salvation, therefore, was not the end but rather "the beginning of a useful life." Thus, evangelical religion made social reform a moral imperative. If social evil resulted from individual sin and selfishness, then progress came from re-forming individuals by religious conversion. The reformer then, was obligated to convert the nation rather than to attempt to legislate it into benevolence.[17]

Revivalism

The dominant force in nineteenth-century American Christianity was revivalism. Revivalism promoted religious diversity in several ways: it fostered many divisions, thus directly creating sect and cultic groups, and it produced a dynamic atmosphere conducive to the rise of new religious bodies. For example, revivalism helped pave the way for Spiritualism, the Shakers and Mormonism. As Bruce Shelley notes, revivalism was preaching aimed at individuals with the intent of bringing about instantaneous, conscious conversion. Individuals were confronted with God's fearful "judgment upon their sins of indifference, infidelity, and immorality" and were infused with an overwhelming sense of guilt. "Sin and hell were painted in vivid tones, producing fear and dread in the minds of the listener." The preacher then pointed sinners to God's forgiveness and urged them to repent of their sins and be "born again" by God's Word.[18]

The revivalistic movements of the early nineteenth century met rigid resistance from conservative clergy, who opposed their methods more than their theology. Nonetheless, revivalism's sweep across the country buried the opposition. By 1860, all major Protestant denominations had accepted in varying degrees the spirit and doctrines of evangelical Christianity. Many people believed that revivalism, or "a state of continuous awakening," was and should be the standard condition of American Christian life. The nineteenth century began with the frontier revivals and ended with great urban campaigns for souls led by Dwight L. Moody. During these years, revivalism was not merely a type of Christianity in America; it became the standard expression of Christianity in America. By the first half of the century, a new religious consensus had arisen. Evangelical Calvinism had been transformed into a practical, if not always theological, evangelical Arminianism with emphasis on human free will. Along with the other major religious reorientations in American history, this one produced fanatical fringe sects.[19]

Religious Pluralism

American society between 1820 and 1870, as Russel Nye indicates, was a "disputatious, competitive, and individualistic society, changing and expanding," and subject to a number of inner tensions. Religion, a very important part of that society, reflected similar developments and characteristics. Intense debates over doctrine, revivalistic methods and slavery divided Christians. Since religion was disestablished, there was no way by law for churches to impose uniformity on their members. Church life depended on the voluntary support of a committed laity. Thus Americans had to try to find principles or positions that would draw wide support. When this failed, "dissenters broke off to form new sects or split the old ones; in other cases, where by compromise or reorganization churches avoided division, there was still change."[20]

Religious diversity was on the increase during the nineteenth century. Yet this development should not be overstated. The new sectarian bodies formed through the frequent religious divisions were for the most part Protestant. As Martin Marty indicates, church-state disestablishment "did not mean loss of dominance by already dominant groups and did not prevent a kind of reestablishment of religion in the mores, ethos, or customs." Indeed, a de facto Protestant establishment existed into the twentieth century. "For a hundred years or more, Americans made little of pluralism." Early national America had primarily a "Protestant pluralism"—a variety of Protestant groups. Catholics, Continental Protestants and later Eastern Orthodox and Jewish people experienced prejudice despite the law's protection.[21]

Nevertheless, the years before the Civil War witnessed cracks in this Protestant empire. Exceptions to Protestant dominance did exist, and they shall be the focus of this study of religion during the antebellum period. Catholicism presented the greatest threat to Protestant spiritual dominance. Millions of Catholics poured into America with the Irish and German migrations of the 1840s and 1850s. Universalists and Unitarians had been visible in America since the eighteenth century. Many of the Founding Fathers were acknowledged Freemasons, and would be claimed in later decades as early leaders of American Rosicrucianism. Transcendentalism and many commune movements advocated some radical ideas. The esoteric views of Emanuel Swedenborg attracted some followers.[22]

Other new religious movements came on the scene. In an age when the sensational attracted people, there was an enormous interest in Spiritualism and many food and health cults. There also existed a surge of concern for specific dates for the coming millennium, leading to the Millerite movement and eventually to the Seventh-day Adventists. Mormonism was a new religion that emerged during the antebellum period, one that would become world-famous and successful. Though Protestant and revivalistic, the several antidenominational "restorationist" movements that arose in the pre-Civil War era must be regarded as innovative and distinct. Some of these groups that stood outside the Protestant establishment were short-lived. Others, however, endured well beyond the pre-Civil War years, some even to the present.[23]

4

Early
Metaphysical & Occult
Movements

T he pre- and post-Civil War years are not good lines of demarcation
for metaphysical and occult activities, for these practices and beliefs
maintained a line of continuity throughout the nineteenth century
and formed the basis for similar developments in the later part of the twentieth century. Occult and metaphysical activities have something of a life of
their own. To be sure, they reflect American culture and the wider social
influences, but because they represent something of a religious sideshow or
"alternative reality," they are not subject to cultural gyrations as much as
some Christian sectarian groups and even mainstream denominations have
been. Consequently, in this section I will focus only on the groups that either
began or became prominent during the antebellum period: Transcendentalism and Spiritualism.

When defined in the context of metaphysical movements, the term *metaphysics* has a different meaning than it does as a division of philosophy.
As a movement, it stands for the deeper realities of the universe, the practical application of that absolute Truth of Being in daily affairs. It is a
practical type of philosophy considered to be both scientific and religious.
Transcendentalism is usually regarded as a forerunner of the metaphysical
movements. The term *metaphysics* was first used in the mid-nineteenth
century to describe the New Thought movement, which developed from the
experiences and philosophy of Phineas P. Quimby. The term is also applied
to kindred organizations such as the Church of Divine Science, the Church

of Religious Science and the Unity School of Christianity, and to groups whose goals differed from those of New Thought such as the Spiritualists, the Theosophists and later proliferations.[1]

J. Stillson Judah believes that the metaphysical movements form one side of the nation's cultural profile and that most of them shared fifteen pervasive characteristics. First, "as allies of the Transcendentalists, the 'metaphysicians' revolted against the creedal authority of organized Protestant churches" and sought a new level of individual freedom. Second, nearly all adherents of the metaphysical movements "became united in the central belief that the inner, or real, self of humanity is divine." Each individual has his or her "spark of divinity." Therefore, they rejected the Christian belief that human beings are created in God's image but do not share his divine nature.[2]

Next, these metaphysicians did not generally want "to be considered as theists." Instead, most of them embraced the "concept of an impersonal God, a God of science, often called by such names as Christ Principle, and Infinite Principle." Fourth, the majority of these groups viewed God as being related to humanity and the world "in a quasi-gnostic or dualistic manner." Such obvious dualism, however, usually gave way to a monistic view of a God who encompasses all reality. They believed that God is completely immanent, rejecting the Christian emphasis upon divine transcendence. Consequently, some metaphysical bodies arrived at a type of humanism in which human beings become masters of their own fate.[3]

Fifth, metaphysical groups differed over their relationship to Christianity—some regarded themselves as Christian, while others did not. In varying degrees all embraced the moral teachings of Jesus, but in their thought they separated Jesus the man "from the Christ or Christ Principle," which they believed is united with God and is every individual's inner nature. Six, these movements rejected the traditional Christian position that every human being is a sinner, "standing under God's judgment and in need of repentance and forgiveness." Accordingly, the Christian doctrines of grace and atonement were irrelevant and thus generally absent. Seventh, the metaphysics regarded God "as all good, so that evil, including sickness, is considered to be unreal or the absence of good."[4]

An eighth characteristic was pragmatism. All metaphysical philosophies focused less on belief than on testing principles by experience. Ninth, metaphysical leaders tended to place "their emphasis upon self-realization,

knowledge, or spiritual science instead of upon faith or works." Tenth, all
the metaphysical movements sought scientific verification for their claims
and religious experiences. Such evidence would be proof that their philosophy brought meaning to life. In this approach, the metaphysical groups
were like most fringe religions in the nineteenth century. Eleventh, like Zen
Buddhism and Yoga, "most metaphysical groups offer a psychological approach to reality." Therefore, they increasingly presented a kind of "monistic, religious psychotherapy for self-fulfillment" and improved health to the
American upper-middle class.[5]

Twelfth, the metaphysical movements tended to be optimistic, focusing
on God's love and human goodness. They believed in universal personal
immortality through continual progression in the heavenly worlds or
through reincarnation. Thirteenth, some metaphysical groups promoted the
acquisition of material things, believing that God freely gives to all who
follow his laws. In this, a degree of hedonism has been fostered among some
groups. Fourteenth, most metaphysical bodies believed in the "inner meaning of words beyond their dictionary definition—a meaning that cannot be
discovered empirically" but must be revealed intuitively. This approach is
known by several terms, "such as the spiritual, metaphysical, or occult
interpretation." Finally, all metaphysical movements placed an emphasis on
healing through the spirit or mind.[6]

The major concepts in the nineteenth-century metaphysical movements
bear a strong resemblance to those of many occult and metaphysical groups
in the late twentieth century. In fact, they contained the working principles
of the modern-day occult and metaphysical movements. As indicated earlier, the old occult based on witchcraft and astrology went into a decline
in the eighteenth century, only to be revived in a new form among educated
people in the nineteenth century. The basis for this new occultism and its
metaphysical counterpart was established by the renowned American
Transcendentalists.[7]

Transcendentalism

The nineteenth-century occult and metaphysical movements had many
roots. Transcendentalism, with its facets of Neoplatonic, Eastern and Swedenborgian philosophy, contributed to the broad spectrum of metaphysical
movements. So did the occult philosophy that flourished in eighteenth- and
nineteenth-century France, with its smatterings of Neoplatonic and quasi-

gnostic ideas joined to cabalistic, astrological and Hermetic philosophy. The spirit of freedom that abounded in nineteenth-century America expressed itself in the individualism of the new religious movements, including the occult and metaphysical groups. This freedom often expressed itself in new divine revelations to select individuals, who in turn began new religious movements.[8]

The ideas of a monistic, mechanistic, impersonal deity drew on several eighteenth-century sources, including Newtonian science and aspects of Jonathan Edwards's philosophy with its Calvinism excised. The God of these metaphysical movements has been regarded as a utilitarian deity who grants desires according to his spiritual laws. A similar pragmatism and optimism also could be found in American orthodox Christianity. The early metaphysical leaders placed great emphasis on intuitive religious experience as the way to truth, a trend that bore resemblance to the revivalistic atmosphere of the nineteenth century.[9]

During the second quarter of the nineteenth century, New England Transcendentalism played an important role in the awakening of the American spirit. The Transcendentalists, by means of their sublime mysticism, envisioned direct contact between the individual soul and its Creator. Western itinerant evangelists demanded that their converts make a similar contact. Transcendentalism is difficult to define. Lacking a definite creed, Transcendentalism was at once a mystical religion, a faith, a philosophy and an ethical way of life. In general, it emphasized the spiritual over the material.[10]

According to Catherine Albanese, Transcendentalism arose "at the radical fringe of Unitarian liberal Christianity." Most Transcendentalists were from Boston and educated at Harvard. Many were also ministers. Beginning in 1836, they met in a loosely structured group for discussion about philosophical, literary and religious issues. Their leader was Ralph Waldo Emerson (1803-82), who in 1836 published a book called *Nature,* giving "the Transcendental movement its gospel." Central to this book was "a new form of the ancient theory of correspondence." The Transcendentalists looked to nature to teach them spiritual truths. By a study of nature they believed they could "uncover the secrets of their inner selves and a corresponding knowledge of divine things." Other prominent Transcendentalist figures include Henry David Thoreau (1817-62), Margaret Fuller (1810-50) and Theodore Parker (1810-60).[11]

An issue that concerned most Transcendentalists was the Oversoul. Their interest in the great World Soul of the Neoplatonists, to which individuals were bound, took them in an unusual direction. Despite being "conservative" in many ways—that is, economically prosperous and Federalist in politics—the Transcendentalists experimented with nontraditional ways of living, sometimes in communes. Whether in communes or not, the Transcendentalists moved down the road toward saving knowledge, a journey in which each person must turn within and develop the qualities necessary for harmony with self and universe.[12]

In forming this new teaching, the Transcendentalists, like many with occult and metaphysical interests, were eclectic. As Albanese says, "they mixed together elements from Oriental sources, from Neoplatonic philosophy, from European Romantic writers, and from the metaphysical system of Emanuel Swedenborg." The Transcendentalists borrowed the Hindu idea that the "world, God, and human beings all participated in one substance and that, beyond the illusion of matter, lay the reality of spirit." From Neoplatonism they acquired a similar teaching about humanity's unity with Oversoul, in which every soul has its being. The Transcendentalists joined the European Romantics in "the revolt against the Enlightenment, which had exalted reason and law." Therefore, the Transcendentalists desired to escape the Unitarian church and "to find religion in the unstructured freedom of nature and the inner self."[13]

Transcendentalism's impact on groups and individuals outside the religious mainstream in America has been significant. It was the forerunner to several nineteenth-century occult and metaphysical movements, such as New Thought and Christian Science. Less obvious but significantly, Transcendentalism represented the first serious endeavor in American history to retain the spiritual experience of the Christian faith without the substance of its belief. Transcendentalism claimed a basic innocence for humankind, substituted a direct intuition of God or truth for any form of revelation and foresaw a future of indefinite but certain glory for humanity. In doing so, the Transcendentalists encouraged the rise of many romantic notions about nature—notions that have become an essential part of the American experience over the last century or so. Also, according to Robert Ellwood, because of the impeccable intellectual credentials of its principal thinkers, Transcendentalism has done more than any other force to legitimate the many varieties of alternative spiritualities in America.[14]

Spiritualism

The breathtaking changes of the nineteenth century helped to produce many occult and metaphysical movements in America. Only a few can be mentioned here; the most prominent one prior to the Civil War was Spiritualism.[15] While the beginnings of organized Spiritualism are usually traced to the rappings heard by the Fox sisters in 1848 in Hydesville, New York, communication with the dead is a phenomenon found in many cultures since ancient times. The Old Testament records the incident of the "witch" or, more accurately, the "medium" of Endor. Trance-speaking people, believed to be possessed by demons rather than by spirits of the dead, have been common within Western civilization. Of course, throughout history many people have believed in haunted houses and poltergeists (spirits that allegedly play pranks on people). The first séance—that is, a "sitting" with a medium through whom the spirits reveal themselves—occurred at least as early as 1762.[16]

Modern Spiritualism owes much of its initial vigor to Franz Mesmer and his French successors. The immediate prototype of the modern séance can be traced to Mesmer. At his séances people hoped to be magnetized—hypnotized and cured of their illnesses—as they sat around a tub, each holding onto the hand of the next person as well as onto a rod extending from the tub. Introduced from France in 1836 and often called animal magnetism, mesmerism was believed to depend on the magnetic transference of a universal fluid from one individual to another. While mesmerism figured in the growth of several other occult and metaphysical movements, it demonstrated trance states similar to those in which contact with the spirits was likely to happen.[17]

Andrew Jackson Davis (1826-1910), whose writings would provide a theoretical grounding for Spiritualism, came into contact with mesmerism. He claimed to have made contacts with the spirits of Galen, a famous doctor from antiquity, and Emanuel Swedenborg. Davis saw the world as one of eternal progress, with spirits on various planes, closer to or farther from the earth. Thus contact with spirits, especially spirits close to the earth plane, seemed a realistic possibility to Davis.[18]

There were other forerunners of Spiritualism in America. Swedenborg, of course, deeply influenced several occult and metaphysical groups, including Spiritualism. Transcendentalism also had a widespread impact on the alternative-reality tradition in the nineteenth century. To a large extent, the

Spiritualists derived their attitude toward the supernatural from the Transcendentalists.[19] In their religious exercises and ecstatic dances, the Shakers often had been visited by spirit beings from the world beyond, including William Penn, George Washington, American Indians and Chinese. John Chapman (1774-1847), better known as Johnny Appleseed, distributed Swedenborgian literature, thus introducing to many individuals the occult tradition that would provide Spiritualists with an explanation for ultimate things, including activities in the spirit world.[20]

Modern Spiritualism began in 1848. Interest in it rose sharply during the 1850s and declined during the Civil War years. After the Civil War Spiritualism experienced a recovery, fed by the wish of many people to communicate with those who had perished during the war. Many Americans were caught up in a Spiritualist craze, often using a modified Ouija board called a planchette. This recovery continued until the late 1870s. Though the declared number of Spiritualists did not significantly decline in the late nineteenth century, their inflated claims to religious and even scientific legitimacy came to be taken less seriously throughout the larger society.[21] The first permanent national organization, the National Spiritualist Association, was not established until 1893, well after the period when Spiritualism had attracted the most public attention. Since then Spiritualism has experienced many schisms and the formation of new Spiritualist bodies.

Though Spiritualists are generally a tolerant lot, they have divided primarily over two points of contention: the doctrine of reincarnation and the question of whether they should be considered Christian. Reincarnation, being easily linked to communication with dead spirits, spread rapidly in Spiritualist circles. The National Spiritualist Association rejected belief in reincarnation and attempted to curb it, with many schisms coming as a result. Davis, the most prominent spokesman for the early Spiritualists, denied Christianity, even in its most liberal form, preferring the authority of his own revelations to that of Scripture. The National Spiritualist Association took a similar stand. However, some mediums claimed to be Christian and interpreted many of the miracles found in Scripture as psychic events of Spiritualism. Spiritualist organizations continued to divide over such disputes even into the post-World War II era.[22]

Spiritualism as a definite religious movement was a product of the nineteenth century, reflecting many of the cultural trends of that era. The many people who went to séances believed that communication with the spirits of the dead was possible with help from human mediums. Many of the individuals who attended were elderly and even prominent people who were mourning the death of a loved one. Most of the mediums were women. To the many who became involved in it, Spiritualism offered a legitimate approach to religion in the new age. During a time when the ancient truths of religion were being called into question, Spiritualism gave empirical evidence, a demonstration that could be seen and heard, that people lived on in a world beyond this one. At a time when science was gaining strength, Spiritualism, along with some other nontraditional religions, tried to emulate the scientific method; more important, it often copied scientific language. Specifically, Spiritualism utilized an occult form of scientific language to explain strange occurrences—the materialization of spirits and appearance of strange objects at séances. Spiritualists opened their meetings to objective investigators who would verify the reality of the apparitions and communications. Actually, Spiritualism sought a fusion of science and religion, not unlike that which had existed in the occult tradition prior to the scientific revolution.[23]

Spiritualism also mirrored nonscientific aspects of nineteenth-century culture. It began in the "Burned-Over District," the region in Upstate New York that had experienced an overabundance of revivals during the first decades of the century. After these awakenings had exhausted themselves, other alternatives moved in to fill the gap. The revivals helped pave the way for Spiritualism. For example, phenomena evidenced in the revival services, such as strange, rapturous speech, made the trance process in mediumship appear less unusual. Spiritualism also owed aspects of its anticlericalism and antidenominationalism to the revivals. Spiritualists' camps inevitably caught the contagion of religious excitement that the revivals spread through antebellum America. Closely associated with the revivals was the frontier spirit. The person on the frontier was an individualist, unfettered by traditional beliefs and prone to unorthodox ideas.[24]

Other nonscientific aspects of American culture had an impact. Spiritualism fell under the influence of the notions of perfectionism that abounded during this time. Perfectionism, as I have noted, impacted many of the social reform movements of the age. Like evangelical Protestantism, though for different reasons, Spiritualism appealed to many of the advocates of reform during the pre-Civil War years.

The Romantic spirit abounded at this time. People often viewed formal religious institutions with impatience and sought inner authority by means of direct experiences of contact with spirits. They understood these contacts to be with the outer perimeters of the natural world, beyond the boundaries set by mainstream religious organizations. Such tendencies fed naturally into Spiritualism. Like the Transcendentalists, the Spiritualists regarded the world as one and taught that there were close connections between the spiritual and material realms, though the spirit world was higher and more important.[25]

Over the course of time, Spiritualism underwent some development. According to Catherine Albanese, "two kinds of mediumship grew up—mental and physical." Mental mediumship concerns psychic happenings when the medium reaches a trance state—that is, a condition when his or her mind ceases to function and a controlling spirit takes its place. By the twentieth century, psychic practices had acquired standard forms. The medium might respond to questions written on small pieces of paper and submitted to a spirit. Another option was for the medium to practice psychometry—that is, get "in touch with the vibrations of a physical object" so he or she could learn "about the people (now dead) who had touched it in the past." Another method available to the medium was to prophesy by reading auras, bands of light emanating from every human being. Auras supposedly record an individual's life history, thus "enabling a spirit to make predictions."[26]

Physical mediumship involves spirits' taking on a material form at a séance so that they can be heard, seen and perhaps felt. The rappings at Hydesville were an early example of this. As time went on, physical manifestations became more elaborate. At séances spirits overturned tables and sent objects flying. "In automatic writing, spirits used the hand of the medium to write their message," and in a related method, independent writing, they wrote on paper without any physical guidance. At other times, spirits made an object disappear in one place only to rematerialize it in another. By the twentieth century, "an elaborate system had been worked out utilizing spirit guides," called Spirit Doctors, to give advice on spiritual subjects. Sometimes mediums even developed healing gifts.[27]

Interest in Spiritualism rose as this phenomenon became associated with aspects of nineteenth-century American culture, but it declined when this linkage weakened after the 1870s. Spiritualism's attempt to present itself as a rational religion did not quite succeed. Despite twenty years of activity, it had failed to gain the scientific credentials it sought. With the end of the crusade against slavery, the force of the social reform movement diminished in the postbellum period. Spiritualism also began to lose credibility as a reform movement. In the twentieth century, Spiritualism is characterized by social indifference. Frauds and scandals also dealt serious blows to Spiritualism. The public found they had been tricked in several cases, and they did not like it. Spiritualism had made impressive gains during its peak years, but it could not establish a coherent organization, and this created many problems. One immediate result was that Spiritualism could not police its frauds.[28]

5

Religious
Communalism

C ommunal social orders are but an aspect of the sectarian impulse
that has flowed through religious history. Separation is basic to the
nature of a sectarian group. All religious sects have been called out
of the world in one way or another, but not all of these bodies have adopted
a communal style of organization.

What made the nineteenth-century American communitarians different
from other sectarians was not so much a contrast in structural principles
(e.g., myth, leader, ethics, ritual) as the extreme to which the communitarians implemented these principles. Catherine Albanese says that the most
important difference resides in their adoption of a communal lifestyle, by
which "they challenged the two great principles of social independence—
private property and sexual exclusivity in the family."[1] Also, many of these
groups adhered to some doctrines or practices that were either unorthodox
or quite bizarre and thus could be labeled as cultic. My study will focus on
these groups, especially the Shakers, the Oneida Perfectionists and the Universal Friend. In one way or another these groups advocated an unusual
sexual orientation or pushed the doctrines of perfectionism, socialism and
millennialism to extremes.

Communal groups existed in earlier European history. The monastic
orders were communal. Yet these orders served the interests of the wider
church community, whereas the nineteenth-century bodies existed to attend
to the interests of their own members. Some groups in the Radical Refor-

mation, especially the Hutterites, lived in religious communes. In America, necessity pushed the Pilgrims into such a pattern for a time. The German sects, including the Mennonites, often gravitated toward such a social system, and some openly adopted it. The early nineteenth century brought a resurgence of this communitarian impulse, manifesting itself in the most diverse ways among both anticlerical freethinkers and Christian enthusiasts.[2]

Historically, the greatest wave of community-building in America occurred in the 1840s; another such wave developed in the late 1960s and early 1970s. According to Rosabeth Moss Kanter, "three kinds of critiques of society have provided the initial impulse for the utopian search: religious, politico-economic, and psychosocial." The religious category can be subdivided. Beyond the clearly religious bodies, there existed utopian groups that had religious origins but had strayed from this original motivation.[3]

There were three discernible stages of community-building. The earliest American communitarians began with the desire to live according to spiritual and religious values, rejecting the sinfulness of the established order. The next major utopian critique of established institutions was politicoeconomic, emerging with the increasing dislocation and poverty that developed in the wake of the Industrial Revolution. People sought the small socialist community as a refuge from the evils of the factory system. In the latter half of the twentieth century most communes were based on a third motivation, the psychosocial critique, which "revolves around the alienation and loneliness of modern society." Individuals joined communes in order to get in touch with their fellow humans and end their isolation. These three impulses more or less match up with the three historical waves of American utopian communities: "the first lasted from early days to about 1845," when religious themes prevailed; "the second, stressing economic and political issues, ran from 1820 to 1930," flourishing in the 1840s; and "the third, the psychosocial period, emerged after World War II" and became important especially in the 1960s.[4]

The religious communes, or at least those originating from religious impulses, are the concern at this point. Though these groups were diverse, most evidence some general characteristics. Many of these American bodies had their roots in European separatist and pietist sects, who sought a haven from persecution by the dominant churches and a place where they could build their own communities according to their own beliefs. Even among

73

the sects that had originated in Europe, however, most members were refugees from other American sectarian or revivalist bodies. Backsliding, apostasy and schisms were problems faced by most newly formed religious bodies. Many believed that isolation and segregation into unitary communities would be an effective way to counter such tendencies. Convinced that they had discovered a unique and exclusive way to salvation and for alleviating the world's problems, many sectarians desired to build new homes far from the contaminating influence of the older faiths and modern civilization. To both Europeans and Americans, the frontier provided land, livelihood and solitude for such religious experiments.[5]

For these communal groups, spiritual ideals were paramount. At times they adopted communalism only because of economic necessity, in order to permit the community to retreat to its own territory to live and practice its religion together. Yet even where communalism was chosen out of necessity, it often became an end in itself, something for which religious sanctions were established. The sect leaders soon discovered that it made the group's separation more complete and that it definitely improved their ability to control the lives of their members. In addition to the religious benefits, there were some decided economic advantages to a planned economy of cooperative enterprise. If well managed, these religious enterprises often became prosperous. Many members prized this economic security more than they did their independence and opportunity for individual gain.[6]

These communal bodies shared some other traits. Frequently these groups united around a single charismatic individual who provided direct access to a deity. The path to perfection was embodied in his or her presence. Most of the early communal sects were pietistic, basing their faith on a literal interpretation of the Bible. They took as their model the early Christian church, with its emphasis on a community of believers possessing all things in common. They emphasized their separateness, rejecting the dogmas and hierarchies of the dominant churches.[7]

Whatever their national origins, these communal bodies grew up on American soil and reflected American culture. The perfectionism so prevalent in antebellum America found its way into the communal sects. Even if they did not believe that society could be perfected, they endeavored to build for themselves a perfect or ideal way of life in their cloistered communities. To a large extent, most of these groups were millennialists. In one form or another, they placed considerable emphasis on the return of Christ.

Moreover, some communalists were openly spiritualistic, and most of them had confidence in miracles. Most communal bodies were similar in that their membership consisted largely of poor, ill-educated, trusting people who were obedient to autocratic leaders. Exceptions to these generalizations were the communities whose major objectives were social and only marginally religious. Experiments such as Bronson Alcott's Fruitlands, John Humphrey Noyes's Oneida Community and the Transcendentalists can be seen as part of the transition from religious to socialistic communalism.[8]

The Shakers

If the Mormons are not classified as a communitarian movement, the United Society of Believers in Christ's Second Coming, better known as the Shakers, were America's most successful and enduring communal group. At any rate, they were probably the most interesting. The Shakers migrated from England, where they had had connections with the so-called Shaking Quakers. Ann Lee Stanley (1736-84) was the group's founding spirit. She migrated with eight followers to America in 1774. Upon arrival, poverty forced the little group to disband for two years. However, in 1776 the Shakers reconvened near Albany, New York, where economic problems prompted them to organize into a socialistic Christian community, although such a social structure previously had not been part of their beliefs.[9]

Until 1779 the Shakers had no evangelistic outreach. Then came an event that would establish their pattern of growth during the nineteenth century. In a revival some "New Light" Baptists were spiritually moved but not entirely satisfied. They visited the Shakers and were converted. Thereafter Shakers began a concerted outreach into communities where revivals previously had occurred. To those who had been converted but needed direction and meaning in their lives, the Shakers provided the answer—they were to leave the world and join the true millennial church. In 1784 Mother Ann died, but capable leaders replaced her. They continued to make deep inroads in revivalist groups, especially the Freewill Baptists. The real yield, however, came when the Second Great Awakening created ideal spiritual conditions in both the West and New England. Between 1830 and 1850, the period of its greatest size and vitality, the church consisted of about six thousand persons living in nineteen communities.[10]

Many of the doctrines prevalent in revivalistic circles were part of the Shaker beliefs. Nevertheless, they articulated some unique teachings. Mother Ann believed that God is a dual personality, that the masculine side of that personality had been made visible in Christ, and that in her lifetime a second incarnation of the Holy Spirit had appeared—the feminine element of God, which continued the work done by Christ. Like the Mormons and Christian Scientists, the Shakers taught that God was a Father-Mother deity, a bisexual being. They considered Christ to be a spirit, appearing first in a masculine form in Christ and then much latter in Mother Ann. The Shakers said that this bisexuality is reflected throughout nature, even in the angels and in Adam.[11]

The Shakers maintained beliefs common to other marginal religions in the nineteenth century, but their emphasis on bisexuality gave such doctrines a distinctive twist. The Shakers were a millennial church. But for them, the Second Coming of Christ had already occurred, being consummated through Ann Lee, who was the feminine incarnation of God. They believed that the millennium was at hand and they were the vanguard or intercessory remnant whose prayers and example would direct all humankind into a state of sanctity and happiness. Their mission was to gather in the elect, who could achieve perfection and salvation by denying the flesh. They were universalists, believing that God would punish the wicked only for a season and then bring a final salvation for all humanity. Perfectionism was an integral part of Shaker doctrine. In the moral demands they placed upon their remnant they were legal perfectionists, emphasizing twelve classic virtues including celibacy.[12]

The roots of the Shaker doctrine of celibacy go back to Ann Lee's sufferings in childbirth. She became convinced that sin had begun with Adam and Eve's sex act in the Garden of Eden, and that ever since then sexual relations had been the root of all of sin. Men and women could achieve salvation only by overcoming their fleshly desires. The Shakers felt that they alone, among the world's peoples, were carrying out God's will. If this Shaker dogma prevailed, the human race would be eliminated; but such a possibility presented no problem for the Shakers, for they believed that since the millennium was at hand there was no real reason for the continuance of humankind. In addition to this important doctrine, the Shakers were the first Spiritualists, communicating with the departed. For a decade or so after 1837, public séances were a very important part of their corporate life. They also expounded the Christian duty of pacifism and, as Mary Baker Eddy would later teach, the power of the spirit over physical disease.[13]

As Albanese points out, the religious beliefs of Ann Lee's followers received their strongest expression in the Shaker ritual. Beginning "in the ecstatic and uncontrollable physical movements of the Shaking Quakers," the Shaker dance became a communal dramatization. If God was a dual person, represented by Jesus Christ and Ann Lee respectively, "then the formal dance of the male and female members of the community revealed that they were members all of one body," reflecting the divine community. Similarly, if the millennium was soon to begin, "or had already begun in the coming of Ann Lee," then the Shaker dance enacted the story of the millennium. In the dance, barriers between this world and the next came down, and the Shakers experienced the rhythms that would "govern the millennial kingdom." As the Shaker dancers continued their stylized movements late into the night, they experienced such ecstasy that they experienced a mystical union with one another in God and Mother Ann.[14]

In social and economic organization the Shakers resembled many other communal groups. Though individual Shakers were commanded to be humble, the society became both arrogant and exclusive, largely because the Shaker Church considered itself to be the sole agency of salvation. Comfortable in the belief that they were among the chosen few, individual Shakers submitted to a form of church autocracy that facilitated the close communal life required by their faith. Individuals submitted their desires to the good of the community, and decision-making belonged to a small group in the Shaker hierarchy. Ultimate authority in the Shaker Society resided in the ministry of the church at Mt. Lebanon, New York, which was self-perpetuating with one elder (male or female) as its head. The Shaker way of life was not democratic. However, the Shakers' recognition of the duality of life and the equality of the sexes became evident in the fact that each ministry consisted of the same number of each sex. Economic communalism grew naturally out of the Shaker religious philosophy. They reasoned that in order to practice celibacy, they had to live apart from the world. And to live apart successfully, it was necessary to abolish private property. They exalted manual labor, worked hard and developed some highly valued skills. The peak of Shaker prosperity came in 1830-60, the years in which their numbers also were the greatest.[15]

William Kephart describes the decline of the Shakers. They peaked about the time of the Civil War. Thereafter, membership declined—at first slowly, then more rapidly. By the turn of the century, entire Shaker communities were collapsing. By 1925, most of the remaining groups had disintegrated, and by 1950 only a few hardy souls remained. Many factors prompted this decline. Even before the Civil War, the American economy was in a state of change. The old handicraft system, which had allowed the Shakers to flourish, was being replaced by the factory system. The Shakers could not compete with the assembly line. With the coming of the automobile, separation broke down and isolation had run its course. Church leadership declined, and there was economic mismanagement. Celibacy was part of the problem. The celibate orders in Catholicism represent only a small percent of the church's membership. But with the Shakers "the entire organization was involved, and when the rate of conversions declined, the end was just a matter of time." Finally, over the decades they lost a certain vitality of spirit. The economic and worldly considerations of communalism became predominant.[16]

Oneida Perfectionists

The Oneida Community, founded by John Humphrey Noyes (1811-86), was a very successful and widely publicized communitarian experiment with evangelical roots. Noyes is an example of how a Christian radical can be created in the excitement of an evangelical revival. Noyes came from an upper-class family in Vermont; after a spiritual experience at a revival, he became involved in religious and social activities. The doctrine of perfectionism, that human beings could be without sin, propelled his activity. The belief in human perfectibility was not new with Noyes, but he established the first sect with such a belief as its major tenet. Moreover, he gave this doctrine some radical twists that were unacceptable to even the evangelical revivalists, let alone the larger society. He claimed that with conversion came a complete release from sin, and he believed himself to be morally perfect.[17]

Noyes linked perfectionism with the optimism, socialism and millennialism of the age. The basis of his perfectionism resided in his postulation that Christ's Second Coming had occurred in A.D. 70. Thus, liberation or redemption from sin was an accomplished fact for followers of Jesus, who were perfect beings. Noyes studied the teachings of contemporary socialists and the religious and economic activities of the Shakers and Brook Farm. He firmly believed that socialism without religion was unworkable, but that combined with perfectionism it could not fail. He came to view socialism as the means by which Christian love would bring in the kingdom of heaven on earth.[18]

Both personal experiences and religious convictions served to make Noyes doubt the morality of ordinary family relationships. Because four of his children were stillborn and his wife suffered greatly in childbirth, Noyes came to question both the justice of man's domination over woman and the nature of sexual intercourse. Furthermore, because Christ indicated there would be no marriage in heaven, there must be something wrong with the ordinary institution of marriage. Moreover, Noyes believed that the traditional family relationship bred injustice, competition and dissension. Thus family life must be reconciled with Christian socialism through a new type of "marriage system."[19]

This new marriage arrangement was based on the twin practices of male continence and complex marriage. Male continence was a system of birth control, based on self-control, in which men would refrain from ejaculation until the completion of their sexual activity. Male continence in turn made possible complex marriage, a form of communal marriage in which every male was husband to every woman in the community and every female was wife to every man. Thus, the only requirement for sexual relations was a mutual agreement between members. Behind this appearance of sexual license resided an asceticism: any exclusive relationship, or "special love," between any two members of the community was prohibited. The Oneida Community perceived that in the outside world sexual relationships had become a source of divisiveness, preventing members of Christ's community from loving one another. In their society, complex marriage would allow sex to become a bond of community that mirrored the heavenly unity.[20]

These thoughts received concrete expression in the communities Noyes established, first at Putney, Vermont (1840-47), and more significantly at Oneida, New York (1848-79). In Putney the community's neighbors, who could not accept Noyes's ideas on marriage and sex, forced him to leave for Oneida; there the perfectionists enjoyed their best years. The Oneida community had firm rules and discipline, but no despotism existed. The members worked hard and prospered, but they practiced no rigorous asceticism; they ate well and enjoyed pleasures such as cultural productions. In general, the members were a contented lot. The twin pillars of complex marriage and communism of property diffused some powerful human drives—sexual passion and economic ambition—and thus removed key sources of anxiety. Furthermore, in monastic fashion members of the Oneida community engaged in the regular practice of mutual criticism. In this activity, the erring individual was given criticism, advice and encouragement by the entire community or a select committee. These moral and emotional purges proved so successful that for the Oneidans they became a treatment for illness, which they regarded as having spiritual origins.[21]

Despite the prosperity and success of the Oneida communal experiment, it came to an abrupt end. The Oneidans' numbers did not decline. But their attacks on the monogamous family brought great external criticism, and internal problems brought the community's demise. The Oneida group moved steadily toward secular communitarianism, and acute internal discord destroyed its sense of community, the very backbone of its existence.[22]

Universal Friend
Originating in the "Burned-Over District" of New York, the Society of the Public Universal Friend was the earliest indigenous American communitarian movement. This group so closely resembled the Shakers in its origins and major beliefs that contemporaries believed a deliberate imitation had taken place. Nevertheless, from the beginning the two movements were quite separate. Jemima Wilkinson (1752-1819), the daughter of a prosperous Quaker farmer in Rhode Island, founded this group. Unusual circumstances surrounded the beginnings of the Universal Friend. At eighteen Wilkinson reportedly died of the plague. Her body grew cold but then warmed up, and she began to speak. The voice coming from her claimed that Jemima Wilkinson had indeed "left the world of time," and that now her body would function as a vehicle for the Spirit of Life from God, which came to be known as "The Publick Universal Friend."[23]

For over forty years "The Friend" operated from within that body. During the first fourteen years she traveled primarily in the Northeastern states, where she won many converts. According to Robert Ellwood, her doctrine was generally orthodox, "save for a lack of respect for lawful marriage." She frequently persuaded her followers "to leave spouses who were not equally dedicated to 'The Friend.' " Gradually she came more and more to counsel complete chastity.[24]

Wilkinson's dramatic presence enabled her to attract many followers. Strikingly tall, with dark hair, passionate eyes and a lovely complexion, she wore a long white robe. Two associates, Sarah Richardson and James

80

Parker, usually accompanied her. Allegedly Richardson was the prophet Daniel, operating in the female line, while the spirit of Elijah spoke through Parker, who dressed in prophet's robes. At the public meetings of "The Friend" these individuals dropped to the ground in rapture, describing visions of heaven as the Spirit prompted them, and "The Friend" pleaded the love of God with a winning voice.[25]

"The Friend" had wealthy followers who lavished her with this world's goods, which she was not averse to displaying. In fact, by the end of her traveling ministry she rode around in an open coach shaped as an upturned half-moon, with seats of gold tapestry and panels engraved with the letters *UF*. Many of her followers regarded her as the returned Christ, a viewpoint she neither confirmed nor denied.[26]

In the early 1790s, "The Friend" ended her itinerant ministry and settled with many of her followers in the Finger Lake area of New York State. Here she and her followers reported frequent wonders, visions and exchanges with the world beyond time. But as time passed, dissensions and apostasy, especially in respect to celibacy and communal property, shook the community. Some supporters remained faithful until her death in 1819, which brought further disruption to the community. Some adherents who had believed her to be immortal were distraught, while others were disappointed by her failure to return in three days. Still, the organization remained intact until 1863, and some devotees continued by occult means to contact "The Friend" until near the end of the century.[27]

6

**Mormonism
& the
Christadelphians**

A ny story of fringe religions in the early nineteenth century should
not ignore the Mormons and Christadelphians. These two movements are not related and have little in common except their status
as alternative religions. From obscure beginnings, the Mormons have not
only survived but thrived, and are currently a large religious body. On the
other hand, the Christadelphians barely exist in America as a small fringe
religion. Though they began in America, the Christadelphians currently
have their greatest strength in Britain.

Both Mormons and Christadelphians teach doctrines that run counter to
orthodox Christianity. Beyond this, the specifics of their beliefs have little
in common. Thus, the Mormons and the Christadelphians have been placed
in the same chapter because they do not fit well into the other categories
of early-nineteenth-century fringe religions.

Mormonism
The Church of the Latter-day Saints, better known as the Mormons, is one
of the most important, successful nontraditional religions in American history. Still, it is a religious phenomenon that nearly defies classification.
Mormonism is the best-known product of the early-nineteenth-century impulse to form sectarian and communitarian bodies. In its early history,
Mormonism conformed to what is often characterized as a sect, though its
followers exhibited some cultlike behavior; it still manifests many of these

traits. Mormonism stood in opposition to the atomistic individualism of an American society that fostered competition and conflict. Instead, it promoted a utopian communitarian vision that challenged the political, economic and social values of early national America.[1]

The deep-seated changes brought about by economic adjustments, numerical growth, internal fighting, external hostilities and heroic deeds by leaders and rank and file alike make irrelevant the usual categories for explaining religious activity. It is difficult to determine whether Mormonism is a sect, a cult, a new religion, a denomination, a church, a people or an American subculture. In fact, at different times and in different places observers have seen the Latter-day Saints as all of these. For example, sociologists Rodney Stark and William Bainbridge say that Mormonism, being a deviant religious tradition, fits their definition of a cult. However, in Utah Mormonism is the dominant religion. Yet there are schismatic Mormon groups in Utah that other Mormons regard as sects. Still, Mormonism should be regarded as a new religion and not a Christian spinoff. While the Mormons maintain a number of beliefs that are rooted in the Christian tradition, they also have incorporated many distinct doctrines that stand outside the bounds of the Christian faith. Because of Mormonism's additional scriptures and unique beliefs, it must be seen as a movement that has never been part of historic Christianity.[2]

Few religious groups have had a more tumultuous and controversial history than the Mormons. The movement began in the 1820s in western New York State, an area known as the Burned-Over District because it had experienced numerous religious revivals. Never in American history has one geographical area witnessed so much religious fervor. The area was permeated by the rapid coming and going of new revelations, Bibles, preachers and prophets. The followers of William Miller declared that the end of the world was soon to come. The Shakers formed a nearby commune and rejected sex and marriage. New revelations prompted Jemima Wilkinson to build her colony of New Jerusalem. John Humphrey Noyes established a community at Oneida Creek. The modern Spiritualist movement began with the Fox sisters and their system of rappings. All this unusual religious activity occurred in western New York roughly between 1825 and 1850. In this area even the older denominations such as the Baptists, Methodists and Presbyterians were torn by dissent and schism.[3]

Into this religious turbulence came Joseph Smith (1805-44). He was born into less than promising circumstances. His father experienced several failures in farming. In 1816 the family moved to New York, where they were no more successful. The young Smith tried his hand at treasure-hunting and money-digging, where failure continued to dog him. In the early years, Smith and his family also engaged in a variety of occult activities, especially the use of divining rods, seer stones, ritual magic, astrology and talismans. In doing so Smith was reflecting the magical worldview so prevalent at this time. But Smith had a revolutionary experience: he was led by the angel Moroni to discover the Golden Plates, which contained a written testimony to the spiritual history of early America. Smith also claimed that he was directed to two stones, the Urim and Thummim, which enabled him to translate what came to be known as the Book of Mormon.[4]

Supplementing the Bible as sacred scripture, the Book of Mormon describes the lives of the "lost tribes of Israel" who migrated to America before the birth of Jesus. It covers the years from 600 B.C. to A.D. 421. According to the Book of Mormon, Jesus appeared to these people after the resurrection and established a church among them. And Smith claimed to be reviving this church. According to Smith, no other churches had divine authority; his authority came directly from God, and he was ordained by John the Baptist.

As Catherine Albanese notes, Joseph Smith and his followers saw their movement "not simply as a restoration of the primitive church," as the Radicals of the sixteenth century had hoped for, "but also as a restoration of the ten tribes of Israel." The Book of Mormon, therefore, "established the Hebraic origins of the American Indians and supplied America with a biblical past. Its revelation was cast as history, and the nature of Smith's inspiration shaped the character of the group which grew up around him." Time and history began to possess significance in their own right. Therefore, for early Mormonism deed and action became the essence of religion, and they expressed this religious insight in a number of ways.[5]

Furthermore, for the Mormons revelation was not a thing of the dead past. It lived on in the present because God continued to speak to the prophet Joseph Smith and his successors, even after the Book of Mormon had been translated. These extraordinary revelations usually occurred at times of crisis, when the young church particularly needed divine guidance. Indeed, as Ruth Tucker notes, the belief in continuing revelation is "one of the pivotal doctrines of the Mormon religion." Without this doctrine, Smith and later Mormon leaders would have lacked the authority needed to control the church and to institute changes in the church's doctrine and practices—changes that seemed to contradict the church's previous positions.[6]

Smith and his followers moved to Kirkland, Ohio, where an entire congregation joined them. From there they moved to Missouri, then to Nauvoo, Illinois, where they prospered but aroused their neighbors' animosity. Smith was killed by a mob in Illinois in 1844.

When Smith died, the church divided into several groups, two of which are particularly important. The largest group followed Brigham Young (1801-77) to Salt Lake City, Utah. There they tried to erect a theocracy—a religiopolitical state in which one ultimate set of authorities governed both secular and sacred affairs. These early theocracies made near-total demands on the saints. Upon entering the faith, each Mormon was required to surrender all goods to a bishop, who then would give back for use what each family needed. The need for an extensive irrigation system, which demanded the community's full commitment to make it work, gave a operational base both to communitarian ideas and to the authority of the church's leaders. Though the importance of polygamy to Mormonism has often been exaggerated, they openly practiced this doctrine in the Utah area from 1852 to 1890.[7]

The termination of polygamy in 1890 was one of the more traumatic upheavals to occur in Mormon history. Prompted by the Edmunds-Tucker Act, which gave the Mormons little choice, the church issued a manifesto banning polygamy. Many Mormons ignored the ban, so that divisions arose in the church. For the many who complied with the edict, the effect was devastating: husbands lost their wives, and women who were no longer wives lost their homes. Of perhaps greater significance, a central doctrine of Mormonism had been renounced. One of Mormonism's most distinctive features gradually faded into the past. After this time, the Mormons came more and more to identify with the America of Main Street.[8]

Central to Mormonism was the belief that the material world was sacred and ultimate. They did not regard God as the omnipotent and infinite creator of humanity and the universe. Rather, God was once a man, who later achieved divinity, as any human being can. He did not totally control the world, but was a God of time and space who did not impede human freedom and could not prevent evil. Individuals can become gods by successfully living through the testing period of mortality on earth. If they do well, each can become a god presiding over his or her own world: there are many worlds and many gods.[9]

In Mormon belief, God is the literal father of human souls. God is a polygamist who mates with female deities to produce an abundance of spirits or souls, who continue to exist in a spirit realm. In order for these souls to have an opportunity to become divine, they must become embodied—be born as human beings. Mormons regard it as a duty to have many children, in order to embody as many souls as possible. The practice of polygamy enabled even more souls to become embodied. Moreover, since it was possible for Mormons themselves to become "as gods," they were moving in the direction of a polytheism in which divinity, as a principle, would be embodied in many gods. In fact, polytheism is central to Mormon teaching, which asserts that the planets in the universe are each governed by a different god. The god of this planet is Elohim, and he had a wife who bore his offspring. Of course, these gods, which the Mormons became, continued to possess material bodies. Because of such a teaching, the human body held a privileged status. The Mormons regarded their bodies as temples and thus made prohibitions against the use of alcohol, tobacco and caffeine.[10]

In respect to reflecting American culture or being separationists, the Mormons have been paradoxical. According to Albanese, their history has embodied the tensions that exist between the manyness and oneness in religious bodies—that is, the dominant religion and the many minority groups. In their restoration of the gathered community and on religious action and righteous living, the Mormons resembled some sectarian groups of the Radical Reformation. Yet in other ways they did not reject the dominant culture—they sacralized it. They were American in their religious vision and its enactment. "Like all sectarians, they were exclusivistic and still mission minded. Like all sectarians, they demanded total commitment in a radical lifestyle. Yet paradoxically, their exclusivity often led them to the center of the political process." To preserve their separation they had to gain worldly power, which would enable them to erect their own societies, independent of the secular government around them.[11]

Similar ambiguities can be found in other aspects of Mormonism. In fact, parts of Mormon belief and culture are more "American" than American mainstream religion. Mormons quickly evidenced an interest in the history of American Indians. Their millennial belief held up America as the promised land and a place where the New Jerusalem could be erected. After all, America is where the lost tribes of Israel chose to migrate. Such an emphasis reflected the nationalism (including the concept of manifest destiny) and the optimism of American society, and the postmillennialism so prevalent in nineteenth-century religious circles. Yet even the Mormons' patriotism contained a central paradox. They considered themselves, as they still do, good and typical Americans. But at the same time, they saw themselves as different from Americans. From their perspective, they held the country to its highest standards, but they did not see other Americans as maintaining these ideals.[12]

Their millennialism also demonstrated these tensions. At first Smith taught an apocalyptic, premillennial eschatology, but this faded as the Mormons began to concentrate more on building Zion as a place than on determining a date for the millennial kingdom. The Mormons expected their cause to triumph through a cataclysmic judgment rather than the gradual conversion of the world. They waited anxiously for the fulfillment of the signs of the times, while they also labored mightily to build the New Jerusalem in Utah. Furthermore, the Mormons intertwined their expectations that America would be the millennial country with the belief that the saints would reign in isolation in Zion.[13]

In several other ways Mormonism mirrored the culture of antebellum America. The frontier spirit was evident. As in the case of several other communitarian groups, the movement of the Mormons west paralleled the westward movement in the United States. R. Laurence Moore points out that in an age when science was gaining respectability, the Mormons tried to "objectify" their differences between themselves and other Americans by the importance assigned to the discovery of the golden tablets and the Book of Mormon. Furthermore, their emphasis on the sacredness of matter should be linked to the material success so prevalent in much of the nineteenth-century America.[14]

Modern Mormonism continues to manifest many ambiguities. Although theocracy officially gave way to statehood for Utah in 1896, an informal fusion of church and state lingered on. Meanwhile, the church continued to be a masterpiece of organizational efficiency, a mighty empire in the West led by a president who inherited the prophetic mantle of Joseph Smith. The twentieth century brought wealth and respectability for the Mormons, and in many ways the movement changed, in Thomas O'Dea's words, "from 'near-sect' to 'near nation.' " Yet the Mormons continued to retain so much of the heritage of their past that they still constitute an important American subculture.[15]

Strangites

Many groups have split off from the major Mormon body, the Church of Jesus Christ of Latter-day Saints, or have arisen independently. In the late twentieth century at least eighteen Mormon bodies still exist.[16] Prior to the Civil War several groups were born out of the turmoil following the death of Joseph Smith. Only two will be mentioned, the Church of Jesus Christ (Strangite) and the Reorganized Church of Jesus Christ of Latter-day Saints.

Many new religions die after the death of their founder. While the Strangites are not quite extinct, they declined rapidly after the death of their colorful founder, James Jesse Strang (1813-56). The year 1844 was a turning point for Strang: Joseph Smith baptized him, and he was ordained to the Melchizedek Priesthood. The church then requested that he go and examine the Burlington, Wisconsin, area as a potential new home for the Mormons. While Strang was in Wisconsin, Smith was killed. Strang later claimed that on the day of Smith's death an angel of the Lord appeared and anointed him the successor to the fallen prophet. Strang also insisted that he received a letter from Smith, dated shortly before his death, naming Strang as his successor and designating Voree, Wisconsin, as the new gathering place of the Saints. After hearing these claims, the twelve apostles of the parent church excommunicated Strang.[17]

Nevertheless, Strang and his followers were undeterred. They proselytized throughout the Midwest, especially publicizing the purported revelation in which an angel had ordained Strang to be Smith's successor. Strang's followers increased, numbering some two thousand at his Voree community; William Smith, the brother of Joseph Smith, was among them. The organization of the Church of Jesus Christ was effected in June 1845. While Strang's following was smaller and less dedicated than that of Brigham Young, the numbers were still impressive. By 1846 Strang's group numbered some ten thousand, as compared to fifteen thousand for Young. But after much dissension, in part because Strang was something of a charlatan, desertions from the highest ranks began.[18]

As a consequence, Strang relocated his group to Beaver Island in northern Lake Michigan. Here he set up a theocracy, crowning himself king. He proceeded to mix religion and politics, being elected in 1852 to the Michigan legislature, a position from which he endeavored to build his own self-governed Mormon territory. By 1856, the Church of Jesus Christ was the largest of the Mormon groups that did not follow Brigham Young. But tragedy struck, ending Strang's ambitions. He was assassinated by some discontented members, and the movement rapidly dwindled, becoming little more than an oddity to outsiders. Yet by as late as 1977, three congregations and a few hundred members still existed.[19]

Reorganized Church of Latter-day Saints

After the death of Joseph Smith, the Mormon movement split in a number of directions. The largest faction comprised those who accepted Brigham Young as their prophet and followed him to Utah. The next largest Mormon body rejected Young's leadership and later migrated to Missouri. This faction, which included Smith's widow, became known as the Reorganized Church of Jesus Christ of Latter-day Saints. Of the several Mormon groups emerging out of the turmoil following Smith's death, aside from the Utah church, the Reorganized Church has been the most stable and successful in respect to long-term growth.[20]

After the trek west by the main Mormon body, remnants of the Saints remained in the East and the Midwest. From such people came the Reorganized Church, which was officially established in 1860. The prime movers of the new church were Jason Briggs, Zenos Gurley and William Marks. While loyal to the Mormon Church, these men renounced the leadership of Brigham Young and gathered together people of a similar persuasion. Briggs claimed to have had a revelation in which God had promised a new leader. Gradually Briggs became convinced that Joseph Smith III (the prophet's oldest living son, a nineteen-year-old boy who lived in Nauvoo, Illinois, with his mother) was the promised "mighty" leader.[21] At this time other Mormon groups were seeking an alternative to Young's leadership, and during the next year and a half they joined the "Young Joseph" movement formed by Briggs. In 1852 these "Reorganizers" convened and formed the "New Organization." They decided Joseph Smith III should lead the new church. At first Young Joseph refused the presidency, but in 1859 he accepted. Thus, in 1860 the "New Organization" became the Reorganized Church of the Latter-day Saints.[22]

Stiff challenges confronted Smith. For the Reorganized Church to prosper, it needed an identity based on issues that went beyond opposition to Brigham Young and to polygamy. The church's stance was a conservative one. Thus, on most issues the Reorganized Church came to occupy a position between Utah Mormonism and standard Protestantism—a position it continues to maintain in the late twentieth century. On a number of important points, the Reorganized Church agrees with the Utah Church. The Reorganized Church reveres Joseph Smith and accepts all the scriptures that he wrote. Also, its statement of faith is very close to that of the Utah Mormons. But on several points the Reorganized Church holds that the Utah Church has fallen into error. The Reorganized Saints shun any identification with the Utah Mormons, regarding Young as a false teacher. The Reorganized Church also rejects the most controversial teachings of Joseph Smith: plural marriage, temple rites and the plurality of gods.[23]

The church's headquarters are in Independence, Missouri. It operates colleges and maintains an intensive missionary effort throughout the world, resulting in a global membership of about a quarter of a million. In recent years the Reorganized Church has moved closer to evangelical Christianity, emphasizing justification by faith and deemphasizing the role of Joseph Smith.[24] Despite these changes, the church has not joined the ranks of orthodox Christianity.

Christadelphians

The Christadelphians are a nontraditional religious group begun by John Thomas (1805-70) during the first half of the nineteenth century. Unlike other movements originating at this time, the Christadelphians were not communal, nor did they engage in any unusual sexual relationships. They did, however, manifest cultic characteristics in respect to their doctrine and restrictive social prohibitions.[25]

The Christadelphians have been regarded by some as forerunners of the Jehovah's Witnesses because of the many doctrinal similarities between the two groups, but there were apparently no direct links between them. While Bryan Wilson regards them as an early Adventist group, Gordon Melton places them in the Baptist family because of their close connections with the Disciples of Christ. Charles Lippy sees them as part of the larger Restorationist and Adventist movements, which were quite active before the middle of the nineteenth century.[26] At any rate, the Christadelphians are an eclectic religious body with diverse roots.

John Thomas studied medicine in London and emigrated to North America in 1832. About this time he abandoned medicine to study Scripture and preach the forthcoming end of the age. Thomas wrote a number of books, expounding his own scheme of biblical exegesis. He engaged in debates with the Millerites and Mormons, and for a time attached himself to the followers of Barton Stone and Alexander Campbell, a group that became known as the Disciples of Christ. Nevertheless, Thomas was a contentious man and found it difficult to accept the ideas of others. When his studies of the Bible led him to deny many of the tenets of the Disciples of Christ, they cut him off from their fellowship.

Thomas insisted that the central message of Scripture was the hope of the kingdom that would come with the second advent of Christ, which he believed to be imminent. Recanting previous errors, he had himself rebaptized and then denied fellowship to any who disagreed with his teachings. In particular, Thomas rejected the concepts of soul, heaven and hell, and although not unitarian, he fiercely renounced the doctrine of the Trinity.[27]

Unlike many leaders of early-nineteenth-century fringe religions, Thomas denied having any special inspiration. He believed the Bible to be inerrant and his commentary on Scripture no more than that of a serious student. He denied having any special inspiration and categorically rejected the idea that he was a prophet. He even repudiated the idea of guidance by the Holy Spirit: the Word of God, as recorded in Scripture, was the only way in which God spoke to people in Thomas's age. Nevertheless, he gathered a number of persons who shared his convictions and formed them into an "ecclesia," or assembly of believers. From about 1814, ecclesias began to be formed in many parts of North America as well as in Great Britain. In order to secure deferment from military duties during the Civil War, the movement had to take a name; "Christadelphians," explained as meaning "brothers in Christ," was chosen.[28]

In respect to theology, the Christadelphians manifested characteristics similar to those of the Unitarians and Adventists. In the steps of their founder, they regarded the Bible as the sole authority for their faith and rejected the immortality of the soul. They were antitrinitarian, believing the Scriptures teach that Christ is not God the Son, but the son of God; not preexistent, but born of Mary by the Holy Spirit. The Holy Spirit was not a divine person but the name for the power of God in action. The devil was not a personal being; instead, Satan was a personification of sin in the flesh. The death of Christ was not an atonement, but expressed the love of the Father in a sacrifice for sin. Salvation came through good works and the acceptance of Christadelphian doctrines and baptism. Consequently, only Christadelphians could be saved to eternal life, and if they failed to live the truth, not all of them would be saved.[29]

Christadelphians believed that the promises of the Scriptures related first to the Jews and only subsequently to those who accepted Christ's later offer to become joint heirs with him. Therefore, Christadelphians were people who had voluntarily chosen to become Jews. In fact, the early Christadelphians followed Jewish events very closely, donating to Jews' needs and doing all they could do to help them return to Palestine. The Christadelphians rejected any teaching of "heaven beyond the skies," instead believing that the saved will live on a renewed earth. Therefore, they emphasized the earthly promises made to Abraham and Israel and expected the returning Christ to reign permanently in Jerusalem.[30]

The Christadelphians maintained an impressive ethic, basing their social and moral teachings closely on Scripture. While the use of alcohol was not strictly prohibited, excessive drinking was strongly proscribed. Associating with ungodly people or frequenting taverns would certainly result in excommunication. Christadelphians did not vote in civil elections, and they refused to accept public office. While they maintained conscientious objection to military service, they were not opposed to war. In fact, the Christadelphians rejected a number of attempts to eliminate international conflict, including leagues for peace, because they regarded wars among nations as clearly part of the divine plan.[31]

While the Christadelphians engaged in evangelism in obedience to Scripture, they remained well segregated and have become a largely self-recruiting group. In Britain in the 1970s they numbered between twenty and thirty thousand; there are currently several thousand elsewhere in the English-speaking world. In the late 1980s, there are probably fewer than six thousand adherents in North America. Though the Christadelphians never took hold in the United States, there is some indication that they are attempting a comeback in their native country.[32]

PART III

Cracks in the Protestant Empire: The Civil War to World War II

The decades between the Civil War and World War II were less active in respect to the rise of new religions than were the early nineteenth and late twentieth centuries. Nevertheless, this era witnessed extensive occult and cultic developments. Economic and social conditions helped to promote such activities. Industrialization, urbanization and secularization continued at a rapid pace. Millennialism again played a role in the rise of fringe religions. The influx of many immigrants, intense racial discrimination and the challenge of both the natural and social sciences also contributed to the growth of new religions. Theosophy, New Thought, Christian Science and other occult and metaphysical movements arose. Eastern religions now become more visible. Christian deviations included such new religions as the Jehovah's Witnesses and the Worldwide Church of God. The early twentieth century saw the rise of many black sects and cults in response to the racism of the age.

American Culture
in the Late
Nineteenth Century

T
he Second Great Awakening ushered in a period of evangelical
ascendancy. In the middle third of the nineteenth century, roughly
the years 1830-60, conservative evangelical Protestantism dominated the religious scene in the United States. Protestantism clearly must be
regarded as the religious mainstream until the post-World War II era,
though by then some cracks had already developed in this "Protestant empire." The first half of the nineteenth century witnessed the rise of several
American religious groups that had no direct connection with the Protestant
Reformation. They include the Shakers, Disciples of Christ, Mormons,
Adventist and Spiritualist groups and others. The monolithic Protestant
character of American Christianity could no longer be taken for granted.[1]

The Religious Setting
After the Civil War, immigration strengthened the Roman Catholic minority. Deadly conflict wrecked several of the older Protestant denominations,
especially the Lutherans and Presbyterians. Within Protestantism, evangelical preeminence was being challenged as early as the 1870s by new intellectual currents, and by 1930 liberalism had supplanted evangelicalism as
the Protestant mainstream. Christian Science and other cult groups appeared, draining strength from the old-line Protestant bodies. Robert
Handy has shown that by the turn of the century "the supremacy of the
Protestant forces was under heavy attack and on the wane." In fact, the

passage of the Prohibition amendment represented the last time Protestantism could muster up the political clout to impose its rigorous standards on
the nation as a whole. "When in 1928 the Democratic Party nominated a
Roman Catholic, Alfred E. Smith, for the presidency, the end of the Protestant era in the United States was clearly in sight." The end came in 1960
when the American people elected another Catholic, John F. Kennedy, as
president with no really serious resistance on religious grounds.[2]

Still, American evangelical Protestantism was extraordinarily well adapted to the popular ideals and patterns of late-nineteenth-century American
life: patriotism, manifest destiny, Anglo-Saxon self-confidence, the common person's social and economic aspirations, and peaceful community life.
By 1890, the Methodists and Baptists were numerically and theologically the
most dominant of the Protestant bodies. The Presbyterians were third, with
the Christians and Disciples of Christ and the Congregationalists following.
Many small sects and groups maintained similar views. But even if these
bodies are not counted, in 1890 mainstream denominations made up about
80 percent of American Protestantism and approximately 55 percent of the
total religious population.[3]

Beyond these numbers, several unifying threads are interwoven in the
development of the mainline denominations. These bodies were distinguished by their deep roots in the Reformed or Calvinistic lineage. Beyond
this Reformed legacy, for the most part American evangelical Protestantism
had accepted, as an essential aspect of its being, the ideas and practices of
revivalism. Particularly crucial was the doctrine of revivalism that made a
conversion experience the essential mark of the true Christian. Such an
emphasis resulted in a gradual erosion of ethics—a trend that had begun
even in the colonial era but was not manifest until after the Civil War.[4]

Two other unifying threads are discernible: Arminianism and the mission
of America. Nearly synonymous with revivalism was Arminianism, a theological tendency that developed from internal disputes in the Dutch Reformed Church but whose dissemination in America came primarily
through the Methodists. Because revivalism emphasized human free will,
the doctrines of predestination and human depravity passed from favor. In
turn, a deluge of emotionalism and sentimentality in religion poured forth.
Also, secular ideas of democracy and the rights of the common person
reinforced Arminianism and further reduced the distinctions between the
clergy and laity. A second basic thread was the nearly universal belief that

the United States had a mission to extend its political, economic and religious influence throughout the world. Many Protestants believed the kingdom of God would be realized in American history. These intellectual commonalities had a socially unifying factor—the basis of Protestantism could be found in the middle-class churches of rural and small-town America during the first quarter of the twentieth century.[5]

Sydney Ahlstrom points out that during the later nineteenth century several religious groups were left unsatisfied by this mainstream tradition, and some were openly hostile to it. Most obvious were the outspoken advocates of agnosticism, socialism, free religion or at least the end of the de facto Protestant establishment. While more moderate, the liberals and social gospelers were similarly disturbed, and they sought to relate the Christian faith and practice to the urgent needs of the modern world. According to William McLoughlin, however, the liberals did not remain a minority group for long. They challenged the evangelical establishment and, by the 1920s, united religion and science in a new consensus that lasted until the early 1960s.[6]

A third group noted by Ahlstrom are those whose particular claims or ethnic background, or in some cases both, placed them outside the Old Protestant mainstream. Mennonites, Mormons, Christian Scientists, Unitarians and other divergent movements fall into this category, but it consisted primarily of blacks, Jews, Lutherans, Roman Catholics, Eastern Orthodoxy and a few other large bodies who "consciously resisted wholesale assimilation or were refused the opportunity." The fourth group was a large interdenominational movement consisting of those who protested against innovation in religion. This movement came to be known as fundamentalism. Most of its adherents were troubled by the decline of the old-time religion with its accent on conversion, but their chief concern was doctrinal. Fundamentalists of all social ranks and geographical areas were distressed by "the advance of theological liberalism and the passing of Puritan moralism."[7]

The groups in Ahlstrom's fifth category more distinctly separated themselves from mainstream Protestantism than most fundamentalists did. A desire for Christian perfection and fullness of the Spirit led these groups "to schism and sectarian withdrawal." They became Holiness or, "if more radical in their innovations, Pentecostal churches." Whereas this movement drew its adherents largely from among the lower classes and the uneducated, it was primarily a protest against the conformity, complacency and middle-class respectability of mainstream Protestantism. However, most of these sectarians came to share the fundamentalists' concern for biblical inerrancy. Moreover, the Second Coming of Christ "loomed large in their thought."[8]

A possible sixth group is the alternative-reality tradition—that is, the occult and metaphysical bodies and the Eastern religions coming to America. This tradition had an existence of its own and was not so much a reaction to or a dissatisfaction with the Protestant mainstream as were the other five groups mentioned. Its adherents, however, constituted an important part of the growing pluralism in the years between the Civil War and World War II.

It is groups three, five and six that concern this study. Some divergent bodies in these categories maintained peculiar claims and practices and evidenced occult and cultic characteristics.

The major religious forces of the first half of the nineteenth century continued with some modification in the last half. Millennialism was still potent after the Civil War. Postmillennialism related well to manifest destiny, the continuing emphasis on nationalism that coincided with America's growing economic power, and the social gospel. Premillennialism and some unorthodox millennial views were often associated with groups outside of the Protestant mainstream. The dispensational variety of premillennialism emerged on the American scene and became popular in fundamentalist circles. The Seventh-Day Adventists and Jehovah's Witnesses proposed a millennialism less easy to categorize. Perfectionism was a major ideological force in the Second Great Awakening, in the growth of Methodism and among several of the communitarian bodies. It even brought about some Methodist schisms in the antebellum period. After the Civil War, perfectionism gained momentum in the Holiness revival.

Such a religious setting was conducive to the growth of occult and cultic groups. Religious pluralism was on the increase. Moreover, because of the revivalistic impulse, American religion was alive and dynamic. Such pluralism and vitality produced several religions new to America and many split-offs within traditional Christianity. Most obvious were the occult, metaphysical and Eastern religious groups. Theosophy, New Thought, Christian Science and related groups made their presence known. Hindu, Buddhist and Islamic bodies emerged on the scene. The decline of the evangelical consensus produced a number of protest movements, especially fundamentalism, Pentecostalism and the holiness churches. While these Christian movements were not cultic, they produced a number of splitoffs that can be labeled cults. Included in these groups would be the Jehovah's Witnesses, the Worldwide Church of God, the Jesus Only Movement and several black cults.

Social and Economic Conditions

The Civil War can be regarded as a watershed between the old and the new America. By general consensus, modern America is said to have emerged some time between 1865 and World War I, the years when industry, the telegraph and the railroads developed extensively and when the national government became secure in relationship to governments of the various states. During this period the American people became much more heterogeneous. The advent of modern science drastically altered the intellectual climate, and the quickening pace of industrialization created new centers of power in national life.[9]

The changing composition of the population was one of the conspicuous contrasts between the old and the new America. The demographic revolution produced by immigration had a heavy impact on the spiritual self-consciousness of the American people. Though the number of foreign-born residents surged dramatically prior to the Civil War and increased thereafter, the influx did not peak until the years between 1901 and 1910. Not surprisingly, during the later decades of the nineteenth century the American people were feeling the increased impact of the country's ethnic and religious pluralism.[10]

In the late nineteenth century great influxes of people came to America from Southern, Central and Eastern Europe. These individuals were not as easily assimilated into the American culture as were immigrants from Northern and Western Europe. Moreover, many of these immigrants brought with them their Roman Catholic, Eastern Orthodox or Jewish faith. Though in far smaller numbers, individuals outside the Judeo-Christian heritage began arriving in America toward the end of the nineteenth century. Muslims came from what are now Syria, Lebanon, India, Pakistan and Poland. Adherents of Hinduism came from India, while Buddhists arrived from China and Japan.[11]

Many Americans reacted to this massive influx with fear, hostility and prejudice. The late nineteenth and early twentieth century was not a happy time for ethnic and racial minorities in the United States. Segregation had a legal basis in the Supreme Court's *Plessy v. Ferguson* decision. Racist prejudice was the standard attitude toward the Chinese. The Bolshevik Revolution aroused the fear that Eastern European immigrants would bring communism with them.

American nativist impulses perhaps climaxed during this period. The Ku Klux Klan was reorganized in 1915 and reached its peak membership in 1923. Americans believed that they were economically and socially threatened by various minorities. Such an influx, they believed, would bring an end to the Protestant Anglo-Saxon dominance. After the war, such attitudes led to severe restrictions, culminating in the Johnson-Reed Act of 1924, which based immigration quotas on proportions of the U.S. population as it had been in 1890. These measures directly lashed out at the growth of Jewish, Catholic and Orthodox communities, and Eastern religions from India and China. Thus the flow of non-Protestant religions from other lands slowed considerably, not to be revived again until after World War II.[12]

Sydney Ahlstrom tells us that the new immigrants adjusted to the American religious situation in several ways. Some immigrants were members of a state church in Europe. These individuals usually maintained either an active or a nominal relationship with their native church or slipped out of the religious scene. A second type consisted of the immigrating sectarians— those who sometime in their history had broken from the state churches and formed more rigorously disciplined communities. The Mennonites migrating from Russia at this time are a classic example. In America these immigrants usually remained sectarians, at least in the years following their arrival. A third category consisted of immigrants who were "incipient sectarians"—that is, those who were deeply dissatisfied with the established church but had not broken from it while in Europe. In America they usually identified with congregations in the free-church tradition. A fourth type consisted of those in the Christian tradition who for various reasons organized new autonomous churches, some exhibiting cultic characteristics. A fifth group was composed of those outside the Judeo-Christian tradition who either remained true to their native religion or formulated offshoots from it.[13] The fourth and fifth categories have had considerable impact on the cults and alternative religions.

Another development of the post-Civil War era that became a permanent feature of American life was a marked shift in the center of power. Prior to the war, the agrarian democracy envisioned by Thomas Jefferson still dominated, although even then the lure of the city had begun to attract individuals of spirit and ambition. Within a generation after the Civil War the United States was transformed from a predominantly agricultural to a manufacturing nation. By 1890 the factory had outdistanced the farm as the country's chief producer of wealth, and by 1920 the population's center of gravity had shifted decisively to the cities.[14]

For religion this urban trend had two particularly devastating and related consequences. First, large segments of the new urban population—whether migrants from the country to the city or immigrants from Europe—had little contact with the Protestant churches. In fact, many were Catholic, Jewish or Eastern Orthodox. Second, in respect to religious affiliation, urban growth created a serious cleavage in the city population. While those able to afford churches were well churched, people who could not were either unchurched or set up alternative religions. In fact, some of the unchurched even regarded church people as their economic oppressors. Such a perception helped to foster the rise of many black sects and cults. This dramatic exodus of Protestant churches from the growing areas of American cities revealed both serious problems in the crumbling Protestant establishment and increased movement toward a pluralism that promoted the growth of fringe religions.[15]

The Intellectual Climate

Another difference between the old and the new America was a dramatic change in the intellectual climate. Geology, pioneered by Charles Lyell (1797-1875), presented a version of the origin and history of the earth that seemed to conflict with the Genesis story. Lyell challenged the biblical account on geological grounds because of the records which the rocks preserved. Needless to say, controversy ensued. And the matter did could not stop with geology—in part because the fossil records and geological estimates of the earth's great age made developmental theories of biological evolution increasingly plausible.

Yet the greatest challenge to traditional Christianity and the chief symbol of the new intellectual revolution was the new biology, as set forth by Charles Darwin (1809-82). Darwin unquestionably became the nineteenth century's Newton, and his theory of evolution through natural selection became the century's cardinal idea. The idea of evolution did not begin with Darwin, of course, and it was to be carried even further by others. The writings of Herbert Spencer (1820-1903) carried the implications of evolutionary thinking into social theory. The doctrine of evolution became a unifying philosophical principle that was applied to all phenomena—social structures, economic developments, race relations and the growth of nations.[16]

With evolutionary ideas penetrating every realm of thought, a new history began to be written, based on the application of evolutionary theories of learning to the theories of the past. In turn, this new historical understanding bolstered the developing "higher criticism" of the Bible, first in Germany and then in Britain and America. Higher criticism studies Scripture from the standpoint of literature, as if the Bible were any other ancient book whose credentials and accuracy had to pass the tests of historical methods. This approach resulted in conclusions that shook orthodoxy. Among other things, the critics generally agreed that Moses did not write the first five books of the Bible, that the apostle John did not write the Gospel of John (and that it was not good history) and, of central concern, that the life of Jesus was different from the story portrayed in the Gospels.[17]

The years after 1830 also witnessed an extensive development of the social sciences. Before the nineteenth century, nearly all efforts to analyze the social environment were restricted to history, economics and philosophy. The first of the new social sciences was sociology, originated by Auguste Comte (1798-1857) and elaborated by Herbert Spencer. Next came the founding of anthropology, and about 1870 psychology was broken off from philosophy and cultivated as a separate science. After the beginning of the twentieth century, psychologists divided into a number of conflicting schools, with behaviorism and psychoanalysis the two major ones. Behaviorism, originating in the work of the Russian Ivan Pavlov (1849-1936), is an attempt to study the human being as a purely physiological organism—that is, reducing all human behavior to a series of physical responses. Psychoanalysis, founded by the Austrian Sigmund Freud (1856-1939), interprets human behavior mainly in terms of the subconscious or unconscious mind.[18]

These new social sciences maintained some assumptions about human behavior and existence that conflicted with orthodoxy. Yet they did not present such an immediate challenge to Christianity as did the new sciences, the new approach to history, and higher criticism. The impact of the social sciences, especially psychology, on religion would be tremendous in the

102

post-World War II era. In fact, psychology blended with Eastern religions produced many of the psychoreligions and self-help groups that sprang up during the 1970s and 1980s.

One area of the social sciences, parapsychology, had a closer relationship with fringe religions prior to World War II. J. B. Rhine defines parapsychology as the "science of psychic abilities." Parapsychology, at times called psychic research, relates to studies that "enable individuals to make contact with the world around them without the aid of their senses and muscles." It is the systematic inquiry into whether human minds receive information in ways that bypass the normal channels of sensory communication, or interact with matter in ways not yet comprehensible to physical science. The two main categories of parapsychology are extrasensory perception (ESP) and psychokinesis (PK), with each having its subdivisions.[19]

Parapsychology has always had a close relationship with religion, especially with the occult. This situation was created when the advance of science produced skepticism regarding religious supernaturalism. Naturalistic theories arose in an attempt to account for the miraculous. Early examples of this include mesmerism, Swedenborg's spirit communication, hypnosis, Spiritualism and Christian Science in nineteenth-century America. In particular, parapsychology sprang from Spiritualism, for it was believed that mediums were gifted with telepathy.

Psychology departments in America and Europe during the late nineteenth century began to research telepathy. But it was the work of J. B. Rhine, beginning at Duke University in 1927, that gave parapsychology its scientific legitimacy. Nevertheless, whether parapsychology is science or the occult is still hotly argued, and the fact that many parapsychologists in the 1960s were closet occultists using science to promote a preconceived religious position further complicated the problem.[20]

American religious groups responded to the new intellectual currents, especially modern science and higher criticism, in several ways. Existing sects, whether already in America or migrating in, usually remained withdrawn religious bodies. By and large they ignored or resisted the new intellectual trends and did not undergo many changes. Occultic groups, which were outsiders already, appeared to move in two directions, sometimes simultaneously. Some clung to their traditional beliefs and practices as if the new science did not exist. Higher criticism, of course, was irrelevant to them. Other occult bodies utilized "pseudoscience" to give empirical evi-

103

dence to their beliefs. Some new groups with occultic characteristics, such as Christian Science, came into being claiming to be scientific. In fact, as R. Laurence Moore notes, "virtually every new American religion of the late nineteenth and early twentieth centuries has offered to prove itself by empirical and objective standards."[21]

A third response was schisms, the creation of new sectarian bodies from mainline denominations. Rather than accommodate their faith to the world, many evangelicals chose to resist the new intellectual currents, even if it meant separating from the mainline denominations and establishing new religious bodies. Examples of this option include the groups associated with the fundamentalist, Holiness and Pentecostal movements. Even many of these sectarian groups sought to prove themselves empirically. For example, Pentecostals believed that healings and tongues-speaking overtly demonstrated the operation of the Holy Spirit. Fundamentalists sought to "prove" the Christian faith by scientific claims.[22] The cults related to these Christian movements also evidenced similar tendencies—both separation from society and some attempt to support their claims by rational or scientific means.

A fourth response was theological liberalism. According to Bruce Shelley, Protestant liberalism "engaged a problem as old as Christianity itself: how do Christians make their faith meaningful in a new world of thought without distorting or destroying the gospel? The Apostle Paul tried and succeeded. The early Gnostics tried and failed." Many individuals in the mainline churches were faced with a difficult choice. They could hang onto evangelicalism and sacrifice current standards for intellectual respectability. If they were to retain intellectual respectability, it seemed they must either abandon Christianity or modify it to meet the standards of the day. For many the latter choice seemed the only live option—but at a price. Liberalism, it would seem, replaced evangelicalism as the consensus by 1930 and became the mainstream.[23]

This movement had two names, *liberalism* and *modernism,* both reflecting its two primary emphases. The movement was liberal in that it stressed freedom from tradition and modern in its focus on adjustment to the modern world. While the movement encompassed a wide variety, some idea of its outlook can be gained by considering three of its methods for saving the Christian faith from the modern intellectual onslaught. First, liberals responded to intellectual challenges by deifying the historical process. This meant that God revealed himself in history and was incarnate in the development of humanity. Liberals felt that the old orthodox Christian idea of a God somewhere beyond the universe was unacceptable to the modern mind. So they stressed divine immanence, the idea that God dwells in the world and works through natural processes. Liberals believed the kingdom of Christ to be the continuing manifestation of the power of God to alter human relationships. To them the Bible was not an encyclopedia of dogma, but a record of the religious experience of an ancient people.[24]

The second and third strategies of liberalism, to a large extent, separated Christianity from the intellectual arena. Thus the liberals sheltered important aspects of the Christian heritage from the challenge of modern thought. The liberals emphasized the ethical component of Christianity. The crucial test for the Christian faith was lifestyle, not doctrine. Liberals reasoned that while traditional theology might collapse before the blistering blasts of modern criticism, the ethics of Jesus would survive. The practical outcome of such ethical emphases came in several varieties, but social concern in the form of the social gospel was the most prominent. The third approach common to the liberal defense of Christianity was the belief that religious feelings went to the very core of Christianity. As in their emphasis on ethics, liberals contrasted religious feelings with the religion of reason, dogma or some literal interpretations of the Bible. Historical criticism and science could not challenge a religion of feelings and intuition, something residing outside the confines of reason. Liberal Christians followed the Romantic and liberal sentiments of their day by allowing science to reign freely in its own domain, while insisting on a realm of religious truth that science could not touch.[25]

These three liberal emphases influenced alternative religions in several major ways. Many people rejected liberal theology, regarding it as a perversion of the historic Christian faith. Thus schisms developed and sectarian bodies were formed, largely related to fundamentalism, but also within the Holiness and Pentecostal movements. These sectarian movements in turn spawned some cultic bodies that went beyond the confines of Christian orthodoxy. Second, some radical new religious movements were not conservative bodies but stood at the opposite end of the religious spectrum, having much in common with liberalism. For example, Christian Science grew out of some of the same impulses that produced Protestant liberalism. Third, liberalism's bifurcation between religion and the intellectual realm helped to create a setting for the explosion of the new religions of the 1960s.

Cardinal characteristics of these new religious movements were feelings, experience and subjectivity as opposed to doctrine, theology and learning by the cognitive process.[26] Fourth, liberalism's emphasis on divine immanence—that is, God's indwelling of the world—is vital to the worldview of occult and Eastern religions. Thus, in several ways liberalism helped pave the way for the surge among occult and Eastern religions that occurred after World War II.

8

Nineteenth-Century
Occult &
Metaphysical Movements

As I have already explained, the Civil War is not a good watershed for demarcating historical trends in the occult and metaphysical tradition in America. Certain trends ran through the entire nineteenth century. Spiritualism experienced a surge of activity after the Civil War and World War I, and along with Transcendentalism, it provided the foundation for some occult and metaphysical movements that developed in the late nineteenth century. But the years from the Civil War to the mid-twentieth century did witness some new developments, including the arrival of Theosophy, New Thought and Christian Science. Theosophy and New Thought have in turn produced many splitoffs and related religious bodies.

Theosophy
Theosophy must be regarded as one of the most important occult movements in America. It began in the nineteenth century, partially growing out of Spiritualism. The guiding spirit and principal founder of Theosophy was Helena Petrovna Blavatsky (1831-91), or H.P.B., as her friends and followers affectionately called her. Born in Russia of a well-to-do aristocratic family, she was a woman of great mystery and complexity, clearly composed of several personalities, all of them extreme. Opinions of her are also polarized. Some call her a fraud and a con artist, while others praise her as a sage of sages; to some she was a compulsive liar, others consider her a rare psychic. As a child she was difficult and unmanageable, and if her

account is true, her psychic development began during her early life, because even then she had invisible playmates and believed in superhuman and subhuman spirits.[1]

After a short and unfortunate marriage to General Blavatsky when she was seventeen, she ran away to become a wanderer through many lands. In 1851 she traveled to London with her father. She claimed that here she first viewed her "Master," a man from the East with a commanding presence. Then for almost thirty years H.P.B. virtually disappeared from sight, the exception being 1858-64, which she spent in Russia with her family. If she can be believed, for the rest of these years Blavatsky traveled widely over the world, contacting masters and shamans in places such as Mexico, Egypt, Canada and inner Asia, with Tibet as her ultimate goal. She arrived there in 1864 and spent three years undergoing initiations with her masters. In many ways, H.P.B. can be seen as the archetype of the magus, with her remarkable birth and childhood, esoteric and mysterious personality, wide travels and supernormal powers.[2]

In 1874 Blavatsky came to the United States to defend the validity of Spiritualistic phenomena. Here she met Colonel Henry Steel Olcott, who became a cofounder of the Theosophical Society. Olcott (1832-1907), a well-known lawyer, had been interested in Spiritualism for many years. While Blavatsky was the spiritual leader of Theosophy, Olcott provided its organization. In 1875 these two, along with William Q. Judge (1851-96) and a group of others, formed the Theosophical Society to discuss ideas regarding ancient lore, supernatural phenomena and the expansion of human powers of mind and spirit. From their statement of intentions it was clear that knowledge was the key issue for Theosophists. Indeed, *theosophy,* in the generic sense, is another name for the occult tradition of knowledge about the inner workings of the divine.[3]

The history of the Theosophical Society was never smooth. The society was formally established in New York in 1875. During these early years most members were Spiritualists, being attracted to the society by Madame Blavatsky's writings and by the prospect of seeing the phenomena they believed she could produce. However, she seems to have lost interest in such phenomena; instead she began writing her first book, *Isis Unveiled,* which was published in 1877. Soon many Spiritualists left the organization, viewing Blavatsky as a foe of "true" Spiritualism. The New York period ended in 1878, when Madame Blavatsky and Colonel Olcott sailed to India.[4]

Eventually a Theosophical headquarters was established at Adyar in Madras, India. The society spread throughout Europe and America. After Madame Blavatsky's death in 1891, however, the American society broke with the Adyar headquarters. Katherine Tingley, who became the head of the American society, established a noteworthy Theosophical center at Point Loma, in San Diego, California, which endured for over forty years. Meanwhile, in a short while the Adyar society regained its lost ground and came to embrace most American Theosophists. During the first thirty years of the twentieth century, C. W. Leadbeater and Annie Besant dominated this group. Another significant development at this time was the refinement into a schematic hierarchy of the concept of the Masters. In fact, during this period Krishnamarti, a young Indian boy, was promoted as likely to become the World Teacher for this era. Until he renounced the claim in 1929, this prospect caused considerable excitement.[5]

During the first half of the twentieth century, Theosophy underwent considerable fragmentation. In the 1978 edition of the *Encyclopedia of American Religions* J. Gordon Melton lists forty-three Theosophical-related groups, many of which came into existence before the end of World War II.[6] Thus only some broad trends and significant groups can be noted. According to Robert Ellwood, the many devolutions from Theosophy fall into two general classes. First, there are what he called the "right wing" groups, which "reject the alleged extravagance and orientalism of evolved Theosophy, in favor of serious emphasis on its metaphysics and especially its recovery of the Gnostic and Hermetic heritage." These bodies have a Western focus and hold that the love of India and its mysteries, which developed after *Isis Unveiled,* was inappropriate for a Western group. This class includes several neognostic and neo-Rosicrucian bodies plus the Anthroposophy of Rudolf Steiner. Second, there exists what may be termed "left wing" Theosophical schisms, "generally based on new private revelations from the Masters not accepted by the main traditions." In this category are Alice Bailey's groups, "I AM" and, in a way, Max Heindel's Rosicrucianism.[7]

The source for all these developments was and still is the teachings of Madame Blavatsky, particularly those found in *The Secret Doctrine.* From her published works and those of Olcott one can discern a three-stage development in Blavatsky's philosophy. These stages largely relate to her responses to Spiritualism and the doctrine of reincarnation. During the first stage, which lasted until 1875, she defended Spiritualism. From 1875 to 1879 she began to attack Spiritualism, but still opposed the doctrine of reincarnation. Only after her return from India in 1879 did a fully developed philosophy of Theosophy appear, one that included reincarnation.[8]

J. Stillson Judah says that Theosophy, "like the other metaphysical groups, claims to be a philosophy, a religion, and a science." Functioning as a science, it attempts to uncover hidden spiritual laws, while still insisting that eventually natural and spiritual laws will be discovered to be one. Operating as a religion, Theosophy endeavors "to be nonsectarian, nondogmatic, and the ground of every religion." Consequently, Theosophy sees "all religions as essentially the same, but separated from one another only by the dogmas and encrusted superstitions."[9]

Madame Blavatsky's ideas were complex, but Robert Ellwood has distilled several features from her teachings. First, the magic and mystery of the ages uncovered by Blavatsky cannot be attributed strictly to supernatural sources. Instead, these entities relate "to laws and forces as natural as gravitation but far less well known." These powers are the ones that flash through all things. Second, the two substances of spirit and matter permeate the universe. Spirit is primary in that it is closer to the Universal Mind and Universal Soul and in that it contains the ideas that give form to matter. Nevertheless, matter is also very important. Such a teaching about spirit and matter is complex and more than a crude dualism. Yet early Theosophy displayed a distinctly antimaterialistic face in its focus on "the priority of spirit and the divine spark within each expression of life." This emphasis arose because the early Theosophists regarded science as the blatant materialism of their day, "hardly better than the shallow orthodoxy of the churches."[10]

Third, Ellwood says, Theosophy upheld the existence of a basic universal truth, which is contained in myths and legends and concealed within the conventional religious teachings of all peoples. Thus Theosophy was syncretistic, "affirming that the 'ancient wisdom' was to be found, at least in bits and pieces, worldwide." Theosophists opened themselves to the spiritual truths of many religious traditions. Yoga, alchemy and even Catholic sacramentalism could play their part in an individual's infinite journey.[11]

Fourth, Blavatsky saw a universe composed of matter, spirit and consciousness to be in a continual process of evaluation. Such an idea moved Theosophical thought, along with its Platonic, cabalistic and Eastern sources, into a dialogue with modern Darwinism. In Theosophical teaching evolution is holistic, "involving both biological organisms and the subtler entities of the realm of spirit." Moreover, individual and planetary evolution is really a series of initiations rather like those of the mystery schools in the occult tradition, and like the notion of rebirths. Last, for the early Theosophists "such 'sciences' as astrology, clairvoyance, or control of physical appearances through 'mayavic' (magic) power were quite important." For them, these "sciences" prefigured a use of the subtle force whose reality and control they were learning.[12]

Basic to understanding the many varieties of Theosophical experience is its rejection of materialism, but not of natural law. Theosophy regards materialism (the equation of the physical with the totality) as the fundamental error that needs to be combated. Theosophy really has two dimensions. One side approximates a cult of the marvelous, an enchantment with psychic phenomena and with apparitions of the Masters. On the other side is a strongly mentalist philosophy, one that regards the mind as the basis of life. Both can be seen in the life and work of Helena Blavatsky. Both reject the presuppositions of materialism.[13]

Beyond these main features, certain specific Theosophical teachings are commonly identified with occultism and Eastern spirituality. Theosophy maintains an impersonal concept of God, essentially that of Hindu pantheism. God is the one uncreated, universal, infinite and everlasting Cause. Blavatsky rejected the idea of a personal, extracosmic and anthropomorphic God. She saw God as the Absolute or Absolute Principle. Moreover, Theosophy is profoundly pantheistic. Its proponents argue that there is only one life, one consciousness and one power: God's life, which is immanent in all aspects of existence. Theosophy, however, makes a distinction between God as infinite existence and God's manifestation as a revealed God evolving and guiding a universe. Beneath this supreme God who has several natures are other lesser cosmic beings, who are its agents.[14]

The perfectibility of human nature is one of Theosophy's central principles. Human beings represent a phase of the general evolutionary process that is constantly going on in the universe. Humanity is regarded as a spark of divine fire, an elementary spiritual substance belonging to the monadic world. The individual is a fragment of the group soul, demonstrating its ego in three ways: in the spiritual world as Spirit, as intuition in the intuitional world and in the mental world as intelligence. Moreover, individuals have not one body but many, including an astral body. The astral body consists of matter with higher vibrations than the physical, and emits various colors, visible to a clairvoyant, in accord with one's emotions. The astral body is the vehicle of feelings and desires through which an individual has consciousness on the astral plane during sleep.[15]

As Theosophy developed, reincarnation assumed an important place in its teachings. Once a soul has become individualized as a human being, Theosophy teaches, it never returns to the animal stage but continues to progress. When the soul reincarnates, it may not be in the same ethnic race or remain in the same locality. The process of reincarnation proceeds until the person's karma permits him or her to attain a superhuman state. At this point, one may direct one's own destiny by deciding whether or not to accept Nirvana. Instead of accepting Nirvana, one may choose to remain close to this world to help humankind.[16]

As Catherine Albanese notes, Theosophy drew from many diverse sources, especially Neoplatonism and Gnosticism. Buddhism and Hinduism also made significant contributions to the movement, especially in the knowledge imparted by the Mahatmas to Madame Blavatsky. In fact, "the movement may be perceived as a spiritual pilgrimage of discovery to the East, a search by 'strangers' in America for their religious home abroad." Yet the Theosophical Society was an eclectic organization, combining much from the Western occult masters as well as from the Eastern teachers. Furthermore, in the American religious climate, in which popular Swedenborgianism, Transcendentalism, Spiritualism and mesmerism had all prospered, "it absorbed elements from these movements and made them its own."[17]

Theosophy has had an importance in modern history that is often overlooked. The writings of Madame Blavatsky and others inspired several generations of occultists, to the extent that Theosophy has been called "the mother of the occult" in modern America. Moreover, the movement played a remarkable role in assisting the peoples of nineteenth-century Asia in the restoration of their own spiritual heritage. The Theosophists were among the few non-Easterners who were interested in Eastern scriptures. Furthermore, Theosophists played a role in advancing the cause of India's independence in the twentieth century. Theosophy's most important cultural impact in the West was on the so-called Irish Renaissance. W. B. Yeats, George Russell (A.E.) and other such writers were significantly influenced by the Theosophical vision, some even being members of the society itself.

Such writers made Theosophy a vehicle for a visionary presentation of the occult tradition and ancient wisdom to the modern world.[18]

Theosophical-Related Bodies

Alice Bailey (1880-1949) founded a devolution of Theosophy, the Full Moon Meditation tradition. Born into an upper-class English family, she was an ill-adjusted and headstrong child. Following a brief marriage and a miserable breakup, she came to Theosophy. Her fiancé, Foster Bailey, and she became dissatisfied with Theosophy, and in 1923 they established the Arcane School in New York, out of which emerged the Full Moon Meditation tradition. Alice Bailey produced a long series of books whose teachings closely resemble those of Theosophy. After 1949 the movement splintered, and a number of Full Moon Meditation groups emerged. Having grown out of Theosophy, the movement acquired its own flavor. It gave a show of modern rationality and scientism, together with a blending of an eschatological hope in the second advent and One World idealism. The movement peaked in the early postwar years and experienced both difficulty and success in adjusting to the spiritual climate of the sixties and seventies.[19]

Rudolf Steiner (1861-1925), born of Austrian Catholic parents, had an early attraction to occultism that led him to Theosophy. But Theosophy's Eastern orientation and its focus on marvelous occurrences bothered Steiner. He believed that emphasis should be placed on scientific study of the spiritual world and human initiations into it. Also, Steiner regarded Christ as a more important symbol of the spiritual world than any Eastern master. In 1912 Steiner established a new fellowship within the Theosophy Society, but this group soon became an independent organization—the Anthroposophical Society. Steiner was a charismatic individual who allegedly had clairvoyant and psychic powers. He taught that spiritual consciousness was the fundamental reality of the cosmos and that humanity had originally shared in such an awareness. While matter is real, it is derivative from spirit. Thanks in part to the efforts of a former evangelical pastor, Friedrich Rettelmeyer (1872-1938), Anthroposophy developed a definite Christian bias, even basing its worship on the Protestant model.[20]

As has been indicated earlier, Rosicrucianism has a long history, dating to at least the seventeenth century. In the twentieth century, however, Rosicrucianism is chiefly identified with two organizations: the Rosicrucian Fellowship and the Ancient and Mystical Order Rosae Crucis, or AMORC

113

as it is usually abbreviated. Carl Louis van Grosshoff (1865-1919), who used the pen name Max Heindel, founded the Rosicrucian Fellowship in 1907. Of the two major Rosicrucian organizations, this one was the older and the one more influenced by Theosophy. In fact, the common Theosophical beliefs of world evolution, secret initiation, reincarnation, invisible helpers and elder brothers became basic to the Rosicrucian Fellowship. The atmosphere, however, is all Western, and there is special emphasis on healing and astrology. Moreover, churches in the Rosicrucian Fellowship have something of an old-fashioned Protestant atmosphere.[21]

The other Rosicrucian group, begun in 1915 by H. Spencer Lewis (1883-1939), is far larger. AMORC claims to be not a religion but a worldwide "fraternal organization" in the Masonic mode. As such, its objective is to teach a philosophy and practices that help a person to tap into ordinarily latent faculties to improve his or her abilities and lead a better life. More than most occult and metaphysical groups, AMORC is geared to a popular audience. AMORC has been fairly well accepted in America, in part because its structure and ritual, and some of its terminology, are similar to those of Freemasonry.[22]

One of the more important movements inspired by Theosophy during the first half of the twentieth century was "I AM." The "I AM" movement emerged in the 1930s under the charismatic leadership of Gary Ballard (1878-1938). Born in Kansas, Ballard had long been interested in occultism, including the practice of Spiritualism and the study of Theosophy. In 1930 he had his first contact with the hidden world. One of the Masters appeared to him in the California woods, imparting to him wisdom from the ancient past. Ballard then accepted most of the teachings of Theosophy, including its worldview. Nevertheless, "I AM" teachings have certain distinctives. In particular, they have nationalistic overtones, emphasizing the American setting. The Masters are not found only in faraway Egypt or Tibet; they also reside in the American West, especially at Yellowstone, Mt. Shasta and the Grand Tetons. The "I AM" movement also made rich use of color, vividly decorating its bookstores and centers.[23]

The most important teaching of the "I AM" movement is that the "Mighty 'I AM' Presence" is both God and immediately available. A host of Ascended Masters, including Jesus and Saint-Germain, play a mediating role between the "I AM" and human beings. The goal of human life is ascension. Through various steps and procedures, a person ascends to join the Ascended Masters. "I AM" reached large numbers in the 1930s but started to decline with Ballard's death in 1939. Ballard's wife had claimed that he had become an Ascended Master. So when he died rather than ascending as many had expected, it was too much for many believers. Also, the movement was discredited by some fraudulent money-raising tactics. Nevertheless, "I AM" is still alive today, with Mt. Shasta as its major center.[24]

The Liberal Catholic Church is a body founded by Theosophists; many of its members are Theosophists. James Ingall Wedgewood founded the Liberal Catholic Church in London in 1916. During the first decade of the twentieth century, mysticism had become a popular subject among Anglicans. Into this mystical atmosphere came Theosophy. Liberal Catholic doctrine endeavors to interpret the apostolic faith of Christianity as an example of the ancient mystical wisdom elucidated by Madame Blavatsky and Annie Besant. Liberal Catholicism then teaches an esoteric interpretation of Christianity in the context of the Catholic rather than Protestant tradition. The early leaders of the movement took pains to affirm Christian symbols, while attaching a Theosophical meaning to them. All vestments, colors, liturgical forms and altar articles were given mystical meanings. Like Theosophy itself, Liberal Catholicism has suffered from personality problems and divisions. As of 1978 there were seven Liberal Catholic bodies and related groups.[25]

New Thought

Even before Theosophy had attracted the attention of some Americans, the foundations were being laid for The Movement, or New Thought, as it came to be known. Ellwood says that this late-nineteenth-century development "is not so much a cult or a church in itself as a type of teaching which has influenced a number of groups." New Thought's tenets are the basis of several churches, including Unity, the Church of Religious Science and the Church of Divine Science. In addition, several varieties of what is labeled as "metaphysical," or even "positive thinking," have flowed from this tradition and its major writers—Horatio Dresser, Phineas Quimby, Thomas Troward, Ralph Waldo Trine and Ernest Holmes.[26]

New Thought took many forms. As opposed to Spiritualism and Theosophy, it stressed metaphysical concerns without occult elaboration. Like Spiritualism and Theosophy, however, New Thought was diffuse; it lacked boundaries and could not be confined to a specific religious body. The basic assumption of New Thought is that mind is fundamental and causative. New Thought can be regarded as a modern Western adaption of this concept, because it emphasizes that every event is an internal, nonmaterial idea. New Thought shares one of Theosophy's major ideas, that the inner reality of the universe is mind and idea. But it rejects a major tenet of Theosophy: New Thought does not point to the Ascended Masters as the minds that make things happen, but to the mental potential of every individual.[27]

New Thought relates well to American culture, for it has appealed to the practical and material side of American life. In very concrete ways, New Thought teachers have attempted to demonstrate how thoughts of health, wholeness and success can create equivalent material realities. Assuming that mind is the basis of the physical world, altering one's thoughts should bring changes in the physical world. Even if an individual's thoughts focus on a specific objective, such as acquiring a new job, these thoughts will bring such a reality into existence. Beyond such obvious material benefits, the healing of mind and body has always had an important place in the New Thought movement. In respect to style, New Thought's approach resembles that of liberal Protestantism: liberal theology, nonradical lifestyle and social opinion, and an optimistic atmosphere.[28]

New Thought's distant roots may be in German idealism and New England Transcendentalism, especially in Hegel and Emerson. But it was the teaching and healing practice of Phineas P. Quimby (1802-66) that provided the immediate impetus for New Thought. Quimby was a mental healer who also played an important role in the life of Mary Baker Eddy (1821-1910). Two factors encouraged the development of New Thought ideas in Quimby's mind. As a young man he developed an interest in mesmerism, and he was in poor health. Quimby was cured by Lucius Burkmar, a person who could diagnose and heal disease while in a hypnotic trance. Impressed by his experience, Quimby studied its meaning and concluded that Burkmar's healing depended on one's inward belief, which controlled one's state of sickness or health. Thus Quimby embarked upon a career dedicated to healing the sick.[29]

Though Quimby was above all a practical man who desired to heal people, he also took pains to analyze the basis of inner healing. As result of this study, he came to reject the use of mesmerism and came under a Swedenborgian influence. J. Stillson Judah has shown that there are large areas of agreement between Quimby and the Spiritualist Andrew Jackson Davis, who were both influenced by Swedenborgian ideas. They agree that God (pure mind or spirit) is wisdom and humankind's real nature. But Quimby focused on healing, not on world evolution and life after death as did Davis and Madame Blavatsky. Quimby taught that human beings had a spiritual nature and were the inhabitants of a world higher than this one. Also, he regarded the soul as in direct relationship with the divine mind. Consequently, Quimby concluded that people were healed because of the operation of the divine spirit on a human soul. They experienced an awakening by which they became aware of their inner spiritual nature. Quimby identified the vehicle of this awakening with several sources. Sometimes he related it to a wisdom or science called the Christ; in at least one instance he designated his teaching as Christian Science.[30]

Second only to Quimby in importance to New Thought is Warren Felt Evans (1814-89), a former Methodist minister. Evans first met Quimby in 1863, the same year he became a Swedenborgian. Because Evans was suffering chronic illness, he sought Quimby's assistance and received healing. With Quimby's encouragement he opened his own healing practice. Evans became a far more systematic theoretician for the emerging New Thought movement. By 1869 he had written his first book, *The Mental Cure,* in which he said that disease results from a loss of mental balance which in turn affects the body. Illness is the translation into flesh of a wrong idea in the mind, and the way to get well is to think rightly, thus restoring the harmony between the human spirit and the divine.[31]

Some of Evans's other ideas were important to New Thought. While his concept of God resembled the Neoplatonic idea of the One, he attempted to incorporate Christianity into his teachings. Evans saw the Christ Principle as an emanation from the One that is present within every person. Moreover, union with this Christ Principle, the divine spark within, brings health and wholeness. But above all, Evans believed in the power of suggestion in healing. He stressed the power of conscious affirmation, and his thinking in this regard turned New Thought toward the practice. The result of this for later New Thought was significant. Mind cure meant that the sick individual must think positively, affirming health in deliberate internal statements.[32]

New Thought continued to develop, especially in its organizational aspects, in the later nineteenth century. The mere existence of Christian

117

Science helped in the growth of New Thought. Some people who read Mary Baker Eddy's *Science and Health with Key to the Scriptures* (1875) were in turn attracted to Evans's writings. By the 1880s, many of Evans's followers and Quimby's former patients were convinced that thought was the greatest power in the world and that harmony with Divine Thought, or Mind, was the key to all health and happiness. By the 1890s mental science had become known as New Thought, and it became an organization. While most people in the movement did not see themselves as forming a separate church, New Thought now was distinguished from the older theology of mental science.[33]

Of even more importance to the growth of New Thought was the formation of the Metaphysical Club in Boston in 1895. This organization became the center for national and international development, intending to reach the world with the message of New Thought. An International Metaphysical League had emerged by the turn of the century, and beginning in 1915 international New Thought congresses were held annually. As the twentieth century proceeded, an organization called the International New Thought Alliance continued to provide leadership, while the Unity School of Christianity emerged as the best known of the New Thought institutions. Furthermore, specific New Thought denominations such as Religious Science, based in Los Angeles, and Divine Science, headquartered in Denver, helped to propagate the ideas of the movement.[34]

According to Albanese, a continuing theme has been New Thought's ambivalence about existing in separate churches. New Thought, as a saving knowledge, has been more "individual than communal in its emphasis." Like most occult and metaphysical movements, it eventually led to "inwardness and private religious experience." Thus, New Thought's greatest impact has come through its publishing endeavors. Many of its books have become well known in the self-help market. Even more important, New Thought has infiltrated liberal Protestantism to the extent that many in the religious mainstream absorbed its ideas and values and spread them. Norman Vincent Peale (b. 1898) is an example. Millions of people outside the movement learned of mental healing and the success ethic from his book *The Power of Positive Thinking* (1952). A series of writers less famous than Peale brought a similar message. The fundamental assumptions of the occult tradition can be found in New Thought. Yet in the end, its optimism, individualism and confirmation of the gospel of health and prosperity "dissolved the sense of mystery that surrounded occultism," while at the same time blending "occultism unobtrusively with American culture in the main-stream."[35]

New Thought Groups

Aside from Christian Science, J. Gordon Melton lists thirty-one New Thought bodies, many which were established after World War II. This study will note briefly only three major groups established before the mid-twentieth century. The only New Thought body with strength and a national organization in all parts of the country is the Unity School of Christianity. Founded in 1889 by Charles and Myrtle Fillmore, this largest of the New Thought bodies is headquartered in Kansas City, Missouri. From the very onset, Unity claimed that it had no intention of founding a new sect or denomination. In fact, it still insists that it is a school, not a church or a sect. Still, the Unity groups may easily be seen as churches with their own local membership, meeting places, ministers and book of rituals covering procedures for baptism, Communion, worship, marriage and funerals. Even so, Unity insists that it does not aim to take anyone out of his or her own church. Most of its work is done through its literature, which circulates widely among the Protestant, Catholic and Jewish bodies.[36]

Melton says that in respect to beliefs, "Unity is distinctive within the New Thought movement on two points: an emphasis on Jesus as the Christ and reincarnation." Apart from these two concepts, Unity teachings closely resemble those of the other New Thought bodies. Despite incorporating several aspects of Hindu teaching, Charles Fillmore was one of the most Christ-centered teachers in New Thought. He regarded Unity as "Scientific Christianity" and Christ as the Word, the perfect expression of God. While Fillmore taught reincarnation, he did not emphasize it. Still, reports say that he considered himself to be a reincarnation of the apostle Paul.[37]

In 1889, two movements merged to form the Divine Science Federation International. One movement was headed by Malinda Cramer and the other by Nona L. Brooks and her sister Fannie James. These two movements were distant from one another and based on the experiences of two women, Cramer and Brooks, who were unknown to each other. For twenty-five years Malinda Cramer had been an invalid. Then, in 1885, she discovered metaphysical truth and was healed in San Francisco. She became a teacher of the science of health; in 1888 she chartered the College of Divine Science and began to publish *Harmony,* a monthly periodical. Fannie James and

Nona Brooks moved to Pueblo, Colorado, where Brooks was cured of a throat condition. Her healing came through the realization of the omnipotence of God. Then James began to teach classes, while Brooks began to treat people. They moved to Denver. In 1889 Cramer made her first trip to Denver, where she discovered that her ideas corresponded with those of Brooks and James. A long-term cooperation began. In 1898, the two groups incorporated as the Divine Science College. The work grew slowly, first in the West and then in the East. In fact, it took until 1957 for the Divine Science Federation International to be formed as a merger of cooperative Divine Science organizations.[38]

The cornerstone of Divine Science teaching is the omnipotence of God. God fills all, is infinite Spirit and is the one and only substance. This reality is the basis of all Divine Science thinking. The omnipotence, omnipresence and omniscience of God demonstrate the unreality of evil, which has no independent existence. Evil exists only because individuals support its existence by their belief. Creation is both the self-expression of God and Spirit. Divine Science postulates that humankind is the very likeness and image of God, at one with the Creator. The individual realizes eternal life only by realizing the true nature of self.[39]

The Church of Religious Science emerged later than any of the major groups considered to be part of the New Thought movement. In the early years, it did not label itself New Thought or identify with the New Thought movement. In fact, some early members of the Religious Science movement deny that they were ever "New Thoughters." Despite differences in some important respects from other New Thought groups, Religious Science did maintain certain beliefs and characteristics that matched New Thought. A partial list includes its concept of humankind as divine, the centrality of Mind, its insistence on the immanence of God to a point scarcely to be distinguished from pantheism, its practice of metaphysical healing and its clear distinction between the Jesus of history and the Christ. Moreover, Religious Science is a member of the International New Thought Alliance and has participated in its activities for years.[40]

Ernest Holmes and his brother Fenwicke grew up in a devoutly religious home. Early in their careers they became interested in metaphysical thought. In 1917 they founded the Metaphysical Institute in Los Angeles and began a periodical, *Up Lift*. Their first books were published two years later: *Creative Mind* by Ernest and *The Law of Mind in Action* by Fenwicke.[41]

By 1927 Ernest had a wide base, from which he founded the Institute of Religious Science. The institute continued to grow, especially in the West, with the name *Church* being affixed to new branches. In 1949, after some reorganization, the Church of Religious Science was created, with the word *United* added later.

The basic teachings of the United Church of Religious Science are located in the four chapters of *Science of Mind,* published in 1928. According to Holmes, freedom is the birthright of every person. The love and the law of God, which are perfect, are the answer to human problems. "Science of Mind" is a study of God, the power and intelligence behind creation. The path to freedom is to learn of God, his love and law, and to apply what is learned. Religious Science regards this application as a scientific process, not something mysterious or supernatural.[42]

Christian Science

Christian Science, a religion founded by Mary Baker Eddy (1821-1910), is currently in decline. Yet it is still a nationally recognized movement with substantial strength in America.[43] In many ways Christian Science reflected the culture of late-nineteenth-century America, but it is usually regarded as an alternative or nontraditional religion, a minority religion, a sect, a new religion or an established cult.

There are several reasons for such labels. First, in several areas of belief and practice Christian Science differs significantly from what is regarded as normative in American culture. The major tenets of Christian Science are not in harmony with those of orthodox Christianity, or even the mainstream of Western Christianity, despite Eddy's claim to reinstate primitive Christianity and its lost element of healing. Second, much of what has been written concerning Christian Science is highly partisan, either positive or negative, thus contributing to exaggerated claims about the movement. Third, Christian Science has gone through conflicts, being criticized and scorned until its adherents have become hypersensitive and defensive, even against the well-substantiated judgments of impartial scholars concerning their religion.[44]

At least two other factors have fostered such views of Christian Science, especially the cultic label: Eddy's authoritarian personality and Christian Science's occultic connections. Mary Baker Eddy's actions and words contributed to the public opinion of her as a cult leader. She regarded herself as "God's mouthpiece" on matters pertaining to Christian Science. Her style was very authoritarian; she required her followers to refer to her as "our leader." Within Christian Science circles her word was not challenged. Furthermore, a mystical aura surrounded Eddy. Having acquired considerable wealth, she lived in luxurious seclusion, a situation that fostered many apocryphal stories of her larger-than-life feats.[45]

Christian Science's relationship to the occult is more open to question. Eddy disavowed any connection between Christian Science and the occult. On the surface, this would appear to be correct. Yet as a young woman she had had considerable interest in spiritualism. Of more importance, M.A.M. (malicious animal magnetism) became a fundamental teaching of Christian Science. Eddy argued that her physical afflictions were caused by the malicious thoughts of others—that is, a type of black magic.[46]

A major point of controversy is the relationship of Christian Science to New Thought. Christian Science claims to be in possession of unique truth revealed in its founder, Eddy, and thus has chosen to sharply dissociate itself from the New Thought movement. Yet any comparison between New Thought and Christian Science in respect to major points of belief demonstrates how close Christian Science is to New Thought.

This statement, of course, is not to contend that Christian Science and New Thought are identical, for in a number of areas they differ significantly. For example, the Christian Scientist conviction that Eddy's teachings constitute a final revelation has produced an authoritarianism not found in New Thought. Next, negativism has dominated Christian Science—its members tend to be very fearful—while a prevailing optimism exists in the New Thought movement. Third, Christian Science categorically rejects the use of medical remedies, while most adherents of New Thought are not absolutely opposed to cooperation with physicians in the treatment of disease, though they prefer nonmedical means of healing. Moreover, Christian Science is much more organized and institutional than is New Thought. Still, despite some sharp differences between the two, they are facets of the same general thought movement, sometimes described as the metaphysical movement.[47]

Mary Baker was born in Bow, New Hampshire, in humble surroundings and was reared a strict Congregationalist by her parents. Until her twenty-second year, her young life was marked by frequent emotional and physical illnesses. In an attempt to remedy these problems, the then-infant science of mesmerism was frequently applied to her case, with some success. Mary Baker was married three times, the last at age fifty-six to Asa G. Eddy, a successful businessman, whose name she retained. The first and third marriages ended in death, the second by divorce.[48]

The real history of Christian Science, however, cannot be told unless Phineas P. Quimby is considered. It was from this man, most non-Christian Science writers believe, that Eddy received the beginnings of her ideas on healing, though she did add to Quimby's thought and even modified it significantly. Yet the official Christian Science view is that Quimby was only a mesmerist healer and that Eddy acquired little from him; instead, she gave him ideas, which later became the basis of the New Thought movement. But as Charles Braden indicates, "there can be no doubt that Mrs. Eddy was deeply and favorably impressed by Quimby and his ideas." She believed that Quimby had healed her, and she became his adoring disciple, lavishing him with praise. In later years Eddy's recollections of Quimby were not as positive. After Quimby's death she began to develop her own system of spiritual healing, built on the principle that mind is the only reality and matter is an illusion. She said that Christ had healed by his spiritual influence, and this art she claimed to have rediscovered by revelation of the Scriptures.[49]

In *Science and Health,* which enjoyed immense success and went through many editions until her death in 1910, Eddy stated her principles and her healing methods. Suffering and death are the effects of false thinking, which consists of a mistaken belief in the existence of matter. Health, therefore, is to be restored not by medical treatment but by applying right thinking to the illusions of the patient.[50]

Eddy began the Christian Scientists Association in 1876 and chartered the Church of Christ, Scientist, three years later. The Metaphysical College was founded in 1881. From that time Christian Science spread, especially in the English-speaking countries, and also in Germany. In 1892 the church received its present organization. At the center stood the First Church of Christ, Scientist, of Boston, which became known as the mother church. Other Christian Science churches are regarded as branches, although each is independently governed. Eddy incorporated the doctrines and bylaws of the church into the church manual of 1895. Since her death the organization has been in the hands of a board of directors, who hold their office for life and appoint their successors. The organization's leading publication, *The Christian Science Monitor,* a well-respected newspaper, is one of its principal assets.[51]

Theologically, Christian Science does not agree with the basic tenets of traditional Christianity. While it utilizes the theological terms of historic Christianity, it gives metaphysical meanings to these words. The pillars of authority for Christian Science are the Bible and Eddy's writings, but Eddy's writings are preeminent. Church members regard her writings as divine revelation. The Bible is seen largely as a book of allegories and is to be interpreted through her words. For the Church of Christ, Scientist, the most important authority is *Science and Health,* which Eddy said contained the perfect word of God and was therefore divine and infallible in its teaching.[52]

Christian Science maintains a monistic view of God. God is Divine Principle, not the supreme being of Christianity. God is mind, and mind is all. Christian Science's great truth is that God as spirit is all in all. Everything is mind or spirit—or, rather, there is no reality except mind or spirit. Mind or spirit is truth, love, power, life and goodness. Materiality is evil, sin, sickness, death and unreality. *Trinity* in Christian Science doctrine relates to the threefold nature of Divine Principle or God: truth, life and love. God, Christ and the Holy Spirit are not persons.[53]

Since Jesus of Nazareth is a physical man, he cannot be identified with God in Christian Science teaching. Only Christ, as the principle of mind, is identified with God. Christian Science rejects any notion of a physical incarnation of Christ, insisting that Mary conceived Christ only as a spiritual idea. Given that God is mind and spirit, and nothing exists that is not spirit, it follows that there can be no matter or flesh; these are only illusions. Therefore, Christ did not possess a body. He did not die on a cross or rise from the grave. In fact, when Jesus left the grave, he knew that he had not died and that no person could die. Each individual must acquire such knowledge, for salvation comes from an understanding of the illusory character of death. Salvation to the Christian Scientist is gaining the understanding that a human being's life is wholly derived from God the Spirit, and is not mortal and material.[54]

According to Christian Science, humanity is created in God's image as spirit and mind and is good. Therefore, human beings are incapable of sin and immune to sickness and death. Humanity is regarded as equal with God in respect to his origin, character and eternity. Church doctrine insists that heaven and hell are present states of a person's thoughts, not real future dwelling places. Nevertheless, while laying claim to such metaphysical idealism, Christian Science tolerates marriage and such things as money and

food, since in the imperfection of their faith human beings do not completely accept the fact that God, or Mind, is all.[55] (As I have noted, Mary Baker
Eddy herself was thrice married, and she had great interest in the acquisition
of money.)

The central claim of Eddy and Christian Science is that she has restored
to Christendom the power of healing lost since the early days of the church.
Indeed, the chief attraction of Christian Science lies in its seeming power
over disease and mental conflict. Nevertheless, Christian Science should not
be seen as a faith-healing religion. Because Christian Science regards all
forms of illness as an illusion, it makes no claim to *heal* sickness in any strict
sense. Christian Scientists claim that their healing is not mental—that is,
only a phase of the action of the human mind, which in some unexpected
way results in the cure of disease. In fact, Charles Braden notes a contrary
perspective: "the physical healing of Christian Science results now, as in
Jesus' time, from the operation of divine Principle, before which sin and
disease lose their reality in human consciousness and disappear as naturally
and as necessarily as darkness gives place to light." If Mrs. Eddy is correct
and "the cause of so-called disease is mental, a mortal fear, a mistaken belief
or conviction" regarding the power of ill-health, then the remedy is to "get
rid of the mistaken belief."[56]

One may free him or herself of an erroneous belief without going through
formal church channels. People have read *Science and Health* on their own,
and many claim to have found health in this way. However, the usual course
of action is to receive help from a practitioner. Such a person has received
special training concerning how to rid supposed sufferers of their errors,
thus providing a cure.[57]

Throughout the world, Christian Science services are simple and uniform.
A distinctive of Christian Science is that its message is never preached. The
church has no clergy or priesthood, no preachers and sermons. Rather, the
emphasis is upon the uniform lesson-sermons, which are read aloud from
the Bible and *Science and Health,* without comments, explanations or interpretations, by readers elected from the congregation. This procedure was
decreed by the founder. In this way the Christian Science tenets received
from readings are not embellished, and Mary Baker Eddy's special status
is protected. Eddy was and still remains the first and last word about the
truth of Christian Science.[58]

The beliefs of Christian Science set it apart from the mainstream of nineteenth-century Protestantism, giving it a sectarian and even cultic character. Nevertheless, other characteristics of Christian Science resemble those of nineteenth-century culture and even the religious mainstream. Christian Science did not draw its membership from the socially downtrodden but included many educated and wealthy people, as have other metaphysical groups. Also, Christian Science mirrored some of the same impulses that gave birth to Protestant liberalism. For example, it embodied an idealism that was, in a sense, an extreme form of positive thinking. Furthermore, most moral teachings of Christian Science are the ones commonly accepted by the major denominations.[59]

Albanese notes some other important ways in which Christian Scientists showed themselves to be citizens of nineteenth-century America. First of all, they designated themselves as "Christian Scientists." In a century that had witnessed impressive advances in science, the use of the word *science* carried much status. Christian Science claimed that its healings, "like scientific experiments, were repeatable procedures" and thus demonstrable. These healings "could be counted on, so long as one had studied and practiced correctly." Thus Eddy placed her new teaching into a scientific framework. Second, Mary Baker Eddy built an organizational edifice as American as the business structures of the Gilded Age. The Christian Science organization "became a masterpiece of technical efficiency," with bureaucratic principles rivaling those in the "structures built by John D. Rockefeller and Andrew Carnegie."[60]

Third, the American backdrop to Christian Science was mirrored in Eddy's life and the movement she spawned. In many ways, her problems were shared by others in the Gilded Age. This was a time of spiritual malaise beneath the surface brilliance of a prosperous America. It was an America of anxieties and tensions: recovery from the Civil War, great industrial growth, new waves of migrations, an increase of cultural pluralism and intellectual challenges to the supernatural aspects of Christianity. Into such a world Eddy brought a movement whose message "provided some form of resolution for the key anxieties of the era." She offered her followers "a bastion of security in the Mother Church," a purposeful life that could be lived alone when urbanization was breaking down community values, and "a telling rebuttal to a male-oriented America that had denied a public place to women and their concerns."[61]

Early
Eastern Groups

T his study does not regard Hinduism, Buddhism and Islam as cultic or occultic. They are world religions. Nevertheless, like Christianity, these world religions have spawned cultic bodies. While these spinoffs would not necessarily be regarded as cultic in their native settings, they are new religions in America. They have brought new beliefs and new cultures to America. Thus, in sociological terms, some Eastern groups in America can be regarded as cultic. The early Eastern religious groups are usually closely related to the world religions that parented them and thus often escape the cult label, which was not widely employed in the years before the 1920s. Yet they laid the foundation for the outbreak of Eastern cults that contemporary America has witnessed.

This section will not only deal with the early Eastern transplants but also provide a brief background to Hinduism, Buddhism and Islam. For if one is to understand the beliefs and practices of Eastern cults, one needs a basic knowledge of Eastern world religions and their worldviews.

Eastern Contacts

While hard evidence is meager, it has been conjectured that Hinduism and Buddhism have had some influence on Neoplatonism. If one accepts this not unreasonable assumption, then the entire alternative-reality tradition in the West always has had at least some indirect contact with India.[1] As William McNeill contends, contacts between the East and West picked up in the sixteenth century, after having been in a decline from about A.D. 500 to 1500.[2] Americans began to show interest in Eastern religions about 1700, several centuries after Europeans had begun to be attracted to them. This American fascination with Eastern religious and philosophical ideas gradually accelerated, becoming well advanced by the end of the nineteenth century.[3]

America's gradual awakening to Eastern faiths did not occur in a vacuum. Rather, it developed as a part of the wider development of alternative religions, as an aspect of extended cultural contacts and in relation to certain political decisions. The strongest factor until at least the late nineteenth century was the growth of the alternative religious tradition. Occult and metaphysical groups interacted with Eastern faiths and became the primary avenues for introducing Eastern religion and thought to America.

Unitarianism must be regarded as the most important early vehicle for bringing Eastern religion to public attention in America. The Unitarian Church forged an alliance with several Hindu groups and brought the first Hindu teachers to America. The Transcendentalists, particularly Ralph Waldo Emerson and Henry David Thoreau, delighted in Eastern thought and did much to promote it in America. The Theosophical Society helped to popularize Asian religions. Being a blend of Hinduism, Spiritualism, Buddhism, occultism and rationalism, Theosophy presented an extraordinary amalgam of the new and old, the West and East. William James, who founded the American Society for Psychical Research in 1884, and his brother Henry were interested in Eastern religions and drew a following for this pursuit. Astrology with its Eastern perspective became more respectable in the late nineteenth century.[4]

The emergence of the alternative religious tradition in the West was fittingly symbolized by the 1893 World Parliament of Religions, where for the first time representatives of all the major world religions gathered in Chicago for dialogue on many issues and a sharing of belief systems. Yet generally Americans did not discover Eastern religions through personal contacts. Instead, the American knowledge of religions from the East came largely from the printed page. For most Americans in the nineteenth century, the convergence of East and West was primarily a literary enterprise and an intellectual experience. To be sure, New England merchants traded in China and India, Protestant missionaries had contact with Asian peoples, and members of the Theosophical Society found their way to the East, but most conceptions of Eastern religion were forged by the written word. Travel between the United States and Asia, by either Americans or Asians, was quite minimal.[5]

Herein can be found a major difference between the nineteenth century and the contemporary scene. In the last half of the twentieth century, the exchange between America and the East has been direct. American soldiers, businesspeople and students have traveled to the East, while Asians have steadily arrived in the United States. Contemporary Americans have a much greater opportunity to explore the Eastern religions firsthand.[6]

Though an influx of Asians had arrived in late-nineteenth-century America, a series of exclusion acts in the early twentieth century cut immigration and denied the possibility of citizenship to Asians already in America.[7] Gordon Melton says these acts had two effects on alternative religions. "First, they cut off the trickle of Eastern teachers coming to the United States and effectively limited the spread of Hinduism and Buddhism. Second, the exclusion of Asian teachers shifted the mode of transmission of Asian teaching. After World War I such teachings were filtered" (and often distorted) "through the writings of American occult teachers." During the first half of the twentieth century, a number of Americans attracted disciples by their claims to secret wisdom, actually a combination of Eastern and Western occult thought.[8] This situation of limited direct contact with Eastern religions would, of course, change in the last half of the twentieth century, when America's cultural pluralism was enhanced by a new influx of Asians.

According to Carl Jackson, the reaction to Asian thought is closely connected to the peculiar religious climate of nineteenth-century America. Though vigorous on the surface, American Christianity faced a serious crisis in the latter part of the century. Individuals' misgivings regarding Christian beliefs played a pivotal role in promoting a positive response to Asian ideas. In fact, "an affirmative reaction to Oriental religion was often a vote against doctrinaire Christianity, not a vote for an alternative religious system. The more critical American thinkers became of the tribalism of traditional Christianity, the more sympathetic many became to Oriental religions." In this reaction one can detect another difference between the nineteenth- and twentieth-century responses to Asiatic religions. In the post-Christian era of the late twentieth century there is little pressure to embrace the Christian faith. Therefore, Americans are exploring the meaning of Eastern ideas because they are interested in them, not because they are rebelling against the church. The nineteenth-century response, however, came more out of a negative reaction to Christianity.[9]

Hinduism as a World Religion

Hinduism is a very ancient religion, and so diverse as to nearly defy definition. It lacks an individual founder, a definite relationship to an authoritative scripture and any set of issues around which it might orient itself. In fact, Hinduism ranges from a profoundly philosophical understanding of the nature of the universe and humanity to popular devotion to one or another of the gods in many small sects and cults. Still, there are themes common to the various Hindu religious movements, and it is possible to speak of Hinduism as a single religion.[10]

Hinduism has grown up on the Indian subcontinent over a period of three millennia. Hindus relate to a common history—that of India. They do hold certain ideas in common, such as beliefs in reincarnation and karma, and they do practice certain disciplines, the most common being yoga. Two writings, the Vedas and Upanishads, have a particular value for Hindus, although they seldom function as authoritative books as do the Bible and the Qur'an.[11]

The central belief of Hinduism is that there is one Universal Spirit, or Eternal Essence, without beginning or end, called Brahman, which means the World Soul. The World Soul is the three-in-one-God called Trimutri, consisting of Brahman the creator, Vishnu the preserver and Shiva the destroyer. Humanity is not considered to be outside the World Soul, but part of it.

Over the centuries, many Hindus have considered that the world is one reality and the appearance of separation is an illusion. Behind the material world in which people live is a vast power or impersonal force. The Hindus think of this power as the basic reality in the universe, and they call it Brahman. Matter, which promotes a sense of distinctiveness and separation, contains less reality than people commonly assume. In fact, the doctrine of maya states that the world is a grand illusion. Most important, residing within each human being is the Atman, the spark of sacred power that unites individuals to Brahman. And since God is the Atman in each person, as people attain the realization of personal divinity, they see the relativity and contingency of all that had seemed to be reality—including each person's own body, feelings and thoughts.[12]

This understanding of reality, called monism, was not accepted by all Hindus. Some Hindu sects maintain a form of dualism, insisting that spirit and matter are eternally different and separate. Others hold that the soul can never become one with God. Yet it is monism that gives Indian thought its characteristic flavor, and it has become the fundamental attraction of Hinduism for Westerners.[13]

The belief in transmigration also separates the Eastern faiths, including Hinduism, Buddhism and Jainism, from the religions of the West. This doctrine may be seen as a watershed, broadly dividing the great religions of the world. Hinduism maintains that the soul inhabits many bodies in its journey through the cosmos until it reaches its final goal, union with the World Soul. While Judaism, Christianity and Islam generally teach that humanity is a special creation, possessing an immortal soul that is denied to the lower animals, Hinduism believes that all living things have souls. These souls are essentially equal, being distinguished only through *karma,* or the effect of previous deeds, which conditions successive rebirths in different types of bodies.[14]

Hinduism is more than a set of beliefs. In fact, religious experience and especially religious discipline are high priorities with most Hindus. Catherine Albanese indicates that in Hinduism there are three broad paths to God. First is the "path of devotion," called *bhakti.* The god-centered culture of India expected that each individual would express personal worship to at least one of India's many gods and goddesses. The second route to God is the "way of action." The basis of Indian society is the class or caste system. Each individual is born into a particular class and thus acquires a birthright, a set of prescribed obligations and action. "The religious way of action taught that each person must live according to the law for his or her caste." The faithful performance of the duties required by one's state in life, called *karma,* will lead to a rebirth in a higher state in the next lifetime. The third path to God is the "way of knowledge." As in the occult and metaphysical traditions, knowledge involves more than the acquisition of information and the exercise of rational thought. Instead, it entails an understanding of the basic meaning of life, "a total realization in mind, heart, and body of the universal being of Brahman." This knowledge, called *jnana,* is gained through a serious cultivation of inner states of mind. There are various techniques and disciplines to facilitate this knowledge, which leads to mystical experience.[15]

Hindu Groups in America

Of all the Eastern faiths, Hinduism has had the greatest influence on American religion. An important reason for this is that Britain began to colonize India during the seventeenth and eighteenth centuries. Unlike Japan and China, which largely closed their doors to Westerners until the nineteenth century, India made possible considerable religious interaction between Hinduism and Christianity. Thus before any Hindu leaders attempted to establish a religious body in the United States, Americans were drinking at the well of Indian wisdom.[16]

The three sides of Indian Hinduism arrived in America in separate waves. First and most influential, of course, has been the philosophic, impacting American thought early in the nineteenth century. The centrality of this emphasis was affirmed by the first Hindu religious organization established in the West, the Vedanta Society. Next to arrive were the yoga groups, as if to provide a tangible means for obtaining the promises of Vedanta. Last, and primarily after World War II in the Krishna Consciousness group, has come bhakti, devotional Hinduism.[17]

Two major Hindu groups arrived in America before World War II, the Vedanta Society and the Self-Realization Fellowship. The Vedanta Society was the most influential of these groups, and the only Hindu body established in America before 1900. The society grew out of the vision of Sri Ramakrishna (1836-86) and the work of his prime disciple, Swami Vivekananda. Ramakrishna never traveled beyond northern India, and he knew nothing of Western learning. But after his death, Vivekananda shaped his movement into an international witness to Hinduism, committed not only to the mystical ideal of Ramakrishna but also to action in the world. In 1893 Vivekananda arrived in America and began to teach his universal religion. He made a great impression in the World Parliament of Religions, and for two years he traveled throughout the United States, lecturing and gathering members. In 1895 he founded the Vedanta Society and presented Hinduism to Americans in a form they were likely to understand.[18]

When Vedanta came to the United States, it introduced Americans to India's most prevalent type of monistic religious philosophy. Vedanta represents an intellectual approach to Hinduism, appealing to the college-educated. As Vedanta societies offered lectures on Vedanta philosophy and literature, the way of knowledge, or jnana, became primarily the way of intellectual understanding. Yet in both India and America, the way of action, karma, was also important to the movement. The way of devotion, or bhakti, while less important, accompanied Vedanta in its temple meetings and was practiced by individual members in their homes.[19]

Melton summarizes the central ideas of Vedanta monistic philosophy in three propositions. First, "reality is universal Love." Love is Vedanta, the goal of all knowledge. Next, "the world is illusion." All varieties of its manifestation are nothing but appearance. Third, "the individual 'I,' or ego, that we feel within us is always identical with the ultimate principle. The self is the same as Reality."[20]

Vedanta attracted upper- and middle-class Americans who had some knowledge of Indian culture and interest in Eastern spirituality. More than any other Hindu movement in America, Vedanta conformed to Christian customs, developing a religious service that included hymns, scripture, prayers and sermons. In particular, many insights drawn from Vedanta corresponded with liberal Protestant teachings concerning the goodness of human nature and the immanence of God.[21]

Vedanta, unlike other Hindu movements, is not built on the teacher-student relationship. In Vedanta, Ramakrishna and Vivekananda are highly esteemed, but they and their successors are not regarded as gurus who direct one's spiritual progress. In Vedanta the personality and presence of the guru are less important than they are in most other Hindu movements. While Vedanta continued into the twentieth century, its intellectual emphasis hampered its growth. The real popularity of Hinduism lay with the newer movements, which stressed yoga as a less intellectual approach to the way of jnana. The ways of karma (action) and bhakti (devotion) were to have their impact, but not until after World War II.[22]

The second major Hindu body to arrive in the United States was the Self-Realization Fellowship. It came to America in 1920, when Paramahansa Yogananda (1893-1952) attended the International Congress of Religious Liberals held under the auspices of the Unitarian Church. For over thirty years Yogananda remained in America, becoming the first Hindu master to teach in the West for such a lengthy period. With a winning personality and a willingness to use American publicity methods to promote his beliefs, he attracted many followers. In 1920 Yogananda formed a small center in Boston. By 1935 his movement had spread to the West Coast, where the Self-Realization Fellowship was formed with national headquarters in Los Angeles. Since then the Fellowship has spread all over the world, including

India. By the early 1970s the movement had forty-four centers in the United States, with about 200,000 people involved in it at various levels.[23]

Instead of being an intellectual Vedantist, Yogananda was a yogi, bringing with him the essential teaching of traditional yoga philosophy, based on the ancient Yoga Sutras of Patanjali (c. 100 B.C.). This philosophy contends that underneath all apparent limitations and frustrations, people are an eternal soul. They have the drive and the capacity for love, joy and power. But because of ignorance they misdirect their energy toward outward things in the material world. As a yogi, Yogananda brought to America not only this teaching but also techniques for implementing it.[24]

The word *yoga* means "union," including the discipline that brings union. Therefore, *yoga* denotes the teaching and practice that endeavor to unify a person's inner being, and the accompanying understanding of the basic unity of all things in Brahman. This self-realization or God-realization entails an experiential union with the divine spark within, and a mystical encounter with the All-Power in the universe.[25]

The way of this self-realization is yoga, which entails a number of scientific techniques for promoting a personal experience of God. The fundamental principles of yoga begin with the body. By means of a series of physical exercises, a person relaxes and stretches away the tensions that obstruct spiritual happiness and peace. The individual learns to keep the body in various prescribed physical postures. As a result, energy shifts from one area of the body to another, allowing the spiritual center to receive the divine energy. Control of breathing induces a quiet that could promote a release into a condition of bliss. Because the object of yoga is mental separation from the material world, such bliss is a state of mind. Meditation techniques, therefore, are basic to yoga. A method for calming a person's thoughts is fixing inwardly on a sacred sound, called a mantra.[26]

In several ways the Self-Realization Fellowship reflected American culture in the first half of the twentieth century. Yogananda employed the vocabulary of modern Western science to interpret to Western audiences the ancient wisdom of yoga. This method was typical of the yoga master in the West. Yoga masters insisted that their methods and philosophy were scientific and supported by the discoveries of Western science. The Self-Realization Fellowship also made accommodations to the dominant Christian culture. The Ten Commandments and the teachings of Jesus and Paul were adjusted to harmonize with the teachings and techniques of the Fellowship.

In fact, Jesus and Paul were regarded as past yoga masters. Even the Fellowship's services were Protestantized, using an invocation, an altar, hymns, announcements and a closing blessing.[27]

Buddhism as a World Religion

Buddhism arose as a reformist movement with roots in Hinduism. Some call Buddhism an export version of Hinduism, just as Christianity can be considered an export version of Judaism. The founder, Siddhartha Gautama (563?-483? B.C.), was born a prince in a small Hindu state in northern India. His early years were a time of pleasure and protection from the real world, especially its evil and suffering. His life changed in 529, when he left the palace and began a wandering quest for the meaning of life. His search ended when he was thirty-five. After extended meditation, he achieved enlightenment as he sat under a fig or "bo" tree. He realized that life consists of suffering, desire causes suffering, and there can be an end to desire. To extinguish desire one had to follow Gautama's path. After his enlightenment Gautama became known as Buddha, the "awakened" or "enlightened" one.[28]

From the very beginning Buddhism emphasized religious wisdom. In its approach to religious wisdom, Buddhism resembled the occult and metaphysical traditions in America and some strands of Hinduism. According to Buddhism, religious wisdom is spiritual insight, an enlightenment acquired not by the cognitive processes of reading and studying but through an emptying of the mind's ordinary and rational content so that light can enter in. While the intellectual content of enlightenment is simple, it contains great depth. Hinduism teaches that the soul or self is identical with God or Brahman. Buddha carries this idea even further. If the self is identical with the one impersonal, universal Brahman, it is also no self or non-Atman in any individualistic sense. An individual is not a personal being but a package of thoughts, sensations and feelings in a state of change.[29]

The teachings of Buddha center on the four basic truths and the eightfold path. The notion of "no self" is a basic clue to an understanding of the four noble truths. First, according to Buddhism, all existence involves suffering. Second, the cause of suffering is desire—that is, the thirst for pleasure, prosperity and continued life. Next, the way to escape suffering, existence and rebirth is to rid oneself of desire. Fourth, to be emancipated from desire, one must follow the eightfold path.[30] This path helps one to end all desire and to achieve Nirvana, which means freedom or emancipation. Nirvana is achieved by meditating and acting in harmony with the spirit of Buddha. When one blows out all the fires of desire and the illusions of self that constrict them, they can break out into a nirvanic ocean and ride the tides of the infinite.[31]

Nearly all Buddhists accepted these basic teachings of Buddha. Yet as time went on and the Buddhist community pondered the meaning of Buddha's message, different understandings of his teachings arose and different forms of Buddhism resulted. India never completely accepted Buddhism. Buddhist teaching spread into other areas of the Far East, and by the third century B.C. it had divided into two great traditions—Theravada and Mahayana Buddhism.[32]

Southern or Theravada Buddhism remained conservative in that it perpetuated the original teachings of the Buddha. Instead of focusing on the community, Theravada emphasizes the individual whose goal is to quench desire completely. In the strict teachings of this tradition, the historical Buddha is revered but not regarded as divine; he was a human being who set an example of what each person might become. Furthermore, Theravada is atheistic, teaching that there is no God to save or condemn people. The ultimate being in the universe is not a divine God; instead, everything goes back to the experience of attaining bliss or pure nonattachment in Nirvana. Theravada is the form of Buddhism of Sri Lanka, Burma, Thailand, Cambodia and Laos.[33]

Mahayana or northern Buddhism developed in China, Tibet, Japan and Korea. It is more flexible than Theravada Buddhism. While respected, the historical Buddha is relatively deemphasized in this version of Buddhism. In fact, the Mahayana school regards anyone who has achieved the experience of enlightenment as a Buddha. It is theoretically possible for anybody to become a Buddha. Therefore, contrary to the atheism of Theravada, Mahayana presents a form of polytheism consisting of many Buddha gods. The hero of Mahayana is not the solitary monk seeking personal enlightenment. Rather, Mahayana exalts an individual, called the *bodhisattva,* who, on the verge of experiencing Nirvana, postpones the time indefinitely in order to serve other human beings.[34]

As Buddhism spread it became quite diverse. Out of the Theravada and Mahayana traditions there arose a number of sects and schools of interpretation. As new spiritual leaders came on the scene, they valued one portion of Buddhist scripture over the rest and interpreted aspects of Buddhist teaching differently. Therefore, the new Buddhist movements focused on different aspects of Buddhism. Furthermore, as Buddhism spread, it took upon itself the national characteristics of each of its adopted countries. Thus the new forms of Buddhism usually had two points of reference: one of the two major schools of Buddhism and national characteristics.[35]

Buddhist Groups in America

Without a knowledge of the international spread of Buddhism, the story of Buddhism in America would be difficult to understand. This is because most Buddhist bodies in the United States represent transplanted forms of the various schools of thought and practice found in Asia, especially Japan. American Buddhists split from these Asiatic groups and formed new bodies, but they are in a minority.[36]

According to Melton, there are three kinds of Buddhist groups in America. "Most are transplanted Chinese, Japanese and other Oriental sects" which keep "contact with a parent body." Such contacts may be institutional or simply the continuation of a teaching. The second type are bodies that have splintered from the transplanted groups. Differences over emphasis, practice, beliefs and race have produced schisms. When a basically Asian body grows by addition of Caucasians, it often splits along racial lines as soon as the Caucasians are numerous enough to form their own group. The third type is the "philosophical Buddhist center" established by one or more leaders who have settled in the United States after studying in Japan.[37]

Though Buddhism made its greatest impact in America after World War II, its presence could be observed prior to this time. Not only had American culture been prepared for Hinduism, but it was also ready for Buddhism. In general, the Transcendentalists drew much of their wisdom from Eastern sources. The Theosophical Society had more direct contacts with Buddhism. Henry Olcott aided the cause of Buddhism overseas and wrote a book discussing the religion for Westerners. His associate, Madame Blavatsky, had a number of Buddhist contacts. Her Tibetan Mahatmas were acquainted with Buddhist practices, and her occult works incorporated Buddhist teachings.[38]

Melton also tells us that the account of Buddhism in America relates closely to the history of Japanese immigration. The Japanese influx to the United States began in 1868, when large numbers of laborers arrived in

Hawaii. A short while later, Japanese immigrants also settled on the West Coast, bringing Buddhism with them. This community grew until a 1907 law limited Japanese immigration.[39]

Many expressions of Japanese Buddhism found their way to America before World War II. For convenience they can be reduced to two types: Pure Land Buddhism and Zen. Buddhism arrived in Hawaii by at least 1889 and in California about a decade later, coming by means of the Jodo Shinshu missionaries. Jodo Shinshu came from the Nishi Hongwanji movement, one of numerous Buddhist sects in Japan and a branch of Pure Land Buddhism. Like all groups in the Mahayana tradition, Pure Land Buddhism taught faith in a Buddha called Amida Buddha. When he experienced enlightenment and became a Buddha, Amida took steps to fulfill his previous bodhisattva vows to establish a paradise or "western kingdom." By trusting in Amida, people could enter the Pure Land after death and there attain enlightenment. To experience this enlightenment, one did not need to develop great meditation techniques or to reach a sinless state. Rather, one had to show gratitude to Amida by calling on him in the formula "Hail to Amida Buddha." Pure Land Buddhism relied on the "other-power" of Amida to attain enlightenment, not the "self-power" emphasized by Theravada and other types of Buddhism.[40]

Of the various types of Buddhism, Pure Land most resembled Christianity. Thus, as Albanese notes, Pure Land Buddhism accommodated itself to American culture during the first half of the twentieth century. From 1899 to 1944 it was "primarily organized by the Nishi Hongwanji sect as the North American Buddhist Mission, and after that date it became the Buddhist Churches of America." Buddhist churches did not exist in Japan. The word *church* was used simply to accommodate American ears. Buddhists made other concessions to the American environment: they began to call their overseer a "bishop" and to have Sunday services and Sunday schools. This Americanization was not unique to the Pure Land, but it was perhaps more pronounced in that group. By the 1970s, the Buddhist Church of America had grown. It was the second-largest Buddhist group in the United States, with about 100,000 people affiliated with it in some way.[41]

The second major form of Buddhism in America was Zen, most notably the Japanese and Tibetan varieties. Though interest in Zen exploded in the years following World War II, it had been introduced in America toward the end of the nineteenth century. Zen is the mystical school of Buddhism, standing in relationship to Buddhism much as contemplative Catholicism does to Christianity and Sufism does to Islam. Zen originated in China as Ch'an Buddhism in the fifth and sixth centuries A.D., arising in the interchange between Buddhist philosophy and Taoist meditative techniques. The founder was Tao-shing (360-434), who brought a mystical dimension to Buddhism. To Buddhist meditative techniques he added the doctrine of instantaneous enlightenment, which provided the mystical element. Instantaneous enlightenment can be described as attaining in one act of illumination the goal of mystical truth.[42]

In the late twelfth and early thirteenth centuries, Zen moved from China to Japan. Here *Ch'an* was transliterated as *Zen,* and it prospered as a combination of Theravada meditation techniques and Mahayana religious philosophy. The objective of Zen was to enable a person to have the experience of enlightenment by means of meditation. In Japanese Zen there arose two major schools, Rinzai and Soto. These two approaches to Zen differed considerably, promoting divergent techniques of meditation and different processes to gain enlightenment.[43]

According to the teachings of Rinzai Zen, enlightenment comes suddenly, being set off by some unusual development that shocks an individual into a different realization of the nature of things. Thus the practice of Rinzai focused on the use of *koans* in meditation. Koans are riddles or verbal puzzles intended to confuse the ordinary mind. The best-known koan is the following question: What is the sound of one hand clapping? A koan is unanswerable by normal reasoning. It was believed that in pondering such a puzzle the mind's grip would be broken, and enlightenment would come as a result.[44]

Zen first reached America in 1893, when a Rinzai monk, Soyen Shaku (1859-1919), addressed the World Parliament of Religions in Chicago. However, the spread of Rinzai Zen throughout America was largely the work of his disciple Daisetz Teitaro Suzuki (1870-1966). After working from 1897 to 1909 as an editor for the Open Court Publishing Company, Suzuki returned to Japan, where he wrote extensively in English about Buddhism. Many of his writings were widely circulated in the United States. When he returned in the fifties, he spoke frequently on university campuses. Suzuki effectively communicated Zen teachings to non-Asian Americans by focusing on themes that corresponded with the contemporary Western philosophy of existentialism. Moreover, he neglected to promote the ritual and discipline associated with the Zen monastic tradition. But it was left to others to establish the Rinzai organization in the United States. Rinzai Zen has had a continuous presence in America since 1928, with the First Zen Institute of America being founded in 1930. Of the two Zen groups, Rinzai is best known. In fact, most Westerners view Zen through the perspective of Rinzai practice.[45]

In the other school, Soto Zen, enlightenment comes gradually by means of a practice that centers on "just sitting." In such a meditation, the mind becomes quiet and emptied of all thought in order that enlightenment might grow. The most obvious difference between Soto and Rinzai is that Soto does not emphasize use of koans to bring about the awakening experience. Soto Zen came to Hawaii in 1903, spreading to the continental United States several decades later. Since the organization of the Zenshuji Mission in Los Angeles in 1922, there has been a continuous presence of Soto in America.[46]

The story of Buddhism in America prior to World War II is not entirely an account of Japanese Buddhism. A number of Chinese migrated to the United States between 1854 and 1883, when legislation restricting their migration was passed. Most Chinese settled on the West Coast; their religion was usually the eclectic form of Buddhism that had been popularized on the Chinese mainland. This version of Buddhism contained Confucian and Taoist elements. Chinese Buddhist centers were erected in several cities, the largest being Buddha's Universal Church, founded in the late 1920s in San Francisco.[47]

Central to the rise of Buddhism in America has been the work of a number of non-Asians who were attracted to Buddhist philosophy and then became advocates to Caucasian audiences. These individuals often became full disciples instead of simply studying Buddhism. At times they gathered other followers around them and formed Western Buddhist societies, the best known being the Friends of Buddhism societies founded in the 1930s.[48]

Islam as a World Religion
Islam is a cousin to Judaism and Christianity that arose in the seventh century A.D.[49] Like them, it originated in the Near East among Semitic people. It is strongly monotheistic and has a holy book that is believed to contain a unique revelation from God. It accepts much of the Old Testament as its own history, claims Abraham as its patriarch and even evidences

some Christian influences. In contrast to Hinduism and Buddhism and resembling Judaism and Christianity, Islam teaches a God who is absolutely different from humanity.[50] Yet Islam carries the notion of transcendence further than do Judaism and Christianity. God's revelation is considered actually a disclosure of his will rather than of his nature, which remains essentially unknown.

John Newport provides a brief summary of Islamic beliefs. *Islam* means "submission to God (Allah)," and *Muslim* means "one who submits." Non-Muslims usually regard the prophet Muhammad as the founder of Islam. However, Muslims take a different view of Muhammad, considering him as God's messenger and the interpreter of the Qur'an, the holy book of Islam. At the age of forty, he began to experience the visions that gave him his prophetic call. Muhammad claimed that the angel Gabriel instructed him to proclaim God's message, and he began to preach monotheism, or belief in one God, while denouncing polytheism as idolatrous.[51]

Muhammad's visions and revelations were written down in the Qur'an. Along with the unrecorded prophecies, or *sunna,* the Qur'an became the foundation for Islam, a new militant religion that was determined to win the world for Allah. The Qur'an differs from the Hebrew-Christian Bible in respect to the time span and method of its reception. The Bible contains diverse material revealed to many people over a period of one thousand years. According to Islamic teaching, the angel Gabriel delivered the Qur'an to one man in private sessions during a period of no more than twenty-two years. The Qur'an is not a history book or a biography of Muhammad. Instead, it is a book about Allah, proclaiming his oneness and sovereignty and humankind's need to submit to him. The sunna is an application of the Qur'an, telling how it is to be used in everyday life.[52]

The fundamental belief of orthodox Islam is a zealous unitarianism. God is undivided and has no partners or associates to share his being. Muslims regard Christianity as a polytheistic religion. Moreover, belief in angels is very important to the Muslim faith, perhaps more than it is to Christianity. Because Islam teaches that God is absolutely different from humanity, there is need for beings between God and humankind to bring God's message to humanity.[53]

Another essential element in the Muslim faith is the belief in apostles or prophets. Islam recognizes many apostles or prophets, including Noah, Abraham, Ishmael, Moses, Elijah and Jesus. Nevertheless, Muhammad is recognized as the greatest one of all. While Islam does not deify Muhammad, he is regarded as the last of the prophets and thus supersedes all his predecessors. Because Islam is the simplest of all religions and the restoration of original monotheism, it claims to be the ultimate religion.[54]

George Braswell writes about the five major practices or "pillars of faith" in Islam. First is a confession: "There is no deity but Allah, and Muhammad is the messenger of Allah."[55] This confession is prayed daily. Second is the practice of prayer five times each day. In preparation for prayer, the Muslim washes hands, arms and feet for ceremonial purification. Prescribed words are spoken and coordinated with genuflections and postures to signify one's relationship to God.[56] The third practice is fasting, which is observed throughout a special lunar month. During this month no food is consumed from sunrise to sunset, and there is no sexual intercourse. Muslims regard fasting as a health measure and see this month as a time to give to the needy and to meditate on God.[57]

Almsgiving, which supports the work of the mosques and provides the livelihood of the clergy, is the fourth practice. The followers of Muhammad are to give certain percentages of their income and possessions to the causes of Islam.[58] The fifth practice is the pilgrimage, or *hajj*. According to the Qur'an, if health and economic conditions are adequate, each Muslim is to make the pilgrimage to Mecca once during his or her lifetime.[59] Some regard the *jihad* as the sixth pillar of Islam. Jihad denotes a "holy effort" or "holy conquest" in the name of Allah. While *jihad* sometimes refers to a Muslim nation going to war against infidels, it is usually used in the context of a missionary effort for the Islamic faith. Muslims are to engage in jihad for Allah. Because this has been taken seriously, Islam has been spread to every continent.[60]

Islamic history demonstrates much unity in doctrinal statements and ritualistic practices. However, since its origins there have been sectarian divisions. The most noted branches are the Sunni and the Shiite. The Sunni branch claimed that Muhammad left no heirs and no individual preferences; its members favored an election of a leader from the community. The Sunni established the caliphate, with the caliph ruling in religious and political matters. *Sunni* means "orthodox" or "traditional"; the Sunni claim to be the true bearers of the Islamic tradition. They emphasize the fundamental authority of the Muslim law and tend to be legalistic. Sunni are the great majority of Muslims and are in all parts of the world.[61]

The second major branch of Islam, the Shiite, is smaller but it has many followers. Shiites differ with the Sunni over the succession issue, claiming that the prophet picked his successor, his cousin and son-in-law Ali. The Shiites believed that the leaders of Islam were to come from the prophet's family; they thus established the imamate and appointed Ali as the first imam. By the end of the ninth century, twelve imams had ruled. The twelfth one vanished, and Shiites believe that he went into occultation—that he is hidden and will return sometime. Until this event, a *mujtahid* or *ayatollah*, acting as an agent of the hidden imam, is to preside over the Islamic community. The Shiites are represented heavily in Iran, Iraq and Lebanon.[62]

The greatest influence on the American cult movements of the late twentieth century did not come from the two major Islamic groups, however, but from esoteric and mystical Islam, known as Sufism. The followers of this tradition are called Sufis. While all Sufis worship the God of the Qur'an and traditional Islam, there are two emphases within the movement. The most orthodox group claims that the proper goal is only to develop a more immediate and direct communion with Allah. A less orthodox group, given to esoteric extravagances, moves closer to pantheistic forms of mystical absorption and almost passes over the line drawn between God and creation.[63]

The origin of Sufism is unclear. We do know, however, that mystical Islam had its practitioners even in the seventh century. This mystical emphasis arose for at least three reasons. First, the Qur'an records incidents in Muhammad's life that can be interpreted as mystical experiences. Second, elements within Islam reacted against the corruption and lifestyles of luxury that had emerged by the eighth century. The Sufis desired a life of simplicity and devotion. Third, there arose a discontent with the abstraction, dryness and legalism of Islamic law and dogma as developed in the tenth and eleventh centuries. Orthodox Islam had obviously failed to satisfy the needs people had for a greater devotional spirit.[64]

Newport points out that "practice or experience is all important for the Sufis." By the eleventh century, the belief that an individual should submit to his spiritual master or guide had gained strength among the Sufis. "The master concept is an Islamic parallel to the Hindu guru." These masters introduced their followers to the inward meaning of the normative devotional practices of Islam such as prayers, almsgiving and fasting. The way taught by these Sufi masters consisted of "three main grades: the novice, the traveler, and the attainer."[65]

Sufi masters organized themselves into orders and developed special techniques for knowing God. At first these Sufi orders centered on a great master and his methods for experiencing the divine. The repetition of the ninety-nine beautiful names of God, aided by prayer beads, was one such technique. These repetitions helped focus the mind on God and produced considerable emotion, which in turn prompted chanting and swaying. The dervish dance was another important technique. In the dervish dance, the individual participates in a rhythmic movement of the body and recitations that induce detachment from the material world and concentration on God. These rhythmic and musical techniques cause some Sufis to collapse in ecstasy and call out in various tongues.[66]

The Sufi orders still exist, and some have had great success in spreading Islam in Indonesia, India and Africa. Also, people outside of Islam have discovered Sufism and have appreciated its qualities. In the West, Sufism has gained a significance beyond its status as an Islamic sect. Modern Sufi leaders contend that Sufi techniques offer a universal process by which humans can encounter God, truth and beauty. These techniques have become an important aspect of the mystical, emotional and nonrational approach to religion that is so prevalent in the late twentieth century. Some of the techniques of the Sufi masters were introduced in the West by Subud, Gurdjieff, and Oscar Ichaza and the Arica movement. However, only since World War II, as a consequence of the counterculture, has Sufism made an impact in America.[67]

Islamic Groups in America
The presence of Islam in American history has been largely hidden. Only since oil shifted much political and economic power to the Arabs in the 1970s has Islam been made visible to the average American. The first Muslims came to the New World in the sixteenth century with the Spanish explorers and slave traders. But significant numbers of Muslims did not begin to enter America until the late nineteenth and early twentieth centuries. When immigration laws changed after World War II, many more Muslim immigrants began arriving. And when oil wealth expanded the budgets of several Arab countries, Muslim students flocked to American colleges and universities by the tens of thousands.[68]

Nearly all the Islamic fringe religions were present in America prior to World War II. Some of the groups related to Sufism—Lovers of Meher

Baba from India and Gurdjieff with Russian origins—arrived before the war. Others, such as Subud from Indonesia and Arica with roots in Bolivia, came after the war. Regardless of the time of their arrival, these groups had little visibility until the surge of the counterculture in the 1960s.[69]

Most of the Black Muslim bodies originated in America before World War II. Several of these groups were set off from American society because of their race and from mainstream Islam because of their beliefs. The Moorish-American Science Temple was one example. Timothy Drew emerged in 1913 as Noble Drew Ali, "Prophet of Islam." Most present-day Black Muslim groups trace their origin to Ali's activity. The teachings of the Moorish Temple are drawn from its Holy Koran, which is not the same as the Qur'an of orthodox Islam. The Temple's Holy Koran enunciates a different version of the creation and fall, the origin of the black race, and opposition to Christianity. Noble Drew Ali believed that only Islam could unite the black people; that the black race is "Asiatic" or Moorish; that Jesus was a black man who was executed by white Romans; and that Moorish-Americans must be united under Allah and his prophet.[70]

The Nation of Islam, the largest of the Black Muslim groups, originated in 1930, but its major growth took place in the late fifties and sixties as the civil rights movement gained momentum. Major changes in the organization took place after 1960. Thus I will give it fuller consideration in a later chapter.

An Islamic offshoot prominent in America both before and after World War II was the Baha'i religion. Muslims generally regard Baha'i as an Islamic heresy. Its greatest difference with Islam is that Baha'i refuses to revere Muhammad exclusively as preeminent among the prophets. Baha'i may contain enough diverse elements to be regarded as a genuinely new religion. The Shiite wing of Islam must be regarded as the most basic root of Baha'i, but there are also Sufi mystical qualities, Zoroastrian influences and even Christian elements.[71] Since its origins it has spread into numerous countries, at times making adaptations to these cultures.

The Baha'i religion originated in Persia, now known as Iran, with a Shiite Muslim named Siyyid Ali Muhammad (1819-50). Like other Shiites, he had grown up in expectation that the hidden imam would return to guide Islam correctly. In 1844 Siyyid Ali Muhammad declared that he was the expected twelfth imam. He gathered disciples and adopted the title of Bab, or "gate." He preached across Persia until the authorities had him imprisoned and executed in 1850.[72] Among his followers was Husayn Ali (1817-92), later known as Baha'u'llah (the glory of God). Husayn Ali came to see himself as the manifestation of God for the present age, the greatest in a long line of prophets. Krishna, Buddha, Zoroaster, Moses, Jesus and Muhammad had been earlier manifestations of God who had proclaimed messages needed in their time. But Baha'is regard Baha'u'llah as the final revelation for the current era, and believe that the second coming of Christ has taken place in his life.[73]

Albanese notes one of Baha'u'llah's key teachings, that "as Islam had been the purification and fulfillment of Judaism and Christianity, Baha'i was the completion of Islam and of all prior religions." Each previous "religion had been the religious expression suited for its era, for revelation in human history had been progressive." But Baha'i was also a genuine new religion that at some time would establish a new world order. The world now "stood at the threshold of an era of universal unity and peace," a new age that would follow the principles of Baha'i. Baha'u'llah also taught the equality of people. Men and women and all races were equal in the plan of God. Such a vision resembled the Christian expectations of the millennium that were so prevalent in nineteenth-century America. It also has similarities to aspects of the New Age movement of the late twentieth century.[74]

Baha'u'llah offered a vision but also advocated a concrete plan. By means of a moral and ritual program, he gave the Baha'i community a sense of its distinctive character. In doing so he created a paradoxical situation: a religion with universalist claims maintained a strong sense of boundary and identity. A special solar calendar of nineteen months of nineteen days contained designated feast and holy days and a period for fasting, as had Islam. Baha'i changed the Islamic practice of prayer, maintaining the custom of prescribed daily prayers, but not five times a day as called for in Islam.[75]

While claims about God's manifestations and the performance of religious practices are important, the main emphasis of the Baha'i religion is ethical and social issues. The Baha'i faith is not exclusive. It reveres all religions as components of God's plan. Baha'i prides itself in being a humanitarian religion and as such emphasizes certain principles for promoting justice and binding people together into a united world. These principles include the shunning of evil speaking; humility and honesty; self-realization; the harmony of science and religion; the repudiation of racial prejudice and nationalism; and the equality of sexes.[76]

The Baha'i faith was publicly introduced to Americans at the World
Parliament of Religions in Chicago in 1893. The following year a group was
formed in Chicago. The first U.S. Baha'i convention met in 1907. Abdu'l-
Baha, Baha'u'llah's son and successor in the movement, spread Baha'ism
around the world. He came to the United States in 1912 and spent eight
months propagating the Baha'i faith. That year he laid the cornerstone of
the Baha'i House of Worship in Wilmette, Illinois. It took forty years to
complete the temple, which was dedicated in 1953.[77]

The Baha'i faith has experienced considerable growth, both in America
and throughout the world. In particular, its message of a new age of peace
and unity appealed to a nation in whose history a millennial hope had
already run. By the mid-1980s Baha'i had about 100,000 adherents in America and an estimated 3.5 million in the world. With its strong organization,
its missionary enthusiasm and its sense of identity, Baha'i thrived on the
hope of becoming a world faith. The Baha'i saw its status as a fringe religion
in America as only a temporary condition. But instead of blending with
American culture, Baha'i desired to persuade Americans to accept its
ways.[78]

The Baha'i faith certainly has had an appeal in the West, especially with
the well-educated and those disillusioned with Christianity. But as a de-
spised stepchild of Islam, it has had trouble in its own backyard. After the
rise of Ayatollah Khomeini to power in 1979, Baha'i was seriously persecuted in Iran. *Time* magazine reported that by 1984 hundreds of Baha'is had
been imprisoned or executed, and that "thousands had lost their homes and
possessions." Baha'i assemblies and cemeteries, and even its holiest shrine
in Iran, the House of the Bab in Shiraz, have been desecrated by mobs.
Christians and Jews in Iran are permitted to practice their faith, but the
Iranian government considers Baha'is to be apostates from Islam and thus
subject to the death penalty.[79]

10

Christian-Related
Bodies

During the late nineteenth century and early twentieth, there arose several developments within evangelical Christianity that would produce numerous fringe religions. These unfoldings were Adventism, the holiness movement, Pentecostalism and fundamentalism. They produced splitoffs and new religions in their immediate context (the years from about 1860 to 1945) and would help to foster nontraditional religions after World War II. These religious movements were not mutually exclusive; in fact, they overlapped considerably. For example, the holiness impulse could be found in Pentecostalism and fundamentalism. Adventist groups might also be fundamentalists. Thus it is no surprise that their spinoffs often manifested characteristics from several groups.

These movements largely produced sectarian groups, setting off an explosion of splits seldom matched in American history. These unfoldings have parented several cultic bodies. Adventism has fostered at least two major cultic groups that are active today: the Jehovah's Witnesses and the Worldwide Church of God. From both the holiness and Pentecostal movements sprang many of the black cults that were so prominent during the first half of the twentieth century. The Jesus Only movement also came out of Pentecostalism. Several post-World War II groups are offshoots of both fundamentalism and Pentecostalism. While these evangelical movements are not "cultic," they proved to be fertile soil for many new religions. Some groups have pushed the distinctives of these evangelical movements beyond the boundaries of orthodoxy and may be regarded as cultic.

In this chapter two Adventist bodies and one Pentecostal group will be examined. Cults related to the holiness and fundamentalist movements will be covered in future chapters.

Adventism

Millennial fever ran high in nineteenth-century America, where this movement is often known as Adventism. The teaching that Christ will return is unescapably biblical and has put its mark on many chapters of church history. Yet as the nineteenth century wore on, a distinctively new concern for Christ's Second Coming arose amid the various anxieties and evangelical enthusiasm of antebellum America. At first the ancient doctrine became the source of great popular expectation, culminating in Millerism. Millerism was the millennial movement led by William Miller, who believed Christ would return in 1844. Until its last years Millerism was a broad movement, welcoming between 50,000 and 100,000 believers from many groups. But with the "great disappointment"—Christ's failure to return as Miller had predicted—millennialism became a force in the creation of sectarian bodies.[1]

Since the belief in Christ's imminent return was no longer widely fashionable, those who espoused it could be found primarily in sectarian bodies. Many such groups elevated this expectation as their central idea. The remnant Millerites, who still expected Christ to return shortly, were forced to draw in upon themselves, forming many Adventist sects.[2] At least forty religious groups, most founded before World War II, can be generally classified as Adventist.

Adventism has developed a worldview with some general theological and sociological characteristics. The roots of many American Adventist bodies go back to Miller, the Baptist lay preacher. So it is no surprise to discover that popular Baptist theology has had a significant influence on Adventism. Two general features dominate Adventist theology. The central focus, of course, is the Second Coming of Christ to establish his millennial reign. Second is an emphasis on the Old Testament and Hebrew law; indeed, many groups have embraced the Jewish sabbath and dietary laws. Socially, many members of Adventist groups belong to the lower and middle socioeconomic classes. The Adventist worldview attracts members of a distressed class who despair of obtaining status and wealth through the present order.

149

Therefore, they seek escape through a divine intervention that will destroy the "worldly classes" and elevate the "saints" to a position that they normally could not attain.[3]

According to Gordon Melton, "following any apocalyptic failure such as the Millerite disappointment of 1844, there are several options open to the faithful followers." One alternative is to disband the group and return to normal life. Spiritualization is a popular option: "the process of claiming that the prophecy was in error to the extent of its being seen as a visible historical event, and the attempt to reinterpret it as a cosmic, inner, invisible, or heavenly event." A final alternative for "disappointed apocalyptics is to return to the source of revelation (the Bible, a psychic-prophet, or an analysis of contemporary events) and seek a new date." A less committed form of this option is to set a vague new date, such as in "the near future."[4]

After the "great disappointment," leaders rose and fell as they projected new dates and had to live with their failures. Few of these individuals spawned groups that lasted beyond the new predicted dates. The Seventh-day Adventists resorted primarily to the spiritualization option and have since become a major sect. At first the Jehovah's Witnesses projected a new date; when this failed, they spiritualized it. In doing so, they perpetuated themselves, becoming what can be best described as an established cult. The Worldwide Church of God has made fewer predictions regarding the Second Coming, but its members also have had their prophetic expectations dashed.

The Second Coming of Christ is not emphasized only in Adventist bodies. Other sectarian groups found in the holiness, Pentecostal and fundamentalist movements regard it as an important doctrine. But the primary identity of these bodies centers on beliefs other than eschatology. Thus, the current discussion will be limited to two Adventist groups that are generally regarded as cultic—the Jehovah's Witnesses and the Worldwide Church of God.

A few words, however, need to be said about a significant omission: the Seventh-day Adventist Church, one of the oldest, largest and best-organized of the Adventist bodies. In keeping with the focus of this study, only unambiguously cultic bodies will be discussed in detail. Whether the Seventh-day Adventists are a sect, a cult or a denomination is a matter of intense controversy. Some evangelical scholars have insisted that they are cultic. Others have claimed that they are not. Some scholars have reviewed the institutional development of the Seventh-day Adventists and asked whether this onetime sect has now become a denomination.[5]

This study will regard the Seventh-day Adventists as a sect. To be sure, they possess some cultic characteristics. The Seventh-day Adventists have added a significant number of new and deviant teachings to the Christian tradition. They uplift a prophetic teacher, Ellen G. White, and come close to making her teachings a "third testament." Some of their prophetic positions and their teaching on the "Investigative Judgment" have pushed at the boundaries of Christian orthodoxy. In particular, the Investigative Judgment doctrine, which diminishes the work of Christ on the cross by emphasizing his continuing atoning work, stretches the limits of orthodoxy. The Seventh-day Adventists maintain some other beliefs and practices that give them a pronounced sectarian character, not only in the nineteenth century but also in the late twentieth. In particular, their maintenance of the sabbath and rigid dietary practices separate them from most of Christian society.[6]

Yet, by and large, Seventh-day Adventists maintain an orthodox position regarding the important doctrines of the inspiration and authority of the Scriptures, the deity of Christ, the Trinity, the bodily resurrection and Second Coming of Christ, and the way of salvation. While the Seventh-day Adventists may have some cultic characteristics, this study assumes them to be an established, institutionalized sect that is set off from society by certain peculiar beliefs and practices.

The Holiness Movement
The holiness movement originated in the United States in the 1840s and 1850s as an endeavor to preserve and propagate John Wesley's teachings on entire sanctification and Christian perfection.[7] The movement did not gain momentum, however, until the late nineteenth century, when it spilled out of the Methodist church to form a bewildering profusion of sectarian organizations. The movement experienced phenomenal growth from about 1880 to about 1935, becoming international in character and spawning other offshoots such as Pentecostalism.[8]

Many holiness bodies have traveled down the familiar path from sect to denomination. By the late twentieth century, many have shed their sectarian character, settling down to a stable life as a permanent part of the American religious landscape. Then why include the holiness bodies in a study of the cults? The label *cult* cannot be attached to any but some extremely aberrational holiness and Pentecostal groups.

The holiness movement contained innovative elements and may be regarded as an old religious impulse that spawned new religious bodies. The liberals were not the only Protestants who met the challenges of the day with religious innovations. Some conservative Protestants also offered new directions in response to developments of the time. The holiness movement may be understood as a major evangelical innovation, one that stood as a mirror image of a modernist theme: the stress on morality. Unlike religious liberalism, however, the holiness movement did not emphasize innate human goodness as the key to morality. Instead, its members asserted that nothing less than a dramatic work of the Holy Spirit could cleanse the heart of sin.[9]

The basic notion of going on to Christian perfection was not new with Wesley or the holiness movement. The desire to follow Christ's call "Be perfect, therefore, as your heavenly Father is perfect" (Mt 5:48) has caused many divisions in Christianity. In the late nineteenth century, it resulted in the "holiness churches." These churches made the drive for holiness or perfection their primary emphasis. One result of this drive was separation from Christians who did not make perfection a major priority. Therefore, in the holiness movement the drive for perfection produced a separatist tendency that reached explosive proportions in the last years of the nineteenth century. This "come-outer" movement produced many sectarian bodies and even sowed the seeds of more cultic groups.[10]

Pentecostalism

Pentecostalism may be the largest mass religious movement of the twentieth century. Along with its more recent outgrowth, neo-Pentecostalism or the charismatic movement, Pentecostalism is the most significant of the new or innovative religious movements in the twentieth century, even being designated as the "Third Force in Christendom."[11] The distinguishing mark of Pentecostalism is a religious experience, usually called the Pentecostal experience, which entails receiving the gift of speaking in an unknown tongue as a sign of the baptism of the Holy Spirit. In Pentecostalism, this baptism usually comes as an experience subsequent to conversion and is regarded as the Holy Spirit's coming to dwell in an individual believer. From the idea of this baptism of the Holy Spirit and speaking in tongues emerged the belief in the current operation of the gifts of the Holy Spirit manifested in the New Testament church.[12]

The practice of speaking in tongues has occurred periodically through church history. Most people probably associate it with modern Pentecostalism, which was born in Kansas at the turn of the twentieth century. Pentecostalism appears to have developed from the confluence of several religious traditions, the most important being the holiness movement. Tongues-speaking and faith healing, the hallmarks of Pentecostalism, may be seen as a radicalization of the holiness doctrine of the "second blessing," or entire sanctification. Individuals in the holiness tradition found it hard to demonstrate empirically that they had received the second blessing, but Pentecostals could point to tongues-speaking as evidence of the reception of the Holy Spirit. This ability to provide a tangible expression of the indwelling of the Holy Spirit gave Pentecostalism its great impetus.[13]

Many holiness people believed that attaching tongues to Holy Ghost baptism had biblical warrant. But it should not be forgotten that speaking in tongues erupted on the American scene at a time when many religious groups felt the need to empirically validate their beliefs and experiences. Faith healing should also be seen in this context. In an age when science challenged Christianity, tongues-speaking and faith healing were seen as "signs and wonders" to bolster Christian faith.

Pentecostalism cannot be explained solely as a social phenomenon. Nevertheless, social factors played a major role in shaping this new religious movement. From a general perspective, Pentecostalism may be seen as a small segment of a widespread, long-term protest against the whole thrust of "modernity": the modern urban-industrial capitalistic society. Pentecostalism arose at the end of a century in which science and technology, through urbanization and industrialization, had significantly changed all aspects of life. Accompanying these revolutions in the means of production were the growth of large, impersonal social institutions. Moreover, these revolutions facilitated both social and geographic mobility, allowing vast numbers of people to move from continent to continent, from farm to city and from one lifestyle to another.[14]

Pentecostalism made its strongest appeal to those who had difficulty coping with these massive changes, especially to individuals in the lower echelons of society. These people were disappointed; their worldly hopes had repeatedly been frustrated. Pentecostal meetings, which were charged

153

with emotion, provided a real sense of relief from oppressive, frustrating and even bewildering social circumstances. In these meetings individuals who were otherwise poor, uneducated and powerless experienced a sense of power that provided compensation for their status in life. Because of its supernatural source, they regarded such an experience as "real power," greater than the power of the rich and worldly.[15]

After a slow start, the Pentecostal message caught fire and spread across the United States. Many of the new Pentecostal denominations originated as indigenous churches with little contact with other organized bodies. Yet a number came about through controversy or schism. It was inevitable that such a vigorous movement would suffer controversy and division in its formative stages. Pentecostalism has been noted for its many submovements, most of which can be regarded as sectarian bodies.[16] One significant controversy, however, concerned the Trinity. Out of this problem came the Jesus Only movement, a development that produced many groups that can be described as cultic in both social and theological characteristics.

Beyond such overt heresy, much misunderstanding about Pentecostalism was caused by extremists within the movement, some sectarian and some cultic. The practice most damaging to the image of Pentecostalism probably has been the rite of "snake-handling," a bizarre custom performed by mountain groups that are not connected with the major Pentecostal bodies. Other spectacular, but unusual, practices fostering misunderstanding and public criticism include speaking in tongues, interpretation of tongues, the "laying on of hands" for divine healing, the "holy laugh" and the "holy dance." To the Pentecostals these practices were considered to be sure signs of the Holy Spirit's touch. But to an unbelieving public, they were seen as signs of madness and fanaticism.[17]

Fundamentalism

Fundamentalism has many definitions, some broad and some restrictive. According to George Marsden, in American religion fundamentalism can be best defined as "militantly antimodernist evangelical Protestantism." Though fundamentalism's roots go back much earlier, the name was not coined until 1920. It soon came "to describe all types of American Protestants who were willing to wage ecclesiastical and theological war against modernism" in religion and the cultural changes that modernists welcomed.[18]

Fundamentalism's status as a fringe movement is somewhat in question. Along with the holiness and Pentecostal movements, fundamentalism should be seen as a Protestant protest against modernity, especially its new intellectual and cultural directions. Yet it was less radical and more establishment than either the holiness or Pentecostal movements. As Marsden also points out, "fundamentalism has had a strikingly paradoxical tendency to identify sometimes with the 'establishment' and sometimes with the 'outsiders.' "[19] This paradox has been present in the movement at all times, but has been more pronounced in certain periods.

Fundamentalism spawned many sectarian groups from about 1920 to 1950. Moreover, in the last half of the twentieth century, fundamentalism combined with tendencies derived from the Adventist, holiness and Pentecostal movements has parented several cultic bodies and other fringe groups that are difficult to classify.

Scholars have interpreted fundamentalism in a variety of ways. It has been defined as essentially a social reaction to the forces of modern urbanized, industrialized America.[20] But though social factors are important, fundamentalism is primarily a religious phenomenon.[21] George Marsden regards it as a "sub-species of American revivalism." It sprang from the complex and tangled roots of several nineteenth-century traditions: revivalism, evangelicalism, pietism, Americanism and several variant orthodoxies, including dispensationalism, holiness teachings, Baptist traditionalism and Princeton theology.[22] At no time were any of these traditions coextensive with fundamentalism.

The two fundamentalist characteristics that most influenced cultic groups were biblical literalism and dispensationalism. Selective teachings of the Bible were applied in a most literal way. Dispensationalism viewed history as divided into several distinct ages, determined by the ways God tested humankind in respect to obedience to his will. It also gave a new wrinkle to Bible prophecy. Rejecting the prevailing postmillennialism, which taught that Christ's kingdom would grow out of spiritual and moral progress, dispensational premillennialists insisted that the churches and culture were declining and that Christ's kingdom would come only after he personally returned to rule.[23]

Jehovah's Witnesses

The Jehovah's Witnesses are one of the most radical, successful and well publicized of the Adventist bodies and may be regarded as an established cult. Actually, the Jehovah's Witnesses are the most prominent of about a dozen "Russellite" groups, which are in turn part of the larger Adventist movement. Charles Taze Russell (1852-1916) began a Bible Student movement that spawned a number of groups, including the Jehovah's Witnesses.[24]

Because the Jehovah's Witnesses repudiate many cardinal Christian doctrines and even the Christian church itself, many people question their status as a Christian body. Nevertheless, they have Christian roots and consider themselves to be the only "true" Christians. As Gordon Melton notes, Russell's views were strongly influenced by Adventism. After the "great disappointment" of 1844, new leaders arose to project new dates for Christ's return. One such date was 1874. When this projection failed, Russell spiritualized it and set a new date. He believed that *parousia* (the Greek word translated "return") meant "presence" and concluded that, in 1874, Christ's presence had begun. The new date, 1914, would mark the end of the "time of the Gentiles" and the beginning of God's rule on earth.[25]

Russell broke with the Adventists and, in 1884, founded Zion's Watchtower Tract Society. In 1896 the society became known as the Watchtower Bible and Tract Society, and in 1908 the organization's headquarters were moved to Brooklyn, New York. Through voluminous writings and extensive speaking, Russell promoted his version of a modified Adventism.[26]

"Pastor" Russell had a number of character defects. His monumental ego prompted him to make outlandish claims about himself, even allowing his followers to categorize him with Paul, Wycliffe and Luther. He was charged with fraudulent activities and perjured himself in court. Not surprisingly, today's Jehovah's Witnesses disclaim any connection with Russell and dislike being branded "Russellites." Yet evidence proves that he founded and organized the Jehovah's Witnesses and that his doctrines provide the basis for their beliefs.[27]

Joseph Franklin Rutherford (1869-1942) succeeded Russell as president of the Watchtower Bible and Tract Society in 1917. When Rutherford became president of the society, a power struggle ensued and several Russellites left, starting a number of smaller sects. He warned them that they would suffer destruction if they failed to return to the fold. Rutherford increased his control over the movement so that when he died at age seventy-two, the Jehovah's Witnesses had become an autocratic, hierarchical organization.[28]

Ruth Tucker notes several contrasts between Russell and Rutherford in style and belief. Russell had depended heavily on his personal charisma to shape his followers. Under his leadership the Witnesses were a decentralized Bible society. Rutherford, however, "used organizational strategy and fear tactics" to change the society into a tightly controlled structure, "which he later referred to as a 'Theocratic Government.' " There were also doctrinal differences between Russell and Rutherford, especially in respect to eschatology. Rutherford "downplayed the year 1874 in favor of 1914; he then focused on 1925 for 'the completion of all things.' " That "the completion of all things" did not come in 1925 became a serious problem for the Witnesses. Many had quit their jobs and sold their homes in the expectation that they would soon be living in an earthly paradise.[29]

In 1942 Nathan Homer Korr (1905-77) became the next leader of the Watchtower Bible and Tract Society; he served as president until his death. He was a capable administrator, and during his presidency the Jehovah's Witnesses focused on the training of their people, especially improving their techniques for door-to-door witnessing. In 1958 Korr promoted mass gatherings of Witnesses at the Polo Grounds and Yankee Stadium, events that gained considerable media attention. Under his leadership international missions became quite important. The society's membership spread from 54 countries to 210, and membership increased from 113,000 to 2,000,000. But perhaps the most important development under Korr's tenure was the change from individual to corporate leadership. In effect, the society became a collective oligarchy.[30]

Frederick William Franz (born 1893) became the organization's president at Korr's death in 1977. But soon rumblings of dissent became audible in all ranks of the society, from the Kingdom Halls (local places of worship) to the headquarters itself. In part, this grew out of the disconfirmation of 1975. In 1966, the society's leaders had predicted that the world would end in 1975. When the year passed without the coming of Armageddon, dissent bubbled over. In 1978 some thirty thousand Witnesses were expelled, and the hierarchy tightened its control over the rank and file in order to root out "apostates."[31]

Whether one sees the Jehovah's Witnesses as a cult or a sect depends on how important one considers theology as a criterion. They grew out of the Christian tradition, but on major points of doctrine they stand outside orthodoxy. While Jehovah's Witnesses are not a well-educated lot, they endeavor to subordinate the teachings of Scripture to reason, rejecting anything in the Bible that is beyond human understanding. Such an approach has led the Witnesses to deny most traditional Christian beliefs, especially the doctrines of the Trinity, the deity of Christ and the Holy Spirit. Like the ancient Arians, they are staunch unitarians. The Witnesses also reject the traditional beliefs concerning Christ's bodily resurrection and Second Coming.[32] Instead, they teach that the Second Advent has already occurred, in three stages. Christ came in 1874 and spiritually resurrected the dead members of the 144,000 remnant class, who were to be immortal. Stage two came in 1914, when the time of the Gentiles ended and Christ began his reign. Finally, in 1918 Christ came into the spiritual temple and began his judgment of the nations. None of these events were physical or visible. The Witnesses are now awaiting not the return of Christ, but the battle of Armageddon.[33]

The Jehovah's Witnesses are set off from the Christian tradition by their unorthodox beliefs; their lifestyle also erects some enormous barriers to any meaningful interaction with society. Considering their numbers, they are one of the most separationist of the noncommunal fringe religions. In this their sectarian character becomes quite evident. Since Satan dominates the world, especially the institutional aspects of business, politics and religion, dedicated Jehovah's Witness separate themselves from social institutions and seek safety in the New World Society. Jehovah's Witnesses will not salute the flag, stand for the national anthem, vote, hold a government office, serve in the armed forces of any nation, actively participate in a labor union or another secular organization, or develop close relationships with non-Witnesses.[34]

According to William Whalen, the list of things opposed by the Jehovah's Witnesses is impressive: "Catholicism, Christmas trees and observances, Communism, evolution, higher education, liquor, lodges, Protestantism, Mother's Day, Sunday Schools, tobacco, the United Nations, and the YMCA." Their children "will generally avoid birthday parties, Christmas and Easter celebrations, school organizations, and college." Blood has a special place among the taboos of the Jehovah's Witnesses. Since blood supposedly contains the principle of life, committed Witnesses will not eat meat that has not been properly prepared, such as in the kosher ritual. Moreover, their resistance to blood transfusions has led to lawsuits and unfavorable publicity. The Witnesses also object to modern psychotherapy.

As might be expected, few of them are college-educated.[35]

The world of the Jehovah's Witness centers on the activities of the local Kingdom Hall. Individuals may hold secular jobs to support their families, but they must invest considerable time in the work of the society, so much that they have little time left for other activities. There is no such thing as a nominal Jehovah's Witness—that is, an inactive member whose name is simply on the membership roll. The society regards every baptized member as an ordained minister. Above and beyond the five regular meetings held each week in the Kingdom Hall, the average Jehovah's Witness puts in eleven hours per month in door-to-door preaching.[36]

The Jehovah's Witnesses are paradoxical, but to a lesser extent than the Seventh-day Adventists. From its earliest years the Watchtower Society has displayed a clear sectarian character. Its demanding practices and doctrines have appealed primarily to social outsiders. Moreover, a number of its dogmas have placed it beyond the bounds of traditional Christian orthodoxy. Still, in some ways the Jehovah's Witnesses have reflected the surrounding culture, particularly that of the late nineteenth century. Their basic impulses resemble those of the innovative Protestant movements that grew out of conservative revivalism. In its strict ethical teachings, Russellism was much like the growing premillennialist movement. Russellism can also be seen as a religious protest movement that came in the same context as Populism, which was challenging the dominance of big business and big government in late-nineteenth-century American society.[37]

The paradox has also emerged in more recent years. Since the 1960s there has been considerable discontent among the Witnesses. In part, they are dissatisfied with their authoritarian leaders, who allow no questioning of the society's beliefs. The rank and file has experienced some disillusionment over the unfulfilled public forecasts of the end of the world. But more important, since the sixties many Witnesses have been influenced by themes current in the American culture: autonomy, individual freedoms, protest, liberation movements and success.[38] In a society with increasing emphasis on technology, education and pluralism, to what extent will the Jehovah's Witnesses adapt to cultural demands? Their ability to adjust in a rapidly changing and mobile age is being called into question.

The Worldwide Church of God

Another well-known, successful Adventist group is the Worldwide Church of God. Founded in 1933 as the Radio Church of God by Herbert W. Armstrong (1892-1986), a former advertising man, the movement not only has survived but appears to be prospering in the early 1990s. Though its roots can be traced to the Adventist movement, the Worldwide Church of God has been viewed as a mixture of Seventh-day Adventism, Jehovah's Witnesses, Judaism, Mormonism and British Israelism.[39]

The Worldwide Church of God has been described as "an off-shoot of an off-shoot of an off-shoot" of the Seventh-day Adventist Church.[40] In the early nineteenth century, a popular idea was that churches should be called simply "Church of God." One reason for the rise of this notion was that "Church of God" was a nonsectarian label. But as several groups began to utilize the name, modifiers had to be used to distinguish them. During the nineteenth century, a number of Adventist groups employed the "Church of God" label.[41]

In 1866 several members broke from the Iowa Conference of the Seventh-day Adventist Church and formed a new sect, the Church of God (Adventist). But disagreements prompted another separation, resulting in the start of still another sect, the Church of God (Seventh Day). This group, which would be one step removed from the Worldwide Church of God, was the "off-shoot of an off-shoot" that the Armstrong family joined. This body ordained Armstrong, and he conducted his first revival in 1933. No existing church being suitable for him, Armstrong soon left the Church of God (Seventh Day) and began a church three steps removed from Seventh-day Adventism. He called this church the Radio Church of God, but later renamed it the Worldwide Church of God.[42]

Armstrong's talents for copyrighting and merchandising, once devoted to business, were now turned to religion. In 1934 Armstrong began to publish a magazine, which has subsequently been called *The Plain Truth*. This publication and his radio broadcasts grew during the 1930s. In 1941 he gave his broadcast program the name by which it is still known, "The World of Tomorrow." The church and the radio broadcasts continued to expand, and in 1947 Armstrong opened Ambassador College in Pasadena, California. With the addition of Radio Luxembourg in 1953, Armstrong's organization went international.[43]

During the next twenty years, the church experienced significant growth. In 1957 Armstrong's son Garner Ted moved into the limelight, speaking on most broadcasts and becoming a nationally recognized radio and television figure. The church's international outreach also expanded, with "The World of Tomorrow" now being heard in French, Spanish and German. The circulation of *The Plain Truth* increased, and two additional Ambassador College campuses opened. In 1968 the name of the Radio Church of God was changed to its present name, the Worldwide Church of God.[44]

The church experienced two decades of spectacular growth, but as Melton notes, serious problems then arose. Beginning in 1972, the church entered a period of intense controversy that did not abate until the mid-1980s. Within the Worldwide Church there existed the "widespread expectation that 1972 would signal the beginning of God's kingdom" and a time of turmoil, so that the "true church" would be forced into hiding. This expectation, of course, went unfulfilled. Garner Ted Armstrong became an object of controversy, leaving the air for unknown reasons, only to return four months later. In 1973 some structural changes occurred, with the church reorganizing at the regional level and embarking on a new course of openness.[45]

In 1974 a serious scandal struck the Worldwide Church of God. Several charges of sexual misconduct were leveled at Garner Ted Armstrong. Compounding this problem, there developed an internal theological dispute over the remarriage of divorced members and the date for Pentecost. The intensity of the conflict reached serious proportions when a number of ministers resigned to begin independent offshoots of the Worldwide Church of God. Furthermore, Garner Ted and a lawyer, Stanley Rader, who managed the church's business affairs, clashed in public. A consequence of this dispute was Garner Ted's departure in 1978 to begin the Church of God International. Adding to this conflict, Herbert Armstrong, who had previously condemned remarriage for divorced people, married a young church secretary who had been divorced. By 1984 he would in turn divorce this woman. To further compound these problems, in 1979 some former members filed suit against the church leaders on behalf of the church, claiming financial mismanagement. As a result, the church was placed under a temporary court-ordered receivership.[46]

By the mid-eighties the Worldwide Church of God appeared to be recovering from these controversies. Some five to ten thousand members had left, but they had been replaced by new converts, and membership stood at approximately 100,000.[47] In January 1986, Herbert Armstrong died at age ninety-three. Garner Ted, his heir apparent, has his own organization and remains estranged. Joseph Tkack, who had been director of church administration, became the new leader. How well the Worldwide Church of God will do after the death of its leader remains to be seen. Still, the immediate years since Armstrong's death have been surprisingly upbeat. The movement has grown, and there appears to be a new openness to outsiders and a readiness to reassess the church's doctrine and practices. The church appears to be modifying its views regarding members' seeking medical attention, racial equality, setting dates for prophetic events, and British Israelism.[48]

But whether the church's doctrinal changes are substantial or cosmetic remains to be seen. Despite the recent changes, for most of its history the Worldwide Church of God was an organization dominated by one man—Herbert W. Armstrong. From the very onset, Armstrong regarded his movement as having a unique position among all churches, being the "true" church, and believed that he was specially chosen to be God's messenger for the modern age. His authoritarian leadership was a key factor throughout the church's history.[49]

In respect to both its theology and its social characteristics, the Worldwide Church of God can be seen as a fringe religious group. It is often regarded as an established cult.[50] The origins of the Worldwide Church of God go back to Seventh-day Adventism, and it accepts many of that group's doctrines, though other influences also are evident. In harmony with Adventist teaching, the Worldwide Church of God regards the Bible as the infallible Word of God and affirms God as Creator and Father, and Christ as divine. But the church vehemently denies the Trinity. Instead there are two Gods: God the Father, the Father of Jesus Christ; and the God of Abraham, the Creator of heaven and earth—the God who became Jesus Christ. Jesus is God, but not an eternal God as orthodox Christianity teaches. Instead, he is the firstborn in the family of God. The Holy Spirit also is not God. Rather, it is God's power, shared by both God the Father and Christ. The Worldwide Church of God believes in a plurality of gods, contending that all humans have the potential to become gods.[51]

Like Seventh-day Adventism, the Worldwide Church of God is sabbatarian, holding that the command to keep the sabbath has never been nullified. As Ruth Tucker writes, "For Armstrong the issue of Sabbath keeping became the ultimate test of faith." In fact, he went beyond "the Seventh-day Adventists in his insistence that true faith could not be demonstrated unless the Sabbath was maintained." In keeping with the Old Testament emphasis of the Worldwide Church of God, Armstrong believed that various Old Testament festivals still should be observed (such as Passover, the Days of Unleavened Bread, Atonement, Trumpets). On the other hand, traditional holidays such as Valentine's Day, Easter, Halloween and Christmas were condemned as pagan practices.[52] Armstrong's followers share some of the Adventists' dietary practices, including abstaining from ham, pork, clams, lobster and shrimp in conformity with Old Testament regulations. They prohibit smoking but allow drinking in moderation.[53]

Basic to the beliefs of the Worldwide Church of God is an understanding of its position and role in history. Such an understanding was derived from Armstrong's acceptance of British Israelism (or Anglo-Israelism). Armstrong's church is the most prominent proponent of this unusual school of biblical interpretation. The basic idea is that after the dispersion of the ten lost tribes of Israel, they migrated to northern Europe, where they became the ancestors of the Saxons who invaded England. Thus the people of England (and, by extension, the United States and the peoples of the British Commonwealth nations) are the literal descendants of the ten lost tribes of Israel. So Britain and the United States occupy a special place in respect to God's promises and blessings.[54]

The Worldwide Church of God, as Melton indicates, has "adopted the dispensational view of the history of the Church of God." The seven churches of Revelation 2—3 are considered to be the seven church ages. "The Worldwide Church is identified as the Church at Philadelphia, which was to appear just before the endtime events described in the Book of Revelation." It was widely believed that the Tribulation would start in 1972 and that the church would have to flee the United States. Many members still expect Christ to return in the 1990s.[55]

The Worldwide Church of God regards itself as the one and only true church since the time of the apostles. It denounces the Protestant and Catholic churches for propagating pagan beliefs and practices. In the opinion of the Worldwide Church of God, the corruption of the Christian church began early, setting in shortly after the death of the last apostle. For eighteen and a half centuries the gospel was not preached, but now it has been restored in the message of the Worldwide Church of God. Members of this "only true" church are expected to support it faithfully, contributing 20 percent of their annual income to its work.[56] Despite considerable institu-

163

tionalization and effective use of the media, in the late twentieth century the Worldwide Church remains a marginal religious group.

The Jesus Only or Oneness Movement

In 1913 a serious schism nearly destroyed the fledgling Pentecostal movement. It grew out of the "Pentecostal unitarian" question, also called the "Oneness" or "Jesus Only" issue. Out of this controversy a nontrinitarian movement developed. This movement spread rapidly among the Pentecostals, eventually forming about twenty-five religious bodies, the largest being the United Pentecostal Church. The Oneness message had a particular appeal among black people and eventually claimed about one-fourth of all Pentecostals. The movement does, however, include large numbers of whites, and its distinctive is its nontrinitarian stance, not its racial makeup.[57]

The Jesus Only Pentecostals are rarely discussed in studies of cultic groups. They are a large movement that has spread around the world through massive missionary endeavors. Yet the Oneness Pentecostals maintain several beliefs, especially a denial of the doctrine of the Trinity, which set them apart from other Pentecostal groups and the larger Christian community. They deny the preexistence of Christ. Jesus Only Pentecostals believe that Jesus was himself the Father. They also argue that tongues is a necessary sign of salvation and that baptism in Jesus' name is a requirement for salvation. Oneness Pentecostals believe that they are the only people who will go to heaven.[58] They also carry some social restrictions further than does mainstream Pentecostalism. When both theological and social criteria are employed, the Jesus Only movement can be seen as sufficiently deviant to be regarded as cultic.

The Oneness movement did not slide slowly into heresy; its proponents deliberately chose to depart from orthodox Christianity. And it has upheld this distinctive heresy for more than seventy years. The Oneness Pentecostals deny the Trinity and uphold the oneness of God. Jesus is identified with God the Father, God the Creator and the bodily presence of God. The Holy Spirit is considered to be not a third person within the Trinity but the spirit and power of God and Christ. The Oneness doctrine rests primarily on the words of Jesus, "I and the Father are one" (Jn 10:30). God the Father and the Holy Spirit are regarded as mere manifestations of Christ.[59]

According to Tucker, this doctrine is emphasized largely "in the rite of baptism." In light of the conviction that God and the Holy Spirit are manifestations of Christ, "converts are baptized only in the name of Jesus." When the movement first emerged, many of its supporters insisted that miracles had taken place in Jesus' name. Many believed "that God had given a 'new revelation' concerning the name of Jesus, which almost had a magical aura about it." They believed baptism could not be valid unless "it was done in the name of Jesus only." Many people were impressed by this "new revelation," and they began to search Scripture for some new teaching regarding the name of Jesus. This research brought a dramatic change to Pentecostalism, one moving a large segment of the movement beyond the bounds of orthodoxy.[60]

The Jesus Only Pentecostals are not a nontrinitarian movement in the same category as the Unitarians. They have social characteristics that separate them from much of traditional Christianity. These traits are general to most early Pentecostalism and are typical of many sect groups. But when combined with the Oneness movement's doctrinal deviations, they reinforce its cultic characteristics. While there are differences in lifestyle prohibitions among the many Jesus Only groups, they have much in common. They disapprove of their members' engaging in the following activities: theater attendance, dances, mixed bathing, cutting one's hair (for women), the use of makeup, wearing any apparel that immodestly exposes the body, any worldly sports or amusements, listening to unwholesome radio programs and music, and watching television. While the Oneness groups affirm loyalty to the government, they usually prohibit their members from serving in combat during war. Also, members cannot consciously affiliate with unions or secret societies.[61]

In the second decade of its existence, the new Pentecostal movement faced a critical issue. At a 1913 Los Angeles camp meeting, R. E. McAlister, a popular preacher, spoke out on the issue of baptism, forcefully insisting that in the apostolic church baptism was performed not with a trinitarian formula but in the name of Jesus Christ. Despite much opposition, McAlister's message found favor with John C. Scheppe and Frank J. Ewart. Scheppe's emotional acceptance of the "new" idea had a powerful impact on the camp. He claimed to have been "given a glimpse of the power of the blessed name of Jesus." Afterward, Ewart joined McAlister in a revival meeting in Los Angeles and began to note results whenever he called upon the name of Jesus.[62]

In Pentecostal circles, the notion of baptism in the name of Jesus went

165

back to at least 1902. It was in 1913, however, that the idea began to spread rapidly, and a number of prominent Pentecostal leaders were baptized in the name of Jesus. The "New Issue," as people began to call it, was soon related to a denial of the Trinity and to the notion that while God is a threefold being—Father, Son and Holy Spirit—there is but one person, Jesus Christ. This teaching penetrated the Pentecostal movement until it became the issue of the day. It caught on rapidly among Pentecostals because of the apparent supernatural method of its revelation, its promise of additional power to those who accepted it, and its emphasis on the name of Jesus.[63]

The recently organized Assemblies of God was hit hard by the controversy. Many of its leaders defected. The issue came to a head in 1916, and the Assemblies of God adopted a strong trinitarian stance in its statement of beliefs. As a consequence, 156 ministers were expelled from the church and many assemblies were lost.[64]

The era of formation of Oneness churches began. In early 1917, expelled proponents of the Oneness doctrine organized the General Assembly of the Apostolic Assemblies. They shortly merged with the smaller, racially integrated Pentecostal Assemblies of the World, a West Coast Oneness body that had been organized in 1914. In the 1920s and 1930s a number of new Oneness bodies were formed. In 1945 the major white Pentecostal proponents of the Oneness doctrine merged to form the United Pentecostal Church International. This is the largest Jesus Only Pentecostal group, claiming in 1986 an American membership of nearly half a million. In the post-World War II era, several smaller Oneness Pentecostal bodies were formed.[65]

11

Black
Religious Groups

T he rise of the black churches in the last half of the nineteenth century and the early decades of the twentieth century paralleled significant changes in the African-American social and political environment. By this time the United States had lost its will to carry out the intent of the Emancipation Proclamation. The series of bills and constitutional amendments designed to safeguard the rights of blacks had become dead letters. As a result, two changes came to the black community which were as significant as nineteenth-century emancipation. First of all, the setting was transformed by an immense movement of blacks from Southern farms to cities of both the North and the South. Seventy-five percent of the blacks had become city dwellers by the last quarter of the twentieth century. Second, there emerged the voice of black nationalism, which aspired to make black freedom a reality. African-Americans expressed their peoplehood in a series of nationalistic movements, including the promotion of black culture and theology and Marcus Garvey's back-to-Africa strategy.[1]

Catherine Albanese tells us that the tremendous transformation in location, status and occupation for the African-Americans who moved to industrial cities had "considerable implications for black churches." As blacks were confronted with "strange and hostile urban forces," they developed "a sense of rootlessness and alienation." Moreover, social divisions became more pronounced, with "upper, middle, and lower class blacks more clearly defined." These social differentiations were reflected in styles of worship and church organizations. Upper-class African-Americans tended strongly toward membership in churches of predominantly white denominations, especially the Episcopal, Presbyterian and Congregational. The black middle class also made these affiliations, but remained far more loyal to the black denominations, especially the African Methodist and Baptist churches. Lower-class blacks largely identified with these two churches as well. The Baptist and African Methodist churches offered blacks a sense of religio-cultural identity, even as they conformed to the decorum of mainline Protestant churches. On the whole, during the early twentieth century, over 90 percent of black church members were affiliated with some version of the Baptist or Methodist church.[2]

Black Sects and Cults

The social groups in the black religious tradition that experienced the most drastic changes were the very poor and the recent migrants to the city. Some gravitated to the new holiness and Pentecostal movements, while a number of cults in Northern cities attracted others.

Fringe religious groups often have a particular appeal to members of the urban underclass who are overwhelmed by the impersonality of city life and overt discrimination. Sydney Ahlstrom gives several reasons for this. Economic factors supply one explanation: the poor are often attracted to fringe religions. The "small size and intimate atmosphere" of these bodies is a factor. Furthermore, these religious groups provided an outlet for "imaginative leadership." Throughout history, the church has "provided leadership opportunities for the lowly born." Among blacks in the urban ghettos, with few opportunities to exercise their talents, religious institutions became an important avenue by which charismatic individuals could exercise their leadership abilities.[3]

Drawing a meaningful distinction between sects and cults is as difficult with black groups as it is with white bodies. The black *sect* has more continuity with past Christian tradition. Black *cults* are more radical departures, often virtually new religions with new doctrines and new grounds for authority, including new messiahs. Joseph Washington points out that while "the Bible is basic to the black sect types, the black community is the fundamental core of most black cults." He also contends that the black sect typically concentrates on the world to come as a compensation for lack of desired power in this world. But the black cult tends to seek secular realization of black social power.[4]

On the whole, the black holiness and Pentecostal churches must be regarded as sect-type bodies. Except for a few aberrations, such as the Jesus Only movement, which saw the Trinity as an error, the holiness and Pentecostal movements fell within the orthodox Christian tradition. African-Americans played a large part in the origins and growth of these two movements. Holiness and Pentecostal doctrines and churches have addressed the needs of oppressed and disinherited people all over the world. It was natural for poor urban blacks to identify with these religious bodies.[5]

In the small communal settings of storefront and residential churches of the holiness and Pentecostal bodies, African-Americans found a religious expression that resembled the black religion of slave times. The emphasis the holiness and Pentecostal churches placed on emotions and the presence of the Spirit appealed to blacks who desired a form of transcendence through ecstasy. The inspired style of preaching found in these churches was familiar to blacks. For their part, blacks brought to the holiness and Pentecostal churches a heritage of spirituals, which when combined with blues and jazz helped to produce a new style of music called gospel. Finally, these churches taught the doctrine of perfection or holiness and required that their followers pursue a sanctified, disciplined life. In this way, the holiness and Pentecostal churches provided a stable religious framework for people living in the midst of urban chaos.[6]

The various denominations and sectarian groups spawned by the holiness and Pentecostal bodies by no means represented the only religious impulse that took institutional form in the urban ghettos. The hopeless conditions in which urban blacks lived also led to far more drastic innovations, especially the founding and development of small cults. If independence and pluralism characterized the holiness and Pentecostal bodies, this was even more so for the new urban cults that multiplied rapidly in storefronts and local residences. Several religious impulses influenced the new black cults. Some drew their beliefs and practices from forms of Spiritualism and voodoo. Yet close ties existed between these cults and the churches, especially the holiness and Pentecostal bodies. Pentecostalism emphasized tongues-speaking. This gift presented evidence that one was a charismatic person—that is, filled with the Holy Spirit. Individuals so blessed often followed the leading of the Spirit, left the church and, with great authority, started a separate religious movement. At times these bodies were close enough to the parent church to be labeled as sects. On other occasions, the inspired man or woman received a "new revelation" and used charismatic authority to produce a religious body that departed significantly from the Christian tradition.[7]

Thousands of small black cults sprang up during the first third of the twentieth century. They drew from various religious traditions, including Islam, Judaism, Spiritualism and Christianity. Many members of black cults had been left dissatisfied by the holiness and Pentecostal bodies; they represent the left wing of this movement. But the core attraction of most black cults was not a distinctive drawn from a particular religious tradition but its ability to meet practical needs. According to Washington, "the distinction between Afro-Americans who followed cults and those who were Pentecostals or independent Baptists had little to do with the extent to which superstition, magic or inherent religion lingered." Rather, the primary difference lay between those who remained loyal to a tradition or a particular ritual "and those who looked to religion to give concrete evidence of making a difference in the daily round" of life.[8]

To a large extent, black cults may be seen as reactions to the extreme poverty of African-Americans at the turn of the century. As Washington also notes, "The black cult-type is not merely a religious movement. It is a political, social and economic entity as well." These cults seek power to free their people "from material, economic, moral, and political want." God is the primary source of this power, but the search "for immediate power may lead to the creation of a black prophet or black messiah." Such an individual is to provide a "piece of the pie in the sky," not only for the future but also in the present. "The messiah is not coming in the future, he has come and is the future." Though this messiah cannot meet all the concrete needs of the cult, he or she does bring some tangible benefits to the flock and serves "as a token of what is to come." This future hope may be a new land, as the Black Muslims desire, or it may be the interracial fellowship of the Father Divine movement, which some blacks saw as an expression of the kingdom of God on earth. Whatever the destiny or the messiah, the people have specific projects in which they are currently involved as well.[9]

During the 1920s and 1930s numerous black cults emerged, especially in the urban ghettos. The three receiving the most attention have been the Nation of Islam, the Peace Mission of Father Divine and the United House of Prayer. All three were products of the discrimination of the interwar years. But the Nation of Islam did not take off until after World War II, and is better seen in the context of the civil rights movement. Thus a more detailed examination of the Black Muslims will come in a later chapter.

The Universal Peace Mission Movement of Father Divine

During the first half of the twentieth century, the black cult gaining the most publicity was the Peace Mission of Father Divine. In fact, Gordon Melton says that no "cult" group gained more attention in the period between the two world wars than did Father Divine's movement. During this interwar period, "the word 'cult' was first used by social scientists," and the Peace Mission was often mentioned as a "typical example of a cult." The Peace Mission was highly eclectic. It drew motifs from perfectionism, New Thought, the holiness movement and the Adventists and combined them with new elements as to constitute a small but distinct religion.[10]

The Peace Mission was founded by Father Major J. Divine (1878?-1965). What little is known about his life prior to 1914 is a matter of disagreement. The story that is most widely accepted by those outside the movement is that he was born George Baker in Georgia around 1878 or 1880. He evidenced an interest in religion very early in life, but the turning event occurred when he was approximately twenty and serving as a part-time minister in Baltimore. Here he met Father Morris, an itinerant minister who called himself "the Father Eternal." He began his own church and made George Baker his "Messenger," or second person.[11]

The two split in 1912, and Baker gathered his own following in Valdosta, Georgia. Here Baker's teachings included a mixture of practical religion and mysticism: if an individual were truly at one with the Spirit of God, health and material blessings would follow. Most likely Baker acquired these ideas from several sources, including mind-cure teachings, which were part of New Thought, and the perfectionism of the holiness movement. Forced to leave Valdosta, he emerged in Brooklyn in 1914. Five years later he moved to Sayville, Long Island, where he lived quietly until 1931. During this time he evangelized and drew a small following, including some whites.[12]

In 1931 an event occurred that gave Father Divine national visibility. Some minor complaints prompted the police to arrest him for disturbing the peace. Father Divine regarded the entire incident as racially motivated. Therefore he refused bail, pleaded not guilty and was tried and convicted.

171

The judge meted out a harsh punishment—a year in jail. But the judge, who appeared to be a healthy man, died two days later. From his cell, Father Divine announced that the judge's death was not of natural causes; "I hated to do it," he said. This event encouraged his followers to see him as divine, and the Peace Mission began to publish accounts of disasters that came upon those people who opposed Father Divine's program.[13]

Encouraged by the events in Sayville, and with the Depression almost at its worst, in 1932 Father Divine moved his group to Harlem. Here the Peace Mission enjoyed a decade of expansion. By now he had considerable status in the black community, and proceeded to expand the Peace Mission in response to the dire situation created by the Depression. The Mission provided housing, cheap food, employment and a new lifestyle for its members. In a small but important way, Father Divine had brought the kingdom of heaven to many poor blacks, and in doing so he reinforced the notion that he was God.[14]

Mounting legal problems forced Father Divine to transfer his headquarters and residence to Philadelphia, where the Peace Mission continued to prosper. His first wife had died, and in 1946 he married Edna Rose Ritchings, a white Canadian. He died in 1965; his body is still enshrined in Philadelphia. At the time of his death the major concentrations of the Peace Mission were in Philadelphia and New York, but there were farms in New York State and other programs in several Western and Northern cities.[15]

After Father Divine's death, Mother Divine, his wife, became the leader of the movement and proceeded to administer its global operations. The movement had its greatest growth during Father Divine's life, but still exists as a number of independent church corporations, businesses and religious orders interrelated by the participants' belief in Father Divine and his teachings. As of the early 1980s, four congregations still met in Philadelphia, three in the New York area, two in California and one each in Switzerland and Australia.[16]

The beliefs and practices of the Peace Mission came from several sources and reflected such an amalgamation. In various degrees, three major tenets can be detected. First and foremost were Father Divine's personal characteristics: his flamboyant personality, his excessive extravagance and his presumed divinity. Although he did not explicitly teach that he was God, he allowed his followers to arrive at that conclusion and to act accordingly. Augmenting his alleged divine status is the Peace Mission teaching that

Father Divine met all the biblical prophecies for the coming of the Jewish messiah and the Second Coming of Christ. God has Father and Mother dimensions, which are personified in Father and Mother Divine and provide the basis for one human brotherhood. The movement even has a holy text. Father Divine's words, transcribed by secretaries and published in the *New Day,* have the authority of sacred scripture. According to some sources, he made claims to immortality, saying that neither he nor his genuinely devout followers would grow sick and die.[17]

According to Peter Williams, Father Divine's alleged divine status had many implications for his movement. He maintained a lifestyle appropriate for one possessing divinity. To the disappointment of the Internal Revenue Service, it was never proved that he had any personal wealth, though he lived lavishly "on the largesse of his followers." He required complete obedience and loyalty from his disciples, and to a great extent they complied. They repudiated "all ties with the outside world and all continuity with their previous lives." Those followers who had families had to either bring them into the movement or sever ties with them. The members were to turn all their income and personal wealth over to the movement. In turn, they received room and board in the Peace Mission's houses and restaurants and a modest allowance for other expenses. As is the practice in some Catholic religious orders, the members "received new spiritual names such as Sweet Angel, or Beautiful Peace."[18]

To those outside the movement and who thought along the lines of Western logic, Father Divine's claim to divinity seemed outlandish and absurd. Yet his followers could point to a modest level of evidence to sustain their belief. Many in the movement did not approach the issue of Father Divine's divinity logically. Williams points out that the Peace Mission represents "a withdrawal from the logic and mores of everyday American life into a separate world governed by a communistic economy, a regime of asceticism" and a leader whose behavior dramatically contrasted with the "expectations of conventional Christianity." Father Divine's apparent ability to perform "miracles" came as confirmation of his divine power to the faithful. They were not left without tangible evidence. Father Divine "claimed that he could bring down violent retribution upon those who opposed the Movement." Indeed, some remarkable coincidences in which disaster befell his opponents shortly after his maledictions seemed to support these claims. Father Divine's ability to provide "food and security for the unemployed and comfort to the emotionally dispossessed" was seen as a powerful and tangible confirmation of his divine power. Even his lavish banquets for his followers were seen as modest proof of his divine power.[19]

A second motive was Father Divine's perception of the plight of the downtrodden, particularly African-Americans. Melton says that he envisioned a "total economic and religious program to reform the individual and restructure society." Members of the Peace Mission saw America as the birthplace of the kingdom of God and longed for the day when America would live up to such ideals. They equated "the Kingdom with the principles of true Americanism, Brotherhood, Democracy, Christianity, Judaism, and all other true religions." According to the teachings of the Peace Mission, all individuals are equal in the sight of God, and therefore all deserve the material necessities of modern society, plus such basic rights as the pursuit of life, liberty and happiness.[20]

Father Divine wanted a new heaven on earth for his followers, and, in a limited measure, he provided one. He went beyond most religious leaders in blending the spiritual and physical realms. Father Divine taught the doctrine of peace on earth, provided food and shelter at a minimal price, helped blacks to find employment and opened the doors of the Peace Mission to white followers as well. He allowed no discrimination within the confines of his movement. While he rigidly segregated men and women, integration by race was as strict. The Peace Mission maintains a communal organization. All possessions are owned by the group, and all properties are maintained by the members without pay for their work. Father Divine provided benefits for his people in the material realm and advocated social change because he believed in American values and the country's ability to change. Nevertheless, in reality, his movement functioned primarily as a counterculture. Bringing little actual change in the surrounding society, it substituted a spiritual order with some material blessing for a reordered society.[21]

A third motive concerns certain emphases drawn from the holiness and New Thought movements. Drugs, tobacco and alcohol were banned, and a disciplined lifestyle, including complete celibacy, was encouraged. The imprint of New Thought can be seen in the movement's belief that sin, sickness and death are consequences and signs of spiritual malfunction, and that the Spirit-filled person normally should not experience such problems.[22]

The appeal of Father Divine came from his balance between the universal and the particular. While he presented a utopian vision, he went to great lengths to meet the particular needs of the downtrodden for food, shelter and employment. Father Divine denied the reality of race, just as Mary Baker Eddy had refused to accept the existence of sickness and death. Thus he gained white as well as black converts and declared his goal to be a deracialized America. Many other black movements responded to their desperate urban situation with actions that actually intensified racial tensions. In contrast, Father Divine sought to modify such conflicts. A related reason for Father Divine's appeal is that he, more than any other of the ghetto's innumerable cultists, built on a faith in American society and its capacity for change. By referring often to the nation's democratic values, he struck a responsive chord among blacks and whites.[23]

United House of Prayer for All People
Another case of a black cult formed around a black charismatic leader who assumed a divine status was the United House of Prayer for All People. This group was a rival of the Peace Mission of Father Divine and is often compared to it. Whatever one may think of Father Divine's presumption to divine status, his Universal Peace Mission did have many redeeming social qualities. The same cannot be said for the United House of Prayer.

The United House of Prayer was the creation of Bishop Charles Immanuel Grace (1881-1960). "Sweet Daddy Grace," as his followers affectionately called him, was the cornerstone of this religious movement. He believed himself to be as important as Father Divine and to occupy a similar status. His names, Immanuel (God with us) and Grace (the gift of God), indicate his self-perceived importance: that he was God in the midst of his followers. In the House of Prayer Daddy Grace was substituted for God and was worshiped as such, exemplified by genuflection and prayer before his picture.[24]

Grace had a humble background. He came from Portugal or the Azores, of parents who were said to be black and Portuguese. With flowing hair and a bronze color, he claimed to be white and often spoke patronizingly of the blacks who were baptized into his church. His church had its origin in the South, where Grace worked for years on a railroad job. In 1925 he began preaching and gathered followers to himself. His ministry spread, and his churches sprang up on the Eastern seaboard, with Washington, D.C., serving as the headquarters.[25]

The House of Prayer was a cult of the holiness and Pentecostal type, teaching the necessity of conversion and subsequent sanctification, the intervention of the Holy Spirit, and the usual moral restrictions. Actually, however, the beliefs came down to worshiping and serving Daddy Grace. The central characteristics of the House of Prayer were worship of Daddy Grace, fundraising to support his lavish lifestyle, and services marked by physical and emotional frenzy.[26]

As Sydney Ahlstrom points out, "the basic tenet of the House of Prayer is the sovereign power of its bishop," Sweet Daddy Grace. From him "all blessings flow," but unlike the blessings of Father Divine, his were intangible: healings on occasion, but often ecstasies of the spirit, various ceremonial honors and "the vicarious pleasures of sharing in Sweet Daddy's sumptuous life." What traces of Christianity remained in the House of Prayer "suggest an extreme form of Pentecostalism." Worship was a time when members joyously celebrated the person of Daddy Grace. They sang to the rhythmic beat of tambourines and drums, with dancers moving erotically and in an emotional frenzy, proclaiming, "Oh Daddy! Daddy, you feel so good!" The meetings were an emotional marathon. Scores of worshipers constantly fell on the floor. After lying prostrate for a while, they usually rose suddenly, crying excessively, singing and dancing throughout the House of Prayer.[27]

From its members the House of Prayer demanded two things: servile obedience and a willingness to part with money. Daddy Grace was the undisputed leader. He demanded unquestioning obedience from all his preachers and church members. The preachers were to carry out the instructions of the bishop, preach, conduct services and—probably most important—raise money. During each service there were numerous high-pressured collections. Rewards were given to individuals who raised the most money. Beyond soliciting and donating money, members were encouraged to purchase products that supposedly had spiritual or magical qualities. Some claimed that Daddy Grace soap would not only cleanse the body but also reduce fat and heal. Daddy Grace writing paper would improve an individual's writing skills and assist him or her in composing a good letter. If placed on the chest, *The Grace Magazine* would completely cure a cold or even tuberculosis. Other commodities included Daddy Grace toothpaste, tea, coffee, hair pomade, face powder, talcum powder, shoe polish, cold cream, cookies, badges, emblems, banners, uniforms and so forth.[28]

In a word, the House of Prayer was a business enterprise for Daddy Grace, whose success came from his ability to manipulate spiritual thirst into a system of self-aggrandizement. As a consequence, its social and moral impact was virtually nil, and it did little to alleviate the condition of poor blacks. Like an old trickster, Daddy Grace took from his people and profited greatly from them. In return, his people received great emotional and spiritual experiences. The success achieved by the House of Prayer seemed to depend on two related factors. The most depressed elements of the black community had deep psychic needs, and a charismatic leader had the ability to satisfy some of those needs through splendid parades, lively meetings, majestic pomp in worship, and public baptismal services that utilized fire hoses.[29]

The death of Daddy Grace in 1960 brought a great crisis to the House of Prayer, as the death of a leader often does to cultic groups. For a while, it seemed that conflicts between rival successors and tax litigation would bring an end to the House of Prayer and scatter its twenty thousand or so members. After a year or two, however, Bishop Walter McCollough became the leader of the church. While he assumed Daddy Grace's powers, he did not claim to be divine. Under McCollough's leadership the church has assumed a more traditional Pentecostal stance. In 1969, in Washington, D.C., he dedicated an impressive new headquarters with an adjoining home for elderly people. In the same year he staged more fire-hose baptisms and a grandiose parade, suggesting that the church would continue to emphasize the flamboyant and could still win a lively following. Yet by the late sixties, the temper of the ghetto had changed. With the rise of black militancy, such self-serving religious charades were subjected to increasingly severe criticism.[30]

177

PART IV

Eastern Groups
in Post-Christian
America

In America during the last half of the twentieth century, Christianity has not been the definer of cultural values that it had been in years past. As a consequence, the latter part of the twentieth century has been designated "the post-Christian era." During this time new religions have abounded. Many of them have had little or no connection with the Judeo-Christian tradition. While these fringe religions exhibit great variety, they can be seen as a response to different aspects of American culture. This section focuses on the marginal groups connected with the Eastern religions, often designated as Eastern cults. Eastern religions have been visible in America since the nineteenth century. But there has been a virtual invasion of Eastern spirituality since the 1960s, partially in response to the relaxation of immigration laws and partially as a result of the West's susceptibility to Eastern ideas.

12

Religious Innovations
in Post-Christian
America

During the 1960s and 1970s a number of new religions paraded across the American scene, in such profusion that Americans believed that they were being invaded by the cults. Fringe religions became fodder for television talk shows and news specials. Stories about the occult and cults made the front covers of *Time* and *Newsweek*. Scores of books with titles such as *The Cults are Coming, Strange New Religions* and *New Gods in America* aroused interest. A flood of scholarly publications on cults came from the pens of academicians. During much of the 1970s attention was directed toward groups associated with the counterculture, popularly called sects, cults and the occult. As the counterculture waned, interest moved in directions more acceptable to middle America: the human potential and New Age movements. Meanwhile, on the other side of the religious spectrum, a conservative revival was taking place in the form of an evangelical awakening.

To be sure, many of these religious innovations were not new. They had deep roots in Western culture and American history. In particular, Transcendentalism, Spiritualism, Theosophy, New Thought and the Eastern religions have been the precursors of many fringe groups in the late twentieth century. And many current Christian deviations have sprung from nineteenth-century movements. The myth that the cults and sects of the late twentieth century came from nowhere must be shattered. America has had a rich tradition of religious pluralism from which these so-called new religions have emerged.

The American tradition of religious pluralism notwithstanding, something different happened in the 1960s. As Robert Wuthnow points out, "few decades have given rise to as many religious movements as the late 1960s and early 1970s." By the late 1970s some sources estimated that "the number of local new religious groups in America might number in the thousands, with some of the larger movements claiming adherents in the hundreds of thousands."[1] These decades stand out as one of the great periods of religious experimentation in Western history, with some similarities to the Hellenistic era, the sixteenth and early seventeenth centuries in Europe, and the 1830s and 1840s in America.[2]

By the mid 1980s, however, observers recognized that a mass movement toward the fringe religions was not going to occur, and that earlier statistics concerning these movements might have been inflated. The countercultural aspect had peaked at least ten years earlier, and interest now centered on various quasi-religious movements. Still, the numbers of people in these groups must be taken seriously. The most sober estimates in the 1980s list several hundred thousand people as members of alternative religions,[3] while some experts claim that the total of these groups is between two and three million.[4]

Whether the higher or lower figures are accurate, the importance of these new religions transcends their numbers. The significant growth of the new religions in the 1960s and 1970s reflects the quantum leap in religious and cultural pluralism that has taken place in recent America. The increase in marginal religions is also connected with anxieties brought on by rapid social and economic changes in postwar America. A sociocultural revolution took place, and many Americans were dissatisfied with the conditions that developed. Some of the reactions were conservative, some radical; they were visible in ethics, morals, economics, social arrangements and religion. The marginal religions must be seen as one of these reactions to rapid change.

Society in Change

Forces of both continuity and change were active in post-World War II America. Historians have tended to focus on the enormous change, ignoring the fact that such forces had already been active for much of the twentieth century. During the sixties many elements in American society exploded; thus this period is often seen as a revolutionary decade, a watershed in American society. Such observations are essentially true. But the sixties were also a time when the "chickens came home to roast." This turbulent decade served as a catalyst to forces already in motion. Long-term economic, moral, theological and cultural processes were brought to a crisis point by rapid social change and the tremendous economic expansion that Americans had experienced and carelessly enjoyed during the affluent years following World War II.[5]

The 1950s are generally seen as a conservative and affluent period. A popular president, Dwight Eisenhower, presided over the peak of a postwar economic boom. The friendly policies of his administration helped to promote a decade of unprecedented industrial growth. Middle America shared in this prosperity, enjoying a steady rise in living standards. The Soviet Union had the atomic bomb; Japanese and European economies were recovering from the war. Still, America was not yet seriously challenged either economically or militarily. Not surprisingly, the prevailing mood was complacency. Nevertheless, in the late fifties many premonitory signs could be seen on the horizon. Certain attitudes and interests of the fifties presaged the secularizing theologies of the sixties. The unrest of the black community in the late fifties was a sign of what was to come. President Eisenhower's speech concerning the growing power of "the military-industrial complex" gave hints of the next decade's radical protests.[6]

The years from the election of John F. Kennedy in 1960 to 1975, when Gerald Ford inaugurated the bicentennial era, were tumultuous and traumatic. According to Sydney Ahlstrom, "never before in the nation's history have so many Americans expressed revolutionary intentions and actively participated in efforts to alter the shape of American civilization in almost every imaginable aspect"—from religion to the political process, from art to the economic order, from health to diplomacy. These years were a watershed in American history. American society was severely shaken and in many ways permanently transformed.[7]

Urbanization, science and technology brought much of this change. Rampant, unregulated urban and industrial growth had begun to create difficulties with which American political and fiscal practices could not cope. Technological and scientific advances had seemed to have no bounds. In the face of sensational scientific achievements, dramatized by the moon landing and heart transplants, transcendent reality had faded from view. Consequently, for many the idea of the supernatural had lost its force. Theodore Roszak speaks of the impact of technology on society, particularly its role in creating a counterculture. The advance of science and technology, along with urban growth, depersonalized human relationships, creating a thirst for community and intimacy that for some could be quenched in fringe religious groups. The great emphasis on science, technology and cold rationality caused a backlash. A shift in epistemology, our way of learning, could be detected. Research and cognitive methods began to be replaced by experience and intuition. Such means of acquiring truth are, of course, central in many fringe religions.[8]

Gordon Melton notes significant changes in the scientific community during the twentieth century—changes that affected nontraditional religions. As indicated previously, parapsychology had been born in the 1920s and had had a close relationship with fringe religions before World War II. In the 1960s the lines between parapsychology and the occult became increasingly blurred, with some parapsychologists engaging in occult activities. This development, of course, was not new. On numerous occasions in Western history science and the occult have overlapped.

Second, the discovery of LSD had quasi-religious implications. Though invented in 1938, this mind-altering drug only became popular and widely available in the 1960s. Soon psychedelic experiences became identified with the search for religious ecstasy. The mainline and evangelical churches "opposed the use of psychedelic substances on moral grounds," but alternative religions have taken a variety of positions in respect to psychedelic experiences. Some, such as The Farm, have tended to accept them. Most groups tolerated them, while others (such as Hare Krishna and the Jesus People) promised to provide a better, nondrug-related ecstasy.[9]

Third, "a revolution in psychiatry and psychology" has opened avenues to alternative religions. The twentieth century produced a number of psychological systems different from the psychoanalytic approach of Freud and the behaviorism of John Broadus Watson (1878-1958). Some of these systems drew from the occult and became familiarization tools and legitimizing agents for some fringe religions and quasi-religions. The ideas of C. G. Jung (1875-1961) provide the best example. Jung became a student of the occult, and his concept of archetypes supported modern neopaganism and magic. Less known is the Italian psychiatrist Robert Assagioli (1888-1974), who assimilated aspects of Theosophy and developed psychosynthesis, a system intertwined with ideas from Alice Bailey's Arcane School. Even more important, on a broader scale "humanistic psychology took a positive turn toward religion and religious experience." Psychological principles and techniques became surrogates for traditional religious beliefs and practices. Combined with Eastern thought and practice, this humanistic psychology "gave birth to the human potentials movement," which has fostered many new quasi-religions.[10]

The 1960s also witnessed drastic alterations in social and political relations. Most important, the situation that had long supported Protestant dominance and white Anglo-Saxon Protestant (WASP) ascendancy in American life came under serious challenge. Cracks in the Protestant establishment had been visible by the turn of the century, but they now opened into gaping fissures. Immigration patterns brought many new voters who repudiated this Protestant ascendancy. In 1961 the Protestant lock on the presidency ended, and a Roman Catholic entered the White House. This, combined with the ending of the Counter-Reformation by Vatican II, drastically altered the old Protestant-Catholic relationships.[11]

What the voters did not do the Supreme Court accomplished. In the fifties and sixties the Supreme Court removed crucial legal supports from the power structure of the white Protestant establishment. Segregation became illegal. The court supported the principle of one person, one vote. Also, the court outlawed the use of Christian ceremonies in the public schools. And of great significance, black America, first through the vehicle of the civil rights movement and then later under the banner of Black Power, began to demand an end to the historic inequalities that had characterized African-Americans' existence. Though not as violent and divisive as the civil rights and antiwar movements, feminism and environmentalism challenged some of the most fundamental assumptions of Western culture: that men dominated women and that humanity could act with impunity toward nature.[12]

President Lyndon Johnson's decision to escalate the Vietnam War provided the supreme catalyst for all these challenges to the American system. Cynicism toward the political establishment erupted into violence. Some saw the war's escalation as the betrayal of a political promise. Others believed that the war would be used as an excuse for government to avoid implementing civil rights. And among youth there developed a level of hostile feeling toward the establishment that was probably unique in America's history. College students and others agitated for nearly half a decade. To cap off this period, America experienced a series of traumas: Watergate, the resignation of President Nixon and the collapse of the American-backed regime in Vietnam.[13]

All these developments, writes Ron Enroth, helped to foster an apocalyptic mentality in American society at large. This mood was very strong in both secular and religious sectors during the 1960s and 1970s. "The invention of the atomic bomb began the . . . apocalyptic mood." The widespread concern with environmental pollution was a manifestation of the apocalyptic mindset. Apocalypticism was political as well. During the sixties and seventies many believed "that the American government [was] beyond reforming and must be destroyed totally in order for something new and better to take its place." While such an apocalyptic mood could be discerned within many groups, "it was perhaps the strongest in the counterculture." As a consequence, religious groups with a Western background that came out of the counterculture tended to be radical and apocalyptic.[14]

A very important component in the growth of the new religions in the sixties and seventies was the expansion of cultural pluralism, primarily by means of increased contacts with the East. During the first two decades of the twentieth century, immigration laws had reduced the flow of people from the Orient to a trickle. This had changed dramatically after World War II. The war against Japan, military involvement in Korea and Vietnam, and all the contacts that world leadership entailed, to say nothing of a creeping secularism, had expanded American pluralism beyond its Judeo-Christian confines.[15]

According to Melton, several specific events triggered a new flow of contacts with Eastern religions. First, at the conclusion of World War II "America imposed religious freedom on Japan as a condition of peace." As a result of this new freedom, many formerly suppressed religious groups spread rapidly, and hundreds more emerged; some of them found their way to America. Second, India gained independence in 1948. As members of the British Commonwealth, Indians had the freedom to travel to the West. "Among these travelers were swamis and gurus." Third, after the Chinese Revolution many religious leaders fled atheistic rule. In 1965 President Johnson overturned the Oriental Exclusion Act and allowed Chinese immigrants to enter the United States. The result was staggering: a massive human flood from Asia. Melton says that this "change in the limits of Asian immigration is the single most important factor in the rise of new religions in America."[16]

The counterculture of the 1960s is usually seen as the immediate catalyst for the rise of fringe religions. But as the counterculture declined in the seventies, many of the new religions connected with the counterculture also receded. Martin Marty lists several reasons for this development. First, joining such groups was no longer in vogue. Second, countercultural sects and cults had a high dropout rate, and the individuals leaving were not replaced with new converts. Next, certain incidents such as the mass suicide of Jamestown stigmatized all cults and drove people off. Four, some declining groups were drastically altered in their appearance and practices, becoming more acceptable to society but also less noticeable. Finally, evangelicals, Catholic Pentecostals and Hasidic Jews cut into the recruiting market of the cults. These groups offered young people intense experiences, authority in their lives and group identity.[17]

As social, economic and political changes brought an end to the counterculture, the cults and occult slipped from public view. This did not signal an end to the new religions, but the passing of a phase. By the late seventies this shift could be discerned. Attention had shifted from the cults and occult to several quasi-religions and psychoreligions, especially the groups associated with the human potential and New Age movements.

Several reasons can be given for this change. First, the political activism of the late sixties and early seventies had given way to a more conservative era. The flame of political and social reform now burned low. People were now more interested in career advancement and personal fulfillment than in remaking American society. Second, the affluence of the sixties had declined. The luxury of experiment ended with the economic downturn of the 1970s, and young people conformed to society in order to further careers that might assure them of prosperity in difficult times.[18]

The new religions that are popular in the 1980s, namely the human potential and New Age movements, better match these political and economic trends than the counterculture groups did. Self-fulfillment and personal transformation are important goals for individuals in these quasi-religious movements. Furthermore, in the 1970s conservative religion made a comeback. Evangelicals came to national prominence, and fundamentalists became politically active. These developments also paralleled the political and economic trends of the seventies.[19]

It would be a mistake, though, to push the contrasts between these periods too far. Many of the changes that occurred in the sixties became institutionalized. Aspects of countercultural lifestyles such as permissive sex and the use of drugs became common, even the norm in some segments of society. The elimination of racism and sexism in American society became public policy. The stripping away of moral authority from major American social institutions—government, law, business, religion, marriage and the family—has not been reversed. In the late 1970s and the 1980s there was no simple return to conditions prior to the sixties.[20]

Christopher Lasch and others have painted a stark contrast between the sixties and seventies. The sixties are seen as morally generous and politically active; the seventies, in contrast, are portrayed as an apolitical decade when people were preoccupied with self.[21] Peter Clecak has challenged this interpretation, arguing that there was more continuity between the two decades than meets the eye. The quest for personal fulfillment was at the forefront in both periods. People may have approached it differently in the two decades, but the quests had many similarities.[22] It would also be a mistake to exaggerate the contrasts between the cults and sects of the counterculture and the quasi-religions of the seventies and eighties. To be sure, there are many differences, but self-fulfillment was important in both movements.

Major Developments in the Religious Setting

There have been four major, related religious developments in America since 1960: the rise of the new religions, the revival of conservative religion, the decline of liberalism and the privatization of religion. As I have indicated, the new religions came in two overlapping phases: those of the youthful counterculture and the quasi-religions. These new religions sprang from the same milieu as did other major religious developments and can be best understood in this context. Moreover, these fringe movements manifested many of the same characteristics as did other bodies, particularly the conservative ones.

A resurgence of conservative religion came in the 1970s. The churches that grew in the late sixties and seventies were virtually all conservative— Protestant evangelical and fundamentalist, neo-Pentecostal, Seventh-day Adventist, Jehovah's Witness, Mormon and Orthodox Jewish bodies. Though these groups have obvious theological differences, they all manifest what Dean M. Kelley calls "traits of straitness": demanding, absolutist beliefs, social and moral conformity, and a missionary spirit.[23] The emergence of the "electronic church," with its vast network of television programming, popular preachers and broad-based support, can be seen as a new form of conservative religion. Moreover, the politicization of religious conservatism and the formation of organizations like the Moral Majority can be seen as a new religious development.[24]

The fringe religions share several important characteristics with the conservative groups, especially the evangelicals. Both sought authority in a world of intellectual chaos. Both groups placed a heavy emphasis on religious experience. Further, both reacted to the mainline religions and to the pluralization and secularization of society. The new religions and the conservative groups attracted people who were discontented with the chaos of pluralism, the hallmark of modernity. People sought authoritative teachings instead of the babel of ideological voices that tend to cancel one another out. Such individuals were also intolerant of *moral* pluralism—the many competing claims to values and to definitions of right and wrong.[25]

However, people sought to satisfy their craving for intellectual and moral authority not through abstract propositions, but through experience. Mainstream modern religiosity has seldom ministered to the thirst for experience, but the new religions and much of evangelicalism have emphasized experiential dimensions of faith. Public opinion polls have noted a surge toward experiential religion. With few exceptions, fringe religions minister to this need. The "born again" experience is basic to evangelicalism. According to a 1976 Gallup poll, one out of every three Americans had been "born again." Some evangelical groups also emphasize other experiences such as tongues-speaking and fervent feelings of devotion.[26]

The growth of the new religions and the conservative bodies accompanied the decline of liberalism. As noted by Wade Roof and William McKinney, during the sixties and seventies "religion was flourishing on the right and left fringes but languishing in the center." Individuals experimented with "new religions and various quasi-religious and spiritual therapies." In quest of their own spiritual pursuits and in rebellion against old authorities, many young, well-educated people turned to meditation techniques and mystical faiths. In a world out of kilter, the turn inward in quest of self-enlightenment seemed the correct thing to do. On the other extreme, many conservative faiths, "seeking to restore the traditional ways of believing and behaving, were prospering as well." Against the new faiths of the young were the old faiths of history. Yet both the new religions and conservative faiths rode the crest of a tide of experiential faith sweeping the country.[27]

Meanwhile, the groups in the middle—the culturally accommodating and more liberal versions of the Catholic, Jewish and Protestant faiths—were in a state of serious decline. Wrenched from all sides, the liberal religious center could no longer maintain its numbers and influence. Differences increased between the religious and secular worldviews, and between those seeking inner truth and those espousing a more traditional, God-centered religious order. William McLoughlin sees liberalism as the religious mainstream, the consensus from the 1920s to the 1960s. But in the sixties American culture once again suffered "from a crises of legitimacy." The system was under pressure "to adjust its institutions and central value systems to alleviate strains created by the changing social situations."[28]

Did the evangelical revival and the Reagan-Bush years signify a new conservative consensus? Daniel Yankelovich says that tomorrow will not look like the conservative past. A cultural revolution has changed the rules of American life, moving the nation into uncharted territory. McLoughlin contends that American culture has been in a state of crisis since 1960 and will continue in it until sometime in the 1990s, when he predicts that a new consensus will form. Roof and McKinney insist that there is currently no single dominant religious influence. Instead, many religious ideological forces are seeking to exert influence.[29]

Liberalism declined for many reasons, largely because its claims failed the test of reality. Scholars such as Freud and Jung had raised doubts regarding the rationality of human existence. The neo-orthodox theologians challenged the optimism of liberalism, insisting that history points to the depravity of human nature. On the other side, Michael Harrington pointed out that the liberal welfare state has not solved the problem of poverty. Events—the rise of Mussolini, Hitler and Stalin to power, the atrocities of Nazism and communism, World War II and the Korean War and, most frightening, the possibility of a nuclear holocaust—were not kind to liberalism either. Salvation no longer seemed securely locked into the advance of science and modernism. Liberal Protestantism's cherished faith in progressive education and rationality appeared to be naive at best.[30]

The trend toward greater individualism in religious choice and practice— the privatization of faith—is important in modern history. Historically, individualism has been an important value in American culture, and in contemporary society basic psychological and social transformations have made it more so. That religion remains a matter of personal choice or preference has deep roots in American history. This religious individualism has been reinforced, of course, by cultural pluralism, political democracy and capitalism.[31]

A new voluntarism arose in the 1970s and 1980s. While this voluntarism embraced many of the older themes of individualism found in American history, it differed substantially. Previously, individualism had usually rested within the context of a religious and cultural consensus and thus had a certain direction. As the old cultural and religious synthesis of the Eisenhower years unraveled, the value system within the country shifted dramatically. In the sixties, support for public piety and patriotism no longer held. Life in the modern world had become fragmented. As the American way of life lost its idealism, the deep-seated quest for personal fulfillment gained momentum. Many Americans could not find wholeness and meaning in the institutions and values of the prevailing society. So they turned inward.[32]

As Thomas Luckmann points out, religion has become "invisible," a private affair, something to be worked out within the confines of an individual's life experiences. Each person is expected to fashion, from the available resources, a system of sacred meanings and values in accord with personal needs and preference.[33] According to Wade Roof, such a privatized religion knows little of communal forms and needs little institutional support. While it may provide meaning for the individual believer, "it is not a shared faith."[34]

This quest for fulfillment as a matter of individual experience had implications for all segments of American religion, but especially the new religions and spiritual therapies. Most individuals in the conservative religious bodies considered personal fulfillment to be a consequence of Christian salvation, something to be acquired only by faith in the life and death of Jesus Christ. Whether fundamentalist, evangelical, neo-Pentecostal or holiness Christians, they stressed the continuing and personal benefits of their faith. Even many within the liberal mainstream sought personal fulfillment, often through spiritual therapies. Growing numbers of both laity and clergy took part in workshops on personal growth and meditation techniques. Many charismatics within Catholicism and liberal Protestantism placed a high priority on spiritual growth. Since the sixties and seventies the political and social climate has changed considerably. Nevertheless, the themes of personal freedom and individual fulfillment gained strength in the 1980s because the baby boomers carried them into mainstream culture.[35]

Privatized religion and the quest for personal fulfillment fit perfectly with many new religions. The occult and metaphysical versions of the new religions do not always issue in group life. Many of their ideas are propagated through the mail or private readings. Lonely people who never attend church or cult meetings may be informed by this means. In astrology and in groups such as Spiritualism, Scientology, astrology and est, the focus is on self-fulfillment rather than any social dimension. Similarly, it must be recognized that much in Eastern religions is private and invisible and not a social force. Even in their collective aspects, the practical, ritual and behavioral correlates receive most of the attention. Eastern movements with a strong appeal to individualism and privatization are Transcendental Meditation, Zen and yoga.[36]

The quasi-religions and spiritual therapies made the strongest appeal to those interested in self-fulfillment. In fact, many in these groups equated salvation with fulfillment, something that could be found only within the self. Individuals in these movements employ techniques to promote spiritual growth or, in more secular terms, to awaken inner awareness. Whether the movement is humanistic or religious in orientation, personal fulfillment is the primary objective of all its activities. The major concerns are how a particular technique can lead to greater self-realization and how spiritual enlightenment can be obtained. In fact, a number of these spiritual therapies are intended for mass consumption and are packaged and marketed for wide audiences.[37]

In the free religious marketplace of the sixties, seventies and eighties, which groups are the fringe or marginal religions? The new religions—that is, the cults and sects of the counterculture—are obviously on the fringes of American religion. So are the Eastern religions, the occult and the quasi-religions, including spiritual therapies and the New Age movement. These have drawn most of their adherents from the educated middle class, not the socially deprived. Nevertheless, in some cases their members are alienated from society. Also, the beliefs and practices of many of these groups are far removed from the Christian tradition.

In the late 1980s and early 1990s no religious body held a dominant position. Instead, many groups are competing for influences. Nevertheless, liberal Protestantism (despite its decline in members and influence) and Catholicism are usually still regarded as the religious mainstream. Though the religious center is weakened, these bodies do occupy the middle ground on many social and ideological issues.

But what about the evangelical and fundamentalist bodies? The evangelical mainstream and the moderate fundamentalist bodies currently reflect an accommodating posture. Once rigid and hostile toward society, Protestant conservatism has generally become more culture-affirming. Today only the most separationist of the fundamentalists are on the fringes of American religion. Vastly different from the "holy rollers" and "fightin' fundies" of America's revivalistic past, contemporary evangelicals take an intellectual stance more consistent with modern rationality and tend to maintain behavior that is in good taste. Moreover, any religious movement that can claim the loyalty of the three presidential candidates in the 1980 election (Carter, Reagan and Anderson) cannot be dismissed as a marginal phenomenon.[38]

The Watershed of the 1960s

The 1960s marked a turning point in American religious life. The confluence of so many widespread changes led Martin Marty to speak of a "seismic shift" in the nation's religious landscape.[39] Sydney Ahlstrom regarded the 1960s as a time when the "old foundations of national confidence, patriotic idealism, moral traditionalism, and even of historic Judaeo-Christian theism, were awash. Presuppositions that had held firm for centuries—even millennia—were being widely questioned."[40]

Robert Bellah defines civil religion as a complex of symbolic meanings that many Americans share and that unite them in a moral community.[41] The upheaval and turbulence, the emergence of many new sects and cults, and the deep sense of disillusionment in the 1960s had a shattering effect on civil religion. To many the United States was no longer a beacon of hope to the world. The image of America as the chosen nation, the new Israel, had been smashed. The old public faith that once unified Americans around national values and purpose was deemed by many to be hollow and deceitful. Polls indicated that church attendance declined during the 1960s, and more and more Americans believed that religion was losing its importance. As a consequence, the terms *post-Protestant* and even *post-Christian* were used to describe American society. These phrases are not misleading or simplistic if they are used to point out that other forces have displaced

193

Protestantism, and perhaps even Christianity in the broader sense, as the primary definer of cultural values and behavior patterns in the nation.[42]

Religious pluralism has a long history in America. Despite a de facto Protestant establishment that lasted well into the twentieth century, American religion has not been monolithic. In addition to Catholicism, Eastern Orthodoxy, Judaism and Eastern religions, the religious landscape has been dotted with many other marginal religions. Nevertheless, for over a hundred years such pluralism had little impact on American culture. As Roof and McKinney write, "In self perception, if not in fact, the United States was a white country in which Protestant Christianity set the norms of religious observance and moral conduct." WASP influence "shaped much of public life."[43]

The Constitution of 1789 legally disestablished religion on a national level. As a result, pluralism has been around for a while. But it did not pose much of a problem throughout most of the nation's history, when a common core of Protestant values could be taken for granted.[44] All of this began to change during the twentieth century. After World War I the old WASP order was challenged by a growing pluralism. Protestantism now had to accommodate other faiths. Robert Handy speaks of these developments during the 1920s and 1930s as a "second disestablishment." From the 1920s to the 1960s the United States had become, in Will Herberg's words, a "Protestant-Catholic-Jewish" country.[45]

Yet not until the 1960s did the realities of an extended pluralism become apparent. Cultural pluralism had mushroomed. Immigrants from Asia and Latin America poured in, expanding America's cultural horizons. The ease of travel and communication also played a role; Americans traveled abroad much more. Middle-class Americans had been in the military all over the world. Foreign students with appreciation for other religions came to North America in droves.

The extended pluralism was moral as well as cultural. As American culture became more secular and rational, diversity in moral values and lifestyle also increased. The liberal consensus had been shattered by the 1960s, and thereafter religion lost much of its strength as an integrative influence in America. America no longer had a moral core. When a moral core still existed, pluralism in morals and values had not seemed so threatening. Now, lacking a common religious culture, groups contend with each other for power and influence. The debate over morals and values has crystallized around two camps: moral traditionalists versus those advocating a more libertarian and secular position.[46]

The controversy over values is centered in two basic social institutions: the family and the school. Throughout the seventies, conservatives generally opposed the Equal Rights Amendment and the extension of legal rights to homosexuals, while favoring a ban on abortion. In the schools, they supported prayer in the classroom and condemned the teaching of evolution and the use of "humanist" textbooks. These conservatives seek to turn the country around and to restore a Christian America. Meanwhile, secularists push for greater openness, insisting that individuals are fully capable of choosing for themselves what to believe and how to make moral choices. On the surface the secularists appear to be more accommodating and less dogmatic than the conservatives. Yet many of them pursue their values— racial and gender equality, the ERA, affirmative action, freedom of choice in respect to abortion—with the same vigor and intolerance that conservatives manifest. As a consequence, America in the 1980s is morally polarized.[47]

The pluralism in culture and values was accompanied by an explosion of fringe religions. Amid the many developments of the sixties and seventies, America's traditional spiritual institutions were tested and found wanting. The new religions stepped in and filled spiritual, social and emotional voids left by many of society's overburdened institutions. Many individuals, especially among the youth, sought radical solutions to problems in politics, education, economics and social relations (love, courtship, family and community). It was, therefore, only natural for the youth to turn to radical religious solutions as well—otherworldliness, secluded communalism, mysticism, the occult, Eastern religions and the cults.[48] In the words of Daniel Bell, "Where religion fails, cults appear."[49]

When the Age of Aquarius receded from view, the religious situation did not return to normal. Many individuals now turned to less radical but still unconventional outlets—the quasi-religions and spiritual therapies. (Roy Wallis calls these nontraditional groups "world affirming religions."[50]) By the 1980s the religious order was deeply fragmented. According to Roof and McKinney, the developments in American religion after the 1960s may be regarded as a "third disestablishment": an expanded pluralism in which there is less of a religiously grounded moral basis for society.[51]

For over one hundred years, the main intellectual currents in American society have assumed that religion would continuously—and inevitably—lose influence as a result of the process of modernization. Many have argued that urbanization, industrialization and new intellectual currents have made religion outmoded. Various political and social agencies now provide many of the services once furnished by religious institutions. Psychology, sociology and science now answer questions regarding human existence that were once the exclusive domain of religious thought. Yet the surge of new religious groups and the revival of conservative religion have called this secularization thesis into question. There appears to be a deep and abiding human need for the transcendent, the sacred, and the emotional and social aspects of religious life. In part, the rise of fringe religions since the 1960s reflects this craving.[52]

13

The Turn East:
Why Now?

Rudyard Kipling once declared, "East is East and West is West, and never the twain shall meet." This often-quoted line has a somewhat hollow ring in the late twentieth century. Today the East is turning West, and West is turning East. Millions of Asians are looking to the West for technology and science, political systems and cultural forms. At the same time, the West is experiencing a deep spiritual crisis—one that has prompted millions of Westerners, especially Americans, to "look East" in search of meaning in life.[1]

Since the nineteenth century Eastern religion and philosophy has been a growing presence in America. But beginning in the 1960s, interest in Eastern spirituality grew to a level that is without precedent in American religious history. Just how many Americans have been involved in this "turn East" is difficult to say. Estimates vary widely, in part because the Eastern movements greatly exaggerate their numbers, in part because there are various levels of interest in Eastern spirituality. The actual number of adherents is small, at most 100,000-200,000. But there are other levels of involvement. Several millions of Americans have encountered some form of neo-Eastern thought or devotional practice. Many practice, whether regularly or sporadically, some form of meditation. Of the many people who practice the martial arts, some go beyond the techniques of self-defense into their underlying Buddhist philosophy.[2] The influence of Eastern worldviews is even more difficult to measure, but they have left marks on philosophy, psychology, health care, business practices, education and religion.

Robert Ellwood places Eastern religions in America in two categories: those imported by the large number of Asian immigrants who have migrated to American shores, and those focusing on spiritual seekers of a Western background. The disposition of Buddhism, Hinduism, Islam and other Asiatic religions differs considerably according to category. Among the immigrants and their descendants who have not become Christians, religion is a quiet aspect of their identity, deeply embedded in family and community life and in traditional practices. On the other hand, for Westerners "the journey to the East represents a spiritual adventure," often entailing severing familiar ties, finding a new community, and having new experiences.[3]

Ellwood also says that when a religion lacks such sociological "supports as family, community and ethnic identity" it must compensate for these deficiencies, often through an emphasis on subjective spiritual experience. Thus, the Asian religions oriented to Americans emphasize "such practices as chanting and meditation" believed to promote spiritual experience. They also "tend to create intentional communities or more formal associations, which offer strong subjective support through charismatic leadership and close relationships" among members. This category of Eastern religion stresses authority, the power of the guru leader and such practices as meditation, instead of weddings, funerals and other family rituals.[4] It is the Eastern religions adapted to Western adherents, often called neo-Orientalism, that will be the focus of this study.

Social and Religious Factors

Why has an interest in Eastern religions grown significantly in recent years? Why are Americans attracted to Eastern spirituality? As I indicated earlier, Asiatic religions have had a long history in the United States. The influence of their ideas and worldview has come largely through occult and Theosophical teachings. There has also been a direct presence of Eastern religions since the nineteenth century. Thus, by the early twentieth century Asiatic religions had established a solid foothold in America, a foundation for the spurt of Eastern spirituality that was to come.

Gordon Melton notes the staggering impact of President Lyndon Johnson's decision to rescind the Oriental Exclusion Act, placing "Asian immigration quotas on a par with those of Western Europe." Not only did millions of Asian immigrants come to America, but Eastern religious teachers arrived also. The growth of alternative religions in the United States, especially the neo-Eastern ones, "can be traced to the movement of Eastern teachers to take up residency in America beginning in 1965." A partial list would include Swami Prabhupada of ISKCON in 1965, Yogi Bhajan of Sikh Dharma in 1968, Swami Rama of the Himalayan Institute in 1970, Maharaj Ji of the Divine Light Mission in 1971 and Sun Myung Moon of the Unification Church in 1972.[5]

After the barrier to Asian immigration was lifted in 1965, Eastern religions changed in at least one important area: they began to exhibit a missionary spirit. Hinduism, Buddhism and other Asiatic religions traditionally have not been characterized by a strong missionary zeal. Inspired by the example of Christian missions to their homeland, however, Asian immigrants, under the guidance of a number of gurus, set out to remake American religion when the door opened in 1965.[6] The Eastern religious groups vigorously reached out to Americans, at times making adaptations to American culture, at times zealously spreading their ideas.

This newfound missionary zeal coincided with changes in the West. The intellectual and cultural climate of America had been prepared for Eastern religions and philosophy. As Robert Wuthnow notes, by the 1960s Eastern religions had received enough exposure in North America to give them a certain legitimacy.[7] Eastern ideas spread by means of academic courses, books and other forms of communication. Of considerable importance, the popular response to Asiatic religions can be traced directly to the publication of a variety of English-language materials on these subjects. Melton points to the belief in reincarnation as a yardstick by which to measure the acceptance of Eastern ideas. "In the 1880s when the Theosophical Society began to champion the idea in the West, few supporters could be found. By 1980, twenty-three percent of the American public professed some belief."[8]

In part, the favorable acceptance of Eastern ideas in America is linked to changes in Western thought patterns, especially the weakening of traditional Christian ideas and Western dualism. Os Guinness believes an important factor in the acceptance of Eastern thought is that Eastern ideas dovetail in many areas with post-Christian Western thought, especially in respect to the views of God, humanity and nature.[9]

By the 1960s Western Christianity had been weakened by liberalism's emphasis on divine immanence, its minimizing of human depravity, the death-of-God theology and the mystical thrust of modern religion. William

McLoughlin points out several ways in which the counterculture of the 1960s departed from its Christian, Western and even American intellectual moorings. It rejected dualistic views of humanity and God, humanity and nature, this world and the next—views that had been deep-rooted in Western thought. Judeo-Christian theology, which portrays the world as sinful and humanity as profoundly sinful and separated from God, lost much of its appeal. Thus it became much easier for people to accept many Eastern ideas. Eastern philosophy endeavors to make human beings "feel at home in the universe." The "holism" of Eastern thought—that is, the unity of humanity with God and nature—appealed to those who had been turned off by the divisions, dualism and individualism inherent in the Western worldview. Humankind's "duty is not to get from this world to the next" nor to fight a constant battle against internal and external evil but to pursue a unity between themselves and nature. "To lose one's self in a sense of oneness with nature or harmony with the universe is truly to find one's innermost being."[10]

The rationalism, materialism, enslavement to technology and hectic pace of Western life was rejected by many. They "turned East" because of their disdain for the hard-driving, aggressive American ethic, "which placed so much emphasis on personal aggrandizement and materialism. Where American life seemed so hectic and disordered, Eastern culture offered calm and order." Eastern philosophy appealed to those who questioned the Western definitions of time and space, energy and matter. In place of the linear, step-at-a-time Western approach to time, there emerged "a new sense of timelessness—a preference for measuring life in terms of eternity rather than in terms of the near future."[11]

Personal Factors
Harvey Cox sees the reasons for the "turn East" in more personal terms. He believes that the "East turners" are not really different from most people. They are searching for the same things that most Americans desire; they have simply "chosen a more visible and dramatic way of looking." For many East turners "the need for just plain friendship is the chief motivation" for joining a neo-Oriental group. They are "looking for the warmth, affection and close ties of feeling" they have not found at school, at work or even at home.[12]

Another element stressed by Cox and others is the quest for the experiential or practical aspect of religion. The East turners want "a real personal encounter with God or the Holy," or simply with life, other people and nature. Only direct religious experiences will do. They are tired of sermons or homilies and the abstract approach to religion taken by most American churches. For them all of this is rather like "dull, boring cold coffee." To many, attending a church service is like poring over the label on a can of food instead of opening the can and eating the food.[13]

Many of the neo-Eastern religions have stepped in to fill this void. While Western religions stress beliefs or codes of ethics, sometimes at the expense of the experiential element, Eastern groups in America began at the level of practice. Jacob Needleman contends that the better-known Eastern teachings have preserved the "instrumental aspect of religion." They come to people "with such things as meditation techniques, physical and psychological exercises and tend to emphasize the necessity of a guru or master."[14] They keep ideas to a minimum. They recognize that practice and direct experience are keys to the kingdom—a point that has been largely ignored by many Western religions.

Because Western religion has largely forgotten its instrumental forms, it has been challenged not only by Eastern religions but also by the science of psychology. Western religion has focused on abstract exhortations, commandments and prescriptions but has not told people how to be able to follow them. As a consequence, the church is perceived as not being able to effect the essential improvement of human life. With Western religion stripped of the reason people turned to it in the first place, many have looked to psychology as a practical form of religion in the modern secular world. Psychology is seen as much more efficient than religion in solving human problems. Thus, in this regard psychology and the neo-Eastern religions have much in common. They both have stepped into to fill a gap left by Western religion. They both have a *self* focus. Their goal is primarily release from suffering—my own suffering as well as the sufferings of humanity.[15]

Other individuals have turned East in search for authority. These people are not so much looking for the instrumental or practical side of religion. Faced with what Alvin Toffler called "overchoice"—a vast array of ideas and moral codes from which to choose—these people suffer from a kind of "choice-fatigue." They thirst for an authority that will reduce their choices and make them less stressful. They have turned East to find a truth, a teaching or a message that they could trust. Their quest for authority often ends at the feet of a particular guru or swami whose charismatic power and wisdom can radically alter their lives.[16]

Though the neo-Eastern religions and their adherents reject key aspects of Western culture, they also reflect certain trends in American religion, often in an exaggerated way. Their emphasis on fellowship, community, experience, practical results and authority can be found not only in many other nontraditional religious bodies but also within the growing evangelical denominations. The experiential aspect of Christianity, not doctrine or ethics, must be regarded as the primary focus of many evangelical, fundamentalist and charismatic bodies. Moreover, many of these groups have authoritative leaders who have mesmerized their followers and established religious empires. Though a vast theological gulf separates these evangelical and charismatic bodies from the neo-Eastern religions, both categories of groups have capitalized on America's religious thirst for fellowship, experience and authoritative leadership.

14

Hindu, Sikh
& Jain-Related
Bodies

In the period between the two world wars, as Robert Ellwood indicates, a new set of Eastern religions appeared which shared the basic ideas of the older groups. But these newer bodies also evidenced "a freer, more expansive and more praxis-oriented style, usually centered on a flamboyant, charismatic personality." Such a trend was not limited to Hinduism, but could be detected in the offshoots of most Eastern religions. The Krishnamurti enthusiasm in Theosophy, the Meher Baba movement, the Self-Realization Fellowship, the "I AM" offshoot of Theosophy, and the First Zen Institute typify a trend during these years. Within these groups there was "less reading and more doing, fewer didactic lectures and more warm relationships" and more following of remarkable personalities. These tendencies, already observable between the two wars, were taken much further after World War II.[1]

The Hindu groups certainly reflected the trend away from the cognitive and toward the experiential and praxis side of religion, especially in respect to following the charismatic personality. The way of knowledge, or jnana—largely the way of intellectual understanding—gave way to the other two paths of Hinduism. The way of action, or karma, and the way of devotion, or bhakti, made much headway, especially after the 1960s. In fact, of the two major Hindu groups that arrived in America before World War II, Vedanta and the Self-Realization Fellowship, it was the latter that represented the wave of the future. More than Vedanta with its intellectual emphasis, the Self-Realization Fellowship pointed in the direction of the individual religious experience that would become the pattern in the later twentieth century.[2]

More indirectly, the way of action also had an influence on developments in postwar America. The teachings and example of Mohandas Gandhi, the political and spiritual leader of India in its struggle for independence from Britain, influenced the civil rights movement in America, inspiring the non-violent civil disobedience of blacks. In this case, karma became a type of social action required by a sense of justice.[3]

Transcendental Meditation

Numerous Hindu-related groups, at least forty-five, have dotted the American religious landscape during the twentieth century. The ones that have gained the most visibility since the 1960s would seem to be transcendental meditation, Hare Krishna, the Divine Light Mission and, most recently, the Rajneesh Foundation International. The most numerically successful and perhaps the most controversial is the movement popularly known as transcendental meditation (TM) and officially called the World Plan Executive Council. According to TM sources, over a million Americans have participated in its program. This figure needs to be understood in light of the reality that many of these individuals have membership in other religious bodies, and many did not continue with TM.[4]

Whether TM is a religion or not is a point of controversy. The World Plan Executive Council denies that it is a religion. In 1978 the U.S. District Court in New Jersey ruled to the contrary and banned its teaching in New Jersey schools. My study, of course, will regard TM as a religion. In fact, TM exists in the interface of Eastern religions and the human potential and New Age movements and shares elements with both. Also, TM has retained much from the Hinduism that gave it birth. The work begun by Yogananda and later Vivekananda prospered after 1960, especially in the TM organization. In several ways, this popular movement of the sixties and seventies has followed in the footsteps of the Self-Realization Fellowship.[5]

While Guru Dev is regarded as the founder or modern rediscoverer of TM, its real exponent became Maharishi Mahesh Yogi. Biographical facts about Maharishi's early life are sketchy. It is uncertain whether he was born in 1911 or 1918. More certain is the information about his life after 1940, when he took a bachelor's degree in physics from Allahubad University.

Rather than pursue a career in science, he withdrew to a monastery and began an intense study of Hindu philosophy and meditation practices or yoga. His favorite teacher was Guru Dev, a famous spiritual leader in an Indian monastery. Three years after Guru Dev's death, Maharishi emerged to proclaim to his own people his version of Hindu wisdom, later known as transcendental meditation.[6]

Because India had an oversupply of spiritual masters, Maharishi's message did not receive an outstanding reception. He thus launched a spiritual regeneration movement to spread Guru Dev's teachings in more fertile areas. After some stopovers in other parts of the world, in 1959 he arrived in California and established the Spiritual Regeneration Foundation, a non-profit religious organization. The appeal of his new religion came in its offer of peace, happiness and spiritual growth through a system of deep meditation. Maharishi then returned to India, where he focused on training teachers for his movement. The Spiritual Regeneration Foundation remained the only TM organization until 1965.[7]

Over the next several years Maharishi made annual world tours, visiting the United States and other countries. He contacted TM centers and followers throughout the West and began speaking on college campuses. The resulting student interest prompted the formation in 1965 of the Student International Meditation Society (SIMS), the most successful branch of the work. With his white beard, long gray hair and twinkling eyes, Maharishi not only appealed to many college students but also attracted many celebrities to meditation. The Rolling Stones, the Beatles, Shirley MacLaine, Mia Farrow, Samantha Jones (a celebrated model), Bill Walton (a basketball star), Joe Namath (a football star) and others tried TM and gave Maharishi mass-media coverage. By the late sixties, TM had mushroomed into a fad among teenagers and young adults. The basic TM course had been taken by nearly a million people.[8]

But then the Maharishi's popularity sagged. Having moved back to India in 1970 to reconsider his entire strategy, he soon came up with a new version of TM. In 1972 he proclaimed a "World Plan," a strategy that has guided TM since that time. The objective of the World Plan is to take the movement's comprehensive understanding of knowledge and life to the entire world. Transcendental meditation is but the practical and popular aspect of this understanding. Maharishi now promoted TM as a science, not a religion, more in psychological language than in spiritual terms. He desired to avoid a conflict over church-versus-state issues and to gain a wider audience and broader support base, including even government funds and endorsements. To the general public Maharishi attempted to sell himself as a psychological therapist and scientific genius. Nevertheless, his disciples regarded him as a guru teaching the ancient yoga, wisdom and spiritual philosophy of India.[9]

The goal of the World Plan has been to establish academies of science, meditation centers, a university and consultation services with world governments, and to train many teachers. In 1974 Maharishi bought the campus of Parsons College, a former Presbyterian school in Iowa, and opened it as Maharishi International University. TM's World Plan has some very ambitious components, especially its desire to establish a world government for the "Age of Enlightenment." According to Maharishi, not only can meditators improve their personal lives, but mass meditation can influence global developments and facilitate social change. He contends that if only 1 percent of a community or country meditates, the other 99 percent will benefit. If 5 percent meditate, there will be remarkable social transformation. According to Maharishi, the practice of meditation will usher in the Age of Enlightenment. He has invited all types of governments to permit his World Government of the Age of Enlightenment to solve their problems, whether they be political, economic, social or religious.[10]

As George Braswell says, TM found favor not only among individuals but also among American institutions. The U.S. Army used TM programs to combat alcoholism and drugs. In New Jersey, the state department of education provided a TM course for high schools. Programs for TM teachers have been funded by the National Institute of Mental Health. TM is popular with college students; it is taught on over three hundred campuses, often at taxpayer expense. Leading college publications such as the *Harvard Law Record* and *Yale Alumni Magazine* have published articles endorsing TM.[11]

The World Plan suffered several major setbacks in the mid-seventies. After the peak year of 1975, the number of new people taking TM courses dropped significantly.[12] Confronted with this decline, the TM leadership announced an advanced program which purported to teach meditators to levitate and to vanish at will. Such claims have tarnished the scientific image of TM, which it still doggedly strives to maintain, and has caused the organization to suffer a credibility gap.[13] An even more telling blow came in 1978, when a federal court ruled that TM was a religious practice and thus subject to the establishment clause of the U.S. Constitution. As a result, TM not only lost federal funds but also could not be taught in the public schools, thus losing one of its major markets.[14]

Since then TM's progress has slowed significantly in the United States. Nevertheless, it remains a solid organization with more than three hundred World Plan Centers and tens of thousands of active meditators in America. In fact, in the late 1980s TM launched an ambitious program: the Maharishi Heaven on Earth Development Corporation. This enterprise hopes to establish fifty "noise-free, pollution-free and stress-free" communities in North America. TM continues to experience growth in other areas of the world.[15]

Transcendental meditation, as Gordon Melton notes, is "the basic practice" taught by the World Plan Executive Council. It is "a simple system of meditation, basically consisting of daily meditation using a *mantra,*" a word that is repeated as one sits in silence. A mantra consists of sounds or words which are believed to have a magical effect when spoken with an intent in mind. Meditation with mantras is not a recent development, having been used by Hindu teachers for centuries. Maharishi, however, "advocated the use of a single mantra" which is given to the student when he or she takes the basic TM course. He contends that in TM the silent, or psychic, repetition of the mantra enables a person to enter into new spiritual realms.[16]

The initiation ceremony, when the seed mantra is implanted in the mind, is the most important step in learning TM. Braswell describes the ceremony. The initiate brings a white cloth, three fruits and six flowers. She or he next removes shoes, enters "a candlelight and incense-filled room" and bows before the picture of Guru Dev. The teacher repeats the words of the ceremony, the *puja,* a Vedic hymn venerating the line of gurus from which Maharishi descended.[17]

The candidate is then given his or her individual mantra, whispered by the teacher. The mantra must be kept secret. After this ceremony the initiate is prepared to meditate on the mantra for twenty minutes twice a day. The candidate is asked to return to the teacher for "checking sessions" to make certain that the meditation is being performed correctly. Beyond the basic TM course, there are a number of advanced courses.[18]

Much of TM's appeal lies in the fact that it requires little effort. The methods of TM differ from other meditation techniques because they require no strong or sustained concentration. In fact, if you try hard you will fail. Central to TM is the teaching that meditation helps people reach the very basis of joy and thus enhances their enjoyment of life. A major emphasis is that transcendental meditation is a natural process that provides a relaxing interlude in a busy schedule. Partly because of this marketing emphasis, only a small percent of those who took up TM have chosen to go on to advanced courses. The advanced studies often entail withdrawal from day-to-day life and living in an ashram with like-minded devotees. The key to TM's success is that it does not require such an overarching commitment.[19]

The World Plan claims that the practice of TM will have a phenomenal effect on many aspects of one's life. Supposedly, the regular practice of TM can produce changes in the body that will produce an amazing array of physical and mental benefits, including improved resistance to disease, better psychological health, a reversal of the aging process, increased intelligence, improved academic performance and higher job productivity. In sum, the practice of TM can completely change a person's life.[20]

The World Plan has encouraged scientists to take the basic TM course and test the results. But scientific findings concerning the results of transcendental meditation have been mixed. Psychologists have verified some of its physical effects, but have demonstrated that the same results could have come from a variety of other techniques as well.[21] Nevertheless, from the World Plan's perspective, these scientific findings have established the foundation for a total worldview, the Science of Creative Intelligence. Included in this science is knowledge and experience of the range and application of creative intelligence. Creative intelligence is the flow of energy in the universe, a concept resembling what some other Eastern religions have called the Absolute or the Divine. This reveals that the underlying philosophy of the entire movement is Hindu monism.[22]

The World Plan intends to extend the knowledge and experience of creative intelligence throughout the world by offering solutions to basic human problems. Its ultimate objective is to develop the full potential of the individual and to eliminate many of the world's social, political, economic and environmental problems. The primary method for accomplishing these objectives is to spread transcendental meditation throughout the population. The previously noted World Government of the Age of Enlightenment is another vehicle.[23]

TM achieved a measure of numerical success during the seventies. Yet it has also been the source of much controversy. As Melton points out, "TM's claims for scientific substantiation have been challenged on several levels," particularly by the scientific community. Next, a coalition of critics, mostly evangelical Christians and individuals interested in the separation of church and state, contested the use of state funds to spread TM. Last, "critics have charged the TM movement with an element of deception," especially in its claims to be a science rather than a religion and in its extravagant claims of success.[24]

Like many other fringe religions, TM has mirrored trends evident in other areas of American religion and culture. There is the movement away from cognitive aspects of religion and the emphasis on experience, practice and the personality of the leader—tendencies also evident in many segments of evangelical Christianity. Some Americans prefer a religion that requires little effort and commitment and are thus attracted to TM. As David Haddon says, in the heyday of the mid-seventies TM could be seen as "the McDonalds of meditation because of its extravagantly successful packaging of Eastern meditation for the American mass market."[25] TM has fit well into an American culture that is obsessed with both science and self-improvement. Maharishi shrewdly discerned that in America science was regarded as the highest authority. He therefore presented TM as a scientifically verified, effortless technique of self-improvement totally unrelated to religion.

The interface between aspects of psychology and Eastern religions is close. In modern America psychology has come to perform many of the functions once enacted by religion and thus has become a quasi-religion. At its peak, TM capitalized on such a development. Further, TM echoes the millennial overtones that have been a long-standing motif in American religious history. The World Plan intends to change individuals and to relieve problems that have plagued humankind for centuries. In its embrace of these utopian objectives TM can legitimately be regarded as a type of millennial New Age movement.

Hare Krishna

The most visible of the Eastern religions in America was the International Society for Krishna Consciousness (ISKCON), better known as the Hare Krishna. In the United States, Hare Krishna is often seen as a "new religion" or a "cult." While it is new to the United States, having been launched here in 1965, it is an old tradition going back to at least the sixteenth century. Since the late 1960s this organization's members are often seen in major cities of the United States and elsewhere, dressed in colorful robes, selling magazines, books and incense, and constantly chanting their mantra: "Hare Krishna." As a consequence of its visibility, ISKCON has come to represent the invasion of Eastern religions into American life in the 1970s. The reaction to the movement, therefore, has been extreme, ranging from humor and satire to great hostility.[26]

In a broad sense, most Hindu movements in North America have their roots in the Vedanta tradition, which teaches that the divine within can be realized through meditation and yoga techniques. ISKCON differs from the Hindu mainstream in several ways. It is a prominent example of bhakti, the way of devotion. Grounded in the dualistic teachings of a sect begun by a Bengali saint named Chaitanya Mahaprabhu (1486-1533), Hare Krishna has broken from the traditional monism and polytheism of popular Hinduism. Actually, ISKCON philosophy contains both dualistic and monistic elements, so that J. Stillson Judah describes it as "incomprehensible dualistic monism." The focus of this devotional movement's worship is Lord Krishna, a Hindu deity whom his followers regard as a supreme personal God. Members of ISKCON are Krishna monotheists. The more orthodox Hindu groups consider ISKCON's perception of Krishna as the lord, the supreme personality, the absolute truth and the complete whole to be heretical. Brahma, Vishnu and Shiva are seen as expressions of Krishna. All other gods, even the god of Judaism, Christianity and Islam, are Krishna also, but people are not aware of it.[27]

Chaitanya gained a following when he began preaching salvation through constantly chanting the name Hare Krishna. He combined a life of intense devotional activity focused upon chanting and dancing with the ascetic ideal of monasticism. Though his movement experienced a decline after his disappearance in 1534, it experienced revivals led by a succession of teachers in the seventeenth and nineteenth centuries. Out of the nineteenth-century revival came the founding of the Gaudiya Vaishnava Mission, along with a number of other missions, and ISKCON.[28]

A. C. Bhaktivedanta Swami Prabhupada (1896-1977) was born in Calcutta. In 1920 he graduated from the University of Calcutta and began work as a manager of a chemical plant. In 1922 his life took a turn when he met Bhakti Siddhanta of the Gaudiya Vaishnava Mission and accepted him as his guru. Bhakti Siddhanta charged Prabhupada with the task of carrying Krishna consciousness to the West. For years his primary activities in this regard had to do with producing English-language material for ISKCON. The Asian Exclusion Act was rescinded in 1965, when Prabhupada was nearly seventy years old. At this time he began his missionary activity in the West, starting a work in New York City. At first he appealed only to a few hippies. But the next year witnessed the opening of a center and the launching of a magazine, *Back of Godhead.* By 1967 a center was opened in San Francisco, and the movement experienced a period of steady growth.[29]

Prabhupada led the movement until his death in 1977. He had come to the United States with little income and few followers. Less than ten years later, the same swami had ridden in a chauffeured Mercedes to a Hare Krishna celebration in San Francisco, where more than ten thousand were assembled. By 1970 the work had a global dimension, having spread to Canada, England, Germany, Australia and Japan. In 1982 ISKCON reported fifty centers in the United States, including a number of vegetarian restaurants and several farms. By the mid-eighties, the movement's global figures included more than 175 centers, 3,000 initiated members and 500,000 lay members. Though not a large movement, ISKCON remains a stable organization with an international outreach, a publishing arm and a business interest.[30]

During his lifetime, Prabhupada directed the movement personally. To head off leadership conflicts, before his death he appointed twenty commissioners to administer the ISKCON organization. Twelve of these commissioners had special responsibilities to make disciples as he had done, to be responsible for a particular area of the world and to appoint temple presidents who would administer individual temples. These temples are organized on a strict schedule, beginning before sunrise. Each hour of the day is filled with worship, chanting and assigned tasks.[31]

Although members of ISKCON contend that Krishna consciousness is incomprehensible to the intellect, the movement does have an agreed-upon set of beliefs and practices, which have as their purpose devotion (bhakti) to Krishna. John Newport summarizes these beliefs and practices. First, Krishna is considered to be "the highest personality of the godhead. Devotion and love of him will bring Krishna consciousness or bliss." Next, because Krishna is far removed from the average person, "a spiritual master is needed." This master comes from a line of succession going back to

Chaitanya. Prabhupada, of course, is "god's representative for our time." Third, human beings have a spiritual nature like Krishna's. "The soul is individual and at the same time part of the divine soul." Yet each person also has a material body composed of lower energy. In fact, the material world, including the human body, is maya or illusion. "The material world is superficial and unreal." Thus one should wage war against one's body.[32]

Fourth, "to be delivered from the illusory world, one must develop Krishna consciousness." Certain techniques, largely related to the senses, help a devotee to be completely aware of Krishna. The chanting of the mantra is the most important ritual of the ISKCON liturgy. The mantra is composed of Sanskrit words: "Hare Krishna, Hare Krishna, Krishna, Krishna, Hare, Hare, Hare Rama, Hare Rama, Rama, Rama, Hare, Hare." These words are the holy names of the Lord. Hare is a "form of the word for the energies of god. Krishna is the name of the supreme lord. Rama is an earlier divine descent of Krishna." It is believed that chanting will place the devotee in tune with the supreme energy of Krishna. The chant, sung to the accompaniment of tambourines, cymbals and drums, also rejuvenates an individual's pure consciousness. "The instruments provide transcendental sound vibrations," helping to burn away karma and human ignorance. Behind chanting is the idea of a homology between sound and reality. Sounds can function as direct links to the sacred, enabling one to experience God directly.[33]

Each ISKCON devotee is "to chant at least sixteen rounds of the mantra daily." A round is regarded as "singing the mantra once on each of the 108 prayer beads." By utilizing the beads, a devotee is using his or her touch as a means to remember Krishna. The repetition of the mantra helps to shut out the external world. Hare Krishna chanting has been criticized as "a form of psychological conditioning."[34]

Another religious act is eating. ISKCON devotees call meals "prasadam or love feasts." Each day only two "yoga diet meals" are eaten. The diet is strictly vegetarian: no fish, meat or eggs are permitted. Before the food is eaten, it is offered to Krishna in a religious ritual. "Eating the food is an act of devotion, an aid to god-consciousness, and a way of remembering Krishna through the sense of taste." According to ISKCON's beliefs, Krishna's energy floods the body of the devotee when the food is digested.[35]

Worshiping and attending to the needs of several deity statues is another ritual act, called the *aratrika* ceremony. The statues are given flowers, incense and food and are symbolically bathed and dressed. "Such an act recalls Krishna's memory through sight." The smell of flowers and incense is another dimension to remembering Krishna. Devotees do not regard the images as idols, but believe that Krishna incarnates into the figure representing him and is "physically present in the aromatic fragrances."[36]

Though ISKCON does have an identifiable set of beliefs, best seen in its ritual, it would be a mistake to overemphasize this aspect of the movement. Instead, the devotional and experiential aspects of its ideology and practices must be underscored. The tenets of ISKCON's philosophy are to be lived and experienced rather than argued and debated. The whole purpose of the movement's philosophy and actions is devotion to Krishna and the development of Krishna consciousness. Devotees believe that the movement has provided them with truths that are timeless and absolute. Yet the Vedic knowledge of Hare Krishna is transcendent and cannot be understood through cognitive study. It can be studied, but study will only take one only so far. Rather, the absolute knowledge and insight offered by ISKCON must be acquired through personal experience. When it is, a person can "feel" it. Conversely, rational arguments about truth have little value; logic only leads to disagreement, never to one path or one answer, but to many paths and answers.[37]

When devotees join ISKCON, they not only accept a set of beliefs but also a semimonastic life marked by a disciplined asceticism. Among new religious groups ISKCON is properly classified as a *world-rejecting* group. Perhaps no religious group breaks more emphatically with American culture—in its dietary, material, social and religious practices—than Krishna consciousness. Hare Krishna calls for a radical change in lifestyle. All facets of the convert's prior identity are surrendered when he or she enters ISK-CON.[38]

The Hare Krishna lifestyle is distinctive and austere. Male converts must shave their heads (supposedly hair is for the sole purpose of sexual attraction). A shining scalp is a sign of submission to Krishna. Only a pigtail, which Krishna will use to pull the devotee into heaven, is left on the back of the head. Clothes, money and personal effects are given to the temple. Personal finances are superfluous, since all the member's needs—food, clothes and travel—are supplied by the movement. Moreover, the devotee is assigned a new Sanskrit name. The initiate is also given a set of Hindu robes (yellow or orange), which are to be worn at all times. These changes in appearance are fortified by a rigorous set of prohibitions: sex outside of marriage, gambling, drugs, cigarettes, alcohol and meat are strictly forbidden.[39]

Since most American members came from prosperous homes, their commitment to a life of poverty and ascetic denial is particularly dramatic. Devotees give up a great deal, renouncing most pleasures from their previous lives. But most traumatic is the severance of contacts with nondevotees. This cutting off from people outside the ISKCON community has caused serious tension, particularly with family members of devotees.[40]

In the Hare Krishna movement, there are several stages and levels of commitment. First is the preinitiation stage, which usually lasts about six months. At initiation the devotee is put through an elaborate process. In this ceremony, the convert is given his or her new Sanskrit name and three strands of neck beads. Upon these 108 beads, which resemble Catholic rosary beads, the "great mantra" is chanted. The devotee must wear these beads until death. The next step comes about six months after the initiation: the devotee is now eligible to become a brahmin. At the initiation service, the men are given a sacred thread to be worn over the chest, and both men and women receive a secret mantra, to be chanted three times a day. The next step in the ISKCON organization is *sannyasi*. Women are not eligible for this stage, which is reserved for especially devoted men. Because of the dedication required, few men reach this holy stage.[41]

ISKCON members may live in the temple compound or outside. However, to live at the temple one must observe strict vows and take responsibilities for temple life. Those who live outside the temple may or may not follow the vows. The 1980s saw an increase of Hare Krishna "laity," those who live and work outside the communes or ashrams but are committed in various degrees to the movement. By the mid-eighties, ISKCON's new laity far outnumbered the movement's core membership.[42]

According to Newport, the full-time devotee's daily routine is "based on a pattern that comes from India. All senses are to be engaged in the service of Krishna. Thus, to this end each hour is carefully planned." Though schedules vary according to a member's duties in the temple, a general pattern does exist. This schedule would begin at 3:00 or 3:45 a.m. Until about 9:30 or 10:00 a.m., the time is filled with chants or prayers. The devotee spends the next two hours on the street, chanting and selling. The afternoon is usually taken up with more of the same street work. The evening hours, until 9:15, are occupied with chanting and studying. Retirement time comes at 10:00 p.m. Six hours is the maximum time allowed for sleep.[43]

Even the sex life of ISKCON members is structured. While celibacy is preferred, marriage is permitted. Outside of marriage sex is taboo. But even in the marital context severe restrictions exist. Married couples may engage in sex only once a month, the night devoted to fertility in the Vedas. But even on this night, before sex is permitted, the spouses must purify themselves by chanting for five or six hours.[44]

Why has this relatively small new religion gained converts and so much attention? Why are people attracted to ISKCON? In part, it is because of the movement's dramatic visibility on the streets and at airports. But the total picture is more complex. On one hand, Hare Krishna symbolizes the youth revolt of the 1960s. It was closely identified with the counterculture and became some young people's vehicle of protest against materialistic lifestyles in the sixties and early seventies. On the other hand, a central theme underlying commitment to ISKCON was the rejection of the pursuit of pleasure, and drugs were proscribed. In this sense Hare Krishna was in fundamental opposition to the larger counterculture, which emphasized personal experience and individualism. The discipline of Krishna consciousness represented a conservative reaction to the passionate assertion of self so prevalent in the 1960s.[45]

Hare Krishna developed in the same context and grew for many of the same reasons as the charismatic and conservative Christian groups in the sixties and seventies. Like fundamentalist Christian bodies, ISKCON emphasizes commitment, discipline, hardship and authoritative teachings. As with the charismatic sects, central to Hare Krishna are ecstatic experiences generated by a verbal encounter with their god. Moreover, ISKCON meets the same need for community and fellowship as do many of the conservative Christian bodies.[46]

Though Hare Krishna rejects the pursuit of pleasure, it does incorporate aspects of this need, but within a community. To many devotees the mantra had a hypnotic quality that seemed to parallel the experience of using hallucinogenic drugs. Chanting the mantra promoted feelings of ecstasy, but within a community—something often absent in the drug experience. Another difference is evident. Though chanting often evoked feelings previously experienced only through drugs, the Hare Krishna movement stressed participation, not the resignation and passivity of the drug culture.[47]

Hare Krishna exhibits intolerant, undemocratic qualities. To an outsider these traits are perhaps the least attractive aspects of the movement. Yet to the devotees these qualities are absolutely necessary. They have made a great and very difficult decision that has wrenched them out of the mainstream of Western life and made them objects of hatred and ridicule. As a consequence, the devotees must feel that they and they alone are in possession of truth and that the rest of the world is made up of fools.[48]

According to Gregory Johnson, the ideology and practices of ISKCON made sense once one granted a crucial assumption: "the present age was undergoing a decisive transformation, characterized by unprecedented confusion and turmoil." The course of events had demonstrated that previous beliefs had failed. Therefore, people were now in pursuit of a spiritual absolute that would take them beyond chaos, strife and war. In promoting these positions, ISKCON devotees claimed "that the world was near the end of the materialistic age of Kali-Yuga, the final cycle of a four-cycle millennium." If enough people could be changed, the current age would be concluded and a "new age of peace, love, and unity would be discovered."[49]

While ISKCON is monastic and separationist, it aims to usher in a new age. The vehicle for bringing in this new age is the transformation of the consciousness of millions of people. Of great importance, this transformation would be a psychological one, developing in the minds of individuals rather than through changed institutions. ISKCON maintains that the rewards for practicing bhakti yoga discipline are great: eternal bliss and protection by Krishna. Beyond these individual benefits, social and political problems are expected to fade away once the population is unified by Krishna consciousness.[50]

What is ISKCON's future in America? It is a small but stable organization with several strengths. It has a committed core membership. Its strong support in India provides a home base for its worldwide organization. Moreover, ISKCON has weathered the stress caused by the death of its leader better than many other new religions that have lost their founders.[51]

Yet ISKCON faces several problems that could threaten its survival. In America it has ceased to grow numerically. As the counterculture faded and fragmented, Hare Krishna lost its most lucrative source of recruits. Furthermore, to survive, ISKCON needs to achieve more economic stability, an issue that is related to its evangelistic activities. Internally, several problems exist. There has been infighting among the successors to Prabhupada that could erupt in a schism. Also, there is the ongoing tension over whether ISKCON should make itself more accommodating to society or remain a strict separationist group. While there is little danger that Hare Krishna will soon become a tolerant, world-accommodating religious movement, it has taken a few steps in that direction. Such action is viewed as compromise by those who insist on the traditional strict standards.[52]

The Divine Light Mission

Few movements have grown and declined as quickly as the Divine Light Mission, flashing across the American religious scene like a meteor. The Divine Light Mission is a global organization committed to the propagation of Guru Maharaj Ji's Knowledge (with a capital K), which is acquired through experience rather than cognition. Though the Maharaj Ji maintains an international operation, at the time of this writing he has his headquarters in Miami Beach. The Divine Light Mission functions as a group of organizations engaged in numerous activities, all connected by their general aim of service to the Maharaj Ji. On the whole, there is nothing orderly about the operations of the Divine Light Mission, and in recent years in the United States it has experienced a significant decline in both numbers and national exposure.[53]

Guru Maharaj Ji, the central figure in the Divine Light Mission, was born in Hardwar, India, in 1957 into a family of gurus. His father, Sri Hans Maharaj Ji (d. 1966), founded the movement. Sri Hans Maharaj Ji was regarded as a *satguru,* or Perfect Master, and the young Maharaj Ji and his three brothers grew up in India with the expectation that they would demonstrate spiritual gifts. In his early years Maharaj Ji supposedly revealed unique talents, extraordinary spiritual sensitivity and superb discipline. Thus at the age of eight, when his father died, Guru Maharaj Ji rather than his eldest brother was named satguru and became (at least symbolically) the head of the Divine Light Mission.[54]

By the time he had reached the age of twelve, Maharaj Ji was making thousands of converts at his Divine Light ashram on the Ganges River. In 1969, he sent forth his first missionary, Mahatma Guru Charanand, to gain converts in London. In 1970, after finishing the ninth grade, Maharaj Ji withdrew from school and began to take his Knowledge (enlightenment) to the world. He began this mission by riding through New Delhi in a golden chariot, attracting over a million spectators to pay homage to the young Perfect Master. On this occasion,he declared that he would bring peace to this world, exploding what his disciples call his Peace Bomb.[55]

In 1971 Maharaj Ji left India for the West, appearing first in Glastonbury, England. In the same year he was invited to the United States by several American "preemies," or followers, who had received Knowledge from the movement in India. Maharaj Ji has demonstrated a great deal of independence throughout his life, and though his mother (referred to as the "Holy Mother") disapproved, he took the trip anyway. He was thirteen when he arrived in Denver, which he selected as the location for his national and international headquarters.[56]

Hopes were high in the early 1970s for a spiritual revolution that would realize the dreams of rebellious youth: a world of peace where people cared for each other. Along with the rapid expansion of other various spiritual movements that had sprung up across the country, the Divine Light Mission grew in numbers. Maharaj Ji aroused considerable interest among hippies and college-age youth, especially in the Colorado area. His preemie missionaries spread the word of this adolescent holy man's existence, the local counterculture responded enthusiastically, and soon the local movement began a rapid growth phase. By the end of 1973 an estimated fifty thousand persons had received the Knowledge; most, however, moved on in their spiritual quest or simply returned to the counterculture. Nevertheless, several hundred centers as well as over twenty ashrams sprang up. Social service facilities opened, and two periodicals were begun. At this point the movement's supporters were quite enthusiastic about its future.[57]

After a sensational beginning in North America, a series of disastrous events combined with the decline in the counterculture to bring a numerical decline in the Divine Light Mission in the United States. The big event, known as Soul-Rush or Millennium 1973, was held in the Houston Astrodome. Promoted by devotees as "the most important event in the history of the world," this festival was scheduled to usher in the millennium described in the book of Revelation. Eighty thousand people were expected to attend, but Millennium '73 did not live up to its billing. Although admission was free, only between twelve and twenty thousand people showed up for the event. The huge debt incurred for this ill-fated extravaganza forced the Divine Light Mission to cut its staff and programs.[58]

Other problems came. In India, Maharaj Ji's secretary was charged with trying to smuggle jewels past customs. In the United States some of his followers fractured the skull of a reporter who had previously thrown a pie in the guru's face. But the hardest blow came in 1974 when, at age seventeen and contrary to his mother's wishes, Guru Maharaj Ji married his older Caucasian secretary. He presented her as the reincarnation of the goddess Durga, a ten-armed, tiger-riding deity. Nevertheless, since the Maharaj Ji had previously encouraged his followers to pursue the path of strict celibacy, his marriage shocked them. Some estimates say that the very core of the movement, between 40 and 80 percent of the ashram preemies, defected over the Maharaj Ji's marriage.[59]

This marriage also brought to a breaking point the dispute between the Maharaj Ji and his mother in India. He had already begun to do things that upset his mother, including speaking a hippie vocabulary, wearing Western clothes and a fashionable hairstyle, and adopting an affluent lifestyle complete with limousines and a mansion. Coming on top of his deemphasis of Hindu elements in the Divine Light Mission, his marriage was the last straw. His mother revoked his satguru title and took control of the Divine Light Mission in India. Maharaj Ji replied that Perfect Masters are born, not made, and returned to India to take his family to court. The court awarded him control of the movement in every country except India. Even though he retained much of his global organization and the support of the remaining American preemies, the Divine Light Mission of Guru Maharaj Ji was suddenly cut off from its home base in India.[60]

Since the mid-1970s, the Divine Light Mission has lost much of its Hindu flavor. Few people refer to the Maharaj Ji as the Lord of the Universe, and expectations for a coming millennium have been totally abandoned. The movement evidenced some vitality in the late 1970s, experiencing a brief internal revival. Some preemies apparently returned to the ashrams, and the Maharaj Ji was once again hailed as a quasi-divine personality. Nevertheless, the period of growth had clearly ended. The movement in America peaked in 1974 and has never approached its earlier size and wealth. While still growing in other parts of the world, by the late 1970s the Divine Light Mission in the United States had almost disappeared from public view. Its headquarters is now in Miami Beach, Florida, and it claims about ten to twelve thousand members in America.[61]

The roots of the Divine Light Mission can be found in Sant Mat, meaning the way of the saints, a variant of the Sikh religion which owes much to

Hinduism. As David Bromley and Anson Shupe explain, the Divine Light Mission does not maintain a complex theology. Contrary to the monotheistic beliefs of the Hare Krishnas, who worship Krishna as God, the theology of the Divine Light Mission is monistic. "There is One Reality in which everyone exists. All distinctions are therefore illusory." Maharaj Ji's theology also has been characterized as "syncretic, individualistic, and loose." The major focus is "receiving Knowledge, that is, understanding the primordial energy or source of life, which is also the Divine Light." A special "imitator" or movement teacher provides this Knowledge, and its full implications are subsequently explored in "daily meditation and in *satsang*— *spiritual* discourses on the Knowledge given by Maharaj Ji or other teachers."[62]

Other than its emphasis on Knowledge, the Divine Light Mission has developed few beliefs, and it has no scriptures. The Knowledge is believed to be the foundation for all major religions, which means that all are true— a belief that obscures the distinctions between the Divine Light Mission and other Eastern groups. At one time devotees regarded the Maharaj Ji as a living avatar (the incarnation of a Hindu deity) and referred to him as Lord of the Universe. Among the preemies there existed a vague millennial expectation that the Maharaj Ji's presence signaled an impending change in the universe. These beliefs, however, received little development. Bromley and Shupe write that the lack of a sophisticated theology "may be one reason why many young people were initially attracted to the movement, but paradoxically it may also help explain why they found so little in the movement to hold their commitment."[63]

The spectacular rise and sudden decline of the Divine Light Mission in America was closely related to the personal problems of its leader and certain cultural trends in the United States. As with many new religions, the fortunes of the Divine Light Mission rose and fell with those of a charismatic personality, in this case a boy guru whose revelations to his devotees transcended theology and philosophy. Indeed, rational thought is the supreme enemy of the inner peace preached by the guru. Reflecting a tendency in modern American culture, most new religions emphasize experience over beliefs, but the Divine Light Mission pushed this trend even further, regarding "mind" as the obstacle to bliss and something to be denounced in no uncertain terms.

When a religious movement's existence is almost entirely dependent on experiencing peace and bliss, its membership becomes unstable and in constant need of replenishment. The Divine Light Mission can be seen as a child of the counterculture, drawing many of its members from this source. With the end of the counterculture and the diminishing use of psychedelic drugs, the Divine Light Mission lost a reservoir of young people who had been available for conversion.[64]

The Rajneesh Foundation International
The spectacular rise and fall of the Bhagwan Rajneesh as a major Indian guru in the United States occurred over a short space of time—May 1981 to November 1985. The fortunes of the Rajneesh Foundation, as a post-counterculture movement, were tied not so much to a shift in culture as to the escapades of its founder. Rajneesh jumped into the spotlight when he moved his movement's headquarters to a large tract of land in Oregon, creating major conflicts with the local inhabitants and legal authorities that gained the attention of the national news media. The controversies surrounding the movement and the Rajneesh's legal difficulties resulted in the decentralization of the movement in America by late 1985.[65]

The founder of the Rajneesh Foundation is referred to as Bhagwan Shree Rajneesh by his followers. *Bhagwan* is a term connoting honor, used commonly for God. *Shree* means master, a title of respect for great teachers. Rajneesh is the proper name of the founder, who was born Rajneesh Chandra Mohan in central India in 1931.[66] Even as a child he evidenced mature spiritual qualities, claiming to have first experienced *samadhi* (enlightenment) at the age of seven. Later he attended the University of Jabalpur, where he received his B.A. in 1951. He attained his master's degree in philosophy at the University of Saugar in 1957.[67]

Rajneesh claims that at the age of twenty-one, during his student days at the University of Saugar, he experienced complete enlightenment. This enlightenment did not immediately end his academic career. From 1957 to 1966 he held two academic posts in philosophy. He began to travel and speak to people about his experience and the teachings that had grown out of it. He was an eloquent speaker and an advocate of controversial religious views, often making irritating and offensive statements about religion, politics and sexual attitudes. In short order he acquired a reputation as a spiritual rebel. In 1966 he resigned his academic position at the University of Jabalpur in order to concentrate on his meditation retreats and speaking career. In 1969 he stopped traveling and settled down in Bombay with a group of dedicated disciples. Around 1970 the first Westerners developed an interest in his teachings and began to come to his Bombay apartments. Then, in 1974, Rajneesh established an ashram in Poona, India, and founded the Rajneesh Foundation. It was at Poona that Rajneesh took the name Bhagwan.[68]

During the years Rajneesh spent in Poona (1974-81), he became one of the best-known unconventional gurus in India. But as Melton indicates, problems arose. More traditional proponents of Indian religion "expressed strong disapproval of his reinterpretation of *sannyas,* the renounced life, and of the public displays of affection shown by his disciples both at the ashram and on the streets of Poona." Rajneesh's ashram embraced many aspects of Western culture, thus becoming less attractive to indigenous Indians. Not only did his approach to religion embrace Western characteristics, but some observers say that 80 percent of the ashram's residents were foreigners. His following among Westerners also grew outside of India, with centers appearing in Australia, Europe and North America.[69]

In the late seventies and early eighties, events in India began to pressure Rajneesh to move to the United States, a step that he took with considerable reluctance. Hostility toward his ashram in Poona and a falling-out with the Indian government prompted the move. In May 1981 he moved to the United States, first to his center in New Jersey. Two months later he acquired a sixty-four-thousand-acre ranch near Antelope, Oregon, which for a time served as his world headquarters. Within a year, a group of two hundred followers had moved to the ranch and begun to construct Rajneeshpuram, a newly incorporated city which was to house four to six thousand people by the turn of the century.[70]

Rajneeshpuram, which means "essence of Rajneesh," was to be a model community and home for up to two thousand permanent devotees. These devotees, called *sannyasins,* worked for their lodging and food and the opportunity to practice meditation near the Bhagwan himself. Eventually, this community was to be self-sufficient. To the hills of Oregon Rajneesh drew a corps of professionals—doctors, lawyers, city planners, agriculture experts and skilled tradespeople—from various countries to create a farming cooperative. In addition, the community contained a hotel and forty other commune businesses, including a pizzeria, a beauty salon and a bookstore. The sannyasi worked the farm and the businesses, while thousands of visitors, some exploring life with the Bhagwan, paid to stay in Rajneesh-puram.[71]

Activities in and around Rajneeshpuram became the focus of great con-troversy, which played a role in the Bhagwan's departure from America. Rajneesh's open approach to sex, prompting some to call him the "swami of sex," gave the movement a dubious reputation though it was a point of attraction for some devotees. Prior to 1979, acts of physical aggression had taken place in Rajneesh's encounter groups around the world. Though the physical violence largely stopped after 1979, verbal expressions of pent-up anger still characterized these groups. Both the sexual activities and the aggressive outbursts brought the movement hostile criticism. But Rajneesh was attacked perhaps more for his open show of wealth than for his con-troversial teachings. He took daily Rolls-Royce rides, and his luxury cars numbered almost one hundred by 1985. Such problems strained the social and political fabric of the Oregon community, culminating in the resigna-tion of Ma Anand Sheela (Silverman), his secretary and close associate. She was accused of inventing "Rajneeshism," supposedly a distortion of the Bhagwan's teachings.[72]

Tensions between Rajneesh's Big Muddy Ranch and the local community at Antelope attracted the attention of the national media. His followers overran the area and had bitter conflicts with local residents. Rajneesh's disciples won the mayor's office and a majority of seats on the city council of Antelope. The ranch won a legal battle for incorporation, only to have its charter overturned by the Oregon state court of appeals. In 1984 efforts to deport the Bhagwan were thwarted; in 1985 he was indicted for immi-gration fraud, and for reasons unknown he departed from Oregon. Federal agents caught up with Rajneesh in North Carolina; believing that he was attempting to leave the country illegally, they arrested him. The matter was settled by a plea bargain. Rajneesh pleaded guilty to two felonies, paid a fine of forty thousand dollars and agreed to be deported. He went home to India and established a new center there.[73]

Estimates of the size of Rajneesh's movement vary. In 1984, before his serious problems, he claimed a worldwide following of 250,000. In the Unit-ed States there were about ten to twenty thousand disciples in over one hundred centers. Shortly after the fall of Rajneesh in 1985, it was announced that the ranch would be shut down and the property, including his Rolls-Royces, sold. A court also ruled that the incorporation of Rajneeshpuram violated principles of separation of church and state, amounting to religious control of a municipal government. These developments resulted in the decentralization of the Rajneesh Foundation in America, with Rajneesh's followers returning to the loose structure which had existed prior to the Bhagwan's arrival. It appears, however, that the Rajneesh Foundation in other countries was only marginally affected by the developments of 1985, with most followers expressing their faith in Rajneesh. Rajneesh died of heart failure in India in 1990. What impact his death will have on the international aspects of his movement remains to be seen.[74]

What was Rajneesh's mission? He believed that the world has a serious sickness. In 1979 he warned: "If we cannot create the 'new man' in the coming twenty years, then humanity has no future. The holocaust of a global suicide can only be avoided if a new kind of man can be created."[75] This new humanity could be formed only through enlightenment, or Buddhahood. His mission was to bring enlightenment to humanity, beginning with his followers.[76]

What are Rajneesh's teachings? Strictly speaking, he was not a Hindu but a Jain. Jainism developed in India during the sixth century B.C. However, he moved well beyond the Jain tradition and is perhaps the most eclectic of all the recent swamis from India.[77] In fact, as Melton points out, Rajneesh endeavored to create "a new religious synthesis which brings elements of all the major religious traditions together with the new Western techniques of inner transformation and therapy (many borrowed directly from humanistic psychology)."[78]

In his blending of Western psychology and Eastern wisdom, Rajneesh built on the human growth movement that had developed in California in the 1960s. This development attracted individuals such as Alan Watts and Baba Ram Dass (Richard Alport), a onetime colleague of Timothy Leary of the LSD culture. Human growth centers rose up in Europe, and the name of Rajneesh was mentioned in them. These centers and the proponents of an East-West blend of psychology, philosophy and consciousness-altering techniques prompted people to travel to India to learn from Rajneesh. Such an amalgamation was made easier because in traditional Eastern thought psychology and philosophy are not sharply distinguished from each other.[79]

The basis for Rajneesh's teachings and practices was his monistic worldview. Eckart Floether describes the ideas that are built on this foundation. Distinctions between the Creator and creation do not exist. All reality consists of a single quality or essence, called by a number of names—God, Brahman, Silence, Void. "Thus everything can be called God. To exist is to be divine." Rajneesh argued that the mind prevents people from seeing the oneness of all things, causing them to divide up reality into artificial dichotomies. Human beings do not realize that they are truth (or God) because they are unenlightened or ignorant.[80]

Another problem is the ego, which human beings mistakenly believe to be their true self. Rajneesh said that a person's "true self is God, understood as emptiness or void." Humankind's struggle is with the ego, which also strives for "fulfillment and survival of the self." Thus it is necessary to abandon the ego.[81]

Rajneesh contended that in a strict sense "humanity needs no deliverance or salvation." Even at their worst, people are still divine. People live in needless misery and fear. He promised that "these negative experiences will vanish and enlightenment will occur" when people understood that there is "no duality of God and non-God."[82]

The path to enlightenment is the personal mystical experience. If people are to experience God (or Buddhahood) and achieve enlightenment, Rajneesh argued, the mind could not be involved in the process. Thus "he leans heavily on the doctrine of the void: the more nearly we are passive and empty, the more closely we approximate God." The objective of his workshops, meditations, lectures, therapies and even sex groups was "to bring about this state of emptiness," creating the mindless person. The mindless individual is the enlightened one: he or she has "no past, no future, no attachment, no mind, no ego, no self."[83]

Rajneesh taught that modern humanity is severely repressed, especially in respect to sex. His meditation and therapeutic techniques often have as their objective the release of the individual from the prison of modern life. His best-known procedure may have been "dynamic meditation," which had five stages. All participants wore blindfolds or were asked to close their eyes. Stage one entailed hyperventilating, a process that helped one to build up energy. The next stage involved primal screaming, which consisted of shouting, shaking, dancing, singing, laughing and beating the floor. In stage three, the participants jumped with hands above their heads, shouting the mantra. Stage four saw an end to the action. When the music stopped, the participants stood completely still for fifteen minutes. In the last stage they relaxed with the flow of music and engaged in something of a celebration.[84]

According to Rajneesh's teachings, the way of enlightenment is broad. But in practice he restricted the process, keeping it quite narrow. Though he kept his personal contact with his followers to a minimum, he was the enlightened one, the path to enlightenment. While he mentioned other avenues to enlightenment, he also noted that they had come through past masters, who are now dead. In our day enlightenment is possible only through the living master, Rajneesh himself. He is the object of surrender that enables a person to overcome ego and to attain enlightenment. Rajneesh, therefore, is "I am the Way" to his followers.[85]

In several ways the Rajneesh Foundation has mirrored the American culture of the 1980s. Rajneeshism attracted many refugees from the counterculture, especially those who merged Western psychology with Eastern spirituality. The Rajneesh Foundation can be seen as a New Age group. It is an aspect of a growing 1980s movement toward the convergence of Eastern religion and Western psychology. Moreover, like other New Age groups, Rajneeshism evidences the long-standing millennial thrust so prevalent in American history and has capitalized on the thirst for experience so dominant in modern American religion.

15

**Buddhist
Groups**

B uddhism arrived in America in the late nineteenth century and
enjoyed a significant presence during the first half of the twentieth
century. In many ways Buddhism grew after World War II on the
foundation laid by the earlier groups. The two most prominent Buddhist
bodies in postwar America are Zen and Nichiren Shoshu. Zen has had a
lengthy history. Both of the major schools of Zen Buddhism, Rinzai and
Soto, had arrived by the early decades of the twentieth century, and I have
already described them in that historical context. Though Zen was not new
to postwar America, it achieved its greatest growth during the 1950s and
1960s and must be regarded as one of the most important Eastern religions
associated with the counterculture. Nichiren Shoshu also has a long history,
going back to thirteenth-century Japan. But, unlike Zen, it did not arrive
in the United States until after World War II. Despite its recent arrival,
however, Nichiren Shoshu has experienced considerable growth.

Zen Buddhism

Historically Zen has been seen as a form of Mahayana Buddhism. *Zen* is
derived from the Sanskrit word meaning "meditation." A person meditates
in order to experience *satori*—that is, enlightenment. Because satori resides
in a realm beyond the intellect, it cannot be described. Experience is basic
to Zen. The point of Zen is to experience a reality beyond the rational world
or be in a condition beyond the intellect.[1] According to George Braswell,

five key words encompass an understanding of Zen: *zendo, zazen, satori, mondo* and *koan*. The place where meditators meet is called the zendo. Zazen is the "practice of meditation," which comes in various forms. Satori is "the enlightenment itself." Zen uses several techniques by which to transcend rational thought. Mondo is one of these methods; it is a "form of question and answer between the Zen master and the pupil." Koan is a phrase or word "insoluble by the intellect." It resembles a riddle or puzzle, "but it has no rational answer."[2]

Zen became a major symbol of the spiritual counterculture in the fifties, before LSD and maharishis and astrology had come forward to share this new milieu. Postwar interest in Zen was too extensive to be attributed to one line of transmission. Nevertheless, the most important influence on American Zen was probably the writings of D. T. Suzuki, rather than any Western source. Suzuki, along with his American wife, Beatrice Lane Suzuki, and a number of Westerners who learned Zen from him—Hubert Benoit, Alan Watts, Hubert Humphries, Edward Conze—produced a vast number of books on Buddhism. These writings have largely been responsible for Zen's appeal to the West.[3]

The fact that Suzuki and his followers produced more English-language literature than all the rest of Buddhism put together no doubt gave this form of Buddhism an edge over its spiritual competitors. Suzuki's lectures at Columbia University early in the 1950s ignited an intense intellectual interest in Zen. Robert Ellwood says that the strengths of Zen in the West—namely, its emphasis on universality, psychological awareness and freedom—and also its weaknesses—its impatience with discipline and a limited concern for the practice of monastic Zen—stem from the inclinations of Suzuki and his disciples.[4]

In the late fifties, a number of San Francisco writers and artists including Jack Kerouac (1922-69), Allen Ginsberg (b. 1926), Gary Snyder (b. 1930) and Alan Watts (1915-73) produced a new version of Zen. They combined the ideas of Suzuki with those of other sources to form an eclectic "Beat Zen." According to Catherine Albanese, as a group these men "drew on the side of Rinzai teaching in which the suddenness of enlightenment became a celebration of spontaneity and emotional freedom." Beat Zen, therefore, pursued liberation at the expense of other aspects of the Rinzai tradition, especially its "rigorous and ascetic meditation practices."[5]

Zen's greatest thrust in America came through the beatniks of the 1950s.

Kerouac chronicled many of the activities of the beat generation in his most famous work, *On the Road,* a novel that captured the beginnings of rebellion in a new postwar generation. The link between this rebellion and Zen Buddhism is described in another of Kerouac's books, *The Dharma Bums.* For the "dharma bums" or "Zen lunatics," the rhetoric of the Eastern faith became an expression of their displeasure with American values and a legitimation of their "hip" lifestyle.[6]

After Suzuki, the West's leading proponent of Zen was Alan Watts. This Englishman became the chief popularizer of Zen in America, even being dubbed by some "the Norman Vincent Peale of Zen." His relationships with formal Buddhist groups were quite marginal, for he did not identify himself with any Zen movement or even call himself a Buddhist. In fact, he practiced meditation only sporadically. Nevertheless, one of Watts's many books, *The Way of Zen* (1957), represents the most readable and understandable introduction to Zen in English, at least from the perspective of the Suzuki tradition. Watts offered Zen to the average American as something more than a religion. In a visionary, emotional style he stressed the "otherness" of Zen and presented it as a new way of life, a revolution in inner awareness. Watts glossed over the hard monastic discipline of Zen, disdaining the "skinhead military zip" of many Japanese monks. Instead, he focused on what intrigues most Westerners when they first turn to Zen: a new holistic "view of life" that cannot be comprehended by people's normal mental processes.[7]

Gary Snyder did not popularize Zen to the extent that Watts did. Instead, as Albanese points out, he "moved beyond the Romanticism of Watts to investigate the meaning of Zen with greater rigor." He connected Zen's meaning with what he found in some expressions of primitive spirituality. With a background in literature and anthropology and considerable knowledge of Native American religions and ecological issues, he wrote poetry expressing the "themes of interdependence among all living creatures." For one work, *Turtle Island,* Snyder received the Pulitzer Prize in poetry. But he was not satisfied to learn Zen from such a distant vantage point. So he traveled to Japan, where he learned the language and lived in a monastery for a period of intense training in order to better understand Zen. Snyder, more than the other proponents of "Beat Zen," brought the two sides of Zen—"its meditative discipline and its spontaneity"—together.[8]

More formal, traditional aspects of Zen also grew in post-World War II America, often in connection with Soto Zen and the establishment of Zen centers. A leading center was the one in San Francisco that opened in 1961 under the leadership of Shunryu Suzuki (1904-71), a priest from the Soto lineage. Having begun as a small group of approximately thirty people, this Zen center flourished in the 1960s, even establishing several branches in the Bay area. Ten to twelve other Zen centers have been established throughout America since the Korean War and after the Zen enthusiasms of the fifties. These centers have explored a variety of ways for practicing Zen in America. In general, they have served as places where people might spend either short or extended interludes away from society and receive intensive training in Zen.[9]

From the Soto school there developed a movement that combined both Soto and Rinzai techniques. The great modern figure in this development was Hakuun Yasutani (1885-1973), and his most prominent American disciple was Philip Kapleau (b. 1912). Having visited Japan several years earlier, Kapleau became seriously interested in Zen when he attended D. T. Suzuki's lectures at Columbia University. In 1953 he returned to Japan, where he met Yasutani. Upon returning to the United States in 1966, after absorbing much from Yasutani, he opened a major Zen center in Rochester, New York.[10]

Yasutani's teachings are evident in Kapleau's book *The Three Pillars of Zen* (1965). Of the Western Zen books, this publication has had an influence second only to that of the writings of Suzuki and Watts. In fact, Kapleau balanced Suzuki and Watts's emphasis on the relationship between master and student by his focus on the traditional practice of zazen (sitting meditation). At his Zen center he attempted to Americanize Zen, utilizing the English language, adapting the rituals to American culture and wearing Western clothes during meditation.[11]

Since the late 1950s, the faddishness of Zen has worn off. Its self-discipline, austerity and simplicity did not fit well in the extravagant "do-your-own-thing" atmosphere of the sixties. But a few years earlier, as beatniks gathered in dreary apartments to discuss philosophy over cheap wine, Zen had seemed to be the primary avenue of religious protest against Western values. By the seventies Zen had moved from the coffeehouses of Greenwich Village to Zen centers, where it was practiced on a more serious basis. In these centers Zen prospered and grew during the 1970s. It has experienced a decline since then, but it must still be regarded as a stable alternative religious movement.[12]

Zen Buddhism has had its moment in the sun and remains attractive to many Americans. Ellwood suggests two reasons for this continued viability. First, Zen is paradoxical. On one hand it has "conspicuously played the role of an exotic import," attracting many who were turning East. On the other, it has been "the most readily assimilated of the Eastern imports in America." By and large, Zen has maintained "a supplemental or noncompetitive relationship" with Western thought, religion and culture. Its enjoyable art, conceptual flexibility and numerous English publications have placed Zen in a position to make a mark on Western culture, better than any other form of Buddhism.[13]

Second, like many nontraditional religions, Zen has capitalized on Americans' seemingly unquenchable thirst for the experiential and nonrational aspects of religion. The primary objective of Zen is "to induce an experience which stops the activity of the monkey mind" with its constant bouncing from one subject to another. Rather than presenting a deliberate challenge to Western thought, Zen "throws sand in the mind's gears and brings it up against a blank wall."[14] In fact, for some individuals the Zen experience has become a replacement for drugs. Many of the American young people who now pursue Zen were once on drugs. Jacob Needleman says that most of the American students he interviewed at a Zen center spoke of their prior experience with drugs. Drugs had opened up to them the possibilities which became realized in Zen practice. It would seem that drugs gave them "a taste or glimpse of enlightenment." Satori (enlightenment) then becomes a substitute for drugs.[15]

A variety of other factors lie behind the appeal of Zen. George Braswell gives us a partial list. Some individuals are attracted to Zen because they see it "as a religionless religion with no transcendent authority, no binding scripture, and no legislation of morality." Zen has appealed to others because of "its various therapies for the mind, emotions, and body." Some people believe that meditation postures enhance their physical health. Some have "chosen to apply Zen's emphasis upon silence, discipline, order, and meditation techniques to their own spiritual awareness and development, and to practice Zen in this way along with their involvement with other religious communities." Such people would distinguish between Zen techniques and Zen Buddhism, utilizing the former while not embracing the later.[16]

Nichiren Shoshu (Soka Gakkai) of America

The Nichiren Shoshu religion and its lay organization, Soka Gakkai, officially go by the name Nichiren Shoshu Academy—in the United States, Nichiren Shoshu of America (NSA). Of the several religious groups that developed from the work of the Buddhist teacher Nichiren Daishonin, Nichiren Shoshu must be considered the most successful. Currently it is the largest Buddhist body in America. Nichiren Shoshu is a noncommunal but aggressively proselytizing type of Mahayana Buddhism; its aim is to transform the world by changing individuals in accordance with its interpretation of Buddhism, regarded by its most dedicated followers as "true" or "orthodox" Buddhism.[17]

Most of Nichiren Shoshu's doctrine and its basic rituals can be traced back to thirteenth-century Japan and the person of Nichiren Daishonin (1222-81). The NSA teaches that Buddha predicted the arrival of a special teacher in the thirteenth century A.D. to present the true form of Buddhism for the new age. NSA followers insist that Nichiren fulfilled all conditions set forth in this prophecy. In Nichiren's day Japan was in turmoil, beset with internal disorder and threatened by outside invaders. Moreover, Buddhism seemed too complex to the average person and was losing influence. During this critical period, on April 18, 1253, Nichiren delivered a chant that had allegedly never been heard before. The chant was "Nam-Myoho-Renge-Kyo," meaning "Hail to the Lotus Sutra," and contained what he regarded as the basic substance of Buddha's teachings. Instead of chanting "Hail to Amida Buddha," people now were to praise the Lotus Sutra, which revealed the basic laws of nature and would help them to discover their own Buddha nature within.[18]

Motivated by the belief that he had come upon the secret to happiness and enlightenment, Nichiren set out to save the world. He soon proposed a simpler approach to worship and chanting. For his followers he became the Buddha of the new age, attacking the government for not keeping the Buddhist dharma and suggesting that Japan would collapse if it did not convert. Despite a fanaticism and prophetic zeal unusual among Japanese religious figures, Nichiren did not attract a large following during his lifetime. Nevertheless, over seven centuries later and in many parts of the world "Nam-Myoho-Renge-Kyo" is being chanted and promoted with a zeal characteristic of its founder.[19]

According to NSA teachings, religious authority has been handed down from Nichiren in a direct line of succession to a present abbot in the movement. Nevertheless, during the seven hundred years since the death of its founder several Nichiren sects have arisen, three of which are in the United States. The movement had only modest growth until after World War II, but the first half of the twentieth century witnessed several developments important for the modern-day revival called Nichiren Shoshu. In 1928 two Japanese men, Tsunesaburo Makiguchi (1871-1944) and Josei Toda (1900-58), became converts to Nichiren Shoshu. Two years later they founded Soka Gakkai, the lay organization for Nichiren Shoshu members. Soka Gakkai, meaning Value-Creating Education Society, was based on Nichiren's idea of chanting.[20]

Makiguchi, an elementary-school principal, began writing a number of books on values and education. In 1937 he became the society's first president. Unfortunately, Nichiren Shoshu's teachings conflicted with the policies of the militaristic Japanese government. Also, Nichiren Shoshu refused to merge with other Nichiren sects. Thus the movement dwindled in numbers, and Makiguchi was placed in prison, where he died in 1944.[21]

Toda then became the organizational driving force behind the movement, taking steps to rebuild Soka Gakkai after World War II. In the process he gave the movement its modern shape. Using Nichiren Daishonin's book *Kachiron* as an official text, he extended the organization's goal from education to facilitating peace in the world and bringing happiness to all people. In 1951 Toda became the president of the rejuvenated Soka Gakkai organization.

Postwar Japan witnessed many changes, including an increase in religious freedom. This permitted a phenomenal flowering of religious cults and sects. In such an environment, Toda employed a controversial method of evangelism called *shakubuku* (break and subdue) to build the membership. By the time of his death in 1958, Soka Gakkai claimed a membership of 750,000 in Japan.[22]

In 1960 Daisaku Ikeda (b. 1928) became the movement's third president. Since coming into this position of leadership, Ikeda has given Nichiren Shoshu and Soka Gakkai an international dimension, spreading it around the world. With a militaristically organized, high-spirited corps of youthful devotees spearheading its propagation efforts, Soka Gakkai began to gain ascendancy over its competitors. By 1970 it had become an important religious and political force in Japan, with an approximate membership of ten million and its own political party (Komeito, or Clean Government). In addition, it claimed an international following of about one million, with the largest and most active branch in the United States.[23]

After World War II, the Nichiren Shoshu faith began to show up in the United States, arriving with Japanese immigrants (especially the brides of American servicemen) and American military personnel who had developed an interest in the movement while stationed in Japan. Ikeda came to the United States in 1960 to rally and organize Nichiren Shoshu members. But the real work for Nichiren Shoshu in American was done by Masayasu Sadanaga, who had migrated to the United States in 1957 to prepare for Ikeda's visit. He began to contact members, gradually establishing networks and organizing Soka Gakkai in Washington, D.C. Sadanaga became the director of the work in America, founding the Los Angeles headquarters in 1963 (the first outside of Japan) and, by 1968, a national headquarters in Santa Monica, California. To facilitate growth among Caucasian Americans, Sadanaga began to Americanize the movement, even changing his name in 1972 to George Williams.[24]

The Americanization of Nichiren Shoshu has been an important factor in its growth. It has attracted more Westerners than any other Japanese religion in America. Until 1964 the organization remained Japanese in membership. The period of 1965-69 was a time of rapid expansion, with the conversion of large numbers of non-Japanese Americans.[25] By the mid-seventies the organization in the United States had grown to more than 200,000 variously committed followers, most of whom were Westerners. Of the Western converts, about 60 percent were between twenty-one and forty, and nearly a third had a Roman Catholic background. Also, more Latin Americans and blacks joined Nichiren Shoshu than any other Buddhist group. Although the movement peaked in the seventies and began to decline in the eighties, it is still the largest Buddhist movement in the United States.[26]

The Americanization of Nichiren Shoshu has taken many paths. In Nichiren Shoshu, East has met West. The doctrine is Buddhist, but the methods and movement have been shaped to suit American culture. The Soka Gakkai meeting halls, called *kaikans,* began to be called "community centers." Following adverse publicity in the American media, the Japanese name Soka Gakkai fell into disuse, and the name of the movement became Nichiren Shoshu of America, or NSA. In Japan, Nichiren Shoshu treated religion and politics as nearly inseparable, with a close harmony between the Buddhist dharma and the law of the emperor. It was assumed that government should be the primary institution to bring happiness to all. At one point Soka

Gakkai was the third largest political party in Japan. In accordance with the American emphasis on the separation of church and state, however, NSA has tended to avoid politics.[27]

Nichiren Shoshu's accommodation to American culture has also come in more subtle ways. During the time of social change in postwar Japan, many new religions were unleashed. These religious, including Nichiren Shoshu, found a receptive and somewhat similar climate in America. The authentic quest for spiritual subjectivity that overtook America in the sixties and seventies left open an inviting door for Nichiren Shoshu and other new religions. Nichiren Shoshu's emphasis on religious experience found a welcome home in America.

Yet there was a shift between the spiritual climate of the 1960s and that of the 1970s in the United States. While religion in both decades placed a premium on experience, in the sixties it tended to be more expansive compared to the somewhat inward-looking mood of the seventies. In such a context, as Ellwood notes, "Nichiren Shoshu of America entered into a period of retrenchment and change." Though it had met the needs of many who were alienated with American values during the sixties, "it could not compete with evangelical Christianity." Evangelicalism not only offered the experiential element but was also a "symbolic bearer of the American spiritual heritage."[28]

Nichiren Shoshu does have points of resemblance with American culture. It has sympathies with the American obsessions with the here-and-now and with materialism. When compared to other imported Eastern religions such as ISKCON and Zen, Nichiren Shoshu appears to be extremely worldly and materialistic. Instead of promising transcendence of the material world, as do most Eastern imports, Nichiren Shoshu focuses on the attainment of personal regeneration and happiness in the present, largely through the acquisition of spiritual, physical and material benefits. Thus, the philosophy of the NSA may be regarded as largely utilitarian and secular, even humanistic. All the promises of religion are made to apply to this world. All divine potential is within human beings and can be unleashed. Modern psychology is investigating similar ideas about the scope of human capability through the study of states of consciousness, transpersonal psychology and so forth.[29]

Yet there is a social side to Nichiren Shoshu. Its doctrine holds that individuals cannot be happy until humankind as a whole is well-off. As a consequence, NSA has a utopian thrust similar to that of American millennialism and the New Age movement. NSA's ultimate social objective is to create a happy, peaceful world. However, its method resembles that of many conservative evangelical groups: the world will improve when individuals are changed. For Nichiren Shoshu, the "one way" to achieving these objectives is the practice of chanting "Nam-Myoho-Renge-Kyo."[30]

Unlike many Eastern imports, Nichiren Shoshu is not "laid-back" and quietly meditative. Rather, it is aggressively missionary and evangelistic. Like some strains of American evangelicalism and fundamentalism, NSA promoted its ideals fervently and insists that it is the only "true and proven" religion. But when its aggressive methods became less acceptable in the seventies, a change could be detected. NSA shifted its focus from the immediate material benefits to be gained from chanting to the more serious aspects of Buddhist philosophy, especially touting the chanting experience as a release of creative potential.[31]

Like the Unification Church, Nichiren Shoshu reinforces American patriotism. It has resocialized people who were formerly alienated from American culture by giving them a positive image of American society. NSA has taken a positive attitude toward neatness, respect for parents, work, capitalism and the American past. At its major centers the American flag is visibly displayed, and pageants on American history have had a leading place at NSA conferences.[32]

What are the teachings of Nichiren Shoshu? Despite the presentation of many philosophical insights in lectures, NSA representatives insist that it has no mandatory doctrine. Yet certain beliefs do come to the fore. Nichiren Shoshu regards itself as the true version of Buddhism. It claims to enable an individual to find enlightenment (Buddhahood), or the fulfillment of life within society. Its primary purposes are to chant, achieve one's personal goals and develop humanity to levels beyond the tenets of any creed.[33]

According to Hideo Hashimoto and William McPherson, three doctrines seem to be most relevant for achieving these objectives: *shakubuku, daimoku* and *kosen-rufu*. Shakubuku, or conversion, is "an act of mercy" intended to "rid a person of . . . worries" and provide him or her with everlasting happiness. Shakubuku has been associated with the movement's rapid growth. But the militant recruiting methods linked to shakubuku have brought some notoriety to the NSA and a high turnover rate among new members. Thus its importance has declined in the United States.[34]

The central practice of Nichiren Shoshu is chanting, and the "doctrine of *daimoku* is the religious basis of this practice." According to Nichiren Shoshu teachings, "Nam-Myoho-Renge-Kyo" captures the essence of the Lotus Sutra, the primary text of Nichiren Buddhism. Chanting these words can bring enlightenment, harmony with the universal law and even tangible benefits ranging from a new car to a better job. In both the morning and the evening one chants "Nam-Myoho-Renge-Kyo" many times and recites parts of the Lotus Sutra.[35]

Kosen-rufu is defined as propagating the Buddhism of Nichiren Shoshu to "achieve peace and happiness" for all humanity. This doctrine is "the basis of many political and ideological positions" maintained by Nichiren Shoshu. Nichiren Shoshu sees itself as leading humanity into a new civilization, in which peace and harmony will flourish. The goal of Nichiren Shoshu is world peace. This will be achieved around the year 2200, after enough people have been transformed by the practice of Nichiren Shoshu and a "Third Civilization" of humankind has been established.[36]

1 6

Islam-Related
Groups

O ften less noticeable in the United States than Buddhism or Hinduism, Islam arrived at an earlier date, for Muslim traders and immigrants came during colonial times. But not until the late nineteenth and early twentieth centuries did Islam establish a sizable presence in America, and the real surge of Islam in the United States did not come until after World War II. Much of this growth was linked to the arrival of immigrants and students. Exact figures are difficult to come by, but it has been estimated that by 1990 there were nearly five million Muslims in North America.[1]

Most of these Muslims were related to "orthodox" Sunni and Shiite Islam and have been primarily ethnic—that is, they have an Arab ancestry. Nevertheless, Islam has drawn adherents from other segments of the American population, especially from the black community. Also, many unconventional offshoots of Islam exist in America. Though not as prone to the formation of sectarian and cultic groups as Hinduism and Buddhism have been, Islam has produced a number of splinter groups. Many people who are not attracted to orthodox Islam have been drawn to its mystical wing, known as Sufism. Of the Sufist groups in America, the most influential have been the Sufi Order, brought by Hazarat Inayat Khan (1881-1927) in 1910, and Sufism Reoriented, a movement centered on the teachings of Meher Baba (1894-1969). Post-World War II America has seen other groups that have drawn their inspiration in various degrees from Sufism. They include Subud, Gurdjieff and Arica.[2]

The two largest Islamic offshoots in America are the Baha'i World Faith and the Nation of Islam. These movements are quite eclectic, however, having diverse religious and social origins. Baha'i has had a long presence in America, being well established before World War II. Though its greatest growth in the United States occurred after the war, its faith and institutional structure had long been in place. The movement is stable and seems likely to endure. The Nation of Islam, on the other hand, should be seen more as a postwar development. Its origins were in the 1930s, but its effective beginnings did not come until after the war. Also, the movement has experienced some earth-shaking changes in recent years.

Black Muslims (The American Muslim Mission)

When one reads or hears of "Black Muslims," most likely the reference is to the Nation of Islam, the movement headed for years by Elijah Muhammad. But the matter of names is more complicated than this. There have been other Black Muslims. When the first Black Muslim came to America is not known. Islamic centers had developed in Africa south of the Sahara before the slave trade began, and some of the slaves brought to America were Muslims. While no direct connection can be made between them and the modern Black Muslim groups, some slaves even in the nineteenth century maintained their Muslim faith. During the first half of the twentieth century, three Black Muslim groups developed: the Moorish-American Science Temple, the Ahmadiyya movement and the Nation of Islam. The Nation of Islam has been the dominant group, and in this study it will be referred to as "the Black Muslims." However, the Nation of Islam has changed its name several times since the death of Elijah Muhammad in 1975, first to "World Community of Islam in the West" and currently to "American Muslim Mission." To complicate matters further, a major split-off from the original body since Elijah Muhammad's death, led by Louis Farrakhan, still goes by the name "Nation of Islam." Also, during the sixties and seventies, several smaller Black Muslim sect groups developed.[3]

The Black Muslims constitute a black protest movement closely related to changing social conditions such as the urbanization of blacks, racial tensions and the spirit of black nationalism. In fact, the Nation of Islam is more an expression of social protest than it is a religious movement. Eric

Lincoln says that "religious values are of secondary importance" to the Black Muslims. "They are not part of the movement's basic appeal." Instead, the Nation of Islam's ultimate attraction is the opportunity to identify with a group strong enough to cast off the domination of the white race—and perhaps even subordinate it in turn.[4]

Peter Williams contends that "the designation Islam," which the movement gave itself, was "based more on a desire for symbolic identification with an exotic non-Western religion and culture" associated with Africa than on "a substantive espousal" of traditional Muslim doctrines.[5] More specifically, the Black Muslims are closely related to two social contexts: the 1920s and 1930s, which gave birth to the movement, and the 1950s and 1960s, which provided the catalyst for its greatest growth.

The early twentieth century witnessed an immense migration of blacks from Southern farms to Northern cities, where they crowded into ghettoes. When World War I ended and jobs became less plentiful, their temporary welcome wore thin, and racial tensions increased. Their hope for a better life in the North faded, and blacks became desperate during the 1920s and 1930s. Their shift in location and occupation, added to already crushing discrimination, was a traumatic experience for black Americans. With traditional family, church and community structures torn asunder, many urban blacks turned to nontraditional religious groups as a means of coping with reality.[6] The best known of these bodies that flourished between World Wars I and II were Father Divine's Peace Mission and Sweet Daddy Grace's United House of Prayer.

Another of these black religious movements, in some ways in a class by itself, was the Nation of Islam. The Black Muslims brought several religious and cultural streams into one movement. They successfully combined an affirmation of Islam with an appeal to black culture. Moreover, perhaps more than any other cultic group they became a protest movement, emphasizing black nationalism and militantly denouncing the white race.[7]

One of these streams, black nationalism, has its roots in the "African dream" of Bishop Henry Turner and the later work of Marcus Garvey (1887-1940), a Jamaican whom the Black Muslims recognize as a pioneer. Garvey's objective was to raise the self-esteem of blacks everywhere. He called for a literal rather than imaginary return of blacks to their African homeland. His intentions were rather like those of the Zionists of his day; in fact, he deliberately utilized the Jewish story of a people in exile awaiting a return to the land of their rightful origins. Though his dreams went un-fulfilled, he did awaken the spirit of African nationalism among the urban masses.[8]

A second and more direct stream seems to have connected the Black Muslims and the Moorish Science Temple of America. Its founder, Timothy Drew, departed from Garvey's form of black nationalism and declared that blacks should drop the name Negro and declare themselves to be Moors with "Asiatic" origins. When Drew died in 1929, the movement splintered, and one of the claimants to lead the group was Wallace D. Farad (or Wali Farad Muhammad). In 1930 he began to gather a following and allegedly claimed to be an occasional visitor in Mecca and a reincarnation of Drew. At first Farad (who was at the time believed to be a prophet, but who was after his departure recognized as Allah himself) met with small groups in homes. As his fame spread, he established the Temple of Islam in Detroit and then a second one in Chicago, where Robert Poole, his most trusted follower, was in command.[9]

Farad boldly attacked the white establishment, declaring that his follow-ers were not "Negroes," a term invented by whites, but rather "Black Men." Furthermore, he insisted that blacks were not Americans but Asiatics, and that Christianity was a religion of the white race contrived for the enslave-ment of nonwhite peoples. Farad declared Islam to be "the natural religion" of blacks and the only faith by which they could find freedom, justice and equality. Farad was the prophet who led blacks toward the millennium, but in 1934 he disappeared mysteriously.[10]

Fred Williams says that the Nation of Islam under Farad had many resemblances with Father Divine's Peace Mission Movement. Both Divine and Farad came out of obscurity to begin a new faith. "Each appealed to alienated and unemployed urban blacks." Both men rejected, explicitly or implicitly, the basic teachings of Christianity and substituted their own beliefs and rigorous practices. "Each also developed a successful network of cooperative business institutions which provided the movements with financial support." Both individuals required their followers "to repudiate their former lives and to confine their associations solely within the context of the movement." Despite these similarities, the Nation of Islam charted a course that was different from the Peace Mission Movement's.[11]

A second chapter in the story of the Nation of Islam, which Sydney Ahlstrom describes, began when the leader of the Chicago temple became dominant. He was Robert Poole (1897-1975), renamed Elijah Muhammad, whose authority rested on the "claim that the will of Allah himself had been communicated to him" and published in *The Supreme Wisdom* and consecutive issues of *Muhammad Speaks*. These writings teach that the Nation of Islam will lead the blacks of North America to their "true inheritance as members of the ancient tribe of Shabazz," which considers Abraham to be its patriarch and to which the nonwhite people of the world belong. "Caucasian people are an inferior, latter-day offshoot of the Black Asiatic Nation." African-Americans' self-hatred and negative regard for black culture must be replaced with a strong positive image and a sense of triumphant nationhood. Black Muslim doctrine is millennial, insisting that God already has come, there is no life after death, and "heaven and hell are only two contrasting earthly conditions." The hereafter, which will begin about A.D. 2000, is but the end of the present "civilization of the Caucasian usurpers, including the Christian religion." This age will be followed "by the redemption of the Black Nation" and its glorious dominion over all the world.[12]

Having gradually become the dominant figure in the movement, Elijah Muhammad, as well as a number of his followers, went to prison during World War II because he refused to kill on any orders but Allah's. In a practical sense, the Nation of Islam can be dated from 1946, when Elijah Muhammad resumed leadership of a group undergoing a numerical decline. In the postwar years, especially from 1955 to 1964, the movement experienced its greatest growth, achieving a membership of about 100,000 disciplined followers. In the atmosphere of the late 1950s and early 1960s, which had been changed by the civil rights movement, the Nation of Islam spread to almost every American city with a sizable black population. The black ghetto, with its crime, filthy streets and crowded apartments where life is cheap, was the principal context of Muslim recruitment. Here the voice of social protest, challenging the downtrodden and criminals to recover their self-respect and repudiate the dominant white culture and its religion, did not go unheard.[13]

The sectarian character of the Black Muslims evidenced itself in many ways. According to Eric Lincoln, the Nation of Islam has been a protest movement "directed at the whole value construct of white Christian society," a society in which the Black Muslims consider themselves "an isolated and unappreciated appendage. Hence, the burden of their protest is against their 'retention' in a society where they are not wanted." The Black Muslims have sought to abandon the fundamental principles of American society and to substitute what they perceive to be new principles, new values and a new creed based on the primacy of a nation of blacks called to a manifest destiny under a black god. This radical ideology sets the nation of Islam apart from other black protest movements and religious groups.[14]

The attraction and importance of the Black Muslims resides not in any hidden doctrines or secretive rituals, but in their publicly declared social and moral teachings, particularly their demanding standards of family responsibility, personal behavior and occupational stability. From the followers of Elijah Muhammad much is required. They must give unquestioned obedience to the Messenger of Allah, attend meetings on a regular basis and pay at least a tithe. Despite their rejection of standard American values, writes Ahlstrom, the Black Muslims' prohibitions of sexual immorality, alcohol and drugs and their demands for respect of women in patriarchal families and for occupational responsibility resemble the standards of the "Puritan-American mainstream." In this sense the Black Muslims have adopted many "moral standards of the Caucasian devils" and can be regarded as a "cultural sect calling blacks out of their sub-culture."[15]

Meanwhile, the Black Muslims developed strained relations with traditional Islam. Many members of orthodox Islam insist that the "racism of the Black Muslims," as well as Elijah Muhammad's claim to authority, contradicts the basic nature of the "most interracial of world religions." Yet some Arab leaders have shown honor to prominent individuals in the Nation of Islam.[16]

As Ahlstrom also indicates, the growth of the movement "testifies to the alienation and despair bred by racial discrimination" in the United States. In this sense, the Black Muslims serve as a "bridge between the escapist cults and the main tradition of black militancy." While in theory the movement presents a message of deliverance for blacks, in reality it is "an island of disciplined security that is at once radical and bourgeois."[17]

The individual who most effectively presented the message of the Nation of Islam was the charismatic Malcolm X (1925-65), born Malcolm Little in Omaha, Nebraska.[18] His father was a Baptist preacher who had supported Marcus Garvey. While in prison for burglary from 1946 to 1962, Malcolm Little became a convert to Black Islam. After his release he became the dynamic and energetic messenger of the movement in New York City and throughout the nation. However, Malcolm X progressively became alienated from the Chicago version of Black Islam, particularly after his personal experience with the Islam of Mecca. In 1964 he broke with the Black Muslims, establishing the Muslim Mosque and the secular Organization of Afro-American Unity, both of which sought to arouse and unify the movement for black liberation. In February 1965 he was assassinated in Harlem. Nevertheless, by means of his posthumously published speeches and autobiography he continued to be a prophetic voice of black emancipation.[19]

Following Malcolm X's death, Elijah Muhammad designated Louis Farrakhan to be his chief lieutenant, appointing him to Malcolm's former positions, national minister for the Nation of Islam and minister of the Harlem temple. During the 1970s the Nation of Islam experienced considerable growth, acquiring many business enterprises and establishing more temples. By the mid-1970s, the Black Muslims had gained wide acceptance throughout black America as a reasonable religious alternative for blacks. Young blacks desiring dignity and a new status were attracted to the movement. Well-known sports figures, such as the heavyweight champion Muhammad Ali, joined the movement, bringing it wider publicity. But problems loomed on the horizon. Considerable tension existed between factions within the Nation of Islam and between the Nation and other Muslim groups in America. Moreover, by the early 1980s it was obvious that the organization faced massive financial problems.[20]

These already developing problems were compounded by the death of Elijah Muhammad in 1975. His son, Wallace Muhammad, assumed the Nation's leadership the day after Elijah's death. Wallace had been active in the Nation of Islam since his youth. But he knew of his father's shortcomings and had been friends with Malcolm X, even sharing some of his ideas. Wallace Muhammad, therefore, began to change some of the beliefs and practices of the Black Muslims. Downplaying his father's idiosyncratic doctrines and strident racism, he began to move the Nation more toward the mainline Islamic tradition. The Nation of Islam began to call itself the Bilalian Muslims, and in 1976 it adopted a new name, the World Community of Islam in the West (WCIW).[21]

In the 1980s Wallace moved the Nation of Islam further in the direction of orthodox Islam and traditional American culture. The symbol of the American flag turned up on the organization's printed material, and its schoolchildren began to pledge allegiance to the flag. Further Americanization could be seen in the 1980 decision to change the WCIW's name to the American Muslim Mission. Wallace adopted the name Warith Deen Muhammad. The move toward orthodox Islam is evident in other changes. Temples became mosques, ministers became imams. Chairs were taken from the temples, and worshipers were required to sit on carpeted floors. The season of Ramadan, when the Islamic faithful fast, was observed according to the Muslim lunar calendar.[22]

All of this Americanization and Islamization of Wallace's organization was too much for some Black Muslims. The movement's always-present schismatic tendencies came to the surface. The 1976 decision to admit whites was what drove Farrakhan from the organization. By 1978 he had formed his own Muslim movement, which still used the original name, the Nation of Islam, and has remained true to the literal teachings of Elijah Muhammad. Farrakhan continues to advocate the combative racism and black separation that characterized the movement in the 1960s. He still calls white people "devils" and believes that blacks must have a separate nation within the United States. He also maintains the Fruit of Islam, a Black Muslim paramilitary organization.[23]

By the mid-1980s the future of this indigenous expression of Islam in America remained uncertain. A financial crisis exists for the American Muslim Mission. Some members disagree with the direction of the movement. Court cases and dissension within the ranks of the imams have caused further problems. Moreover, Wallace Muhammad and Louis Farrakhan still differ in their interpretation of Elijah Muhammad's message, and Black Muslims must decide which of them is his true heir.[24]

Meher Baba

Meher Baba, or the Lovers of Meher Baba, is the name given to a loosely constructed movement around Meher Baba. For the most part this movement is not highly structured; it consists of many more or less autonomous groups. There are, however, several formal associations of Baba Lovers, including the Society of Avatar Meher Baba in New York City and Sufism Reoriented in San Francisco. There is also the important Meher Spiritual Center in Myrtle Beach, South Carolina.[25]

The Meher Baba movement falls within the Sufi tradition. Sufism grew out of mystical Islam, or as William Petersen puts it, "an Islam more directed by the heart than by the head." But as it developed in India "it became syncretistic, adopting views from Hinduism, Buddhism and Christianity as well as Islam." Sufism has remained "more emotional and mystical than rational and mental." Meher Baba's writings reflect this diversity, combining Islamic monotheism with a Vedantic sense of divine nondualism and immanence, and Sufi devotionalism with the ideal of love for God.[26]

Meher Baba was born Merwan Sheriar Irane in Poona, India, in 1894. In 1913 he met Hazarat Babajan, an ancient Muslim woman, one of five "Perfect Masters of the Age." (Meher Baba contends that at all times five Perfect Masters, or God-realized souls, exist for the spiritual guidance of the world.) She gave him God-realization, and another Perfect Master, Upasni Maharaj, gave him "gnosis" or divine knowledge, the addition of which meant he had attained spiritual perfection.[27]

There followed for Meher Baba, as Needleman indicates, a lengthy, difficult "process of returning to normal consciousness while still retaining the ecstasy of being one with God, and the awareness of all levels of reality in the universe." Meher Baba's disciples contend that the course of his life on earth "involved this simultaneous participation in the highest and lowest states of human existence." On one hand he retained the spiritual pinnacle of being one with God. On the other he returned "to full consciousness of the world of illusion," the world in which all people live. This process of "coming down," that is, restoration to full normal consciousness, took about seven years.[28]

He brought together his first intimate disciples in 1921, and soon founded an ashram near Bombay. These first disciples gave him the name Meher Baba, which means "Compassionate Father." In the next few years he established a colony near Ahmednagar called Meherabad. This colony remains the spiritual and geographical center of the worldwide movement. Besides spiritual activities, Meher Baba's work in his colony involved building shelters for the poor, caring for the sick and establishing free schools and hospitals.[29]

Meher Baba was best known for "the Silence." In 1925 he voluntarily chose not to speak for the rest of his life. At first he communicated with an alphabet board, from which he also dictated many discourses and messages that have been attributed to his name. In 1956, however, while still maintaining "the Silence," he discontinued use of the board and limited his communication to an expressive system of hand gestures.[30]

Why "the Silence"? There is considerable speculation among his followers over this question. The Silence remains the greatest mystery about Baba.

He claimed to have embraced the Silence because his followers already had sufficient words and action needed to be taken. Meher Baba said, "I have come not to teach, but to awaken." But the primary reason may have been more than this. Needleman says, "He kept the Silence so that he could break it." Meher Baba claimed that his breaking the Silence would be a miracle, "the most significant event in the history of humanity."[31] "When I break my silence," he said, "the impact of my love will be universal and all life in creation will know, feel and receive of it."[32] Thus, as the years went by, his followers waited in great expectation.

But in 1969, instead of speaking, Meher Baba "dropped the body" (as Baba Lovers speak of death). Because he had said that he would break the Silence before he died, his followers were baffled. Some had believed he was going to break his silence in the Hollywood Bowl engagement of 1931 or the special 1962 East-West gathering which he called "strictly for My Lovers." Within the movement one school of thought holds that he did break his silence, but no one was able to hear it. Still others believe that he will yet break the Silence.[33]

Meher Baba visited the United States six times. The first occasion came in 1931, when he made contacts with the Sufis of the Sufi Order. Correspondence was opened with Baba, and the organization guided many Sufis toward him. Among his early American followers were some upper-class women, including Elizabeth Patterson, a prominent businesswoman; Princess Norina Matchabelli, an actress and wife of a diplomat; and some movie stars. Patterson spearheaded the Myrtle Beach work, which culminated in the building of the major Meher Baba spiritual center in 1952. In 1956 Baba himself dedicated the center, and it was opened to the public.[34]

In India, Meher Baba's followers number in the hundreds of thousands. Until the sixties, however, his disciples in the United States were few and largely middle-aged. In the late 1950s, young people began to go to the Myrtle Beach Center for short stays. During the mid-sixties, many American hippies developed an interest in Meher Baba. Some of this attention was linked with the heightened interest in "Eastern" mysticism which accompanied the drug culture. On the other hand, some of the interest in Meher Baba was connected with his forthright opposition to the use of psychedelic drugs.[35]

Thomas Robbins has demonstrated that Eastern mystical movements operating in America, including Meher Baba, "recruit partly from young persons who have previously experimented with psychedelic drugs." Meher Baba and other such groups "serve as a 'half-way house' between the drug culture and reassimilation into conventional society." Since mystical experiences and drug sensations share certain elements, "the former can operate as a substitute gratification for the latter." On one hand, Meher Baba opposed the use of drugs. On the other, his writings contain elements that harmonize "with the 'psychedelic' emphasis on inner exploration." While the Meher Baba group has staunchly opposed drugs, it has provided a nonchemical mysticism for those moving from the drug culture to more conventional society.[36]

Though Meher Baba's attraction in the 1960s was primarily to the youth, he did not appeal exclusively to the hippie segment. Many relatively straight youth joined the movement. In fact, among his followers can be found scientists, professors, psychologists, industrialists, businesspeople and actors.[37]

The boundary lines between Meher Baba and other religions are not sharp. As Dick Anthony and Thomas Robbins have demonstrated, "the Baba movement is somewhat inclusive and nonsectarian." Baba's disciples contend "that God takes many forms," and this belief bestows a measure of "legitimacy on other religions which are viewed as varied modes relating to Meher Baba." Many Baba followers are convinced that he was a force behind the revival of older religious traditions (Hare Krishna, Buddhism, Christianity) which took place in the sixties and seventies. Yet most "Baba Lovers" are somewhat estranged from organized religion, whose rituals and ceremonies Baba compared to the shell surrounding the "kernel of true spirituality."[38]

In the Meher Baba tradition, spirituality is not defined in terms of any special religious technique such as a particular prayer, form of meditation or ritual chant. Therefore, the relationship between Baba and his disciples is not determined by a prescribed set of operations. Instead, the relationship is geared to particular circumstances. Baba is seen as ministering to the special needs of each follower.[39] Aside from restrictions on the use of drugs and premarital sex, Meher Baba set down few rules for his followers. There is a sort of moral pluralism or built-in antinomian tendency in the movement, whereby a number of lifestyles are acceptable because of the individualistic interpretations of Baba's teachings. Some followers tend to be self-indulgent, though most maintain a stable lifestyle. The focus of the movement is the person of Meher Baba, not any set of doctrines. His followers have the liberty to emphasize the aspects of his message that relate most to their needs.[40]

In fact, some of the American Baba Lovers follow their leader only on the basis of emotion. Needleman thinks Baba Lovers "live by their feelings" and strongly rely on intuition as a source of knowledge. In other words, the heart, rather than the mind, is the center of knowledge.[41] In his *Discourses* Baba stated, "Love and Happiness are the only important things in life, and they are both absent in the dry and factual knowledge which is accessible to the intellect."[42] According to Robbins and Anthony, "the essence of Meher Baba's universal message is love which, in its purest form arises in the heart . . . in response to the descent of grace from the Master." Meher Baba comes to humanity bringing this grace and awakening love in people. His followers view him as the "loving Master." Thus, in this case "the medium is the message."[43]

The focus of the Baba movement is clearly emotions and feelings. Nevertheless, Meher Baba's teachings do contain some definite ideas drawn from Sufism and elsewhere. As Ellwood says, "Clearly his chief concept was the cult of the holy men so central to Sufism and one strand of Hinduism." This tradition believes that "a certain number of the true holy men or 'Perfect Masters' are always alive in the world." The various manifestations of their religious belief and practice are unimportant. The necessary thing is to discover these Perfect Masters, or be found by them, and then to "love and serve them, and emulate them. In them is all grace and love."[44]

Meher Baba said that "there are at all times five Perfect Masters in the world." These Perfect Masters recognized him as an avatar, a Hindu word "meaning divine descent or incarnation." While these five God-realized masters are to be held in great esteem, an avatar is greater, being a self-revelation of God himself. Meher Baba was clear in this regard. He said: "There is no doubt of my being God personified. . . . I am the Christ." About every seven hundred years humanity is blessed with the presence of an avatar. Past avatars include such individuals as Buddha, Krishna, Jesus, Muhammad and other great religious leaders. However, Baba claimed that his own avataric form was the last incarnation of this cycle of time, and hence the greater manifestation.[45] Such claims may sound outrageous, but they are the foundational beliefs for thousands of his followers worldwide.

Membership figures for the Meher Baba groups are difficult to determine.

The movement is loosely constructed, and commitments to the teachings of Meher Baba vary considerably from individual to individual. Globally, Baba has many followers, especially in India. In 1971 Peter Rowley estimated that the movement had some seven thousand adherents in America. Though the organization grew in the sixties, by the mid-seventies it was in decline for several reasons. Perhaps the most basic factor was the waning of the counterculture, which had brought youth into the movement in the 1960s. Also, the expectations of many of Baba's followers had been dashed when he "dropped the body" before breaking the Silence. A lesser reason may lie in the fact that Baba Lovers are not usually aggressive in their proselytizing. They do not chant in the streets as do Hare Krishna devotees or witness as the "Jesus freaks" did.[46]

Gurdjieff-Ouspensky Groups (G-O)

The Gurdjieff movement has drawn from many sources: Sufi, Buddhist, Christian and occult are all mixed together. Yet Sufi and occult elements seem to be the most pronounced. The founder of this movement was George I. Gurdjieff (1872-1949), one of the most remarkable, mysterious individuals associated with fringe religions. Nat Freedland regards this obscure figure as "the most far-reaching occult theorist of the twentieth century." Robert Ellwood says Gurdjieff has "probably influenced Western cults and esotericism more than any other modern figure except Madame Blavatsky."[47]

Gurdjieff's theories became widely known through his greatest disciple, P. D. Ouspensky (1878-1947), a well-known Russian mathematician. His *In Search of the Miraculous* is regarded as the best systematic presentation of Gurdjieff's ideas.[48] Combining the names of Gurdjieff and Ouspensky, the religious bodies studying their teachings are often called G-O groups. J. G. Bennet was Gurdjieff's chief English follower. In reading the writings of Gurdjieff, Ouspensky and Bennet, one cannot always tell where Gurdjieff's thought leaves off and where the others' begins. Moreover, at times their systems and ideas are incompatible.[49]

As is common among occult figures, the details of Gurdjieff's early life are shrouded in obscurantism and questionable fantasy. He was born in Russia near the Persian border. At an early age, he became interested in astrology and spiritualism, and studied all types of supernatural phenomena. Gurdjieff traveled throughout the Middle and Far East—including the old standby for professional occultists, Tibet—learning much from Sufism and Tantric Buddhism. He met what he claimed was a hidden Sufi order that had preserved an occult tradition. Later, he brought its insights and techniques to the West.[50] Gurdjieff was also a keen businessman, making money from nearly every thing he did. In Russia he operated or invested in restaurants, stores, cattle, oil wells, fisheries and more.[51]

However, he had all of these experiences before he was thirty-five years old. Then he moved to Moscow on the eve of the Bolshevik Revolution. Though many Russians were preoccupied with other things at this time, his lectures attracted an impressive assortment of philosophers, scientists and other intellectuals. One of them was Peter D. Ouspensky, who had traveled widely in search of what he believed to be the "ultimate truths" of the occult tradition. While Gurdjieff was intuitively unpredictable, Ouspensky was systematic and logical, and he brought these elements to the movement.[52]

Because of the turmoil caused by the Revolution, Gurdjieff and some of his disciples retreated to his home territory in the Caucasian Mountains and eventually to other European countries. After roaming throughout Europe, he finally settled at Fontainebleau, France, in 1922. There he founded the Institute for the Harmonious Development of Man.[53]

At the institute, life revolved around the personality of Gurdjieff. He was an authoritarian who often made unreasonable demands. One of his principal ideas was that humanity had become complacent and could advance spiritually only by having this smugness shattered, especially through menial, back-breaking tasks. Thus, the Institute fostered an almost monastic existence, involving hard work, strict discipline and "spiritual gymnastics"—that is, spiritual exercises and dances.[54]

Gurdjieff's ideas were propagated by several means, especially through his two books, *All and Everything* and *Meetings with Remarkable Men*.[55] The writings of his principal disciple, Ouspensky, have been read even more widely; Ouspensky's book *The Fourth Way* has been particularly influential.[56]

The Gurdjieff system came to the United States in 1924, when a group from Fontainebleau toured the country, presenting the "sacred gymnastics." Gurdjieff's students now began to spread his teachings throughout the world. But the going was slow. His teachings were esoteric, intended to be understood only by a select group. Thus until 1959, ten years after his death, his writings were shared with only his dedicated followers.[57]

Rowley estimates that by the early 1970s there were about five thousand disciples of Gurdjieff in America. Considering the fact that several factors have prevented and will continue to prevent G-O from becoming a mass movement, this figure is remarkable. First, his teachings are difficult to comprehend. Second, Gurdjieff chose to emphasize techniques that involve toil and mental strain rather than mystical illumination. Third, his disciples seldom evangelize. They tell the outside world very little about Gurdjieff. Instead, they prefer to tantalize people with small amounts of knowledge and information so that only those serious about pursuing Gurdjieff's ideas will enter their groups. In fact, the entire Gurdjieff movement has something secretive about it.[58]

The occult explosion of the late sixties and early seventies did revive a considerable interest in Gurdjieff. Books about him that had been out of print for twenty years now sold well at occult shops. He became a popular fad on quite a few college campuses. With this exception, the emphasis of the Gurdjieff movement has been quality, not quantity.[59]

Gurdjieff groups have no central organization, but the name and tradition have considerable influence. Gurdjieff's ideas are perpetuated by a number of teachers and groups. Some of these disciples are in a line of succession going back to the Fontainebleau school, while others have developed independently. The most important and serious group in America is the Gurdjieff Foundation, established in 1953 by Lord Pentland. This organization, which keeps in touch with the major Gurdjieff bodies abroad, is headquartered in New York City and has affiliated groups around the country. There is one other Gurdjieff organization functioning in the United States, the Gurdjieff Work of W. A. Nyland. There are also several parallel organizations; the best known is the Prospers, founded in 1956 in Florida by Phez Kahil and Thane Walker.[60]

Gurdjieff's key idea was that those who fail to train themselves to be fully "awake" are sleepwalking through life. Thus, the central concept in his teachings pertains to his methods of arousing a person's dormant consciousness or potentiality. Gurdjieff described his approach as "the Fourth Way." Gurdjieff and Ouspensky say there are there are four levels of human consciousness, but most people exist in only two of them. They spend their time either asleep or awake. But Gurdjieff encourages his disciples to explore higher levels of consciousness, which he calls "objective consciousness" and "self-consciousness."[61]

A person can move up to the next level not by increasing logical knowledge, but by acquiring psychological wisdom. According to William Petersen, when Gurdjieff and Ouspensky spoke of psychology they were not referring to the work of individuals like Freud and Jung "but merely to the study of oneself," the "I." This "I" is "extremely prominent in their teaching." The difficulty is that people "do not really know themselves." They have no goal in life. Also, the "I" of most people is constantly changing and causing confusion. Thus, it might be said that "salvation to a follower of Gurdjieff is finding one's permanent 'I.' "[62]

The "self-awareness" found on the fourth level is described by John Newport. It can be prompted by experiences such as physical labor, music and dance. The "waking-up" experience entails a period of careful instruction and guidance from a teacher, followed by the student's supreme effort. The ingredients needed for "waking up" are deliberate suffering, a strict master and a support group of fellow students.[63] For Gurdjieff, physical labor was an important technique for awakening. At his institute all people, rich and poor, engaged in hard manual labor under his direction. His program also entailed the regulation of food consumption. At the institute, the prescribed diet was generally strange and sparse. Moreover, students had to endure intense physical and emotional testings, including the use of therapeutic irritation and abuse. Evening activities entailed listening to speeches and participating in "sacred gymnastics." Employing techniques from the Sufis, the people would dance ecstatically, often whirling. The meetings of contemporary G-O groups follow a similar pattern, employing discussions, music and Eastern-style sacred dancing.[64]

In terms of numbers, G-O groups are not large. Yet Gurdjieff's influence in the United States continues, and he is now recognized as one of the most important of the West's early gurus. On one hand, he regarded the life of the average person as largely pointless. On the other, he taught positive techniques for change, some recognizable as the seeds for contemporary therapeutic developments. Encounter groups, T-groups, Transactional Analysis, Erhard Seminar Training, Synanon games and others are significantly indebted, usually unknowingly, to the unusual experiments in human relations and personal growth that Gurdjieff inaugurated at his institute in France.[65]

PART V

The Occult, Psychic Groups & the New Age Movement in Post-Christian America

P ost-Christian America has witnessed an outburst of quasi-religions—groups whose status as full-fledged religions is open to question. These groups vary greatly, but all maintain occult-mystical worldviews.

The late 1960s and early 1970s saw an occult explosion. This occult revival came in two forms. Traditional occult activities such as astrology, divination and witchcraft staged a comeback. But more important, an occult-metaphysical worldview began to be widely accepted in the West. By the mid-seventies a shift could be detected. The traditional occult activities were being supplemented by new expressions of the occult. The New Age movement, one of the most popular new religions of the 1980s, can be viewed as the occult dressed in clothing acceptable to modern America. In fact, the New Age movement has penetrated the most affluent and socially prominent levels of American society. Closely related to the New Age movement is the vast array of psychospiritual groups. In the late twentieth century, some aspects of psychology have taken on religious dimensions. Psychological surrogate religions have adopted an Eastern-mystical worldview and psychospiritual techniques to trigger quasi-religious experiences.

17

Twentieth-Century
Occult &
Metaphysical Movements

In 1967 *Hair* exploded like a bomb on the American cultural scene. This hit musical production revealed to the "straight" world something ignored for centuries except by the astrologers: One age in world history is ending, and another is about to begin. The generation now living is destined to witness the fading of the Age of Pisces—mystically, the era of Christianity—and the first glimmerings of the Age of Aquarius. Astrologers maintain that every 2,170 years or so the sun's spring equinox (day and night of equal lengths) shifts by one zodiac sign and a new age begins. The occult worldview holds that with the current shift, science, religion and art will become one and usher in the Age of Aquarius, a new golden era of peace, brotherhood and progress.[1]

Tame as *Hair* may seem by today's standards, this playfully perverse celebration of an often-debased social situation marked the return of occultism to the public scene. This movement had been well under way with the reproductions of old horror films in the fifties, the publication of *Rosemary's Baby* and with the syndicated predictions of Jeane Dixon. But in the late sixties and seventies, the occult became a passion for some and a fad for many. *Time's* cover story of March 21, 1969, "Cult of the Occult," gave an indication of the large number of people involved in the occult phenomenon. During 1969 and 1970, *Harper's Bazaar, Esquire* and *McCall's* had special issues on the occult revival. Many institutions of higher learning, including prestigious universities, began to offer courses on aspects of the occult. Universities and institutes sponsored research on parapsychological phenomena.[2]

Interest in the psychic sciences and in matters weird and sensational became widespread. Psychic healers made extravagant claims. People were fascinated with spiritualism. Many witches came out of the closet. But the greatest barometer of the occult explosion was the mushrooming interest in divination—that is, discerning the future. Tarot, I Ching, palmistry and Ouija boards were in vogue, along with astrology.

In *The Morning of the Magicians,* Louis Pauwels and Jacques Bergier estimate the number of professional astrologers in America during the early seventies at thirty thousand. Astrological columns were carried in at least two of every three daily newspapers (a few decades earlier fewer than 90 of America's 1,750 papers had had similar columns). The reappearance of the occult in the seventies was not limited to the United States. It was a world-wide phenomenon. It had never declined in much of the Third World, and Europe also witnessed an increased interest in the occult.[3]

The Occult Explosion

Did all of this activity indicate an explosion of the occult? There is a widely held view that in the seventies America experienced an occult revival.[4] The word *revival* means the renewal of something that was (or was perceived to be) dead, decadent, dormant or deficient. The idea of an occult revival presupposes a preceding period in which the occult was unimportant or moribund. Did such a period exist? A vital tradition of occultism and meta-physical movements developed in the nineteenth century and continued into the twentieth. As with any religious movement, the occult has its peaks and valleys. Apparently, what occurred in the 1970s was a peak of popular interest in the occult.[5]

In the past two hundred years, there have been a number of other peaks, though perhaps not as widespread or as publicized. According to Robert Galbreath, principal examples "include the impact of Swedenborgianism, mesmerism, secret societies, and phrenology in Western Europe" during the late eighteenth and early nineteenth centuries; the rise of spiritualism in America in 1848 and its spread to Europe; "the popularity of Theosophy and psychical research" by the 1880s, of Asian religions following the World Parliament of 1893, of ritual magic and divination in the early twentieth century; and the growth of cults and astrology in the 1930s.[6] The occult has had a substantial presence in America for the last century and a half. What happened in the 1970s in respect to the occult was an unprecedented peak in public attention, publishing and organizational activity. Of greater importance, the occult worldview is becoming widely accepted in the 1970s and 1980s, far more than in previous years and perhaps to a degree unprecedented since the seventeenth century.

This so-called occult explosion entails two tendencies, one focusing on specific phenomena and the other on a worldview. These two emphases are not mutually exclusive; they entail considerable overlap. First is the renewed interest in certain occult practices (the occult "arts"). Most popular are astrology and the many forms of divination (cartomancy, crystal-gazing, palmistry, Ouija boards, prophetic dreams and visions, psychometry, numerology, I Ching and others). Other familiar occult practices and focuses that one might encounter include witchcraft, Satanism, spiritualism (necromancy), magic, paranormal experiences, unidentifiable flying objects and perhaps an occasional monster.

Ron Enroth says that collectively these occult phenomena have laid claim to the following distinctive characteristics. One, they disclose and communicate information unavailable to humans through normal means—that is, the five senses. Two, they place persons in contact with untapped powers and paranormal energies. Three, "they facilitate the acquisition and mastery of power in order to manipulate or influence other people into certain actions."[7]

Occult activities are practiced by both individuals and groups. The occult lends itself to private activity, and this may be where most of the action takes place. In general, many of the new religions resemble Thomas Luckmann's "invisible religions," but the occult carries this trend even further. Though there exist metaphysical churches, opportunities to worship with swamis, and even occult organizations, fellowship and community are not central. The occult is an invisible religion because it is private, personal and not regularly institutionalized or monitored by priests or contained in organizations. Thus, it cannot be mapped. If community is not central, symbols, sacramental objects and rituals are.[8] Performing the correct procedures is vital to obtaining results in the occult.

But not all occult activities are without an organizational structure. There exist groups in which occult practices are so central that scholars have classified them as occult bodies. Some examples include witch covens, Satanist groups, Theosophical societies, Rosicrucian orders, Swedenborgian-ism and a vast array of Spiritualist bodies.[9] Many Eastern cults, some metaphysical bodies and the human potential and New Age movements utilize occult and quasi-occult practices, but not enough that scholars would label them "occult."[10]

Of perhaps greater significance for the last third of the twentieth century is the second tendency in the occult revival: the widespread acceptance of the occult worldview in the West. The occult-metaphysical worldview has many expressions, especially in the Eastern cults, the human potential and New Age movements and many psychotherapies. This alternative to the Judeo-Christian view of reality has several general components, which are described by Ron Enroth. First is "the promise of godhood" and the divinity of humanity. Nearly all forms of occult philosophy insist that the true or real human self is synonymous with God. Next, occult philosophy generally says that "all is one, God is everything (pantheism)." There exists only one reality (monism), and thus "everyone and everything in the material world is part of the Divine." Consequently, there is no difference between the natural and supernatural, good and evil, God and Satan.[11]

A third component is that "life's purpose is to achieve awareness of the Divine within": self-realization. The way to salvation—that is, enlighten-ment, illumination or union—comes by experience, not by rational knowl-edge. It is the "path to *gnosis,* the seeking of experiential knowledge through metaphysical insight." Fourth is the notion that "humankind is basically good." Evil is only an imperfection or illusion. The root of the human dilemma is ignorance, not sin. An enlightened person will rise above moral distinctions. Thus, individuals do not need redemption or forgiveness as the Judeo-Christian tradition teaches. Only self-realization is needed. Finally, self-realization that comes via spiritual techniques leads to power. It puts the divine-human in charge. By utilizing spiritual techniques such as chant-ing, yoga and meditation, and by applying universal laws, the "realized being" becomes master of his or her own reality and can influence the lives of other people.[12]

By the mid to late seventies, a shift in the direction of the occult could be detected. The early occult explosion, from the late sixties to the mid-seventies, was closely related to the counterculture and the use of psyche-delic drugs, and was largely a youth phenomenon. The most prominent tendency in this part of the occult explosion was a dabbling in occult practices, especially astrology and divination. In fact, to many the occult was something of a pop religion, a fad of the youth culture, a means to proclaim the new Aquarian Age. As the more radical countercultural context disappeared, however, the occult arts mostly receded from public view, while many occult groups lived on as isolated cults or attained a respectable presence in society.[13]

Closely related to this acceptable social position was the second occult tendency, the widespread acceptance of the occult worldview. The occult worldview and some of the more subtle occult arts penetrated the respectable ranks of society and became the foundation for the human potential and New Age movements. The preoccupation with self-awareness and self-actualization presupposes the acceptance of many occult principles. Many corporations and therapy centers have had their employees and clients engage in self-awareness exercises. In its higher forms, the modern occult is unquestionably a quasi-religious movement, an attempt to find substantiation of the abilities that traditional occultism has always insisted were hidden within the human mind.[14]

Why did this so-called occult revival occur in the 1960s? Though the occult emerged for most of the same reasons that the other new religions did, there were some specific twists to this development. As Jeffrey Russell has demonstrated, from a broad historical view "interest in the occult has grown significantly in periods of rapid social breakdown, when establishments cease to provide readily accepted answers and people turn elsewhere for assurance." Periods for which this generalization seems accurate are the third century A.D., which witnessed the decline of Roman society; the late Middle Ages and Reformation era, when the medieval synthesis was collapsing; and the twentieth century. But for the roots of the current occult revival, one must turn to the nineteenth century. As indicated earlier, this century was congenial to occult-metaphysical developments, including Transcendentalism, Spiritualism, the Shakers, Theosophy, New Thought, Christian Science and many Eastern faiths. Moreover, the first half of the twentieth century witnessed the rise of many prominent occultists, including George I. Gurdjieff, P. D. Ouspensky and Edgar Cayce.[15] Hence, by the last third of the twentieth century there existed a vital tradition from which the occult and metaphysical movements could draw.

Catherine Albanese points out that many people were "prepared by American culture to turn toward self" and the universe in their pursuit for religious certainty. The Protestant tradition had generally supported the importance of knowledge or belief in religion. Then the liberal wing of Protestantism had modified this approach. It "stressed the presence of God everywhere" and underscored American optimism concerning the innate goodness of human nature. Liberalism's "diffusiveness and lack of strong boundaries" helped people to adjust to the idea of living comfortably without rigid religious guidelines. The holiness tradition, also, had fostered a perfectionism that "could easily be linked to metaphysical views." At the same time, the urban and corporate organization of society weighed against the development of strong community life. Of necessity, in their everyday lives individuals began to depend more on internal resources. Thus, the occult and metaphysical movements blended into the cultural mainstream. Because they often lacked organization, they became difficult to count. Because their message had a superficial resemblance to general cultural currents, they became difficult to identify. By the late twentieth century it seemed that vast numbers of people had an "occult or metaphysical skeleton" somewhere in their closet.[16]

American culture had paved the way for the occult-metaphysical movements. Yet as Albanese also tells us, these movements still had to deal with ordinary life. Occult practices had to be perceived as having the capacity to satisfy daily needs. "Astrology gave people a sense of identity" and assisted them in establishing secure relationships with others. Self-help literature helped people to take steps toward improved prosperity, health and happiness in their daily situations. "Psychics offered physical healing and spiritual advice" on how to deal with everyday problems. People thought that by knowing the future they could change it, "take the steps necessary to avoid harm" or restore balance to life. Communicating with a dead mother could assist a person with a current problem. "Abiding by Theosophical rules could enable someone to gain confidence in self and the universe." Renewed health and good fortune could come from the practice of New Thought. To Americans, the practicality of the occult was important. People believed that engaging in occult and metaphysical activities was a way to stimulate energies that would bring useful results.[17]

In a less tangible way, occult and metaphysical movements met a deep spiritual thirst—and this is a major part of their attraction today. By the late twentieth century, scientific and secular forces have drastically diminished a sense of the supernatural, the transcendent, the sacred and the immortal in American life. Because of their worldview and their desire to validate their activities, many occultists reject a concept of the supernatural.[18] Nevertheless, they engage in a quest for other aspects of the transcendent, whether they be the forces of nature or of the hidden depths of the mind. Occultism, with its long history of unorthodox beliefs and practices, is above all a declaration of the existence of powers emanating from beyond. Thus it can be seen as a counterreligion in quest of aspects of transcendence that lie outside the Judeo-Christian tradition.[19]

The occult-metaphysical movements have been described as countercultural. It is more accurate, however, to say that they exaggerated certain existing tendencies within American religion and culture so that they seemed strange and unusual.[20] The passion for divination in the sixties and early seventies had its parallel in evangelical Christianity. Many evangelicals, spurred on by Hal Lindsey's book *The Late Great Planet Earth,* engaged in a flood of predictions concerning the Second Coming of Christ and events of the last times. This preoccupation with "Christian tea leaves" became a fad among many conservative Christians. The apocalyptic mood brought on by anticipation of the Age of Aquarius had its counterpart in the secular community as well. In the seventies and eighties, environmentalists and many nuclear pacifists envisioned the destruction of the planet. The AIDS epidemic furthered the apocalypticism, conjuring up visions of a plague akin to the Black Death.[21]

The occult's insistence that experience is the path to knowledge and enlightenment also had its parallel in the larger society. A major epistemological shift, particularly in religion, had taken place. The cognitive processes had been dethroned, and experience was the new king. The many religious therapies associated with the human potential and New Age movements closely resembled their secular counterparts. Indeed, many developments in psychology rested on occult-metaphysical assumptions. Furthermore, the emphasis that certain groups with an Eastern-occult worldview place on health and wholeness has been a widespread fad.[22]

Astrology

Most of the occult arts practiced in modern America have their roots deep in antiquity or European history. Though they may have been adapted to the modern world, they are not new. Occultists claim that the forces behind the modern occult arts were accessible to primitive people. Before the Age of Reason, these arts in various forms were widely practiced.[23] From the eighteenth century to the mid-twentieth century, they largely fell into disuse among educated segments of society. During this interval the occult arts still had a home among the uneducated, but were regarded as superstition by the larger society. In the 1960s the occult arts staged a comeback among all ranks of society, but especially among those disenchanted with American culture.[24]

Astrology was undoubtedly the most popular aspect of the occult revival in America. During the sixties it came in like a whirlwind. It peaked as a fad during the seventies, but on a much higher plateau than it had occupied before this surge.[25] A moderate interest in astrology appears to be a permanent feature of life in the industrialized West. Many astrology devotees, in all levels of society, still seek the advice of the stars. This was brought out by the disclosure in 1988 that astrology had been embraced within the highest level of American society, the White House.

Despite the popularity of astrology, many modern astrologers tend to hold themselves apart from the rest of occultism. They see astrology as an overlooked science, as precise as medicine—which, like horoscope-making, also requires intuitive personal skills. Some even believe that science must catch up with astrological truth. More metaphysically oriented astrologers, however, are less interested in the precise techniques for divining the future than in relating evidences of the stars' effects on human destiny to the overall workings of a universal plan.[26] In fact, as John Kerr indicates, "modern astrology only claims that the stars show trends, but do not determine actual behavior, which is up to each person's free will." A fatalistic individual may discover aspects of astrology that reinforce his or her desire to be controlled, but this distortion is in the believer's perception, not in astrology.[27]

The original astrology of Chaldea began with a close link to religion and maintained this relationship up to the time of the Macedonian conquest of this area. As it spread throughout the Near East, it merged with the syncretistic religions of the Hellenistic world, gradually losing its religious core and becoming Western astrology. As a magical science and no longer a religion, astrology occasionally could coexist with other religions, if they accepted magical beliefs outside of their own systems.[28]

The next major shift came in the seventeenth century. Until then astrology had occupied the position of a magical religion. The religious and political institutions now denounced astrology as superstition and relegated it to the ghetto of occultism. In the eighteenth and nineteenth centuries, having lost its legitimacy, astrology (along with palmistry, telepathy, clairvoyance and alchemy) encountered both social and legal repression. Therefore, it took two forms during this period. First, it became diffused through society as superstitious folk beliefs. Second, it became clandestine and occultic, taught by secret societies and esoteric sects.[29]

The backdrop for the comeback of astrology in the post-World War II era can be found in the nineteenth century and the first half of the twentieth. The use of astrology by Spiritualism and Theosophy in the last century and the popularity of astrology in Germany between the two world wars helped set the stage for the Age of Aquarius.[30] But according to Claude Fishler, it was not until "hope in the omnipotence of science" to find answers for human problems had diminished, "not until religion had also weakened," not until individualism had spread through the ranks of society that a mass astrology could emerge. Around 1930, the mass media brought astrology out of occultist obscurity. "Mass astrology was born with newspaper horoscopes, and from here progressed very rapidly," even though it did not square with the philosophy and religion of the modern world.[31]

Several individuals are closely related to the comeback of astrology in the twentieth century. Leon McBeth says that the first professional astrologer in the United States was probably Evangeline Adams, who in the 1920s began an astrology studio in New York City. Her clientele included the millionaire financier J. P. Morgan, "who paid her handsomely for monthly astrological forecasts to help guide his business ventures." Following in her train have come such popular astrologers as Carroll Righter and Sydney Omar, whose columns ran in about 550 daily newspapers.[32] Though better known for other occult activities, the "sleeping prophet" Edgar Cayce enunciated fascinating astrological doctrines while in trances. He has been a major figure in popularizing many areas of the occult, including astrology. On a more secular level, beginning in the 1920s there were attempts to bolster the scientific validity of astrology. Most individuals engaged in this enterprise were Europeans, but some Americans were involved.[33]

Marcello Truzzi says that the astrological revival associated with the Age of Aquarius has occurred on three levels of involvement. On the first and most superficial level can be found "the occasional reader of newspaper and magazine astrology columns." The vast majority of astrology believers are in this category. At the second level of involvement can be found "those people who have some knowledge of the mechanics of astrology." These people often have personal horoscopes cast. Unlike those on the first level, the believers on this plane have some understanding of the special astrological language and reasoning of astrology. Those involved with astrology in the first two categories seem to take a somewhat playful attitude toward it.[34]

On the third level of astrological involvement are people who have become "involved in the literature of the field and usually cast their own horoscopes." Unlike individuals operating on the first two levels, astrology believers in this category are not "primarily concerned with advice or prediction." For these individuals, astrology's complex, symbolic depth presents them with a "meaningful view of their universe and gives them an understanding of their place in it." They employ astrology as a way to establish their identity. For these people, astrology constitutes a worldview far more reminiscent of religion than of science. In fact, they usually "speak of their belief system, not as a science like physics, or astronomy, but as an art or as one of the occult sciences."[35]

Divination

Divination is the endeavor to forecast the future or to discover secret knowledge by means of some operator or instrument. Popular forms of divination in the modern world include the Ouija board, tarot cards, I Ching, palmistry, crystal-ball gazing, numerology, dreams and predictions by prophetic figures. In antiquity not all astrology was divination, nor is it in the modern world. When astrology is principally a method for character analysis, it is not divination. But endeavors to foretell the future by astrological methods, known as astromancy, may be regarded as divination. Most newspaper astrological columns are primarily astromantic, to the extent they pretend to give advance advice regarding probable events according to the position of the planets on a particular day.[36]

Throughout history, divination has been the most popular of the occult arts, largely because both rulers and common people desperately desired to know what the future held. However, by the middle or late nineteenth century interest in divination had declined so significantly that it resided in the "basement" of the occult arts. This decline coincided with dramatic advances in science and the beginning of reliable statistical analysis, both of which proved to be more reliable indicators than divination. Nevertheless, divination still functions in the modern world in many forms, some of which have a touch of pseudoscience.[37]

In the ancient world, animal entrails were a primary means to indicate the future, and official state diviners had high status in society. The ancients viewed divination not so much as coercive revelation as part of religion. It was an attempt to discover the will of the gods. In medieval Europe, the divination arts fascinated people in most segments of society. The various forms of divination were regarded both as a unity and as a type of magic. One person, called a magician or magus, could perform most types of divination. In modern times, the occult practitioner usually specializes in one of the branches of the art. There are relatively few comprehensive "magicians" in the medieval sense.[38]

Some forms of the occult arts have come on hard times. Crystal-ball gazing, also called crystomancy or scrying, has become a type of show business often practiced by gypsy types. Enjoyed as entertainment, it has clearly taken a major step down from its past stature. Earlier crystal-ball gazers took their art seriously, praying, burning candles and entering into a trance state in which they managed their divinations. In the trance, the crystal gazers allegedly communicated with transcendent forces. Few modern practitioners have entered a trance; they usually settle for telling clients about the "tall-dark-handsome man" in their future.[39]

Palmistry also has fallen on difficult times in the modern age. It is currently something of a game, described in cheap manuals. While palm readers may engage in some pretensions about contacting forces from "the Beyond," most do not go into a trance state. Rather, they usually engage in a simple palm examination, looking at major lines and interpreting what these variations say about one's future. At times the results are striking. The survival of palmistry is something of a feat in itself. But even more significant is its increasing use by physicians and law enforcers. Fingerprinting, of course, is commonly employed by both agencies. Dermatoglyphics, the science of studying the hands of newborn infants for signs of cryptic defects, has made strides. This relatively new procedure is based on the fact that some infants who later demonstrate symptoms of retardation have distinctive lines on their hands at birth. So it is not strange to see such age-old occult arts as phrenology (study of the skull), graphology (character analysis by studying handwriting), physiognomy (discovering character by outward appearance) and palmistry upheld to some degree under the rigorous testing of modern science. These enterprises have sufficient basis in the experience of humankind to resist hasty denunciation.[40]

For many centuries, cards also have been a popular device for divining the future. The early decks that came to Europe in about the fourteenth century had seventy-eight cards. They contained two parts—the fifty-six cards of the Minor Arcana (prototypes of modern playing cards) and twenty-two cards of the Major Arcana. The Major Arcana cards, which do not appear in the modern deck, were called tarots or *triomphes* (trumps) because they had a higher value. The seer or magician would lay out the cards, interpret their sequence according to what they symbolized, and then predict what the future held for his or her client. Because the cards have mystical associations, mostly originating from cabalism, tarot-reading is more sophisticated and complicated than palm-reading.[41]

In the sixties and seventies, the Ouija board sold almost as fast as Monopoly and was perhaps the most popular parlor game in America. The occult-sounding name is a combination of the French and German words for "yes." Robert Fuld, building on a venerable belief in the magical tradition, marketed the game in the 1890s. World War I and the Depression years were the peak sales periods, but after a slight decline during the Eisenhower years, the game made a striking new surge in the 1960s. A Ouija board features a marker that moves across the board and points toward words that imply answers. The user places his or her hand on the marker and concentrates on a particular question. Nearly unnoticeable muscular movements cause the marker to glide over the board until it comes to rest on a letter. This is repeated until the message is spelled out.[42]

What makes this happen? Edmund Gruss tells us that three explanations have been given. One, "all that comes through the board originates in the conscious or subconscious mind of the operator." Two, much of what comes through on the board reflects the conscious or subconscious mind of the operator, but "the remainder is communication with the spirits of the dead." Three, a considerable amount that comes through the board "reflects the conscious or subconscious mind of the operator, but a small portion is contact with evil spirits (demons)"—not the spirits of the deceased.[43]

Another type of fortune-telling popular among youth is I Ching. Essentially, I Ching is a book, not a religion, translated from the Chinese; its title means "Book of Changes." The book is so difficult to comprehend that one needs an interpreter. I Ching is an ancient Chinese book of divinations that leads one to gain guidance for action by tossing coins or sticks. Flipping coins appears to be a random way of deciding anything. Yet to the Chinese, nothing occurs by accident; everything has a meaning. Coin-tossing has a deep meaning because it rests on the old Chinese idea that the universe is divided into two complementary forces, yin and yang. The yang is the male force, a spirit-substance that begins things. The yin is a female force that completes things, giving substance to what the yang has started. Carl G. Jung's preface to the first Western translation of I Ching was published in 1949. Sales were slow from then until the 1960s, when they soared.[44]

Most forms of divination depend on some intermediary procedure or instrument—cards, crystal balls, numbers, dreams, omens and so forth. But there is another type of divination that requires only the prophetic powers of a charismatic individual. This is called intuitive prophecy. The best known of the twentieth-century prophets were Edgar Cayce and Jeane Dixon.[45]

Edgar Cayce (1877-1945) is well known for many occult activities, including his prophecies. This "sleeping prophet" founded the Association for Research and Enlightenment (ARE) in 1931. The association still continues his work, especially by promoting his writings on physical healing, astrology, prophecy, diet, reincarnation and interpretations of biblical history. While in a self-induced trance Cayce would make pronouncements on many subjects. Some events he predicted successfully include the Great Depression, the union of Austria and Germany, the death of two American presidents while in office, the Russian-German clash, and the end of World War II in 1945. Before his death that same year, Cayce predicted many catastrophic events that would begin in 1958 and run through the end of the century, when California would break apart and slide into the Pacific and the lost civilization of Atlantis would rise again. Years after his death, his popularity endures.[46]

During the 1960s Jeane Dixon became an American legend, largely because of her accurate predictions and her politically sensitive position in Washington. Already well known for her many correct prophecies, she became an international figure when it was learned that she had forecast the assassination of John F. Kennedy and had attempted to caution him against taking his fatal trip to Dallas. Her other accurate predictions, made well in advance of their denouement, include the assassinations of Martin Luther King Jr. and Bobby Kennedy; the partition of India; the fall of China (three years in advance); the launching of Sputnik; the Alaskan earthquake of 1964; the calling for the Second Vatican Council a year before it happened; the deaths of Franklin D. Roosevelt, Gandhi, Marilyn Monroe, Churchill, Nehru, John Foster Dulles and Dag Hammarskjöld; and Truman's, Eisenhower's and Nixon's elections. These accurate forecasts must be seen, however, in light of the fact that Dixon has also had a number of *incorrect* predictions. A list includes her denial that Jacqueline Kennedy would remarry; that Russia would invade Iran in 1953 and Palestine in 1957; that World War III would begin in 1958; that Russia would be first to land a man on the moon; and that Lyndon Johnson would be the Democratic nominee in 1968.[47]

America has numerous seers and prophets. But as Richard Woods notes, "Jeane Dixon shares with Edgar Cayce the major acclaim of the new occultists," in part because of her disclosure relative to the "Child of the East, a boy born on February 5, 1962, the day of the great Aquarian conjunction." She saw this child as revolutionizing the world's religions and governments. His power would reach its zenith in 1999, "when a terrible holocaust will shock the world's peoples into a true renewal." At first Dixon regarded this child as a new messiah, but then she decided that he was the antichrist.[48]

The status of Cayce and Dixon has ignited considerable controversy. While the occultists applaud them, they have been attacked by traditional Christians. Cayce's pronouncements on astrology, reincarnation and the life of Christ and Dixon's employment of occult paraphernalia, including crystal balls, palm-reading, cards and astrology, have drawn fire. The source of their prophecies, writes Woods, is the focal point of the controversy. None, not even Cayce and Dixon themselves, "claim that these American prophets were divinely inspired as were Elijah and Isaiah." It has been argued that these prophets derived their predictions from "natural" or demonic prophecy, or that God is using them as he did Balaam, the prophet of Baal.[49]

Witchcraft

During the 1960s and 1970s, witchcraft and Satanism were the forms of occultism that followed astrology in gaining public attention. The large number of popular books and articles published on these subjects attests that period's upsurge of interest in them.[50] The revival of medieval witchcraft is odd and perplexing to most modern Americans. We are told of love spells, drug rituals, sex rites, nude dancing, secret societies, and charms and amulets—activities and objects that are strangely out of place in a scientific-technological society. Throughout history, however, certain phenomena never seem to lose their appeal. They have managed to fascinate much of humanity over the centuries. Witchcraft is one of these ancient mysteries that will not go away. The image of witches as old hags with conical hats, broomsticks, warts on their noses and evil, cackling laughs has not entirely faded from the popular mind. The wicked witch in *The Wizard of Oz* and Walt Disney's wicked queen in *Snow White* are part of a long tradition, going back to the thirteenth century, which has embedded such an image in the minds of people.[51]

What is witchcraft, and why has it endured? First of all, witchcraft is not Satanism. Although these two phenomena are often believed to go together, they actually represent two entirely different belief-systems, and each has a variety of forms in the late twentieth century. Modern witchcraft is a religion based on the revival of paganism. It is not the heretical witchcraft that existed in Europe from the fourteenth to the seventeenth century. Instead, modern witchcraft regards itself as a throwback to the ancient, pre-Christian religion of Europe. Being pre-Christian, this religion had nothing to do with the devil described in Christian doctrine. Yet all neopagans are not witches. Modern witchcraft has a second component: magic. Thus, as Jeffrey Russell notes, a modern witch is a pagan who, in addition to worshiping the pre-Christian gods, practices some variety of magic.[52]

Why the revival of witchcraft after World War II in Europe and the United States? First, witchcraft in one form or another has survived through history. Its various forms include simple sorcery, which exists the world over, and the combination of sorcery and Christian heresy known as Satanism or diabolism. Even pagan beliefs and practices have survived, though not as a coherent religion as Margaret Murray has contended. A revival was possible, then, because enough aspects of witchcraft have survived. Second, for over a century a sequence of events, which will be examined shortly, facilitated the revival of witchcraft. Third, the increase in witchcraft in the post-World War II era is but an aspect of the larger occult revival and must be seen in this context.[53]

Modern neopagan witchcraft has its more immediate roots in nineteenth-century Romanticism. The Romantic elevated feeling and imagination, and the magician made more systematic use of the same forces. As the century progressed, neopaganism developed a closer working relationship with the occult, utilizing many of the occultic arts. In Britain in the late nineteenth century, a group of Masons founded the Order of the Golden Dawn, by far the best known of the many esoteric groups that emerged at this time. Though this order ceased to exist shortly after World War I, it shaped the thinking of many individuals who have since been influential in occult circles, including Aleister Crowley (1875-1947). Crowley, a notorious magician and occult figure in Britain, powerfully influenced Gerald Gardner, the founder of modern witchcraft.[54]

Robert Ellwood divides the neopagan movement into two broad categories: "the magical groups, deeply influenced by the model of the Order of the Golden Dawn . . . and Crowley; and the nature orientated groups." In the first category are the "more antiquarian" bodies that celebrate occultic phenomena, such as levitations and apparitions. The nature-oriented groups tend to be "more purely romantic," preferring woodsy settings to incense and altars. They plant trees, dance and celebrate the goddesses of nature. Modern witchcraft lies somewhere between these two groups.[55]

Several publications in the late nineteenth and early twentieth centuries powerfully impacted the rise of modern witchcraft. Neopagan witchcraft has roots in the historical tradition of Jules Michelet, who argued that European witchcraft was the survival of an ancient religion. This influenced Sir James Frazer's *The Golden Bough,* Margaret Murray's *Witch-Cult in Western Europe* and the works of other writers and anthropologists. The publication of Charles Leland's *Aradia,* which argued for the continuous existence of pre-Christian witchcraft, was an important step in the development of neopaganism. Murray's work, published in 1921, further developed Leland's argument. Though Murray's ideas are not supported by the evidence, they remained in vogue and provided a further stimulus for the witch revival.[56]

By the end of World War II, witchcraft had already become a reality in the mind of Gerald Gardner (1884-1964). Gardner is regarded as the father of modern witchcraft, though some scholars accord this title to Crowley because of his heavy influence on Gardner. Gardner's books, especially his *Witchcraft Today,* are considered to be the basis of modern witchcraft, and Gardnerians still flourish.[57] Jeffrey Russell points out the two types of Gardnerians: "those claiming direct apostolic succession from Gardner's original coven" and those with different origins but "whose ideas are clearly derivative from Gardner." Besides these Gardnerians, there are a wide variety of neopagans in Britain and America with no lineage and little organization beyond the local coven. The centrality of the Goddess in Gardnerian beliefs has made witchcraft attractive to some feminists. Estimates in 1980 indicate that "possibly fifteen percent of modern witches—more in America than in England—are neopagan feminists."[58]

Modern witchcraft is diverse, and generalizations are difficult to make. Therefore, statements beginning "Witches believe . . ." or "Witches do . . ." really mean that *many* witches "believe" or "do." Russell offers one description of modern witchcraft. As noted earlier, witches are pagans who practice magic. The characteristic most widespread among modern witches is their love and veneration of nature. For most of them, the Deity exists in nature. In fact, some types of witchcraft are really versions of pantheism. The primary deity for witches is the Goddess, "the deity of nature perceived as an earth Goddess, a moon Goddess, and a fertility Goddess." She has a threefold nature: warrior, mother and hag of darkness and rebirth. The Goddess is called Astarte, Isis, the Magna Mater and many other names. Some feminist witches worship only the Goddess, but "most worship both the Goddess and her consort, the horned god." While some witches do not acknowledge other gods and goddesses, others are polytheistic, worshiping the whole pantheon within which the horned God and Goddess are given the preeminent place. "Virtually all witches firmly reject the Judaeo-Christian tradition." Though not many witches are virulently anti-Christian, "they have embraced the term pagan and made it a term of honor."[59]

Central to witchcraft is the practice of magic. Witches practice many different kinds of magic, including divination, astrology, incantations and herbology. In divination they employ devices common to the occult: tarot, crystal-gazing, the pendulum, necromancy and interpreting dreams. In nearly all cases, these varieties of magic are "worked to fulfill the witches' will for benign or at least morally neutral purposes"—commonly called white magic. Some witches employ negative magic, so-called black magic, but they are not usually well received by their peers. The difference between black and white magic has to do with the user's intent rather than his or her technique. Witches also claim a high degree of psychic sensitivity and power, but this can no longer be defined as magic, since what used to be called extrasensory perception is now beginning to be established as a natural phenomenon.[60]

As Russell points out, many modern witches also hold to reincarnation, which they claim is derived from the Celtic or Druid tradition. Actually, in Western religions reincarnation is at best a marginal doctrine, and it has only a small place in the Celtic or Druid system. "The witches' belief in reincarnation comes from Gerald Gardner," who drew it from the spiritual environment of his time, particularly the growing interest in Eastern religion. Yet witches and the Eastern religions do not perceive reincarnation in the same way. In the Eastern tradition, the soul may advance toward nirvana or drop back to lower levels, in keeping with the spiritual merit of the individual. In witchcraft, however, "the soul simply returns to earth."[61]

Gardner stated a rule for witches: "No one can be a witch alone, because working together increases magical power." Many witches ignore this regulation and work alone. Most modern witches enter covens, however, because they believe that "no one is really a witch unless he or she is initiated." After a careful preinitiation screening, a witch is initiated into the Craft and he or she is admitted to the activities of the inner court. The witch is now committed to secrecy. Secrecy and exclusiveness are a pattern in the Craft, in part because "secrecy is magical," in part because of a "well-founded fear of persecution." This exclusiveness presents a problem for witchcraft. Witches are few in number and would like to make converts, but generally they do not proselytize.[62]

Modern witches utilize a number of tools, symbols and meetings to further the interests of the Craft, writes Russell. The most important tool is the "athame, a black-handled, double-edged dagger used to cast and consecrate the circle of worship and to invoke the God and Goddess." The athame is also a phallic symbol, representing "the power of the will." The second most significant tool is the chalice, the feminine symbol of receptivity. Witchcraft commonly employs sexual symbols. They are not intended to be pornographic; rather, they are "rooted in the pagan love for the earth and its growing things, and in the powerful symbol of sexual union as cosmic integration." Each year witches observe eight major sabbats or festivals. The sabbat, a religious ceremony commemorating the seasonal changes, is open to prospective new members for socializing, worship and celebration. In addition to the sabbats, witches hold closed meetings, generally called esbats, which are limited to initiates.[63]

Some neopagan witches say their numbers are in the millions. More sober estimates range from 20,000 to 100,000 worldwide. Witchcraft is still largely "a white, middle-class movement, and most witches are relatively well educated." Women hold a two-to-one ratio over men, and the imbalance is increasing. Most witches are urban dwellers, ranging in age from teens to early thirties. Neopagan witch groups are in the Western tradition, and many of them take pride in this fact. In their independence of gurus and desire to take responsibility for their own lives they differ from many who follow Eastern religions. They are very creative and independent people.[64]

Satanism

In the late sixties, Anton LaVey, head of a San Francisco group known as the Church of Satan, was quoted as saying, "The Satanic Age started in 1966. That's when God was proclaimed dead, the Sexual Freedom League came into preeminence, and the hippies developed as a free sex culture."[65] On one hand, marking 1966 as the beginning of a "satanic age" is something of an exaggeration. On the other, the attention the devil has received lately would have shocked Enlightenment rationalists, who believed two hundred years ago that they had buried him. LaVey is correct in saying that many underground groups devoted to devil worship sprang up in the mid-sixties.

Several forms of Satanism infiltrated the culture of the late sixties and early seventies, often in apparently innocuous forms. Millions watched Anton LaVey on the Johnny Carson show, wearing a horned hood, brandishing a ceremonial-magic sword and proclaiming the Satanic creed: "Evil spelled backwards is live." In 1970 LaVey published *The Satanic Bible,* which in less than a year became a bestseller on college campuses. In the same period the Hell's Angels were rampaging across the nation. Meanwhile, a community of black-cloaked youth from London established themselves in urban centers in America. Members of their Process Church of the Final Judgment, who cannot be considered Satanists in any strict sense, regard Satan, Lucifer and Jehovah as the three gods of the universe.[66]

The general populace was more familiar with other types of Satanism: *Rosemary's Baby* (filmed in 1968) and *The Exorcist* (1973), late-night horror shows on television, bizarre stories of animal mutilations, and persistent rumors of clandestine Black Masses being said in an abandoned church or in someone's living room. The occult revolution would have seemed a bit tame if the devil had not had a visible role in it. There is no necessary connection between the occult and Satanism. Yet it would have seemed strange if Satanism were not explicitly implicated in the occult revival.[67]

Satanism is not the same as any form of witchcraft. The pact with the devil, so central to historical or diabolical witchcraft, has played a part in the revival of some forms of Satanism. Yet as Russell notes, modern Satanism is quite different from diabolical witchcraft. To a greater extent, today's neopagan witches reject Satanism. Modern witches say that since they reject Christianity, it is unreasonable to suppose that they worship the Christian devil.[68]

The basic distinction between witchcraft and Satanism lies in their relationship to Christianity. Modern neopagan witches do not consider themselves to be a Christian heresy or breakoff. Conversely, Satanists see themselves as in an alliance with Satan, either literally or symbolically (many Satanists are atheists). Witchcraft exists as an independent religion, much like other non-Christian religions. It stands as an alternative to the Christian faith, as do Hinduism and Buddhism. Yet Satanism could be described as a kind of inverted Christian sect. It draws on Christianity, but aims to overthrow the Christian deity in favor of his adversary. Satanism stands in a polemical relationship to Christianity in both belief and ritual, using Christian elements but changing them and giving them different meanings.[69]

Despite these substantive differences, several factors make it easy to lump witchcraft and Satanism together. Witches and Satanists share in a common magical worldview. Also, many Satanists have openly identified with witchcraft. For example, LaVey entitled one of his books *The Compleat Witch*. The publications of evangelical Christians often have failed to distinguish between witchcraft and Satanism. This misconception has deep roots, going back to the age of the witch trials, when witchcraft was defined as having a pact with Satan.[70]

After the decline of diabolical witchcraft in Europe during the seventeenth century, several kinds of occult phenomena that resembled Satanism were evident in the subsequent centuries. The Black Mass was celebrated in France and England, although it never amounted to much. The Hellfire Clubs engaged in orgies more than devil worship. Aleister Crowley took pride in his outrageous anti-Christian antics, calling himself "the Wickedest Man Alive," "666" and "The Great Beast." These and similar activities fell short of real Satanism—that is, actual worship of the devil.[71] Nevertheless, they foreshadowed many aspects of modern Satanism, which for the most part also falls short of Satan worship.

As with witches, there are two broad types of modern Satanists: those acting as individuals and those functioning in groups. About the former little is known. Apparently, some individuals have made a pact with the devil, but they do not make this widely known. Despite some publicity, Satanists in America have always been few in number, and by the mid-1970s their strength appeared to be waning even further.[72] Some sources, especially mental health workers, contend that Satanism began to make a comeback in the late eighties. They argue that evidence of Satanic ritualistic abuse has surfaced during therapy sessions. Nevertheless, the level of Satanic activity in modern America is a matter of debate.

The issue seems to center on what is regarded as Satanist. Those who believe Satanism to be on the rise usually define the term broadly to encompass a wide range of bizarre activities. On the other hand, those taking a narrow view of Satanism, limiting it to activities expressly related to the devil, tend to see it as a static or declining movement. Still, Satanist groups continue to exist, and for their numbers they demonstrate considerable diversity.

Marcello Truzzi identifies at least four varieties of modern Satanists. The first type—probably the least common but also the closest to authentic Satanism—are Satanic groups that follow what they regard as a nonheretical interpretation of Christianity "in which Satan is perceived as an angel still to be worshipped." This sort of "white Satanism" probably comes out of the gnostic tradition. A second type "consists of sex clubs that incorporate Satanism and some of its alleged rituals." The attraction here is the sexual aspects of the celebrated but artificial "black mass." A number of these groups are flagellation societies or sado-masochist clubs.[73]

A third Satanic variety grew out of the "acid culture" of the sixties. Represented by the much-publicized Charles Manson group that murdered Sharon Tate in 1969, this type has received much notoriety. It is, however, "much more rare than the newspaper headlines would imply." Manson's religion is one of torture and death ruled by the man who called himself Satan and the Devil. In some mysterious way, Manson appears to have believed that Christ and Satan, good and evil, were to be unified, probably in himself. But these Satanist groups are almost totally nontraditional, making up "their brand of Satanism as they go along." Like the sex clubs, their emphasis is not on occultism at all; in their case, they focus on the use of narcotics.[74]

The fourth variety, constituting the largest and most publicized of the Satanist groups, is the Satanic Church in America. Headed by high priest

Anton LaVey and based in San Francisco, the Satanic Church has spread to urban centers across the United States. By 1977 it claimed more than ten thousand members. Ironically, the Church of Satan embodies little of true Satanism, which entails the worship of Satan, the ancient "deity" that Christianity has (in their view) mistakenly or maliciously identified with the devil.[75]

LaVey's type of Satanism has basic themes that stand in contrast to Christian values: self-assertion, the gratification of humanity's physical and mental nature, and an antiestablishment attitude. In fact, these Satanists do not believe in Satan or the devil in any real sense. They believe in magic, but define it simply as obtaining changes in accordance with one's will. The power of magic comes not from without, but from within. The purpose of Satanism is to acquire and control, and one does this by openly admitting and accepting one's passions. Satanism believes that the seven cardinal sins of Christianity are to be encouraged as vehicles for accomplishing one's desires. The Church of Satan views human nature from the vantage point of extreme Machiavellianism and cynical realism. Satanism's blatantly selfish, brutal philosophy is based on the belief that human beings are inherently selfish, violent creatures.[76]

The Church of Satan actively rejects spirituality and mysticism of any sort. Instead, it espouses an elitist, materialist and basically atheistic philosophy. Satan constitutes a worship of one's ego. Yet unlike most atheism, the Church of Satan interprets symbolic spiritual entities as powerful emotional forces. As Truzzi indicates, not only does this form of Satanism reject "the existence of anything supernatural or spiritual, but it even condemns any narcotics, hallucinogens, or other agents that might separate rational people from their material environment." The Satanist "does not seek to escape reality"; he or she seeks "full control of reality" and is willing to use all forces—even irrational elements—that can help achieve desired ends. In contrast to the acid-culture Satanists, who attempted to alter their consciousness through drugs and mysticism, the Church of Satan opposed the hippie culture.[77]

Psychic and Spiritualistic Phenomena

Determining what is occult and what it is not is generally difficult. The problem becomes compounded when a study of psychic and spiritualistic phenomena is undertaken. Psychic and spiritualistic phenomena are in the occult grab bag, encompassing a wide range of phenomena not easily placed elsewhere. A partial list would include Spiritualism, several types of psychic experiences falling under the general label of extrasensory perception (ESP), ghosts and poltergeists, astral projections, levitations, apparitions and possibly even reincarnation. Depending on one's point of view, with the exception of ESP, most of this list could be categorized as spiritualist phenomena. The issue concerns the source or sources of these phenomena: fraud, imagination, psychic factors, supernatural forces or some combination thereof.

Spiritualism, of course, has had a long history, having become an identifiable movement in the nineteenth century. It has had its ups and downs throughout its 140-year history, often fluctuating in relationship to circumstances and historical trends. Because Spiritualism is a highly decentralized movement, membership figures are always suspect. Moreover, many more people are loosely associated with spiritualistic activities than are indicated by organizational statistics. They are spiritualists with a lower-case *s,* choosing not to formally identify themselves with any one of the branches of the Spiritualist Church.[78] Moreover, the element of fraud, which has been endemic in Spiritualism, also makes membership statistics questionable.[79]

Given these reservations, it seems reasonable to say that because of fraud and other factors Spiritualism was in a decline during the late nineteenth century, only to experience a growth period after World War I. This growth arose largely from two factors: people's longings to contact loved ones killed in the war and mediums' claims of ability to psychically contact the spirits of the dead. A similar growth had occurred after the Civil War, as bereaved families endeavored to contact their deceased loved ones. In the 1920s, séances, table-rapping and fortune-telling were mischievous but exciting diversions from reality. During these years Arthur Ford, a Disciples of Christ minister, became involved in Spiritualism, claiming to have a spirit-guide named Fletcher who was a French-Canadian killed in World War I. Ford continued to function as a medium for about fifty years. But the impact of his teachings was not felt immediately, and the 1920s revival of Spiritualism was short-lived. The Depression turned people's thoughts toward more mundane interests, so that Spiritualism was in retreat until the mid-1960s.[80]

Spiritualism returned to the public limelight in the 1960s for several reasons. In part its return accompanied a broader interest in occult phenomena that had surfaced during this decade. Spiritualism had much in common with other fringe religious movements of the sixties, drawing people who were dissatisfied with traditional religion. In fact, the average Spiritualist in modern America had some knowledge of the Rosicrucians, Yoga, New Thought, flying saucers and other occult and Eastern ideas, and at times they even joining related groups. Yet the notion of social deviance can be pushed too far; most Spiritualists were loyal to middle-class values.[81] In part, the revival of spiritualism in America in the 1960s appears to have been part of a wider movement. The largest body of Spiritualists in the world exists in Brazil, where Spiritualism has reached epidemic proportions, with at least ten million adherents. There are approximately one million Spiritualists in other Latin American countries.[82]

In part, Spiritualism gained public attention in the 1960s because of the activities of some prominent individuals. Some credit for the revival of Spiritualism must go to Arthur Ford. Major credit must go to Episcopal Bishop James A. Pike for making Spiritualism a media event. In 1966 his son Jim Pike killed himself. Bishop Pike visited several mediums, including Ford, Era Twiggy and George Daisley, trying to establish communication with his deceased son. In 1967 Pike had a séance with Arthur Ford on Canadian television. This séance was repeated on a number of other stations, bringing Spiritualism into the homes of millions of Americans and becoming something of a modern classic of psychic documentaries. Pike's book on Spiritualism, *The Other Side,* was a bestseller for many months and helped arouse interest in paranormal phenomena.[83]

In modern America about 150,000 Americans officially claim Spiritualism as their religion. They do not like to be labeled as occultic. In addition to séances they have regular church services, which often resemble those of the Protestant denominations. The interest in Spiritualism, however, goes beyond what church figures indicate. Gallup polls tell us that millions of Americans believe that human beings can communicate with the dead. Yet, for a religious movement of nearly a century and a half, Spiritualism can boast few accomplishments. Its primary claim is that Spiritualism proves human immortality. But even if communicating with the spirits of a few deceased people is genuine, this fails to prove that all human beings survive death. Moreover, Spiritualism is not a cohesive movement. The larger movement's failure to rid itself of openly operating pockets of fraudulent leaders has prevented its acceptance as a bona fide religion in many quarters.[84]

Associated with Spiritualism as phenomena that communicate across time and space among the living are psychic experiences. As George Braswell indicates, "there are various kinds of psychic experiences which contemporary science has no established criteria to evaluate." Research on extrasensory perception (ESP) goes back to J. B. Rhine of Duke University. Included in ESP are such phenomena as precognition, telepathy and clairvoyance. Precognition allows an individual to be aware of an event before it occurs. Telepathy concerns the interaction between two minds or bodies, and the acquisition of knowledge without the aid of known sensory functions. In clairvoyance the individual's mind or body interacts with some event and gains knowledge without the aid of normal sensory functions. Research continues, but investigators' conclusions regarding these psychic happenings are still tentative.[85]

Whether ESP is occultic is a difficult question. On one hand, like hypnosis, ESP is the object of serious scientific research, and a breakthrough may not be too far in the future. On the other hand, as Robert Moore points out, parapsychology is still regarded by the scientific community as "a marginal activity." This is not helped by the fact that many parapsychologists in the 1960s were occultists who came out of the closet and turned to "drugs, astral projection, reincarnation, and Eastern forms of meditation—all in the name of tracking psi phenomena."[86] Furthermore, as Robert Wuthnow demonstrates, followers of the new and quasi-religious movements of the 1960s and 1970s have a higher tendency to be involved in ESP than members of conventional religion.[87]

Ghosts and poltergeists are related phenomena in the realm of Spiritualism. Braswell says that "there are ghosts of the living and of the dead." A ghost of the dead may haunt a house, but when it leaves the house remains essentially the same. Poltergeists are another kind of ghost of the dead. They are noisy spirits who may move, throw or destroy objects. They wreak havoc, and the buildings they inhabit are never the same. Astral projection is more a ghost of the living. It is based on the idea that the living human body has two forms—physical and astral. "The astral body is composed of finer matter. It can be separated from the physical body at times of sleep and travel over time and space." Various explanations have been given for these phenomena. Ghosts are seen as hallucinations, as human auras (the cloud projected from the body, lingering after death); as the dead themselves on the way to their reward, or as sent by God or Satan on a special mission. Psychic explanations are usually given for astral projections.[88]

Reincarnation, also connected with Spiritualism, is a belief in the preexistence of souls and their reincarnation into different bodies throughout history. The Western world has never fully embraced the idea of reincarnation, but it has occupied a major position in the belief structure of Eastern religions and has had its pockets in Western thought. Plato referred to it; it flourished briefly among the Origenists of the third and fourth centuries. Many professed Christians claim to believe in it. In fact, the doctrine of purgatory is a version of reincarnation, since it is basically a belief that the soul can be purified after death.[89]

In post-World War II America, several developments have done much to promote interest in reincarnation. A book published in the mid-1950s popularized the subject and initiated a controversy over it. Morey Bernstein hypnotized Virginia Burns Tighe by a technique called age regression, taking her back to what seemed to be a previous life as Bridey Murphy in nineteenth-century Ireland.[90] Other factors are the mushrooming interest in Eastern religions in America, nearly all of which espouse reincarnation, and the influx of Asian peoples to the United States.

UFO Cults
Rodney Stark and William Bainbridge tell us that flying-saucer cults are based on the expectation of "contacts with spiritually advanced races from outer space." Some leaders in the UFO tradition actually claim to have taken "trips to other planets and to have gained great mystical wisdom" in the company of the space visitors, referred to as the space brothers. Flying-saucer groups are very new, all existing bodies having been formed since 1950. The movement peaked during the 1950s and 1960s and appears to be waning. Few new groups have been formed since 1970.[91]

Though unidentified flying objects (UFOs) are new, there is some precedent for them. In the eighteenth century, Emanuel Swedenborg reported having conversations with beings from outside the solar system. During the nineteenth and early twentieth centuries, some people, primarily psychics, claimed to have met visitors from other planets. They wrote about these contacts and publicized their writings throughout the psychic community. Along with contemporary UFO phenomena, these claims of earlier contacts with extraterrestrial beings provide a background for the modern UFO cults. UFO bodies and Spiritualism bear some similarities, for these types of groups employ the same methods of communication: vision and marvelous journeys, trance speaking and writing, séance circles and telepathy.[92]

The modern history of UFOs began on June 24, 1947. On this day in the state of Washington, Kenneth Arnold saw nine bright disks moving like "saucers" in front of his plane. Since that time, tens of thousands of people around the globe claim to have seen UFOs. Most of these reports have been answered by "conventional" explanations, but approximately 10 percent of them have not been explained by scientific analysis and traditional reasoning. These mysterious sightings have been the subjects of scientific controversy and have prompted occult explanations.[93]

In the early years, even the UFO proponents rejected occult answers and instead appealed to laws of physics. So long as reports of the phenomena remained fairly logical and understandable, ufologists argued their case within the accepted perimeters of scientific inquiry. Their approach was similar to that of the nineteenth-century Spiritualists, who endeavored to make spirit communication credible. Both the Spiritualists and the UFO adherents relied on external facts rather than on inward states of mind. But in 1952, UFO sightings took on another dimension when George Adamski claimed that a UFO occupant met and talked with him. He wrote several books on the subject, and many other reports of contacts with visitors from other planets followed.[94]

Some of the contactees (those contacted by the UFO occupants) continued to seek answers about the nature of the UFO visitors. But a second group gave the UFOs an occult dimension. Having made contact with what they claimed to be extraterrestrial beings, they committed themselves to telling others the message of the space people. The movement had acquired a religious dimension. Gordon Melton says that through these early contacts, the space people began to articulate a message. While it varied over the specifics, the general thrust was the same. The space people were more highly evolved beings who were coming to aid the occupants of Earth. "They brought a message of concern about the course of man, whose materialism is leading him to destruction." However, the space people offered a means of salvation. Humankind could avoid the coming destruction by following their message of love. Space people are said to be constantly nearby, paternalistically guiding the people of Earth.[95]

Continued claims regarding UFO appearances, especially of occupants' contacts with people, heightened interest and led to several further developments. Many began to search for UFOs in history. It has been speculated that some of the wonders of antiquity, such as the pyramids and Stonehenge, were beyond the knowledge of the period and thus had to be produced by visitors from outer space. Others turned to the Bible, especially the book of Ezekiel, as evidence of contacts by extraterrestrial visitors. More recent writers have even speculated that the human race is descended from space beings rather than from the lower forms of mammals.[96]

In addition to individuals' efforts to spread the message of hope brought by space beings, several people who supposedly were in telepathic contact with UFOs began to gather followers around them. These bodies often modeled themselves after the Theosophical and I AM groups. Also, in the 1950s some early New Age groups began to proclaim messages that allegedly came from the saucer world. Nearly all these groups were formed in the 1950s and 1960s, the most notable exception being the Bo and Peep cult, which was founded in 1975 and drew the attention of both the media and the academic community. With few exceptions, these UFO groups maintained the central UFO message and practiced a variety of occult activities.[97]

18

The New Age
Movement

T he New Age currently features Shirley MacLaine, faith healers,
channelers, space travelers and crystals galore. Millions of Americans are trying to learn about their former lives, cure illnesses
without medicine, meet travelers from other galaxies, know the unknowable
and engage in "personal transformation." In the eighties, New Age ideas and
practices penetrated American culture at many levels. They caught on with
celebrities, middle-aged hippies, therapists, church leaders and personnel
executives. In fact, perhaps the greatest number of new religious movements
in the eighties fit into the category of New Age groups.[1]

Description and Definition
What is the New Age movement? Voltaire once remarked that the Holy
Roman Empire was not holy, not Roman and not an empire. The title "New
Age movement" is a little like this—it is misleading. The New Age is not
new, and its members do not make up a movement. Despite its popularity,
the New Age is difficult to define. It is highly eclectic, encompassing a wide
range of fads, rituals and beliefs. Some individuals endorse some parts,
some accept other aspects. Only for special events, such as the highly publicized "harmonic convergence" in August 1987, do believers in crystals or
I Ching gather with believers in astral travel, shamans, tarot readers and
Lemurians. (On the day of the harmonic convergence, some twenty thousand New Agers gathered at sacred sites from Mount Shasta to Central

Park to create harmony by chanting together.) Because of this diversity, statements made by some representatives of the New Age may not hold for all those associated with it. Furthermore, the New Age movement exalts change and evolution; thus many of its ideas and practices are shifting.[2]

The New Age movement can be seen as a broad, diverse cultural trend, reflecting many of the anxieties and aspirations of Americans in the years after the decline of the counterculture. Otto Friedrich says that the New Age can also be regarded as "a cloudy sort of religion," a quasi-religion, "claiming vague connections with both Christianity and the major faiths of the East, . . . plus an occasional dab of pantheism and sorcery." The goals and methods of the New Age resemble those of other religions, such as the endeavor to respond to the believer's spiritual concerns with the promise of an afterlife or, in the case of the New Age, an improved life on earth. Moreover, the New Age requires its followers to believe in things that cannot be proved scientifically—channeling, for example. Yet the "underlying faith is a lack of faith" in the orthodoxies of Christianity, rationalism, high technology, routine living and the political establishment. Somehow, New Agers believe that there must be "some secret and mysterious shortcut or alternative path to happiness and health."[3]

According to Ted Peters, in simplest terms the New Age movement is a "diversified stream of coalitions, organizations, and individuals all striving to induce a new age of enlightenment and harmony in our society." What unites these groups is their desire to promote a new worldview and to revitalize humanity on the basis of a combination of Eastern religions, humanistic ethics, the human potential movement and holistic health ideas. This mindset, this way of understanding reality, writes Brooks Alexander, is "the worldview of occult mysticism, articulated in secular terms." Thus, the New Age movement is an "ancient wisdom, expressed with a modern vocabulary."[4]

The New Age also can be seen as a millennial movement. As Alexander notes, "the heart of the New Age message is the conviction that humanity is poised between two epochs, or ages." New Agers believe that humanity is "at a crossroads, that the human condition is in a desperate state." But instead of despairing, they believe that humanity is on the verge of changes that will "transform our society, our behavior, and even our nature." The impending age is expected to bring a new stage in the evolution of humanity, not physically, but psychologically, spiritually and socially.[5]

Historical Development

J. Gordon Melton says that "the New Age Movement can best be dated from 1971." By that time, various strands had come together and a self-conscious movement became visible. The New Age had a periodical, *East-West Journal,* and various organizational forms and directories. Even in the 1960s, however, small groups had begun to call themselves "new age" and adopt some of the components that would characterize the movement in the 1970s.[6]

The New Age movement has had many precursors. It has some roots in the long tradition of Western millennialism, and in some ways resembles a secular postmillennialism.[7] But the New Age is more complicated than this. Its roots can also be seen in previous attempts to find points of convergence between East and West. As Douglas Groothuis notes, New Age thought is not necessarily "reducible to the classical Eastern religions." Instead, the fusion of certain neopagan, occultic and Eastern ideas with traditional "Western religious thought has produced a hybrid spirituality. It takes the essence of Eastern religions but retains some elements of the Western, Judeo-Christian worldview. What results is a mutation."[8]

In varying degrees, such a convergence can be seen in individuals and groups at the fringes of Western science and religion. On the European scene during the medieval and early modern periods, such a list would include the alchemists, gnostics, cabalists, hermetics, Meister Eckhart, Pico della Mirandola, Jacob Boehme and Emanuel Swedenborg.[9] Melton provides us with a glimpse of the same process in the United States. Here, Transcendentalism was probably the first movement to synthesize the newly discovered Eastern wisdom with Western thought. Transcendentalism was the first significant religious movement in American culture to have a substantial Asian component. The emergence of Transcendentalism marked the beginning of the alternative religious tradition in America, which has existed alongside the more dominant Christian bodies. This alternative tradition has integrated mysticism and Eastern wisdom with Western values, especially "individualism and success orientation."[10]

Transcendentalism passed its focus on Eastern religions and mystical experience to several other popular nineteenth-century movements: Theosophy, Spiritualism, Christian Science and New Thought. Within these movements Transcendentalism merged with "Western occult thought and the new mental healing movement," which had come to America with the followers of Franz Mesmer. During the nineteenth and twentieth centuries, the alternative-reality tradition has fragmented into many factions, which in turn have produced more subgroups. And the members of these various organizations, especially those of Spiritualism and New Thought, provided much of the "initial support for the New Age vision" when it emerged.[11]

The influence was not all in one direction. Just as Westerners were learning about Eastern religious thought, Eastern religion was feeling the impact of Western ideas, largely coming from Western governments and Christian missions. Hinduism, in particular, modified itself to become a "Protestant" Hinduism. It stripped itself of many "deities and accretions . . . so offensive to Western monotheists," adapted its gatherings to resemble those of a Christian congregation and became more receptive to Western knowledge.[12]

During the nineteenth century, Theosophy also furthered the integration of Eastern thought into Western life. In particular, Theosophy became the major vehicle for transmitting the concept of reincarnation. Another Theosophical concept became a basic component of the New Age perspective: a vision for the essential unity of religion. Theosophists furthered the unity concept by proposing "the vision of a coming new world religious teacher, who would teach the nations the new truth, which was being revealed to the theosophical leaders by the spiritual masters."[13]

Throughout Western history there have been periods of religious hunger followed by much criticism of the church and accompanying revivals. However, in the 1960s a highly unusual situation existed. For the first time in centuries, religious hunger "coincided with the presence of a number of Eastern religious teachers and a new wave of sophisticated mystical-occult teachers, many with an eastern flavor to their teachings." As I have noted earlier in this book, the repeal of the Asian immigration exclusion acts brought an influx of Easterners, many of whom were religious teachers. And as Melton points out, "the last years of the 1960s witnessed the launching of a major missionary effort by the Eastern religions toward the West." This effort was not centrally coordinated, but grew out of an idea popular within all the Eastern religious communities: the West is ready for and in need of wisdom from the East.[14]

The roots of the New Age movement travel back through Western history and have important Eastern connections. There are, however, some more immediate developments, resting on an occult and Eastern worldview, that are basic to the New Age movement. New Age ideology is built upon the

counterculture's foundation. The counterculture of the sixties offered people a doorway into the new and the untried—imported Eastern religions,
hallucinogenic drugs and the occult. A number of sects and cults flourished
in the climate of the counterculture, most setting up "alternate altars." A
variety of yogis and gurus promised enlightenment; meditation became popular; Hare Krishnas chanted; witches danced in the woods; and a generation
became acquainted with non-Christian spirituality. A generation of young
people also attempted to elevate consciousness through both organic and
synthetic drugs. Marilyn Ferguson sees drugs as promoting an interest in
alternative realities and considers the psychedelic movement of the sixties
as a critical step in the later development of the New Age movement.[15] The
occult, in both its worldview and its specific practices, powerfully impacted
the counterculture, and this influence was passed on to the New Age movement.

To see the counterculture of the 1960s as but a passing trend is an error,
writes Groothuis. While a number of the outward forms of its protest are
things of the past, "many of its deepest claims have simply changed cos-
tume" and are now regular parts of modern culture. The "love-ins," Eastern
religious disciplines, drugs and occultism that were open but irregular in the
sixties became "well integrated into the general culture by the mid 1970s."[16]

The ideology, practices and objectives of the counterculture did not vanish, but the methods of implementation changed drastically. "The radicalism and enthusiastic protest of the sixties gave way to a more . . . integrated
view that developed in the 1970s." Having learned something about Eastern
spirituality and philosophy in the 1960s, grown-up hippies did not abandon
their pantheistic outlook. "They simply accommodated it to certain social
conventions." They may have cut their hair, but they did not change their
worldview. Instead of separating from society or trying to tear society down
by violent protest, they often joined the culture and infiltrated it from
within, hoping to change it this way. Other refugees from the counterculture
had little hope of changing society. Stung by the excess of the 1960s, they
reorganized without fundamentally changing their views. Instead, "they
turned inward in the hope of personal transformation," an objective that is
basic for the New Age movement.[17]

As the counterculture was receding into the nation's cultural memory,
two other developments—the human potential and holistic health movements—became visible. On one hand, these movements provide an impor-

tant backdrop for the New Age. On the other, they are essential *components* of the New Age, two vital networks of this decentralized movement. They both have focused on some aspect of self-fulfillment, a principal objective of the New Age.

Harriet Mosatche defines the human potential movement (or emotional growth movement) as "an umbrella concept used to encompass many different kinds of therapeutic techniques and offerings. There are group and individual therapies, mental and physical techniques, and various combinations of each whose purposes purport to be enhancement of psychological growth within the person and the breakdown of barriers between people."[18] Like the New Age itself, the human potential movement must be seen as a general rather than specific social movement. As Roy Wallis notes, it consists of a collection of "independent groups, leaders, communication media, etc., which display no common structure of authority or membership" and which manifest a divergence of purpose and practice. Yet these groups and individuals recognize that they have "a common commitment to the attainment of personal growth by self-directed means."[19]

Carl Rasche says that psychoreligiosity is the "use of psychological principles and techniques as surrogates for traditional religious beliefs and practices." According to him, "this is what the Human Potential movement is all about."[20] It is, as Barbara Hargrove points out, a form of "personal salvation through the methods of humanistic psychology."[21]

Though the immediate origins of the human potential movement may be traced to sensitivity training in the late 1940s and the National Training Labs at Bethel, Maine, it has precursors farther back in American history. As Rasche also notes, the human potential movement may be seen as following in the steps of the earlier "mind cure" movement, whose proponents, from Mary Baker Eddy to Norman Vincent Peale, promised "health, wealth, and happiness for confused, lonely, and self-doubting people." At variance with the "mind cure" school in style and rhetoric but not in substance, "the Human Potential movement is a multilayered and eclectic blend of the new clinical psychologies with a dash of watered down Zen Buddhism, Yoga, or other forms of Oriental mysticism." The Christian cast of much "mind cure" thinking is largely absent in the human potential movement, but the basic gospel remains the same: God is within the self; enrichment comes from discovering the self; and the transfiguration of society is through "the reintegration of individual psyches."[22]

290

As an organized body of knowledge, psychology came in the nineteenth century toward the end of the Romantic revolt against the Enlightenment. Psychology in America has developed primarily along the rigorous scientific lines of the behavioral school. But in the human potential movement, psychology has taken up more Romantic and organic themes. Because the Romantics emphasized freedom, spontaneity and feeling, one constant theme in the Romantic movement was inwardness, or absorption in one's own mental and spiritual life. During the 1960s something akin to a new surge of Romanticism extended across America. With it came an emphasis on exploring the frontiers of one's inner life. To turn inward was a way to "turn on." The inner world was seen as good and perhaps even divine.[23]

As Catherine Albanese points out, the new psychologies that encouraged this turning inward were "distinguished in several ways from the therapies of the past." Most important, they did not endeavor so much to heal the mentally ill as to bring ordinary people with usual problems "to the perfection of their capacity for happiness and creativity." Second, while the traditional psychologies had their basis in "the authoritarian model of the relationship between doctor and patient," the new therapies often have stressed different patterns: the community of peer relationships and the self-help techniques, like meditation, of some Eastern religions. Next, while the older psychologies employed a technical, scientific language, the new forms used a somewhat religious vocabulary borrowed from the Eastern faiths. Finally, while the older therapies were seen as temporary processes, the new psychologies were devoted to the cultivation of techniques that should be used for a lifetime.[24]

There are a number of therapies, groups and training programs whose committed participants would regard themselves as part of the broad human potential movement. These include encounter groups, Gestalt awareness training, Transactional Analysis, sensory awareness, primal therapy, bioenergetics, massage, humanistic psychology, psychosynthesis, est, Arica training, transcendental meditation, biofeedback, psychic healing, mind-control training and yoga. These disciplines, organizations and therapies do not function in isolation. In fact, a hallmark of the movement is the extent that they interact, overlap and borrow from each other. Growth centers such as Esalen are at the heart of the movement; organizations like Synanon are more marginal. Of the disciplines, Gestalt therapy probably contains traits that are most characteristic of the movement.[25]

Perhaps the most respected theorist of the human potential movement is Abraham Maslow (1908-70). At the center of his psychology Maslow placed several Romantic themes, especially Jean-Jacques Rousseau's ideas on the natural innocence and goodness of human beings, who need only to be freed from the fetters of social regimen and authority. Thus Maslow did not advocate a restructuring of the socioeconomic system; instead, individuals within it should have their "self-actualizing" capacities enhanced, whereupon the system would reform itself. Self-actualization entailed self-directed action and the full use of one's talents and capacities. For Maslow, the step after self-actualization was a condition that he termed the "peak experience." The peak experience, closely resembling the mystical experiences of several religious traditions, would eliminate an individual's sense of separation from the natural order so that he or she felt at one with the universe and at the same time intensely aware of life all around.[26]

Some aspects of the human potential movement are alien to American culture and may be regarded as Eastern imports. Yet the movement is very American, reflecting some impulses associated with the religious mainstream. First, from the vantage point of numbers, the movement has numerous adherents, penetrating many ranks of society from the professions to popular culture. Second, the human potential movement expresses the perfectionism that has arisen in many areas of American culture—the millennial ideal of a perfect society, Methodist theology, Pietism and the successes of the age of progress. Third, the human potential movement places importance on right feeling, as had revivalism, the Transcendentalists and the metaphysical groups.[27]

Another important aspect of the New Age and its emphasis on personal transformation is the holistic health movement.[28] The pioneer work in this realm occurred in the late 1960s, primarily by the Menninger Foundation and by several individual researchers, and focused on the physiological effects of transcendental meditation and yoga. Nevertheless, this unusual and new approach to health did not become a recognizable subject of study until the mid-1970s.[29]

What is holistic health? As Paul Reisser notes, the holistic health movement defies definition. No single group, organization or type of practice represents this movement. Moreover, it is constantly being reshaped by its practitioners, who include scientists, physicians, osteopaths, chiropractors, sociologists, psychologists, healers, mystics, nurses and laypeople. Organizations that promote or practice holistic health range from large establishments with impressive budgets and facilities to some marginal storefront operations. At its most basic level, the goal of holistic health is not only to treat physical sickness but to provide a comprehensive approach to health, one that cares for the body, mind and spirit.[30]

In many cultures and throughout most of history, diagnosis and cure of physical problems were entrusted to individuals with magical and supernatural connections. For thousands of years mystics, faith healers, gurus and shamans sought to treat illnesses by a variety of procedures, ranging from incision to exorcism. Only in the recent past has the study of the human body and approach to disease been largely removed from a supernatural context. In Western civilization, the scientific method gradually came to dominate the approach to health and disease.[31]

In recent years, the health-care system of the United States has come under attack from a range of critics. It has been seen as too costly, unfair to the poor, sexist, racist and generally inadequate. This attack on Western medicine is but one aspect of a more widespread condemnation of technology. In the holistic health movement, Western medicine is confronted with a new challenge. This movement says that the modern health-care system has lost touch with issues that concern the human soul and spirit, and it seeks to bring these issues back into the practice of medicine. It calls for a radical revolution in our thinking about medicine and disease. Such a revision entails opening up modern medicine to paranormal phenomena and reuniting it with its mystical heritage.[32]

Behind these changes is a worldview similar to that underlying the human potential and New Age movements. This worldview is a loose combination of elements drawn from occultism, mysticism, animism and spiritism, blended with concepts derived from modern paranormal research. Though any method of promoting health or preventing disease has the potential for being holistic, some alternatives to Western medicine are more prevalent than others. Some examples are acupuncture, biofeedback, homeopathy, iridology, a variety of massage and body-work therapies, meditation, and nutritional therapies.[33]

Vision and Beliefs
The foundation of the New Age Movement rests more on a vision and an experience than on a particular belief system. In fact, as a decentralized

movement, it contains contradictory ideas, often articulated by its most prominent spokespersons. As Elliot Miller says, most New Agers would deny the reality of ultimate truth. To them, experience and intuition are the final authorities. "Truth is intensely personal and entirely subjective. Underlying much New Age thinking is a relativistic assumption that anything can be true for the individual, but nothing can be true for everyone." Therefore, the movement should be approached from the vantage point of its goals and ideals rather than by the beliefs it maintains.[34]

As Melton points out, "the central vision of the New Age" is a "radical mystical transformation" on a personal level. The individual awakens to new realities such as the development of new potentials within him- or herself, the experience of psychological or physical healing, the discovery of psychic capabilities, a new view of the universe or an intimate experience within a community.[35] Marilyn Ferguson says that while this personal transformation is a journey, it is usually triggered by a spontaneous mystical or psychic experience, often brought on by participation in psychotechnologies. Psychotechnologies are the methods of biofeedback, meditation, contemporary psychotherapies, self-help networks, seminars such as est and Silva Mind Control, and such systems as Arica, Theosophy and Gurdjieff. These psychotechniques do not contradict reason but transcend it, enabling the individual to place great trust in intuition. The transformed individual now has a new mind that has the potential to help humanity remake itself.[36]

The essence of the New Age is that the vision of the transformed individual is imposed on the world. When a sufficient number of individuals become enlightened, particularly those in positions of influence, they are expected to transform society by means of a decentralized system of networks. Therefore, as Melton writes, "the New Age is ultimately a vision of a transformed world, a heaven on earth, a society in which the problems of today are overcome and a new existence emerges." The power to transform both individuals and society comes from universal energy, which has been given many names—odic force, mana, orgone energy, prana, holy spirit or the healing force.[37]

This vision of transformed individuals remaking society has its parallels in American religion, especially in varieties of the evangelical tradition. To be sure, the resemblances are cultural, pertaining to methodology rather than to theology or substance. Nevertheless, both New Agers and evangelicals believe that the individual must be transformed, one by a mystical experience triggered by a psychotechnique, the other by a conversion through the power of the Holy Spirit.[38] Both groups believe that individuals must be transformed before society can be significantly changed. Both the New Age movement and evangelicalism have a millennial thrust. New Agers optimistically believe that humanity is on the verge of a new age, one in which the current world's problems will be solved. Evangelicalism historically has been divided between pre- and postmillennialism, but both camps envision a future golden age.

This transformationist vision should not be misunderstood. It is not merely social change or the improvement of our current society. According to Robert Burrows, New Agers believe that the collapse of the old age and the birth of a new one "coincides with a radical paradigm shift: a shift in the way reality is perceived." The rationalism so embedded in the Western psyche by Descartes and Newton was the old paradigm. New Agers contend that the new paradigm is heralded by the "new physics"—that is, the "contemporary Western hybrid of the old mysticism." Like the mystics of old, New Agers trace the evils of the social order "to a decidedly nonmystical frame of mind." While the old paradigm has strapped humanity to this world, in the new paradigm the world will break out into infinity, soaring to its highest potential.[39]

Though the New Age movement focuses on the experience of individual transformation and the coming of a new era in human history, most of its adherents do affirm certain concepts and ideas. These beliefs are not uniform among all followers, nor are they criteria for participation in the movement. New Age spirituality, the framework for many of its prominent ideas, is the convergence of East and West. As indicated earlier, the New Age maintains an occult-Eastern mystical worldview, but one that has been made palatable to Western culture. The New Age, as Groothuis points out, "repudiates the world-denying or ascetic approach" so prevalent in Eastern mysticism and the occult. Rather, it prefers a world-affirming, even hedonistic lifestyle in which personal transformation (or enlightenment, as the Eastern religions would say) is "fully compatible with worldly success." In fact, "Western optimism and belief in progress pervade the New Age spirituality—something often foreign to classical Eastern religions." It is this optimism that enables the New Agers to anticipate the transformation of our current world.[40]

When the New Age arrives, unity will prevail, particularly in religion and politics. In this New Age, it is expected that one universal religion will be recognized by most people. This one religion will be highly eclectic, borrowing from all present religious traditions and assuming many different forms. But whatever its various components, the same mystical faith will be the basis of each form. This one universal faith will concentrate on exploration of the inner being, self-knowledge and the continuation of the transformative process that began with the initial entry into the New Age.[41] As a result of this focus on continual transformation, New Agers will proceed on a *sadhana,* a spiritual path. For many, this is to be a lifetime commitment to practices taught by a certain teacher. Actually, it normally takes more than one lifetime to complete this spiritual journey. Thus the belief in karma and reincarnation becomes important for most New Agers as the long-term context in which the individual can complete his or her spiritual progression. Several lifetimes in a physical body will be needed to accomplish the necessary moral and spiritual development.[42]

In respect to their concept of God, most (but not all) New Agers are monistic pantheists. They believe that all is one. Everything that exists consists of one and the same essence or reality. New Agers assume that this ultimate reality is neither dead matter nor unconscious energy. It is Being, Awareness and Bliss. They identify God with the ultimate unifying principle, which binds the whole together, and the power which gives it a dynamic. They regard God and the world as one reality. Other New Agers, however, prefer a form of dualism which regards the spiritual entity as ultimately good and real and matter as evil, something that should not be in the spiritual-mystical life. In respect to Christ, many New Agers separate the historic person Jesus of Nazareth from the Christ or the Christ-consciousness that Jesus attained. Jesus, Krishna, Buddha and other great religious leaders have been the most unmistakable bearers of the Divine or Christ-principle. In the New Age movement, individual worship usually centers on meditation and other transformative practices intended to increase one's self-awareness. On the more corporate level, New Age worship is closest to that of Sufism, which respects all religions while attempting to discover the understanding of the cosmos that provides the basis for each faith.[43]

The root idea of the New Age—oneness, unity and wholeness—extends beyond its religious views. In the New Age there is to be not only one universal religion but also, as Melton indicates, "an allegiance to the planet and the human race, which will supersede loyalties to . . . nation, race, or religion." As a consequence, important concerns will be peace, ecology, models for cooperative living, natural foods, processes of physical and mental healing, and global politics. In this concern for the planet and for social change, New Agers have set themselves apart from "more traditional occultists who tended to avoid social activism."[44]

In keeping with its vision, New Age politics is essentially transformationist. Marilyn Ferguson says, "The political system needs to be transformed, not reformed." Such transformation requires not merely a change of political structure but a new consciousness. Traditional political ideologies must be transcended so that a new political worldview can be developed.[45]

What is the New Age political agenda? Ferguson describes New Age politics as neither left nor right, but calls it a kind of radical center. It is "not neutral, not middle-of-the road," but instead claims "a view of the whole road." What this means is not completely clear. Actually, the New Age appears to have spiritualized a left-of-center political *agenda,* while favoring a right-of-center *approach* to political issues. As the radicalism of the counterculture declined, many political activists turned inward for solutions and spiritualized their agenda. Thus, many New Agers still psychologically struggle for peace, nuclear disarmament, ecological issues, male and female equality, and internationalism. These objectives are not to be achieved by means of a strong centralized government but through a more right-of-center approach—decentralized networks.[46]

Despite the New Age movement's disapproval of political centralization, some of its adherents speak of a one-world political order, which will be led by transformed individuals and thus will be hierarchical in nature. Though the New Age contends for a new economic order that would redress the current unequal distribution of wealth, its adherents are generally prosperous and success-oriented.[47]

In the 1980s the New Age appeared to be gaining momentum and visibility. Is it merely the latest passing religious fad? On many specifics, it may be. But, as Melton contends, since the New Age movement "represents an updating of the longstanding occult and metaphysical tradition in American life," its future may be bright. Also, it has emerged in America at a time when the Christian tradition is less dominant and the climate is quite receptive to occult and mystical ideas. While obvious occultism is still not palatable to many moderns, the New Age packages its occult philosophy in culturally attractive wrappings. It enlists science, psychology, medicine and other aspects of established culture to further its claims. In keeping with the occult tradition, the New Age views itself as "scientific" and sees its world-view as supported by the funding of science. Also, the social status of many New Agers is of considerable help. They are often of an affluent social group, and they use their influence to further the objectives of the movement.[48]

19

Psychospiritual
or Self-Improvement
Groups

Since the 1960s, millions of Americans have embarked on a journey of self-discovery and self-improvement. According to Ron Enroth, a multitude of new mind-body therapies have sprung up and "blended into the stream of America's consumerism in recent years." Some, such as swimming, aerobics, jogging, cycling and weight loss, are largely aimed at improving overall health through physical fitness. Others, such as bioenergetics and rolfing, focus on mind-body interaction, emphasizing physical and psychological treatments that unlock physical tensions. Still others, such as Scientology, est and Silva Mind Control, concentrate on psychospiritual concerns.[1]

This new world of personal growth has become subject to much abuse and exploitation. The programs emphasizing physical fitness, whose results are more subject to verification, are not nearly as prone to abuse as are the psychological, emotional and spiritual therapies. In their longing for self-improvement, as Flo Conway and Jim Siegelman say, America's searchers have had no way of "interpreting their experiences." They have not been able to separate "the truly spiritual from the sham, or of distinguishing genuine personal growth from artificially induced sensation." As pointed out in the book *Cults and Cons,* the message of these therapies is often something like this: "You are not now OK, but after you take our course, participate in this group, et cetera, you will be OK."[2]

Consciousness Revolution

Many of these psychological, emotional and spiritual therapies are part of a large, culturally pervasive movement called the consciousness revolution. This movement may turn out to be the twentieth-century psychoreligious counterpart of some of America's past religious awakenings. Kenneth Woodward says that in broad terms "the consciousness revolution represents a convergence of modern Western psychotherapy with the ancient disciplines of Eastern religions." The movement endeavors to put "seekers progressively in touch with themselves, with others, with nature and . . . with the fundamental forces of the cosmos." Its practitioners, methods and rhetoric run the gamut from the serious to the sham. The movement's ranks include thousands of psychotherapists and psychologists and legions of gurus, swamis and babas. Moreover, the movement inevitably has "attracted a sleazy new breed of self-anointed 'facilitators' who tamper dangerously with other people's psyches"—plus some charlatans who falsely feed unrealistic hopes for health, happiness and holiness.[3]

The consciousness revolution relates to several aspects of American culture. It reinforces several traditional American beliefs, especially the certainty of human progress, the inherent goodness of humanity and the innate alterability of character. Jacob Needleman says that "the new consciousness takes the constitutional right to the pursuit of happiness and gives it a metaphysical twist." The idea of happiness has been transformed "from getting what you want into changing who you are." Behavioral scientist Jean Houston "sees the exploration of consciousness as the latest new frontier in American cultural history." As Americans put astronauts into outer space, we are now launching "psychenauts into inner space."[4]

Others, however, see the consciousness movement as being hastened by a decline of faith in family, church and government. Encounter groups meet personal needs by offering instant intimacy in a society where mobility works against lasting relationships. Author Peter Marin sees the new consciousness therapies as but an aspect of the "new narcissism." They are a way "to avoid the demands of the world." The self replaces community, relationships, neighbors and God. Psychiatrist Perry London says that body therapies "service people's sensory needs in a culture where leisure is so prolific that it must be made elegantly meaningful to be deeply savored." Theologian Albert Outler sees the "loss of the sacred" in our society as generating an excess of self-centered substitutes, ranging from "the inner directedness" of Carl Rogers and Abraham Maslow to the "hard-eyed ego-centrism of Werner Erhard."[5] The mystical elements of the consciousness revolution offer an experience of the sacred that has largely vanished from many of the churches of America.

One popular handbook on the consciousness revolution claims that in North America there are more than eight thousand ways to "awaken." This estimate may be an exaggeration. Nevertheless, as Woodward claims, "the consciousness revolution, once confined to the youthful counterculture, has mushroomed into a mass movement, particularly popular with the more affluent individuals of society who can afford the time and money to develop their inner depths."[6] Ranging from inexpensive yoga classes at the YMCA to luxurious "awareness" cruises in the Caribbean, a vast network of therapeutic outlets is available to millions of Americans who are dissatisfied with their lives, looking for a direct experience with God, or just plain bored. The movement has "produced a lucrative market for packaged programs" designed to produce enlightenment. A partial list includes Silva Mind Control, est, transcendental meditation, Scientology, Synanon and Arica training. These programs have promised a "new you to anyone who can pay for it."[7]

Much of this discussion on the consciousness revolution is reminiscent of what has been said previously about the New Age and human potential movements. These three movements closely overlap and are indebted to each other. Self-fulfillment is the objective of all three. Though the human potential movement is an essential part of the New Age, the two are not synonymous. The New Age is a broader movement. While building on the objective of self-fulfillment, it has other goals as well, including the vision of a new age in which the entire world takes another path. It also tends to be more mystical and occultic than the human potential movement, though these elements are actually present in both.

The consciousness revolution is more closely related to the human potential movement. Indeed, it grew out of the human potential movement, and the two share many characteristics. But the consciousness revolution is more eclectic, drawing on an even wider range of sources. Aspects of the consciousness revolution appear to have more spiritual, mystical and cosmic dimensions. The religious segments of the consciousness revolution most closely relate to transpersonal psychology, which is an outgrowth of the human potential movement.[8]

In the 1950s Abraham Maslow and others challenged the two dominant styles of psychoanalysis—Freudian analysis, which regards human behavior as largely determined by deep-seated biological drives, and behaviorism, which holds that people can be reduced effectively to a collection of stimulus and response mechanisms. As John Allan points out, Maslow established a "third force" in psychiatry: humanistic psychology. He based this new approach on the "assumption that the human being is basically not a collection of neuroses nor a bundle of conditioned reflexes, but good and instinctively inclined towards improving himself." The focus of humanistic psychology is not on treating the mentally ill but on helping the well improve themselves, largely by means of peak experiences that transcend the psychological barriers to self-improvement.[9]

As might be expected, humanistic psychology gave birth to a "fourth force": transpersonal psychology. This "fourth force" takes as its area of study those points at which the human consciousness extends into a mystical union with "cosmic consciousness." It began with the belief that humanity has a spiritual nature, and that no psychological explanation of human nature could be complete without taking into account this dimension. "Transpersonal psychology believes that within everyone exists a center of energy which is the core of one's existence." This core has been called "the Self, the Soul, the Atman." It is the key to one's growth, awareness and expansion, and the job of the transpersonal psychologist is to help this central core to "integrate itself and release its energy." In doing this, the psychologist may use "religious and esoteric techniques, and the perspectives of yoga, Zen or Buddhism."[10]

Is the consciousness revolution a religious movement? At its furthest frontier, as represented by transpersonal psychology, the consciousness revolution can be regarded as at least a quasi-religious movement. Woodward argues that "it brings Western psychotherapy 180 degrees from Freud's rejection of immortality as an illusion to an almost Buddhist rejection of the concrete world as illusion." A sense of the transcendent is present in transpersonal psychology, but the perspective is different from that of the Judeo-Christian tradition. One may have a direct experience with the divine without any necessary reference to God or revelation. As in the New Age, the emphasis is on me. I am the catalyst of change for myself. I am the focal point of my own universe. I have the potential to be divine, creating and experiencing my own reality. As a cultural movement, "the consciousness revolution feeds on the romantic notion that inner experience alone can transform reality" and that anyone can shape his or her life "into a perfect work of art." As a religious phenomenon, "it signals a return to gnosticism, which always disparages common humanity in the name of higher truths."[11]

There is much overlap among the Eastern religions, the New Age and human potential movements, and the Theosophical-occult groups. Thus, many of the religious bodies so far encountered in this study can be placed under the broad umbrellas of the New Age and human potential movements and are also part of the consciousness revolution. They have been placed in different categories in this study, however, because their roots are found in specific Eastern religions and metaphysical groups. Transcendental Meditation, the Rajneesh Foundation, Zen Buddhism, Divine Light Mission, Sufism, Meher Baba, Theosophical and occult bodies, and New Thought metaphysics have in varying degrees been associated with the milieu of the New Age and human potential movements.[12] There are, however, groups in this milieu that have their origin more in Western bodies than in Eastern religions. A partial list would include Scientology, Silva Mind Control, est and Synanon. Arica and Eckankar have been considerably influenced by Eastern thought, but they are eclectic enough that they should not be regarded as Eastern bodies.

The Church of Scientology
Some observers would not regard Scientology as a religion. Ruth Tucker tells us that the Church of Scientology, like Unity, does not require new members to terminate their previous church relationships. "Attending church services is not a high priority." As with many New Age-oriented groups, the emphasis is on "self improvement or self actualization, not on worship." In fact, Scientology church buildings consist of classrooms and offices. But if one allows for an expansive definition of religion, Scientology, along with many of the psychospiritual groups, can be classified as a religion. Scientology bills itself as an "applied religious philosophy." It cannot be placed in any exclusive category such as science, religion, philosophy or technique, but combines aspects of them all. Thus, as Gordon Melton points out, Scientology must be seen as "one of the few genuinely new religions to originate in the United States during the twentieth century." And it is certainly a controversial religion. During the nearly forty years of Scientology's existence, it has been in continuous conflict with the government and other opponents.[13]

Though Scientology is unique, it did not develop in a vacuum. It displays a direct continuity with many themes in American culture, especially in its interest in technology. In particular, Scientology follows a long American tradition of attempting to legitimate religion through science, or to market religion as scientific. In fact, Scientology began as a therapy and evolved into a religion. Its founders understood that in a predominantly secular culture, ultimate human concerns could be addressed in a "therapeutic" and "scientific" way rather than from the usual religious perspective. Though the core themes and values of Scientology evolved from an Eastern and occult worldview, they come to the public in a Western technological package. In this Scientology follows a line from the medieval alchemists to such nineteenth-century groups as New Thought and Christian Science. In fact, even turn-of-the-century evangelical dispensationalists based their methods of interpreting Scripture on a Baconian system of science.[14]

Frank Flinn calls Scientology a technological Buddhism. A Scientologist, he claims, "is a first cousin to the Buddhist." The basic Scientological term "clear" approximates "the Buddhist concept of *bodhi,* which describes 'the one awake' or 'enlightened one' " who has gained release from the entanglement of existence and illusion. The process of becoming "clear" will be described later, but suffice it to say that it resembles a Buddhist step transmuted by Western technology.[15]

Scientology itself has given rise to many groups and practices. The Process, Dianology, Abilitism and Amprinistics were early, short-lived schismatic offshoots. While Scientology and the human potential movement do not acknowledge their connections, they have some close ties. In fact, the origins of some human potential groups can be traced directly to their founders' involvement with Scientology. Mind Dynamics, est, Lifespring and Silva Mind Control are indebted to Scientology's teachings. More important, as Brooks Alexander claims, "Scientology began packaging and marketing Human Potential concepts." Scientology, and its predecessor Dianetics, began a pattern of emphasis and development that has been the hallmark of many human potential teachings—that is, addressing ultimate human concerns from the vantage of science and therapy instead of religion. In addition, Scientology has inspired some occult movements such as Eckankar.[16]

The history of Scientology is closely tied to that of its founder, L. Ron Hubbard (1911-86). Elron, as he was affectionately known by his followers, occupies a place in the mind of Scientologists parallel to Joseph Smith's in Mormonism and Mary Baker Eddy's in Christian Science. Many Scientologists venerate him. In fact, Hubbard managed to create a personality cult that seemed to thrive on his eccentricities. His pictures and quotations from his writings decorate the walls of Scientology meeting places. In matters of Scientology belief and practice, Hubbard was regarded as infallible during his lifetime. Outsiders have contrasting views of him. Some see him as an earnest, honest, sincere guy. To others he was the greatest con man of the century.[17]

Hubbard was born in Nebraska but grew up in rural Montana. His father's naval career took the Hubbard family to the Far East for long tours of duty in China and Japan. Here young Ron encountered several Eastern influences that helped form his emerging philosophy. An even more recognizable influence came when a navy doctor exposed the young boy's mind to Freudian ideas. After returning to the United States, he attended George Washington University for a year (1931-32). After this he led a scientific expedition to the jungles of Central America and began a successful career as a writer. Though he wrote in several genres, he is best known for his science fiction.[18]

At the start of World War II, Hubbard began his service in the navy. According to Scientology sources, he was wounded in the South Pacific and spent almost a year in the hospital. Critically ill and crippled, and twice pronounced dead by doctors, he recovered to live a healthy life. During the years after his recovery, Hubbard synthesized the ideas that later became Dianetics and finally developed into Scientology. Hubbard's life had powerfully influenced the views he was about to propose. It seemed to show a pattern like that of ancient and medieval shamans or cult leaders. He had an unusual childhood, several near-death experiences, a powerful imagination, an expansive worldview and wide travel. Somewhat related to Hubbard's "bigger-than-life" image are his claims of exaggerated achievements, such as a Ph.D. from Sequoia University (a nonaccredited diploma mill) and an expertise in nuclear engineering in spite of having dropped out of college after his sophomore year.[19]

According to George Braswell, in the late 1940s Hubbard's writings attracted the attention of John Campbell, editor of the popular *Astounding Science Fiction* magazine. Campbell believed that Hubbard's ideas and techniques on mind and psychological problems had cured him of a disorder. Thereafter Campbell used his magazine to promote Hubbard's ideas. By 1950, Hubbard had published *Dianetics: The Modern Science of Mental Health.* He also established the Hubbard Dianetic Research Foundation, with headquarters in Elizabeth, New Jersey, and branches in several other cities. Hubbard was becoming popular. *Dianetics* became a national best-seller in 1951, and his therapeutic techniques were in demand. In fact, many informal and independent Dianetics groups sprang up around the country.[20]

After a brief period of growth, difficulties began to arise. The psychiatric and medical communities attacked the practice of Dianetics, denouncing it as potentially dangerous. Furthermore, a host of independent Dianetics groups began to take liberties with Hubbard's thought, combining his ideas with Eastern and occult beliefs and techniques. Hubbard soon found out that he had lost considerable control over his Dianetics practice. Also, as with most popular fads, interest in Dianetics began to wane about the same time.[21]

According to David Bromley and Anson Shupe, Hubbard met these challenges head-on in two ways. First, "he purged his movement of 'amateurs,' 'heretics,' and 'revisionists,' consolidating control . . . over just who would practice Dianetics and how Dianetics would be practiced." Second, believing that Dianetics as a quasi-psychotherapy was on a decline, Hubbard added to it a number of new elements. In 1952 he "created Scientology, a new therapeutic system that incorporated the ideas of reincarnation, extra-terrestrial life, and ultimately a spiritual dimension," which had been lacking in the more psychological Dianetics. Hubbard became convinced that Scientology now possessed enough of a spiritual element to move it "from the category of psychic science into the category of religion." Therefore, in 1953 Hubbard incorporated the Church of Scientology, and in 1955 the first church was established.[22]

Once established, the church grew rapidly, expanding first in the English-speaking world and then throughout Europe by the late 1960s. In 1959 Hubbard established his residence and the church's headquarters at Saint Hill Manor in Sussex, England. But trouble often follows growth. With the establishment of an international church, a global network of members, financial investments and training centers, the church became involved in conflicts with tax authorities. Most serious was the revocation of the tax-exempt status of the Founding Scientology Church in Washington, D.C., and the Food and Drug Administration's seizure of what it claimed to be the church's unapproved instruments for the diagnosis and treatment of disease.[23]

As a consequence of these problems, the church's organization underwent changes. The year 1966 saw the establishment of the office of the Guardian. This office had the twofold task of protecting Scientology from attacks by its external critics and maintaining correct teachings and practice within the church. Shortly thereafter, Hubbard adopted a new behind-the-scenes role within the church, resigning all official positions and devoting his life to the further research and development of Scientology. A ship was purchased and renamed *Apollo,* and Hubbard moved on board, making it his research facility. In the same year the Sea Org (organization), an elite social group made up of the church's most committed members, was established.[24]

The ensuing years saw further developments in the church's organization. Local churches and missions chartered by the Church of Scientology offered the basic Scientology courses. Some even offered work leading to the state of "clear." Advanced work, however, had to be taken elsewhere. Research for more advanced levels of Scientological work took place at the Sea Org. Other organizations, currently located in Los Angeles and Clearwater, Florida, were created to run and operate the advanced courses.[25]

Problems continued to plague the Church of Scientology and its founder. The Internal Revenue Service demanded some six million dollars in taxes and penalties for the years 1970 through 1974, claiming that the income in question had not been used for church purposes. But for a while problems with the government took a back seat to conflicts with the public. Several books attacking the church were published. The church considered some so harmful and libelous as to merit lawsuits, the most famous being *The Scandal of Scientology* by Paulette Cooper. Also, a number of former members filed suits against the church, claiming that it swindled or even kidnapped them. Some of these suits and problems were related to Scientology's alleged methods of controlling its members and preventing defections from the church. Disloyal members, known as "Suppressive Persons," supposedly were threatened verbally and even physically; they were labeled as criminals, communists or sexual deviants. Allegations were made of physical beatings and forced incarcerations.[26]

Gordon Melton says that possibly the most scandalous events in the church's controversial history began in 1977. The FBI raided the Washington, D.C., and Los Angeles churches and seized many files and documents.

They produced information indicating that the church maintained files "on people it considered to be actually or potentially unfriendly and that there had been various attempts to infiltrate anti-cult organizations." Supposedly, Hubbard had an espionage system that included over five thousand covert agents. As a result of this raid and other investigations, a number of top Scientologists, including Hubbard's third wife, were convicted of theft of government documents and sent to prison during the early 1980s. This entire episode did much to destroy the church's credibility.[27]

To compound these legal problems, Hubbard vanished in March 1980. Some were sure that either he had died or he had become mentally incapacitated. The Church of Scientology was confused over the whereabouts of its founder at a time when it had many legal and tax difficulties. Hubbard's son, who in 1972 had changed his name from L. Ron Hubbard to Ronald E. De Wolf, took steps to have his father declared legally missing so that his assets might be frozen. However, in the early 1980s Hubbard thwarted this plan by reappearing and publishing a series of bestselling novels.[28]

Throughout these controversies with both its public and private critics, the church has complained that it has been unjustly singled out. As Melton points out, the church has responded aggressively to its critics. It had directed social action "toward correcting abuses in areas of medical practice, particularly the mental health field." The church accused the government of an "anti-Scientology conspiracy" and even attacked the IRS in a series of advertisements in *The New York Times*. Over seventy lawsuits have been filed against the IRS. Throughout controversies, the church continued to experience growth. In 1985 it reported about three million members worldwide. This figure includes anyone who has been served by the church in recent years. Active membership is estimated to be about fifty thousand. The group also boasts of seven hundred centers in sixty-five countries.[29]

In the mid-1980s the church attempted to change its negative image by "going mainstream" and adopting a less confrontational stance. One method has been the attempt to recruit celebrities and wealthy professionals through a web of consulting groups that often hide their ties to Scientology. These front organizations have directed their activities toward health care, education, mental health, and drug and alcohol rehabilitation. Scientology also retains a public relations company to help eliminate its fringe-group image. Along with a number of TV ads plugging Hubbard's books, full-page ads calling Scientology a "philosophy" have appeared in such magazines as *Business Week* and *Newsweek*. Since 1985 at least a dozen Hubbard books, printed by a church company, have made bestseller lists. The church has been accused of purchasing large quantities of its own books from retail stores to push the titles onto bestseller lists.[30]

The goals of Scientology are twofold and reflect its relationship with the human potential and New Age movements. Like them, it seeks to improve the well-being of the individual. By the hundreds of thousands, people have come to Scientology searching for improved mental and physical health, a better memory, a higher IQ, a more attractive personality and stronger willpower. Scientology also has a vision for a new world. The ultimate goal of Scientology is a "clear" planet. But this can come only when enough individuals become "clear"—that is, have no neuroses or problems. In this goal, Scientology shows itself to be a New Age group. The new age is to be ushered in when a sufficient number of individuals have been transformed. The earliest indication of a clear planet would be the elimination of crime, war, insanity, drugs and pollution.[31]

What are the beliefs and practices of Scientology? The creed of the Church of Scientology has little to say about the church's unusual teachings, but according to Melton it "reads something like a bill of rights," emphasizing the conditions under which people can best function. The creed stresses "the essential goodness of human beings and the basic drive for survival," two basic assumptions that underlie nearly all the specifics of Scientology's beliefs. The ideas and practices of Scientology can best be understood when the movement is examined in two phases: Dianetics and Scientology.[32]

Dianetics was the scientific phase of the movement. Bromley and Shupe say that its original concern was with "engrams," which were regarded as the source of all problems. Engrams are "psychic scars that inhibit full adult potential and operate much the same as Sigmund Freud's repressed desires that result in neuroses and psychoses or Carl Jung's complexes." Hubbard made a distinction between the analytic and reactive "minds." The analytic mind resembles Freud's conscious mind, while the reactive mind is analogous to Freud's unconscious. The analytic mind, unless upset, functions with precision. Traumatic experiences cause engrams, the sensory impressions of the event, to be embedded in the unconscious or reactive mind. These recorded engrams become the source of most mental and mind-body difficulties until they are removed. Some engrams are produced while the child is still in the womb. A variety of things can produce them: the husband's beating his pregnant wife, violent sexual intercourse, even the mother's sneezing or constipation.[33]

Engrams can be removed through the process of "auditing." The patient, designated as a "preclear," goes to a Hubbard-trained therapist called an auditor. The auditor uses a question-answer therapy process to help the patient look for forgotten shock incidents. The auditor throws out key words, and the preclear's subtle reaction identifies the engram. When the patient has confronted and relived the engram and the negative impressions that it conjures up, it is pushed out of the reactive mind. At this point physical and mental problems disappear, and the preclear is on his or her way to being clear. Though Dianetics resembles psychoanalysis, it goes further, taking the preclear back beyond early childhood and exposing experiences that supposedly occurred in the womb.[34]

In the early months of the Dianetics therapy, hundreds of thousands of people—many of them well-educated and intelligent—were drawn into the movement. Hubbard became nationally prominent. *Dianetics* sold over a million copies. But then problems began. The goal of Dianetic therapy was for an individual to reach the level of "clear," named for the button on a calculator that erases all previous calculations. But few clears were produced during the 1950s. A few individuals claimed to have incredible experiences, ranging from extra-long lives to the regrowth of extracted teeth in the gums to unprecedented resistance to common viruses. However, evidence to support these claims was scanty.[35]

Dianetics claimed to be primarily scientific. This meant that its lofty premises must stand up to tests of verification, but that did not happen. Thus, necessity forced Hubbard into the realm of religion, where claims do not necessarily have to be verified. Hubbard then moved down the path of the supernatural and the occult, claiming to have discovered new truth.[36]

Scientology is the supernatural or occult phase of the movement. According to Bromley and Shupe, "the creation of Scientology added a cosmic dimension . . . that elevated Dianetics from (in its critics' view) a bastardized psychoanalysis to a candidate for religious status." In *Scientology: The Fundamentals of Thought,* Hubbard revealed a new truth: the existence of Thetans. John Newport describes the Thetan as "the real you" as over against the body or mind. Thetans are spiritual properties of immortal heavenly beings who lived eons ago and are now trapped in human bodies. Thus, at the core a person is "a fallen immortal god or Thetan." When a Thetan enters an individual's body, "it brings with it all the engrams of millions of years of previous existence. Thetans are reincarnated over trillions of years." As a result, one must clear out or eradicate the engrams of past lives. Such engrams may have come from a falling off the wooden horse in Troy, a blow received from a medieval knight, a gunshot wound during the French Revolution or a dramatic death in a sinking ocean liner.[37]

The goal of Dianetics was to clear the engrams from one's current life, including the time spent in the womb. Attaining this objective meant that one was a "clear." The goal of Scientology, however, is to erase the engrams of a million earlier lifetimes. If a person achieves this new aim, he or she will be an Operating Thetan (OT). Such a position means that one has broken the shackles of this universe and has almost supernatural powers. The sociologists Rodney Stark and William Bainbridge argue that "clear" (and by extension OT) is "not a state of personal development at all, but a social status conferring honor" within the Scientology system and "demanding certain kinds of behavior from the person labeled clear."[38]

Many Eastern religions have taught the innate divinity of humanity. But Hubbard insisted that he alone had discovered the spiritual technology to unshackle this divinity and help people recover their heritage as gods. In the 1950s Scientology introduced a new device for liberating the enslaved Thetan. This instrument, called an E-meter, measures the extent to which an object resists an electrical current.[39]

In the auditing session, the preclear with troublesome engrams holds a can in each hand. These cans are fastened to the dial of a machine, through which a small amount of electricity passes to each can. The auditor asks the preclear questions regarding problem areas. If a particular question excites emotion in the preclear, the needle will fluctuate. The patient is then to bring into the open the engram shock of this past experience. When the needle stops moving, this particular engram is erased from the preclear's unconscious mind. Auditing is the central practice of Scientology and is akin to confession in the Catholic Church.[40]

After much time and expense, it is possible to eradicate all engrams in this life. Preclears go from stage to stage until eventually they are clear. But the process does not have to end here. There are several levels beyond clear. The ultimate goal for anyone going beyond clear is to become an Operating

Thetan. To locate within oneself and dissolve engrams that are billions of years old requires the efforts of a dedicated Scientologist. The Operating Thetan not only is free from all problems but also has supernatural powers, including the ability to have "out-of-body" experiences, practice clairvoyance, and even create the substances making up the universe, or MEST (matter, energy, space, time). Beyond bringing individuals to the clear or Operating Thetan status, Scientology would like to transform the world. This objective will be achieved only when the planet is "clear," a task that only Scientology can accomplish.[41]

Scientology appeals to a certain type of person. Like most of the self-improvement and psychospiritual groups, Scientology appears to attract people who have failed to achieve their social and intellectual aspirations. One must have money to enroll in a Scientology program. It is expensive, costing more than college tuition. The preclear must also be willing to embark on a concentrated course of study that is closely controlled by a leader.[42] Moreover, Scientology draws those seeking Eastern-occult spirituality in the garb of Western technology and psychology.

In Scientology one can recognize a major theme and a minor theme of American culture: fascination with technology and, to a lesser extent, with the alternative spiritual tradition. The entire objective of Scientology is to move candidates through its levels, self-discoveries and breakthroughs to a maximum restoration of spiritual oneness. Perhaps the most distinctive aspect of this new religion is that it spells out the steps and techniques by which one progresses from the mundane to the mystical. Many individuals find the current American religious scene too murky and ill-defined. They are looking for clear signposts along the path of their spiritual quest. Scientology meets this need by precisely outlining and defining nearly everything. It sees itself as a "spiritual technology." In a unique way Scientology incorporates much from Eastern religious teachings, science fiction concepts, modern psychological terms and basic occult ideas.[43]

Scientology's current status is somewhat paradoxical. While the church has size and organizational strength, it faces many challenges. Hubbard's death has raised questions about its leadership. The current leader of Scientology is David Miscavige, a second-generation church member and a high-school dropout. Though many cults fail to outlast their founder, Scientology has prospered since Hubbard's death in 1986. The net worth of the church and its front organizations has increased significantly, and membership has risen. Yet the church has been sued over a number of issues including fraud, extortion, coercion, capital flight and the illegal practice of medicine. A number of foreign governments (e.g., Canada, Spain, France, Italy and Germany) have moved vigorously against the organization's activities. Moreover, recent research into Hubbard's life and accomplishments has challenged the truth of his claims regarding college studies, travels and wartime combat experience. Thus, despite much success, clouds of dissension, embattlement and legal controversy hang over the church's future.[44]

Est (the Forum)

During the 1970s and 1980s hundreds of thousands of people testified of dramatic changes in their lives. They reported that they had solved marital problems, lost weight without strenuous efforts, eliminated physical problems, established better relationships with people, improved their employment and as a result felt better about God, sex and themselves. Most of these individuals credit Werner Erhard and his demanding sixty-hour training program, formerly called est.[45]

What is est? The word, when spelled with lower-case letters, refers to Erhard Seminars Training, an organization that is now officially known as the Forum. *Est* is also Latin for "it is," two little words that have considerable meaning for the movement. Est may be the ultimate self-improvement method. Kenneth Woodward claims that Erhard Seminars Training is "the *Reader's Digest* of the consciousness movement—a distillation of every self-help technique from Dale Carnegie to Zen, packaged for quick consumption."[46] Psychologist Herb Hamsher has called it "one of the most powerful therapeutic experiences yet devised."[47]

Est is no ordinary California cult. Rather, as John Clark points out, it is "a form of secular salvation." It is "secular" because it is not identified with any formal religion. In fact, est denies being a religion at all. Yet est does propound a worldview and does have religious overtones. Since its purpose is to alter one's epistemology and instill a monistic or pantheistic belief in impersonal divinity, est qualifies as religious in the expansive use of the term. "Est even brings 'salvation' in the sense of deliverance from difficulty, not in the sense of redemption from original sin" as in the orthodox Christian story. Clark compares the est process with the Christian revival. Though the doctrines are quite different, the actual results are on the surface similar. "The est trainer convinces you that your life does not work . . . and then offers you transformation," while the revivalist points out your sin and offers you salvation. In either case, "the release is experienced by acceptance of what is already there, not by embarking on a discipline."[48]

Yet est is more than a powerful therapy or a religion. It is also a multimillion-dollar educational corporation. Est began in 1971, and in its first ten years it trained over 325,000 people in the United States, Europe, Asia and the Middle East. Much has been written about est, including over five hundred magazine articles and more than a dozen books, each selling over a million copies. Est operates nationally with the efficiency of a crack brigade and shows promise for continued expansion. As one of the New Age and human potential groups, est was suited to the climate of the eighties. With the waning of the idealism of the counterculture, est was right at home with narcissism. In an age when self-improvement has taken on the dimensions of a quasi-religion, est has expanded rapidly.[49]

Est's growth and popularity are in part due to the type of people it attracts. Along with most New Age groups, it appeals to the upwardly mobile, those who may have something in life but want more. There are no est churches, but that doesn't stop the evangelistic efforts of est's fanatical followers. The message of est is circulated primarily by word of mouth. Because many est graduates are in education, business and communications, the philosophy of the movement has spread rapidly. Erhard says that "the real thrust and goal of est is to put 'it' into education." Apparently this effort is paying off. Approximately 15 percent of the individuals trained at est seminars are in education. Moreover, est has received federal funding to teach its ideas at the elementary-school level—to both teachers and students.[50]

Like many New Age groups, est is making a determined effort to affect American society. Est's strategy for achieving this objective is to influence the nation's key institutions and to pull important people into the movement. In addition to focusing on education, Erhard has projected est into the law-enforcement field and has been teaching both criminals and police. He has a particular desire to influence the clergy, offering them a 50-percent discount to attend his seminars.[51]

The list of prestigious people connected with est is impressive. Graduates of its seminars include such celebrities as Joanne Woodward, Jerry Rubin, Yoko Ono, Polly Bergen, Carly Simon and Olympic gold medalist John

Curry. Singer John Denver wrote a song about est and even called Erhard a "god." On est's advisory boards have been such important professionals as several Warner Brothers executives, a president of NBC Radio, a vice president for Coca-Cola, a deputy mayor of New York City, an administrator for the Federal Energy Administration and other high-ranking executives. In addition, est has been endorsed and even joined by prominent lawyers, physicians and psychologists.[52]

Where did this unusual and successful movement come from? Any answer to this question must begin with the life story of the founder of est. Werner Erhard was born John Paul (Jack) Rosenberg in 1935 in Philadelphia. His father was Jewish but converted to his mother's Episcopal faith. In 1952 his formal education ended when he graduated from high school. After high school, Rosenberg held jobs in various fields, including construction and car sales, and married his high-school girlfriend. They had four children.[53]

When he was twenty-four, Rosenberg tired of responsibility and abandoned his family, taking off with a woman named Ellen, who later became his second wife. This marriage produced three children. On the way to St. Louis one day, Rosenberg decided to take on a new identity, changing his name to Werner Erhard. He pieced this name together from the names of two prominent Germans, the first from a physicist and the last from an ex-chancellor.[54]

Erhard spent the next few years in Washington State and California, engaged in sales work and studying the techniques of the consciousness revolution. These activities helped to shape his future. He was responsible for training and supervising salespeople, an experience from which he would later draw for est. He tried many of the new consciousness techniques on the people he trained. During this time, Erhard's psychospiritual and occult involvement was extensive. He was closely associated with Scientology and Mind Dynamics, an enterprise utilizing self-hypnosis mind control to develop psychic power. In addition, Erhard studied or became involved in telepathy, abilitism, Zen Buddhism, Subud, hypnosis, martial arts, yoga, Gestalt, Silva Mind Control, Dale Carnegie, psychocybernetics, encounter therapy, transpersonal psychology and more.[55]

One day as Erhard was driving on a freeway near the Golden Gate Bridge, he had a Damascus Road experience. In one flash of insight, he claims, he saw what was right and wrong with his life. He became aware that his life was not working and that he was the source of his own difficulties. At a later time he summarized the insight with this statement: "What is, is, and what was, was, and what isn't, isn't." Est, meaning "it is," began with this experience. Est is the result of Erhard's earlier research into the previously mentioned psychospiritual-occult disciplines and his "conversion" experience.[56]

From such humble beginnings, est mushroomed into one of the most successful of the self-improvement/psychospiritual groups of the 1970s and 1980s. Though est has serious critics in both the religious and the psychological communities, scores of people have testified that it has dramatically transformed their lives.[57] On an individual level, Erhard's charismatic, hypnotic personality has catapulted him up the ladder of success. He maintains a lifestyle befitting a monarch. He works and lives in two magnificent houses, drives a Mercedes and flies leased planes. He claims to have summarized his lifestyle and philosophy on his license plate: "SO WUT." Despite his avowedly casual approach to life, though, he has continued to research and develop his controversial approach to self-improvement.[58]

The chief focus of the est organization is an intensive sixty-hour seminar held in the convention centers of major hotels across the country. Some 250 to 300 people attend each training session over two consecutive weekends. The goal of the seminar is for the participants to "get it." The price for getting it in the mid-eighties was five hundred dollars per head—a price that brings $100,000 to $120,000 (less expenses) into the coffers of est for each seminar.[59]

Est training is designed to create an environment in which individuals are forced to experience their inner selves in a way that radically alters all previous conceptions of self and the world. In the words of Erhard, "We want nothing short of a total transformation. . . . All we want is to change the notion of who you are."[60] The official objective of est training, says Erhard, is to transform one's ability "to experience living so that the situations you have been trying to change or have been putting up with, clear up just in the process of life itself."[61]

Est utilizes several psychologically powerful and often devastating techniques to accomplish this transformation. These methods, as Stanley Dokupil and Brooks Alexander point out, are devised to strip from the trainees "every facade, 'game,' belief or mechanism that they have used (consciously or unconsciously) to disguise their true selves." Est training synthesizes elements from several Eastern and occult philosophies, Silva Mind Control,

Scientology, substantial "Nietzschean will-to-power," American business know-how and Marine Corps bravado. Especially striking is est's resemblance to Zen. According to Robert Ellwood, est "could be seen as the ultimate Americanization of Zen, for . . . the gist of it is Zen, but the language is wholly American."[62]

What results from these techniques is a punishing and at times brutal seminar which forces people to come to grips with their lives in a way that they would not do under normal conditions. At the very onset, the complete authority of the trainers is established. Two years of training have given them expertise in methods of control and domination. They use a variety of techniques of intimidation to accomplish this objective. The trainer screams: "You can't win in here. Nobody wins except me, unless I decide to let you win. . . . You're all assholes and I'm God. Only an asshole would argue with God. I may let you be God too, but that'll come later."[63]

Much of the training consists of sitting for long hours in straight chairs, listening to an est trainer expound the estian philosophy. As Dokupil and Alexander note, the "conditions of training have many parallels with a POW camp." At the beginning, trainees agree to complete the seminar irrespective of problems that may arise. Guards stand at the doors. Theoretically you may leave, but practically you feel so intimidated that you do not dare. You do not know the time, because you have surrendered your watch. You cannot "go to the bathroom, eat, drink, chew gum, smoke, or speak (unless spoken to or sharing with the entire group)." Sometimes the est leader resembles a Marine Corps sergeant, using strong, coarse language. You are subjected to constant cursing and other verbal abuse. At other times, the trainer may remind you of a wise old philosopher or a successful business executive, but always he is the leader to whom you have submitted yourself totally and utterly.[64]

All of this psychological shock treatment is linked to physical exhaustion. Sessions can be as long as sixteen hours, at times lasting until 3:00 a.m. with few breaks. As the time passes, a variety of physical distractions may set in: full bladder, backache, hunger, nausea, drowsiness. Est training distorts the basic stimulus-response mechanisms of moving, eating, sleeping, going to the bathroom and smoking cigarettes.[65]

This fairly brutal physical and mental conditioning is intended to undo any preexisting belief system the trainee has. Erhard regards "belief as a disease." In fact, beliefs prevent individuals from living life to the fullest.

As one est trainer told his trainees, "We're gonna throw away your whole belief system. . . . We're gonna tear you down and put you back together."[66] Like Zen, est places emphasis on experience and emotions and attacks the intellect. According to est, the mind "makes you become more and more what you always have been." You take self-improvement courses and read how-to books and you become more proficient, but nothing has basically changed. You need to lay siege on the mind and confront it openly, and the seminar is the means by which this is done. Brainwashing may be too strong a term to apply to such methods, but they certainly can be regarded as intensive indoctrination. Even Erhard says that est techniques are "mind blowing." The mind is given something it cannot handle.[67]

If est is so successful at removing any beliefs one might have had before going into the training, what is offered to replace them? Est gives the trainee an experience first and foremost, but it is an experience based on a world-view or belief system. Trainees must chose between submitting their wills to the trainer and leaving the session. Confronted with two undesirable choices, most individuals turn inward toward the self. They usually have a direct experience of the self, followed by an explanation of the experience from the trainer; this explanation is tantamount to a new belief system. Most individuals who participate in the program "get it" (the life-changing experience). They report a euphoric freedom from past encumbrances, the ability to be open, straightforward and honest, an increased ability to assert themselves and a general enthusiasm about life.[68]

Underlying this experience are several key teachings or ideas, which John Newport summarizes. First, est teaches "that the world has no meaning or purpose"—an idea that can be found in Zen Buddhism. Second, est says "that the mind imposes artificial meanings and purposes on the world." The mind misleads people into responding as if the real world corresponded to these self-imposed belief systems. Est teaches that every system of meaning imposed by sources outside one's mind, such as parents, church and school, is really an illusion. As indicated, the objective of many exercises in the seminar is to get people to abandon their belief systems. When this is done, one can experience truth according to est. "The truth is: You are. . . . This is natural knowing. It is beyond believing, thinking, feeling, sensing, or doing. An enlightened person is one who has learned how to experience the world directly."[69]

A third important teaching is that each person is completely responsible for his or her own life. As an individual, "you are the cause of your own world." You must accept life precisely as you experience it, and then acknowledge that you are responsible for the way you experience it. If individuals blame others for a situation, "they attribute cause to that other person or situation." People then become "the effect of that person or situation" and have lost control of their own lives. Basically, this means that one's own experiences are the cause of ultimate reality. Objective truth does not exist. It is only an illusion. If individuals create reality, they are nothing less than God. Indeed, Erhard's view is that human beings are God. Self is all there is. To pay attention to anything else is to focus on an illusion. Such ideas of God and reality are essentially Eastern.[70]

Newport tells us that the final step or teaching in est is to show trainees how they can create their own subjective universe of ideas, emotions and sensations. "This is called 'getting it.' When you get it, you understand that others can no longer control you." If everything in life is an illusion, you have the option of choosing your illusion. "You can create or recreate your own experience. You, therefore, control your world." But a necessary condition for having this experience or getting it is for est trainees to create an "inner space." The space to which one retreats in order to immerse oneself in one's own consciousness is called an inner space.[71]

The tremendous success of est has occurred largely without direct publicity or advertising. This is because est presents concrete, definitive answers to basic human questions, especially those related to self-definition. The definition given to self affects all aspects of human existence. Thus the therapeutic power of est resides in its ability to provide trainees with an experience that radically redefines the self. Est graduates testify that this redefinition has resulted in concrete changes in their lives. They claim to have higher energy and improved self-image, to be less anxious and dependent and to assume more responsibility for their actions.[72]

In 1985, Erhard changed the name of est to "the Forum." The Forum is not substantially different from est. Ruth Tucker says that the changes made by Erhard are largely cosmetic, for the philosophy of the Forum is essentially that of est. The seminars have been repackaged to improve their appeal to large businesses and corporations. The Forum, Erhard claims, will increase one's personal effectiveness and give one a decisive edge in all endeavors. The essential ingredient, the one that gives a decisive advantage, is the Forum's somewhat vague emphasis on "getting in touch with 'being.' "

Another idea important to the Forum is "finding the questions." The notion that the "solution is better than the problem or the answer is better than the question" must be abandoned. "The Forum is about living in the question," which is much more powerful than having the answer, because answers close down other possibilities. In early 1991, Erhard sold the Forum to a group of employees, who now operate the organization.[73]

Silva Mind Control

In addition to Scientology and est there are many other psychospiritual/self-improvement groups. The best known that have not been examined elsewhere in this study are Silva Mind Control and Synanon. In many ways these groups are not religious in nature. But they fit well the previously mentioned pattern of a psychotherapy group that has adopted occultic, supernatural or mystical methods in order to achieve its lofty goals of self-improvement.

Like most self-improvement bodies, Silva Mind Control promises many tangible benefits: increased happiness and creative energy, weight loss, improved family relationships, a more relaxed life and even psychic powers. These and more can be gained by taking the forty-eight-hour course in Silva Mind Control.[74]

Though Silva Mind Control began in the United States, it is heavily indebted to a number of Eastern and Western sources. It is the product of Jose Silva, a Mexican-American who lacked a formal education. Silva was born in 1914 in the Texas border town of Laredo. Largely self-educated, he learned electronics and ran a radio repair shop, which supported his twenty-six years of research in mind control. During his five-year military term Silva studied psychology, especially hypnosis and parapsychology. After returning home at the close of World War II, Silva used his parapsychological research to help his ten children improve their ability to learn. After more years of study Silva developed his basic Mind Control course. In 1963 he started formal Mind Control classes in Mexico. Since then the movement has spread until the Mind Control organization became worldwide in its outreach. Its headquarters, however, are still in Laredo, Texas.[75]

To begin Silva Mind Control at its basic level, one takes four sequential courses, involving forty-eight hours over a four-day period. Class size usually ranges from five to twenty people. The training is heavy, but unlike est, it is pleasant and soothing. No one screams. Drugs and biofeedback machines are not used. From the very beginning, the trainee is taught to relax.

The basic method of instruction is "voice programming," which verbally guides trainees to lower their brain-wave frequencies.[76]

The heart of Silva Mind Control centers on utilizing the alpha-level brain wave. During waking hours, most people operate on the beta wave. This corresponds to the outer consciousness level, associated with tension, anger, physical activity and work routines. The name given to the inner consciousness is "alpha wave." It is associated with inspiration, tranquillity, creativity, concentration, learning and memory. The trainee is taught to use the alpha level to achieve dynamic results. Silva Mind Control teaches you to relax. But it claims to do much more. Its methods can awaken a person's psychic powers. This is based on the assumption that everything is, ultimately, "energy" or "mind," and that an individual can get in touch with this "energy" within him- or herself and have access to all knowledge.[77]

Religious dimensions emerge when the trainee is introduced to the psychic and occult aspects of Silva Mind Control. Students are guided to the level at which they can perform acts of healing, hypnosis, clairvoyance, ESP, mind-reading and so forth. Silva Mind Control also teaches that invisible psychic advisers can be called up to tell the student what to do. Who or what these psychic counselors are is a matter of debate. Both secular and religious critics of Silva Mind Control say that these spiritual guides may be disguised spiritual forces of evil. Such a view would see Silva Mind Control as bordering on Spiritualism. In any case, many Silva techniques are similar to those associated with the New Age Movement, and thus Silva Mind Control can be categorized as part of the New Age.[78]

Synanon

Synanon is another example of a psychotherapy group that evolved into a quasi-religion. Synanon did not begin as a religion and may still fail to qualify according to rigid criteria. Yet there are definite elements of religiosity in the movement. Richard Ofshe identifies the four stages of Synanon's evolution. It began as a voluntary association but became a therapeutic community, then a social movement, and eventually a religion.[79]

Synanon started as a self-help organization for alcoholics and drug abusers. The movement was begun by Chuck Dederich under inauspicious circumstances. Dederich was born in Ohio, dropped out of Notre Dame and then drifted around the country, becoming involved in several jobs and marriages. By the mid-1950s his travels had taken him to California. Drunk

321

and broke, he sought help from Alcoholics Anonymous. Then, using his unemployment money, he began his own treatment center. He offered harsh, dictatorial treatment tactics to alcoholics and addicts. The core elements in his treatment programs were manual labor and group support systems. With this as a basis, as Paul Chalfant indicates, Dederich started "seminars and prolonged encounter sessions in a type of reality training, which eventually became known as the Synanon 'Game.' " The Game consisted of techniques designed to strip down a person's defense mechanisms and uncover the real person. Synanon received many contributions from wealthy sponsors and government grants. It soon developed into a multi-million-dollar organization with centers across the country.[80]

Confronted with high rates of recidivism and a need to restructure the movement, in the mid-1960s Dederich began allowing nonaddicted outsiders to live in the Synanon community. These outsiders were ordinary men, women and children who gravitated to Synanon not for its reputation for rehabilitating addicts but for its communal, nonviolent, highly ordered lifestyle. These individuals contributed much to the community, bringing to it much-needed business and organizational skills. They were expected to liquidate all their assets and turn over the proceeds to the community.[81]

Other changes came. The Synanon Game began to incorporate violence. Dederich argued that self-defense was needed to defend the community from abusive outsiders; he also advocated the use of force against insiders who wished to defect from the community. Leaving the community was seen by those inside it as "betraying Chuck." This was considered an unpardonable sin. Increasingly the founder, Chuck Dederich, took on the status of a secular god. As Synanon became more religious in its outlook, the adulation of Dederich increased. At times he wore priest's robes, and his wife declared herself to be the "High Priestess of Synanon."[82]

Cultic characteristics continued to develop in Synanon. Members were required to surrender the right to bear their own children. Many vasectomies were performed. In addition, Synanon members swapped spouses and participated in physical-fitness programs, including karate. The Ouija board became part of Synanon's encounter sessions, and messages from the dead conferred a religious significance on Synanon's mission and reinforced the founder's authority. As Synanon failed to substantiate its therapeutic claims, mysticism became dominant. Soon Synanon declared itself a religion, and Dederich became the highest spiritual authority in the organization.[83]

PART VI

Christian Bodies in Post-Christian America

In post-Christian America many Eastern and occult groups have attracted the public's attention. Still, post-World War II America has seen many fringe Christian groups come and go. Most of these bodies fall within the bounds of Christian orthodoxy and should be regarded as sectarian groups. Yet some of them were significantly deviant and bizarre enough to receive the cultic label. They differ from Eastern and occult groups in that they generally embrace a Judeo-Christian worldview or have had some historic connection with the Christian church. In fact, most of these aberrational Christian bodies evolved from evangelical or fundamentalist Christianity. In addition to manifesting cultic social characteristics, these groups distort aspects of orthodox Christian beliefs.

20

The
Christian
Background

N ew and old Christian groups in postwar America are innumerable. Many of these bodies can be regarded as fringe religions—that is, sects or cults. In respect to Christian bodies, the distinction between sect and cult becomes extremely problematic. As a consequence, the groups studied in this section will be limited by two criteria. The religious bodies must be new to post-World War II America. Moreover, they must not only manifest the social characteristics of a cult but also be obviously heretical or deviant in doctrine. There are simply too many evangelical and fundamentalist splitoffs to ignore the criterion of theological orthodoxy.

Even when these two standards are used, the study must be selective. It will be limited to three realms: the Unification Church, the People's Temple and the more cultic groups in the Jesus People movement—the Way and the Children of God.

This study has used the terms *aberrational Christian* and *Christian fringe group* generically. Both terms connote a wide range of Christian bodies that depart from the normal faith and practices of the Christian tradition. Included in these categories are Christian bodies that meet the criteria previously established for designating cultic groups. But I have also used the terms *aberrational Christian* and *Christian fringe groups* to denote Christian bodies that display the social characteristics of a cult while remaining essentially orthodox. Some of these bodies could legitimately be categorized as sect groups, but others are more difficult to classify.

A contemporary example of such a group would be the Faith Assembly, also called the Glory Barn. This is a Pentecostal fringe movement founded by Hobart Freeman and located primarily in the Midwest. Freeman received his theological training in evangelical seminaries and taught at Grace Theological Seminary in Indiana until he was fired for theological reasons. According to Ruth Tucker, his group is controversial in a number of ways. It advocates faith healing to the extent of avoiding the use of medical doctors, eyeglasses and hearing aids. It opposes birth control and sexual foreplay, and urges members to cancel their insurance policies. The Faith Assembly ensures conformity to these practices by setting members up to spy on one another, by authoritarian leadership and by becoming exclusive—that is, claiming to have a corner on salvation. Despite such cultlike characteristics, the Faith Assembly remains essentially orthodox in respect to the major Christian doctrines.[1]

Tucker also notes other such authoritarian and separationist fundamentalist groups. Some examples are the Fundamentalist Army, the Community Chapel, the University Bible Fellowship, Maranatha Christian Churches, First Community Church of America and the Northeast Kingdom Community Church.[2] While such groups often manifest cultic characteristics, this study will not classify them as cults. They will remain outside the purview of this study.

Dualistic Groups

Christian fringe groups can be distinguished from the Eastern new religions by means of their worldviews and ethical systems. Christian groups are dualistic. Not only do they separate God from his creation, but they also emphasize aspects of traditional moral absolutism in a strident, exaggerated manner. On the other hand, monistic elements predominate in the new Eastern cults in America and have pervaded the human potential movement and other therapeutic groups. Monistic bodies usually present a view of the universe in which an ultimate metaphysical unity or "oneness" dissolves polarities and conveys an illusory quality to the material world. Consequently, the monistic movements often emphasize subjectivistic and relativistic moral systems.[3]

Sociologists Thomas Robbins, Dick Anthony and James Richardson subdivide dualistic religious movements in contemporary America into "neofundamentalist" and "revisionist" syncretic groups. Neofundamentalist bodies such as those in the Jesus movement "usually emphasize some mode of biblical literalism combined with an affirmation of the imminence of apocalyptic events foretold in the Bible." Revisionist syncretic groups, such as the Unification Church with its strong Manichaean elements, usually combine many ingredients and are "oriented towards the establishment of an authoritarian theocracy."[4]

Both of these dualistic types generally advocate political and social conservatism. In part this is because "they are locked into a traditional conception of evil as violations of absolute negative taboos." Liberal attempts to reform society through government programs are perceived as a form of satanic interference with personal responsibility. Dualistic groups seem to have "a greater appeal to persons from rural or urban lower middle-class backgrounds" and to persons with a conservative religious orientation. Also, with the exception of Hare Krishna, it is generally the "stringently dualistic and apocalyptic quasi-Christian groups" such as the Alamo Foundation, Children of God, the Unification Church and the People's Temple which tend to function as total social institutions and are accused of brainwashing converts.[5]

Evangelical Origins

Most aberrational Christian groups originating in America had their earliest roots in evangelical piety. The leaders of many contemporary Christian cults come from solid church backgrounds. Victor Wierwille, founder of The Way, was an evangelical Reformed pastor and served as an adjunct professor at an evangelical college. Moses David (David Berg), leader of the Children of God, was raised in an evangelical home, pastored a Christian and Missionary Alliance church and for a time was even involved in a Christian television program. Jim Jones, founder of the People's Temple, was "born again" in a Nazarene church and later pastored an interdenominational congregation and a Disciples of Christ church. Sun Myung Moon, founder of the Unification Church, was raised in an evangelical Presbyterian home in Korea.[6]

Harold Bussell gives several explanations for evangelical Christianity's spawning of so many aberrational groups. One is that evangelicalism contains many elements that are basic to the emergence of cultic bodies. In its reaction against liberalism, rationalism and naturalism, evangelicalism has overemphasized the subjective experience. Gospel songs, personal testimonies and even sermons all "reflect the importance placed on the subjective approach to faith and life." Such an emphasis on subjectivity is basic to the appeal of the cults. Next, evangelicals are fascinated by individuals who claim to have new spiritual insights. At times these insights are merely the latest fad; at times they lay the foundation for a new religious group. Nearly all cult leaders, of course, offer some "new" spiritual insight.[7]

Third, both evangelical "Christians and cult members place high spiritual value on group sharing." With both groups, the basis for community life is the discussion of one's hopes, fears, problems and even sins. In our society and culture, people are encouraged to "let it all hang out." For some people this need for group sharing is met by their church. Others, however, turn to encounter groups and even religious cults. Closely related is the search by many evangelicals for "the 'ideal' Christian community," modeled after the New Testament church. Many cults, of course, "describe themselves as ideal communities; they promise perfect fellowship."[8]

Fifth and most basic, many evangelicals and cult members "seem to need and want an authority figure with charisma." Many Christians evaluate pastors, evangelists and teachers on their leadership, strength, persuasive words and moving presentations. But such a wish list is not confined to the local congregation. "Almost every major, successful, contemporary parachurch ministry is built around a single personality, who is able to attract a coterie of dedicated followers." Society looks for such qualities in its political leaders, who must portray an image of strength and be articulate.[9]

David Wells says that there is a pattern to the development of Christian cults. First, an individual emerges with a new "insight." This insight or new interpretation is then developed by a minority group "in opposition to the local church or the prevailing orthodoxy." Once a subgroup becomes entrenched around a new insight, "devices to protect that minority" are quickly developed, including a subcultural language to explain the new interpretation, "a tight organization" that rebuffs outsiders and unites insiders, and an unquestioning loyalty to the leader, who, in his isolated cultic world, is "placed beyond reproach, criticism or discipline."[10]

Such an emphasis on authoritarian leadership, as Wells also notes, is not limited to the "cultic accretions on the fringes of evangelicalism." In a less threatening form, it can be detected closer to the center of evangelicalism. Authoritarian leadership can be found in some of the huge Bible Belt churches whose entire operation centers on the dominating personality of one pastor. These charismatic leaders have also "created personal kingdoms in which the 'king' [is] beyond discipline." Similar leadership could be seen in certain television and radio preachers. In their cases, the normal channels of denominational and congregational accountability were frequently circumvented, and the individual acquired the power that millions of dollars can bring. In the early 1980s, estimates placed radio audiences at 115 million weekly and television at 14 million. While the income of an established denomination was about twenty to thirty million dollars per year, the big-name evangelists grossed about sixty to eighty million each. "This new form of 'church' centered on powerful and talented individuals" and rested on certain tendencies within evangelical Christianity: an indulgence in rampant individualism, which tends to minimize the communal aspects of the church; a deep suspicion regarding church structures; and a naive acceptance of authoritarian leaders who claim to be God's mouthpiece. Until a series of financial and personal scandals rocked the empires of some well-known television evangelists in the late 1980s, these kingdoms went largely unchecked.[11]

Current Status

What is the status of these aberrational Christian bodies? Are they growing, or are they in decline? No satisfactory generalization can be made in answer to these questions. On one hand, as Dean Kelley and other scholars have demonstrated, conservative Christian bodies experienced growth during the 1960s and 1970s. Among the growing groups were several nonorthodox Christian groups, such as the Mormons and Jehovah's Witnesses, plus several suspect bodies like the Seventh-day Adventists.[12] Along with this surge of growth among conservative Christians came an increase in aberrational evangelical-fundamentalist groups. On the other hand, the fountainhead for many fringe Christian bodies, especially those associated with the Jesus People, was the counterculture. The passing of this phenomenon meant that the major source for new recruits was also gone. Thus, many of these quasi-evangelical or fundamentalist bodies either went into decline or merged with more stable like-minded groups; some even ceased to exist.[13] Still, new aberrational Christian bodies are always making their appearance.

The so-called established Christian cults are those aberrational bodies that have endured past the first generation and have established something of a permanent place in the American religious landscape. Most prominent among these groups in modern America are the Mormons, the Jehovah's Witnesses and the Worldwide Church of God. Other fringe religions such as Christian Science, Spiritualism, Theosophy and Rosicrucianism must also be called established cults, but they cannot be classified as Christian.

On the whole, the pattern in contemporary America for the established Christian cults has been growth mixed with considerable internal discord and problems. Mormonism grew significantly during the seventies and eighties and currently enjoys great wealth and an expanding influence. Yet this fast-growing religion faces many difficulties. It has been criticized for its aging, authoritarian male leadership, its attitude toward women and blacks, its appetite for political involvement, and the serious gaps between its doctrinal claims and archaeological evidence. The Jehovah's Witnesses also experienced considerable growth during the decade of the seventies. But the problems for the Witnesses remained formidable, including the defection of many members, dissatisfaction with authoritarian leadership, disillusionment concerning the failures of the organization's prophetic predictions, and challenges presented by American culture to its extreme separationist stance. The pattern of growth and internal dissension could also be seen in the Worldwide Church of God. The scandals associated with Garner Ted Armstrong's departure and Herbert Armstrong's divorce rocked the church. Embarrassment over the failure of the church's apocalyptic pronouncements and the death of its founder presented problems. But by the mid-eighties the church had apparently coped with these difficulties.[14]

The status of the aberrational Christian bodies new to post-World War II America is mixed. The decrease in news-media coverage of these groups can be misleading. The phenomenon has become so common that it is no longer newsworthy except when bizarre incidents arise. The number of extremist fundamentalist-separatist groups has grown and will probably continue to grow in the future. Yet these bodies give little promise of becoming large movements. Moreover, first-generation aberrational Christian groups that are about thirty to forty years old have had surges of growth, but currently their membership is either in decline or stagnant. Also, many of these bodies have experienced internal and organizational problems. The Unification Church, The Way and the Children of God exemplify such general trends.[15]

21

The Unification
Church

T he Unification Church is one of the most controversial new religions to arrive on the contemporary American religious scene. This
organization's full name is The Holy Spirit Association for the
Unification of World Christianity. Its members are called "Moonies," sar-
castically so by its opponents and affectionately so by Sun Myung Moon
himself. Because the Unification Church has stirred up much controversy,
it has received far more media attention than its small numbers would seem
to warrant.

One might question whether the Unification Church can even be considered an offshoot of Christianity. In fact, Moon's theological distinctives
prompt many Catholic and Protestant theologians to contend that the Unification Church cannot be called Christian. Nevertheless, Moon did come
out of a Presbyterian background, and the Unification Church claims to be
Christian. The Unification Church might be regarded as Christian in the
sense that the Mormon Church is. William Whalen makes several parallels
between Mormonism and the Unification Church. Like the Unification
Church, Mormonism "accepts a new revelation in addition to the Bible (the
Book of Mormon), a latter-day prophet (Joseph Smith, Jr.), and an assortment of beliefs unknown to the vast majority of Christians (secret temple
rites, baptism for the dead, polygamy and the like)."[1] Neither the Unification Church nor Mormonism can be regarded as Christian in the sense of
maintaining the basic doctrines of the Christian faith.

Actually, the Unification Church is unique in that it rests on a modern interpretation of the Christian Bible by an individual from the Far East. While Christian cults exist in the non-Western world, few have made their way to America. The Unification Church is clearly a new religion, not simply because it began in 1954 but because its theology definitely represents an interpretation of the Christian tradition that had not existed previously.[2] The Unification Church's beliefs are a syncretic mixture of many religious impulses. The recipe for Moon's religion combines ingredients from Eastern and Western belief systems, seasoned by mysticism from Moon's own revelations. Unification theology is a strange combination of pseudo-Christian, mystical, psychological, philosophical and charismatic ingredients. So much is this the case that the Unification Church might be seen as an alternative to Christianity rather than a variation of Christianity.[3]

Most aberrational Christian bodies withdraw from society and have few expectations for changing the world. Though the Unification Church is an exclusive, totalistic society, it does have a much broader vision. Arthur Paisons tells us that it "is a messianic movement" whose leader, the Reverend Sung Myung Moon, is, according to his followers, "the Lord of the Second Advent, the Central Figure" through whom all humanity can enter the kingdom of heaven on earth. "The Church is a 'world-saving' movement, seeking to establish one unified family." Uniting people of all religions is a central theme of the movement. The church aims to usher in a new age, a new world moral order in which all religions are unified within itself. The church's goals are theocratic. It intends to overcome separation of church and state and religious pluralism in America and to make itself the only official religion. Some evidence indicates that the church desires to impose its ideas on all institutions—religious, political, scientific, social, industrial—in many societies. The church seems to aspire to become, either overtly or covertly, the dominant religion in the world.[4]

Any movement that desires to transform the world needs both large numbers of dedicated followers and considerable wealth to carry out its mission. Therefore, the Unification Church emphasizes evangelism. It aggressively recruits members, a practice for which it has received its harshest criticism. The church has attempted to build up its economic base by many means, ranging from members' selling flowers on the streets to the purchase of large business complexes. At the same time the church is securing a solid financial foundation, it is attempting to protect its adherents from contamination by the wider society by returning them to live with other church members in a controlled environment. The Unification Church has the difficult task of "being in the world without being of the world." It must maintain its unique standards until it achieves its goal of transforming the world.[5]

A Brief History

Any history of the Unification Church must begin with its founder, Sun Myung Moon. He was born in 1920 in a rural town of what is now North Korea. In many ways, the Unification Church reflects its Korean origins. Korea has produced various semi-Christian cults, sixty by one recent count. The Unification Church happens to be the one that has gained the most attention in America. Moon's parents were humble farm folk and members of a Presbyterian church. But he also had other early religious influences. From his youth he had a mystical bent and a strong interest in clairvoyance. He attended a Pentecostal church as a high-school student, at a time when the Korean Pentecostals were predicting that a new messiah would come to their nation. This idea would greatly influence Moon's thinking. On Easter 1936, when he was sixteen, Jesus appeared to him in a revelation, telling him that he had been the one selected to complete Jesus' unfulfilled mission.[6]

After receiving this life-altering vision, Moon entered into a period of intense inner struggle and searching that lasted from 1936 to 1946. During this time he completed high school and went to Japan to study electrical engineering. These studies probably influenced Moon's interest in numerology, a subject that found its way into his theology. Moon's basic religious views received their shape during these years. He reports that God disclosed to him the purpose of history, the inner or spiritual meaning of the Bible and the purpose of the universe. Moreover, during the same time Moon claims to have been in communication with some of the great spiritual leaders of the past, receiving insights from Buddha, Moses and Jesus.[7]

In 1946, Moon claims, he came upon the key to all of humankind's problems: Satan had sex with Eve in the Garden of Eden. Moon became convinced that he was God's chosen instrument to reverse the fall of humanity caused by Eve's sin. In line with this new commission and his conviction that he was divinity, a new Messiah, Moon changed his name to Sun Myung Moon (meaning Shining Sun and Moon). Judging that Moon's claims were heretical, in 1948 the Presbyterian Church of Korea excommunicated him.[8]

Moon launched his career as an independent preacher in 1948. North Korea had become communist, and Moon was arrested for preaching and sent to prison camp, where he stayed until United Nations forces liberated the camp in 1949. After fleeing to Pusan in the south, he again began to preach. Here he found time to write the first draft of *Divine Principle,* the book he says contains the essence of his revelation from God. In 1957 the first edition was published. By 1954 his ministry began to bear tangible fruit, as those responding to his message became officially organized into the Unification Church. Growth came slowly, but by 1958 the movement sent out its first missionary to Japan. This small beginning would eventually produce a strong Japanese branch of the church.[9]

In 1955 the South Korean authorities arrested Moon on charges of practicing Pikaruna, a blood-cleansing sex ritual, with women of his own congregation. The case was dropped, however, because the government could not get enough witnesses to testify against Moon. According to John Newport, Pikaruna is based on the belief that because "original sin came through Eve's sexual intercourse with Satan," a woman could have sex three times with Moon (the perfect man) and thus "liquidate her original sin." After intercourse with Moon a woman achieved a perfected status, and male church members could have sexual relations with her and liquidate their own sin. Couples experiencing "this blood cleansing [could] produce perfect children." If practiced widely enough, such a ritual could save the world.[10]

Given the implications of Moon's theology, it was absolutely necessary for him to find the wife who would be the perfect mother for humanity. His first marriage had ended in divorce, but in 1960 he married Han Ja Han and began the task of completing the unfulfilled physical aspect of Christ's mission, which included marriage and a family. Over the next twenty years, Moon's wife bore twelve children, the last in 1981.[11]

The Unification movement was a product of the social, economic and religious climate of post-World War II Korea. The removal of the religious restrictions that had been imposed by the occupying Japanese and the post-war political and economic chaos provided the context for a stream of religious innovations. The country was in the grips of a serious economic depression, and communist and anticommunist forces were polarizing the Korean people. As a consequence, Korean society witnessed the rise of a number of religious groups led by charismatic leaders who combined elements from folk, Christian and Confucian traditions. According to Ruth Tucker, these new religions had a popular appeal in that their doctrines had a distinctively this-worldly focus. They offered not only the hope of salvation and human perfectibility but also the hope of "achievable prosperity." It is important to understand that Moon's movement was only one of many such religious groups in Korea at this time.[12]

Moon's missionaries reached Japan in 1958, and one year later his doctrines arrived in the United States. Young Oom Kim established the first American Unification commune on the West Coast. During the 1960s, Moon visited the United States several times. On a 1964 trip Moon attended a séance conducted by the Spiritualist medium Arthur Ford. At this séance, Ford's spirit guide Fletcher designated Moon as a New Age teacher who brought a message for the end of time. During his visits to America, Moon spoke frequently of his familiarity with the spirit world. Themes from mysticism, Spiritualism and the occult became important aspects of Unification thought. Like many unorthodox cults that have arisen since World War II, then, the Unification Church has borrowed from the occult.[13]

As the Unification Church grew and spread across the globe during the 1960s, other related developments took place. Moon experienced success in business, acquiring considerable wealth from a variety of enterprises. He also intensified his philosophical and emotional opposition to communism, lending his support to many anticommunist activities. His vigorous anticommunist campaign in the mid-1960s earned him the support of South Korea's President Park.[14]

During the 1960s the church in the United States grew slowly. Under the leadership of Young Oom Kim, David S. C. Kim and Colonel Bo Hi Pak, centers were established near universities, a periodical, *New Age Frontiers,* was begun, and political activities got under way. In 1972 Moon received a revelation to move his headquarters to the United States. He launched this move by conducting a series of rallies in major American cities. Growth of the American church, as Gordon Melton notes, was spurred by Moon's move to the United States. "During the years 1972 to 1976 it grew from a few hundred members to around 6,000. International headquarters were established in New York City and missions were initiated throughout the world." The Unification Church opened centers in most states and began intense fundraising efforts to give the church a solid financial basis. In 1975 the church established the Unification Theological Seminary to train its future leaders.[15]

To further his broad vision and gain acceptance for his church, Moon made major efforts to penetrate various levels of American society. He acquired two major newspapers, one in Washington, D.C., and one in New York. He has attempted to broaden his ecumenical appeal by joining with other churches to combat certain social problems. He financed the production of a Hollywood film about the Korean War. He also has sought acceptance from the scholarly world by sending select church members to top graduate schools and by organizing a Washington think tank, a peace academy and numerous academic conferences.[16]

To accomplish its goals of world evangelization and the infusion of the world with the ideals of the kingdom of God as perceived by Moon, the Unification Church has established many organizations. There are many structures for the purpose of evangelism, the most important of which is the Collegiate Association for the Research of Principles (CARP). The church has also established many religious, political, charitable and cultural organizations to unite members and nonmembers to further shared ideals. These limited goals range from the search for unity in religious and scientific values to promoting religious liberty. The secondary objective of such organizations is to create a favorable impression of the Unification Church and to make it more acceptable to mainstream America. Critics of the church often regard these organizations as fronts for the church.[17]

While all of this activity has been going on, the Unification Church has never been far from controversy. While some controversies have revolved around accusations made by the church's opponents, especially the anticult movement, others have been stirred up by Moon's support of unpopular causes. During the Watergate crisis, Moon supported Nixon. In a congressional committee's probe of South Korean influence-peddling in Congress, Moon became a target of investigation. But the major controversy that affected nearly every facet of the church during the 1980s was Moon's trial and conviction for tax evasion. After exhausting all avenues of appeal, he spent thirteen months in jail during 1984-85. Other controversies concerned allegations regarding the church's devious methods of recruiting members.[18]

Beliefs

Within the Unification Church, as Melton indicates, considerable theological pluralism exists around a nucleus of shared belief and practice. In part, this situation has developed because Moon's teachings themselves constitute a strange religious mixture; in part it came about because the belief structure of the church changed drastically during the 1970s. These changes came because of the pressure of unrealized prophetic expectations and the growing theological sophistication that had developed at the Unification seminary. The church had maintained an "apocalyptic hope of great changes prophesied for 1957, 1976, and 1981." Such expectations "gave way to a long term perspective in which the work of building the kingdom," begun by the Lord of the Second Advent, would be achieved over a lengthy period of time.[19]

Tucker says that like many new religious groups in modern America, the Unification Church has placed considerable emphasis on "doctrines of the end times." But unlike most of the other groups, which promote a version of premillennialism, Moon's church has advocated a form of postmillennialism. Instead of looking for a cataclysmic end of history, the Unification Church sees the last days as a time when human beings will turn away "from the selfishness of the past" to a future of God-centeredness.[20]

J. Isamu Yamamoto divides the core teachings of the Unification Church into three areas: "the first Adam, the second Adam and the Lord of the Second Advent." Based on the concept of yin and yang, there is a fundamental theme underlying these teachings. "All concepts are broken down into dualities of which male and female is the thread that sews them all together."[21] The duality of creation is found in the relationship between man and woman. There was a dual aspect to the fall of humanity: a spiritual and physical fall. Salvation contains the same spiritual and physical aspects. The political configuration pits communism and democracy against each other.

The first Adam and Eve were God's initial creations who fell into sin. They were supposed to establish the kingdom of heaven on earth through their offspring. "The goal of creation was thwarted, however, by Adam and Eve's sin." Eve's beauty attracted Lucifer, and he entered into a sexual relationship with her. Their sexual intercourse constituted the spiritual fall of humanity. When Eve became involved in this illicit relationship with Lucifer, "she received spiritual insight and realized that she had violated the purpose of creation." She then had sex with Adam in an endeavor to restore her relationship with God. This second relationship constituted the physical fall of humanity. So both the spiritual and the physical aspects of the Fall were closely connected with sexuality.[22]

The Fall also had political implications. A result of Eve's affair with

Satan was the birth of Cain, an individual who symbolized humanity's relationship with Satan. "The political configuration of this relationship has culminated in Communism." Abel was the fruit of Eve's love affair with Adam and symbolizes humanity's relationship with God. Democracy is the political configuration of this relationship. Therefore, "Communism is the expression of Satan and democracy the expression of God." Still, Moon believed that even democracy could not solve all the world's problems. A third alternative to democracy and communism was needed. This option, of course, was the Unification Church, which has a new vision and a systematic worldview grounded in truth and absolute values.[23]

The second Adam was Jesus Christ, who died on the cross because of the faithlessness of the Jews. While the Unification Church rejects orthodox views of Christ's atonement, bodily resurrection and virgin birth, it regards Christ as more than a great teacher. The church claims that Jesus is the Christ, the Messiah, a human being and not a supernatural person, who came to establish the kingdom of heaven on earth. God took several steps to prepare the world for Jesus. To make people ready for the coming of the Messiah he sent Malachi to the Jews, Buddha and Confucius to the Asian world and Socrates to the Hellenistic world. All religions and cultures were to unify under the acceptance of Jesus.[24]

However, the crucifixion of Jesus tragically frustrated God's plan for humanity. John the Baptist's ignorance regarding the providence of God discouraged the Jews from believing in Jesus. Moon's *Divine Principle* "does not claim that Jesus sinned or failed to obey God." Rather, Jesus realized that the Jewish nation would not accept him as their messiah and "took the only course available to him." When Jesus ascertained that he could not bring about both the spiritual and the physical salvation of humanity, "he resolved to take the cross" to pay for humankind's spiritual salvation. If Jesus had not been crucified, he would have "found the perfect mate and founded God's perfect family on earth, thus accomplishing both the spiritual and physical salvation."[25]

The Lord of the Second Advent, as J. Yamamoto says, is the Messiah who must come to establish the kingdom of heaven on earth. Because Jesus failed to marry and produce the perfect family, another messiah is needed to complete the physical aspect of salvation. *Divine Principle* places much emphasis on the number 2,000, which "provides the key to the coming of the Lord of the Second Advent." It states that the time between Abraham and Jesus was two thousand years, during which time God prepared the world for the first coming of the Messiah. Thus, for two thousand years since Jesus, God has been preparing the world for the second coming of the Messiah. The clear implication is that the Messiah could come at any moment "if he has not already arrived." In addition, *Divine Principle* states that the Messiah will be born in the East and through a process of elimination concludes that Korea is the country, the "Third Israel."[26]

Divine Principle does not state that Moon is the Messiah. In fact, until recently neither Moon nor the majority of his followers would publicly declare that he is the Messiah. A 1991 newspaper report did say that Moon had declared himself to be the Messiah. But experts on the Unification Church say that this statement is no more revealing than previous statements by Moon, which strongly imply that he is the Messiah. In addition to indicating the time and place of the Messiah's birth, *Divine Principle* notes the requirements for the Messiah. He must be born a complete human being, conquer sin and evidence God's masculine nature. Moreover, he must marry a woman who manifests God's feminine characteristics. The Lord of the Second Advent will thus complete the half of the messianic mission that Jesus did not.[27]

Human beings also play a role in the salvation of humanity. They take part in the world's restoration by positioning themselves with the Messiah. Such an alignment can be achieved by participating in a process called indemnity. Through the indemnity process, people prepare themselves for entrance into the restored kingdom. Indemnity is a form of salvation by works in which individuals must atone for their sins through specific acts of penance. After John the Baptist frustrated Jesus' mission, he restored himself by going through a process of indemnity—that is, by fasting for forty days in the wilderness. During the time of indemnity, people observe absolute celibacy and perform sacrificial work. At the conclusion of this period, Moon matches each "Moonie" with an appropriate mate. The couple is then married in a ceremony performed by Moon and his wife. Involved in the consummation of the marriage is a ritual that dramatically reenacts the process of indemnity and restoration. In Korea, this ritual gave rise to rumors that Moon had engaged in sexual improprieties.[28]

The work of the Unification Church, according to Gordon Melton, "is the establishment of the Kingdom of God on earth." This task is to be accomplished by its members who have been blessed, that is, married by

Moon. The physical salvation begun by Moon becomes apparent through "the children born to the blessed couples and the spread of the Kingdom ideal of one human family transcending nationality and race."[29]

These marriages are often performed in mass weddings, which have occurred in 1969, 1975, 1982, 1988 and 1992. The size of the weddings has increased each time, ranging from 777 couples in 1969 to 20,000 couples in 1992, with each number carrying a symbolic meaning. Outsiders view the weddings as extravaganzas orchestrated for publicity reasons. Actually, they are based on Unification teachings, especially on the concept of perfection and the emphasis on the ideal family. The couples promise to become a model of love before society and the world. Of the couples married in 1988, the vast majority were pairs with different national origins.[30]

Recruiting

The aspect of the Unification Church arousing most intense controversy has been its recruiting methods. On one hand, scores of critics have accused the church of brainwashing and deception. Many ex-Moonies have told stories about the organization's methods of mind control, long hours of work and poor living conditions. Supposedly recruits are "entrapped" in a total society that turns its members into "zombies" or "robots." Families have been split and lawsuits filed over the church's recruiting methods.[31]

Yet the Unification Church has its defenders, including many in the academic community. These scholars argue that the anticult movement has exaggerated the negative aspects of the Unification Church's recruiting methods, spreading rumors of atrocities and social evils. According to these scholars, the anticult movement's charges regarding "kidnapping and brainwashing" are largely sensationalism. Moreover, they say, the recruiting techniques of the Unification Church are not that different from those used by other new religions and the more strident evangelical/fundamental groups.[32]

Undoubtedly the anticult movement *has* exaggerated the negative aspects of the Unification Church's recruiting methods. It is also true that the Unification Church is making major attempts to improve its image in America. Thus, the church is less aggressive in its recruiting tactics. Nevertheless, the testimonies of many former Moonies would seem to indicate that the church's recruiting can be legitimately criticized. First, the Unification Church appears to practice deception in its recruiting methods. Second, the church seems to use forms of mind manipulation that go beyond even the hard-sell persuasion tactics of some evangelical or fundamentalist bodies. Many ex-Moonies claim that they were programmed to the point that they had little freedom of choice.[33]

Response to American Culture

The Unification Church can be seen as a reaction to certain trends in American society. Though its appeal has been countered by its negative image, it seems to fill a void in American culture and meet certain individual needs. Modern America is marked by both rampant individualism and the breakdown of the traditional family. Society is becoming increasingly fragmented and pluralistic. There is no dominant set of values, interests and meanings. Some individuals desire to escape such a secularized mass society. Thus a need has arisen for a kind of collective based on strong religious values that will serve as a surrogate family and establish strong moral guidelines.[34]

Moon's movement is a response to the cultural fragmentation of mass society. Thomas Robbins says that "the Unification Church is stridently 'collectively oriented.' " Its interests transcend individual salvation and focus on more collective matters. At present the church functions primarily as an authoritarian commune that controls the lives of its members extensively. Its long-term goals are also collective and totalistic. The Unification Church is a theocratic movement that ultimately desires to create one family, unify all religions and transform the world in accordance with its visions. Pluralism in religion and values is regarded as an evil that must be terminated.[35]

The birth and growth of the Unification Church is clearly related to certain political trends. The church was born in the political climate of the Cold War and the Korean War. Its greatest growth occurred in the early 1970s. The late sixties and early seventies were a time when patriotism was being challenged by many groups in America. National loyalty could no longer be assumed. The Vietnam War and Watergate especially rocked the American psyche. By this time Robert Bellah had described American civil religion as "an empty and broken shell." Civil religion can mean several things, but, as Robbins notes, it usually rests on the "assumption that America is or should be an instrument of divine providence."[36]

Moon's movement is staunchly patriotic and regards communism as the mortal enemy, opposing it with considerable emotion. But as Robbins points out, it is "the atheism rather than the collectivism of Communism" that the Unification Church opposes. In respect to collectivism, Moon has borrowed a lesson from Marxism and sees his movement "as the prototype for a coming worldwide collectivist society." It has appealed to individuals who were alarmed by the "trampling of the flag" and by the spread of international communism. Though Moon regards Korea as the "chosen nation," he has restored America's divine mission. America providentially leads the forces of democracy against "Satanic" communism. The ultimate goal of the Unification Church is the unification of all religions around the Divine Principle and the subsequent establishment of the kingdom of heaven on earth. A key element in this mission is winning human hearts from the "false ideology" of communism, which embodies Satan's plan to unify humanity in subjection to himself. The millennium "will occur when 'atheistic' Communism is completely defeated and the world is united into a benevolent theocracy with Reverend Moon at its head."[37]

Future Direction
What kind of future does the Unification Church have? By the mid-1980s, the church's membership stood at about five thousand in the United States and much more in Korea and Japan. Throughout the globe it has missionaries and centers in approximately 120 countries. Yet the Unification movement has never taken off in the United States. What are the problems? The church is not well received in American society. It is perceived as a terror cult that has been guilty of brainwashing recruits, fostering political conspiracies and acquiring great wealth. Moreover, the Unification Church has failed to persuade many people that its new and radically different version of Christianity is really Christian at all. Another problem is the language barrier. For the Lord of the Second Advent to need a interpreter to convey religious "truth" is seen as an incongruity. Lastly, as Tucker notes, the Unification Church does not seem to be delivering on its claims. Its prophecies of doom have not come about. "The millennium has not been ushered in by a Messiah from Korea and there has been no unification of the world's religions."[38]

Like most first-generation religious movements, the Unification Church is undergoing considerable change. Its future depends on how it handles these changes. To counter its poor popular image, the church has made major efforts to be accepted by the religious and academic communities. A benchmark event occurred in 1982, when more than half of the American church members were married in several mass weddings. The leadership of the church now rests with these people, especially those being trained at the seminary. In what direction will they take the church? Most first-generation new religions have a succession crisis when its leader and founder passes from the scene. How will the Unification Church handle Moon's death?[39] Moreover, a major pillar in the theology of the Unification Church has been its opposition to communism. Communism has unraveled in Eastern Europe and the Soviet Union and is changing its face elsewhere. The exact impact this development will have on the Unification Church remains to be seen. Yet at the time of this writing the Unification Church, along with the Jehovah's Witnesses, the Worldwide Church of God and the Mormons, appear to be exploiting this situation. Specifically, the Unification Church is moving into Eastern Europe, sending missionaries and establishing its economic enterprises.[40]

22

The People's Temple

erhaps the most bizarre religion-related incident of the twentieth century occurred in Jonestown, Guyana, in November 1978, when more than nine hundred people committed suicide or were murdered because of their involvement with the People's Temple and its leader, Jim Jones. Within a short time numerous newspaper and magazine articles were written on the subject. In addition, many scholarly articles and books, hours of television and radio coverage, and several movies have been produced about this gruesome occurrence.[1]

Ronald Flowers says that during the seventies two incidents combined to reinforce the negative image of cults—the belief that they are evil and unwholesome for society. In 1971 a jury convicted the Charles Manson "family" for murdering Sharon Tate and some of her friends. During the trial, the bizarre behavior of the Manson family became known to the public: the group had lived in a desert commune, used drugs freely, appeared to worship Manson and engaged in unconventional and promiscuous sexual behavior. Even more than the Manson episode, however, the mass suicides in Jonestown "horrified the nation and brought to public attention the evil potential of cults." These two "dramatic examples of cult membership gone wrong" prompted a widespread revulsion against cults.[2]

Jonestown, for all its gruesome power to shock, has its religious (or quasi-religious) precedents. Even in respect to mass suicide, Jonestown has its rivals. Defending the fortress of Masada against the invading Roman legions in A.D. 73, the Jewish Zealots chose suicide over submission. Nearly a thousand people died. Yet this event really does not compare to Jonestown. The Zealots were confronted with a choice between slavery or slaughter. Thus, in their case suicide had more of a rationale than it did at Jonestown. In seventeenth-century Russia Orthodox dissenters, called the Old Believers, refused to accept the liturgical reforms enacted by the Russian Orthodox Church. Over a number of years about twenty thousand peasants abandoned their fields and burned themselves in protest. Prior to World War I, in what was then German East Africa, witch doctors of the Maji-Maji movement convinced tribespeople that they had the power to turn German bullets into water. As a consequence, they revolted and were slaughtered.[3]

Characteristics

The disaster in Guyana is often explained by treating the People's Temple as typical of the many new religions or cults in American society. It is assumed that the People's Temple was like these other groups in important ways. But as Gordon Melton notes, the People's Temple was not a cult or a new religion in any traditional sense. "It was a full member of a mainline church," the Disciples of Christ, though it subsequently "degenerated into something not recognizable by reference to its parent body."[4] Sociologists Rodney Stark and William Bainbridge argue that the People's Temple "began as an emotionally extreme but culturally traditional Christian sect, then evolved into a cult." As Jones's vision became more radical, the church began to make a revolutionary break from American society and culture.[5]

James Richardson points out several specific areas in which the People's Temple differed from most "new religions" of modern America. Most notable were the time of inception and the characteristics of the members. Most new religions gaining media attention in modern America developed in the late 1960s and early 1970s. "The social, demographic, political and economic conditions of the 1960s combined to produce a situation extremely conducive to the inception of new religions." Developments such as the Vietnam War, the civil rights movement and the drug subculture influenced the broader cultural atmosphere. The People's Temple originated in a profoundly different milieu, having begun in the 1950s in the Midwest "as a reaction to a cultural situation that was extremely racist." The People's Temple began later than did Father Divine's group and the Black Muslims, and it was not exactly like these black sects and cults. Nevertheless, in respect to the cultural context of its point of origin the People's Temple had more in common with the black groups of the first half of the century than it did with the new religions of the 1960s and 1970s.[6]

The members of the People's Temple were generally different from members of other new religions. With the exception of the Unification Church, with its policy of integration, the target population for most new religions has been educated individuals from the white middle class. This social group, however, "did not provide the bulk membership in the People's Temple." The People's Temple was 70-80 percent black, and most of its members came from the lower classes. Moreover, in contrast to most new religions, whose recruits tend to be individuals, the People's Temple "attracted many entire families," including a good proportion of children.[7]

Richardson draws parallels between the People's Temple and the Father Divine Movement. Jones visited Father Divine's center in Philadelphia and studied his methods. Despite some clear contrasts between these two groups, in many ways Jones mimicked Divine's organization. Therefore, in this sense the "People's Temple was not really new at all." Rather, it was "something of a perverted extension of a long tradition of urban blacks affiliating with sects and cults that offered them some 'this worldly' relief" from their suffering.[8]

In still other respects, the People's Temple differed from the new religions of the 1960s and 1970s. On the whole, these new groups were not as tightly centralized or authoritarian as was the People's Temple. Most new religions control their members by a degree of social and geographic isolation. So did the People's Temple. But for most groups social and geographical isolation becomes diminished as time passes. With the People's Temple it increased, and eventually the church moved to Guyana, where the members were totally cut off from contact with nonmembers. The People's Temple's theology or ideology was also quite different. As I will explain more fully later, Jones emphasized three practices: racial equality, socialism and collective suicide.[9] These principles were not basic to most of the new religions.

All of this is not to say that the People's Temple did not share many characteristics with the new religions and cults of the sixties and seventies. Some of the differences were a matter of degree. Generalizations are always hazardous, but in one way or another the People's Temple and the new religions shared the following traits: both had charismatic, authoritarian leaders; both exercised a considerable degree of social control over their members through physical isolation; both encouraged their members to take a dim view of society, even inspiring fear of outsiders.

Some sources even go so far as to question how much the Jonestown incident had to do with religion, particularly the Christian religion. Charles Krause says that although Jones's traditions came from fundamentalist Christianity, "he held to no conventional Christian notion of God." Jones was first a Marxist who held that religion's trappings were useful only for social and economic objectives. But Barbara Hargrove, though admitting how embarrassing the People's Temple was to the Disciples of Christ, says that it was "a recognized congregation" in the denomination.[10] The soundest position is probably to say that the People's Temple was a religious movement, but that it evidenced significant differences from most new religions of its period and that Jones was more Marxist than Christian. It must also be noted that Jones rejected the orthodox doctrine of the Trinity and embraced a unitarian notion of God.

A Brief History

James Warren Jones was born in Lynn, Indiana, in 1931. The major industry in this small town of about one thousand is casket-making. This area of Indiana was a stronghold for the Ku Klux Klan. It is alleged that Jones's father had Klan connections, but this has not been proved. At any rate, the family was poor. Jones's father, a railroad man, worked only occasionally after being wounded in World War I, and his mother had part-time employment at a factory in a nearby town. In 1945 his parents split up, and Jones moved with his mother to Richmond, sixteen miles away.[11]

Raised as a Methodist, Jones evidenced an interest in religion from the early years of his life, often "playing church" and "holding services." In particular, he would conduct pet funerals. On one occasion he held an intensely dramatic service for a dead mouse. Before entering his teens, Jones came under the influence of a neighbor, a devout member of the Nazarene Church, and supposedly experienced a conversion. Having natural leadership qualities, he attracted friends and began to tell them what to do, even disciplining them at times. Most of all, he preached to them, sometimes disturbing his listeners with vivid descriptions of sinners burning in hell. While Jones had been fascinated with preaching since childhood, he first mounted a real pulpit when he was fourteen and employed at a local hospital. Some of his black coworkers invited him to present a sermon at their church.[12]

After moving to Richmond with his mother, in 1949 Jones graduated from high school and married Marceline Baldwin, a nurse. He briefly attended college, but soon left for Indianapolis to form his own church. He attended night school at Butler University and, ten years later, earned a degree in education. In 1953 he founded the nondenominational Christian Assembly of God church. Jones began an urban ministry to the poor that included soup kitchens, day-care facilities and drug counseling. As he would do later in his Indianapolis People's Temple, Jones stressed racial equality, a position that was unpopular in the conservative Midwest of the 1950s and 1960s. In 1956 he opened the People's Temple in Indianapolis. Despite the unpopularity of his stand against racism, his operation was regarded as a legitimate church. It affiliated with the Disciples of Christ, and in 1964 he was ordained as a minister in that denomination.[13]

These early years were very important for the direction Jones and the People's Temple would take. Jones integrated his church and personally adopted eight children, including blacks and Koreans. He became active in civil rights and adopted his pastoral style to appeal to blacks and lower-class whites. Jones visited many ministers to learn from their style. In particular, he was impressed with Father Divine's control over his followers. He also became active in politics in Indianapolis, serving on the human rights commission. His public and religious activities soon drew hostile fire from the segregationists in his area. The persecution that he and his church underwent may have led to the strong paranoia and insecurity that eventually triggered the Guyana massacre. During this time Jones also became disillusioned with the American economic and social system. For reasons that are not entirely clear, he subsequently became a passionate advocate of socialism.[14]

In 1965 Jones moved to Ukiah, California, taking with him one hundred members of his Indianapolis People's Temple. According to a vision that he claimed to have had, the United States would soon be decimated by a nuclear holocaust. Because of the protected Redwood Valley, Ukiah was supposedly one of the ten safest places in the world from a nuclear fallout. In search of such a haven, Jones had previously visited Brazil and what was then British Guiana (now Guyana). From 1965 to 1972 Jones and his followers lived and worked in the vicinity of Redwood Valley, establishing a home for boys and three convalescent centers.[15]

Jones moved his headquarters to San Francisco in 1972 and started attracting local blacks to his church. Here he began a newspaper and a radio broadcast; he was appointed to the San Francisco Housing Authority, becoming chairman of this body in 1977. During this time the temple grew rapidly. Jones started a third church in Los Angeles and continued to operate the original People's Temple in Indianapolis. In all these locations, his churches focused on a social outreach that attracted poor inner-city blacks and a small number of liberal whites. However, as David Bromley and Anson Shupe note, Jones intended to do more than minister to the poor and oppressed. He wanted to change the American economic system "along the lines of socialism." In addition to his involvement in local politics, he began to gain some national recognition for his efforts. He received appreciative letters from Rosalynn Carter, Senators Henry Jackson and Hubert Humphrey and HEW Secretary Joseph Califano, among others. One interfaith group named him one of the one hundred "most outstanding" American clergy in 1975. In 1977 he won the Martin Luther King Jr. Humanitarian Award. By the mid-seventies Jim Jones was indeed riding high.[16]

As the People's Temple grew, Jones' megalomania soared and his services became stranger and stranger. As Paul Chalfant writes, he began to denounce the Bible and the outside world, perform fraudulent miracles, require followers to call him "Dad" or "Father," demand more involvement in temple activities, require members to give their possessions to the temple and insist that members of his inner circle sign loyalty oaths. More and more he preached of coming nuclear holocausts, imminent earthquakes and an approaching race war between blacks and whites. At various times Jones claimed to be God, the reincarnation of Christ and Lenin, and to have the power to bring the dead back to life. Church discipline turned into brutal beatings of erring members. "In 1976 he tested his first suicide drill on Planning Commission members" (the inner circle), explaining that it was a test of their loyalty. He told them that "the wine he had given them was poison and that they had but one hour to live."[17]

Such extremism set in motion the immediate events that led to the move to Guyana. Possibly as a result of Jones's outrageous behavior, several members withdrew from the People's Temple. Because of some alleged beatings and bizarre accidents, these former members urged Congressman Leo Ryan to begin an investigation into the activities of the People's Temple. In 1973 Jones and several followers visited Guyana, and one year later they began a small commune for agricultural production. Meanwhile, Jones's extremism had attracted media attention in San Francisco. In particular, *New West* magazine published an account, based on the stories of former members, that castigated the People's Temple. After failing to block this story, in 1977 Jones and approximately eight hundred followers migrated to the Guyana jungle and expanded the commune. From Guyana, Jones resigned his position as director of the San Francisco Housing Authority and focused on his operation at Jonestown.[18]

Jonestown was a commune of twenty-seven thousand acres located about 150 miles from Georgetown, the capital of Guyana. The socialist government of Guyana had offered a sanctuary to Jones and his followers because of his political views and his intention of establishing an agricultural enterprise. During the 1960s a number of individual Americans had moved to socialist countries protesting their countries' policies. News of a group of nearly one thousand black and white Americans who had openly rejected America and migrated to a socialist country could have been a public relations disaster for the United States. Such an event could have furthered America's image in the developing world as an oppressor of the disadvantaged. But the mass deaths shifted the focus of analysis away from social and ideological issues. Jones was simply written off as a mentally unbalanced fanatic.[19]

Life in Jonestown was very harsh, with conditions resembling those of a concentration camp. By day residents worked eleven hours in the broiling sun with few breaks. By night they attended endless reeducation meetings and listened to sleep-destroying harangues booming over the camp's public address system. Their living quarters were overcrowded. Their diet was monotonous, consisting of rice and gravy. Disciplinary measures and punishments were more harsh than they had been in California. A sin such as drinking a glass of wine was punishable by public beating. Even the children were not exempt. Their misbehavior resulted in such harsh punishments as being tied up and left in the jungle for the night, or being dropped into a well of water, to be pulled out when they screamed for forgiveness. Jonestown has been described as "a nightmare" by some of those who escaped.[20]

Jones was accused of smuggling drugs and weapons into the camp to control potential runaways and other unruly members. When stories of these deeds and other atrocities leaked out, relatives of the residents persuaded Congressman Ryan to lead an investigation. After some negotiations with People's Temple lawyers, Ryan, along with two aides, nine journalists and several others, went to Jonestown, arriving on November 17, 1978. Following a time of questioning, several residents slipped notes to Ryan's investigative team, indicating that they wanted to leave the commune. An hour-by-hour account of the ensuing events has been chronicled by many sources. Suffice it to say that on November 18 some defectors and the investigative team were ambushed and killed as they were leaving the commune. That night more than nine hundred persons, including many children, committed suicide or were murdered by drinking or injecting poison. Evidence suggests that Jones either shot himself or was shot by a close aide.[21]

Ideology

Most government investigators and journalists interpret the Guyana situation psychologically. They say that Jones was crazy and the people were brainwashed. Jones may have been insane, depending on how the term is used, and the people may have been persuaded to commit suicide by a charismatic personality who exercised immense control over them. But behind the tragedy at Jonestown was an ideology or theology. As John Hall points out, the People's Temple should be regarded as an apocalyptic movement.[22] The apocalyptic mood of the larger American society during the 1960s had its impact on Jones, especially the racial strife, the political unrest and the perceived impending nuclear holocaust.

While the roots of the People's Temple can be traced to the revivalistic evangelical tradition, by the time of Jonestown the group had come to resemble an otherworldly, apocalyptic cult. Hall claims that Jones's group shared with other apocalyptic groups a pessimism about "reforming social institutions in this world." Though he supported various progressive causes, he had little hope for their success. Yet his prophetic views were more radical than those of most millennial groups: "he focused on an imminent apocalyptic disaster rather than on Christ's millennial salvation." His eschatology contained tensions over the choice of fighting the "beast" (the American social and economic system) or collective flight from the impending disaster to set up a kingdom of the elect. The People's Temple was more "directed toward the latter possibility."[23]

Even while in Indiana, Jones had adhered to an apocalyptic worldview.

351

He had moved his followers to Redwood Valley on the rationale that this area would survive a nuclear holocaust. During the California years, Jones's apocalyptic vision turned to the predictions of "CIA persecution and Nazi-like extermination of blacks." In California the People's Temple gradually developed certain communal characteristics. By the time of Jonestown, "the People's Temple more and more [had come] to exist as an ark of survival." The mass exodus from California began in 1977, when the People's Temple came under closer investigation by the media. Such scrutiny was perceived by the church as CIA persecution. In this the Temple bears some superficial resemblance to a number of the Protestant sects that arrived in the wilderness of North America beginning in the seventeenth century. The Puritans, Shakers, Rappites, Moravians, Lutherans and many others came to America in order to "escape religious persecution in Europe by setting up theocracies where they could live out their vision of an earthy millennial community."[24]

The People's Temple shared some social characteristics with other apocalyptic groups: harsh disciplinary practices, charismatic leadership, mechanisms for social control and the perspective that society at large was evil. Nevertheless, the People's Temple was distinctive among most apocalyptic groups for three reasons: its racial integration, its ideological communism and its theology of suicide.

Racial equality was an integral part of Jones's overt "theology," even if this point was partially negated by the fact that whites dominated the authority structure of the People's Temple. Throughout his ministry, as Hall indicates, Jones consistently sought to transcend racism by peaceful means. He worked for racial harmony in his Indiana ministry, forming an interracial congregation in the 1950s. That endeavor met much resistance, and this persecution was one reason for the exodus to California. The extent to which Jones actually achieved racial equality in his operations is open to question. Nevertheless, the People's Temple promoted racial harmony more than the larger society and mainstream religious bodies did.[25]

Hall notes another key element in Jones's theology: his commitment to socialism or communism. Jones's reasons for adopting socialism are unclear. It may have been related to his condemnation of American society as racist. As with his views on racial equality, Jones had evidenced a socialism-oriented philosophy early in his professional career, and in his own way he set out to implement this view. Many apocalyptic and otherworldly groups have practiced a religiously inspired communism, "usually a 'clerical' or 'Christian' socialism." However, few if any have dabbled with the communist theories of Marx and Engels. Jim Jones and his staff considered themselves to be socialists in the Marxist tradition. According to his wife, Marceline, Jones regarded himself as a Marxist who "used religion to try to get some people out of the opiate of religion." On one occasion Jones intimated that he had been a member of the U.S. Communist Party in the 1950s. Jones's move to Guyana was predicated not only on his vision of an impending nuclear disaster but also on his communist orientation.[26]

As time went on, Jones's communist ideology came to dominate what was left of his traditional Christian faith. While he was clearly more religious than the leaders of the early-nineteenth-century socialist sects, he did not believe in a God who answers prayer, and at times he even preached a form of atheism. He also believed in reincarnation. According to Hall, Jones apparently used the "outward manifestations of conventional religious activity"—sermons, revivals, faith-healing—to draw people into an organization that had a different orientation. Support for this view can be found in the fact that Jones ceased to perform miracles and cut off other religious activities once he arrived in Jonestown.[27]

The third key aspect of Jones's beliefs was his theology of suicide. This ideology sharply distinguished the People's Temple from other new religions and apocalyptic groups. Where Jones acquired this idea is uncertain. Perhaps it stemmed from his paranoid personality. Or maybe it developed over the persecution that he encountered because of his insistence on racial equality and socialism. We do know that he adopted the gruesome term "revolutionary suicide" from Huey Newton, the Black Panther activist who wrote a book to advocate "dying for a cause." While Newton saw collective suicide as an act of defiance to further the socialist cause, however, Jones exalted the idea to almost a sacramental status.[28]

There exists the common notion that the people who committed mass suicide at Jonestown or elsewhere were simply crazy. This view cannot survive close scrutiny. As Richardson notes, "Jones opposed individual suicide but advocated collective suicide as a possible and logical outcome of being attacked by forces opposed to his efforts." As with other cases of mass suicide in history, the event at Jonestown was " 'dying for a cause' for the more politically oriented," while for the more religious "it was achieving 'other worldly salvation.' "[29]

Hall claims that many apocalyptic sects or cults promise a theocratic haven on earth in which their members can "escape the 'living hell' of society at large." Many of Jones's followers appeared to have joined the People's Temple with such a hope in mind. For the blacks in particular, the temple promised some immediate relief from persecution rather than some other-worldly hope. But as the persecution mounted and defectors from the temple increased, it became doubtful whether Jones could establish such a haven in the United States. He was thus "reduced to decrying the web of 'evil' powers" that had entrapped him and searching for another postapoc-alyptic sanctuary—that is, one that would survive the impending catas-trophe. He went to Jonestown hoping to find such a haven. But he could not be sure that Jonestown was the promised land. He did not "trust the Guyanese government" and was "considering seeking final asylum" in the Soviet Union or Cuba.[30]

But even this hope came unraveled when he became convinced that the church's enemies were about to descend on Jonestown. Jones could not pretend to have achieved any victory over his enemies. In his mind, the People's Temple could only "abandon the apocalyptic hell by the act of mass suicide." The opponents of the temple would then be shut out. They could not undo what had already been undone. "There could be no recrim-inations against the dead." Moreover, this mass suicide "could achieve the other-worldly salvation Jones had promised his more religious followers."[31]

The holocaust at Jonestown must be seen as one of the worst human disasters in the late twentieth century. Beyond the immediate loss of lives there were other repercussions. Anticultists adopted an "I told you so" attitude. Some attempted to portray the People's Temple as the typical cult. Socialists and communists all over the world distanced themselves from Jones's group. Scholars of a liberal persuasion made attempts to see Jones as a casualty of the repressive American social and economic system. Per-haps the Disciples of Christ experienced the most embarrassment. The tem-ple severely bruised the denomination, but did not scar it for life. After the mass deaths, the People's Temple obviously had no future. Though several thousand members remained in California and Indiana, within a year the church officially ceased to exist.[32]

23

Aberrational
Groups in the
Jesus Movement

S ome may say that the Jesus movement began with Jesus and that
the entire history of Christianity is really a history of this movement. Nevertheless, in the current use of the term, "the Jesus movement" refers to a modern social phenomenon involving numerous young
people whose religious activities revolved around a strict literal interpretation of the Bible and other trappings of conservative Christianity. The phenomenon began in the mid-1960s and continued in a modified and reduced
form into the 1980s.[1] The Jesus movement largely falls within the framework of evangelical and fundamentalist Christianity, and thus is not a subject for this book. Yet several Jesus groups were more deviant and exhibited
cultic characteristics. For background on these more radical bodies it will
thus be necessary to examine the Jesus movement as a whole.

The Jesus People
The Jesus movement was highly diverse, a fact illustrated by the number
of names and organizations associated with the movement. The more common generic names are Jesus People, Street Christians, Jesus Freaks and
God's Forever Family.[2] The organizations with identifiable leaders and locations fall into four broad categories: individual churches, parachurch organizations, campus organizations and communal groups. Beyond these
there are a number of individuals and organizations who are on the pe-
riphery of the movement. A partial list of the better-known organizations

linked to the Jesus movement would include Calvary Chapel, Bethel Tabernacle, Jesus People's Army, His Place, Christian World Liberation Front, East Coast Jesus People, Jews for Jesus, Children of God, the Alamo Christian Foundation and The Way. Though the Jesus movement reached many parts of the country, the capital of the Jesus revolution was California, especially Hollywood.[3]

The decade of the 1960s represented a time of cultural dislocation and sociopolitical upheaval. Protests exploded over many issues, and these protests assumed the form of a new social movement, "the counterculture." Quite often the religious aspect of this counterculture came in the shape of Eastern mysticism, new forms of self-awareness and spiritual narcissism. Yet the counterculture had its Christian expression in the Jesus people.

Most of the "Jesus freaks" were recruits from the wider youth movement of the 1960s. Jack Balswick thus claims that "they represent a counterculture within a counterculture." The Jesus people were "double dropouts." On one hand, as part of the counterculture, they differed with some of the values of straight society. On the other hand, they were at "variance with many of the values" of the broader youth culture. As products of their generation, they exhibited counterculture characteristics: subjectivism, informality, spontaneity and the symbols of a hippie lifestyle: "long hair, beards, rock music, cast-off clothes, and a questioning of the American way of life." Yet because of their connection with fundamentalism, the Jesus people rejected key aspects of the counterculture: the use of drugs, alcohol and tobacco; sexual promiscuity; and general moral relativism.[4]

As Ron Enroth notes, these countercultural Christians had little background "exposure to organized Christianity." They were drawn into the fold through the passionate evangelism of ex-drug addicts, street preachers, middle-aged ministers and social dropouts who had "only marginal ties with the institutional church." The movement grew until its heyday in the early 1970s, reaching perhaps 300,000 members. "A kind of grass roots diversity manifested in widely scattered subgroups, which lacked a single leadership structure and clear-cut goals," characterized the Jesus people and their successor movements.[5]

The movement's diversity and its rapid decline since the mid-1970s resulted in considerable polarization between its various elements. One segment of the movement, related to the "more moderate surviving core," adopted a culture-affirming outlook and drifted toward established evangelicalism.

Churches such as Calvary Chapel and the Vineyard Christian Fellowship in southern California exemplify the evolution of "hip churches" into mainstream evangelicalism. The second trend can be found in the "more clearly cultic, isolationist, culture-rejecting extremist groups that emerged out of the turmoil of the 1960s." The Children of God, The Way and the Alamo Christian Foundation illustrate this direction.[6]

As the Jesus people grew older, most of them cut their hair, traded their jeans for business suits and left their communes for single-family homes. With the fading of these outward symbols, the Jesus movement appeared to pass into history. In the late 1980s, however, the Jesus movement still exists. Though the extremes of the secular counterculture eventually disappeared, certain influences and values have endured. The same can be said for the Christian counterculture. Some Jesus-people residential communities still exist. In these groups interest in communal living, diverse modes of worship and simplicity and naturalness continue. But more important, the spirit of the Jesus movement is alive and has found its way into the larger evangelical subculture, especially in the Pentecostal and neo-Pentecostal branches of evangelicalism. Some of the central themes of the psychedelic culture of the sixties have been enfolded into evangelicalism, especially the emphasis on experience, anti-intellectualism, informal worship and new styles of music. For example, Maranatha! music helped establish contemporary Christian music, which is now a multimillion-dollar industry and has caught on in mainline evangelical circles.[7]

A less obvious influence of the Christian counterculture was its role in assisting in the creation of new forms of witness. Perhaps the greatest influence of the Jesus people can be found in a segment of evangelical Christianity which Richard Quebedeaux has termed "the Young Evangelicals." Jesus people who are now twenty years older still reflect the diversity of their earlier years. Many have stepped quietly into mainstream evangelicalism. Some, however, have gravitated toward the "evangelical left." These former Jesus people have shed aspects of their evangelical-fundamentalist background and have been deeply influenced by the social and political struggles of the 1960s. As a consequence, they emphasize a gospel with strong social dimensions. The Christian World Liberation Front and its publication, *Right On* (now *Radix*), was an important vehicle for bringing the spirit of the Jesus movement to the "evangelical left." *Sojourners* (formerly *The Post American*) is also a magazine bringing the "radical" countercultural faith into modern evangelicalism.[8]

Despite its diversity, the Jesus movement did espouse a general set of beliefs and a common mindset. In the Jesus movement two streams flowed together: the counterculture and the fundamentalist expression of evangelical Christianity. On the surface these were two opposing movements. Yet, as Robert Ellwood points out, there was a three-way continuity between the Jesus movement and traditional evangelicalism, and between both of them and the counterculture. The clear points of contact between these movements were subjectivity, an alienation from the dominant culture, a conversion psychology and an apocalyptic hope.[9]

On a more specific level, the beliefs of the Jesus movement had the characteristics of fundamentalism. Perhaps it might be better to say that its articles of faith were Jesus-centered and Bible-centered. While the beliefs of the Jesus people focused on the person of Christ, the other persons of the Trinity were also accepted, particularly the Holy Spirit. They regarded the Bible as inerrant and applied it literally. As in most conservative and fundamentalist groups, proof-texting was popular. They viewed God as an omnipotent deity who continuously intervenes in human affairs to work his will. Such a belief contributed to the movement's emphasis on signs and miracles.[10]

As Ron Enroth, Edward E. Ericson Jr. and C. Breckenridge Peters have indicated, "the single most important teaching of the Jesus People is the simple gospel"—the message that Jesus saves. But what does Jesus save— the soul or the whole person? Is salvation merely an escape from hell, or does it involve service to God and the world? To these and related questions the Jesus people usually gave superficial answers, typical of the "simplistic mentality" of fundamentalism. The simple plan of salvation was seen as the whole solution to a wide range of problems. This "doctrinally unsophisticated approach that Jesus People [took] toward the Bible [had] many ramifications" for the movement.[11]

One of the most prominent views of the Jesus people was that the world is in its last days. Everything in the Jesus movement—views on evangelism, politics, culture, history, the church—was influenced by this apocalyptic mindset. In fact, the Jesus people not only reflected the apocalyptic mentality so prevalent in the 1960s but carried it further. Most Jesus people could not imagine themselves growing old and dying a natural death. They fervently believed that they were God's chosen instruments to give the world one last chance to repent. Though the Jesus people had many differences on how and when the world would end, an apocalyptic theme unified the movement.[12]

The Jesus people minimized doctrine. James Richardson and Rex Davis say that the central focus of the movement was on experience, and that "beliefs themselves [furnished] only a way of interpreting the experiential" side of life.[13] Enroth offers a major reason that the Jesus people were so experience-oriented: they were part of the counterculture and carried this emphasis into the Jesus movement. The words *trip* and *high* were synonymous with *experience*. "To be high on drugs means to have a drug-induced experience. To be high on Jesus means to have a certain religious experience," one that was strikingly similar to the emotional experience induced by drugs.[14]

Enroth carries his point further. Reason has always played a vital role in Western civilization. The counterculture, to a large extent, was a revolt against Western civilization and its emphasis on reason. Many counterculture adherents concluded that they would have to go outside the Western tradition to find meaning in life and to satisfy their religious yearnings. Thus many such youth turned eagerly to drugs and Eastern mysticism. While the Jesus people remained within the Christian fold, they rejected its rational emphasis. The working relationship between faith and reason so prevalent in the Christian tradition was totally foreign to the Jesus people.[15]

This focus on experience has had several results and related trends. The other side of the Jesus people's experience-oriented Christianity was a strident anti-intellectualism. They delighted in quoting out of context such Bible passages as "Hath not God made foolish the wisdom of this world?" (1 Cor 1:20 KJV). Many Jesus people even claimed to read only the Bible or certain devotional guides. As one might suppose, the Jesus people placed little value in education. Beyond what was necessary to read the Bible and evangelize, education was a waste of time. They rejected the notion that education is a tool to cultivate the intellect or to broaden one's horizons.[16]

Being anti-intellectual, the Jesus people were also anticultural. Enroth says that they exemplify H. Richard Niebuhr's "Christ-against-culture approach" to the relationship between Christianity and human culture. Many Jesus people fell under the influence of Watchman Nee's radical rejection of all forms of culture, whether it be politics, education, literature, science, art, law, commerce or music. Some even regarded culture as satanic. Such an outlook promoted in much of the Jesus movement "a radical separation of Christianity from culture." Closely related to the anticultural stance of the Jesus people was their antisocial attitude. Some Jesus people demon- strated an awareness of the world and social issues. But by and large they emphasized "individual conversion to the almost total neglect of the social dimension of the gospel." The Jesus people were also antihistorical, a characteristic that they shared with the larger counterculture. From their Christian perspective, they saw time "collapsed between the period of the Book of Acts and the present day," with little of any value in the intervening period.[17]

Closely related to the experience orientation of the Jesus movement was one of its most distinctive characteristics: an involvement in Pentecostalism. In various degrees, charismatic phenomena prevailed within the Jesus movement. While speaking in tongues was not the focal point of Jesus-people theology, this practice was quite common within the movement. Glossolalia can give the participant an experiential high, rivaling a drug high. Because Jesus people claim to experience God's presence in their lives, they took an accepting attitude toward divine healing. Jesus people everywhere repeatedly cited examples of divine healing, sometimes with a casualness that suggested they took such occurrences for granted. The attention the Jesus people gave to the supernatural was evident in their frequent references to visions and in their strong sense of the presence of evil and demons.[18]

The Jesus people must also be seen as a social movement. Enroth, Ericson and Peters define a social movement "as a large-scale, widespread, informal effort" by a substantial number of people to modify the existing social order. The Jesus movement was an unorganized social movement. It had neither a single leadership structure nor a clearly articulated set of goals. What unity the movement had came in its "shared sense of mission—a compelling desire to bring people to Jesus." Sociologists of religion have regarded the Jesus people as a revitalization movement. Such a movement involves more than reform or renewal. It is more revolutionary, involving reaching out into the unknown for new patterns rather than simply a return to the familiar.[19]

Because of their emotional excesses, the Jesus people were on the fringe of American evangelicalism. Nevertheless, with few exceptions, the Jesus movement can be regarded as within the boundaries of evangelicalism. The two most notable exceptions were the Children of God and The Way. The Christian Foundation of Tony and Susan Alamo might also be placed in this category. The Christian Foundation evidenced many cultic manifestations, especially in its social characteristics. It was one of the more fanatical, totalitarian communal groups in the Jesus movement. The Christian Foundation was accused of deceiving recruits into joining the movement and then forcing them to live under poor conditions, including working for no wages. In contrast, the group's charismatic leaders, Tony Alamo and Susan Alamo (who died in 1982), lived in royal splendor. The religious beliefs of the Christian Foundation, however, were not far removed from those found in other Jesus people groups. Its teachings were largely those of fundamentalist and Pentecostal Christianity. A heavy emphasis was placed on hell and fearing God, the use of the King James Version of the Bible, the soon return of Christ and excessive emotionalism. However, Tony Alamo gained notoriety with the belief that his embalmed wife would rise from the dead. After being charged with child abuse in 1988, he was a fugitive until he was arrested in July 1991.[20]

The Children of God (Family of Love)

The Children of God were the most controversial of the Jesus people groups. Springing from the social crises of the late 1960s, they were born of the counterculture. In 1979 the Children of God changed their name to the Family of Love. Their founder, David Berg, was an early leader in the revival brought on by the Jesus people. Even within the Jesus movement, the Children of God were an extremist group. Because they strayed beyond the confines of orthodox Christianity, they became the first group to be ostracized by the mainstream of the Jesus people movement.[21]

Fervently apocalyptic, the Children of God were driven by their belief in the imminent end of the world. Despite having a name that connoted hope and optimism, they were really children of despair and disillusionment, holding little hope for America. Drawn from the counterculture, the early recruits of the Children of God were typically middle-class youth who had used drugs and were alienated from American society.[22]

David Brandt Berg was born in 1919 into an evangelical family. Both of his parents were involved in the ministry: his father was a minister, his mother was an evangelist. Berg himself served for a time as a minister in the Christian and Missionary Alliance Church, a conservative holiness denomination. After being forced out of a pastorate in Arizona, Berg developed a fierce contempt for the organized churches in America. His message of criticism of the establishment structures of America, withdrawal from the world and commitment to a Jesus revolution appealed to street people.[23]

The Children of God had their beginnings in 1968, when Berg took over a coffeehouse in Huntington Beach, California, that had been established by the Pentecostal minister David Wilkerson. Berg's ministry in Huntington Beach, which he called Teens for Christ, attracted people who had abandoned drugs in favor of the old-time religion. He conducted Bible-study classes and soon had several youth living at the coffeehouse. They became the nucleus of the Children of God. Based on a study of Acts 1—5, Berg persuaded the small group to break all ties with "the system" and to live in a commune, holding all things in common. From these early years, Berg's message was one of total commitment, the imminence of the millennium and hostile attacks on the materialistic, capitalistic, individualistic world his group had left.[24]

In 1969 Berg claimed to have received a revelation that California would shortly sink into the sea as a result of an earthquake. As a consequence, he and his followers left California for Tucson, where the group grew from fifty to seventy-five. After several months they split into four teams to spread their message across America; one team reached Canada several months later. By now the group had begun to take a more organized form.[25]

But the wanderings continued. The entire membership met in Virginia, where Berg informed them of some of his secret revelations. One of these, which Gordon Melton describes, was called "Old Church, New Church," and concerned an adulterous affair Berg had with his secretary. Rather than repent, he attempted to justify the liaison theologically, comparing his wife and secretary to models of the church. "God had abandoned the old denominational church" for the new church (the Jesus revolution). So Berg "abandoned his wife, who, like the old church, had become a hindrance to God's work," for a new love. "This theological metaphor of his sexual life led to the development of sex as a major ingredient of the Children's life and thought." Berg now spoke of America "as the Great Whore" and of "an understanding of revolutionary Christian love that involved communal sex."[26]

The Children of God continued to journey across America, receiving a great deal of media attention as they demonstrated against American society while dressed in red sackcloth and ashes, bearing staves and wearing yokes. They attended such events as the funeral of Senator Everett Dirksen (who had gained their favor because of his advocacy of Bible-reading in the schools) and the conspiracy trial of Jerry Rubin. It was during this "exodus" that they picked up the name Children of God and Berg became known as Mo, Moses or Moses David.[27]

In 1970 Fred Jordan, an independent Pentecostal radio and television preacher, gave the Children permission to move onto his properties. These included a ranch near Thurber, Texas, and two sites in California. Berg hoped to establish large, self-sufficient communes that would attract recruits from throughout the country. In turn, Jordan intended to have the Children of God promote his work by appearing on his radio and television programs. However, the marriage of convenience between Berg and Jordan, who had had previous tensions, broke down, and Jordan evicted the Children from his properties.[28]

By 1971 Berg had already concluded that his plan for several large colonies needed modification. In order to reach the world's population more rapidly, he now advocated the establishment of smaller, widely scattered colonies. The Children of God thus dispersed around the nation in some forty colonies of no more than a dozen. Though Berg was still the ultimate leader of the Children, he began to delegate authority over daily operations to members of his family. He took up directing the evolving doctrine of the scattered flock by means of letters, which came to be known as "Moses Letters" or simply "Mo-letters."[29]

Firmly convinced of the coming downfall of America, by the early 1970s Berg had left the country, and some Children followed him. One Mo-letter warned that a comet, Kohoutek, would destroy America. Typical of most apocalyptic groups, the Children of God went wild and believed that this comet represented the final sign of America's doom and a fulfillment of prophecy. Spurred in part by the possibility of this destruction, by the mid-1970s most of the Children had left America. Though they believed that the whole world would end soon, they were obsessed with the total downfall of America in particular, most likely through a communist takeover. They moved in small groups to Europe, Asia, Africa, South America and Australia. At this time they claimed more than four hundred colonies throughout the world and about four thousand disciples.[30]

During this period of the dispersion of the Children of God, Berg strayed progressively further from Christian doctrines and practices. He came to see himself more as a prophet, and his prophecies, which increasingly were seen as coming from disembodied spirits, assumed the dominant role in molding the group's ideas. According to Ruth Tucker, Berg's occult involvement now became more evident. "He began speaking in tongues with the help of Abrahim, a 'spirit guide' " Berg had acquired at a Gypsy camp. Berg openly bragged of other "spiritual contacts with the dead." A partial list of these individuals would include "his parents, William Jennings Bryan, Martin Luther, Peter the Hermit, the Pied Piper, Ivan the Terrible, Anne Boleyn and many other historical figures." Besides his personal spirit contacts, "Berg claimed that the entire Children of God movement had a guardian angel of sorts—Abner, a faithful member who had died" and now served as the group's personal representative in the courts of heaven. Moreover, on at least one occasion Berg claimed to have had an out-of-body experience in which he was visited by a departed spirit.[31]

After 1974 Berg extended his increasingly radical ideas about sexual freedom to include the most controversial practice of the Children of God, "flirty fishing." In a Mo-letter, Berg ordered the women of the group to use their sexual appeal to gain new members—to become fish bait, hookers for Jesus. This practice began in London, but Berg feared opposition from the English authorities and took some female disciples to Tenerife, a Spanish island off the coast of Morocco where the tourist lifestyle was wide open. Tucker tells us that at Tenerife "the technique of 'FFing,' as Mo calls it, was developed and refined into practically an artform." Berg set forth guidelines for the Children of God's religious prostitution in a pamphlet entitled "The Flirty Little Fishy," where 101 admonitions for this work were enumerated. In his 1979 annual report Berg stated that his "FFers" had now "witnessed to over a quarter-of-a million souls, loved over 25,000 of them and won about 19,000 to the Lord." "Flirty fishing," while not entirely discontinued, began to decline in the late 1970s after venereal disease played havoc with the group.[32]

The practice of using sex to recruit new members increased the negative image of this extremist group. The death of over nine hundred members of the People's Temple furthered such a perception, for some people saw the Children of God as candidates for a similar tragedy. Berg, therefore, took some steps to improve the group's image. He reorganized the Children of God, replacing the colony structure with a family model. He gave the group its present name, the Family of Love, and told followers to call him "Dad."[33]

For most of the group's brief history, the organizational and authority structure of the Children of God resembled a pyramid, with Berg at the top, followed by apostles, elders and deacons. Within such a general pattern, several structural shifts can be detected. During 1968 and 1969, before settling at Jordan's Texas ranch, the Children of God most resembled a wandering remnant. When the Children settled in Texas during 1970 and 1971, they maintained a large colony and saw themselves as "The New Nation," patterned after the tribes of Israel and the Gypsies. The years after their ejection from Jordan's Texas Soul Clinic were a phase of dispersion, when the Children lived in small colonies throughout the world. In 1979 Berg radically altered the group's structure. He disbanded the existing colonies into small family groups and gave the group a new name, the Family of Love, to further this type of organization and image. The modern Children of God movement thus operates under a looser, more decentralized structure than in the past.[34]

As Melton points out, the Children of God began "as a conservative holiness Christian group" related to the Jesus movement. Berg's "ideas about the imminent end of the world, God's abandonment of worldly structures (governments, churches, economic systems), the coming Jesus revolution, and communalism" were extreme "but by no means unacceptable" to the larger Jesus movement. But as the Children of God evolved, "they thoroughly left orthodox Christian belief and practice." This departure began when Berg assumed "the role, and not just the image of Moses." To the Children he was a "prophet of the end time." His Mo-letters replaced the Bible as the group's primary authority. Berg's personality—though he has been a shadowy figure, secluded from the membership at large—has dominated the Children of God through its history. As Tucker writes, he claims to speak "for God as Moses" and to "rule a theocracy as King David." Despite some decentralization, Berg is in "unquestioned control of every aspect of his world wide network."[35]

As Moses had done, Berg declared war on what he regarded as the evil system of his day. In his fanatical hatred for the United States, he twisted biblical prophecies to prove that America was the "Great Whore" of Revelation whom God would destroy. The Children of God generated intense bitterness toward the Christian churches, including the Jesus people, for their "hypocritical, do-nothing" religion. Perhaps the Children directed their most intense hostility toward the American family. While most individuals in the Jesus movement experienced a serious generation gap, the Children of God made it a central doctrine. Interpreting literally the biblical passages that speak of children hating their parents, the group encouraged recruits to view their parents as enemies.[36]

End-time prophecy was very important to the Children of God. Above all they were a millennial group, expecting the soon return of Christ and his thousand-year rule. They saw the present system, especially that of the Western world, as so corrupt that no reformation was possible. It had to end before a new order could begin. The final collapse, writes Tucker, "will come when Communism takes over the western nations and paves the way for the anti-Christ." Under this individual's rule, professing Christians will deny the faith and "receive the mark of the beast" mentioned in the book of Revelation. But the Children of God will stand "as God's faithful remnant of 144,000." The Children of God expect something like the posttribulational rapture, with the saints being persecuted during the tribulation and drawn up into heaven at the end. But in some ways "Berg's eschatology was similar to dispensational premillennialism" with its emphasis on the coming tribulation and rapture. In still other ways, his eschatology—especially his date-setting and exclusivism—resembles those of the Jehovah's Witnesses and the Worldwide Church of God. For the impending end, Berg has a precise countdown beginning with the "End of the Time of the Gentiles" in 1968 and culminating with the rapture in 1993. After Christ's return, the Children of God will serve as important officials during the millennium.[37]

The Children of God, as Melton notes, "assumed the role of the harbinger of God's New World." They were to pave the way by serving as a "living example of a totally new loving society." One sign of their role was "their new sexual ethic." They equated love with sex. As a result, "the free expression of sexuality, including fornication, adultery, lesbianism (though not male homosexuality), and incest, were not just permitted but encouraged." The Children of God had brought the sexual revolution, so prevalent in the counterculture, into their religious practices. As an end-time prophet, Berg claimed authority to teach such new truth, regardless of its biblical support. "He even discarded the traditional concept of the Trinity and adopted a belief in universal salvation."[38]

The domestic and economic organization of the Children of God has shifted several times during its brief existence. Thus generalizations regarding life in the organization are difficult. Yet some patterns can be discerned on most levels. The Children of God are clearly an authoritarian organization that places an enormous emphasis on the divine appointment of its leaders and the need for immediate and complete submission to authority. The life of the convert is carefully controlled. Communication with parents is severely restricted. Mail is censored, and telephone calls are monitored. To make it difficult for parents to find their children, new converts have their names changed and are moved from commune to commune. Life in a colony is generally spartan. While the food is adequate, there are few luxuries. Though the Children hate communism, they practice a form of it. They utterly reject capitalism and share most goods. When joining the Children of God, a convert gives the group all personal possessions, and after this they are kept to a minimum. Moreover, the convert must agree to live by the rules, which include no alcohol, no tobacco, no drugs, little time to oneself and little sleep. Work is long and hard, including attending many educational sessions, seeking donations and distributing literature. The Children of God are definitely a totalitarian cult that maintains strict control over nearly all aspects of members' lives.[39]

What is the future of the Children of God? Berg directs the organization from London. For the most part, the Children have abandoned the United States and have centers in over seventy other countries. Though their numbers declined in the late 1970s, their membership appears to have stabilized on a global level during the 1980s. In 1990 their total membership stood at about thirteen thousand worldwide. The Children of God appeared like a meteor on the American horizon because they expressed something of the hopelessness of the counterculture years. They are a strange group, but they are not new. Millennial groups appear during times of stress and change. Even in the context of the counterculture and the Jesus revolution, the Children of God were an extremist group, but that was what attracted some disaffected youth. They catered to the radical mindset so prevalent in the youth culture of the late sixties and early seventies. The Children of God may hang on, but their appeal will be limited.[40]

The Way International

The Way International had its origin in the early ministries of Victor Paul Wierwille. The organization got its start in 1942 with "Vesper Chimes," a radio ministry begun by Wierwille, who then was serving as the pastor of the Evangelical and Reformed Church of Paine, Ohio. The name was subsequently changed several times, first to "The Chimes Hour" and then to "The Chimes Hour Youth Caravan." The name The Way was assumed in 1955, and in 1974 the present name, The Way International, Inc., was adopted.[41]

Though The Way was not well accepted by other Jesus people groups, both scholars and the news media regard it as part of the larger Jesus movement.[42] The Way began well before the Jesus revolution got underway, but it was largely unknown until its association with the Jesus movement. Thanks to coverage by *Life* and *Time,* it became known as one of the Jesus groups. According to Enroth, The Way's direct association with the Jesus people can be traced to Wierwille's "successful procurement of two of the early Jesus freaks, Steve Hufner and Jimmy Doop, to head up The Way East and The Way West." The Way grew tremendously through recruiting young people from the Jesus movement. Nevertheless, The Way's attempts to gain acceptance in the Jesus revolution were not met with complete friendship. Many of the Jesus people regarded The Way as a heretical movement and Wierwille as a false prophet.[43]

Victor Paul Wierwille (1916-85) was born on the family farm in Ohio and grew up in the Evangelical and Reformed Church, which has since become the United Church of Christ. He attended Mission College in Wisconsin, graduating with a B.A. in 1938 and a B.D. in 1940. He pursued graduate studies at the University of Chicago and Princeton Theological Seminary, which granted him an M.Th. in 1941. In 1942 he was ordained, took his first pastorate and began a radio ministry. Two years later he took an Evangelical and Reformed Church in Van Wert, Ohio, where he stayed until 1957.[44]

His experiences and studies during the years at Van Wert shaped Wierwille's thought and ministry. In the early 1940s he claimed to have had a life-changing experience in which God spoke to him audibly. He also undertook an intense program of biblical research that would eventually shape the teachings of The Way. In 1948 he received a Th.D. from Pikes Peak Bible Seminary, an unaccredited mail-order institution that no longer exists. During these years he focused his studies on the Holy Spirit and in 1951 spoke in tongues for the first time.[45]

While his apparently successful ministry at the Van Wert church continued, Wierwille put the results of his research to use and in 1953 began his first Power for Abundant Living (PFAL) class. His research activities did not end here. By the mid-1950s, he began publication of *The Way Magazine* and embarked upon a study of Aramaic. His research led to his acceptance of doctrines contrary to those of the church and to his resignation from the Evangelical and Reformed Church.[46]

From 1957 to his retirement in 1982, Wierwille led The Way organization. The radio ministry and *The Way Magazine* had begun earlier. But in 1957 Wierwille assumed control of his family's farm in New Knoxville, Ohio, and within several years he had made it the official headquarters of The Way. From this base he began his nondenominational ministry, which focused on fellowship, research and teaching. The ministry experienced growth during the early 1960s, but the real acceleration began in 1967 and 1968, when Wierwille made a mission trip to the Haight-Ashbury district of San Francisco. Important relationships were sparked with a number of countercultural young people. Momentum picked up when several of them returned to the farm in Ohio and became leaders in the organization. At the time of the Jesus people revival, The Way drew college-aged youth mostly from the counterculture. During the early seventies, The Way grew considerably and became one of the largest among the groups that have been labeled as cults.[47]

Many institutional developments accompanied this expansion. In 1971 Wierwille initiated the Word over the World Ambassador (WOW) program, which trained and sent young people affiliated with The Way across the United States and to other countries. The same year saw the first gathering of the Rock of Ages Festival, an annual gathering of Way members, and the beginning of the Way Corps, a leadership-training program. In 1974 The Way College of Emporia, Kansas, on a campus that had been a Presbyterian school, was started. The Way Family Ranch in Colorado was also acquired.[48]

Wierwille modeled The Way after a tree, writes George Braswell. "The leaves were Way followers; the twigs were local fellowships; the limbs and trunks represented regional and national bodies; and the roots were the national headquarters in New Knoxville." The first step in joining The Way is usually when an individual takes its basic course, called "Power for Abundant Living." For this course, students must pay tuition. When it is completed, they are encouraged to continue in The Way by taking advanced courses and becoming involved in the organization's programs. Despite a significant institutionalization, as Melton points out, "The Way has not moved to purchase church buildings and organize congregations in the traditional sense." Thus, its membership meets regularly in members' homes and appears "to be largely invisible in the various communities in which it operates."[49]

In 1982 Wierwille retired and was replaced by the Reverend Craig Martindale, though Wierwille, who became president emeritus, exerted considerable influence until his death in 1985. In 1983 The Way International claimed over twenty-six thousand members in the United States, with foreign work beginning in Argentina, Chile, Colombia, Venezuela and Zaire. In that year, about fourteen thousand took the basic PFAL course. The organization offered many advanced courses and published a number of books and a bimonthly magazine. In addition, The Way vigorously continued its basic programs—the Way Corps, The Way Family Corps and the Sunset Corps.[50]

In recent years, however, The Way has come on hard times. To write its obituary would be premature. Yet to many observers the movement seems to be deteriorating. For years The Way has been under external attack. Besides the usual allegations of mind control and brainwashing, two other charges have been directed at The Way. The organization has been accused of training its members in the use of firearms. To date The Way has not engaged in any violence, and beyond the fact that The Way College offered a gun safety course there is little evidence to support such a charge. The second accusation, that the organization teaches heretical doctrines, stands and remains as a barrier to The Way's being accepted by other Christian bodies.[51]

These external problems, however, have not been the major reasons for The Way's decline in recent years. The organization grew in spite of these problems. With the death of Victor Paul Wierwille—the founder, authority, and charismatic leader of The Way—the organization has gone into a transitional period. It has faced a leadership crisis and does not appear to be coping successfully with this problem. The legitimacy of Martindale's leadership was challenged by dissenters within the organization, and he was forced to resign. Amid accusations of intolerance, adultery and mismanagement, visible signs of deterioration have arisen. In 1987 attendance at the annual conference dropped, donations declined by one-third, enrollment at The Way College plummeted, and, even more significant, at least three factions broke from the church. Some individuals in these "alternative ministries" have challenged Wierwille's teachings. In 1989 The Way closed its college in Emporia because of low enrollment. Yet despite these problems, the soon demise of The Way is not expected.[52]

The Way maintains a strange mixture of beliefs. On one hand, it adheres to some views resembling the ancient heresies of Arianism, Monarchianism, Sabellianism and Modalism. On the other hand, it maintains a Pentecostal ultradispensationalism. These two positions are strange bedfellows, even within the context of fundamentalist Christianity.[53]

As noted by Kenneth Boa, the source of authority for The Way is the Bible as interpreted by Victor Wierwille. Wierwille claims that God spoke to him, saying that he would "teach him the true New Testament doctrines as they were originally understood by the first century apostles." Thus "the Doctor" (as he is affectionately called) is regarded by his followers as the first new apostle after Paul, and in possession of "the first pure and correct interpretation of the Word since the first century A.D." What Wierwille regards as his exclusive "recovery of this lost truth" can be found in his many writings and the PFAL courses. In his lectures and writings Wierwille went to great lengths "to create the appearance of scholarship by referring to the biblical languages (Hebrew, Aramaic and Greek) and to church history."[54]

The Way deviates from traditional orthodox Christianity at several points. One of the cornerstones of Wierwille's theology, and the point at which he departs most radically from orthodoxy, is his denial of the Trinity and the divinity of Christ. This point is illustrated in the title of his most popular book, *Jesus Christ Is Not God* (1975). Wierwille argues that the doctrine of the Trinity is polytheistic and thus pagan. Jesus Christ is neither coequal nor coeternal with God, but a created being. The Holy Spirit, according to Wierwille, is not a personal being but the power of God. In these beliefs, The Way aligns itself with the ancient Arians as well as with other antitrinitarian groups, including the modern-day Jehovah's Witnesses and the Worldwide Church of God. In particular, Wierwille's views resemble those of ancient Sabellianism or Modalism: the teaching that God the Father is preeminent and the Son and Holy Spirit are modes of the Father's self-expression and self-revelation.[55]

The Way, as Gordon Melton indicates, also teaches ultradispensationalism, "an approach to Scripture which views the Bible books as products of progressive . . . periods of different administrations of God's relationship to humanity." Dispensationalism arose in the nineteenth century with the Plymouth Brethren and has since spread throughout evangelical Protestantism. "Dispensationalists believe the church presently exists in the dispensation of grace, which began at Christ's resurrection and will continue until his second coming." Ultradispensationalism adds another dispensation between Christ's resurrection and the New Testament church as depicted in Paul's later epistles. "This period of transition is characterized by John's water baptism and its story is told primarily in the Book of Acts." Ultradispensationalism regards Paul's later epistles, especially Galatians, Ephesians, Philippians and Colossians, as the primary documents of the dispensation of grace. Thus Wierwille concludes that the Old Testament and the Gospels are not basic for the modern church and should be used only for education. Following this line of thought, he believed "in one baptism, that of the Holy Spirit," and therefore rejected water baptism.[56]

The Way's teachings on salvation and on tongues also differ from those of evangelical Protestantism. Salvation comes in two stages. The new birth comes first. One does not have to be a follower of The Way to experience the new birth, but such a salvation is incomplete. It offers no power for abundant living, but is primarily a preparation for the second step of salvation—that is, receiving the Holy Spirit. The evidence for receiving the Holy Spirit is speaking in tongues. Thus for The Way, speaking in tongues is for all born-again believers and is a necessary evidence of complete salvation.[57]

In some ways the religious practices promoted by The Way are typical of contemporary cultic groups, but in other ways they are different. As Tucker notes, The Way is not "a puritanical religious movement," shunning worldly activities as do "the Jehovah's Witnesses, the Worldwide Church of God, and the Hare Krishnas." In fact, except for their frequent Bible studies, The Way followers tend to live mostly as other college students do. They drink alcoholic beverages, smoke and play rock music. But in other ways, The Way's religious practices evidence cultic characteristics. "Way followers who leave the fellowship are shunned. The organization is tight, and those who would challenge the authority of the leadership are viewed as dissidents." Also, The Way's intense indoctrination of potential members "has given rise to charges of brainwashing."[58]

What does the future hold for The Way? On one hand, the movement grew in the wake of the counterculture. But unlike other groups of its time, it continued to grow after the counterculture had waned. This came about for several reasons. First and foremost, The Way, except for its heretical doctrines, shares much with fundamentalism and the Pentecostal movement. It maintains a literal, dispensational interpretation of the King James Bible. The Way's focus on tongues has given it an experiential emphasis. After the counterculture declined, fundamentalism and neo-Pentecostalism continued to grow, largely because they meet religious needs for experience, authoritative teachings, fellowship and a conservative lifestyle. The Way was able to meet many needs, and thus it grew. In addition, The Way's many institutional structures have enabled it to grow.

On the other hand, The Way faces some serious problems. Barring a dramatic rejection of Wierwille's teachings, The Way will continue to be repudiated by other Christian bodies. It tends to remain exclusive in a day when religious pluralism is challenging churches to cooperate. But most serious is the leadership problem. If The Way can solve this dilemma, then it can continue to exist and possibly become a sizable established fringe religion as have the Mormons and Jehovah's Witnesses. If it cannot, the future for The Way is not bright.

24

Epilogue

What future do occult and cultic movements have in an age addicted to science and technology? Many such groups have paraded across American history, from the colonial period to the present. Some of these bodies have survived and even prospered. A larger number, however, have not caught on and are now extinct. Nevertheless, there exists considerable continuity between the occult and cultic movements of the past and those of the present. While the specific forms of these groups may change, the substance is often very similar. The occult and cults of the present day have their roots in the past. In fact, quite often the new religions of the present are really old religions wearing a different set of clothes.

Not only must the cults and occult be seen as connected with the past, but they also must be regarded as closely related to the present. Most fringe religions have been shaped extensively by the cultural milieu out of which they arose. Some have adopted and even exaggerated the cultural trends of their day. Such marginal groups do not reject the prevailing currents in American culture. Instead, they embrace selective aspects of American life, push them to extremes and add their peculiar religious dimension to it. Occult and cultic bodies are influenced by their cultural milieu in yet another way: they strongly reject it. They are countercultural, and their major tenets and practices may be seen as a response to what they perceive to be the problems of American society. Not all fringe religions fit neatly into these culture-affirming and culture-rejecting categories. Some have both elements, embracing some aspects of American culture while reacting to others. Either way, these groups have been extensively shaped by their cultural context.

Several factors point to an increased, or at least a stable, activity on the part of occult and cultic groups. First, cultural pluralism continues to abound. In an age of increased globalization, religious pluralism will accelerate. By the late 1980s about 4 percent of the United States population was Muslim, Buddhist or Hindu. There are about as many Muslims as Episcopalians or Presbyterians. The concept of Christendom has given way to the pluralistic society. One can no longer regard America as a nation in which Christianity is the only real religious option.[1] Such an environment will undoubtedly continue to produce two other types of fringe religions in addition to the endless stream of Christian spinoffs: those with primarily an Eastern focus and those that blend Eastern and Western ideas.

Another factor is rapid social change, including perhaps a new world order. The dramatic changes witnessed since the end of World War II will not abate. Futurists claim that the 1990s will be a period of stunning technological innovation, unprecedented economic opportunity, surprising political reform and great cultural rebirth. The decline of communism brought about by the revolutions of 1989 may usher in a new world order and offer society a new worldview. Communism has collapsed in Eastern Europe and in the Soviet Union. The Cold War has ended, and the arms race appears to be over. The Soviet Union has come unraveled, and there currently exists only one superpower, the United States. Thus the new world order will probably see less tension between the major powers, but much infighting between ethnic and cultural groups and increased political fragmentation. An era of globalization has begun in many areas. There is an international call to environmentalism. Former communist countries are experimenting with democracy and market economies. Among nations, the desire for economic cooperation is stronger than the urge for military adventurism.[2] Massive social changes have produced explosions of new religions in the past and will probably do so in the future.

A third factor pointing toward growth in fringe religions is an increased spirituality. While Americans may not always support organized religion, many seek spiritual fulfillment. America is one of the most religious societies in the world. Religious bodies continue to increase. While the center—Catholic and mainline Protestant groups—has shrunk, more decentralized

"Made-in-America" churches (both evangelical and alternative bodies) have flourished. These alternative groups include cults and the quasi-religions often associated with the various self-help groups. In the future the evangelical, conservative and alternative movements give promise of growth.

A fourth element is the rise of irrationality in religion. Modern America has witnessed a paradox. On one hand, we live in a society in which science and technology dominate nearly every aspect of life. On the other hand, American religion has become more subjective and experiential. The counterculture of the 1960s dealt a blow to the rational aspect of religion. Doctrine and theology are regarded as dull, boring and irrelevant to the practice of religion. Instead, the emphasis is on emotions and experience. When it comes to acquiring religious truth, it is being said, we learn by experience and not by the cognitive process. Religion must make us feel good and meet our personal needs, or we do not want it. Because psychology deals with feelings and personal needs, it has become a surrogate religion. This trend in religion toward the subjective and experiential aspects of life shows no signs of abating in the 1990s. If this is the case, the occult and cults will continue to flourish, especially the psychoreligions and the self-help groups.

A fifth consideration is the end of a millennium. Millennial fever has existed in several religious traditions, including Christianity, Islam, Buddhism and Zoroastrianism, as well as in Brazilian and African religions. While some historians have debated how widespread the phenomenon was, most sources report a popular belief in the West that the world would come to an end in the year 1000. If the atmosphere surrounding the end of that first Christian millennium is any indicator, the 1990s may witness many bizarre religious activities.[3]

Richard Erdoes tells us that today people are again speaking of the "Second Coming—the coming of Christ, of the anointed Messiah, of the Tenth Imam, of the Mahdi, even of Buddha." Some neo-Nazis are eagerly "awaiting the reappearance of the Fuhrer" from outer space. A collection of individuals and groups on the margins of society, including "Neo-Nostradamians, Paracelsians, Cagliostroans, Saurcerians, Pyramidians, followers of Edgar Cayce the Sleeping Prophet, of Wanda the Ultra-Aquarian, of Joseph the Hairstyling Augur, and of other sooth-or-gloomsayers," predict that some cosmic cataclysm will destroy the world. This predicted extinction varies from a total obliteration of the universe to only California's being cast into the Pacific by a mighty earthquake. Yet the doomsday mindset is the same.[4]

But it is no longer only the oddballs walking the streets with placards "proclaiming the end of the world who think that this puny planet of ours might not survive the twentieth century." Perfectly rational people, including scientists and Nobel laureates, "predict humankind's demise due to overpopulation, famines, deforestation, pollution, depletion of the earth's ozone layer, or simply the collapse of civilization due to the exhaustion of essential, nonrenewable raw materials."[5] Whether the source be strange or sane individuals, an apocalyptic mentality tends to promote the growth of fringe religions.

On the other hand, the collapse of communism and the diminished possibility of a nuclear holocaust have encouraged a degree of optimism. Such a positive outlook fits into the predictions of many New Age groups, which anticipate not the end of the world but a new and improved age.

Given a continuity with the past, a close relationship to cultural trends and a stubborn refusal to die out, occult and cultic movements will probably have a good future. They may rise and fall with shifts in the cultural landscape, but they will always be with us. Currently, the occult and cults flourishing most are in the more diffuse, subtle forms of the world-transformation and personal-affirmation movements. Given the coming together of Eastern and Western ideas in a pluralistic, post-Christian America, such a trend may continue. Nevertheless, the more strident, separationist forms of the occult and cults will again have their day. They thrive best during times of crisis and tension.

Notes

Chapter 1: Introduction

[1]Rodney Stark and William S. Bainbridge, "Of Churches, Sects and Cults: Preliminary Concepts for a Theory of Religious Movements," *Journal for the Scientific Study of Religion* 18, no. 2 (1979): 118-19.

[2]John Wilson, *Religion in American Society* (Englewood Cliffs, N.J.: Prentice Hall, 1978), 10; Stark and Bainbridge, "Of Churches, Sects and Cults," 117, 119.

[3]Martin E. Marty, *A Nation of Behavers* (Chicago: University of Chicago Press, 1976), 33-34. A similar but not identical approach is taken by Joachim Wach. He says religion has three forms of expression: theological, practical and sociological. See Joachim Wach, *The Sociology of Religion* (Chicago: University of Chicago Press, 1944), 17-34.

[4]Catherine Albanese, *America: Religions and Religion* (Belmont, Calif.: Wadsworth, 1981), 8-9. See also Alan W. Watts, *Myth and Ritual in Christianity* (Boston: Beacon, 1968).

[5]Thomas Luckmann, *The Invisible Religion: The Problem of Religion in Modern Society* (New York: Macmillan, 1967).

[6]Rodney Stark and William S. Bainbridge, "Secularization, Revival and Cult Formation," *Annual Review of the Social Sciences of Religion* 4 (1980): 86.

[7]Albanese, *America,* 6-7.

[8]Charles Glock and Robert Bellah, eds., *The New Religious Consciousness* (Berkeley: University of California Press, 1976), 73-74.

[9]Rodney Stark and William S. Bainbridge, *The Future of Religion* (Berkeley: University of California Press, 1985), 30-31.

[10]Max Weber, *The Sociology of Religion* (Boston: Beacon, 1963), 46-117, 166-83; Ernst Troeltsch, *The Social Teaching of the Christian Churches,* 2 vols. (New York: Harper & Row, 1960), 1:331-43; J. Milton Yinger, *Religion, Society and the Individual* (New York: Macmillan, 1957).

[11]Roy Wallis, *The Elementary Forms of the New Religious Life* (Boston: Routledge

& Kegan Paul, 1984), 9-37; Roy Wallis, *The Rebirth of the Gods: Reflections on the New Religions in the West* (Belfast: University of Belfast, 1978), 6-10.

[12]Bryan Wilson, *Religion in Sociological Perspective* (New York: Oxford University Press, 1982), 101-5, 121ff.

[13]Bryan Wilson, *Religious Sects* (New York: McGraw-Hill, 1970), 26, 28; Bryan Wilson, "Religious Organization," in *International Encyclopedia of the Social Sciences,* 17 vols., ed. David L. Sills (New York: Macmillan, 1972), 13:134; Yinger, *Religion, Society and the Individual,* 417, 419; Bryan Wilson, ed., *Patterns of Sectarianism: Organization in Social and Religious Movements* (London: Heinemann Educational Books, 1967), 9-10; Calvin Redekop, "The Sect from a New Perspective," *The Mennonite Quarterly Review* 39, no. 3 (1965): 206-8; Troeltsch, *The Social Teaching,* 1:102-12; D. A. Martin, "The Denomination," *The British Journal of Sociology* 13, no. 1 (1962): 1.

[14]Robert Ellwood, "The Several Meanings of Cult," *Thought: A Review of Culture and Idea* 61, no. 241 (1986): 212.

[15]Several distinguished sociologists of religion take this approach. See Wilson, *Religion in Sociological Perspective,* 12; Roy Wallis, "Cult and Its Transformation," in *Sectarianism: Analysis of Religious and Non-Religious Sects,* ed. Roy Wallis (New York: John Wiley & Sons, 1975), 40.

[16]Some examples of this theological approach include the following: Walter Martin, *The Kingdom of the Cults* (Minneapolis: Bethany Fellowship, 1965); James W. Sire, *Scripture Twisting* (Downers Grove, Ill.: InterVarsity Press, 1980); Gordon Lewis, *Confronting the Cults* (Grand Rapids, Mich.: Baker Book House, 1966).

[17]Ellwood, "The Several Meanings of Cult," 217.

[18]J. Gordon Melton and Robert L. Moore, *The Cult Experience* (New York: Pilgrim, 1982), 17.

[19]Stark and Bainbridge, "Of Churches, Sects and Cults," 125.

[20]Ronald B. Flowers, *Religion in Strange Times: The 1960s and 1970s* (Macon, Ga.: Mercer University Press, 1984), 91.

[21]Ibid.

[22]Stark and Bainbridge, "Of Churches, Sects and Cults," 125; Stark and Bainbridge, *Future of Religion,* 25.

[23]Stark and Bainbridge, "Of Churches, Sects and Cults," 125; Stark and Bainbridge, *Future of Religion,* 25.

[24]Flowers, *Religion in Strange Times,* 91; Stark and Bainbridge, "Of Churches, Sects and Cults," 125.

[25]Ibid., 125-26.

[26]Ellwood, "The Several Meanings of Cult," 220.

[27]Ronald Enroth, *The Lure of the Cults* (Chappaqua, N.Y.: Christian Herald Books, 1979), 43-44.

[28]Theodore Roszak, "Ethics, Ecstasy and the Study of New Religions," in *Understanding the New Religions,* ed. Jacob Needleman and George Baker (New York: Seabury Press, 1978), 52.

[29]Ellwood, "The Several Meanings of Cult," 214; Ronald Enroth, "What Is a Cult?" in *A Guide to Cults and New Religions* (Downers Grove, Ill.: InterVarsity Press, 1983), 23.

[30]Ronald Enroth and J. Gordon Melton, *Why Cults Succeed Where the Church Fails* (Elgin, Ill.: Brethren Press, 1985), 79, 83.

[31]Mircea Eliade, *Occultism, Witchcraft and Cultural Fashions* (Chicago: University of Chicago Press, 1976), 48.

[32]Marcello Truzzi, "Definition and Dimensions of the Occult: Towards a Sociological Perspective," in *On the Margin of the Visible,* ed. Edward A. Tiryakian (New York: John Wiley, 1974), 243-44; Robert Galbreath, "The History of Modern Occultism: A Bibliographical Survey," *Journal of Popular Culture* 5 (Winter 1971): 726-54; Robert Galbreath, "Explaining Modern Occultism," in *The Occult in America,* ed. Howard Kerr and Charles Crow (Urbana: University of Illinois Press, 1983), 15, 18-19.

[33]Truzzi, "Definition and Dimensions," 244-45.

[34]Ibid.

[35]Andrew M. Greeley, "Implications for the Sociology of Religion of Occult Behavior in the Youth Culture," in *On the Margin of the Visible,* ed. Edward A. Tiryakian (New York: John Wiley, 1974), 297-98.

[36]Enroth, *Lure of the Cults,* 23-35.

[37]Melton and Moore, *The Cult Experience,* 19-20.

Chapter 2: Fringe Groups in the West
[1]Arthur F. Holmes, *Contours of a World View* (Grand Rapids, Mich.: Eerdmans, 1983), 8; Robert Ellwood, *Religious and Spiritual Groups in Modern America* (Englewood Cliffs, N.J.: Prentice Hall, 1973), 42-43; James W. Sire, *The Universe Next Door* (Downers Grove, Ill.: InterVarsity Press, 1976), 22-30.

[2]Ellwood, *Religious and Spiritual Groups,* 42-43; Holmes, *Contours of a World View,* 8; H. B. Kuhn, "Dualism," in *Evangelical Dictionary of Theology,* ed. Walter A. Elwell (Grand Rapids, Mich.: Baker Book House, 1984), 334.

[3]Robert Ellwood, *Alternative Altars* (Chicago: University of Chicago Press, 1979), 7; Ellwood, *Religious and Spiritual Groups,* 42-43; Philip J. Lee, *Against the Protestant Gnostics* (New York: Oxford University Press, 1987).

[4]Frederick C. Grant, ed., *Hellenistic Religions* (Indianapolis: Liberal Arts Press, 1963), xii-xiii; Ellwood, *Religious and Spiritual Groups,* 43; Ronald H. Nash, *Christianity and the Hellenistic World* (Grand Rapids, Mich.: Zondervan, 1984), 18-42.

[5]F. E. Peters, *The Harvest of Hellenism* (New York: Simon & Schuster, 1970), 196-221, 408-45; Robert M. Grant, *Augustus to Constantine* (New York: Harper & Row, 1970), 3-20.

[6]Luther H. Martin, *Hellenistic Religions* (New York: Oxford University Press, 1987), 6-10; Peters, *Harvest of Hellenism,* 196-221; Grant, *Augustus to Constantine,* 3-20.

[7]Grant, *Hellenistic Religions,* xvii, xxxii-xxxv; Paul Johnson, *A History of Christianity* (New York: Atheneum, 1977), 5-8, 28, 43; Harold Mattingly, *Christianity in the Roman Empire* (New York: W. W. Norton, 1967), 17-23; Hans Lietzmann, *A History of the Early Church,* 2 vols. (Cleveland, Ohio: Meridian Books, 1961), 1:154-76.

[8]J. N. D. Kelly, *Early Christian Doctrines* (New York: Harper & Row, 1978), 20-22; Ellwood, *Religious and Spiritual Groups,* 53; M. L. W. Laister, *Christianity and Pagan Culture in the Later Roman Empire* (Ithaca, N.Y.: Cornell University Press, 1951), 22-24.

[9]G. K. Nelson, *Spiritualism and Society* (New York: Schocken Books, 1969), 44; Eliade, *Occultism, Witchcraft and Cultural Fashions,* 56; Mircea Eliade, *Shamanism: Archaic Techniques of Esctasy* (Princeton, N.J.: Princeton University Press, 1964), 4; Ellwood, *Religious and Spiritual Groups,* 11-18; 49-52; Irving Hexham and Karla Poewe, *Understanding Cults and New Religions* (Grand Rapids, Mich.: Eerdmans, 1986), 79-80.

[10]Ellwood, *Religious and Spiritual Groups,* 52-53; Arthur Darby Nock, *Early Gentile Christianity and Its Hellenistic Background* (New York: Harper & Row, 1964), 97-99.

[11]John Stevens Kerr, *The Mystery and Magic of the Occult* (Philadelphia: Fortress, 1971), 16-19; W. B. Crow, *A History of Magic, Witchcraft and Occultism* (North Hollywood, Calif.: Wilshire, 1968), 179; Lawrence E. Jerome, *Astrology Disproved* (Buffalo, N.Y.: Prometheus Books, 1977), 20-32.

[12]Kerr, *Mystery and Magic,* 19-20.

[13]W. H. C. Frend, *The Rise of Christianity* (Philadelphia: Fortress, 1984), 54-74; Johnson, *History of Christianity,* 28, 43; Lietzman, *History of the Early Church,* 1:45-60; Grant, *Augustus to Constantine,* 79-84.

[14]Johnson, *History of Christianity,* 52-53, 57; John C. Gager, *Kingdom and Community* (Englewood Cliffs, N.J.: Prentice Hall, 1975), 68-86; Kelly, *Early Christian Doctrines,* 41-44.

[15]Carl A. Raschke, *The Interruption of Eternity* (Chicago: Nelson-Hall, 1980); Frend, *Rise of Christianity,* 195-200; Grant, *Augustus to Constantine,* 120-30.

[16]Peters, *Harvest of Hellenism,* 656; Grant, *Hellenistic Religions,* xxxiv; Harold O. J. Brown, *Heresies* (Garden City, N.Y.: Doubleday, 1984), 46-50.

[17]Pheme Perkins, *The Gnostic Dialogue* (New York: Paulist Press, 1980), 10-19; Peters, *Harvest of Hellenism,* 649; Edwin M. Yamauchi, "The Gnostics," in *Eerdmans Handbook to the History of Christianity,* ed. Tim Dowley (Grand Rapids, Mich.: Eerdmans, 1977), 98-99; Kelly, *Early Christian Doctrines,* 22-28; Jaroslav Pelikan, *The Emergence of the Catholic Tradition (100-600),* (Chicago: University of Chicago Press, 1971), 85-97.

[18]Kelly, *Early Christian Doctrines,* 87-88; Johnson, *History of Christianity,* 89.

[19]F. F. Bruce, *The Spreading Flame* (Grand Rapids, Mich.: Eerdmans, 1958), 245-46, 248, 256; Pelikan, *Catholic Tradition,* 176; Bruce, *Spreading Flame,* 279-82.

[20]Johnson, *History of Christianity,* 90; Kelly, *Early Christian Doctrines,* 139-40;

Pelikan, *Catholic Doctrine,* 176; Bruce, *Spreading Flame,* 279-82.

[21]Johnson, *History of Christianity,* 90; J. W. C. Wand, *The Four Great Heresies* (London: A. R. Mowbray, 1955), 38-62; J. N. D. Kelly, *Early Creeds,* 3rd ed. (New York: Longman, 1972), 231-34; Kelly, *Early Christian Doctrines,* 226-31.

[22]Robert I. Moore, *The Origins of European Dissent* (New York: St. Martin's, 1977), 1.

[23]Rodney Stark and William S. Bainbridge, *The Future of Religion* (Berkeley: University of California Press, 1985), 108.

[24]Edward Peters, ed., *Heresy and Authority in Medieval Europe* (Philadelphia: University of Pennsylvania Press, 1980), 25; Eleanor Shipley Duckett, *The Gateway to the Middle Ages: Monasticism* (Ann Arbor, Mich.: University of Michigan Press, 1961), 62-121; Johnson, *History of Christianity,* 128, 145; David Knowles, *Christian Monasticism* (New York: McGraw-Hill, 1969), 25-36; Eleanor Shipley Duckett, *The Wandering Saints of the Early Middle Ages* (New York: W. W. Norton, 1959), 15-79.

[25]Moore, *Origins of European Dissent,* 7-8; Johnson, *History of Christianity,* 177, 191-92, 204-7, 214-21; Jaroslav Pelikan, *The Growth of Medieval Theology (600-1300),* vol. 3 of *The Christian Tradition* (Chicago: University of Chicago Press, 1978), 213-15; Malcolm Lambert, *Medieval Heresy* (New York: Holmes and Meier, 1977), 89-90; Jeffrey Russell, ed., *Religious Dissent in the Middle Ages* (New York: Wiley, 1971), 7-8.

[26]Gordon Leff, *The Dissolution of the Medieval Outlook* (New York: New York University Press, 1976), 91-144; J. Huizinga, *The Waning of the Middle Ages* (Garden City, N.Y.: Doubleday, 1954), 17-28, 37-41; 177-85; Barbara W. Tuchman, *A Distant Mirror* (New York: Ballantine, 1978); Philip Ziegler, *The Black Death* (New York: Harper & Row, 1971), 232-79.

[27]Lambert, *Medieval Heresy,* 42-66; Peters, *Heresy and Authority,* 103-7; Russell, *Religious Dissent,* 57-59; Pelikan, *Growth of Medieval Theology,* 229-35, 238-42; Brown, *Heresies,* 253-61.

[28]Marjorie Reeves, *Joachim of Fiore and the Prophetic Future* (New York: Harper & Row, 1976), 1-3, 59-82; Pelikan, *Growth of Medieval Theology,* 301-3; Lambert, *Medieval Heresy,* 182-96; Gordon Leff, *Heresy in the Later Middle Ages* (Manchester, U.K.: Manchester University Press, 1967), 72-74; Norman Cohn, *The Pursuit of the Millennium* (New York: Oxford University Press, 1974), 108-18.

[29]Robert Ellwood, *Mysticism and Religion* (Englewood Cliffs, N.J.: Prentice Hall, 1980), 110-13; Steven Ozment, *The Age of Reform 1250-1550* (New Haven, Conn.: Yale University Press, 1980), 125-34; Georgia Harkness, *Mysticism* (Nashville: Abingdon, 1973), 103-16; Raymond Blakney, translator's preface in *Meister Eckhart,* (New York: Harper & Row, 1941), xx-xxvii; Brown, *Heresies,* 266-68.

[30]Jeffrey B. Russell, *A History of Witchcraft* (London: Thames and Hudson, 1980), 172; Christina Larner, ed., *Witchcraft and Religion* (Oxford: Basil Blackwell, 1984), 77-88.

[31]Russell, *History of Witchcraft,* 72, 172; William Monter, ed., *European Witchcraft*

(New York: John Wiley, 1969); Peter P. Levack, *The Witch-Hunt in Early Modern Europe* (New York: Longman, 1987), 1-22.

32Ellwood, *Religious and Spiritual Groups,* 54-55.

33Ibid., 55-56; Leo Schaya, *The Universal Meaning of the Kabbalah* (Baltimore: Penguin, 1973), 15-20; Francis A. Yates, *The Occult Philosophy in the Elizabethan Age* (London: Routledge & Kegan Paul, 1979), 2-3.

34Ellwood, *Religious and Spiritual Groups,* 55-56; Schaya, *Universal Meaning of the Kabbalah,* 15-20; Yates, *Occult Philosophy,* 2-3.

35Mircea Eliade, *The Forge and the Crucible* (New York: Harper & Row), 169ff.; Ellwood, *Religious and Spiritual Groups,* 56-57; Crow, *History of Magic, Witchcraft and Occultism,* 199-203.

36Henry Kamen, *The Rise of Toleration* (New York: McGraw-Hill, 1967), 7-8, 22, 54-56; Michael Mullett, *Radical Religious Movements in Early Modern Europe* (Boston: Allen and Unwin, 1980), 75, 78-79; Peter J. Klassen, *Church and State in Reformation Europe* (St. Louis: Forum Press, 1975), 10-14.

37Sidney E. Mead, *The Lively Experiment* (New York: Harper & Row, 1963), 104-6; Mullett, *Radical Religious Movements,* 78-79, 81-82; Kamen, *Rise of Toleration,* 156-60.

38Robert Wuthnow, "World Order and Religious Movements," in *New Religious Movements,* ed. Eileen Barker (New York: Edwin Mellen, 1982), 48-65; Charles Y. Glock and Rodney Stark, *Religion and Society in Tension* (Chicago: Rand McNally, 1965), 242-59.

39Wuthnow, "World Order and Religious Movements," 48.

40Philip Lee Ralph, *The Renaissance in Perspective* (New York: St. Martin's, 1973), 214-18; Hugh Kearney, *Science and Change, 1500-1700* (New York: McGraw-Hill, 1971), 52-53; A. B. Hall, *The Scientific Revolution, 1500-1800* (Boston: Beacon Press, 1966), 305-6; Ellwood, *Religious and Spiritual Groups,* 57; David Bakan, *Sigmund Freud and the Jewish Mystical Tradition* (New York: Schocken Books, 1965); Herbert Butterfield, *The Origins of Modern Science* (New York: Macmillan, 1957), 46-47.

41Lewis W. Spitz, *The Renaissance and Reformation Movements* (Chicago: Rand McNally, 1971), 175-78; Paul Oskar Kristeller, *Renaissance Thought* (New York: Harper & Row, 1961), 58-59.

42Yates, *Occult Philosophy,* 2-5, 17-22; John Warwick Montgomery, *Principalities and Powers* (Minneapolis: Bethany Fellowship, 1973), 83-87; Ellwood, *Religious and Spiritual Groups,* 58.

43Wayne Shumaker, *The Occult Sciences in the Renaissance* (Berkeley: University of California Press, 1972), 165-70; Crow, *History of Magic, Witchcraft and Occultism,* 208-9; Titus Burckhardt, *Alchemy* (Baltimore: Penguin, 1972), 19-20.

44Keith Thomas, *Religion and the Decline of Magic* (New York: Charles Scribner's, 1971), 349-50, 358-59, 650; Jerome, *Astrology Disproved,* 53-60; Shumaker, *Occult Sciences,* 16-24.

45William E. Monter, *Witchcraft in France and Switzerland* (Ithaca, N.Y.: Cornell

University Press, 1976), 29-32; Russell, *History of Witchcraft,* 72; H. R. Trevor-Roper, *The European Witch-Craze of the Sixteenth and Seventeenth Centuries and Other Essays* (New York: Harper & Row, 1956), 1-4.

[46]Nachman Ben-Yehuda, "The European Witch Craze of the 14th to 17th Centuries: A Sociologist's Perspective," *American Journal of Sociology* 86, no. 1 (1980): 1-3, 8, 12-13; Russell, *History of Witchcraft,* 72; Trevor-Roper, *European Witch-Craze,* 1-44.

[47]Russell, *History of Witchcraft,* 73, 110-11; Levack, *Witch-Hunt,* 76-77.

[48]Monter, *Witchcraft in France and Switzerland,* 19-20; Russell, *History of Witchcraft,* 73.

[49]Montgomery, *Principalities and Powers,* 104-5.

[50]J. Gordon Melton, *Encyclopedic Handbook of Cults in America* (New York: Garland, 1986), 68-69; Ruth A. Tucker, *Another Gospel* (Grand Rapids, Mich.: Zondervan, 1989), 376, 378; Ellwood, *Religious and Spiritual Groups,* 60-61; Montgomery, *Principalities and Powers,* 104-5.

[51]Peter J. Klassen, *Europe in the Reformation* (Englewood Cliffs, N.J.: Prentice Hall, 1979), 130; George H. Williams and Angel M. Mergal, eds., *Spiritual and Anabaptist Writers* (Philadelphia: Westminster Press, 1957), 23-24; George H. Williams, *The Radical Reformation* (Philadelphia: Westminster Press, 1957), xxiv-xxxi.

[52]See Christopher Hill, *The World Turned Upside Down* (New York: Viking, 1972), 21-23; J. F. McGregor and B. Reay, eds., *Radical Religion in the English Revolution* (Oxford: Oxford University Press, 1984); Michael Watts, *The Dissenters* (Oxford: Clarendon Press, 1978); Katharine R. Firth, *The Apocalyptic Tradition in Reformation Britain, 1530-1645* (Oxford: Oxford University Press, 1979); Paul Christianson, *Reformers and Babylon* (Toronto: University of Toronto Press, 1978).

[53]Kamen, *Rise of Toleration;* Johnson, *History of Christianity,* 331; James D. Hardy Jr., *Prologue to Modernity* (New York: John Wiley, 1974); Franklin L. Baumer, *Religion and the Rise of Scepticism* (New York: Harcourt Brace, 1980), 78-95.

[54]Thomas, *Religion and the Decline of Magic,* 661-64; Roland H. Bainton, *The Reformation of the Sixteenth Century* (Boston: Beacon Press, 1952), 3-6; Steven E. Ozment, ed., *The Reformation in Medieval Perspective* (Chicago: Quadrangle Books, 1971); William Cook and Ronald B. Herzman, *The Medieval World View* (New York: Oxford University Press, 1983).

[55]See Lewis W. Spitz and Wenzel Lohff, eds., *Discord, Dialogue and Concord* (Philadelphia: Fortress, 1977); Justo L. Gonzalez, *The Story of Christianity,* 2 vols. (New York: Harper & Row, 1984), 2:133; R. T. Kendall, *Calvin and English Calvinism to 1649* (Oxford: Oxford University Press, 1979); Dale Brown, *Understanding Pietism* (Grand Rapids, Mich.: Eerdmans, 1978), 15-28.

[56]Ibid., 28-34.

[57]See Herbert M. Morais, *Deism in Eighteenth Century America* (New York: Russell and Russell, 1960); J. Orr, *English Deism* (Grand Rapids, Mich.: Eerdmans, 1934);

Michael H. McDonald, "Deism," in *Evangelical Dictionary of Theology*, ed. Walter A. Elwell (Grand Rapids, Mich.: Baker Book House, 1984), 304-5; Charles G. Singer, "Unitarianism," in *Evangelical Dictionary of Theology*, 1126-27.

[58]Thomas, *Religion and the Decline of Magic*, 631-68.

[59]Galbreath, "Explaining Modern Occultism," 22-23; Jon Butler, "Magic, Astrology, and the Early American Religious Heritage, 1600-1700," *American Historical Review* 84, no. 1 (1979): 317-46; Jon Butler, "The Dark Ages of American Occultism, 1760-1848," in *The Occult in America*, ed. Howard Kerr and Charles Crow (Urbana: University of Illinois Press, 1983); Peter Burke, *Popular Culture in Early Modern Europe* (New York: Harper & Row, 1978), 270-86.

[60]Jeffrey Russell, *Mephistopheles* (Ithaca, N.Y.: Cornell University Press, 1986); Albanese, *America*, 164; Howard Kerr and Charles L. Crow, introduction to *The Occult in America*, 5.

[61]Herbert Leventhal, *In the Shadow of the Enlightenment* (New York: New York University Press, 1976), 265-68; Albanese, *America*, 164-65.

[62]James Webb, *The Occult Underground* (LaSalle, Ill.: Open Court, 1974), 224; Ellwood, *Religious and Spiritual Groups*, 62-63.

[63]Webb, *Occult Underground*, 224-25; Ellwood, *Religious and Spiritual Groups*, 63; Frances King, *The Rites of Modern Occult Magic* (New York: Macmillan, 1970), 25-30.

[64]Webb, *Occult Underground*, 225-26.

[65]Gonzales, *Story of Christianity*, 2:203, 204; Tucker, *Another Gospel*, 381-83; Ellwood, *Religious and Spiritual Groups*, 64-65.

[66]Ibid.

[67]Ibid., 66; Gonzales, *Story of Christianity*, 2:203. See also Emanuel Swedenborg, *The True Christian Religion* (London: Everyman's Library, 1936).

[68]Robert C. Fuller, *Mesmerism and the Cure of American Souls* (Philadelphia: University of Pennsylvania Press, 1982), 1-47; Webb, *Occult Underground*, 228; Ellwood, *Religious and Spiritual Groups*, 68.

Chapter 3: Early National America

[1]Robert Wuthnow, "World Order and Religious Movements," in *New Religious Movements*, ed. Eileen Barker (New York: Edwin Mellen, 1982), 48-49; Sydney E. Ahlstrom, "From Sinai to the Golden Gate," in *Understanding the New Religions*, ed. Jacob Needleman and George Baker (New York: Seabury Press, 1978), 15-16.

[2]Ibid., 15; Richard Kyle, "The Cults: Why Now and Who Gets Caught?" *Journal of the American Scientific Affiliation* 33, no. 2 (1981): 94-95.

[3]Linda K. Pritchard, "Religious Change in Nineteenth-Century America," in *The New Religious Consciousness*, ed. Charles Glock and Robert Bellah (Berkeley: University of California Press, 1976), 297-312.

[4]William G. McLoughlin Jr., *Revivals, Awakenings and Reform* (Chicago: University of Chicago Press, 1978), 98, 113.

[5]Michel Chevalier, *Society, Manners and Politics in the United States: Being a*

Series of Letters on North America (1839; rpt. New York: A. M. Kelley, 1966), 187; Alice Felt Tyler, *Freedom's Ferment* (New York: Harper & Row, 1944), 5-22. See also Arthur M. Schlesinger Jr., *The Age of Jackson* (Boston: Little, Brown, 1945), 306-90.

6Ernest Lee Tuveson, *Redeemer Nation: The Idea of America's Millennial Role* (Chicago: University of Chicago Press, 1968), 91-136; McLoughlin, *Revivals, Awakenings and Reform,* 105-6.

7Robert G. Clouse, "The Views of the Millennium," in *Evangelical Dictionary of Theology,* ed. Walter A. Elwell (Grand Rapids, Mich.: Baker Book House, 1984), 715; Catherine Albanese, *America: Religion and Religions* (Belmont, Calif.: Wadsworth, 1981), 275-76. For a study of social and emotional aspects of the millennial appeal see George Rosen, "Social Change and Psychopathology in the Emotional Climate of Millennial Movements," *American Behavioral Scientist* 16, no. 2 (1972): 153-67.

8J. F. C. Harrison, *The Second Coming: Popular Millenarianism, 1780-1850* (New Brunswick, N.J.: Rutgers University Press, 1979), 4-7; Tuveson, *Redeemer Nation,* 232; Timothy L. Smith, "Righteousness and Hope: Christian Holiness and the Millennial Vision in America, 1800-1900," *American Quarterly* 31, no. 1 (1979): 22-25; James H. Moorhead, "Searching for the Millennium in America," *Princeton Seminary Bulletin* 8, no. 2 (1987): 17-33.

9James F. Maclear, "The Republic and the Millennium," in *Religion in American History,* ed. John M. Mulder and John F. Wilson (Englewood Cliffs, N.J.: Prentice Hall, 1978), 181-96; Moorhead, "Searching for the Millennium," 17-33; Harrison, *Second Coming,* 4-7; Smith, "Righteousness and Hope," 22-25.

10Harrison, *Second Coming,* 4-6; Tuveson, *Redeemer Nation,* 232; Albanese, *America,* 276-77; William Martin, "Waiting for the End," *The Atlantic,* June 1982, 31-32. For a brief description of the various millennial views see Robert Clouse, ed., *The Meaning of the Millennium* (Downers Grove, Ill.: InterVarsity Press, 1977), 7-13.

11Tuveson, *Redeemer Nation,* 232; Albanese, *America,* 276-77; Martin, "Waiting for the End," 31-32; Harrison, *Second Coming,* 4-6; Grant Underwood, "Early Mormon Millenarianism: Another Look," *Church History* 54, no. 2 (1985): 215-29.

12Russel Blaine Nye, *Society and Culture in America, 1830-1860* (New York: Harper & Row, 1974), 71-73; Vernon L. Parrington, *The Romantic Revolution in America (1800-1860),* vol. 2 of *Main Currents in American Thought* (New York: Harcourt, Brace and World, 1927). See also A. O. Lovejoy, "The Meaning of Romanticism for the History of Ideas," *Journal of the History of Ideas* 2 (1941): 257-78.

13Nye, *Society and Culture,* 21-23.

14Rush Welter, "The Idea of Progress in America," *Journal of the History of Ideas* 14 (1955): 401-15; Nye, *Society and Culture,* 22-30; Arthur Ekirch, *The Idea of Progress in America, 1815-1860* (New York: Columbia University Press, 1944); J. B. Bury, *The Idea of Progress* (London: Macmillan, 1928).

15Welter, "The Idea of Progress," 401-15; Nye, *Society and Culture,* 22-30.

[16]Ibid., 36, 289-92; R. Larry Shelton, "Perfectionism," in *Evangelical Dictionary of Theology,* 843; William G. McLoughlin Jr., *Modern Revivalism* (New York: Ronald Press, 1959), 102-3; Bruce L. Shelley, *Evangelicalism in America* (Grand Rapids, Mich.: Eerdmans, 1967), 49; Smith, "Righteousness and Hope," 22-23.

[17]Nye, *Society and Culture,* 36. See also Timothy L. Smith, *Revivalism and Social Reform* (Baltimore: Johns Hopkins University Press, 1980); Donald W. Dayton, *Discovering an Evangelical Heritage* (New York: Harper & Row, 1976), 15-20.

[18]Shelley, *Evangelicalism in America,* 46; Nye, *Society and Culture,* 285-86. See also William Warren Sweet, *Revivalism in America* (Nashville: Abingdon, 1944).

[19]Nye, *Society and Culture,* 287; Shelley, *Evangelicalism in America,* 46; McLoughlin, *Revivals, Awakenings and Reform,* 113; Smith, *Revivalism and Social Reform,* 45-62; Smith, "Righteousness and Hope," 37-38; William G. McLoughlin Jr., "Third Force in Christendom," *Daedalus* 96, no. 1 (1967): 47; Dickson D. Bruce Jr., *And They All Sang Hallelujah* (Knoxville: University of Tennessee Press, 1974); Robert T. Handy, *The Protestant Quest for a Christian America, 1830-1930* (Philadelphia: Fortress, 1967), 7.

[20]Nye, *Society and Culture,* 297. For an excellent study emphasizing the "populist" religious movements see Nathan Hatch, *The Democratization of American Christianity* (New Haven, Conn.: Yale University Press, 1989).

[21]Martin E. Marty, "Interpreting American Pluralism," in *Religion in America,* by Jackson W. Carroll, Douglas W. Johnson and Martin Marty (New York: Harper & Row, 1979), 81; Sydney E. Ahlstrom, *A Religious History of the American People* (New Haven, Conn.: Yale University Press, 1972), 381; Martin E. Marty, *Righteous Empire* (New York: Dial, 1970), 67-130.

[22]Ahlstrom, "From Sinai to the Golden Gate," 13-15; Kyle, "The Cults," 94-95; Oscar Handlin, *The Uprooted* (New York: Grosset and Dunlap, 1951), 130-34; Mary F. Bednarowski, *American Religion: A Cultural Perspective* (Englewood Cliffs, N.J.: Prentice Hall, 1984), 22-25.

[23]Kyle, "The Cults," 94-95; Ahlstrom, "From Sinai to the Golden Gate," 13-15; Bednarowski, *American Religion,* 22-25.

Chapter 4: Early Metaphysical and Occult Movements

[1]J. Stillson Judah, *The History and Philosophy of the Metaphysical Movements in America* (Philadelphia: Westminster Press, 1957), 11-12.

[2]Ibid., 12-13.

[3]Ibid.

[4]Ibid., 14.

[5]Ibid., 15-18.

[6]Ibid.

[7]Catherine Albanese, *America: Religions and Religion* (Belmont, Calif.: Wadsworth, 1981), 172.

[8]Judah, *History and Philosophy of the Metaphysical Movements,* 22-46.

[9]Ibid.

[10]Alice Felt Tyler, *Freedom's Ferment* (New York: Harper & Row, 1944), 47; Russel Blaine Nye, *Society and Culture in America, 1830-1860* (New York: Harper & Row, 1974), 300.

[11]James C. Moseley, *A Cultural History of Religion in America* (Westport, Conn.: Greenwood Press, 1981), 68-71; Albanese, *America,* 172-73; Sydney E. Ahlstrom, *A Religious History of the American People* (New Haven, Conn.: Yale University Press, 1972), 600-606.

[12]Tyler, *Freedom's Ferment,* 48; Albanese, *America,* 173; Catherine Albanese, *Corresponding Motion: Transcendental Religion and the New America* (Philadelphia: Temple University Press, 1977).

[13]Tyler, *Freedom's Ferment,* 48-49; Albanese, *America,* 173; Nye, *Society and Culture,* 301; Ahlstrom, *Religious History,* 605-8.

[14]Robert Ellwood, *Alternative Altars* (Chicago: University of Chicago Press, 1979), 94; Roger Lundin, "Transcendentalism," in *Evangelical Dictionary of Theology,* ed. Walter A. Elwell (Grand Rapids, Mich.: Baker Book House, 1984), 1107.

[15]Ernest Isaacs, "The Fox Sisters and American Spiritualism," in *The Occult in America,* ed. Howard Kerr and Charles Crow (Urbana: University of Illinois Press, 1983), 79-80. R. Laurence Moore questions the extent to which occult elements were present in several nineteenth-century new religions in America, including Spiritualism. See R. Laurence Moore, "The Occult Connection? Mormonism, Christian Science and Spiritualism," in *The Occult in America,* 135-56.

[16]Isaacs, "The Fox Sisters," 79-80; Judah, *History and Philosophy of the Metaphysical Movements,* 50-51.

[17]Ibid., 51; Ellwood, *Alternative Altars,* 91-92; R. Laurence Moore, *In Search of White Crows* (New York: Oxford University Press, 1977), 9; Robert C. Fuller, *Mesmerism and the Cure of American Souls* (Philadelphia: University of Pennsylvania Press, 1982), 1-15.

[18]Ellwood, *Alternative Altars,* 95-98; Judah, *History and Philosophy of the Metaphysical Movements,* 52-56.

[19]Ellwood, *Alternative Altars,* 84-90, 92-94; Moore, *In Search of White Crows,* 25-26.

[20]Albanese, *America,* 175; Ellwood, *Alternative Altars,* 89-91.

[21]Moore, *In Search of White Crows,* 64. Other histories of nineteenth-century Spiritualism include Geoffrey K. Nelson, *Spiritualism and Society* (London: Routledge & Kegan Paul, 1969); Howard Kerr, *Mediums and Spirit Rappers and Roaring Radicals: Spiritualism in American Literature, 1850-1900* (Urbana: University of Illinois Press, 1972); Katherine H. Porter, *Through a Glass Darkly: Spiritualism in the Browning Circle* (Lawrence: University of Kansas Press, 1958); Burton Gates Brown Jr., "Spiritualism in Nineteenth-Century America," Ph.D. diss., Boston University, 1973; Mary Farrell Bednarowski, "Nineteenth-Century American Spiritualism: An Attempt at Scientific Religion," Ph.D. diss., University of Minnesota, 1973.

[22]Judah, *History and Philosophy of the Metaphysical Movements,* 72-89; Robert

Ellwood, *Religious and Spiritual Groups in Modern America* (Englewood Cliffs, N.J.: Prentice Hall, 1973), 135-40.

[23]Albanese, *America,* 175-76; Moore, *In Search of White Crows,* 7-39; Tyler, *Freedom's Ferment,* 80.

[24]Ellwood, *Religious and Spiritual Groups,* 72-73; Whitney R. Cross, *The Burned-Over District* (New York: Harper & Row, 1965); Moore, *In Search of White Crows,* 50-52.

[25]Albanese, *America,* 176; Moore, *In Search of White Crows,* 51, 70-74.

[26]Albanese, *America,* 176; Judah, *History and Philosophy of the Metaphysical Movements,* 67-68.

[27]Albanese, *America,* 176-77; Judah, *History and Philosophy of the Metaphysical Movements,* 68-69.

[28]Moore, *In Search of White Crows,* 65-68, 71-74.

Chapter 5: Religious Communalism
[1]Catherine Albanese, *America: Religions and Religion* (Belmont, Calif.: Wadsworth, 1981), 155; Sydney E. Ahlstrom, *A Religious History of the American People* (New Haven, Conn.: Yale University Press, 1972), 491. See Robert S. Fogarty, *All Things New* (Chicago: University of Chicago Press, 1990), 1-23.

[2]Rosabeth M. Kanter, *Commitment and Community: Communes and Utopias in Sociological Perspective* (Cambridge, Mass.: Harvard University Press, 1972), 1-3; Ahlstrom, *Religious History,* 491-92; Alice Felt Tyler, *Freedom's Ferment* (New York: Harper & Row, 1944), 108.

[3]Kanter, *Commitment and Community,* 3-8.

[4]Ibid.; Tyler, *Freedom's Ferment,* 108-9, 166, 196.

[5]Ibid., 108-10; Kanter, *Commitment and Community,* 3-4.

[6]Tyler, *Freedom's Ferment,* 108-10; Kanter, *Commitment and Community,* 4-5.

[7]Ibid., 4; Tyler, *Freedom's Ferment,* 109-10.

[8]Ibid., 108-10.

[9]For a comprehensive history of the Shakers see Edward Daning Andrews, *The People Called Shakers* (New York: Dover, 1963); Ahlstrom, *Religious History,* 492. See also Henri Desroche, *The American Shakers: From Neo-Christianity to Presocialism* (Amherst: University of Massachusetts Press, 1971); Marguerite Fellows Melcher, *The Shaker Adventure* (Cleveland, Ohio: Western Reserve Press, 1968).

[10]Whitney R. Cross, *The Burned-Over District* (New York: Harper & Row, 1965), 36; Tyler, *Freedom's Ferment,* 140; Ahlstrom, *Religious History,* 492-93; Andrews, *People Called Shakers,* 55-93.

[11]William M. Kephart, *Extraordinary Groups,* 2nd ed. (New York: St. Martin's, 1982), 224; Robert Ellwood, *Alternative Altars* (Chicago: University of Chicago Press, 1979), 74; Albanese, *America,* 155-56; Tyler, *Freedom's Ferment,* 146-47.

[12]Ahlstrom, *Religious History,* 494; Tyler, *Freedom's Ferment,* 146-47.

[13]Kephart, *Extraordinary Groups*, 224-25; Ellwood, *Alternative Altars*, 77-78; Tyler, *Freedom's Ferment*, 146-47.

[14]Albanese, *America*, 156; Ahlstrom, *Religious History*, 494.

[15]Tyler, *Freedom's Ferment*, 148-49; Andrews, *People Called Shakers*, 177-201; Kephart, *Extraordinary Groups*, 209-18.

[16]Ibid., 226-28; Andrews, *People Called Shakers*, 224-40.

[17]Ahlstrom, *Religious History*, 498-99; Tyler, *Freedom's Ferment*, 184-85; Kephart, *Extraordinary Groups*, 93-94; Leonard Bernstein, "The Ideas of John Humphrey Noyes, Perfectionist," *American Quarterly* 5 (March 1953): 157-65; Ernest R. Sandeen, "John Humphrey Noyes as the New Adam," *Church History* 40, no. 1 (1971): 83-87. See also Maren Lockwood Corden, *Oneida: Utopian Community to Modern Corporation* (Baltimore: Johns Hopkins University Press, 1969).

[18]Kephart, *Extraordinary Groups*, 94, 95; Ahlstrom, *Religious History*, 498-99; Elmer T. Clark, *The Small Sects in America* (Nashville: Abingdon, 1965), 141-42. See also Robert Thomas, *The Men Who Would Be Perfect: John Humphrey Noyes and the Utopian Impulse* (Philadelphia: University of Pennsylvania Press, 1977); Allan Estlake, *The Oneida Community: A Record of an Attempt to Carry Out the Principles of Christian Unselfishness and Scientific Race-Improvement* (London: George Redway, 1900).

[19]Albanese, *America*, 158-59; Tyler, *Freedom's Ferment*, 186; Kephart, *Extraordinary Groups*, 95-96; Ahlstrom, *Religious History*, 499; William M. Kephart, "Experimental Family Organization: An Historico-Cultural Report on the Oneida Community," *Marriage and Family Living* 25 (August 1963): 261-71; Sandeen, "John Humphrey Noyes," 87-89. See also Lawrence Foster, *Religion and Sexuality: Three American Communal Experiments of the Nineteenth Century* (New York: Oxford University Press, 1981).

[20]Albanese, *America*, 158-59; Tyler, *Freedom's Ferment*, 186; Ahlstrom, *Religious History*, 499; Kephart, "Experimental Family Organization," 261-71; Sandeen, "John Humphrey Noyes," 87-89.

[21]Kephart, *Extraordinary Groups*, 110-17; Albanese, *America*, 158-59; Ahlstrom, *Religious History*, 499; Tyler, *Freedom's Ferment*, 190-94; Murray Levine and Barbara Benedict Bunker, *Mutual Criticism* (Syracuse, N.Y.: Syracuse University Press, 1975); Constance Noyes Robertson, *Oneida Community: The Breakup, 1876-1881* (Syracuse, N.Y.: Syracuse University Press, 1972).

[22]Ibid.; Tyler, *Freedom's Ferment*, 190-94; Ahlstrom, *Religious History*, 499; Kephart, *Extraordinary Groups*, 136-40.

[23]Tyler, *Freedom's Ferment*, 115-16; Ahlstrom, *Religious History*, 495-96; Ruth A. Tucker, *Another Gospel* (Grand Rapids, Mich.: Zondervan, 1989), 42; Ellwood, *Alternative Altars*, 70.

[24]Ibid., 70; Tyler, *Freedom's Ferment*, 116-17; Tucker, *Another Gospel*, 42.

[25]Tyler, *Freedom's Ferment*, 120; Ellwood, *Alternative Altars*, 70.

[26]Ibid., 70; Tyler, *Freedom's Ferment*, 118-19; Tucker, *Another Gospel*, 43.

[27]Ellwood, *Alternative Altars*, 70-71.

Chapter 6: Mormonism and the Christadelphians

[1]R. Laurence Moore, *Religious Outsiders and the Making of Americans* (New York: Oxford University Press, 1986), 41-43; Sydney E. Ahlstrom, *A Religious History of the American People* (New Haven, Conn.: Yale University Press, 1972), 508.

[2]Rodney Stark and William S. Bainbridge, *The Future of Religion* (Berkeley: University of California Press, 1985), 245-47; Robert Flanders, "To Transform History: Early Mormon Culture and the Concept of Time and Space," *Church History* 40, no. 1 (1971): 108-9; Ahlstrom, *Religious History,* 508; Ruth A. Tucker, *Another Gospel* (Grand Rapids, Mich.: Zondervan, 1989), 49.

[3]Whitney R. Cross, *The Burned-Over District* (New York: Harper & Row, 1965), 211ff.; William M. Kephart, *Extraordinary Groups,* 2nd ed. (New York: St. Martin's, 1982), 233. The usual interpretation of the development of Mormonism in western New York as set forth by Cross has been challenged by revisionist accounts. See Mario S. DePhillis, "The Quest for Religious Authority and the Rise of Mormonism," *Dialogue: A Journal of Mormon Thought* 1 (Spring 1966): 68-88; Mario S. DePhillis, "The Social Sources of Mormonism," *Church History* 37, no. 1 (1968): 50-79.

[4]Klaus J. Hansen, *Mormonism and the American Experience* (Chicago: University of Chicago Press, 1981), 1-44; Ahlstrom, *Religious History,* 502; David Brion Davis, "The New England Origins of Mormonism," in *Mormonism and American Culture,* ed. Marvin S. Hill and James B. Allen (New York: Harper & Row, 1972), 13-28. See also Leonard J. Arrington and Davis Betton, *The Mormon Experience* (New York: Knopf, 1979); Donna Hill, *Joseph Smith: The First Mormon* (Garden City, N.Y.: Doubleday, 1977). D. Michael Quinn, *Early Mormonism and the Magic World View* (Salt Lake City: Signature Books, 1987), 27-77. The occult had its greatest impact on Mormonism during its early years, especially before the publication of the Book of Mormon and the formal organization of the Church of Latter-Day Saints. See preceding citation, pages 192ff.

[5]Thomas F. O'Dea, *The Mormons* (Chicago: University of Chicago Press, 1957), 22-40; Catherine Albanese, *America: Religions and Religion* (Belmont, Calif.: Wadsworth, 1981), 141-42; Kephart, *Extraordinary Groups,* 234-35; Ahlstrom, *Religious History,* 502-3; Flanders, "To Transform History," 111.

[6]Tucker, *Another Gospel,* 58.

[7]O'Dea, *The Mormons,* 41-96, 198-205; Albanese, *America,* 142, 144; Ahlstrom, *Religious History,* 506-7. See also Susa Young Gates, *The Life Story of Brigham Young* (New York: Macmillan, 1930); Wallace Stegner, *The Gathering of Zion* (New York: McGraw-Hill, 1964); W. Samuel Taylor, *Rocky Mountain Empire* (New York: Macmillan, 1978).

[8]Tucker, *Another Gospel,* 72-73.

[9]Albanese, *America,* 142-43; Kephart, *Extraordinary Groups,* 246-47.

[10]Albanese, *America,* 142-44; Tucker, *Another Gospel,* 82.

[11]Albanese, *America,* 142-43; Hansen, *Mormonism and the American Experience,*

113-46; Klaus J. Hansen, "The Political Kingdom as a Source of Conflict," in *Mormonism and American Culture,* ed. Marvin S. Hill and James B. Allen (New York: Harper & Row, 1972), 112-26; Flanders, "To Transform History," 108, 111. See also Marilyn Warenski, *Patriarchs and Politics* (New York: McGraw-Hill, 1978); O'Dea, *The Mormons,* 255-57.

¹²Moore, *Religious Outsiders,* 44-46; Ernest Lee Tuveson, *Redeemer Nation: The Idea of America's Millennial Role* (Chicago: University of Chicago Press, 1968), 179-86; Albanese, *America,* 143-44; J. F. C. Harrison, *The Second Coming: Popular Millenarianism, 1780-1850* (New Brunswick, N.J.: Rutgers University Press, 1979), 176-92; Alice Felt Tyler, *Freedom's Ferment* (New York: Harper & Row, 1944), 95-96; Ernest R. Sandeen, *The Roots of Fundamentalism: British and American Millenarianism 1800-1930* (Chicago: University of Chicago Press, 1970), 48.

¹³Tuveson, *Redeemer Nation,* 179-86; Albanese, *America,* 143-44. The ambivalence in Mormon millennialism has produced disagreement among scholars. See Grant Underwood, "Early Mormon Millenarianism: Another Look," *Church History* 54, no. 2 (1985): 215-29; Timothy L. Smith, "The Book of Mormon in a Biblical Culture," *Journal of Mormon History* 7 (1980): 3-21; Klaus J. Hansen, *Quest for Empire: The Political Kingdom of God and the Council of Fifty* (East Lansing: Michigan State University Press, 1967).

¹⁴Moore, *Religious Outsiders,* 29; Tyler, *Freedom's Ferment,* 95-96.

¹⁵O'Dea, *The Mormons,* 115; Ahlstrom, *Religious History,* 508; Leonard J. Arrington, "Crisis in Identity: Mormon Responses in the Nineteenth and Twentieth Centuries," in *Mormonism and American Culture,* ed. Marvin S. Hill and James B. Allen (New York: Harper & Row, 1972), 168-84; Howard R. Lamar, "Statehood for Utah: A Different Path," in *Mormonism and American Culture,* 127-41; Hansen, *Mormonism and the American Experience,* 205-17.

¹⁶J. Gordon Melton, *The Encyclopedia of American Religions,* 2 vols. (Wilmington, N.C.: McGrath, 1978), 2:8-21.

¹⁷Arrington and Betton, *Mormon Experience,* 89; Tucker, *Another Gospel,* 46; Melton, *Encyclopedia of American Religions,* 2:18.

¹⁸Tucker, *Another Gospel,* 47; Arrington and Betton, *Mormon Experience,* 89; Melton, *Encyclopedia of American Religions,* 2:18.

¹⁹Tucker, *Another Gospel,* 47; Arrington and Betton, *Mormon Experience,* 90; Melton, *Encyclopedia of American Religions,* 2:18-19.

²⁰Tucker, *Another Gospel,* 375.

²¹Arrington and Betton, *Mormon Experience,* 91; Melton, *Encyclopedia of American Religions,* 2:10.

²²Arrington and Betton, *Mormon Experience,* 91; Melton, *Encyclopedia of American Religions,* 2:11.

²³Arrington and Betton, *Mormon Experience,* 92-93; Tucker, *Another Gospel,* 376; Melton, *Encyclopedia of American Religions,* 2:11.

²⁴Tucker, *Another Gospel,* 375-76.

25Bryan Wilson, *Religious Sects* (New York: McGraw-Hill, 1970), 103, 107; Tucker, *Another Gospel,* 46.

26Melton, *Encyclopedia of American Religions,* 1:409; Tucker, *Another Gospel,* 46; Wilson, *Religious Sects,* 103, 106; Charles H. Lippy, *The Christadelphians in North America* (Lewiston, N.Y.: Edwin Mellen, 1989), 25.

27Wilson, *Religious Sects,* 103, 106; Melton, *Encyclopedia of American Religions,* 1:409; Richard Kyle, "Christadelphians," in *Encyclopedia USA,* ed. Archie P. McDonald (Gulf Breeze, Fla.: Academic International Press, 1989), 11:72; Bryan Wilson, *Sects and Society* (Berkeley: University of California Press, 1961), 236-37.

28Wilson, *Religious Sects,* 106; Kyle, "Christadelphians," 72; Wilson, *Sects and Society,* 238-40.

29J. Stafford Wright, "Christadelphians," in *New International Dictionary of the Christian Church,* ed. J. D. Douglas (Grand Rapids, Mich.: Zondervan, 1974), 219; Kyle, "Christadelphians," 73.

30Wilson, *Religious Sects,* 106-7; Wright, "Christadelphians," 219; Wilson, *Sects and Society,* 246-47.

31Wilson, *Religious Sects,* 108-9; Kyle, "Christadelphians," 73; Wilson, *Sects and Society,* 254-58.

32Wilson, *Religious Sects,* 109; Tucker, *Another Gospel,* 47-48; Kyle, "Christadelphians," 73-74; Lippy, *The Christadelphians,* 25.

Chapter 7: American Culture in the Late Nineteenth Century

1Robert T. Handy, *The Protestant Quest for a Christian America, 1830-1930* (Philadelphia: Fortress, 1967), vii-viii; Robert T. Handy, *A Christian America* (New York: Oxford University Press, 1984), 24-56; Sydney E. Ahlstrom, "From Sinai to the Golden Gate," in *Understanding the New Religions,* ed. Jacob Needleman and George Baker (New York: Seabury Press, 1978), 13-15; Martin E. Marty, *Righteous Empire* (New York: Dial, 1970), 121-30; Richard Kyle, "The Cults: Why Now and Who Gets Caught?" *Journal of the American Scientific Affiliation* 33, no. 2 (1981): 94-95.

2Handy, *The Protestant Quest,* vii-viii; Ahlstrom, "From Sinai to the Golden Gate," 14-16; Kyle, "The Cults," 95; Marty, *Righteous Empire,* 144ff.

3Edwin Scott Gaustad, *Historical Atlas of Religion in America* (New York: Harper & Row, 1976), 44; Sydney E. Ahlstrom, *A Religious History of the American People* (New Haven, Conn.: Yale University Press, 1972), 843.

4Ibid., 843-46.

5Ibid.

6William G. McLoughlin Jr., *Revivals, Awakenings and Reform* (Chicago: University of Chicago Press, 1978), 179; Ahlstrom, *Religious History,* 805-6.

7Ibid.

8Ibid.

9Richard Brown, *The Transformation of American Life 1600-1865* (New York: Hill and Wang, 1976), 4. See also Thomas C. Cochran and William Miller, *The Age of Enterprise,* rev. ed. (New York: Harper & Row, 1961); Samuel P. Hays, *The Response to Industrialism, 1885-1914* (Chicago: University of Chicago Press, 1957); Allan Nevins, *The Emergence of Modern America* (Chicago: Quadrangle Books, 1971); Robert Walker, *Life in the Age of Enterprise* (New York: Capricorn Books, 1971).

[10]Ahlstrom, *Religious History,* 749. See also Marcus Lee Hanson, *The Immigrant in American History* (Cambridge: Harvard University Press, 1948); Maldwyn A. Jones, *American Immigration* (Chicago: University of Chicago Press, 1960).

[11]Philip Taylor, *The Distant Magnet: European Emigration to the U.S.A.* (New York: Harper & Row, 1971), 48-65; Catherine Albanese, *America: Religions and Religion* (Belmont, Calif.: Wadsworth, 1981), 197, 205-10; Jack Chen, *The Chinese of America* (New York: Harper & Row, 1981).

[12]Mark A. Noll et al., eds., *Christianity in America* (Grand Rapids, Mich.: Eerdmans, 1983), 374. See also Oscar Handlin, *The Uprooted* (New York: Grosset and Dunlap, 1951), 186-300; John Higham, *Strangers in the Land: Patterns of American Nativism, 1860-1925* (New York: Atheneum, 1971), 131-57, 234-63; Stuart C. Miller, *The Unwelcome Immigrant: The American Image of the Chinese, 1785-1882* (Berkeley: University of California Press, 1969); C. Vann Woodward, *The Strange Career of Jim Crow,* 3rd ed. (New York: Oxford University Press, 1974).

[13]Ahlstrom, *Religious History,* 753-54.

[14]Winthrop S. Hudson, *Religion in America* (New York: Scribner's, 1973), 210-11. See also Sean Dennis Cashman, *America in the Gilded Age* (New York: New York University Press, 1984), 10-46, 110-42; Robert H. Walker, *Life in the Age of Enterprise, 1865-1900* (New York: Capricorn Books, 1971); Zane Miller, *Urbanization of Modern America* (New York: Harcourt Brace, 1973), 25-145; Constance McLaughlin Green, *The Rise of Urban America* (New York: Harper & Row, 1965), 85-106.

[15]Ahlstrom, *Religious History,* 738.

[16]Hudson, *Religion in America,* 210; Mary Bednarowski, *American Religion* (Englewood Cliffs, N.J.: Prentice Hall, 1984), 38-39. See also Cynthia Eagle Russett, *Darwin in America: The Intellectual Response, 1865-1912* (San Francisco: W. H. Freeman, 1976), 1-43, 89-110; Bert James Loewenberg, *Darwinism Comes to America, 1859-1900* (Philadelphia: Fortress, 1969).

[17]R. K. Harrison, "Higher Criticism," in *Evangelical Dictionary of Theology,* ed. Walter A. Elwell (Grand Rapids, Mich.: Baker Book House, 1984), 511-12; Bruce Shelley, *Church History in Plain Language* (Waco, Tex.: Word Books, 1982), 420.

[18]Roland N. Stromberg, *An Intellectual History of Modern Europe,* 2nd ed. (Englewood Cliffs, N.J.: Prentice Hall, 1975), 375-78.

[19]R. Laurence Moore, *In Search of White Crows* (New York: Oxford University Press, 1977), 134-38; J. B. Rhine, "Parapsychology," in *Encyclopedia of the Unexplained,* ed. Richard Cavendish (New York: McGraw-Hill, 1974), 178, 180-82.

[20]Moore, *In Search of White Crows,* 185, 198, 204, 210, 213, 219, 221, 235.

[21]Ibid., 235.

[22]Ahlstrom, *Religious History,* 805-24, 827, 840; R. Laurence Moore, *Religious Outsiders and the Making of Americans* (New York: Oxford University Press, 1986); Arthur M. Schlesinger Sr., *A Critical Period in American Religion, 1875-1900* (Philadelphia: Fortress, 1967), 11-14.

[23]Kenneth Cauthen, *The Impact of American Religious Liberalism* (New York: Harper & Row, 1962), 4-17; Shelley, *Church History,* 416. See also William R. Hutchison, *The Modernist Impulse in American Protestantism* (Cambridge, Mass.: Harvard University Press, 1976).

[24]Noll et al., *Christianity in America,* 322. See also Cauthen, *Impact of American Religious Liberalism,* 209-20.

[25]Noll et al., *Christianity in America,* 322-23. See also Cauthen, *Impact of American Religious Liberalism,* 209-20; Ahlstrom, *Religious History,* 779-80.

[26]Hutchison, *Modernist Impulse,* 258-74; Ronald Enroth, *The Lure of the Cults* (Chappaqua, N.Y.: Christian Herald Books, 1979), 43-44; Cauthen, *Impact of American Religious Liberalism,* 243-48.

Chapter 8: Nineteenth-Century Occult and Metaphysical Movements

[1]G. Baseden Butt, *Madame Blavatsky* (London: Rider, 1925), 2-54; Robert Ellwood, *Alternative Altars* (Chicago: University of Chicago Press, 1979), 107-11; J. Stillson Judah, *The History and Philosophy of the Metaphysical Movements in America* (Philadelphia: Westminster Press, 1957), 92-93. See also Marion Meade, *Madame Blavatsky: The Woman Behind the Myth* (New York: Putnam, 1980); Alvin B. Kuhn, *Theosophy: A Modern Revival of Ancient Wisdom* (New York: Henry Holt, 1930).

[2]Robert Ellwood, "The American Theosophical Synthesis," in *The Occult in America,* ed. Howard Kerr and Charles Crow (Urbana: University of Illinois Press, 1983), 112-15; Robert Ellwood, *Religious and Spiritual Groups in Modern America* (Englewood Cliffs, N.J.: Prentice Hall, 1973), 76.

[3]Ellwood, *Alternative Altars,* 111-12; Ellwood, *Religious and Spiritual Groups,* 76; Charles S. Braden, *These Also Believe: A Study of Modern Cults and Minority Religious Movements* (New York: Macmillan, 1957), 222-26.

[4]Judah, *History and Philosophy of the Metaphysical Movements,* 93-94. See also Bruce F. Campbell, *Ancient Wisdom Revived: A History of the Theosophical Movement* (Berkeley: University of California Press, 1980).

[5]Judah, *History and Philosophy of the Metaphysical Movements,* 109-26; Braden, *These Also Believe,* 237-42; Ellwood, *Religious and Spiritual Groups,* 78.

[6]J. Gordon Melton, *The Encyclopedia of American Religions,* 2 vols. (Wilmington, N.C.: McGrath, 1978), 2:135-75.

[7]Ellwood, *Religious and Spiritual Groups,* 92-93.

[8]Judah, *History and Philosophy of the Metaphysical Movements,* 93.

[9]Ibid., 108-9.

[10]Ellwood, "American Theosophical Synthesis," 118; Judah, *History and Philosophy of the Metaphysical Movements,* 104-7.

[11]Ellwood, "American Theosophical Synthesis," 119-20.

[12]Ibid.

[13]Ellwood, *Religious and Spiritual Groups,* 89-90.

[14]Braden, *These Also Believe,* 243-46.

[15]Judah, *History and Philosophy of the Metaphysical Movements,* 103-108; Braden, *These Also Believe,* 246-50.

[16]Judah, *History and Philosophy of the Metaphysical Movements,* 104-5.

[17]Ellwood, "American Theosophical Synthesis," 120-31; Catherine Albanese, *America: Religions and Religion* (Belmont, Calif.: Wadsworth, 1981), 179; Braden, *These Also Believe,* 243-45.

[18]Ellwood, *Religious and Spiritual Groups,* 97; Braden, *These Also Believe,* 255.

[19]Melton, *Encyclopedia of American Religions,* 2:144-49; Ellwood, *Religious and Spiritual Groups,* 103-5; Judah, *History and Philosophy of the Metaphysical Movements,* 119-33. See also Alice A. Bailey, *A Treatise on White Magic* (New York: Lucis, 1951).

[20]Ellwood, *Religious and Spiritual Groups,* 106-8; Melton, *Encyclopedia of American Religions,* 2:165-67. See Olin D. Wannamaker, *Rudolf Steiner: An Introduction to His Life and Thought* (New York: Anthroposophic Press, 1958); Rudolf Steiner, *Theosophy* (New York: Anthroposophic Press, 1932).

[21]Ellwood, *Religious and Spiritual Groups,* 110-12; Melton, *Encyclopedia of American Religions,* 2:177-83. See Arthur Edward Waite, *The Real History of the Rosicrucians* (Mokelumme Hill, Calif.: Health Research, 1960); Hargrove Jennings, *The Rosicrucians, Their Rites and Mysteries* (London: John Camden Hotten, 1870); H. Spenser Lewis, *Rosicrucian Questions and Answers* (San Jose, Calif.: Supreme Grand Lodge of AMORC, 1969).

[22]Ellwood, *Religious and Spiritual Groups,* 110-12; Melton, *Encyclopedia of American Religions,* 2:182.

[23]Ellwood, *Religious and Spiritual Groups,* 121-25; Melton, *Encyclopedia of American Religions,* 2:155-58; Braden, *These Also Believe,* 257-307. See David W. Stupple, "A Functional Approach to Social Movements with an Analysis of the I AM Religious Sect and the Congress of Racial Equality," M.A. thesis, University of Missouri at Kansas City, 1965.

[24]Melton, *Encyclopedia of American Religions,* 2:155-58; Braden, *These Also Believe,* 257-307; Ellwood, *Religious and Spiritual Groups,* 121-25.

[25]Braden, *These Also Believe,* 308-18; Melton, *Encyclopedia of American Religions,* 2:149-55. See Peter Anson, *Bishops at Large* (London: Faber and Faber, 1964); John Dart, "Liberal Catholic Church Preaches Free Conscience," *Los Angeles Times,* March 23, 1969.

[26]Charles S. Braden, *Spirits in Rebellion: The Rise and Development of New Thought* (Dallas: Southern Methodist University Press, 1963), 9-25; Ellwood, *Religious and Spiritual Groups,* 79; Judah, *History and Philosophy of the Metaphysical Groups,* 176-86. See Horatio W. Dresser, *A History of the New Thought Movement* (New York: Thomas Y. Crowell, 1919).

[27]Braden, *Spirits in Rebellion,* 14-19; Ellwood, *Religious and Spiritual Groups,* 79-80; Melton, *Encyclopedia of American Religions,* 2:56-58.

[28]Ibid.; Ellwood, *Religious and Spiritual Groups,* 79-80; Braden, *Spirits in Rebellion,* 14-19.

[29]Catherine Albanese, "Physic and Metaphysic in Nineteenth-Century America: Medical Sectarians and Religious Healing," *Church History* 55, no. 4 (1986): 497-501; Ellwood, *Religious and Spiritual Groups,* 80; Braden, *Spirits in Rebellion,* 47-88; Albanese, *America,* 179-80. See also Ann Ballow Hawkins, *Phineas Parkhurst Quimby* (Los Angeles: De Vorss, 1951).

[30]Albanese, *America,* 179-80; Judah, *History and Philosophy of the Metaphysical Movements,* 149-54; Braden, *Spirits in Rebellion,* 47-88; Albanese, "Physic and Metaphysic," 499-501. See also Frank Polmore, *Mesmerism and Christian Science* (London: Methuen, 1909); Robert C. Fuller, *Alternative Medicine and American Religious Life* (New York: Oxford University Press, 1989), 50, 60.

[31]John F. Teahan, "Warren Felt Evans and Mental Healing: Romantic Idealism and Practical Mysticism in Nineteenth-Century America," *Church History* 48, no. 1 (1979): 63-80; Braden, *Spirits in Rebellion,* 89-128; Albanese, *America,* 180-81; Judah, *History and Philosophy of the Metaphysical Movements,* 160-67.

[32]Braden, *Spirits in Rebellion,* 89-128; Albanese, *America,* 180-81; Teahan, "Warren Felt Evans," 63-80; Judah, *History and Philosophy of the Metaphysical Movements,* 160-67.

[33]Braden, *These Also Believe,* 130-38; Albanese, *America,* 180-81; Braden, *Spirits in Rebellion,* 129-69; Albanese, "Physic and Metaphysic," 497-502.

[34]Ibid.; Braden, *These Also Believe,* 130-38; Albanese, *America,* 180-81; Braden, *Spirits in Rebellion,* 129-69.

[35]Judah, *History and Philosophy of the Metaphysical Movements,* 192-93; Albanese, *America,* 182; Braden, *Spirits in Rebellion,* 323-405. See Donald Meyer, *Positive Thinkers,* 2nd ed. (New York: Pantheon Books, 1980).

[36]Melton, *Encyclopedia of American Religions,* 2:59-60; Braden, *These Also Believe,* 144, 146-47, 156-79; Braden, *Spirits in Rebellion,* 233-63; Judah, *History and Philosophy of the Metaphysical Movements,* 227-55. See Dana Gatlin, *Unity's Fifty Golden Years* (Kansas City, Mo.: Unity School of Christianity, 1939); Marcus Bach, *The Unity Way of Life* (Unity Village, Mo.: Unity Books, 1962).

[37]Braden, *Spirits in Rebellion,* 233-63; Melton, *Encyclopedia of American Religions,* 2:59-60; Braden, *These Also Believe,* 144, 146-47, 156-79; Judah, *History and Philosophy of the Metaphysical Movements,* 227-55.

[38]Braden, *Spirits in Rebellion,* 264-84; Melton, *Encyclopedia of American Religions,* 2:62-63. See *Divine Science: Its Principle and Practice* (Denver: Divine Science Church and College, 1957); Hazel Deane, *Powerful Is the Light* (Denver: Divine Science College, 1945).

[39]Melton, *Encyclopedia of American Religions,* 2:62-63; Braden, *Spirits in Rebellion,* 282-311.

[40]Ibid., 285.

NOTES

41Melton, *Encyclopedia of American Religions,* 2:60-61; Braden, *Spirits in Rebellion,* 286-311. See Ernest Holmes, *Creative Mind* (New York: Robert M. McBride, 1919); Fenwicke Holmes, *Law of Mind in Action* (New York: Dodd, Mead, 1919).

42Melton, *Encyclopedia of American Religions,* 2:60-1; Braden, *Spirits in Rebellion,* 286-311; Judah, *History and Philosophy of the Metaphysical Movements,* 207-27. See Ernest Holmes, *The Science of Mind* (New York: Dodd, Mead, 1944); Ernest Holmes, *What Religious Science Teaches* (Los Angeles: Church of Religious Science, 1944).

43In 1972 there were more than two thousand Church of Christ, Scientist, groups in the United States, and fewer than one thousand in the rest of the world. By 1987, however, Christian Science gave evidence of being in a significant decline. See James Doane, "Christian Science," in *New International Dictionary of the Christian Church,* ed. J. D. Douglas (Grand Rapids, Mich.: Zondervan, 1974), 221; Kenneth L. Woodward, "The Graying of a Church: Christian Science's Ills," *Newsweek,* August 3, 1987, p. 60.

44Braden, *These Also Believe,* 180; Richard Kyle, "Church of Christ, Scientist," in *Encyclopedia USA,* ed. Archie P. McDonald (Gulf Breeze, Fla.: Academic International Press, 1989), 92-93.

45Ruth A. Tucker, *Another Gospel* (Grand Rapids, Mich.: Zondervan, 1989), 165-66.

46Stephen Gottschalk, *The Emergence of Christian Science in American Religious Life* (Berkeley: University of California Press, 1973), 140-41; Tucker, *Another Gospel,* 157, 174.

47Braden, *Spirits in Rebellion,* 14-24; Albanese, "Physic and Metaphysic," 501-2.

48For more on Eddy's early life see Robert Peel, *Mary Baker Eddy: The Years of Discovery* (New York: Holt, Rinehart and Winston, 1971); Julius Selberger, *Mary Baker Eddy: An Interpretive Biography of the Founder of Christian Science* (New York: Little, Brown, 1980).

49Braden, *These Also Believe,* 184-85; Melton, *Encyclopedia of American Religions,* 2:75; Horatio W. Dresser, *The Quimby Manuscripts* (New York: Thomas Y. Crowell, 1921); Albanese, "Physic and Metaphysic," 499-501; Kyle, "Church of Christ, Scientist," 93.

50For a general background on Eddy and Christian Science see Charles S. Braden, *Christian Science Today* (London: George Allen and Unwin, 1959); Lyman P. Powell, *Mary Baker Eddy: A Life Size Portrait* (New York: Macmillan, 1930); Gottschalk, *Emergence of Christian Science;* John Dewitt, *The Christian Science Way of Life* (Englewood Cliffs, N.J.: Prentice Hall, 1962).

51Ahlstrom, *Religious History,* 1022-23; Mary Baker Eddy, *Science and Health with Key to the Scriptures* (Boston: Christian Science Publishing Society, 1875); Judah, *History and Philosophy of the Metaphysical Movements,* 271-73.

52P. G. Chappell, "Church of Christ, Scientist," in *Evangelical Dictionary of Theology,* ed. Walter A. Elwell (Grand Rapids, Mich.: Baker Book House, 1984), 243; Melton, *Encyclopedia of American Religions,* 2:75; Braden, *These Also Believe,*

399

208-9; Kyle, "Church of Christ, Scientist," 94.
[53]Judah, *History and Philosophy of the Metaphysical Movements,* 274-75; Chappell, "Church of Christ, Scientist," 243; Braden, *These Also Believe,* 200-203; Kyle, "Church of Christ, Scientist," 94.
[54]Braden, *These Also Believe,* 203-6; Judah, *History and Philosophy of the Metaphysical Movements,* 275-80; Kyle, "Church of Christ, Scientist," 95.
[55]Judah, *History and Philosophy of the Metaphysical Movements,* 275-98; Braden, *These Also Believe,* 207; Kyle, "Church of Christ, Scientist," 95.
[56]Melton, *Encyclopedia of American Religions,* 2:76; Judah, *History and Philosophy of the Metaphysical Movements,* 283.
[57]Braden, *These Also Believe,* 212-13; Kyle, "Church of Christ, Scientist," 95.
[58]Braden, *These Also Believe,* 196-97; Doane, "Christian Science," 221-22; Ahlstrom, *Religious History,* 1023; Kyle, "Church of Christ, Scientist," 95.
[59]Braden, *These Also Believe,* 210-12.
[60]Albanese, *America,* 152-53; Gottschalk, *Emergence of Christian Science,* 1-45.
[61]Albanese, *America,* 153-54; Gottschalk, *Emergence of Christian Science,* 1-11.

Chapter 9: Early Eastern Groups
[1]Robert Ellwood, *Religious and Spiritual Groups in Modern America* (Englewood Cliffs, N.J.: Prentice Hall, 1973), 219.
[2]See William H. McNeill, *The Rise of the West* (Chicago: University of Chicago Press, 1963). See also S. Radhakrishman, *Eastern Religions and Western Thought* (New York: Galaxy, 1959).
[3]Carl T. Jackson, *The Oriental Religions and American Thought: Nineteenth-Century Explorations* (Westport, Conn.: Greenwood, 1981), 3.
[4]J. Gordon Melton, "How New Is New? The Flowers of the 'New' Religious Consciousness Since 1965," in *The Future of New Religious Movements,* ed. David G. Bromley and Philip E. Hammond (Macon, Ga.: Mercer University Press, 1987), 49; Ronald Enroth and J. Gordon Melton, *Why Cults Succeed Where the Church Fails* (Elgin, Ill.: Brethren Press, 1985), 120-23; Jackson, *Oriental Religions,* 25, 32, 45-46, 63-64, 157-58.
[5]Ibid., 265.
[6]Ibid.
[7]David M. Reimers, *Still the Golden Door: The Third World Comes to America* (New York: Columbia University Press, 1985), 1-10.
[8]Enroth and Melton, *Why Cults Succeed,* 122-23; Melton, "How New Is New?" 50-51.
[9]Jackson, *Oriental Religions,* 266.
[10]Some basic books on Hinduism include Thomas J. Hopkins, *The Hindu Religious Tradition* (Belmont, Calif.: Dickinson, 1977); H. H. Wilson, *Religious Sects of the Hindus* (Calcutta: Susil Gupta, 1958); A. L. Basham, *The Wonder That Was India* (London: Sedgwick and Jackson, 1954); Marvin Henry Harper, *Gurus, Swamis and Avatars* (Philadelphia: Westminster Press, 1972); Sir Charles Elliot, *Hinduism*

and Buddhism, 3 vols. (London: Routledge & Kegan Paul, 1954).

[11]J. Gordon Melton, *The Encyclopedia of American Religions,* 2 vols. (Wilmington, N.C.: McGrath, 1978), 2:355-56; Hopkins, *Hindu Religious Tradition,* 3-4, 36-63; Malcolm Pitt, *Introducing Hinduism* (New York: Friendship, 1955), 22-26.

[12]A. L. Basham, "Hinduism," in *The Concise Encyclopedia of Living Faiths,* ed. R. C. Zaehner (Boston: Beacon Press, 1959), 225; Catherine Albanese, *America: Religions and Religion* (Belmont, Calif.: Wadsworth, 1981), 203-4; Jacob Needleman, *The New Religions* (New York: E. P. Dutton, 1970), 24-25; Pitt, *Introducing Hinduism,* 12-21.

[13]Albanese, *America,* 204; Basham, "Hinduism," 225; Ellwood, *Religious and Spiritual Groups,* 218.

[14]Basham, "Hinduism," 225; John B. Noss, *Man's Religions,* 5th ed. (New York: Macmillan, 1974), 101-3; R. C. Zaehner, *Hinduism,* 2nd ed. (London: Oxford University Press, 1966), 58-66.

[15]Albanese, *America,* 204-5; Basham, "Hinduism," 241-54; Zaehner, *Hinduism,* 103-46.

[16]Melton, *Encyclopedia of American Religions,* 2:358-59.

[17]Ellwood, *Religious and Spiritual Groups,* 219.

[18]Melton, *Encyclopedia of American Religions,* 2:360; Ellwood, *Religious and Spiritual Groups,* 220-22; Albanese, *America,* 205-6.

[19]Ibid.

[20]Melton, *Encyclopedia of American Religions,* 2:360-61; Ellwood, *Religious and Spiritual Groups,* 224.

[21]Albanese, *America,* 206.

[22]Melton, *Encyclopedia of American Religions,* 2:361; Albanese, *America,* 206.

[23]Ellwood, *Religious and Spiritual Groups,* 225-27; Albanese, *America,* 207; Melton, *Encyclopedia of American Religions,* 2:361. See also Paramathansa Yogananda, *Autobiography of a Yogi* (Los Angeles: Self-Realization Fellowship, 1959).

[24]Ellwood, *Religious and Spiritual Groups,* 225.

[25]Melton, *Encyclopedia of American Religions,* 2:362; Albanese, *America,* 206-7.

[26]Ibid., 207.

[27]Ellwood, *Religious and Spiritual Groups,* 227-29.

[28]John Newport, *Christ and the New Consciousness* (Nashville: Broadman, 1978), 50-51; Melton, *Encyclopedia of American Religions,* 2:393-94; Ellwood, *Religious and Spiritual Groups,* 251. General sources for Buddhism include Maurice Percheron, *Buddha and Buddhism* (New York: Harper & Brothers, 1957); Edward Conze, *Buddhism: Its Essence and Development* (New York: Harper & Brothers, 1959); Clarence H. Hamilton, *Buddhism: A Religion of Infinite Compassion* (New York: Liberal Arts Press, 1952); Hans Wolfgang Schumann, *Buddhism: An Outline of Its Teaching and Schools* (Wheaton, Ill.: Theosophical Publishing House, 1974); J. B. Pratt, *The Pilgrimage of Buddhism* (New York: Macmillan, 1958).

[29]Christmas Humphreys, ed., *The Wisdom of Buddhism* (New York: Harper & Row, 1960), 42-105; Newport, *Christ and the New Consciousness,* 50-51; Henri Arvon,

Buddhism (New York: Walker, 1951), 13-21; Albanese, *America,* 210.

[30]A. J. Bahm, *Philosophy of the Buddha* (London: Rider, 1958), 38-48; Conze, *Buddhism,* 43-48; Arvon, *Buddhism,* 35-44; Melton, *Encyclopedia of American Religions,* 2:394.

[31]Arvon, *Buddhism,* 44-47; Bahm, *Philosophy of the Buddha,* 80-91; Melton, *Encyclopedia of American Religions,* 2:394.

[32]J. Kashyap, "Origin and Expansion of Buddhism," in *The Path of the Buddha,* ed. Kenneth W. Morgan (New York: Ronald, 1956), 3-66; Christmas Humphreys, *Buddhism* (Baltimore: Penguin, 1951), 45-76; Newport, *Christ and the New Consciousness,* 51.

[33]Ananda Maitreya Nayaka Thero, "Buddhism in Theravada Countries," in *The Path of the Buddha,* ed. Kenneth W. Morgan (New York: Ronald, 1956), 113-52; Humphreys, *Buddhism,* 78-129; Albanese, *America,* 211; Newport, *Christ and the New Consciousness,* 51-52.

[34]Susuma Yamayuahi, "Development of Mahayana Buddhist Beliefs," in *The Path of the Buddha,* ed. Kenneth W. Morgan (New York: Ronald, 1956), 153-81; E. A. Burtt, ed., *The Teachings of the Compassionate Buddha* (New York: Mentor Books, 1955), 130-40, 161-69; Conze, *Buddhism,* 119-43; Humphreys, *Buddhism,* 167-77; Albanese, *America,* 211; Newport, *Christ and the New Consciousness,* 51-52.

[35]Melton, *Encyclopedia of American Religions,* 2:396; Albanese, *America,* 212.

[36]Melton, *Encyclopedia of American Religions,* 2:396.

[37]Ibid., 2:401.

[38]Rick Fields, *How the Swans Came to the Lake: A Narrative History of Buddhism in America* (Boulder, Colo.: Shambhala, 1981), 83-118; Robert Ellwood, *Alternative Altars* (Chicago: University of Chicago Press, 1979), 131-39; Albanese, *America,* 212.

[39]Melton, *Encyclopedia of American Religions,* 2:400; Reimers, *Still the Golden Door,* 4-6; John Higham, *Strangers in the Land: Patterns of American Nativism, 1860-1925* (New York: Atheneum, 1971), 129-30, 164.

[40]Fields, *How the Swans Came,* 11-12; Albanese, *America,* 212.

[41]Albanese, *America,* 212-13; Melton, *Encyclopedia of American Religions,* 2:410-11; Alan W. Watts, *The Way of Zen* (New York: Vintage Books, 1957), 68-70.

[42]Ibid., 77-112; Melton, *Encyclopedia of American Religions,* 2:413-14; Ellwood, *Religious and Spiritual Groups,* 251-52; Thomas Hoover, *The Zen Experience* (New York: New American Library, 1980), 2-9.

[43]Albanese, *America,* 213; Hoover, *Zen Experience,* 137-59.

[44]Ibid., 137-49; Watts, *Way of Zen,* 154-73; Albanese, *America,* 213; Needleman, *New Religions,* 40-41.

[45]Albanese, *America,* 213-14; Fields, *How the Swans Came,* 174-84; Needleman, *New Religions,* 41.

[46]Hoover, *Zen Experience,* 151-59; Melton, *Encyclopedia of American Religions,* 2:415-19; Albanese, *America,* 213; Needleman, *New Religions,* 41.

[47]Melton, *Encyclopedia of American Religions*, 2:424-30.

[48]Ibid., 2:401, 434-35; Fields, *How the Swans Came*, 184-91.

[49]For general information on Islam see D. S. Roberts, *Islam* (New York: Harper & Row, 1981); Caesar E. Farah, *Islam: Beliefs and Observances* (Woodbury, N.Y.: Barron's Educational Series, 1968); Alfred Guillaume, *Islam* (Baltimore: Penguin, 1954); John B. Christopher, *The Islamic Tradition* (New York: Harper & Row, 1972); H. A. R. Gibb, *Mohammedanism* (New York: Oxford University Press, 1962); Sayyed Abul A'la Maudoodi, *Towards Understanding Islam* (Lahore, Pakistan: Islamic Publications, 1963).

[50]Guillaume, *Islam*, 10-18; Farah, *Islam*, 28, 31, 85, 87; Norman Daniel, *Islam and the West* (Edinburgh: Edinburgh University Press, 1960), 47-67; Newport, *Christ and the New Consciousness*, 64.

[51]Ibid. For general information on Muhammad's life see E. G. Parrandea, *An Introduction to Asian Religions* (London: SPCK, 1957), 7-11; Guillaume, *Islam*, 20-54; Roberts, *Islam*, 9-29; Fazlur Rahman, *Islam* (Garden City, N.Y.: Anchor Books, 1968), 1-24; W. Montgomery Watt, *Muhammad: Prophet and Statesman* (London: Oxford University Press, 1961).

[52]Newport, *Christ and the New Consciousness*, 64; Kenneth Cragg, *The House of Islam* (Belmont, Calif.: Wadsworth, 1975), 30-43; Rahman, *Islam*, 25-41; Farah, *Islam*, 78-102; H. A. R. Gibb, "Islam," in *The Concise Encyclopedia of Living Faiths*, ed. R. C. Zaehner (Boston: Beacon Press, 1959), 178-80.

[53]Newport, *Christ and the New Consciousness*, 65; Farah, *Islam*, 104-12; Noss, *Man's Religions*, 520.

[54]Newport, *Christ and the New Consciousness*, 65; Guillaume, *Islam*, 88-110.

[55]Christopher, *Islamic Tradition*, 39-40; Roberts, *Islam*, 36, 37; George W. Braswell Jr., *Understanding Sectarian Groups in America* (Nashville: Broadman, 1986), 336-37; Noss, *Man's Religions*, 522.

[56]Braswell, *Understanding Sectarian Groups*, 337; Roberts, *Islam*, 37; Christopher, *Islamic Tradition*, 40-43; Noss, *Man's Religions*, 522.

[57]Braswell, *Understanding Sectarian Groups*, 337; Christopher, *Islamic Tradition*, 44-46; Roberts, *Islam*, 38-39; Noss, *Man's Religions*, 523.

[58]Braswell, *Understanding Sectarian Groups*, 337; Christopher, *Islamic Tradition*, 43-44; Roberts, *Islam*, 38; Noss, *Man's Religions*, 523.

[59]Braswell, *Understanding Sectarian Groups*, 337; Christopher, *Islamic Tradition*, 46-51; Roberts, *Islam*, 39; Noss, *Man's Religions*, 523-24.

[60]Braswell, *Understanding Sectarian Groups*, 338; Farrah, *Islam*, 158-60; Gibb, "Islam," 185-86.

[61]Farah, *Islam*, 184-85; Gibb, "Islam," 180-81; Braswell, *Understanding Sectarian Groups*, 339; Noss, *Man's Religions*, 531-32.

[62]Braswell, *Understanding Sectarian Groups*, 339; Rahman, *Islam*, 207-13; Farah, *Islam*, 161-65; Gibb, "Islam," 180-81.

[63]Newport, *Christ and the New Consciousness*, 66; Phillip K. Hitti, *Islam: A Way of Life* (Minneapolis: University of Minnesota Press, 1970), 54-60; Noss, *Man's*

Religions, 536.

64Newport, *Christ and the New Consciousness,* 66-67; Rahman, *Islam,* 153-62; Ignaz Goldzaher, *Introduction to Islamic Theology and Law* (Princeton, N.J.: Princeton University Press, 1981), 116-66; Gibb, "Islam," 202; Noss, *Man's Religions,* 535-36. Martin Lings, *What Is Sufism?* (Berkeley: University of California Press, 1975), 100-127.

65Hitti, *Islam,* 56-60; Newport, *Christ and the New Consciousness,* 67-68; Rahman, *Islam,* 162-65.

66Newport, *Christ and the New Consciousness,* 68; Gibb, "Islam," 203; Guillaume, *Islam,* 152-54; Idries Shah, *The Sufis* (Garden City, N.Y.: Doubleday, 1971), 294-322.

67Newport, *Christ and the New Consciousness,* 68-69; Melton, *Encyclopedia of American Religions,* 2:345.

68Braswell, *Understanding Sectarian Groups,* 340-41; Melton, *Encyclopedia of American Religions,* 2:339.

69Ibid., 2:343-50.

70Arthur Fauset, *Black Gods of the Metropolis* (Philadelphia: University of Pennsylvania Press, 1971), 41-42, 45-48; Melton, *Encyclopedia of American Religions,* 2:339-40.

71For general information on Baha'i see Gloria Faizi, *The Bahai Faith: An Introduction,* rev. ed. (n.p., 1972); George Townsend, *The Promise of All Ages* (London: George Ronald, 1961); William McElwee Miller, *The Baha'i Faith: Its History and Teachings* (South Pasadena, Calif.: William Carey Library, 1974).

72Ibid., 13-44; Braswell, *Understanding Sectarian Groups,* 352-53.

73Miller, *Baha'i Faith,* 115-65; George Townsend, *Christ and Baha'u'llah* (Oxford: George Ronald, 1957), 69-78; Newport, *Christ and the New Consciousness,* 81.

74Albanese, *America,* 201-2; Miller, *Baha'i Faith,* 138-65; Ruth A. Tucker, *Another Gospel* (Grand Rapids, Mich.: Zondervan, 1989), 286.

75Miller, *Baha'i Faith,* 142-63; Albanese, *America,* 202.

76Tucker, *Another Gospel,* 294-96.

77Melton, *Encyclopedia of American Religions,* 2:352; Miller, *Baha'i Faith,* 191-215.

78Albanese, *America,* 202; Braswell, *Understanding Sectarian Groups,* 354.

79Richard N. Ostling, "Slow Death for Iran's Baha'is," *Time,* February 20, 1984, 76; Tucker, *Another Gospel,* 285.

Chapter 10: Christian-Related Bodies
1Peter W. Williams, *Popular Religion in America* (Englewood Cliffs, N.J.: Prentice Hall, 1980), 128; Jonathan Butler, "From Millerism to Seventh-Day Adventism: 'Boundlessness to Consolidation,' " *Church History* 55, no. 1 (1986): 56-58; James H. Moorhead, "Searching for the Millennium in America," *Princeton Seminary Bulletin* 8, no. 2 (1987): 61. For more on Adventism see Henry C. Sheldon, *Studies in Recent Adventism* (New York: Abingdon, 1915); Edwin Scott Gaustad, *The Rise of Adventism* (New York: Harper & Row, 1974).

²Williams, *Popular Religion,* 128; Sydney E. Ahlstrom, *A Religious History of the American People* (New Haven, Conn.: Yale University Press, 1972), 479; Butler, "From Millerism to Seventh-Day Adventism," 56-58.

³J. Gordon Melton, *The Encyclopedia of American Religions,* 2 vols. (Wilmington, N.C.: McGrath, 1978), 1:461-62; Elmer T. Clark, *The Small Sects in America* (Nashville: Abingdon, 1965), 25-30; William J. Whalen, *Minority Religions in America* (New York: Alba House, 1981), 4.

⁴Leon Festinger, Henry W. Riecken and Stanley Schachter, *When Prophecy Fails* (New York: Harper & Row, 1964), 3-32; Melton, *Encyclopedia of American Religions,* 1:481.

⁵See Anthony A. Hoekema, *The Four Major Cults* (Grand Rapids, Mich.: Eerdmans, 1963); Walter Martin, *The Kingdom of the Cults* (Minneapolis: Bethany Fellowship, 1965); Gordon Lewis, *Confronting the Cults* (Grand Rapids, Mich.: Baker Book House, 1966); Catherine Albanese, *America: Religions and Religion* (Belmont, Calif.: Wadsworth, 1981), 145, 149; Horton Davies, *Christian Deviations* (Philadelphia: Westminster Press, 1985), 42-46.

⁶Rodney Stark and William S. Bainbridge, *The Future of Religion* (Berkeley: University of California Press, 1985), 489; Albanese, *America,* 146-48; Ronald L. Numbers, "Ellen G. White and the Gospel of Health," in *Christianity in America,* ed. Mark A. Noll et al. (Grand Rapids, Mich.: Eerdmans, 1983), 197-99; Geoffrey J. Paxton, *The Shaking of Adventism* (Grand Rapids, Mich.: Baker Book House, 1977).

⁷General sources for the holiness movement include Charles Edwin Jones, *Perfectionist Persuasion: The Holiness Movement and American Methodism, 1867-1936* (Metuchen, N.J.: Scarecrow, 1974); J. E. Searles, *History of the Present Holiness Revival* (Boston: McDonald and Gill, 1887); John Leland Peters, *Christian Perfectionism and American Methodism* (New York: Abingdon, 1956).

⁸Edwin Scott Gaustad, *Historical Atlas of Religion in America* (New York: Harper & Row, 1976), 123; Jones, *Perfectionist Persuasion,* 209-10.

⁹Mark A. Noll et al., eds., *Christianity in America* (Grand Rapids, Mich.: Eerdmans, 1983), 331-32. See also Timothy L. Smith, "Righteousness and Hope: Christian Holiness and the Millennial Vision in America, 1800-1900," *American Quarterly* 31, no. 1 (1979): 21-45.

¹⁰Melton, *Encyclopedia of American Religions,* 1:199; Gaustad, *Historical Atlas,* 122; Vinson Synan, *The Holiness-Pentecostal Movement in the United States* (Grand Rapids, Mich.: Eerdmans, 1971), 53; Frederick A. Norwood, *The Story of American Methodism* (Nashville: Abingdon, 1974), 292-94.

¹¹For general information on Pentecostalism see Walter J. Hollenweger, *The Pentecostals* (Minneapolis: Augsburg Publishing House, 1972); Synan, *Holiness-Pentecostal Movement;* John Thomas Nichol, *The Pentecostals* (Plainfield, N.J.: Logos International, 1966); Jessyca Russell Gaver, *Pentecostalism* (New York: Award Books, 1971).

¹²Melton, *Encyclopedia of American Religions,* 1:243-44; Dennis J. Bennett, "The

Gifts of the Holy Spirit," in *The Charismatic Movement,* ed. Michael P. Hamilton (Grand Rapids, Mich.: Eerdmans, 1975), 16-20.

[13]James N. Lapsley and John N. Simpson, "Speaking in Tongues," *The Princeton Seminary Bulletin* 58 (February 1965): 6-7; Synan, *Holiness-Pentecostal Movement,* 122.

[14]Robert Mapes Anderson, *Vision of the Disinherited* (New York: Oxford University Press, 1979), 223-24; Bryan Wilson, *Religious Sects* (New York: McGraw-Hill, 1970), 72-73.

[15]Anderson, *Vision of the Disinherited,* 114-15; Wilson, *Religious Sects,* 70-72.

[16]Vinson Synan, "Pentecostalism," in *Evangelical Dictionary of Theology,* ed. Walter A. Elwell (Grand Rapids, Mich.: Baker Book House, 1984), 837-38; Synan, *Holiness-Pentecostal Movement,* 117-39.

[17]Ibid., 186-87; Horace S. Ward, "The Anti-Pentecostal Argument," in *Aspects of Pentecostal-Charismatic Origins,* ed. Vinson Synan (Plainfield, N.J.: Logos International, 1975), 107-14.

[18]George Marsden, "Fundamentalism," in *Christianity in America,* ed. Mark A. Noll et al. (Grand Rapids, Mich.: Eerdmans, 1983), 384. For general information see George Marsden, *Fundamentalism and American Culture* (New York: Oxford University Press, 1980); Ernest R. Sandeen, *The Roots of Fundamentalism* (Chicago: University of Chicago Press, 1970); George W. Dollar, *A History of Fundamentalism* (Greenville, S.C.: Bob Jones University Press, 1973); Norman F. Furness, *The Fundamentalist Controversy, 1918-1931* (New Haven, Conn.: Yale University Press, 1954); Louis Gasper, *The Fundamentalist Movement* (The Hague: Mouton, 1968); S. G. Cole, *The History of Fundamentalism* (New York: R. R. Smith, 1931).

[19]Marsden, *Fundamentalism and American Culture,* 6.

[20]Cole, *History of Fundamentalism;* Furness, *Fundamentalist Controversy.*

[21]Ernest R. Sandeen, "Towards a Historical Interpretation of the Origins of Fundamentalism," *Church History* 36, no. 1 (1967): 82; Ernst R. Sandeen, "Fundamentalism and American Identity," *The Annals of the American Academy of Political and Social Science* 387 (January 1970): 57-58.

[22]George Marsden, "Fundamentalism as an American Phenomenon: A Comparison with English Evangelicalism," *Church History* 46, no. 2 (1977): 225-26; Marsden, *Fundamentalism and American Culture,* 5, 224.

[23]For more on dispensationalism see Charles Caldwell Ryrie, *Dispensationalism Today* (Chicago: Moody Press, 1965); Clarence B. Bass, *Backgrounds to Dispensationalism* (Grand Rapids, Mich.: Baker Book House, 1960); Timothy P. Weber, *Living in the Shadow of the Second Coming* (New York: Oxford University Press, 1979).

[24]Melton, *Encyclopedia of American Religions,* 1:481-92; J. Gordon Melton, *Encyclopedic Handbook of Cults in America* (New York: Garland, 1986), 62-67. For a general picture of the Bible Student Movement see Timothy White, *A People for His Name* (New York: Vantage, 1968); Alan Rogerson, *Millions Now Living Will*

Never Die (London: Constable, 1969); William J. Whalen, *Armageddon Around the Corner* (New York: John Day, 1962); Edmund C. Gruss, *Apostles of Denial* (N.p.: Presbyterian and Reformed, 1970).

[25] Wilson, *Religious Sects,* 109-10; Melton, *Encyclopedia of American Religions,* 1:481-82; Kenneth Boa, *Cults, World Religions and You* (Wheaton, Ill.: Victor Books, 1977), 73.

[26] Gruss, *Apostles of Denial,* 38-50; Boa, *Cults, World Religions and You,* 73-74.

[27] Ibid., 74; Gruss, *Apostles of Denial,* 46-49; Hoekema, *Four Major Cults,* 227-28; Ruth A. Tucker, *Another Gospel* (Grand Rapids, Mich.: Zondervan, 1989), 119.

[28] George W. Braswell Jr., *Understanding Sectarian Groups in America* (Nashville: Broadman, 1986), 66-67; Boa, *Cults, World Religions and You,* 74-75; Wilson, *Religious Sects,* 100-111; Gruss, *Apostles of Denial,* 53-66.

[29] Tucker, *Another Gospel,* 125-28.

[30] Braswell, *Understanding Sectarian Groups,* 67-68; Boa, *Cults, World Religions and You,* 75; Gruss, *Apostles of Denial,* 67-72; Heather Batting and Gary Batting, *The Orwellian World of Jehovah's Witnesses* (Toronto: University of Toronto Press, 1984), 41.

[31] Braswell, *Understanding Sectarian Groups,* 68-69; Melton, *Encyclopedic Handbook of Cults in America,* 63-64; Tucker, *Another Gospel,* 130, 132.

[32] Gruss, *Apostles of Denial,* 79-94; Boa, *Cults, World Religions and You,* 75-76; Hoekema, *Four Major Cults,* 255-95; Tucker, *Another Gospel,* 138-39.

[33] Hoekema, *Four Major Cults,* 295-326; Boa, *Cults, World Religions and You,* 77-78; Edwin Scott Gaustad, *Dissent in American Religion* (Chicago: University of Chicago Press, 1973), 115-16; Tucker, *Another Gospel,* 139-40.

[34] Gaustad, *Dissent in American Religion,* 116; Whalen, *Minority Religions,* 64; Tucker, *Another Gospel,* 132-33.

[35] Braswell, *Understanding Sectarian Groups,* 90-93; Whalen, *Minority Religions,* 64; Tucker, *Another Gospel,* 133.

[36] Whalen, *Minority Religions,* 68; Tucker, *Another Gospel,* 136-37.

[37] Braswell, *Understanding Sectarian Groups,* 94; Kenneth L. Woodward, "Are They False Witnesses?" *Newsweek* July 20, 1981, 75; Tucker, *Another Gospel,* 117.

[38] Woodward, "Are They False Witnesses?" 75; Braswell, *Understanding Sectarian Groups,* 94.

[39] Melton, *Encyclopedia of American Religions,* 1:471; William J. Whalen, *Strange Gods* (Huntington, Ind.: Our Sunday Visitor, 1981), 28-29. For general information on the Worldwide Church of God see Joseph Hopkins, *The Armstrong Empire* (Grand Rapids, Mich.: Eerdmans, 1974); Herman Hock, *A True History of the Church* (Pasadena, Calif.: Ambassador College, 1959; Marion J. McNair, *Armstrongism: Religion . . . or Rip-off?* (Orlando, Fla.: Pacific Charters, 1977); David Robinson, *Herbert Armstrong's Tangled Web* (Tulsa, Okla.: John Hadden Publishers, 1980).

[40] Whalen, *Strange Gods,* 29.

[41] Melton, *Encyclopedia of American Religions,* 1:469.

[42]Whalen, *Strange Gods*, 29; Hopkins, *Armstrong Empire*, 37-40; Melton, *Encyclopedic Handbook of Cults in America*, 98.

[43]Ibid., 98; Whalen, *Strange Gods*, 33; Hopkins, *Armstrong Empire*, 49-52; Tucker, *Another Gospel*, 195.

[44]Melton, *Encyclopedic Handbook of Cults in America*, 98-99; Hopkins, *Armstrong Empire*, 48-52.

[45]Melton, *Encyclopedic Handbook of Cults in America*, 99; Whalen, *Strange Gods*, 35-36.

[46]Melton, *Encyclopedic Handbook of Cults in America*, 99; Whalen, *Strange Gods*, 35-36; Tucker, *Another Gospel*, 197-98. For the perspective of the Worldwide Church of God on being placed in receivership see Stanley R. Rader, *Against the Gates of Hell* (New York: Everest House, 1980); Joseph M. Hopkins, "First Amendment Threat Brings WGG Some Improbable Allies," *Christianity Today*, February 8, 1980.

[47]Melton, *Encyclopedic Handbook of Cults in America*, 102.

[48]Joseph M. Hopkins, "Successor Takes Over After Death of Herbert Armstrong," *Christianity Today*, February 21, 1986, 48; Tucker, *Another Gospel*, 215; "Unprecedented Changes Affect Worldwide Church of God," *Christian Research Journal* 13, no. 4 (1991): 5-6.

[49]Tucker, *Another Gospel*, 195-97.

[50]See William J. Petersen, *Those Curious New Cults in the 80s* (New Canaan, Conn.: Keats, 1973), 130-43; Martin, *Kingdom of the Cults*, 295-324; Tucker, *Another Gospel*, 191-216; Melton, *Encyclopedic Handbook of Cults in America*, 95-102.

[51]Ibid., 99-100; Tucker, *Another Gospel*, 212-13; Hopkins, *Armstrong Empire*, 101-17.

[52]Melton, *Encyclopedic Handbook of Cults in America*, 99-100; Hopkins, *Armstrong Empire*, 135-51; Tucker, *Another Gospel*, 205-6.

[53]Whalen, *Strange Gods*, 30-31; Hopkins, *Armstrong Empire*, 149-51.

[54]Melton, *Encyclopedic Handbook of Cults in America*, 100; Hopkins, *Armstrong Empire*, 66-88; Tucker, *Another Gospel*, 207-8; Davies, *Christian Deviations*, 74-85; Whalen, *Strange Gods*, 32-33.

[55]Melton, *Encyclopedic Handbook of Cults in America*, 100; Hopkins, *Armstrong Empire*, 89-100.

[56]Whalen, *Strange Gods*, 30-31, 33; Hopkins, *Armstrong Empire*, 9-10, 53-65; Tucker, *Another Gospel*, 191, 208.

[57]Melton, *Encyclopedia of American Religions*, 1:287-88; Arthur C. Piepkorn, *Holiness and Pentecostal Bodies*, vol. 3 of *Profiles in Belief* (New York: Harper & Row, 1977), 195-96.

[58]Tucker, *Another Gospel*, 385; Synan, *Holiness-Pentecostal Movement*, 220; Gregory A. Boyd, "Sharing Your Faith with a Oneness Pentecostal (Part One)," *Christian Research Journal* 13, no. 4 (1991): 7.

[59]Tucker, *Another Gospel*, 385; Melton, *Encyclopedia of American Religions*, 1:288; Nichol, *The Pentecostals*, 90.

⁶⁰Melton, *Encyclopedia of American Religions,* 1:288; Tucker, *Another Gospel,* 385; Nichol, *The Pentecostals,* 90.

⁶¹Piepkorn, *Holiness and Pentecostal,* 197-216.

⁶²Melton, *Encyclopedia of American Religions,* 1:287-88; Piepkorn, *Holiness and Pentecostal,* 197; Nichol, *The Pentecostals,* 90; Hollenweger, *The Pentecostals,* 31.

⁶³Nichol, *The Pentecostals,* 90-91; Piepkorn, *Holiness and Pentecostal,* 195; Hollenweger, *The Pentecostals,* 33.

⁶⁴Ibid., 34; Piepkorn, *Holiness and Pentecostal,* 195; Nichol, *The Pentecostals,* 91.

⁶⁵Piepkorn, *Holiness and Pentecostal,* 196; Tucker, *Another Gospel,* 385.

Chapter 11: Black Religious Groups

¹Sydney E. Ahlstrom, *A Religious History of the American People* (New Haven, Conn.: Yale University Press, 1972), 1055-56; Catherine Albanese, *America: Religions and Religion* (Belmont, Calif.: Wadsworth, 1981), 125-26; Peter W. Williams, *Popular Religion in America* (Englewood Cliffs, N.J.: Prentice Hall, 1980), 43; Martin E. Marty, *The Irony of It All,* vol. 1 of *Modern American Religion* (Chicago: University of Chicago Press, 1986), 98-106.

²Albanese, *America,* 126; Ahlstrom, *Religious History,* 1056, 1058; Mark A. Noll et al., eds., *Christianity in America* (Grand Rapids, Mich.: Eerdmans, 1983), 346.

³Ahlstrom, *Religious History,* 1059; Albanese, *America,* 126.

⁴Joseph R. Washington Jr., *Black Sects and Cults* (Garden City, N.Y.: Doubleday, 1973), 9-10; Ahlstrom, *Religious History,* 1061.

⁵Arthur C. Piepkorn, *Holiness and Pentecostal Bodies,* vol. 3 of *Profiles in Belief* (New York: Harper & Row, 1977), 93-94; Ahlstrom, *Religious History,* 1059.

⁶Albanese, *America,* 126.

⁷Ibid., 127; Ahlstrom, *Religious History,* 1061.

⁸Washington, *Black Sects and Cults,* 118-19; George Eaton Simpson, *Black Religions in the New World* (New York: Columbia University Press, 1978), 266-67.

⁹Washington, *Black Sects and Cults,* 12-15.

¹⁰J. Gordon Melton, *Encyclopedic Handbook of Cults in America* (New York: Garland, 1986), 93; Ahlstrom, *Religious History,* 1062; Joseph R. Washington Jr., *Black Religion* (Boston: Beacon Press, 1964), 122.

¹¹Robert Weisbrot, *Father Divine* (Boston: Beacon Press, 1983), 9-21; Melton, *Encyclopedic Handbook of Cults in America,* 93; Ahlstrom, *Religious History,* 1062.

¹²Albanese, *America,* 128; Weisbrot, *Father Divine,* 21-30.

¹³Melton, *Encyclopedic Handbook of Cults in America,* 93; Weisbrot, *Father Divine,* 46-50; Kenneth E. Burnham, *God Comes to America* (Boston: Lambeth, 1979), 20-23.

¹⁴Melton, *Encyclopedic Handbook of Cults in America,* 94; Weisbrot, *Father Divine,* 59-82.

¹⁵Ahlstrom, *Religious History,* 1062; Weisbrot, *Father Divine,* 213-15.

¹⁶Melton, *Encyclopedic Handbook of Cults in America,* 94, 96.

¹⁷Washington, *Black Sects and Cults,* 125; Ahlstrom, *Religious History,* 1062; Mel-

ton, *Encyclopedic Handbook of Cults in America*, 94; Albanese, *America*, 128; Burnham, *God Comes to America*, 24-31.

[18]Williams, *Popular Religion*, 44-45; Arthur Fauset, *Black Gods of the Metropolis* (Philadelphia: University of Pennsylvania Press, 1971), 56-58.

[19]Williams, *Popular Religion*, 45-46; Weisbrot, *Father Divine*, 78-88.

[20]Melton, *Encyclopedic Handbook of Cults in America*, 94-95; Weisbrot, *Father Divine*, 122-42.

[21]Washington, *Black Sects and Cults*, 125-27; Albanese, *America*, 128; Melton, *Encyclopedic Handbook of Cults in America*, 95.

[22]Ahlstrom, *Religious History*, 1063; Albanese, *America*, 128-29.

[23]Williams, *Popular Religion*, 47; Weisbrot, *Father Divine*, 189.

[24]Albanese, *America*, 129; Ahlstrom, *Religious History*, 1064.

[25]Fauset, *Black Gods*, 23; J. Gordon Melton, *The Encyclopedia of American Religions*, 2 vols. (Wilmington, N.C.: McGrath, 1978), 1:302; Ahlstrom, *Religious History*, 1064.

[26]Fauset, *Black Gods*, 26, 29.

[27]Ahlstrom, *Religious History*, 1064-65; Albanese, *America*, 129; Fauset, *Black Gods*, 29.

[28]Fauset, *Black Gods*, 22, 24, 29-30; Ahlstrom, *Religious History*, 1064; Albanese, *America*, 129.

[29]Washington, *Black Sects and Cults*, 158-59; Ahlstrom, *Religious History*, 1064.

[30]Melton, *Encyclopedia of American Religions*, 1:302; Ahlstrom, *Religious History*, 1065.

Chapter 12: Religious Innovations in Post-Christian America

[1]Robert Wuthnow, "World Order and Religious Movements," in *New Religious Movements*, ed. Eileen Barker (New York: Edwin Mellen, 1982), 48.

[2]Theodore Roszak, *The Making of a Counter Culture* (Garden City, N.Y.: Doubleday, 1969), 141; Wuthnow, "World Order and Religious Movements," 48; Allan W. Eister, "Cultural Crises and New Religious Movements: A Paradigmatic Statement of a Theory of Cults," in *Religious Movements in Contemporary America*, ed. Irving I. Zaretsky and Mark P. Leone (Princeton, N.J.: Princeton University Press, 1974), 623.

[3]Martin E. Marty, "As the New Religions Grow Older," in *Encyclopedia Britannica, 1986 Book of the Year*, ed. Daphne Daume and J. E. Davis (Chicago: Encyclopedia Britannica, 1986), 370.

[4]"America's Cults: Gaining Ground Again," *U.S. News and World Report*, July 5, 1982, p. 37.

[5]Richard Kyle, "The Cults: Why Now and Who Gets Caught?" *Journal of the American Scientific Affiliation* 33, no. 2 (1981): 95; Sydney E. Ahlstrom, *A Religious History of the American People* (New Haven, Conn.: Yale University Press, 1972), 1091. See also Barbara Hargrove, *Religion for a Dislocated Generation* (Valley Forge, Penn.: Judson Press, 1980), 16-22.

[6]Sydney E. Ahlstrom, "The Traumatic Years: American Religion and Culture in the '60s and '70s," *Theology Today* 36, no. 4 (1980): 507, 510. The late 1950s foreshadowed the upheaval of the 1960s. See Morris Dickstein, *Gates of Eden: American Culture in the Sixties* (New York: Harper & Row, 1977). See also Peter Clecak, "Culture and Politics in the Sixties," *Dissent* 24 (Fall 1977): 440; Ronald B. Flowers, *Religion in Strange Times: The 1960s and 1970s* (Macon, Ga.: Mercer University Press, 1984), 15.

[7]Ahlstrom, "The Traumatic Years," 510-11. See also Milton Viorst, *Fire in the Streets* (New York: Simon & Schuster, 1979); Steven M. Tipton, *Getting Saved from the Sixties* (Berkeley: University of California Press, 1982), 2.

[8]See Sydney E. Ahlstrom, "The Radical Turn in Theology and Ethics: Why It Occurred in the 1960s," *The Annals of the American Academy of Political and Social Sciences* 387 (January 1970): 9, 12; Roszak, *Making of a Counter Culture,* 1-41; Theodore Roszak, *Unfinished Animal* (New York: Harper & Row, 1975), 7-8, 14, 16, 19-20; William Braden, *The Age of Aquarius: Technology and the Cultural Revolution* (Chicago: Quadrangle Books, 1970); Charles Reich, *The Greening of America* (New York: Random House, 1970), 17-19; Hargrove, *Religion for a Dislocated Generation,* 44-45.

[9]J. Gordon Melton, "How New Is New? The Flowers of the 'New' Religious Consciousness Since 1965," in *The Future of New Religious Movements,* ed. David G. Bromley and Philip E. Hammond (Macon, Ga.: Mercer University Press, 1987), 54-55.

[10]Ibid., 55; Carl A. Raschke, "The Human Potential Movement," *Theology Today* 33, no. 3 (1976): 253-54. See also Paul C. Vitz, *Psychology as Religion* (Grand Rapids, Mich.: Eerdmans, 1977).

[11]Ahlstrom, "The Radical Turn," 11; Kyle, "The Cults," 95.

[12]Ahlstrom, "The Traumatic Years," 513; Ahlstrom, "The Radical Turn," 11-12.

[13]Ibid., 12; Ahlstrom, "The Traumatic Years," 512-13.

[14]Ronald Enroth, Edward E. Ericson Jr. and C. Breckenridge Peters, *The Jesus People* (Grand Rapids, Mich.: Eerdmans, 1972), 182.

[15]Robert Ellwood, *The Eagle and the Rising Sun* (Philadelphia: Westminster Press, 1974), 13-14; Ronald Enroth and J. Gordon Melton, *Why Cults Succeed Where the Church Fails* (Elgin, Ill.: Brethren Press, 1985), 124; Kyle, "The Cults," 95.

[16]Enroth and Melton, *Why Cults Succeed,* 124; J. Gordon Melton and Robert L. Moore, *The Cult Experience* (New York: Pilgrim, 1982), 26. See Richard Polenburg, *One Nation Divisible* (New York: Pelican Books, 1980), 205-8; David M. Reimers, *Still the Golden Door: The Third World Comes to America* (New York: Columbia University Press, 1985), 63-90.

[17]Marty, "As the New Religions Grow Older," 371; Martin E. Marty, *A Nation of Behavers* (Chicago: University of Chicago Press, 1976), 135; Hargrove, *Religion for a Dislocated Generation,* 44-47.

[18]Marty, "As the New Religions Grow Older," 371; Mary Ann Groves, "Marginal Religious Movements as Precursors of a Sociocultural Revolution," *Thought* 61,

no. 241 (1986): 267-68; Daniel Yankelovich, *New Rules* (New York: Bantam Books, 1982), 1-4; Daniel Yankelovich, "New Rules in American Life: Searching for Self-Fulfillment in a World Turned Upside Down," *Psychology Today,* April 1981, pp. 39-43; Henry Fairlie, "A Decade of Reaction, Part I," *The New Republic* January 6, 1979, p. 17; Daniel A. Foss and Ralph W. Larkin, "From 'Gates of Eden' to 'Day of the Locust': An Analysis of the Youth Movement of the 1960s and the Heirs of the Early 1970s—The Post-Movement Groups," *Theory and Society* 3 (1976): 56.

[19]Yankelovich, *New Rules,* 1-4; Yankelovich, "New Rules in American Life," 39-43; Fairlie, "A Decade of Reaction," 17; Foss, "From 'Gates of Eden,' " 56.

[20]See Daniel Yankelovich, "A Crisis of Moral Legitimacy?" *Dissent* 21 (Fall 1974): 526-33; Tipton, *Getting Saved from the Sixties,* 29-30.

[21]Christopher Lasch, *The Culture of Narcissism* (New York: W. W. Norton, 1979), 4-5. See also Peter Marin, "The New Narcissism," *Harper's,* October 1975, pp. 45-56.

[22]Peter Clecak, *America's Quest for the Ideal Self* (New York: Oxford University Press, 1983), 5-6.

[23]See Dean M. Kelley, *Why Conservative Churches Are Growing* (New York: Harper & Row, 1972), 53-59; Dean M. Kelley, "Why Conservative Churches Are Still Growing," *Journal for the Scientific Study of Religion* 17, no. 2 (1978): 165-72; Reginald W. Bibby, "Why Conservative Churches Really Are Growing: Kelley Revisited," *Journal for the Scientific Study of Religion* 17, no. 2 (1978): 129-37.

[24]See Gregory T. Goethals, *The TV Ritual* (Boston: Beacon Press, 1981); Paul Anthony Schwartz and James McBride, "The Moral Majority in the U.S.A. as a New Religious Movement," in *Of Gods and Men: New Religious Movements in the West,* ed. Eileen Barker (Macon, Ga.: Mercer University Press, 1983), 127-38; Martin E. Marty, "I Think—On the Electronic Church," *The Lutheran Standard,* January 2, 1979, pp. 11-13; Martin E. Marty, "Television Is a New, Universal Religion," *Content,* January 15, 1981, p. 1; Jeffrey K. Hadden, "The Electronic Churches," in *Alternatives to American Mainline Churches,* ed. Joseph Fichter (Barrytown, N.Y.: Unification Theological Seminary, 1983), 159-77.

[25]Wade Clark Roof and William McKinney, *American Mainline Religion* (New Brunswick, N.J.: Rutgers University Press, 1987), 23, 49.

[26]Ibid.

[27]Ibid., 25, 49; Wade Clark Roof, "America's Voluntary Establishment: Mainline Religion in Transition," in *Religion and America,* ed. Mary Douglas and Steven M. Tipton (Boston: Beacon Press, 1982), 134-39. For more on the polarization of American religion since 1945 see Robert Wuthnow, *The Restructuring of American Religion* (Princeton, N.J.: Princeton University Press, 1989).

[28]William G. McLoughlin Jr., *Revivals, Awakenings and Reform* (Chicago: University of Chicago Press, 1978), 179-80, 211-16; Roof and McKinney, *American Mainline Religion,* 25-26, 29-32, 73.

[29]Yankelovich, "New Rules in American Life," 36; Roof and McKinney, *American Mainline Religion,* 25-26, 29-32, 73; McLoughlin, *Revivals,* 179-85.

[30]Ibid.; Roof, "America's Voluntary Establishment," 134-37. See also Allen J. Matusow, *The Unraveling of America* (New York: Harper & Row, 1984); Daniel Bell, "Liberalism Has Little Further Momentum," *U.S. News and World Report,* December 19, 1980/January 5, 1981, pp. 52-54.

[31]Robert Bellah et al., *Habits of the Heart* (New York: Harper & Row, 1985), 220-25.

[32]Roof and McKinney, *American Mainline Religion,* 45-47; Yankelovich, "Crisis of Moral Legitimacy?" 526-27. See Edwin Schur, *The Awareness Trap* (New York: McGraw-Hill, 1976).

[33]Thomas Luckmann, *The Invisible Religion: The Problem of Religion in Modern Society* (New York: Macmillan, 1967).

[34]Roof, "America's Voluntary Establishment," 132.

[35]Roof and McKinney, *American Mainline Religion,* 49-50, 62.

[36]Roof, "America's Voluntary Establishment," 132-33.

[37]Roof and McKinney, *American Mainline Religion,* 49-50; Roof, "America's Voluntary Establishment," 132.

[38]Roof and McKinney, *American Mainline Religion,* 25, 53.

[39]Martin E. Marty, foreword to *Understanding Church Growth and Decline, 1950-1978,* ed. Dean R. Hoge and David A. Roozen (New York: Pilgrim, 1979), 10.

[40]Ahlstrom, *Religious History,* 1080.

[41]Robert Bellah, *Beyond Belief* (New York: Harper & Row, 1970), 171. See Dick Anthony and Thomas Robbins, "Spiritual Innovation and the Crisis of American Civil Religion," *Daedalus* 111, no. 1 (1982): 215-34.

[42]Kyle, "The Cults," 95.

[43]Roof and McKinney, *American Mainline Religion,* 31, 35.

[44]Ibid., 35.

[45]Robert T. Handy, *A Christian America* (New York: Oxford University Press, 1984), 159-84. See also Robert T. Handy, "The American Religious Depression, 1925-1935," *Church History* 29, no. 1 (1960): 3-16; Will Herberg, *Protestant Catholic Jew* (Garden City, N.Y.: Anchor, 1960).

[46]Roof and McKinney, *American Mainline Religion,* 29-32, 35.

[47]Ibid., 30-31.

[48]Ahlstrom, *Religious History,* 1093-96; Kyle, "The Cults," 95.

[49]Daniel Bell, "Religion in the Sixties," *Social Research* 38, no. 3 (1971): 474.

[50]Roy Wallis, *The Rebirth of the Gods: Reflections on the New Religions in the West* (Belfast: University of Belfast, 1978), 16-17.

[51]Roof and McKinney, *American Mainline Religion,* 38. See also Bellah et al., *Habits of the Heart,* 276.

[52]Arguments regarding the secularization thesis are varied. Some scholars reject it, arguing that religion is on an upturn. Others accept it with modifications. They say that the surge of cults and religiotherapies is a sideshow, inconsequential to modern society. Others say that the many quasi-religions are not really religions and thus do not contradict the secularization thesis. Still others say that new

religions are rising because these groups manipulate people into joining. See Dick Anthony, Thomas Robbins and Paul Schwartz, "Contemporary Religious Movements and the Secularization Premise," in *New Religious Movements,* ed. John Coleman and Gregory Baum (New York: Seabury Press, 1983), 1-8; Daniel Bell, "The Return of the Sacred? The Argument on the Future of Religion," *British Journal of Sociology* 28, no. 4 (1977): 419-49; Martin E. Marty, "The Spirit's Holy Errand: The Search for a Spiritual Style in Secular America," *Daedalus* 96, no. 1 (1967): 99-115; Peter L. Berger, "From the Crisis of Religion to the Crisis of Secularity," in *Religion and America,* ed. Mary Douglas and Steven M. Tipton (Boston: Beacon Press, 1982), 14-24; David Martin, *A General Theory of Secularization* (New York: Harper & Row, 1978); Bryan Wilson, "The Debate over 'Secularization,' " *Encounter* 45 (1975): 77-83.

Chapter 13: The Turn East

[1]For arguments regarding the turn East as a phenomena of major religious and cultural change see Harvey Cox, "Eastern Cults and Western Culture: Why Young Americans Are Buying Oriental Religions," *Psychology Today,* July 1977; Steven M. Tipton, *Getting Saved from the Sixties* (Berkeley: University of California Press, 1982); Charles Glock and Robert Bellah, eds., *The New Religious Consciousness* (Berkeley: University of California Press, 1976).

[2]Cox, "Eastern Cults and Western Culture," 36; J. Gordon Melton and Robert L. Moore, *The Cult Experience* (New York: Pilgrim, 1982), 26-28.

[3]Robert Ellwood, "Asian Religions in North America," in *New Religious Movements,* ed. John Coleman and Gregory Baum (New York: Seabury Press, 1983), 17.

[4]Ibid.

[5]J. Gordon Melton, "How New Is New? The Flowers of the 'New' Religious Consciousness Since 1965," in *The Future of New Religious Movements,* ed. David G. Bromley and Philip E. Hammond (Macon, Ga.: Mercer University Press, 1987), 52. Other Eastern religious leaders taking up residence in America included Sant Keshavadas (Temple of Cosmic Wisdom), Thera Bode Vinita (Buddhist Vihara Society), Tarethang Tulku (Tibetan Nyingmapa), Swami Satchidananda (Integral Yoga Institute), Guradeo Chitrabhana (Meditation International Center) and Vesant Paranjpe (Fivefold Path).

[6]Melton, "How New Is New?" 52-53; J. Gordon Melton, *Encyclopedic Handbook of Cults in America* (New York: Garland, 1986), 110.

[7]Robert Wuthnow, *Experimentation in American Religion* (Berkeley: University of California Press, 1978), 18.

[8]Melton, "How New Is New?" 54; Wuthnow, *Experimentation in American Religion,* 19-22.

[9]Os Guinness, *The Dust of Death* (Downers Grove, Ill.: InterVarsity Press, 1973), 200-210. See also Harvey Cox, *The Feast of Fools* (Cambridge, Mass.: Harvard University Press, 1969), 27-34.

10William G. McLoughlin Jr., *Revivals, Awakenings and Reform* (Chicago: University of Chicago Press, 1978), 199-201; Robert Ellwood, *Religious and Spiritual Groups in Modern America* (Englewood Cliffs, N.J.: Prentice Hall, 1973), 218. For more on the psychological changes in Western culture see Philip Rieff, *The Triumph of the Therapeutic* (New York: Harper & Row, 1966), 48-65.

11McLoughlin, *Revivals*, 199-201. See William Braden, *The Age of Aquarius: Technology and the Cultural Revolution* (Chicago: Quadrangle Books, 1970), 3-17.

12Harvey Cox, *Turning East* (New York: Simon & Schuster, 1977), 95-96, 100; Cox, "Eastern Cults and Western Culture," 39.

13Cox, *Turning East*, 96, 98; Cox, "Eastern Cults and Western Culture," 39.

14Jacob Needleman, "Young America Turns Eastward," in *Religion for a New Generation*, ed. Jacob Needleman, A. K. Bierman and J. H. Gould (New York: Macmillan, 1973), 12-13; Jacob Needleman, *The New Religions* (New York: E. P. Dutton, 1970), 16-18; Jacob Needleman, "Winds from the East," *Commonweal*, April 30, 1971, p. 190.

15Needleman, *The New Religions*, 10-13, 18-19; Needleman, "Young America Turns Eastward," 8-15. For more on the linking of psychology and Eastern religions see William C. Henderson, *Awakening: Ways to Psycho-Spiritual Growth* (Englewood Cliffs, N.J.: Prentice Hall, 1975), 110-202.

16Cox, *Turning East*, 97-98; Cox, "Eastern Cults and Western Culture," 39.

Chapter 14: Hindu, Sikh and Jain-Related Bodies
1Robert Ellwood, "Asian Religions in North America," in *New Religious Movements*, ed. John Coleman and Gregory Baum (New York: Seabury Press, 1983), 18-19.

2Catherine Albanese, *America: Religions and Religion* (Belmont, Calif.: Wadsworth, 1981), 206-8.

3Ibid., 206.

4Ellwood, "Asian Religions in North America," 19; J. Gordon Melton, *The Encyclopedia of American Religions*, 2 vols. (Wilmington, N.C.: McGrath, 1978), 2:377.

5Ibid., 2:377-78; J. Gordon Melton, *Encyclopedic Handbook of Cults in America* (New York: Garland, 1986), 187; Albanese, *America*, 207-8.

6For general information on Maharishi's background see George W. Braswell Jr., *Understanding Sectarian Groups in America* (Nashville: Broadman, 1986), 283; Melton, *Encyclopedic Handbook of Cults in America*, 187-88; John Newport, *Christ and the New Consciousness* (Nashville: Broadman, 1978), 20-21; William J. Petersen, *TM: A Do About Nothing* (New Canaan, Conn.: Keats, 1976), 6-12.

7Braswell, *Understanding Sectarian Groups*, 283-84; Newport, *Christ and the New Consciousness*, 21-22.

8Melton, *Encyclopedic Handbook of Cults in America*, 188; Newport, *Christ and the New Consciousness*, 21, 25; Braswell, *Understanding Sectarian Groups*, 283-84; William J. Petersen, *Those Curious New Cults in the 80s* (New Canaan, Conn.: Keats, 1973), 127.

[9]Melton, *Encyclopedic Handbook of Cults in America,* 188; Braswell, *Understanding Sectarian Groups,* 284; Newport, *Christ and the New Consciousness,* 22; Vishal Mangalwadi, *The World of Gurus* (New Delhi: Viskas Publishing House, 1977), 103-4.

[10]Braswell, *Understanding Sectarian Groups,* 285-86; Newport, *Christ and the New Consciousness,* 24-25; William J. Whalen, *Strange Gods* (Huntington, Ind.: Our Sunday Visitor, 1981), 77; Mangalwadi, *World of Gurus,* 104-6.

[11]Braswell, *Understanding Sectarian Groups,* 287-88; Newport, *Christ and the New Consciousness,* 25-26; Mangalwadi, *World of Gurus,* 106.

[12]William S. Bainbridge and Daniel H. Jackson, "The Rise and Decline of Transcendental Meditation," in *The Social Impact of New Religious Movements,* ed. Bryan Wilson (New York: Rose of Sharon, 1981), 144. Some sources argue that TM declined for two reasons: its attempt to propagate the practice of levitation and the 1978 court ruling against it. Bainbridge and Jackson show that the decline had set in earlier and that TM's foray into levitation was more an attempt to arrest the decline, not a cause of it.

[13]Melton, *Encyclopedic Handbook of Cults in America,* 188; Newport, *Christ and the New Consciousness,* 24.

[14]Bainbridge and Jackson, "Rise and Decline of Transcendental Meditation," 155; Melton, *Encyclopedic Handbook of Cults in America,* 188; John E. Patton, *The Case Against TM in the Schools* (Grand Rapids, Mich.: Baker Book House, 1976).

[15]Melton, *Encyclopedic Handbook of Cults in America,* 188-89; David Haddon, "Transcendental Meditation," in *A Guide to Cults and New Religions* (Downers Grove, Ill.: InterVarsity Press, 1983), 136-37; "TM Continues to Flourish, Despite Legal Battles," *Christian Research Journal* 12, no. 2 (1989): 5. In Europe TM has also peaked. See Reinhart Hummel and Bert Harden, "Asiatic Religions in Europe," in *The Social Impact of New Religious Movements,* ed. Bryan Wilson (New York: Rose of Sharon, 1981), 23; Reinhart Hummel and Bert Hardin, "Asiatic Religions in Europe," *Update,* no. 2 (1983): 3.

[16]Melton, *Encyclopedic Handbook of Cults in America,* 189; Newport, *Christ and the New Consciousness,* 23-24; Gordon R. Lewis, *Transcendental Meditation* (Glendale, Calif.: Gospel Light Publications, 1975), 4-9; Jacob Needleman, *The New Religions* (New York: E. P. Dutton, 1970), 134.

[17]Newport, *Christ and the New Consciousness,* 24-25; Braswell, *Understanding Sectarian Groups,* 284-85; Needleman, *The New Religions,* 134.

[18]Braswell, *Understanding Sectarian Groups,* 285.

[19]Robert Ellwood, *Religious and Spiritual Groups in Modern America* (Englewood Cliffs, N.J.: Prentice Hall, 1973), 232; Daniel Cohen, *The New Believers* (New York: Ballantine, 1975), 81.

[20]Melton, *Encyclopedic Handbook of Cults in America,* 189; Bainbridge and Jackson, "Rise and Decline of Transcendental Meditation," 152.

[21]John W. White, "Second Thoughts: What's Behind TM?" *Human Behavior,* October 1976, pp. 70-71; John W. White, "A Critical Look at TM," *New Age Journal,*

January 1976, pp. 30-35; Melton, *Encyclopedic Handbook of Cults in America,* 191; Whalen, *Strange Gods,* 82.

[22]Melton, *Encyclopedic Handbook of Cults in America,* 189; Mangalwadi, *World of Gurus,* 108-9.

[23]Melton, *Encyclopedic Handbook of Cults in America,* 189-90; Newport, *Christ and the New Consciousness,* 22-23; Braswell, *Understanding Sectarian Groups,* 286-87.

[24]Melton, *Encyclopedic Handbook of Cults in America,* 191-92; White, "Second Thoughts," 70-71; Patton, *The Case of TM,* 63-76; Mangalwadi, *World of Gurus,* 120-21.

[25]Hank Johnston, "The Marketed Social Movement: A Case Study of the Rapid Growth of TM," *Pacific Sociological Review* 23, no. 3 (1980): 333-54; Haddon, "Transcendental Meditation," 136.

[26]Melton, *Encyclopedia of American Religions,* 2:371-72; Melton, *Encyclopedic Handbook of Cults in America,* 159.

[27]Francine Jeanne Daner, *The American Children of Krisna* (New York: Holt, Rinehart, and Winston, 1976), 33-51; Albanese, *America,* 208; Ellwood, "Asian Religions in North America," 19; J. Stillson Judah, "The Hare Krishna Movement," in *Religious Movements in Contemporary America,* ed. Irving I. Zaretsky and Mark P. Leone (Princeton, N.J.: Princeton University Press, 1974), 467-68; Newport, *Christ and the New Consciousness,* 31.

[28]Melton, *Encyclopedic Handbook of Cults in America,* 159-60; J. Stillson Judah, *Hare Krishna and the Counterculture* (New York: John Wiley & Sons, 1974), 33-45.

[29]Melton, *Encyclopedic Handbook of Cults in America,* 160; Judah, *Hare Krishna,* 40-43; Gregroy Johnson, "The Hare Krishna in San Francisco," in *The New Religious Consciousness,* ed. Charles Glock and Robert Bellah (Berkeley: University of California Press, 1976), 32-34; Ruth A. Tucker, *Another Gospel* (Grand Rapids, Mich.: Zondervan, 1989), 269-70.

[30]Melton, *Encyclopedic Handbook of Cults in America,* 162-63; Newport, *Christ and the New Consciousness,* 33; Judah, *Hare Krishna,* 182-84. For some global figures in regard to ISKCON see Rodney Stark and William S. Bainbridge, *The Future of Religion* (Berkeley: University of California Press, 1985), 485.

[31]Melton, *Encyclopedic Handbook of Cults in America,* 162.

[32]Newport, *Christ and the New Consciousness,* 33-4. For a statement listing ISKCON beliefs see Melton, *Encyclopedic Handbook of Cults in America,* 161; Whalen, *Strange Gods,* 88-89; Tucker, *Another Gospel,* 273-74.

[33]Newport, *Christ and the New Consciousness,* 34; Steven J. Gelberg, ed., *Hare Krishna, Hare Krishna* (New York: Grove, 1983), 84; Judah, "Hare Krishna Movement," 473; Braswell, *Understanding Sectarian Groups,* 276; Mangalwadi, *World of Gurus,* 91-92.

[34]Newport, *Christ and the New Consciousness,* 34; Whalen, *Strange Gods,* 88; Mangalwadi, *World of Gurus,* 93-94.

35Newport, *Christ and the New Consciousness*, 34-35; Judah, "Hare Krishna Movement," 471; Judah, *Hare Krishna*, 88-90.

36Newport, *Christ and the New Consciousness*, 35; Judah, *Hare Krishna*, 93-94; Tucker, *Another Gospel*, 275.

37Johnson, "The Hare Krishna in San Francisco," 35-37; Judah, "Hare Krishna Movement," 468-69.

38Ellwood, *Religious and Spiritual Groups*, 243; Melton, *Encyclopedic Handbook of Cults in America*, 161; Johnson, "The Hare Krishna in San Francisco," 39.

39Ibid., 39; Newport, *Christ and the New Consciousness*, 35; Tucker, *Another Gospel*, 277.

40Melton, *Encyclopedic Handbook of Cults in America*, 162; Johnson, "The Hare Krishna in San Francisco," 39.

41Newport, *Christ and the New Consciousness*, 35; Daner, *American Children of Krisna*, 64.

42Braswell, *Understanding Sectarian Groups*, 277, 281; Melton, *Encyclopedic Handbook of Cults in America*, 163.

43Newport, *Christ and the New Consciousness*, 36. For some sample schedules see Daner, *American Children of Krisna*, 39-44; Judah, *Hare Krishna*, 93; Ellwood, *Religious and Spiritual Groups*, 242.

44Newport, *Christ and the New Consciousness*, 36; Daner, *American Children of Krisna*, 67; Tucker, *Another Gospel*, 277.

45Johnson, "The Hare Krishna in San Francisco," 43; Judah, *Hare Krishna*, 79-111; Newport, *Christ and the New Consciousness*, 30.

46Judah, "Hare Krishna Movement," 468; Newport, *Christ and the New Consciousness*, 31, 40. See also Dean M. Kelley, *Why Conservative Churches Are Growing* (New York: Harper & Row, 1972); Dean R. Hoge and David A. Roozen, eds., *Understanding Church Growth and Decline, 1950-1978* (New York: Pilgrim, 1979).

47Johnson, "The Hare Krishna in San Francisco," 44.

48Cohen, *The New Believers*, 94.

49Johnson, "The Hare Krishna in San Francisco," 34; Judah, *Hare Krishna*, 187-97.

50Johnson, "The Hare Krishna in San Francisco," 34-35; Newport, *Christ and the New Consciousness*, 36.

51Larry D. Shinn, "The Future of an Old Man's Vision: ISKCON in the Twenty-first Century," in *The Future of New Religious Movements*, ed. David G. Bromley and Philip E. Hammond (Macon, Ga.: Mercer University Press, 1987), 123, 130.

52Steven J. Gelberg, "The Future of Krishna Consciousness in the West: An Insider's Perspective," in *The Future of New Religious Movements*, ed. David G. Bromley and Philip E. Hammond (Macon, Ga.: Mercer University Press, 1987), 190-91, 194-96, 204; Shinn, "The Future of an Old Man's Vision," 131.

53Jeanne Messer, "Guru Maharaj Ji and the Divine Light Mission," in *The New Religious Consciousness*, ed. Charles Glock and Robert Bellah (Berkeley: University of California Press, 1976), 62; Mangalwadi, *World of the Gurus*, 191.

[54]James V. Downton, *Sacred Journeys: Conversion of Young Americans to Divine Light Mission* (New York: Columbia University Press, 1979), 2-3; Melton, *Encyclopedic Handbook of Cults in America,* 141; Cohen, *The New Believers,* 59.

[55]Petersen, *Those Curious New Cults,* 148-49; Melton, *Encyclopedic Handbook of Cults in America,* 141.

[56]Petersen, *Those Curious New Cults,* 149; Whalen, *Strange Gods,* 103.

[57]Downton, *Sacred Journeys,* 4-5; Melton, *Encyclopedic Handbook of Cults in America,* 142.

[58]Petersen, *Those Curious New Cults,* 150-51; Melton, *Encyclopedic Handbook of Cults in America,* 142; Whalen, *Strange Gods,* 103-4; Downton, *Sacred Journeys,* 6.

[59]David G. Bromley and Anson Shupe Jr., *Strange Gods* (Boston: Beacon Press, 1981), 45; Petersen, *Those Curious New Cults,* 151-53; Whalen, *Strange Gods,* 104.

[60]Bromley and Shupe, *Strange Gods,* 45-46; Melton, *Cults in America,* 142-43; Mangalwadi, *World of the Gurus,* 194.

[61]Whalen, *Strange Gods,* 102-3; Melton, *Encyclopedic Handbook of Cults in America,* 142-43; Bromley and Shupe, *Strange Gods,* 46.

[62]Ibid., 43; Melton, *Encyclopedic Handbook of Cults in America,* 143; Messer, "Guru Maharaj Ji," 53-54; Cohen, *The New Believers,* 61; Mangalwadi, *World of the Gurus,* 195-96.

[63]Bromley and Shupe, *Strange Gods,* 44; Cohen, *The New Believers,* 61.

[64]Downton, *Sacred Journeys,* 223; Cohen, *The New Believers,* 61.

[65]For some examples of the news coverage see Neal Karlen and Pamela Abramson, "Bhagwan's Realm," *Newsweek,* December 3, 1984, pp. 34-38; Julia Duin, "The Guru down the Road," *Christianity Today,* April 23, 1982, pp. 38-40; Neal Karlen, "Busting the Bhagwan," *Newsweek,* November 11, 1985, pp. 26-32; "Goodbye, Guru," *Newsweek,* November 25, 1985, p. 50; Lewis F. Carter, "The 'New Renunciates' of the Bhagwan Shree Rajneesh," *Journal for the Scientific Study of Religion* 26, no. 2 (1987): 159-63.

[66]Arvind Sharma, "The Rajneesh Movement," in *The Future of New Religious Movements,* ed. David G. Bromley and Philip E. Hammond (Macon, Ga.: Mercer University Press, 1987), 115; Braswell, *Understanding Sectarian Groups,* 289.

[67]Sharma, "The Rajneesh Movement," 116; Melton, *Encyclopedic Handbook of Cults in America,* 176; James S. Gordon, *The Golden Guru* (Lexington, Mass.: Stephen Greene, 1987), 21-25.

[68]Melton, *Encyclopedic Handbook of Cults in America,* 176-77; Eckart Floether, "Bhagwan Shree Rajneesh," in *A Guide to Cults and New Religions* (Downers Grove, Ill.: InterVarsity Press, 1983), 44-45; Sharma, "The Rajneesh Movement," 116; Mangalwadi, *World of the Gurus,* 126-27; Susan J. Palmer, "Purity and Danger in the Rajneesh Foundation," *Update* 10, no. 3 (1986): 19-20.

[69]Braswell, *Understanding Sectarian Groups,* 290; Melton, *Encyclopedic Handbook of Cults in America,* 177; Sharma, "The Rajneesh Movement," 117; Carter, "The New Renunciates," 158; Gordon, *Golden Guru,* 38-43.

[70] Melton, *Encyclopedic Handbook of Cults in America,* 177; Sharma, "The Rajneesh Movement," 117; Karlen and Abramson, "Bhagwan's Realm," 34; Carter, "The New Renunciates," 159.

[71] Karlen and Abramson, "Bhagwan's Realm," 36; Suin, "The Guru down the Road," 38-39; Gordon, *Golden Guru,* 99-118.

[72] Karlen and Abramson, "Bhagwan's Realm," 34, 38; Floether, "Bhagwan Shree Rajneesh," 49-50; Palmer, "Purity and Danger," 21-22, 25-26; Carter, "The New Renunciates," 161-62; Gordon, *Golden Guru,* 109-12.

[73] Melton, *Encyclopedic Handbook of Cults in America,* 181; Karlen, "Busting the Bhagwan," 26-32; "Goodbye, Guru," 50.

[74] Melton, *Encyclopedic Handbook of Cults in America,* 179-81; Karlen, "Busting the Bhagwan," 31-32; Carter, "The New Renunciates," 163; "Briefly Noted," *Christianity Today,* March 5, 1990, p. 38.

[75] Quoted from Floether, "Bhagwan Shree Rajneesh," 46, which in turn quotes from *Orange Juice,* a newsletter of the Rajneesh Meditation Center, San Francisco, September 1981.

[76] Floether, "Bhagwan Shree Rajneesh," 46-47.

[77] Sharma, "The Rajneesh Movement," 115-16; Mangalwadi, *World of the Gurus,* 127-28.

[78] Melton, *Encyclopedic Handbook of Cults in America,* 147.

[79] Braswell, *Understanding Sectarian Groups,* 290; Sharma, "The Rajneesh Movement," 118.

[80] Braswell, *Understanding Sectarian Groups,* 291; Floether, "Bhagwan Shree Rajneesh," 51-52.

[81] Ibid., 52-53; Sharma, "The Rajneesh Movement," 118.

[82] Floether, "Bhagwan Shree Rajneesh," 52-53; Mangalwadi, *World of the Gurus,* 132.

[83] Sharma, "The Rajneesh Movement," 120; Floether, "Bhagwan Shree Rajneesh," 53; Mangalwadi, *World of the Gurus,* 128-29.

[84] Braswell, *Understanding Sectarian Groups,* 293; Sharma, "The Rajneesh Movement," 119-20.

[85] Floether, "Bhagwan Shree Rajneesh," 53; Braswell, *Understanding Sectarian Groups,* 291-92.

Chapter 15: Buddhist Groups

[1] Christmas Humphreys, *Zen Buddhism* (New York: Macmillan, 1962), 12-14; George W. Braswell Jr., *Understanding Sectarian Groups in America* (Nashville: Broadman, 1986), 313; Robert Ellwood, *Religious and Spiritual Groups in Modern America* (Englewood Cliffs, N.J.: Prentice Hall, 1973), 258.

[2] Braswell, *Understanding Sectarian Groups,* 313; Humphreys, *Zen Buddhism,* 108-11; Alan W. Watts, *The Way of Zen* (New York: Vintage, 1957), 154-73; Steven M. Tipton, *Getting Saved from the Sixties* (Berkeley: University of California Press, 1982), 97-101.

[3]Ellwood, *Religious and Spiritual Groups,* 259; Rick Fields, *How the Swans Came to the Lake: A Narrative History of Buddhism in America* (Boulder, Colo.: Shambhala, 1981), 204-6. Among D. T. Suzuki's books are *The Training of the Zen Buddhist Monks* (New York: University Books, 1965); *Studies in Zen* (New York: Philosophical Library, 1955); *Essays in Zen Buddhism, First Series* (Boston: Beacon Press, 1952); *On Indian Mahayana Buddhism* (New York: Harper & Row, 1968).

[4]Ellwood, *Religious and Spiritual Groups,* 255, 259; Robert Ellwood, *Alternative Altars* (Chicago: University of Chicago Press, 1979), 147; Fields, *How the Swans Came,* 204-5.

[5]Catherine Albanese, *America: Religions and Religion* (Belmont, Calif.: Wadsworth, 1981), 214; Fields, *How the Swans Came,* 210-17.

[6]Jack Kerouac, *On the Road* (New York: Penguin, 1955); Jack Kerouac, *The Dharma Bums* (New York: Viking, 1958); Ellwood, *Alternative Altars,* 143-45.

[7]Watts, *Way of Zen;* Ellwood, *Alternative Altars,* 153, 157, 165; William J. Petersen, *Those Curious New Cults in the 80s* (New Canaan, Conn.: Keats, 1973), 113; Albanese, *America,* 214.

[8]Ibid., 214; Ellwood, *Alternative Altars,* 149-51; Ellwood, *Religious and Spiritual Groups,* 259; Fields, *How the Swans Came,* 216, 221.

[9]Tipton, *Getting Saved from the Sixties,* 95-97; Albanese, *America,* 214; Ellwood, *Alternative Altars,* 163-64.

[10]Ibid., 162-63; Fields, *How the Swans Came,* 231-34; Albanese, *America,* 214.

[11]Fields, *How the Swans Came,* 239-42; Ellwood, *Religious and Spiritual Groups,* 259; Ellwood, *Alternative Altars,* 162-63; Albanese, *America,* 214.

[12]Ellwood, *Religious and Spiritual Groups,* 255; Braswell, *Understanding Sectarian Groups,* 316.

[13]Ellwood, *Alternative Altars,* 139, 147, 158; Braswell, *Understanding Sectarian Groups,* 316; Watts, *Way of Zen,* 174, 201.

[14]Ellwood, *Religious and Spiritual Groups,* 258; Humphreys, *Zen Buddhism,* 158-60; Tipton, *Getting Saved from the Sixties,* 153.

[15]Jacob Needleman, *The New Religions* (New York: E. P. Dutton, 1970), 44; Petersen, *Those Curious New Cults,* 119-20.

[16]Braswell, *Understanding Sectarian Groups,* 316; Tipton, *Getting Saved from the Sixties,* 133-34.

[17]David A. Snow, "Organization, Ideology and Mobilization: The Case of Nichiren Shoshu of America," in *The Future of New Religious Movements,* ed. David G. Bromley and Philip E. Hammond (Macon, Ga.: Mercer University Press, 1987), 154; J. Gordon Melton, *Encyclopedic Handbook of Cults in America* (New York: Garland, 1986), 171; Albanese, *America,* 215.

[18]Noah S. Brannen, *Soka Gakkai* (Richmond, Va.: John Knox Press, 1968), 61-63; Snow, "Organization, Ideology," 154; Braswell, *Understanding Sectarian Groups,* 317; Albanese, *America,* 215-16.

[19]Snow, "Organization, Ideology," 155; Braswell, *Understanding Sectarian Groups,*

317-18; John Newport, *Christ and the New Consciousness* (Nashville: Broadman, 1978), 56-57; Brannen, *Soka Gakkai,* 61-63.

²⁰Ibid., 73-74; Braswell, *Understanding Sectarian Groups,* 318; Melton, *Encyclopedic Handbook of Cults in America,* 171.

²¹Ibid., 171-72; Brannen, *Soka Gakkai,* 73-75; David J. Hesselgrave, "Nichiren Shoshu Soka Gakkai: The Lotus Blossoms in Japan," in *Dynamic Religious Movements,* ed. David J. Hesselgrave (Grand Rapids, Mich.: Baker Book House, 1978), 131-32.

²²Braswell, *Understanding Sectarian Groups,* 318; Brannen, *Soka Gakkai,* 75-78; Melton, *Encyclopedic Handbook of Cults in America,* 172; Hesselgrave, "Nichiren Shoshu," 136-37.

²³"Japan: The Value Creators," *Newsweek,* July 13, 1964, pp. 40-41; "Japan: Goodness, Beauty and Benefit—But for Whom?" *Time,* May 22, 1964, p. 40; Brannen, *Soka Gakkai,* 75-83; Melton, *Encyclopedic Handbook of Cults in America,* 172; Ted J. Solomon, "The Response of Three New Japanese Religions to the Crises in the Japanese Value System," *Journal for the Scientific Study of Religion* 16, no. 1 (1977): 10-11; Hesselgrave, "Nichiren Shoshu," 138-40.

²⁴Melton, *Encyclopedic Handbook of Cults in America,* 172; Robert Ellwood, *The Eagle and the Rising Sun* (Philadelphia: Westminster Press, 1974), 96-99; Braswell, *Understanding Sectarian Groups,* 318-19; Snow, "Organization, Ideology," 155.

²⁵Hideo Hashimoto and William McPnerson, "Rise and Decline of Sokagakkai in Japan and the United States," *Review of Religious Research* 17, no. 2 (1976): 88.

²⁶Ellwood, *Religious and Spiritual Groups,* 274; Robert Ellwood, "Asian Religions in North America," in *New Religious Movements,* ed. John Coleman and Gregory Baum (New York: Seabury Press, 1983), 20; Braswell, *Understanding Sectarian Groups,* 323-24; Snow, "Organization, Ideology," 155-56.

²⁷"Japan: The Value Creators," 40-41; "Japan: Goodness, Beauty and Benefit," 40; Hashimoto and McPherson, "Rise and Decline of Sokagakkai," 88-89; Braswell, *Understanding Sectarian Groups,* 319.

²⁸Ellwood, *The Eagle and the Rising Sun,* 102-3.

²⁹Snow, "Organization, Ideology," 156; Ellwood, *The Eagle and the Rising Sun,* 94-95, 105-7; Braswell, *Understanding Sectarian Groups,* 319-20.

³⁰Snow, "Organization, Ideology," 156; Ellwood, *The Eagle and the Rising Sun,* 78-79.

³¹Hashimoto and McPherson, "Rise and Decline of Sokagakkai," 90; Ellwood, *The Eagle and the Rising Sun,* 102-3.

³²Ellwood, *The Eagle and the Rising Sun,* 77; Snow, "Organization, Ideology," 165-66.

³³Melton, *Encyclopedic Handbook of Cults in America,* 172; Ellwood, *The Eagle and the Rising Sun,* 77, 103-4.

³⁴Hashimoto and McPherson, "Rise and Decline of Sokagakkai," 89-90; Braswell, *Understanding Sectarian Groups,* 322.

³⁵Ellwood, *The Eagle and the Rising Sun,* 77-78, 103, 107; Melton, *Encyclopedic*

Handbook of Cults in America, 172; Hashimoto and McPherson, "Rise and Decline of Sokagakkai," 90.
[36]Ellwood, *The Eagle and the Rising Sun,* 78-79; Hashimoto and McPherson, "Rise and Decline of Sokagakkai," 90-91; Newport, *Christ and the New Consciousness,* 58, 61.

Chapter 16: Islam-Related Groups

[1]Catherine Albanese, *America: Religions and Religion* (Belmont, Calif.: Wadsworth, 1981), 196-97, 199; Robert Ellwood, introduction to *New Religious Movements in the United States and Canada,* ed. Diane Choquette (Westport, Conn.: Greenwood, 1985), 11; Colin Chapman, "The Riddle of Religions," *Christianity Today,* May 14, 1990, pp. 16-22.
[2]Ellwood, introduction to *New Religious Movements in the United States and Canada,* 11-12; John Newport, *Christ and the New Consciousness* (Nashville: Broadman, 1978), 66-81.
[3]J. Gordon Melton, *The Encyclopedia of American Religions,* 2 vols. (Wilmington, N.C.: McGrath, 1978), 2:339-43; George W. Braswell Jr., *Understanding Sectarian Groups in America* (Nashville: Broadman, 1986), 348-49. See Arthur Fauset, *Black Gods of the Metropolis* (Philadelphia: University of Pennsylvania Press, 1971), 41-51; David Gates "The Black Muslims: A Divided Flock," *Newsweek,* April 9, 1984, p. 15.
[4]C. Eric Lincoln, *The Black Muslims in America,* rev. ed. (Boston: Beacon Press, 1973), 29.
[5]Peter W. Williams, *Popular Religion in America* (Englewood Cliffs, N.J.: Prentice Hall, 1980), 49.
[6]Richard Kyle, "Black Muslims," in *Encyclopedia USA,* ed. Archie P. McDonald (Gulf Breeze, Fla.: Academic International Press, 1985), 6:137; Lincoln, *Black Muslims,* xxiii.
[7]Ibid., xx-xxii; Kyle, "Black Muslims," 6:138; Sydney E. Ahlstrom, *A Religious History of the American People* (New Haven, Conn.: Yale University Press, 1972), 1066.
[8]Williams, *Popular Religion,* 47; Ahlstrom, *Religious History,* 1066; Lincoln, *Black Muslims,* 61-64; R. Laurence Moore, *Religious Outsiders and the Making of Americans* (New York: Oxford University Press, 1986), 190-91. See also E. V. Essein-Udom, *Black Nationalism* (Chicago: University of Chicago Press, 1962); Pierre Crabites, "American Negro Mohammedans," *Moslem World* 23, no. 3 (1933): 272-84.
[9]Kyle, "Black Muslims," 138; Ahlstrom, *Religious History,* 1067; Fauset, *Black Gods,* 47-48; Lincoln, *Black Muslims,* 53-55.
[10]Kyle, "Black Muslims," 138; Lincoln, *Black Muslims,* 70-81; Williams, *Popular Religion,* 40
[11]Ibid., 48
[12]Henry J Young, *Major Black Religious Leaders Since 1940* (Nashville: Abingdon,

1979), 66-72; Kyle, "Black Muslims," 138; Ahlstrom, *Religious History*, 1068; Williams, *Popular Religion*, 50-52. See also Elijah Muhammad, *Message to the Blackman in America* (Chicago: Muhammad Mosque of Islam No. 2, 1965); Elijah Muhammad, *The Fall of America* (Chicago: Muhammad's Temple of Islam No. 2, 1973).

[13]Braswell, *Understanding Sectarian Groups*, 345-46; Kyle, "Black Muslims," 138-39; Ahlstrom, *Religious History*, 1068; Lincoln, *Black Muslims*, xxvi, 116-20; Charles S. Braden, "Islam in America," *The International Review of Missions* 48 (July 1959): 315.

[14]Lincoln, *Black Muslims*, xxvii-xxx; Kyle, "Black Muslims," 139; Williams, *Popular Religion*, 50-51.

[15]Ahlstrom, *Religious History*, 1069; Lincoln, *Black Muslims*, 82-85; Kyle, "Black Muslims," 139-40; Williams, *Popular Religion*, 51. See also Elijah Muhammad, *How to Eat to Live* (Chicago: Muhammad Mosque of Islam No. 2, 1967).

[16]Lincoln, *Black Muslims*, 29; Kyle, "Black Muslims," 140; Ahlstrom, *Religious History*, 1069.

[17]Ibid., 1069-70; Kyle, "Black Muslims," 140.

[18]For general information on Malcolm X see *The Autobiography of Malcolm X* (New York: Grove, 1965).

[19]Young, *Major Black Religious Leaders*, 73-81; Kyle, "Black Muslims," 139; Ahlstrom, *Religious History*, 1068-69.

[20]Braswell, *Understanding Sectarian Groups*, 346-47; William J. Whalen, *Minority Religions in America* (New York: Alba House, 1981), 29.

[21]Braswell, *Understanding Sectarian Groups*, 347-48; Moore, *Religious Outsiders*, 193; Gates, "The Black Muslims," 15; Lawrence H. Mamiya, "From Black Muslim to Bilalian," *Journal for the Scientific Study of Religion* 21, no. 2 (1982): 138, 143-44. Bilal was an African slave who became the first prayer leader for Prophet Muhammad.

[22]Braswell, *Understanding Sectarian Groups*, 347-48; Whalen, *Minority Religions*, 30-31; Mamiya, "From Black Muslim to Bilalian," 143-44, 149.

[23]Moore, *Religious Outsiders*, 193; Braswell, *Understanding Sectarian Groups*, 348; Gates, "The Black Muslims," 15; Mamiya, "From Black Muslim to Bilalian," 141-43.

[24]Braswell, *Understanding Sectarian Groups*, 350, 352; Gates, "The Black Muslims," 15; Mamiya, "From Black Muslim to Bilalian," 149-50.

[25]Dick Anthony and Thomas Robbins, "The Meher Baba Movement: Its Effect on Post-Adolescent Social Alienation," in *Religious Movements in Contemporary America*, ed. Irving I. Zaretsky and Mark P. Leone (Princeton, N.J.: Princeton University Press, 1974), 492; Melton, *Encyclopedia of American Religions*, 2:347.

[26]Robert Ellwood, *Religious and Spiritual Groups in Modern America* (Englewood Cliffs, N.J.: Prentice Hall, 1973), 283; William J. Petersen, *Those Curious New Cults in the 80s* (New Canaan, Conn.: Keats, 1973), 138; Newport, *Christ and the New Consciousness*, 70.

[27]C. B. Purdom, *The God-Man* (Crescent Beach, S.C.: Sheriar, 1964), 15-26; Jacob

Needleman, *The New Religions* (New York: E. P. Dutton, 1970), 80.

28Ibid., 80-81; Purdom, *The God-Man*, 24-26.

29Ibid., 29-33; Needleman, *The New Religions*, 83-84.

30Ibid., 84; Melton, *Encyclopedia of American Religions*, 2:347; Newport, *Christ and the New Consciousness*, 71; Purdon, *The God-Man*, 407-14.

31Needleman, *The New Religions*, 84-85; Purdom, *The God-Man*, 412-14; Ellwood, *Religious and Spiritual Groups*, 282.

32From a pamphlet entitled *Meher Baba's Universal Message.*

33Needleman, *The New Religions*, 85-86; Purdom, *The God-Man*, 413; Ellwood, *Religious and Spiritual Groups*, 283.

34Peter Rowley, *New Gods in America* (New York: McKay, 1971), 120-21; Melton, *Encyclopedia of American Religions*, 2:347.

35Anthony and Robbins, "Meher Baba Movement," 487-88.

36Thomas Robbins, "Eastern Mysticism and the Resocialization of Drug Users: The Meher Baba Cult," *Journal for the Scientific Study of Religion* 8, no. 2 (1969): 300-317. See also Thomas Robbins and Dick Anthony, "Getting Straight With Meher Baba," *Journal for the Scientific Study of Religion* 11, no. 2 (1972): 122-40.

37Anthony and Robbins, "The Meher Baba Movement," 487-88; Needleman, *The New Religions*, 75; Robbins, "Eastern Mysticism," 311.

38Anthony and Robbins, "The Meher Baba Movement," 489-90.

39Robbins and Anthony, "Getting Straight with Meher Baba," 133, 134; Anthony and Robbins, "The Meher Baba Movement," 490.

40Ibid., 490-91.

41Needleman, *The New Religions*, 96.

42Meher Baba, *Discoveries*, 3 vols. (Ahmedegar, India: Adi K. Irani, 1967).

43Ibid., Robbins and Anthony, "Getting Straight with Meher Baba," 133.

44Ellwood, *Religious and Spiritual Groups*, 281.

45Ibid., 281-82; Needleman, *The New Religions*, 75; *Meher Baba's Universal Message.*

46Peter Rowley, *New Gods in America* (New York: McKay, 1971), 121; Ellwood, *Religious and Spiritual Groups*, 285; Anthony and Robbins, "The Meher Baba Movement," 488.

47Nat Freedland, *The Occult Explosion* (New York: G. P. Putnam's, 1972), 37; Ellwood, *Religious and Spiritual Groups*, 159. See also Colin Wilson, *The Occult* (New York: Vintage, 1971), 385-408.

48P. D. Ouspensky, *In Search of the Miraculous* (New York: Harcourt, Brace and World, 1949); Newport, *Christ and the New Consciousness*, 72.

49Ibid., 72; Theodore Roszak, *Unfinished Animal* (New York: Harper & Row, 1975), 138; Petersen, *Those Curious New Cults*, 179-80.

50Melton, *Encyclopedia of American Religions*, 2:348; Petersen, *Those Curious New Cults*, 180, 187; Kathleen Riordan Speeth and Ira Friedlander, *Gurdjieff: Seeker of the Truth* (New York: Harper & Row, 1980), 49-118.

51Ibid., 25-49; Petersen, *Those Curious New Cults,* 181-82; Wilson, *The Occult,* 385-86.

52Needleman, *The New Religions,* 208; Petersen, *Those Curious New Cults,* 181-82; Freedland, *Occult Explosion,* 38.

53Ellwood, *Religious and Spiritual Groups,* 160-61; Christopher Evans, *Cults of Unreason* (New York: Dell, 1973), 209; Needleman, *The New Religions,* 208.

54Ellwood, *Religious and Spiritual Groups,* 161; Melton, *Encyclopedia of American Religions,* 2:348; Thomas de Hartmann, *Our Life with Mr. Gurdjieff* (Baltimore: Penguin, 1972), 35.

55George I. Gurdjieff, *All and Everything* (New York: Harcourt, Brace and World, 1950); George I. Gurdjieff, *Meetings with Remarkable Men* (New York: E. P. Dutton, 1963).

56P. D. Ouspensky, *The Fourth Way* (New York: Knopf, 1957).

57Melton, *Encyclopedia of American Religions,* 2:348; Petersen, *Those Curious New Cults,* 183.

58Rowley, *New Gods in America,* 18; Petersen, *Those Curious New Cults,* 178, 182, 184; Freedland, *Occult Explosion,* 40.

59Ibid., 40; Petersen, *Those Curious New Cults,* 178-79.

60Ellwood, *Religious and Spiritual Groups,* 162, 164-67; Melton, *Encyclopedia of American Religions,* 2:348-49; Rowley, *New Gods in America,* 18.

61Freedland, *Occult Explosion,* 38; Petersen, *Those Curious New Cults,* 185-86; Newport, *Christ and the New Consciousness,* 72.

62Petersen, *Those Curious New Cults,* 185-87; Newport, *Christ and the New Consciousness,* 72.

63Ibid., 72; Freedland, *Occult Explosion,* 38.

64Newport, *Christ and the New Consciousness,* 72-73; Roszak, *Unfinished Animal,* 146; de Hartmann, *Our Life With Mr. Gurdjieff,* 35; Petersen, *Those Curious New Cults,* 180.

65Roszak, *Unfinished Animal,* 139; Newport, *Christ and the New Consciousness,* 73.

Chapter 17: Twentieth-Century Occult and Metaphysical Movements

1Richard Woods, *The Occult Revolution* (New York: Herder and Herder, 1971), 15-16; Nat Freedland, *The Occult Explosion* (New York: G. P. Putnam's, 1972), 118-19.

2Woods, *Occult Revolution,* 15-16; Marcello Truzzi, "The Occult Revival as Popular Culture: Some Random Observations on the Old and the Nouveau Witch," *The Sociological Quarterly* 13 (Winter 1972): 16-17; Freedland, *Occult Explosion,* 14-15.

3L. Pauwels and J. Berger, *The Morning of the Magicians* (New York: Avon, 1973); Woods, *Occult Revolution,* 21-22.

4See Mircea Eliade, *Occultism, Witchcraft and Cultural Fashions* (Chicago: University of Chicago Press, 1976), 58-63; Truzzi, "Occult Revival as Popular Culture," 16-47; Woods, *Occult Revolution;* Freedland, *Occult Explosion;* Edward A. Tiryakian, "Toward the Sociology of Esoteric Culture," in *On the Margin of the*

Visible, ed. Edward A. Tiryakian (New York: John Wiley, 1974), 257-75.

⁵Robert Galbreath, "Explaining Modern Occultism," in *The Occult in America,* ed. Howard Kerr and Charles Crow (Urbana: University of Illinois Press, 1983), 20-21.

⁶Ibid., 21.

⁷Ronald Enroth, "The Occult," in *Evangelical Dictionary of Theology,* ed. Walter A. Elwell (Grand Rapids, Mich.: Baker Book House, 1984), 787.

⁸Martin E. Marty, "The Occult Establishment," *Social Research* 37 (1970): 228; Martin E. Marty, *A Nation of Behavers* (Chicago: University of Chicago Press, 1976), 135, 139-40.

⁹J. Gordon Melton, *The Encyclopedia of American Religions,* 2 vols. (Wilmington, N.C.: McGrath, 1978), 2:83-306; Ronald Enroth, *The Lure of the Cults* (Chappaqua, N.Y.: Christian Herald Books, 1979), 33-35; John Newport, *Christ and the New Consciousness* (Nashville: Broadman, 1978), 148-60; Robert Ellwood, introduction to *New Religious Movements in the United States and Canada,* ed. Diane Choquette (Westport, Conn.: Greenwood, 1985), 7-8.

¹⁰J. Gordon Melton, *Encyclopedic Handbook of Cults in America* (New York: Garland, 1986), 116; Robert Burrows, "Corporate Management Cautioned on New Age," *Eternity,* February 1988, p. 33; Carl A. Raschke, *The Interruption of Eternity* (Chicago: Nelson-Hall, 1980), 105ff.; Carl A. Raschke, "The Human Potential Movement," *Theology Today* 33, no. 3 (1976): 254.

¹¹Enroth, "The Occult," 788. See also John C. Cooper, *Religion in the Age of Aquarius* (Philadelphia: Westminster Press, 1971), 28-31.

¹²Enroth, "The Occult," 788; Raschke, *The Interruption of Eternity,* 105ff.

¹³Eliade, *Occultism, Witchcraft,* 67; Freedland, *Occult Explosion,* 17; Marty, *Nation of Behavers,* 135-36.

¹⁴Richard Watring, "New Age Training in Business: Mind Control in Upper Management?" *Eternity,* February 1988, pp. 30-32; Raschke, "Human Potential Movement," 254-57; Freedland, *Occult Explosion,* 19. See also Colin Campbell, "The Secret Religion of the Educated Classes," *Sociological Analyses* 39, no. 2 (1978): 146-56.

¹⁵See Colin Wilson, *The Occult* (New York: Vintage Books, 1973), 166-68, 384-412; Freedland, *Occult Explosion,* 37-41; James Bjornstad, *Twentieth Century Prophecy* (Minneapolis: Bethany Fellowship, 1969), 69-126; John Godwin, *Occult America* (Garden City, N.Y.: Doubleday, 1972), 100-111; Jeffrey B. Russell, *A History of Witchcraft* (London: Thames and Hudson, 1980), 173.

¹⁶Catherine Albanese, *America: Religions and Religion* (Belmont, Calif.: Wadsworth, 1981), 183-84. See also Os Guinness, *The Dust of Death* (Downers Grove, Ill.: InterVarsity Press, 1973), 280-81.

¹⁷Albanese, *America,* 183-86.

¹⁸Galbreath, "Explaining Modern Occultism," 16.

¹⁹Woods, *Occult Revolution,* 24-26; John C. Cooper, *Religion in the Age of Aquarius* (Philadelphia: Westminster Press, 1971), 33-37. For a discussion regarding

whether there is a counterreligion see John P. Newport, *Demons, Demons, Demons* (Nashville: Broadman, 1972), 20-22.

[20]Albanese, *America,* 184.

[21]Barbara Hargrove, "New Religious Movements and the End of the Age," *The Iliff Review* (Spring 1982): 41-52.

[22]See Kenneth Cinnamon and Dave Farson, *Cults and Cons* (Chicago: Nelson-Hall, 1979); Paul C. Reisser, Teri K. Reisser and John Weldon, *The Holistic Healers* (Downers Grove, Ill.: InterVarsity Press, 1983); Paul C. Reisser, Teri K. Reisser and John Weldon, *New Age Medicine* (Downers Grove, Ill.: InterVarsity Press, 1987); Kenneth R. Pelletier, *Holistic Medicine* (New York: Dell, 1979); Kenneth R. Pelletier, *Mind as Healer, Mind as Slayer* (New York: Dell, 1977).

[23]See Wilson, *The Occult,* 21; Rudolf Steiner, *The Occult Mysteries of Antiquity* (Blauvelt, N.Y.: Rudolf Steiner Publications, 1961); Bernard Bromage, *The Occult Arts of Ancient Egypt* (N.p.: Samuel Weiser, 1953); Richard Cavendish, *The Black Arts* (New York: Putnam's, 1967).

[24]See Robert Wuthnow, *Experimentation in American Religion* (Berkeley: University of California Press, 1978), 42-43, 60, 78-79; Woods, *Occult Revolution,* 16-17.

[25]Truzzi, "Occult Revival as Popular Culture," 18-19; Freedland, *Occult Explosion,* 111, 119; Marty, "Occult Establishment," 223.

[26]Truzzi, "Occult Revival as Popular Culture," 20; Freedland, *Occult Explosion,* 111.

[27]John Stevens Kerr, *The Mystery and Magic of the Occult* (Philadelphia: Fortress, 1971), 39-40.

[28]Claude Fischler, "Astrology and French Society," in *On the Margin of the Visible,* ed. Edward A. Tiryakian (New York: John Wiley, 1974), 283-84.

[29]Ibid., 284; Keith Thomas, *Religion and the Decline of Magic* (New York: Charles Scribner's, 1971), 283-85.

[30]See Jean-Michel Angebert, *The Occult and the Third Reich* (New York: McGraw-Hill, 1975); Robert Ellwood, "The American Theosophical Synthesis," in *The Occult in America,* ed. Howard Kerr and Charles Crow (Urbana: University of Illinois Press, 1983), 120; Leon McBeth, *Strange New Religions* (Nashville: Broadman, 1977), 87; James Bjornstad and Shildes Johnson, *Stars, Signs and Salvation in the Age of Aquarius* (Minneapolis: Bethany Fellowship, 1971), 88.

[31]Fischler, "Astrology and French Society," 284-85; Kerr, *Mystery and Magic,* 15. Bodeman emphasizes the relationship between individualism and the appeal of astrology. See Y. Bodeman, "Mystical, Satanic and Chiliastic Forces in Countercultural Movements," *Youth and Society* 5, no. 4 (1974): 443.

[32]Kerr, *Mystery and Magic,* 13-14; McBeth, *Strange New Religions,* 87; Freedland, *Occult Explosion,* 114-15.

[33]Woods, *Occult Revolution,* 85-87; Freedland, *Occult Explosion,* 119-21; Bjornstad, *Twentieth Century Prophecy,* 71ff.; Charles Ponce, *The Game of Wizards* (Baltimore: Penguin, 1975), 43-44.

[34]Truzzi, "Occult Revival as Popular Culture," 20-21. There are other ways to view

the various levels of astrology in the modern world. See Woods, *Occult Revolution*, 77-78; Bjornstad, *Stars, Signs and Salvation*, 17; Ron Matthies, *The Unopened Door* (Minneapolis: Augsburg, 1971), 22-23.

35Truzzi, "Occult Revival as Popular Culture," 22.

36Woods, *Occult Revolution*, 149.

37Kerr, *Mystery and Magic*, 46.

38Woods, *Occult Revolution*, 147-48; Kerr, *Mystery and Magic*, 46-48.

39Ibid., 49-50.

40Ibid., 50; W. B. Crow, *A History of Magic, Witchcraft and Occultism* (North Hollywood, Calif.: Wilshire, 1968), 310-11; Woods, *Occult Revolution*, 151-55.

41See A. E. Waite, *A Pictorial Key to the Tarot* (New Hyde Park, N.Y.: University Book, 1959); Woods, *Occult Revolution*, 155-58; Kerr, *Mystery and Magic*, 51-53; Matthies, *Unopened Door*, 40-56; Ponce, *Game of Wizards*, 237-40.

42Edmund C. Gruss, *The Ouija Board* (Chicago: Moody Press, 1975), 25-36; Kerr, *Mystery and Magic*, 46; Woods, *Occult Revolution*, 146.

43Gruss, *Ouija Board*, 43-44; Kerr, *Mystery and Magic*, 46.

44Ponce, *Game of Wizards*, 75-116; William J. Petersen, *Those Curious New Cults in the 80s* (New Canaan, Conn.: Keats, 1973), 35-39; Freedland, *Occult Explosion*, 133-34.

45Kerr, *Mystery and Magic*, 59-60. See Jess Stearn, *Edgar Cayce: The Sleeping Prophet* (New York: New American Library, 1969); Jeane Dixon, *My Life and Prophecies* (New York: Morrow, 1969); Jeane Dixon, *The Call to Glory* (New York: Bantam, 1971); Ruth Montgomery, *A Gift of Prophecy* (New York: Bantam, 1965).

46Stearn, *Edgar Cayce;* Woods, *Occult Revolution*, 160-65; Bjornstad, *Twentieth Century Prophecy*, 84-89; Godwin, *Occult America*, 100-111.

47Montgomery, *Gift of Prophecy*, 103, 155, 164, 176; Woods, *Occult Revolution*, 165-67.

48Woods, *Occult Revolution*, 168; Dixon, *Call to Glory*, 160-84; Bjornstad, *Twentieth Century Prophecy*, 46-54.

49Ibid., 56-64; Woods, *Occult Revolution*, 171.

50Some examples include H. H. Ward, "Can Satanists and Christians Talk Together?" *The Detroit Free Press* June 27, 1970, p. 4A; J. Rascoe, "Church of Satan," *McCall's*, March 1970, p. 74; W. W. Weir, "The New Wave of Witches," *Occult*, January 1970, pp. 24-37; P. Blaxham, "The Devil and Cecil Williamson," *The New York Times*, April 19, 1970, p. 5; "The Cult of the Occult," *Newsweek*, April 13, 1970, pp. 96-97; D. St. Albin-Greene, "There May Be a Witch Next Door," *National Observer*, October 13, 1969, p. 24; R. Bone, "We Witches Are Simple People," *Life*, November 13, 1964, pp. 55-62; V. Thomas, "The Witches of 1966," *Atlantic Monthly*, September 1966, 119-25; J. Kobler, "Out for a Night at the Local Caldron," *Saturday Evening Post*, November 5, 1966, pp. 76-78.

51Raymond Van Over, "Witchcraft Today: A Survey," in *Witchcraft Today*, ed. Martin Ebon (New York: New American Library, 1971), 13; Russell, *History of Witchcraft*, 8.

[52]Marcello Truzzi, "Witchcraft and Satanism," in *On the Margin of the Visible,* ed. Edward A. Tiryakian (New York: John Wiley, 1974), 215; Russell, *History of Witchcraft,* 148, 157; Truzzi, "Occult Revival as Popular Culture," 22-23.

[53]Peter P. Levack, *The Witch-Hunt in Early Modern Europe* (New York: Longman, 1987), 232; Russell, *History of Witchcraft,* 152; Lucy Mair, *Witchcraft* (New York: McGraw-Hill, 1969), 225-34. Nugent sees the revival of witchcraft in the modern world as an aspect of the return of Renaissance culture. See Donald Nugent, "The Renaissance and/of Witchcraft," *Church History* 40, no. 1 (1971): 69-78.

[54]Robert Ellwood, *Religious and Spiritual Groups in Modern America* (Englewood Cliffs, N.J.: Prentice Hall, 1973), 190-91; Jeffrey Russell, *Mephistopheles* (Ithaca, N.Y.: Cornell University Press, 1986), 168-213.

[55]Ellwood, *Religious and Spiritual Groups,* 191-92.

[56]Margo Adler, *Drawing Down the Moon* (Boston: Beacon Press, 1979), 46-47; Margaret A. Murray, *The Witch-Cult in Western Europe* (Oxford, U.K.: Clarendon, 1921); Russell, *History of Witchcraft,* 133, 152; Raymond Buckland, *Witchcraft from the Inside* (St. Paul, Minn.: Llewellyn, 1971), 50-52.

[57]See Gerald B. Gardner, ed., *Witchcraft Today* (New York: Citadel, 1955); Adler, *Drawing Down the Moon,* 60-64; Russell, *History of Witchcraft,* 154; Charles Alva Hoyt, *Witchcraft* (Carbondale, Ill.: Southern Illinois University Press, 1981), 136-38.

[58]See Russell, *History of Witchcraft,* 148, 154; Melton, *Encyclopedia of American Religions,* 2:272-82; Adler, *Drawing Down the Moon,* 171-222; Naomi Goldenberg, "Feminist Witchcraft: Controlling Our Own Inner Space," in *The Politics of Women's Spirituality,* ed. Charlene Spretnak (Garden City, N.Y.: Anchor, 1982), 213-18; Naomi R. Goldenberg, *Changing of the Gods* (Boston: Beacon Press, 1979).

[59]Russell, *History of Witchcraft,* 157-59. See Marija Gembutas, "Women and Culture in Goddess-Oriented Old Europe," in *The Politics of Women's Spirituality,* ed. Charlene Spretnak (Garden City, N.Y.: Anchor, 1982), 22-31; Woods, *Occult Revolution,* 115-16.

[60]Russell, *History of Witchcraft,* 161-62; Truzzi, "Occult Revival as Popular Culture," 22-23; Adler, *Drawing Down the Moon,* 150-70; Gordon Fleming, " 'Black' Magic Against 'White,' " in *Witchcraft Today,* ed. Martin Ebon (New York: New American Library, 1971), 62-68.

[61]Russell, *History of Witchcraft,* 161; Buckland, *Witchcraft from the Inside,* 69-70; Adler, *Drawing Down the Moon,* 110.

[62]Russell, *History of Witchcraft,* 162-66; Truzzi, "Witchcraft and Satanism," 216-17; Cavendish, *The Black Arts,* 322-23; Woods, *Occult Revolution,* 117.

[63]Russell, *History of Witchcraft,* 166-68; Adler, *Drawing Down the Moon,* 106-11.

[64]Russell, *History of Witchcraft,* 170-71; Ellwood, *Religious and Spiritual Groups,* 190.

[65]Arthur Lyons, *The Second Coming: Satanism in America* (New York: Award Books, 1970), 7-8; Newport, *Demons, Demons,* 15. For more on Satanism see

Jason Michaels, *The Devil Is Alive and Well and Living in America* (New York: Award Books, 1973); Richard Woods, *The Devil* (Chicago: Thomas More, 1973).

[66]Woods, *Occult Revolution*, 121-22; Freedland, *Occult Explosion*, 148; Richard Woods, "Satanism Today," in *Soundings in Satanism*, ed. F. G. Sheed (New York: Sheed and Ward, 1972), 92; Bodeman, "Mystical, Satanic and Chiliastic Forces," 441.

[67]Woods, *Occult Revolution*, 122; Freedland, *Occult Explosion*, 152; Russell, *Mephistopheles*, 253.

[68]Russell, *History of Witchcraft*, 144. See also Nugent, "Renaissance and/of Witchcraft," 71.

[69]Melton, *Encyclopedia of American Religions*, 2:300; Truzzi, "Occult Revival as Popular Culture," 24.

[70]Melton, *Encyclopedia of American Religions*, 2:300. See Anton LaVey, *The Compleat Witch* (New York: Lancer, 1970). For an example of lumping witchcraft and Satanism together see Nugent, "Renaissance and/of Witchcraft," 71, 75.

[71]Jules Michelet, *Satanism and Witchcraft* (Secaucus, N.J.: Lyle Stuart, 1939), 229ff.; Russell, *Mephistopheles*, 89-91; Woods, *Occult Revolution*, 133-36; Russell, *History of Witchcraft*, 128-31; Richard Cavendish, *The Powers of Evil* (New York: G. P. Putnam's Sons, 1975), 225-28.

[72]Melton, *Encyclopedia of American Religions*, 2:301; Truzzi, "Witchcraft and Satanism," 218. Carl Raschke regards Satanism as the culminating phase of the New Age movement. See Carl A. Raschke, "Satanism and the Devolution of the 'New Religions,' " *SCP Newsletter* 11, no. 3 (1985): 24; Ken Sidney, "Satanism: The Horror and the Hype," *Christianity Today*, November 17, 1989, pp. 48-50; Jerry Johnston, *The Edge of Evil* (Dallas: Word, 1989).

[73]Truzzi, "Occult Revival as Popular Culture," 26; Cavendish, *Powers of Evil*, 221-22. See also William Sims Bainbridge, *Satan's Power* (Berkeley: University of California Press, 1978).

[74]Truzzi, "Occult Revival as Popular Culture," 26-27; Russell, *History of Witchcraft*, 146; Russell, *Mephistopheles*, 253-56.

[75]Melton, *Encyclopedia of American Religions*, 2:303; Truzzi, "Occult Revival as Popular Culture," 27; Russell, *Mephistopheles*, 253-54.

[76]Truzzi, "Occult Revival as Popular Culture," 28; Anton La Vey, *The Satanic Bible* (New York: Avon, 1969), 64-65, 81-86; Felex Bak, "The Church of Satan in the United States," *Antonianum* 50 (1975): 160-63.

[77]Truzzi, "Occult Revival as Popular Culture," 28; La Vey, *Satanic Bible*, 91-95; Bak, "Church of Satan," 162-63.

[78]Geoffrey K. Nelson, "The Members of a Cult: The Spiritualists National Union," *Review of Religious Research* 13, no. 3 (1972): 171-72.

[79]In particular, Stark and Bainbridge challenge the membership figures that show Spiritualism declining significantly in the early twentieth century and then rising again in the 1920s. See Rodney Stark and William S. Bainbridge, *The Future of Religion* (Berkeley: University of California Press, 1985), 253-54. For general in-

formation on Spiritualism see Slater Brown, *The Heyday of Spiritualism* (New York: Hawthorne, 1970); Emma Hardinge, *Modern American Spiritualism* (New Hyde Park, N.Y.: University Books, 1970); Eric Post, *Communicating with the Beyond* (New York: Atlantic, 1946); Herbert G. Jackson Jr., *The Spirit Rappers* (Garden City, N.Y.: Doubleday, 1972).

[80]J. Gordon Melton, "New Churches of the 1920s and 1930s," in *Christianity in America,* ed. Mark A. Noll et al. (Grand Rapids, Mich.: Eerdmans, 1983), 412; Petersen, *Those Curious New Cults,* 58; Kerr, *Mystery and Magic,* 94-95.

[81]R. Laurence Moore, *In Search of White Crows* (New York: Oxford University Press, 1977), 226-27.

[82]William J. Whalen, *Minority Religions in America* (New York: Alba House, 1981), 181; Guy Lyon Playfair, *The Unknown Power* (New York: Pocket Books, 1975), ix-xvi; John R. W. Stott, "Brazil: The Spiritual Climate," *Christianity Today,* April 4, 1980, pp. 32-33.

[83]James A. Pike, *The Other Side* (Garden City, N.Y.: Doubleday, 1968); Petersen, *Those Curious New Cults,* 56; Kerr, *Mystery and Magic,* 102-5.

[84]Melton, *Encyclopedic Handbook of Cults in America,* 85; Petersen, *Those Curious New Cults,* 56; Whalen, *Minority Religions,* 184. Sociologists have difficulties placing Spiritualism in the church-sect typologies. See Geoffrey K. Nelson, "The Spiritualist Movement and the Need for a Redefinition of Cult," *Journal for the Scientific Study of Religion* 8, no. 1 (1969): 152-60.

[85]Richard H. Neff, *Psychic Phenomena and Religion* (Philadelphia: Westminster Press, 1971), 22-29; George W. Braswell Jr., *Understanding Sectarian Groups in America* (Nashville: Broadman, 1986), 252; E. Garth Moore, *Try the Spirits* (New York: Oxford University Press, 1977), 7-20, 68-78.

[86]Moore, *In Search of White Crows,* 221-22.

[87]Wuthnow, *Experimentation in American Religion,* 66, 76.

[88]Moore, *Try the Spirits,* 35-60; Braswell, *Understanding Sectarian Groups,* 252-53; Neff, *Psychic Phenomena,* 131-43; Douglas Hill and Pat Williams, *The Supernatural* (New York: New American Library, 1967); John Warwick Montgomery, *Principalities and Powers* (Minneapolis: Bethany Fellowship, 1973), 140-43.

[89]Woods, *Occult Revolution,* 177-78; Neff, *Psychic Phenomena,* 143; Mark Albrecht, "Reincarnation and the Early Church," *Update* 7, no. 2 (1983): 36-37.

[90]Neff, *Psychic Phenomena,* 144-45; Braswell, *Understanding Sectarian Groups,* 253; Morey Bernstein, *The Search for Bridey Murphy* (New York: Doubleday, 1956).

[91]Stark and Bainbridge, *Future of Religion,* 197-99, 205.

[92]Melton, *Encyclopedia of American Religions,* 2:199; Ellwood, *Religious and Spiritual Groups,* 131.

[93]David M. Jacobs, "UFOs and Scientific Legitimacy," in *The Occult in America,* ed. Howard Kerr and Charles Crow (Urbana: University of Illinois Press, 1983), 218. For the UFO and science question see Paris Flammonde, *The Age of Flying Saucers* (New York: Hawthorne, 1971); J. Allen Hynek, *The UFO Experience: A*

Scientific Inquiry (Chicago: Henry Regnery, 1972); Carl Sagan and Thornton Page, eds., *UFOs: A Scientific Debate* (Ithaca, N.Y.: Cornell University Press, 1972); Jacques Vallee and Janine Vallee, *Challenge to Science: The UFO Enigma* (New York: Ace Books, 1966).

94Jacobs, "UFOs and Scientific Legitimacy," 219, 228-29. For the issue of contacting UFOs see Carol and Jim Lorenzen, *Flying Saucer Occupants* (New York: New American Library, 1967); Brad Steiger, *The Aquarian Revelations* (New York: Dell, 1971); Clifford Wilson, *U.F.O.s and Their Mission Impossible* (Burnt Hills, N.Y.: Word of Truth Productions, 1974).

95Melton, *Encyclopedia of American Religions,* 2:199; Robert W. Balch and David Taylor, "Salvation in a UFO," *Psychology Today,* October, 1976, pp. 58-66, 106; Robert W. Balch and David Taylor, "Seekers and Saucers: The Role of the Cultic Milieu in Joining a UFO Cult," *American Behavioral Scientist* 20, no. 6 (1977): 839-60.

96Melton, *Encyclopedia of American Religions,* 2:200. See Erich Von Daniken's *Chariots of the Gods?* (New York: Bantam, 1971); Josef F. Blumrich, *The Spaceships of Ezekiel* (New York: Bantam, 1974); Irving Hexham, "Yoga, UFOs and Cult Membership," *Update* 10, no. 3 (1986): 12.

97Melton, *Encyclopedia of American Religions,* 2:200-212; Leon Festinger, Henry W. Riecken and Stanley Schachter, *When Prophecy Fails* (New York: Harper & Row, 1964), 33-57.

Chapter 18: The New Age Movement

1Otto Friedrich, "The New Age Harmonies," *Time,* December 7, 1987, p. 62; Barbara Hargrove, "New Religious Movements and the End of the Age," *The Iliff Review* (Spring 1982): 47; Douglas Groothuis, *Confronting the New Age* (Downers Grove, Ill.: InterVarsity Press, 1988), 152-65.

2Douglas R. Groothuis, *Unmasking the New Age* (Downers Grove, Ill.: InterVarsity Press, 1986), 18; Friedrich, "New Age Harmonies," 64; Bill Barol et al., "The End of the World (Again)," *Newsweek,* August 17, 1987, pp. 70-71.

3Richard Blow, "Moronic Convergence," *New Republic,* January 25, 1988, p. 26; Friedrich, "New Age Harmonies," 64.

4Ted Peters, "Post Modern Religion," *Update* 8, no. 1 (1984): 23; Brooks Alexander, "The New Age Movement Is Nothing New," *Eternity,* February 1988, p. 34; Richard Kyle, "Is There a New Age Coming?" *Christian Leader,* January 17, 1989, p. 4.

5Hargrove, "New Religious Movements," 47; Peters, "Post Modern Religion," 23; Alexander, "New Age Movement," 34; Barol et al., "End of the World," 70-71; Kyle, "Is There a New Age Coming?" 4; Ruth A. Tucker, *Another Gospel* (Grand Rapids, Mich.: Zondervan, 1989), 335-36.

6J. Gordon Melton, *Encyclopedic Handbook of Cults in America* (New York: Garland, 1986), 108.

7Hargrove, "New Religious Movements," 46-47; Robert Burrows, "New Age Movement: Self-Deification in a Secular Culture," *SCP Newsletter* 10, no. 5 (1984-85): 1, 4.

[8]Groothuis, *Unmasking the New Age,* 131.

[9]Marilyn Ferguson, *The Aquarian Conspiracy* (Los Angeles: J. P. Tarcher, 1980), 46.

[10]Melton, *Encyclopedic Handbook of Cults in America,* 108-9; Ferguson, *Aquarian Conspiracy,* 47; Alice Felt Tyler, *Freedom's Ferment* (New York: Harper & Row, 1944), 48; Catherine Albanese, *America: Religion and Religions* (Belmont, Calif.: Wadsworth, 1981), 173. See previous material in chapters two, four and eight of this work.

[11]Melton, *Encyclopedic Handbook of Cults in America,* 108-9. See also Catherine Albanese, "Physic and Metaphysic in Nineteenth-Century America: Medical Sectarians and Religious Healing," *Church History* 55, no. 4 (1986): 489-502; J. Stillson Judah, *The History and Philosophy of the Metaphysical Movements in America* (Philadelphia: Westminster Press, 1957), 135-40; Russell Chandler, *Understanding the New Age* (Dallas: Word, 1988), 45-46; Tucker, *Another Gospel,* 321-22.

[12]Melton, *Encyclopedic Handbook of Cults in America,* 109; Carl T. Jackson, *The Oriental Religions and American Thought: Nineteenth-Century Explorations* (Westport, Conn.: Greenwood, 1981), 85-99.

[13]Melton, *Encyclopedic Handbook of Cults in America,* 109-10; Robert Ellwood, *Alternative Altars* (Chicago: University of Chicago Press, 1979), 134-35; Chandler, *Understanding the New Age,* 47.

[14]Richard Polenburg, *One Nation Divisible* (New York: Pelican Books, 1980), 205-8; Melton, *Encyclopedic Handbook of Cults in America,* 107, 110; Kyle, "Is There a New Age Coming?" 6.

[15]Ferguson, *Aquarian Conspiracy,* 89; Groothuis, *Unmasking the New Age,* 38-39.

[16]Ibid., 39-40. See also Jerry Adler et al., "The Graying of Aquarius," *Newsweek,* March 30, 1987, pp. 56-58; Peter Clecak, *America's Quest for the Ideal Self* (New York: Oxford University Press, 1983), 4-8.

[17]The New Age could be regarded as a world-affirming movement. It has not rejected society as did many of the counterculture groups. See Roy Wallis, *The Rebirth of the Gods: Reflections on the New Religions in the West* (Belfast: University of Belfast, 1978), 8-9; Groothuis, *Unmasking the New Age,* 45-46; Robert Burrows, "Americans Get Religion in the New Age," *Christianity Today,* May 16, 1986, p. 17; Kyle, "Is There a New Age Coming?" 6.

[18]Harriet Mosatche, *Searching* (New York: Stravon Educational Press, 1983), 13. See also Kenneth Cinnamon and Dave Farson, *Cults and Cons* (Chicago: Nelson-Hall, 1979), xvi.

[19]Roy Wallis, "The Dynamics of Change in the Human Potential Movement," in *Religious Movements,* ed. Rodney Stark (New York: Paragon House, 1985), 133; Robert C. Fuller, *Alternative Medicine and American Religious Life* (New York: Oxford University Press, 1989), 91-97.

[20]Carl A. Raschke, "The Human Potential Movement," *Theology Today* 33, no. 3 (1976): 253.

[21]Barbara Hargrove, *The Sociology of Religion* (Arlington Heights, Ill.: AHM Publishing, 1979), 275.

[22]Raschke, "Human Potential Movement," 253-54; Donald Meyer, *Positive Thinkers,* 2nd ed. (New York: Pantheon Books, 1980); Hargrove, *Sociology of Religion,* 275; Edwin Schur, *The Awareness Trap* (New York: McGraw-Hill, 1976), 74-80; Paul C. Vitz, *Psychology as Religion* (Grand Rapids, Mich.: Eerdmans, 1977), 69-74. See also William C. Henderson, *Awakening: Ways to Psycho-Spiritual Growth* (Englewood Cliffs, N.J.: Prentice Hall, 1975).

[23]Albanese, *America,* 325; Raschke, "Human Potential Movement," 255.

[24]Albanese, *America,* 325-26.

[25]Donald Stone, "The Human Potential Movement," in *The New Religious Consciousness,* ed. Charles Glock and Robert Bellah (Berkeley: University of California Press, 1976), 93-94. See also Wallis, "The Dynamics of Change," 134-35.

[26]Raschke, "Human Potential Movement," 255; Vitz, *Psychology as Religion,* 23-24; Albanese, *America,* 326; John H. Marx and Joseph H. Seldin, "Crossroads of Crises, Part I: Therapeutic Sources and Quasi-Therapeutic Functions of Post-Industrial Communes," *Journal of Health and Social Behavior* 14 (March 1973): 46-47.

[27]Albanese, *America,* 327-28; Vitz, *Psychology as Religion,* 74-75.

[28]Marilyn Ferguson is enthusiastic about the concept of holistic health and would like to see it legitimized by government programs and recognized by insurance companies. Ferguson, *Aquarian Conspiracy,* 242; Tucker, *Another Gospel,* 347-48.

[29]Brooks Alexander, "Holistic Health from the Inside," *SCP Journal* 2, no. 1 (1978): 6.

[30]Paul C. Reisser, Teri K. Reisser and John Weldon, *New Age Medicine* (Downers Grove, Ill.: InterVarsity Press, 1987), 11; Paul C. Reisser, "Holistic Health," in *The New Age Rage,* ed. Karen Hoyt (Old Tappan, N.J.: Revell, 1987), 55-73; Chandler, *Understanding the New Age,* 162-70.

[31]Reisser, Reisser and Weldon, *New Age Medicine,* 9; Groothuis, *Unmasking the New Age,* 57.

[32]Reisser, Reisser and Weldon, *New Age Medicine,* 9-10; Kenneth R. Pelletier, *Holistic Medicine* (New York: Dell, 1979), 1-22.

[33]Kenneth R. Pelletier, *Mind as Healer, Mind as Slayer* (New York: Dell, 1977), 193ff.; Reisser, Reisser and Weldon, *New Age Medicine,* 10, 12, 20-25.

[34]Melton, *Encyclopedic Handbook of Cults in America,* 112-13. The emphasis on an experience and vision is the thrust of many books about the New Age. See Ferguson, *Aquarian Conspiracy;* Leonard Orr and Sondra Roy, *Rebirthing in the New Age* (Millbrae, Calif.: Celestial Arts, 1977); David Spangler, *Towards a Planetary Vision* (Forres, Scotland: Fendhorn Foundation, 1975); Robert Burrows, "A Vision for a New Humanity," in *The New Age Rage,* ed. Karen Hoyt

(Old Tappan, N.J.: Revell, 1987), 33-51; Elliot Miller, *A Crash Course on the New Age Movement* (Grand Rapids, Mich.: Baker Book House, 1989), 17-18, 207-8.

[35]Melton, *Encyclopedic Handbook of Cults in America,* 113. See also Ferguson, *Aquarian Conspiracy,* 45; Blow, "Moronic Convergence," 24.

[36]Ferguson, *Aquarian Conspiracy,* 85-90, 107-8.

[37]Melton, *Encyclopedic Handbook of Cults in America,* 113; Ferguson, *Aquarian Conspiracy,* 23, 26; Kyle, "Is There a New Age Coming?" 6.

[38]For a discussion of the parallels between the New Age and fundamentalism see Catherine L. Albanese, "Religion and the American Experience: A Century After," *Church History* 57, no. 3 (1988): 349-50.

[39]Ferguson, *Aquarian Conspiracy,* 26-33; Burrows, "New Age Movement," 5.

[40]Groothuis, *Unmasking the New Age,* 132; Melton, *Encyclopedic Handbook of Cults in America,* 113; Irving Hexham and Karla Poewe-Hexham, "The Soul of the New Age," *Christianity Today,* September 1, 1988, p. 19.

[41]Melton, *Encyclopedic Handbook of Cults in America,* 113; Groothuis, *Unmasking the New Age,* 27-28.

[42]Melton, *Encyclopedic Handbook of Cults in America,* 113-14.

[43]Ibid., 114; Groothuis, *Unmasking the New Age,* 141, 144-46; Burrows, "New Age Movement," 5; Miller, *Crash Course,* 16; Ron Rhodes, *The Counterfeit Christ of the New Age Movement* (Grand Rapids, Mich.: Baker Book House, 1990).

[44]Ferguson, *Aquarian Conspiracy,* 415-17; Melton, *Encyclopedic Handbook of Cults in America,* 115.

[45]Ferguson, *Aquarian Conspiracy,* 189-91; Groothuis, *Unmasking the New Age,* 11, 112.

[46]Ferguson, *Aquarian Conspiracy,* 223, 228-31; Groothuis, *Unmasking the New Age,* 112-13. See Douglas Groothuis, "Politics," in *The New Age Rage,* ed. Karen Hoyt (Old Tappan, N.J.: Revell, 1987), 91-106.

[47]Groothuis, *Unmasking the New Age,* 112-13, 116-17; Blow, "Moronic Convergence," 26; Ferguson, *Aquarian Conspiracy,* 223; Chandler, *Understanding the New Age,* 193-203.

[48]Melton, *Encyclopedic Handbook of Cults in America,* 116-17. For another view on the future of the New Age see Groothuis, *Confronting the New Age,* 199-202.

Chapter 19: Psychospiritual or Self-Improvement Groups

[1]Ronald Enroth, *The Lure of the Cults* (Chappaqua, N.Y.: Christian Herald Books, 1979), 29; Kenneth Woodward et al., "Getting Your Head Together," *Newsweek,* September 6, 1976, pp. 56, 60-61. Bioenergetics says that the human body is an energy system and that its energy must flow freely for a person to function properly. This free flow is achieved by a variety of treatments that unlock physical tensions. Rolfing is a form of deep muscle manipulation, focusing on the emotions as well as the body. See also Alan Gartner and Frank Reissman, eds., *The Self-Help Revolution* (New York: Human Sciences Press, 1984); Brock Kilbourne and James T. Richardson, "Psychotherapy and New Religions in a Pluralistic Society,"

American Psychologist, March 1984, pp. 237-51.

[2]Kenneth Cinnamon and Dave Farson, *Cults and Cons* (Chicago: Nelson-Hall, 1979), 40; Enroth, *Lure of the Cults,* 29-30; Flo Conway and Jim Siegelman, *Snapping* (New York: Delta, 1978), 19; Edwin Schur, *The Awareness Trap* (New York: McGraw-Hill, 1976), 43.

[3]Woodward et al., "Getting Your Head Together," 56-57; Donald Stone, "The Human Potential Movement," in *The New Religious Consciousness,* ed. Charles Glock and Robert Bellah (Berkeley: University of California Press, 1976), 93; Cinnamon and Farson, *Cults and Cons,* 41-50.

[4]Woodward et al., "Getting Your Head Together," 56-57.

[5]Peter Marin, "The New Narcissism," *Harper's,* October 1975, p. 48; Woodward et al., "Getting Your Head Together," 57; Albert C. Outler, "Recovery of the Sacred," *Christianity Today,* January 23, 1981, p. 23.

[6]Woodward et al., "Getting Your Head Together," 56.

[7]Ibid., 56-57; Carl A. Raschke, "The Human Potential Movement," *Theology Today* 33, no. 3 (1976): 253-54; Roy Wallis, "The Dynamics of Change in the Human Potential Movement," in *Religious Movements,* ed. Rodney Stark (New York: Paragon House, 1985), 134-35.

[8]John Allan, *Shopping for a God* (Leicester, U.K.: Inter-Varsity Press, 1986), 96; Woodward et al., "Getting Your Head Together," 62; Frances Adeney, "The Flowering of the Human Potential Movement," *SCP Journal* 5, no. 1 (Winter 1981-82): 15-16.

[9]Allan, *Shopping for a God,* 96; Raschke, "Human Potential Movement," 255-56; Adeney, "Flowering," 12-13.

[10]Allan, *Shopping for a God,* 96-97; Woodward et al., "Getting Your Head Together," 62; Adeney, "Flowering," 15-16.

[11]Allan, *Shopping for a God,* 97-98; Woodward et al., "Getting Your Head Together," 62. See Carl A. Raschke, *The Interruption of Eternity* (Chicago: Nelson-Hall, 1980).

[12]Wallis, "The Dynamics of Change," 134-35; Melton, *Encyclopedic Handbook of Cults in America,* 120-21.

[13]Frank K. Flinn, "Scientology as Technological Buddhism," in *Alternatives to American Mainline Churches,* ed. Joseph Fichter (Barrytown, N.Y.: Unification Theological Seminary, 1983), 93; Melton, *Encyclopedic Handbook of Cults in America,* 128; Ruth A. Tucker, *Another Gospel* (Grand Rapids, Mich.: Zondervan, 1989), 310.

[14]Bryan Wilson, *Religious Sects* (New York: McGraw-Hill, 1970), 163; Brooks Alexander, "Scientology: Human Potential Bellweather," *SCP Journal* 5, no. 1 (Winter 1981-82): 27; Flinn, "Scientology as Technological Buddhism," 93, 103; Peter W. Williams, *Popular Religion in America* (Englewood Cliffs, N.J.: Prentice Hall, 1980), 218.

[15]Flinn, "Scientology as Technological Buddhism," 93.

[16]Roy Wallis, "Hostages to Fortune: Thoughts on the Future of Scientology and the

Children of God," in *The Future of New Religious Movements,* ed. David G. Bromley and Philip E. Hammond (Macon, Ga.: Mercer University Press, 1987), 82-83; Alexander, "Scientology," 27; Rodney Stark and William S. Bainbridge, *The Future of Religion* (Berkeley: University of California Press, 1985), 263-64; Roy Wallis, *The Rebirth of the Gods: Reflections on the New Religions in the West* (Belfast: University of Belfast, 1978), 16-17.

[17]Joseph M. Hopkins, "Scientology: Religion or Racket? Part I," *Christianity Today* 14, no. 3 (1969): 6; John Newport, *Christ and the New Consciousness* (Nashville: Broadman, 1978), 83; William J. Whalen, *Strange Gods* (Huntington, Ind.: Our Sunday Visitor, 1981), 63; Harriet Whitehead, "Reasonably Fantastic: Some Perspectives on Scientology, Science Fiction, and Occultism," in *Religious Movements in Contemporary America,* ed. Irving I. Zaretsky and Mark P. Leone (Princeton, N.J.: Princeton University Press, 1974), 549.

[18]George Malko, *Scientology: The New Religion* (New York: Dell, 1970), 30-31; Newport, *Christ and the New Consciousness,* 84-85; Melton, *Encyclopedic Handbook of Cults in America,* 128; George W. Braswell Jr., *Understanding Sectarian Groups in America* (Nashville: Broadman, 1986), 234.

[19]David G. Bromley and Anson Shupe Jr., *Strange Gods* (Boston: Beacon Press, 1981), 46; Newport, *Christ and the New Consciousness,* 84-85; Malko, *Scientology,* 31; Whalen, *Strange Gods,* 66.

[20]Braswell, *Understanding Sectarian Groups,* 235; Melton, *Encyclopedic Handbook of Cults in America,* 128. See L. Ron Hubbard, *Dianetics* (Los Angeles: Bridge, 1950); Roy Wallis, *The Road to Total Freedom: A Sociological Analysis of Scientology* (New York: Columbia University Press, 1977).

[21]Melton, *Encyclopedic Handbook of Cults in America,* 129; Malko, *Scientology,* 58-59; Braswell, *Understanding Sectarian Groups,* 235; Wallis, *Road to Total Freedom,* 83-90.

[22]Ibid., 77-100; Bromley and Shupe, *Strange Gods,* 48; Wilson, *Religious Sects,* 163; "Scientology," *Newsweek,* September 12, 1974, p. 84.

[23]Melton, *Encyclopedic Handbook of Cults in America,* 129, 132; Braswell, *Understanding Sectarian Groups,* 236; "A Farewell to Scientology?" *Newsweek,* August 26, 1968, p. 8.

[24]Melton, *Encyclopedic Handbook of Cults in America,* 129, 131; Wallis, *Road to Total Freedom,* 132-36.

[25]Ibid., 132-33; Melton, *Encyclopedic Handbook of Cults in America,* 129-31; "A Sci-Fi Faith," *Time,* April 5, 1976, pp. 56-57.

[26]Clay Steinman, "Scientology Fights Back," *The Nation,* May 22, 1972, pp. 658-59; Melton, *Encyclopedic Handbook of Cults in America,* 132-33; Tucker, *Another Gospel,* 313-15; Richard Behar, "The Thriving Cult of Greed and Power," *Time,* May 6, 1991, p. 50.

[27]"Scientology: Parry and Thrust," *Time,* July 25, 1977, p. 67; Melton, *Encyclopedic Handbook of Cults in America,* 133; Whalen, *Strange Gods,* 71; Ron Enroth, "Did Two Scientologist Spies Come In from the Cold?" *Christianity Today,* September

.7, 1982, pp. 32-36; Behar, "Thriving Cult of Greed and Power," 50.

[28]Braswell, *Understanding Sectarian Groups,* 237-38; Joseph M. Hopkins, "The Founder of Scientology Is Dead at 74," *Christianity Today,* March 7, 1986, pp. 52-53.

[29]Melton, *Encyclopedic Handbook of Cults in America,* 133-34; "Scientology: Parry and Thrust," p. 67.

[30]Melton, *Encyclopedic Handbook of Cults in America,* 134; Behar, "Thriving Cult of Greed and Power," 50, 52-55.

[31]Whalen, *Strange Gods,* 62, 69; Melton, *Encyclopedic Handbook of Cults in America,* 131.

[32]Ibid., 130; Braswell, *Understanding Sectarian Groups,* 238-39.

[33]Hubbard, *Dianetics,* 51-78; Newport, *Christ and the New Consciousness,* 86-87; Bromley and Shupe, *Strange Gods,* 49.

[34]Hubbard, *Dianetics,* 186-211; Newport, *Christ and the New Consciousness,* 86-87; Bromley and Shupe, *Strange Gods,* 49-50; Wilson, *Religious Sects,* 164.

[35]Bromley and Shupe, *Strange Gods,* 50; Wallis, *Road to Total Freedom,* 86-88; Malko, *Scientology,* 57-60.

[36]Stark and Bainbridge, *Future of Religion,* 269; Wallis, *Road to Total Freedom,* 87-88; Newport, *Christ and the New Consciousness,* 87.

[37]Bromley and Shupe, *Strange Gods,* 50; Wallis, *Road to Total Freedom,* 106-11; "A Sci-Fi Faith," 53; Newport, *Christ and the New Consciousness,* 87-88; Whitehead, "Reasonably Fantastic," 550.

[38]Stark and Bainbridge, *Future of Religion,* 266; Newport, *Christ and the New Consciousness,* 87-88; Bromley and Shupe, *Strange Gods,* 50; Malko, *Scientology,* 106; Bless Donovan, "Scientology: Total Freedom and Beyond," *The Nation,* September 19, 1969, pp. 311-13.

[39]Wallis, *Road to Total Freedom,* 116; Braswell, *Understanding Sectarian Groups,* 240; Newport, *Christ and the New Consciousness,* 89; Malko, *Scientology,* 124.

[40]Wallis, *Road to Total Freedom,* 113-17; Malko, *Scientology,* 77; Newport, *Christ and the New Consciousness,* 87-88; Donovan, "Total Freedom and Beyond," 312-13.

[41]Newport, *Christ and the New Consciousness,* 89-90; Robert Ellwood, *Religious and Spiritual Groups in Modern America* (Englewood Cliffs, N.J.: Prentice Hall, 1973), 171; Malko, *Scientology,* 121-22; Wilson, *Religious Sects,* 164.

[42]Allan, *Shopping for a God,* 84.

[43]Newport, *Christ and the New Consciousness,* 90.

[44]Braswell, *Understanding Sectarian Groups,* 241-42; Tucker, *Another Gospel,* 300-301; Behar, "Thriving Cult of Greed and Power," 51, 56-57.

[45]John Weldon, "est," in *A Guide to Cults and New Religions,* (Downers Grove, Ill.: InterVarsity Press, 1983), 76.

[46]Stanley Dokupil and Brooks Alexander, "est: The Philosophy of Self-Worship," *SCP Journal* 5, no. 1 (Winter 1981-82): 20; Woodward et al., "Getting Your Head Together," 58.

[47]Adelaide Bry, *est: Sixty Hours That Transform Your Life* (New York: Avon,

1976), 200; Tucker, *Another Gospel,* 369.

48John Rudkin Clark, "Secular Salvation: Life Change Through 'est,' " *Christian Century,* November 10, 1976, p. 982.

49Mark Brewer, "We're Gonna Tear You Down and Put You Back Together," *Psychology Today,* August 1975, p. 35; William J. Petersen, *Those Curious New Cults in the 80s* (New Canaan, Conn.: Keats, 1973), 206; Allan, *Shopping for a God,* 98; Marin, "New Narcissism," 46-47.

50Weldon, "est," 76; Petersen, *Those Curious New Cults,* 207; Brewer, "We're Gonna Tear You Down," p. 35.

51Petersen, *Those Curious New Cults,* 207. See Donald Stone, "Social Consciousness in the Human Potential Movement," in *In Gods We Trust,* ed. Thomas Robbins and Dick Anthony (New Brunswick, N.J.: Transaction Books, 1981), 215, 227.

52Kevin Garvey, "The Serpentine Serenity of est," *Christianity Today,* January 21, 1977, p. 13; Weldon, "est," 76-77; Brewer, "We're Gonna Tear You Down," 35.

53Newport, *Christ and the New Consciousness,* 107; Weldon, "est," 77.

54Newport, *Christ and the New Consciousness,* 107; Conway and Siegelman, *Snapping,* 25; Petersen, *Those Curious New Cults,* 205; Brewer, "We're Gonna Tear You Down," 82.

55Weldon, "est," 77-78; Newport, *Christ and the New Consciousness,* 107; Brewer, "We're Gonna Tear You Down," 82, 88.

56Newport, *Christ and the New Consciousness,* 107; Weldon, "est," 77; Petersen, *Those Curious New Cults,* 205.

57Richard P. Marsh, "I Am the Cause of My World," *Psychology Today,* August 1975, p. 38; Susan Cheever Cowley, "est-erical Behavior?" *Newsweek,* May 9, 1977, p. 95; Woodward et al., "Getting Your Head on Straight," 59.

58Newport, *Christ and the New Consciousness,* 107-8; Clark, "Secular Salvation," 981; Brewer, "We're Gonna Tear You Down," 35.

59Dokupil and Alexander, "est," 20; Weldon, "est," 76; Petersen, *Those Curious New Cults,* 206.

60Adam Smith, "Powers of Mind, Part II: The est Experience," *New York Magazine,* September 29, 1975, p. 35; Dokupil and Alexander, "est," 20.

61Weldon, "est," 76; Brewer, "We're Gonna Tear You Down," 36.

62Dokupil and Alexander, "est," 20; Newport, *Christ and the New Consciousness,* 112; Robert Ellwood, *Alternative Altars* (Chicago: University of Chicago Press, 1979), 165.

63Luke Rhinehart, *The Book of est* (New York: Holt, Rinehart and Winston, 1976), 47. For the quotation see Dokupil and Alexander, "est," 20.

64Ibid.; Brewer, "We're Gonna Tear You Down," 39; Petersen, *Those Curious New Cults,* 207-8.

65Brewer, "We're Gonna Tear You Down," 39; Weldon, "est," 78-79.

66Ibid., 84; Brewer, "We're Gonna Tear You Down," 39; Petersen, *Those Curious New Cults,* 208; Tucker, *Another Gospel,* 368. For the quotation see Weldon, "est," 84.

67Ibid. For the quotation see Petersen, *Those Curious New Cults,* 208.

68Dokupil and Alexander, "est," 20-21.

69Newport, *Christ and the New Consciousness,* 108-9; Garvey, "Serpentine Serenity," 14-15; Woodward et al., "Getting Your Head Together," 58.

70Weldon, "est," 85-86; Newport, *Christ and the New Consciousness,* 109-10; Brewer, "We're Gonna Tear You Down," 39-40.

71Newport, *Christ and the New Consciousness,* 110-11; Clark, "Secular Salvation," 984; Marsh, "I Am the Cause, " 38.

72Dokupil and Alexander, "est," 21; William C. Henderson, *Awakening: Ways to Psycho-Spiritual Growth* (Englewood Cliffs, N.J.: Prentice Hall, 1975), 64.

73Tucker, *Another Gospel,* 369; "60 Minutes," March 3, 1991; Yutaka Amano, "Bad for Business," *Eternity,* March 1986, pp. 55-57; "Briefly Noted," *Christianity Today,* April 8, 1991, p. 61.

74Newport, *Christ and the New Consciousness,* 99-100.

75Henderson, *Awakening,* 18; Newport, *Christ and the New Consciousness,* 99-100; Walter Martin, *The New Cults* (Santa Ana, Calif.: Vision House, 1980), 237-38.

76Henderson, *Awakening,* 18; Newport, *Christ and the New Consciousness,* 100.

77Ibid., 100-101.

78Henderson, *Awakening,* 19; Newport, *Christ and the New Consciousness,* 103, 105; Martin, *New Cults,* 243-45.

79Richard Ofshe, "The Social Development of the Synanon Cult: The Managerial Strategy of Organizational Transformation," *Sociological Analysis* 41, no. 2 (1980): 109-15.

80Paul H. Chalfant, Robert E. Beckley and C. Eddie Palmer, *Religion in Contemporary Society* (Sherman Oaks, Calif.: Alfred Publishing, 1981), 307-8; Richard Ofshe, "Synanon: The People Business," in *The New Religious Consciousness,* ed. Charles Glock and Robert Bellah (Berkeley: University of California Press, 1976), 116-19.

81Ofshe, "Social Development of the Synanon Cult," 110-11; Chalfant, Beckley and Palmer, *Religion in Contemporary Society,* 308.

82Ibid., 308, 310; Ofshe, "Social Development of the Synanon Cult," 114.

83Ibid., 113-14; Stark and Bainbridge, *Future of Religion,* 512-13; Chalfant, Beckley and Palmer, *Religion in Contemporary Society,* 309.

Chapter 20: The Christian Background

1Ruth A. Tucker, *Another Gospel* (Grand Rapids, Mich.: Zondervan, 1989), 17-19; Ronald Enroth, *The Lure of the Cults* (Chappaqua, N.Y.: Christian Herald Books, 1979), 28.

2Tucker, *Another Gospel,* 19.

3Thomas Robbins, Dick Anthony and James Richardson, "Theory and Research in Today's New Religions," *Sociological Analysis* 39, no. 2 (1978): 101-3. See also R. Stephen Warner, "Dualistic and Monistic Religiosity," in *Religious Movements in Contemporary America,* ed. Irving I. Zaretsky and Mark P. Leone (Princeton,

N.J.: Princeton University Press, 1974), 199-215; Eileen Barker, "Free to Choose? Some Thoughts on the Unification Church and Other Religious Movements, Part I," *Clergy Review,* October 1980, p. 366.

[4]Robbins, Anthony and Richardson, "Theory and Research," 101. See also Ronald Enroth, Edward E. Ericson Jr. and C. Breckenridge Peters, *The Jesus People* (Grand Rapids, Mich.: Eerdmans, 1972), 16; Robert Ellwood, *One Way* (Englewood Cliffs, N.J.: Prentice Hall, 1973), 86-93, 97-100; Thomas Robbins, Dick Anthony and Thomas Curtis, "The Last Civil Religion: Reverend Moon and the Unification Church," *Sociological Analysis* 37, no. 2 (1976): 121.

[5]Robbins, Anthony and Richardson, "Theory and Research," 101-2. See also Robert Wuthnow, "The New Religions in Social Context," in *The New Religious Consciousness,* ed. Charles Glock and Robert Bellah (Berkeley: University of California Press, 1976), 277, 283-84, 288.

[6]Harold L. Bussell, *Unholy Devotion* (Grand Rapids, Mich.: Zondervan, 1983), 16, 111; Mark A. Noll et al., eds., *Christianity in America* (Grand Rapids, Mich.: Eerdmans, 1983), 473.

[7]Bussell, *Unholy Devotion,* 19-20, 29.

[8]Ibid., 41, 44, 51-52.

[9]Ronald M. Enroth, "The Power Abusers," *Eternity,* October 1979, pp. 23-27; Bussell, *Unholy Devotion,* 62, 65-66. See also Richard Quebedeaux, *By What Authority* (New York: Harper & Row, 1981), 164-69.

[10]Noll et al., *Christianity in America,* 473.

[11]Ibid., 472; Quebedeaux, *By What Authority,* 170-72. See also Gregory T. Goethals, *The TV Ritual* (Boston: Beacon Press, 1981), 33-85.

[12]See Dean M. Kelley, *Why Conservative Churches Are Growing* (New York: Harper & Row, 1972), 65-67; Dean M. Kelley, "Why Conservative Churches Are Still Growing," *Journal for the Scientific Study of Religion* 17, no. 2 (1978): 165-66; David A. Roozen and Jackson W. Carroll, "Recent Trends in Church Membership and Participation," in *Understanding Church Growth and Decline, 1950-1978,* ed. Dean R. Hoge and David A. Roozen (New York: Pilgrim, 1979), 23-28; Wade Clark Roof and William McKinney, *American Mainline Religion* (New Brunswick, N.J.: Rutgers University Press, 1987), 18-21.

[13]See James T. Richardson and Rex Davis, "Experiential Fundamentalism: Revisions of Orthodoxy and the Jesus Movement," *Journal of the American Academy of Religion* 5 (1983): 397; Jack Balswick, "The Jesus People Movement: A Generational Interpretation," *Journal of Social Issues* 30, no. 3 (1974): 23, 27, 30; Steve Rabey, "Remembering the Jesus Movement," *Christianity Today,* November 22, 1985, pp. 53-54.

[14]George W. Braswell Jr., *Understanding Sectarian Groups in America* (Nashville: Broadman, 1986), 51-52, 93-94, 222-23; J. Gordon Melton, *Encyclopedic Handbook of Cults in America* (New York: Garland, 1986), 33-34, 94-96, 99-102. The recent growth of these groups outside the United States has been even more striking. See Ruth A. Tucker, "Nonorthodox Sects Report Global Membership Gains,"

Christianity Today, June 13, 1986, pp. 48-51.

[15]Joseph H. Hopkins, "Cult Specialists Assess Nontraditional Religions in the Mid-eighties," *Christianity Today,* August 9, 1985, p. 54.

Chapter 21: The Unification Church

[1]William J. Whalen, *Strange Gods* (Huntington, Ind.: Our Sunday Visitor, 1981), 53-54; Annette P. Hampshire and James A. Beckford, "Religious Sects and the Concept of Deviance: The Mormons and Moonies," *The British Journal of Theology* 34, no. 2 (1983): 208-29.

[2]Ronald B. Flowers, *Religion in Strange Times: The 1960s and 1970s* (Macon, Ga.: Mercer University Press, 1984), 103; John Newport, *Christ and the New Consciousness* (Nashville: Broadman, 1978), 119; Robert Ellwood, *Religious and Spiritual Groups in Modern America* (Englewood Cliffs, N.J.: Prentice Hall, 1973), 293.

[3]Leon McBeth, *Strange New Religions* (Nashville: Broadman, 1977), 11; Newport, *Christ and the New Consciousness,* 122; Whalen, *Strange Gods,* 55.

[4]Arthur S. Parsons, "Messianic Personalism: A Role Analysis of the Unification Church," *Journal for the Scientific Study of Religion* 25, no. 2 (1986): 141-42; Whalen, *Strange Gods,* 57; Flowers, *Religion in Strange Times,* 105-6. See also David G. Bromley and Anson D. Shupe Jr., *Moonies in America* (Beverly Hills, Calif.: Sage, 1979), 243-56.

[5]Flowers, *Religion in Strange Times,* 106-8; Bromley and Shupe, *Moonies in America,* 169-95.

[6]Ibid., 35-55; James Bjornstad, *The Moon Is Not the Son* (Minneapolis: Bethany Fellowship, 1976), 29-43; Newport, *Christ and the New Consciousness,* 120-21; Whalen, *Strange Gods,* 47-48, 50; J. Gordon Melton, *Encyclopedic Handbook of Cults in America* (New York: Garland, 1986), 194; J. Isamu Yamamoto, *The Puppet Master* (Downers Grove, Ill.: InterVarsity Press, 1977), 15-19.

[7]Newport, *Christ and the New Consciousness,* 120; Melton, *Encyclopedic Handbook of Cults in America,* 193; Yamamoto, *Puppet Master,* 16-18; Bjornstad, *The Moon Is Not the Son,* 32-33; Frederick Sontag, *Sun Myung Moon and the Unification Church* (Nashville: Abingdon, 1977), 78-79.

[8]Newport, *Christ and the New Consciousness,* 120; Bjornstad, *The Moon Is Not the Son,* 32.

[9]Melton, *Encyclopedic Handbook of Cults in America,* 193; Bromley and Shupe, *Moonies in America,* 36-37; Newport, *Christ and the New Consciousness,* 120-21; Sontag, *Sun Myung Moon,* 79-80.

[10]Newport, *Christ and the New Consciousness,* 121; Bjornstad, *The Moon Is Not the Son,* 33-34; McBeth, *Strange New Religions,* 13.

[11]Bromley and Shupe, *Moonies in America,* 41; Newport, *Christ and the New Consciousness,* 121-22; Melton, *Encyclopedic Handbook of Cults in America,* 193; Sontag, *Sun Myung Moon,* 80; Yamamoto, *Puppet Master,* 21.

[12]Bromley and Shupe, *Moonies in America,* 36-37; Ruth A. Tucker, *Another Gospel*

(Grand Rapids, Mich.: Zondervan, 1989), 248-49.

[13] Melton, *Encyclopedic Handbook of Cults in America*, 193-94; Sontag, *Sun Myung Moon*, 80; Newport, *Christ and the New Consciousness*, 121; Tucker, *Another Gospel*, 261-62.

[14] Melton, *Encyclopedic Handbook of Cults in America*, 194; Newport, *Christ and the New Consciousness*, 122.

[15] Braswell, *Understanding Sectarian Groups*, 105-6; Melton, *Encyclopedic Handbook of Cults in America*, 194-95; Bromley and Shupe, *Moonies in America*, 57-58.

[16] Melton, *Encyclopedic Handbook of Cults in America*, 194; Braswell, *Understanding Sectarian Groups*, 107.

[17] Bromley and Shupe, *Moonies in America*, 117-22; Melton, *Encyclopedic Handbook of Cults in America*, 196-97; Braswell, *Understanding Sectarian Groups*, 128-31.

[18] Melton, *Encyclopedic Handbook of Cults in America*, 194, 199. For other examples see Jai Hyon Lee, "The Activities of the Korean Central Intelligence Agency in the United States," in *Science, Sin and Scholarship*, ed. Irving L. Horowitz (Cambridge, Mass.: MIT Press, 1978), 121-37.

[19] Melton, *Encyclopedic Handbook of Cults in America*, 195; Bromley and Shupe, *Moonies in America*, 66.

[20] Mose Durst, *To Bigotry, No Sanction: Reverend Sun Myung Moon and the Unification Church* (Chicago: Regnery Gateway, 1984), 42; Tucker, *Another Gospel*, 255.

[21] Braswell, *Understanding Sectarian Groups*, 113; J. Isamu Yamamoto, "Unification Church," in *A Guide to Cults and New Religions* (Downers Grove, Ill.: InterVarsity Press, 1983), 156-57; Melton, *Encyclopedic Handbook of Cults in America*, 195; Newport, *Christ and the New Consciousness*, 122-23.

[22] Ibid., 123; Yamamoto, "Unification Church," 157-58; Braswell, *Understanding Sectarian Groups*, 113-14; Bjornstad, *The Moon Is Not the Son*, 56-57.

[23] Yamamoto, "Unification Church," 158; Newport, *Christ and the New Consciousness*, 123-24; Sontag, *Sun Myung Moon*, 115; Parsons, "Messianic Personalism," 152-54; Tucker, *Another Gospel*, 259.

[24] Newport, *Christ and the New Consciousness*, 123-24; Yamamoto, "Unification Church," 158; Tucker, *Another Gospel*, 251; Young Oon Kim, *Unification Theology* (New York: Holy Spirit Association for the Unification of World Christianity, 1980), 183.

[25] Yamamoto, "Unification Church," 158-59; Braswell, *Understanding Sectarian Groups*, 114, 118; Newport, *Christ and the New Consciousness*, 124; Bjornstad, *The Moon Is Not the Son*, 58-59.

[26] Yamamoto, "Unification Church," 158-59; Newport, *Christ and the New Consciousness*, 124; Braswell, *Understanding Sectarian Groups*, 120-21; Sontag, *Sun Myung Moon*, 115.

[27] Melton, *Encyclopedic Handbook of Cults in America*, 195; Sontag, *Sun Myung*

Moon, 99; Braswell, *Understanding Sectarian Groups,* 123; J. Isamu Yamamoto, "Sects Target New Areas, Make Subtle Changes," *Christianity Today,* October 22, 1990, p. 52.

[28]Melton, *Encyclopedic Handbook of Cults in America,* 195-96; Braswell, *Understanding Sectarian Groups,* 123-24; Tucker, *Another Gospel,* 252-53.

[29]Melton, *Encyclopedic Handbook of Cults in America,* 196.

[30]Tucker, *Another Gospel,* 256.

[31]David G. Bromley, Anson D. Shupe Jr. and J. C. Ventimiglia, "Atrocity Tales, the Unification Church and the Social Construction of Evil," *Journal of Communication* 29 (Summer 1979): 46, 48; McBeth, *Strange New Religions,* 19-21; David G. Bromley, Bruce C. Busching and Anson D. Shupe Jr., "The Unification Church and the American Family: Strain, Conflict and Control," in *The Future of New Religious Movements,* ed. David G. Bromley and Philip E. Hammond (Macon, Ga.: Mercer University Press, 1987), 307-9; "Unification Church Fails to Stop Lawsuit," *Wichita Eagle,* May 12, 1989, p. 3A; Ronald Enroth, *Youth, Brainwashing and the Extremist Cults* (Grand Rapids: Mich.: Zondervan, 1977), 101-21; Chris Elkins, *Heavenly Deception* (Wheaton, Ill.: Tyndale House, 1980); Steve Kemperman, *Lord of the Second Advent* (Ventura, Calif.: Regal, 1981).

[32]Bromley, Shupe and Ventimiglia, "Atrocity Tales," 42, 52; David G. Bromley and Anson Shupe Jr., *Strange Gods* (Boston: Beacon Press, 1981), 92-127; Eileen Barker, "Free to Choose? Some Thoughts on the Unification Church and Other Religious Movements, Part I," *Clergy Review,* October 1980, pp. 365-68; John T. Biermans, *The Odyssey of New Religious Movements* (Lewiston, N.Y.: Edwin Mellen, 1986).

[33]Newport, *Christ and the New Consciousness,* 134-35.

[34]Parsons, "Messianic Personalism," 147, 157; Thomas Robbins, Dick Anthony and Thomas Curtis, "The Last Civil Religion: Reverend Moon and the Unification Church," *Sociological Analysis* 37, no. 2 (1976): 112-15.

[35]Ibid., 112-16.

[36]Robert N. Bellah, *The Broken Covenant* (New York: Seabury Press, 1975), 142; Robbins, Anthony and Curtis, "The Last Civil Religion," 111-12.

[37]Ibid., 121.

[38]Melton, *Encyclopedic Handbook of Cults in America,* 198; Tucker, *Another Gospel,* 263.

[39]Braswell, *Understanding Sectarian Groups,* 134; Eileen Barker, "Quo Vadis? The Unification Church," in *The Future of New Religious Movements,* ed. David G. Bromley and Philip E. Hammond (Macon, Ga.: Mercer University Press, 1987), 143; Melton, *Encyclopedic Handbook of Cults in America,* 198.

[40]Yamamoto, "Sects Target New Areas," p. 52.

Chapter 22: The People's Temple

[1]Paul A. Chalfant, Robert E. Beckley and C. Eddie Palmer, *Religion in Contemporary Society* (Sherman Oaks, Calif.: Alfred Publishing, 1981), 271-72. This event

dominated the news media for a time, with cover stories in the major national magazines. See Tom Mathews et al., "The Cult of Death," *Newsweek,* December 4, 1978, pp. 38-53; "Nightmare in Jonestown," *Time,* December 4, 1978, pp. 16-21; Judith Mary Weightman, *Making Sense of the Jonestown Suicides* (New York: Edwin Mellen, 1983); Philip Kerns, *People's Temple, People's Tomb* (Plainfield, N.J.: Logos, 1979); Marshall Kilduff and Ron Jovers, *The Suicide Cult* (New York: Bantam, 1978); Kenneth Wooden, *The Children of Jonestown* (New York: McGraw-Hill, 1981); Ethan Feinsod, *Awake in a Nightmare* (New York: W. W. Norton, 1981).

[2]Ronald B. Flowers, *Religion in Strange Times: The 1960s and 1970s* (Macon, Ga.: Mercer University Press, 1984), 86; Lance Morrow, "The Lure of Doomsday," *Time,* December 4, 1978, p. 30.

[3]Ibid., 30; Mathews et al., "The Cult of Death," 40.

[4]J. Gordon Melton, *Encyclopedic Handbook of Cults in America* (New York: Garland, 1986), 244-45.

[5]Rodney Stark and William S. Bainbridge, *The Future of Religion* (Berkeley: University of California Press, 1985), 186-87.

[6]James T. Richardson, "People's Temple and Jonestown: A Corrective Comparison and Critique," *Journal for the Scientific Study of Religion* 19, no. 3 (1980): 241-42; Chalfant, Beckley and Palmer, *Religion in Contemporary Society,* 276.

[7]Richardson, "People's Temple and Jonestown," 242-43. Most of the defectors from the People's Temple were white and fairly well educated. These were the people the media interviewed. Thus, the membership of the People's Temple appeared to be more white than it really was.

[8]Richardson, "People's Temple and Jonestown," 243. See also Joseph R. Washington Jr., *Black Sects and Cults* (Garden City, N.Y.: Doubleday, 1973); Arthur Fauset, *Black Gods of the Metropolis* (Philadelphia: University of Pennsylvania Press, 1971). There were both parallels and contrasts between Jones's movement and that of Father Divine. The most obvious contrast is that in Jones's case a predominantly black group was being led by a white man. For the comparison see Steve Rose, *Jesus and Jim Jones* (New York: Pilgrim, 1979), 81-85.

[9]Chalfant, Beckley and Palmer, *Religion in Contemporary Society,* 276-77; Richardson, "People's Temple and Jonestown," 246-49; John R. Hall, "The Apocalypse at Jonestown," in *In Gods We Trust,* ed. Thomas Robbins and Dick Anthony (New Brunswick, N.J.: Transaction Books, 1981), 181-83.

[10]Charles Krause, Stern Lawrence and Richard Harwood, *Guyana Massacre* (New York: Berkeley Books, 1978), 33-34; Barbara Hargrove, "Informing the Public: Social Scientists and Reactions to Jonestown," paper offered at the Annual Meetings of the Society for the Scientific Study of Religion, San Antonio, Texas, 1979; Chalfant, Beckley and Palmer, *Religion in Contemporary Society,* 276, 278.

[11]"Messiah from the Midwest," *Time,* December 4, 1978, p. 22; Peter Axthelm et al., "The Emperor Jones," *Newsweek,* December 4, 1978, p. 54; Rose, *Jesus and Jim Jones,* 54; Tim Reiterman, *Raven: The Untold Story of Rev. James Jones and*

His People (New York: E. P. Dutton, 1982), 9-21.

[12]Ibid., 22-24; "Messiah from the Midwest," 22; Axthelm et al., "Emperor Jones," 54.

[13]Rose, *Jesus and Jim Jones,* 55; Chalfant, Beckley and Palmer, *Religion in Contemporary Society,* 272; Axthelm et al., "Emperor Jones," 54-55; "Messiah from the Midwest," 22.

[14]Chalfant, Beckley and Palmer, *Religion in Contemporary Society,* 272-73; Reiterman, *Raven,* 43-66; "Messiah from the Midwest," 22; Axthelm et al., "Emperor Jones," 55-56.

[15]Rose, *Jesus and Jim Jones,* 56; Chalfant, Beckley and Palmer, *Religion in Contemporary Society,* 272-73; "Messiah from the Midwest," 22; Axthelm et al., "Emperor Jones," 56, 59.

[16]David G. Bromley and Anson Shupe Jr., *Strange Gods* (Boston: Beacon Press, 1981), 53; Chalfant, Beckley and Palmer, *Religion in Contemporary Society,* 273; Reiterman, *Raven,* 163-71; "Messiah from the Midwest," 22-23; Axthelm et al., "Emperor Jones," 60.

[17]Reiterman, *Raven,* 171-80; Chalfant, Beckley and Palmer, *Religion in Contemporary Society,* 273; "Messiah from the Midwest," 27; Axthelm et al., "Emperor Jones," 50, 60.

[18]Chalfant, Beckley and Palmer, *Religion in Contemporary Society,* 274; Axthelm et al., "Emperor Jones," 60; James Reston Jr., *Our Father Who Art in Hell* (New York: Times Books, 1981), 72-73, 104-9, 205-6.

[19]Bromley and Shupe, *Strange Gods,* 62-63; Chalfant, Beckley and Palmer, *Religion in Contemporary Society,* 274.

[20]Richard Steele, "Life in Jonestown," *Newsweek,* December 4, 1978, pp. 62-66; Chalfant, Beckley and Palmer, *Religion in Contemporary Society,* 274-75; Rose, *Jesus and Jim Jones,* 168-75; Flo Conway and Jim Siegelman, *Snapping* (New York: Delta, 1978), 245-46.

[21]Reiterman, *Raven,* 481ff.; Reston, *Our Father Who Art in Hell,* 276ff.; Chalfant, Beckley and Palmer, *Religion in Contemporary Society,* 275-76; Mathews et al., "The Cult of Death," 38-53; "Nightmare in Jonestown," 16-21.

[22]Hall, "Apocalypse at Jonestown," 173; Rose, *Jesus and Jim Jones,* 93-94.

[23]Hall, "Apocalypse at Jonestown," 174-75.

[24]Ibid., 175-76.

[25]Richardson, "People's Temple and Jonestown," 248; Hall, "Apocalypse at Jonestown," 181.

[26]Bromley and Shupe, *Strange Gods,* 54; Hall, "Apocalypse at Jonestown," 181-82; Robert Lindsey, "Jim Jones—From Poverty to Power of Life and Death," *The New York Times,* November 26, 1978, p. 20; Richardson, "People's Temple and Jonestown," 248-49.

[27]Hall, "Apocalypse at Jonestown," 182.

[28]Bromley and Shupe, *Strange Gods,* 54-55; Richardson, "People's Temple and Jonestown," 249.

29Ibid. See also Reston, "Our Father Who Art in Hell," 270-71.

30Hall, "Apocalypse at Jonestown," 186-89.

31Ibid.

32Edward E. Plowman, "Jonestown: Question Marks Abound One Year After Tragedy," *Christianity Today,* November 16, 1979, p. 45; J. Gordon Melton, *The Encyclopedia of American Religions,* 2 vols. (Wilmington, N.C.: McGrath, 1978), 2:225.

Chapter 23: Aberrational Groups in the Jesus Movement

1Paul H. Chalfant, Robert E. Beckley and C. Eddie Palmer, *Religion in Contemporary Society* (Sherman Oaks, Calif.: Alfred Publishing, 1981), 267.

2Jack Balswick, "The Jesus People Movement: A Generational Interpretation," *Journal of Social Issues* 30, no. 3 (1974): 23; Ronald Enroth, Edward E. Ericson Jr. and C. Breckenridge Peters, *The Jesus People* (Grand Rapids, Mich.: Eerdmans, 1972), 9; "The New Rebel Cry: Jesus Is Coming!" *Time,* June 21, 1971, p. 56.

3Enroth, Ericson and Peters, *Jesus People,* 67-157; Chalfant, Beckley and Palmer, *Religion in Contemporary Society,* 267.

4Balswick, "Jesus People Movement," 23-27; James T. Richardson and Rex Davis, "Experiential Fundamentalism: Revisions of Orthodoxy and the Jesus Movement," *Journal of the American Academy of Religion* 5 (1983): 398-99.

5Ronald Enroth, "The Christian Counterculture," in *Christianity in America,* ed. Mark A. Noll et al. (Grand Rapids, Mich.: Eerdmans, 1983), 469-70; Steve Rabey, "Remembering the Jesus Movement," *Christianity Today,* November 22, 1985, p. 53. Sources differ in respect to the number of Jesus people. Perhaps the range from 200,000 to 400,000 in the United States would be more accurate. See Enroth, Ericson and Peters, *Jesus People,* 15; Balswick, "Jesus People Movement," 24.

6Enroth, "Christian Counterculture," 469; Enroth, Ericson and Peters, *Jesus People,* 41-66; Richardson and Davis, "Experiential Fundamentalism," 404ff.; Les Parrott and Robin D. Perrin, "The New Denominations," *Christianity Today,* March 11, 1991, pp. 29-31.

7Rabey, "Remembering the Jesus Movement," 53-54; Enroth, "Christian Counterculture," 469-70; Richardson and Davis, "Experiential Fundamentalism," 397; Parrott and Perrin, "New Denominations," 29-31.

8Richard Quebedeaux, *The Young Evangelicals* (New York: Harper & Row, 1974), 40, 94-97; Enroth, "Christian Counterculture," 470.

9Robert Ellwood, *One Way* (Englewood Cliffs, N.J.: Prentice Hall, 1973), 18-20.

10Richardson and Davis, "Experiential Fundamentalism," 398; Christopher R. Stones, "The Jesus People: Fundamentalism and Changes in Factors Associated with Conservatism," *Journal for the Scientific Study of Religion* 17, no. 2 (1978): 155-58.

11Enroth, Ericson and Peters, *Jesus People,* 161-64. See also Michael McFadden, *The Jesus Revolution* (New York: Harrow, 1972), 7-10.

¹²Ellwood, *One Way*, 86-93; Enroth, Ericson and Peters, *Jesus People*, 179-87; "The New Rebel Cry," 59; Richardson and Davis, "Experiential Fundamentalism," 399-400.

¹³Ibid., 400-401.

¹⁴Enroth, Ericson and Peters, *Jesus People*, 164-65; Richardson and Davis, "Experiential Fundamentalism," 402. See also Robert Lynn Adams and Robert Jon Fox, "Mainlining Jesus: The New Trip," *Society* 9, no. 4 (1972): 53-54; McFadden, *The Jesus Revolution*, 137-52.

¹⁵Enroth, Ericson and Peters, *Jesus People*, 164-65.

¹⁶Ibid., 168-69; Adams and Fox, "Mainlining Jesus," 54.

¹⁷Enroth, Ericson and Peters, *Jesus People*, 168-76; Adams and Fox, "Mainlining Jesus," 55-56.

¹⁸Richardson and Davis, "Experiential Fundamentalism," 402; Enroth, Ericson and Davis, *Jesus People*, 195-202; "The New Rebel Cry," 59. For a view of the Jesus movement as a segment of the broader neo-Pentecostal movement (charismatic renewal) see James T. Richardson and M. T. V. Reidy, "Form and Fluidity in Two Contemporary Glossolalic Movements," *Annual Review of the Social Sciences*, 1980, pp. 183-220.

¹⁹Enroth, Ericson and Peters, *Jesus People*, 223-34.

²⁰J. Gordon Melton, *Encyclopedic Handbook of Cults in America* (New York: Garland, 1986), 125-127; Enroth, Ericson and Peters, *Jesus People*, 54-65; Ellwood, *One Way*, 83-85; Ronald Enroth, *Youth, Brainwashing and the Extremist Cults* (Grand Rapids: Mich.: Zondervan, 1977), 56-80; "Cult Leader Found, Nabbed," *Wichita Eagle*, July 6, 1991, p. 3A.

²¹Melton, *Encyclopedic Handbook of Cults in America*, 154; Daniel Cohen, *The New Believers* (New York: Ballantine, 1975), 3.

²²Leon McBeth, *Strange New Religions* (Nashville: Broadman, 1977), 48, 52; Enroth, Ericson and Peters, *Jesus People*, 33; Rex Davis and James T. Richardson, "The Organization and Functioning of the Children of God," *Sociological Analysis* 37, no. 4 (1976): 323.

²³Roy Wallis, "Observations on the Children of God," *Sociological Review* 24, no. 4 (1976): 809-10; Enroth, Ericson and Peters, *Jesus People*, 22-23; McBeth, *Strange New Religions*, 48-49; Roy Wallis, *Salvation and Protest* (New York: St. Martin's, 1979), 55-56.

²⁴Wallis, "Observations on the Children of God," 810-11; David G. Bromley and Anson Shupe Jr., *Strange Gods* (Boston: Beacon Press, 1981), 26; Enroth, Ericson and Peters, *Jesus People*, 23; William J. Whalen, *Strange Gods* (Huntington, Ind.: Our Sunday Visitor, 1981), 91.

²⁵Melton, *Encyclopedic Handbook of Cults in America*, 154-55; Wallis, "Observations on the Children of God," 811-12; McFadden, *Jesus Revolution*, 92-94.

²⁶Melton, *Encyclopedic Handbook of Cults in America*, 155; Davis and Richardson, "Organization and Functioning of the Children of God," 323-24.

²⁷Wallis, "Observations on the Children of God," 812; Melton, *Encyclopedic Hand-*

book of Cults in America, 155; Bromley and Shupe, *Strange Gods,* 27; McFadden, *Jesus Revolution,* 94-95; Wallis, *Salvation and Protest,* 56-57.

[28] Enroth, Ericson and Peters, *Jesus People,* 27-31; Wallis, "Observations on the Children of God," 812-13; McBeth, *Strange New Religions,* 49-50; Fred Bruning et al., "Europe's Rising Cults," *Newsweek,* May 7, 1979, pp. 100-102.

[29] Wallis, "Observations on the Children of God," 813-14; Melton, *Encyclopedic Handbook of Cults in America,* 155; Wallis, *Salvation and Protest,* 58.

[30] Wallis, "Observations on the Children of God," 814; Melton, *Encyclopedic Handbook of Cults in America,* 155; McBeth, *Strange New Religions,* 51; Davis and Richardson, "Organization and Functioning of the Children of God," 325-26.

[31] Ruth A. Tucker, *Another Gospel* (Grand Rapids, Mich.: Zondervan, 1989), 233-34.

[32] Richardson and Davis, "Experiential Fundamentalism," 407; Melton, *Encyclopedic Handbook of Cults in America,* 156; McBeth, *Strange New Religions,* 60; Wallis, *Salvation and Protest,* 78-79; Tucker, *Another Gospel,* 237-38.

[33] Melton, *Encyclopedic Handbook of Cults in America,* 156; Joseph Hopkins, "The Children of God: Fewer and Far Out," *Christianity Today,* January 25, 1980, pp. 40-41.

[34] Wallis, "Observations on the Children of God," 823-24; Melton, *Encyclopedic Handbook of Cults in America,* 156-57. See also Davis and Richardson, "Organization and Functioning of the Children of God," 327ff.

[35] Melton, *Encyclopedic Handbook of Cults in America,* 156; McBeth, *Strange New Religions,* 53, 60; Hopkins, "The Children of God," 40-41; Tucker, *Another Gospel,* 236.

[36] McBeth, *Strange New Religions,* 52-55; Whalen, *Strange Gods,* 92-94.

[37] Melton, *Encyclopedic Handbook of Cults in America,* 156; Wallis, "Observations on the Children of God," 818-19; Bromley and Shupe, *Strange Gods,* 29-31; Tucker, *Another Gospel,* 240-41.

[38] Melton, *Encyclopedic Handbook of Cults in America,* 156; Wallis, "Observations on the Children of God," 818-19; Hopkins, "The Children of God," 41.

[39] Wallis, "Observations on the Children of God," 820-22; McBeth, *Strange New Religions,* 55-59.

[40] Joseph Hopkins, "Children of God Cult Records Higher Numbers," *Christianity Today,* November 26, 1982, pp. 40-41; McBeth, *Strange New Religions,* 61; Enroth, Ericson and Peters, *Jesus People,* 54; Dalva Lynch, "Inside the Heavenly Elite: The Children of God Today," *Christian Research Journal* 13, no. 1 (1990): 16.

[41] Melton, *Encyclopedic Handbook of Cults in America,* 204.

[42] J. Gordon Melton, *The Encyclopedia of American Religions,* 2 vols. (Wilmington, N.C.: McGrath, 1978), 2:449; Enroth, Ericson and Peters, *Jesus People,* 152-53; Richardson and Davis, "Experiential Fundamentalism," 404; "The New Rebel Cry," 62.

[43] Enroth, Ericson and Peters, *Jesus People,* 152-53; Whalen, *Strange Gods,* 99;

Kenneth Boa, *Cults, World Religions and You* (Wheaton, Ill.: Victor Books, 1977), 197; Melton, *Encyclopedia of American Religions,* 2:449.

44J. L. Williams, *Victor Paul Wierwille and The Way International* (Chicago: Moody Press, 1979), 17-19; Melton, *Encyclopedic Handbook of Cults in America,* 205; George W. Braswell Jr., *Understanding Sectarian Groups in America* (Nashville: Broadman, 1986), 142-43; Whalen, *Strange Gods,* 97-98.

45Braswell, *Understanding Sectarian Groups,* 143-44; Whalen, *Strange Gods,* 97-98; Melton, *Encyclopedic Handbook of Cults in America,* 205.

46Braswell, *Understanding Sectarian Groups,* 144; Williams, *Victor Paul Wierwille,* 23-24; Boa, *Cults, World Religions and You,* 197.

47Braswell, *Understanding Sectarian Groups,* 144-45; Melton, *Encyclopedic Handbook of Cults in America,* 206; Whalen, *Strange Gods,* 99; Williams, *Victor Paul Wierwille,* 25.

48Ibid., 38-42; Melton, *Encyclopedic Handbook of Cults in America,* 208; Braswell, *Understanding Sectarian Groups,* 163-65.

49Ibid., 146; Melton, *Encyclopedic Handbook of Cults in America,* 208; Williams, *Victor Paul Wierwille,* 31-34.

50Joseph M. Hopkins, "The Way Founder Wierwille Announces Plan to Retire," *Christianity Today,* March 13, 1981, p. 57; Melton, *Encyclopedic Handbook of Cults in America,* 208-9; Braswell, *Understanding Sectarian Groups,* 147.

51Melton, *Encyclopedic Handbook of Cults in America,* 209.

52Keith Tolbert, "Infighting Trims Branches of The Way International," *Christianity Today,* February 19, 1988, p. 44; John P. Juedes, "The Way Tree Is Splintering," *Christian Research Journal* 11, no. 2 (1988): 9-13.

53Enroth, Ericson and Peters, *Jesus People,* 152; Boa, *Cults, World Religions and You,* 200; Melton, *Encyclopedic Handbook of Cults in America,* 206.

54Braswell, *Understanding Sectarian Groups,* 147; Williams, *Victor Paul Wierwille,* 28-30; Boa, *Cults, World Religions and You,* 199.

55Williams, *Victor Paul Wierwille,* 49-73; Melton, *Encyclopedic Handbook of Cults in America,* 207; Braswell, *Understanding Sectarian Groups,* 153-55; Joel A. MacCollam, "The Way," in *A Guide to Cults and New Religions* (Downers Grove, Ill.: InterVarsity Press, 1983), 180-81; Tucker, *Another Gospel,* 224.

56Melton, *Encyclopedic Handbook of Cults in America,* 207; Whalen, *Strange Gods,* 99; Braswell, *Understanding Sectarian Groups,* 151.

57Ibid., 158-59; MacCollam, "The Way," 186-87.

58Tucker, *Another Gospel,* 221.

Chapter 24: Epilogue

1Colin Chapman, "The Riddle of Religions," *Christianity Today,* May 14, 1990, pp. 16-22; John Naisbitt and Patricia Aburdene, *Megatrends 2000* (New York: Morrow, 1990), 276; Terry Muck, "The Mosque Next Door," *Christianity Today,* February 19, 1988, pp. 15-16; Denise Lardner Carmody and John Tully Carmody, *Exploring American Religion* (Mountain View, Calif.: Mayfield, 1990), 351.

[2]Naisbitt and Aburdene, *Megatrends 2000,* 11, 14-15.

[3]Richard Erdoes, *A.D. 1000: Living on the Brink of Apocalypse* (New York: Harper & Row, 1988), viii-ix; Naisbitt and Aburdene, *Megatrends 2000,* 285-86; Ron Rhodes, "Millennial Madness," *Christian Research Journal* 13, no. 1 (1990): 39.

[4]Curt Suplee, "Apocalypse Now: The Coming Doom Boom," *The Washington Post,* December 17, 1989, pp. 131-32; Erdoes, *A.D. 1000,* x; Rhodes, "Millennial Madness," 39.

[5]Erdoes, *A.D. 1000,* x.

Selected Bibliography

This brief bibliography is not a comprehensive list of the sources cited in this study. Instead, here I list books and articles that will be helpful to the individual interested in further reading on the occult, the cults and the historical context in which they developed. For more detailed information regarding the sources utilized, see the appropriate endnotes.

Adler, Margot. *Drawing Down the Moon*. Boston: Beacon Press, 1979.

Ahlstrom, Sydney E. "The Traumatic Years: American Religion and Culture in the '60s and '70s." *Theology Today* 36, no. 4 (1980): 504-22.

Albanese, Catherine. *America: Religions and Religion*. Belmont, Calif.: Wadsworth, 1981.

_____ . *Corresponding Motion: Transcendental Religion and the New America*. Philadelphia: Temple University Press, 1977.

Allan, John. *Shopping for a God*. Leicester, U.K.: Inter-Varsity Press, 1986.

Andrews, Edward D. *The People Called Shakers*. New York: Dover, 1963.

Arrington, Leonard, and Davis Bitton. *The Mormon Experience*. New York: Knopf, 1979.

Baba, Meher. *The Everything and the Nothing*. Berkeley: Beguine Library, 1963.

Bailey, Alice A. *A Treatise on White Magic*. New York: Lucis, 1951.

Bainbridge, William S. *Satan's Power*. Berkeley: University of California Press, 1978.

Barker, Eileen, ed. *New Religious Movements: A Perspective for Understanding Society*. New York: Edwin Mellen Press, 1982.

_____ . *Of Gods and Men: New Religious Movements in the West*. Macon, Ga.: Mercer University Press, 1983.

Basham, A. L. *The Wonder That Was India*. London: Segwick and Jackson, 1954.

Bednarowski, Mary F. *American Religion: A Cultural Perspective*. Englewood Cliffs, N.J.: Prentice Hall, 1984.

Bell, Daniel. "Religion in the Sixties." *Social Research* 38, no. 3 (1971): 447-97.

Bellah, Robert N., et al. *Habits of the Heart.* New York: Harper & Row, 1985.

Bernstein, Leonard. "The Ideas of John Humphrey Noyes, Perfectionist." *American Quarterly* 5 (March 1953): 157-65.

Bjornstad, James. *The Moon Is Not the Son.* Minneapolis: Bethany Fellowship, 1976.

―――. *Stars, Signs, and Salvation in the Age of Aquarius.* Minneapolis: Bethany Fellowship, 1971.

―――. *Twentieth Century Prophecy.* Minneapolis: Bethany Fellowship, 1969.

Boa, Kenneth. *Cults, World Religions and You.* Wheaton, Ill.: Victor Books, 1977.

Braden, Charles S. *Christian Science Today.* London: Allen and Unwin, 1959.

―――. *Spirits in Rebellion: The Rise and Development of New Thought.* Dallas: Southern Methodist University Press, 1963.

―――. *These Also Believe.* New York: Macmillan, 1957.

Braswell, George W. Jr. *Understanding Sectarian Groups in America.* Nashville: Broadman, 1986.

Bromley, David G., and Philip E. Hammond, eds. *The Future of New Religious Movements.* Macon, Ga.: Mercer University Press, 1987.

Bromley, David G., and Anson D. Shupe Jr. *Moonies in America.* Beverly Hills, Calif.: Sage, 1979.

―――. *Strange Gods.* Boston: Beacon Press, 1981.

Brown, Harold O. J. *Heresies.* Garden City, N.Y.: Doubleday, 1984.

Bussell, Harold L. *Unholy Devotion.* Grand Rapids, Mich.: Zondervan, 1983.

Butler, Jon. "Magic, Astrology and the Early American Religious Heritage, 1600-1700." *American Historical Review* 84, no. 2 (1979): 317-46.

Carroll, Jackson W., Douglas W. Johnson and Martin E. Marty. *Religion in America: 1950 to the Present.* New York: Harper & Row, 1979.

Cauthen, Kenneth. *The Impact of American Religious Liberalism.* New York: Harper & Row, 1962.

Cavendish, Richard. *The Black Arts.* New York: G. P. Putnam's, 1967.

―――. *The Powers of Evil.* New York: G. P. Putnam's, 1975.

Clark, Elmer T. *The Small Sects in America.* Nashville: Abingdon, 1965.

Clecak, Peter. *America's Quest for the Ideal Self.* New York: Oxford University Press, 1983.

Cohen, Daniel. *The New Believers.* New York: Ballantine, 1975.

Coleman, John, and Gregory Baum, eds. *New Religious Movements.* New York: Seabury Press, 1983.

Cooper, John C. *Religion in the Age of Aquarius.* Philadelphia: Westminster Press, 1971.

Cox, Harvey. *Turning East.* New York: Simon & Schuster, 1977.

Cross, Whitney R. *The Burned-Over District.* New York: Harper & Row, 1965.

Crow, W. B. *A History of Magic, Witchcraft and Occultism.* North Hollywood, Calif.: Wilshire Book, 1968.

Daner, F. *The American Children of Krisna.* New York: Holt, Rinehart and Winston, 1976.

Davis, Rex, and James T. Richardson. "The Organization and Functioning of the Children of God." *Sociological Analysis* 37, no. 4 (1976): 321-39.

Dixon, Jeane. *The Call to Glory.* New York: Bantam, 1971.

Douglas, Mary, and Steven M. Tipton, eds. *Religion and America.* Boston: Beacon Press, 1982.

Ebon, Martin, ed. *Witchcraft Today.* New York: New American Library, 1971.

Eliade, Mircea. *Occultism, Witchcraft and Cultural Fashions.* Chicago: University of Chicago Press, 1976.

Ellwood, Robert S. *Alternative Altars: Unconventional and Eastern Spirituality in America.* Chicago: University of Chicago Press, 1979.

_____ . *The Eagle and the Rising Sun.* Philadelphia: Westminster Press, 1974.

_____ . *One Way: The Jesus Movement and Its Meaning.* Englewood Cliffs, N.J.: Prentice Hall, 1973.

Ellwood, Robert S., and Harry B. Partin. *Religious and Spiritual Groups in Modern America.* 2nd ed. Englewood Cliffs, N.J.: Prentice Hall, 1988.

Enroth, Ronald. *The Lure of the Cults.* Downers Grove, Ill.: InterVarsity Press, 1987.

_____ . *Youth, Brainwashing and the Extremist Cults.* Grand Rapids, Mich.: Zondervan, 1977.

Enroth, Ronald, et al. *A Guide to Cults and New Religions.* Downers Grove, Ill.: InterVarsity Press, 1983.

Enroth, Ronald, Edward E. Ericson Jr. and C. Breckinridge Peters. *The Jesus People.* Grand Rapids, Mich.: Eerdmans, 1972.

Fauset, Arthur. *Black Gods of the Metropolis.* Philadelphia: University of Pennsylvania Press, 1971.

Ferguson, Marilyn. *The Aquarian Conspiracy.* Los Angeles: J. P. Tarcher, 1980.

Fields, Rick. *How the Swans Came to the Lake: A Narrative History of Buddhism in America.* Boulder, Colo.: Shambhala, 1981.

Flowers, Ronald B. *Religion in Strange Times: The 1960s and 1970s.* Macon, Ga.: Mercer University Press, 1984.

Freedland, Nat. *The Occult Explosion.* New York: G. P. Putnam's, 1972.

Gardner, Gerald B. *Witchcraft Today.* New York: Citadel, 1955.

Gelberg, Steven, ed. *Hare Krishna, Hare Krishna.* New York: Grove, 1983.

Glock, Charles, and Robert Bellah. *The New Religious Consciousness.* Berkeley: University of California Press, 1976.

Gordon, James S. *The Golden Guru.* Lexington, Mass.: Stephen Green, 1987.

Gottschalk, Stephen. *The Emergence of Christian Science in American Religious Life.* Berkeley: University of California Press, 1973.

Groothuis, Douglas. *Confronting the New Age.* Downers Grove, Ill.: InterVarsity Press, 1988.

_____ . *Unmasking the New Age.* Downers Grove, Ill.: InterVarsity Press, 1986.

Gruss, Edmund C. *The Ouija Board*. Chicago: Moody Press, 1975.

Gurdjieff, George I. *All and Everything*. New York: Harcourt, Brace and World, 1950.

Hansen, Klaus J. *Mormonism and the American Experience*. Chicago: University of Chicago Press, 1981.

Hargrove, Barbara. "New Religious Movements and the End of the Age." *The Iliff Review* (Spring 1982): 41-52.

Hashimoto, Hideo, and William McPherson. "The Rise and Decline of Sokagakkai in Japan and the United States." *Review of Religious Research* 17, no. 2 (1976): 82-92.

Hexham, Irving, and Karla Poewe. *Understanding Cults and New Religions*. Grand Rapids, Mich.: Eerdmans, 1986.

Hill, Douglas, and Pat Williams. *The Supernatural*. New York: New American Library, 1967.

Hoover, Thomas. *The Zen Experience*. New York: New American Library, 1980.

Hopkins, Joseph. *The Armstrong Empire*. Grand Rapids, Mich.: Eerdmans, 1974.

Hoyt, Karen, ed. *The New Age Rage*. Old Tappan, N.J.: Revell, 1987.

Hubbard, L. Ron. *Dianetics*. Los Angeles: Bridge, 1950.

Humphreys, Christmas. *Zen Buddhism*. New York: Macmillan, 1962.

Jackson, Carl T. *The Oriental Religions and American Thought*. Westport, Conn.: Greenwood Press, 1981.

Jerome, Lawrence. *Astrology Disproved*. Buffalo, N.Y.: Prometheus, 1977.

Judah, J. Stillson. *Hare Krishna and the Counter-culture*. New York: John Wiley, 1974.

———. *The History and Philosophy of the Metaphysical Movements in America*. Philadelphia: Westminster Press, 1957.

Kanter, Rosabeth M. *Commitment and Community: Communes and Utopias in Sociological Perspective*. Cambridge, Mass.: Harvard University Press, 1972.

Kelley, Dean M. *Why Conservative Churches Are Growing*. New York: Harper & Row, 1972.

Kephart, William M. *Extraordinary Groups*. 2nd ed. New York: St. Martin's, 1982.

Kerns, Philip. *People's Temple, People's Tomb*. Plainfield, N.J.: Logos, 1979.

Kerr, Howard. *Mediums and Spirit Rappers and Roaring Radicals*. Urbana: University of Illinois Press, 1972.

Kerr, Howard, and Charles L. Crow, eds. *The Occult in America*. Urbana: University of Illinois Press, 1983.

Kerr, John S. *The Mystery and Magic of the Occult*. Philadelphia: Fortress, 1971.

Lambert, Malcolm. *Medieval Heresy*. New York: Holmes and Meier, 1977.

Land, Gary, ed. *Adventism in America*. Grand Rapids, Mich.: Eerdmans, 1986.

Lasch, Christopher. *The Culture of Narcissism*. New York: Norton, 1979.

LaVey, Anton. *The Satanic Bible*. New York: Avon, 1969.

Levack, Brian P. *The Witch-Hunt in Early Modern Europe*. New York: Longman, 1987.

Leventhal, Herbert. *In the Shadow of the Enlightenment.* New York: New York University Press, 1976.

Lewis, Gordon R. *Transcendental Meditation.* Glendale, Calif.: Gospel Light, 1975.

Lincoln, C. Eric. *The Black Muslims in America.* Rev. ed. Boston: Beacon Press, 1973.

Lippy, Charles H. *The Christadelphians in North America.* Lewiston, N.Y.: Edwin Mellen, 1989.

Lyons, Arthur. *The Second Coming: Satanism in America.* New York: Award Books, 1970.

McBeth, Leon. *Strange New Religions.* Nashville: Broadman, 1977.

McGregor, J. F., and B. Reay, eds. *Radical Religion in the English Revolution.* New York: Oxford University Press, 1984.

McLoughlin, William G. *Revivals, Awakenings and Reform.* Chicago: University of Chicago Press, 1978.

Mair, Lucy. *Witchcraft.* New York: McGraw-Hill, 1969.

Malcolm X. *The Autobiography of Malcolm X.* New York: Grove, 1965.

Mamiya, Lawrence H. "From Black Muslim to Bilalian." *Journal for the Scientific Study of Religion* 21, no. 1 (1982): 138-52.

Martin, Luther H. *Hellenistic Religions.* New York: Oxford University Press, 1987.

Martin, Walter. *The Kingdom of the Cults.* Minneapolis: Bethany Fellowship, 1965.

_____ . *The New Cults.* Santa Ana, Calif.: Vision House, 1980.

Marty, Martin E. *A Nation of Behavers.* Chicago: University of Chicago Press, 1976.

Mathews, Tom, et al. "The Cult of Death." *Newsweek,* December 4, 1978, pp. 38-53.

Melton, J. Gordon. *The American Encyclopedia of Religions.* 2 vols. Wilmington, N.C.: McGrath, 1978.

_____ . *Encyclopedic Handbook of Cults in America.* New York: Garland, 1986.

Melton, J. Gordon, and Robert L. Moore. *The Cult Experience: Responding to the New Religious Pluralism.* New York: Pilgrim, 1982.

Miller, Elliot. *A Crash Course on the New Age Movement.* Grand Rapids, Mich.: Baker Book House, 1989.

Miller, William M. *The Baha'i Faith.* South Pasadena, Calif.: William Carey Library, 1974.

Montgomery, John W. *Principalities and Powers.* Minneapolis: Bethany Fellowship, 1973.

Moore, R. Laurence. *In Search of White Crows.* New York: Oxford University Press, 1977.

_____ . *Religious Outsiders and the Making of Americans.* New York: Oxford University Press, 1986.

Mosatche, Harriet. *Searching.* New York: Stravon Educational Press, 1983.

Needleman, Jacob. *The New Religions.* New York: E. P. Dutton, 1977.

Needleman, Jacob, and George Baker, eds. *Understanding the New Religions:* New York: Seabury Press, 1978.

Newport, John. *Christ and the New Consciousness.* Nashville: Broadman, 1978.

Notestein, Wallace. *A History of Witchcraft in England.* New York: Thomas Y. Crowell, 1968.

O'Dea, Thomas F. *The Mormons.* Chicago: University of Chicago Press, 1957.

Pelletier, Kenneth R. *Holistic Medicine.* New York: Dell, 1979.

Petersen, William J. *Those Curious New Cults in the 80s.* New Canaan, Conn.: Keats, 1982.

Pike, James A. *The Other Side.* Garden City, N.Y.: Doubleday, 1968.

Purdom, C. B. *The God-Man.* Crescent Beach, S.C.: Sheiriar, 1964.

Raschke, Carl A. "The Human Potential Movement." *Theology Today* 33, no. 3 (1976): 253-62.

―――. *The Interruption of Eternity: Modern Gnosticism and the Origins of the New Religious Consciousness.* Chicago: Nelson-Hall, 1980.

Reimers, David M. *Still the Golden Door: The Third World Comes to America.* New York: Columbia University Press, 1985.

Reisser, Paul C., Teri K. Reisser and John Weldon. *The Holistic Healers.* Downers Grove, Ill.: InterVarsity Press, 1983.

―――. *New Age Medicine.* Downers Grove, Ill.: InterVarsity Press, 1987.

Reiterman, Tim. *Raven: The Untold Story of the Rev. Jim Jones and His People.* New York: E. P. Dutton, 1982.

Richardson, James T. "People's Temple and Jonestown: A Corrective Comparison and Critique." *Journal for the Scientific Study of Religion* 19, no. 3 (1980): 239-55.

Robbins, Thomas, and Dick Anthony, eds. *In Gods We Trust.* New Brunswick, N.J.: Transaction Books, 1981.

Roof, Wade Clark, and William McKinney. *American Mainline Religion.* New Brunswick, N.J.: Rutgers University Press, 1987.

Roszak, Theodore. *The Making of a Counter Culture.* Garden City, N.Y.: Doubleday, 1969.

Russell, Jeffrey B. *A History of Witchcraft: Sorcerers, Heretics and Pagans.* London: Thames and Hudson, 1980.

―――. *Witchcraft in the Middle Ages.* Ithaca, N.Y.: Cornell University Press, 1972.

Sandeen, Ernest R. "John Humphrey Noyes as the New Adam." *Church History* 40, no. 1 (1971): 82-90.

Schur, Edwin. *The Awareness Trap.* New York: McGraw-Hill, 1976.

Shumaker, Wayne. *The Occult Sciences in the Renaissance.* Berkeley: University of California Press, 1972.

Sire, James W. *Scripture Twisting.* Downers Grove, Ill.: InterVarsity Press, 1980.

Sontag, Frederick. *Sun Myung Moon and the Unification Church.* Nashville: Abingdon, 1977.

Spangler, David. *Emergence: The Rebirth of the Sacred.* New York: Dell, 1984.

Speeth, Kathleen, and Ira Friedlander. *Gurdjieff: Seeker of Truth.* New York: Harper & Row, 1980.

Stark, Rodney, ed. *Religious Movements: Genesis, Exodus and Numbers.* New York: Paragon House, 1985.

Stark, Rodney, and William S. Bainbridge. *The Future of Religion.* Berkeley: University of California Press, 1985.

Suzuki, Daisetz. *An Introduction to Zen Buddhism.* New York: Macmillan, 1966.

Thomas, Keith. *Religion and the Decline of Magic.* New York: Scribner's, 1971.

Tipton, Steven M. *Getting Saved from the Sixties.* Berkeley: University of California Press, 1982.

Tiryakian, Edward A., ed. *On the Margin of the Visible.* New York: John Wiley, 1974.

Trevor-Roper, H. R. *The European Witch-Craze of the Sixteenth and Seventeenth Centuries and Other Essays.* New York: Harper & Row, 1956.

Troeltsch, Ernst. *The Social Teaching of the Christian Churches.* 2 vols. New York: Harper & Row, 1960.

Truzzi, Marcello. "The Occult Revival as Popular Culture: Some Random Observations on the Old and the Nouveau Witch." *The Sociological Quarterly* 13 (Winter 1972): 16-36.

Tucker, Ruth A. *Another Gospel.* Grand Rapids, Mich.: Zondervan, 1989.

Tyler, Alice Felt. *Freedom's Ferment.* New York: Harper & Row, 1944.

Wallis, Roy. "Observations on the Children of God." *Sociological Review* 24, no. 4 (1976): 807-29.

————. *The Rebirth of the Gods: Reflections on the New Religions in the West.* Belfast: University of Belfast Press, 1978.

————. *The Road to Total Freedom: A Sociological Analysis of Scientology.* New York: Columbia University Press, 1977.

Washington, Joseph R. *Black Sects and Cults.* Garden City, N.Y.: Doubleday, 1973.

Webb, James. *The Occult Underground.* LaSalle, Ill.: Open Court, 1974.

Weightman, Judith May. *Making Sense of the Jonestown Suicides.* New York: Edwin Mellen, 1983.

Weisbrot, Robert. *Father Divine.* Boston: Beacon Press, 1983.

Whalen, William J. *Strange Gods: Contemporary Religious Cults.* Huntington, Ind.: Our Sunday Visitor, 1981.

Williams, J. L. *Victor Paul Wierwille and The Way International.* Chicago: Moody Press, 1979.

Williams, Peter W. *Popular Religion in America.* Englewood Cliffs, N.J.: Prentice Hall, 1980.

Wilson, Bryan R. *Religious Sects.* New York: McGraw-Hill, 1970.

————, ed. *The Social Impact of New Religious Movements.* New York: Rose of Sharon Press, 1981.

Wilson, Colin. *The Occult.* New York: Vintage, 1971.

Woods, Richard. *The Occult Revolution.* New York: Herder and Herder, 1971.

Woodward, Kenneth, et al. "Getting Your Head Together." *Newsweek*, September 6, 1976, pp. 56-62.

Wuthnow, Robert. *Experimentation in American Religion.* Berkeley: University of California Press, 1978.

—————. *The Restructuring of American Religion.* Princeton, N.J.: Princeton University Press, 1988.

Yamamoto, J. Isamu. *The Puppet Master: An Inquiry into Sun Myung Moon and the Unification Church.* Downers Grove, Ill.: InterVarsity Press, 1977.

Zaretsky, Irving I., and Mark P. Leone, eds. *Religious Movements in Contemporary America.* Princeton, N.J.: Princeton University Press, 1974.

Index

Abdu'l-Baha *147*
Abilitism *304, 315*
Abraham *92, 140-41, 162, 242, 292, 301, 338*
Adams, Evangeline *265*
Adamski, George *283*
Adventism *148-51, 156, 159-60, 162*
Adyar, India *109*
Adyar Society *109*
African Methodist Church *168*
Ahlstrom, Sydney *97, 100, 168, 176, 183, 193, 241, 243*
Ahmadiyya movement *239*
AIDS *263, 326*
Alamo Christian Foundation *327, 356-57, 361*
Alamo, Susan *361*
Alamo, Tony *361*
Albanese, Catherine *19, 47, 65-66, 70, 72, 77, 84, 86, 112, 118, 126, 131, 138, 146, 167, 228-29, 261-62, 291*
Albigensianism *38*
Alchemy *15, 27, 39-42, 44-45, 47-48, 110, 265*
Alcoholics Anonymous *322*
Alexander, Brooks *286, 304, 316-17*
Alexandria *34*
Ali, Husayn *146*
All and Everything 251
Allahubad University *204*
Allan, John *228, 302*
Alport, Richard *224*
American Muslim Mission *239, 245*
Amida Buddha *138, 232*
AMORC (Ancient and Mystical Order Rosae Crucis) *113-14*
Amprinistics *304*
Anabaptism *46*

Anglicans *46, 115*
Antelope, Oregon *222-23*
Anthony, Dick *248-49, 326*
Anthroposophical Society *113*
Anthroposophy *109, 113*
Aquarian Age *49, 261*
Arcane School *113, 185*
Arianism *37, 371*
Arica *144-45, 239, 291, 294, 301, 303*
Arius *36-37*
Arminianism *54-55, 59, 96*
Armstrong, Garner Ted *160-62, 330*
Armstrong, Herbert W. *160-63, 330*
Ascended Masters *114-16*
Assagioli, Robert *184*
Association for Research and Enlightenment (ARE) *269*
Astarte *273*
Astral projections *279, 282*
Astrology *11, 15, 27, 34-35, 39, 41-42, 45, 47, 64, 84, 111, 114, 128, 192, 228, 250, 255, 258-59, 261-66, 269-70, 273*
Astronomy *35, 42, 266*
Atlantis *269*
Ayatollah Khomeini *147*
Babajan, Hazarat *246*
Baha'i religion *145-46*
Baha'u'llah *146-47*
Bailey, Alice *109, 113, 185*
Bainbridge, William *24, 37, 83, 282, 311, 345*
Baldwin, Marceline *348*
Ballard, Gary *114-15*
Balswick, Jack *356*
Baptists *46, 54-55, 75, 83, 96, 170*
Bellah, Robert *193, 341*
Bennet, J. G. *250*
Benoit, Hubert *228*
Berg, David (Moses David) *327, 361-67*
Bernstein, Morey *282*

Besant, Annie *109, 115*
Bethel Tabernacle *356*
Bhajan, Yogi *199*
Bhakti *131-33, 203, 210-11, 216*
Bilalian Muslims *244*
Bioenergetics *291, 299*
Black Muslims. *See* Nation of Islam
Blavatsky, Helena Petrovna (H.P.B.) *107-12, 115, 117, 137, 250*
Boa, Kenneth *371*
Boehme, Jacob *287*
Bolshevik Revolution *100, 251*
Boston *65, 118, 123, 133*
Braden, Charles *123, 125*
Brahman *130-31, 134-35, 225*
Braswell, George *142, 206-7, 227, 231, 281, 305, 369*
Brethren of the Free Spirit *58*
Briggs, Jason *89*
British Israelism *162-63*
Bromley, David *220, 306, 309-10, 349*
Brook Farm *57, 78*
Brooks, Nona L. *119-20*
Buddhism *11, 22, 33, 64, 112, 127-29, 131, 135-41, 198-99, 227-32, 236-38, 245, 248, 251, 276, 290, 302-4, 315, 318, 376*
Burkmar, Lucius *116*
Burned-Over District *69, 80, 83*
Bussell, Harold *327*
Cabala (Kabbalah) *15, 39-40, 42, 48*
Cabalism *40, 268*
Calvary Chapel *356-57*
Calvinism *54, 59, 65*
Campbell, Alexander *91*
Campbell, John *305*
Canada *108, 211, 313, 362*
Carnegie, Andrew *126, 313, 315*

Carter, Jimmy *193*
Catharism *32, 38*
Catholic Church *37, 115, 311*
Cayce, Edgar *261, 265, 269-70, 376*
Chalfant, Paul *322, 349*
Chapman, John *68*
Chicago, University of *368*
Children of God *12, 37, 325, 327, 330, 356-57, 361-67*
China *99-100, 128, 132, 136, 139, 269, 305*
Christadelphians *11, 51, 82, 90-92*
Christian and Missionary Alliance Church *327, 361*
Christian Science *11, 26, 43, 66, 93, 95, 98, 103-5, 107, 117, 119, 121-26, 261, 287, 304-5, 330*
Christian World Liberation Front *356-57*
Church of Christ, Scientist *123-24*
Church of the New Jerusalem *48*
CIA *352*
Clark, John *313*
Cold War *341, 375*
Collegiate Association for the Research Principles (CARP) *336*
Columbia University *228, 230*
Communism *79, 100, 158, 190, 335, 337-38, 341-43, 352-53, 366-67, 375, 377*
Community Chapel *326*
Comte, Auguste *102*
Confession of the Rosicrucian Fraternity *44*
Congregationalists *46, 54, 96*
Consciousness revolution *300-303, 315*
Conway, Flo *299*
Conze, Edward *228*
Cooper, Paulette *307*
Copernicus *42*
Cox, Harvey *200*
Cramer, Malinda *119-20*
Crowley, Aleister *272, 276*
Crystal ball gazing *267*
Cults and Cons *299*
Daishonin, Nichiren *232-33*
Darwin, Charles *101*
Dass, Baba Ram *224*
Davis, Andrew Jackson *67-68, 117, 359*

Dederich, Charles (Chuck) *321-22*
Deism *46*
Democratic Party *96*
Dev, Guru *204-5, 207*
DeWolf, Ronald E. *308*
Dianetics *304-6, 309-11*
Dianology *304*
Disciples of Christ *90-91, 95-96, 279, 327, 345, 347-48, 354*
Discourses *220, 246, 249*
Dispensationalism *155, 372*
Divination *11, 28, 255, 258-59, 261, 263, 266-67, 269, 273*
Divine, Father *170-75, 240-41, 345-46, 348*
Divine Light Mission *11, 199, 204, 217-18, 219-21, 303*
Divine Principle *124-25, 334, 338-39, 342*
Divine Science *62, 115, 118-20*
Divine Science, Church of *62, 115*
Divine Science College *120*
Divine Science Federation International *119-20*
Dixon, Jeane *257, 269-70*
Docetists *36*
Dokupil, Stanley *316-17*
Doop, Jimmy *368*
Dresser, Horatio *115*
Drew, Timothy *145, 241*
East Coast Jesus People *356*
East-West Journal *287*
Eastern Orthodoxy *17, 97, 194*
Ebionites *36*
Eckhart, Meister *38, 287*
Eddy, Mary Baker *76, 116, 118, 121-26, 175, 290, 305*
Edmunds-Tucker Act *85*
Egypt *108, 114*
Eisenhower, Dwight *183, 191, 268, 270*
Electronic church *189*
Elementary spirits *44*
Ellwood, Robert *23, 32, 39-41, 66, 80, 109-10, 115, 198, 203, 228, 231, 235, 249-50, 272, 317, 358*
Emerson, Ralph Waldo *65, 116, 128*
Encyclopedia of American Religions *109*
English Civil War *44*
English Ranters *58*

Enlightenment, The *46-47, 54, 57, 66, 206, 291*
Enroth, Ronald *25, 29, 186, 259-60, 299, 356, 358, 359-60, 368*
Equal Rights Amendment *195*
Erdoes, Richard *376*
Erhard Seminar Training (est) *251, 301, 303-4, 313-20*
Erhard, Werner *253, 301, 313-20*
ESP *103, 279, 281, 321*
est. *See* Erhard Seminar Training
Evangelical Reformed Church *368*
Evans, Warren Felt *117-18*
Ewart, Frank J. *165*
Faith Assembly *326*
Fama Fraternities *44*
Fard, Wallace O. (Wali Farad Muhammad) *241*
Farm, The *101, 184, 222, 369*
Farrakhan, Louis *239, 244-45*
Father Divine. *See* Divine, Father
Ferguson, Marilyn *100, 289, 294, 297*
Ficino, Marsilo *42*
Fillmore, Charles *119*
Fillmore, Myrtle *119*
Finney, Charles G. *56, 58*
First Community Church of America *326*
First Great Awakening *54*
Fishler, Claude *265*
Fletcher *279, 335*
Flinn, Frank *304*
Floether, Eckart *224*
Flowers, Ronald *207, 212-13, 332, 344*
Fontainebleau *251-52*
Ford, Arthur *279, 280, 335*
Ford, Gerald *183*
Forum, The *313, 319-20*
Fox sisters *67, 83*
France *38, 64, 67, 251, 253, 276, 313*
Franz, Frederick William *49, 67, 157, 288*
Frazer, James *272*
Freeman, Hobart *326*
Freemasonry *44, 47-48, 114*
French Revolution *45, 56, 311*

Freud, Sigmund *102, 184,*
  190, 253, 302, 309
Friedrich, Otto *113, 286*
Fuller, Margaret *65, 145*
Fundamentalism *97-98, 105,*
  148, 154-55, 236, 356, 358,
  373
Fundamentalist Army *326*
G-O groups *250, 253*
Galbreath, Robert *28, 258*
Gardner, Gerald *272, 274*
Garvey, Marcus *167, 240-41,*
  243
Gaudiya Vaishnava Mission
  210
Gautama, Siddhartha *135*
George Washington University
  305
Germany *102, 123, 211, 265,*
  269, 313
Ghosts *45, 279, 281*
Ginsberg, Allen *228*
Glory Barn *326*
Gnosticism *32, 35-36, 112,*
  303
Gnostics *36, 38, 104, 287*
Gospel of John *102*
Grace, Charles Immanuel
  (Sweet Daddy Grace) *175-*
  77, 240
Great Britain *91*
Groothuis, Douglas *287, 289,*
  295
Gurdjieff, George I. *250-53,*
  261
Gurdjieff movement *11, 144-*
  45, 239, 250-53, 261, 294
Gurley, Zenos *89*
Haddon, David *209*
Hall, John *159, 351-54*
Hamsher, Herb *313*
Handy, Robert *95, 194*
Hare Krishna (ISKCON) *11,*
  25-26, 184, 199, 204, 209-17,
  235, 248, 250, 327
Hargrove, Barbara *290,*
  347
Harvard *65, 206*
Hegel, Georg Wilhelm
  Friedrich *116*
Heindel, Max *109, 114*
Hellenistic Age *32-34, 36*
Hellfire Clubs *276*
Herbert, Will *102, 160-62,*
  330
Hermes Trismegistus, Book of
  34

Hermeticism *34*
Hinduism *22, 33, 99, 112,*
  127-33, 135, 137, 141, 198-99,
  203-4, 210, 220, 238, 245,
  249, 276, 288
Hipparchus *35*
His Place *356*
Holiness movement *148, 151-*
  53, 171
Holistic health
  movement *292-93*
Hollywood Bowl *247*
Holmes, Ernest *115, 120-21*
Holy Koran *145*
Houston, Jean *218, 300*
Hubbard, L. Ron *304-13*
Hufner, Steve *368*
Human Potential movement
  286, 290-92, 301, 304, 326
Humanistic psychology *185,*
  224, 290-91, 302
Humphries, Hubert *228*
Hutterites *73*
Hydesville *67, 70*
I AM *43, 109, 114-15, 203,*
  284
I Ching *258-59, 266, 268-69,*
  285
Ichaza, Oscar *144*
Ikeda, Daisaku *233-34*
In Search of the
  Miraculous *250*
Independence, Missouri *90*
India *31, 99-100, 108-10, 112,*
  127-28, 130-32, 134-36, 144-
  45, 186, 204-6, 214, 216-19,
  221-24, 245-47, 250, 269
Institute for the Harmonious
  Development of Man *251*
International Metaphysical
  League *118*
International New Thought
  Alliance *118, 120*
Investigative Judgment *151*
Irane, Merwan Sheriar *246*
Irish Renaissance *112*
ISKCON. *See* Hare Krishna
Isis *108-9, 273*
Isis Unveiled *108-9*
Islam *22, 32, 127, 131, 139-*
  47, 170-71, 198, 210, 238-46,
  376
Israel *84, 87, 92, 163, 193,*
  339, 365
Italy *38, 313*
Jabalpur, University of *221*
Jackson, Carl *129*

Jainism *131, 224*
James, Fannie *119-20*
James, William *128*
Japan *99, 132, 136-39, 186,*
  211, 227, 229-30, 232-35, 305,
  333-35, 342
Jehovah's Witnesses *11, 26,*
  37, 56, 90, 93, 98-99, 148,
  150, 155-60, 329-30, 343, 366,
  371-73
Jesus movement *327, 355-61,*
  365-66, 368
Jesus Only Movement
  (Oneness Movement) *11,*
  99, 148, 154, 164-65, 169
Jesus People's Army *356*
Jews for Jesus *22, 356*
Jnana *131-33, 203*
Joachim of Flora *38*
Jodo Shinshu *138*
John the Baptist *84, 338-39*
Johnson, Gregory *216*
Johnson, Lyndon *185-86,*
  198, 270
Johnson, Paul *33, 36*
Johnson-Reed Act *100*
Jones, Jim *205, 327, 344-54*
Jonestown, Guyana *344-45,*
  347, 350-54
Jordan, Fred *363, 365*
Judah, J. Stillson *63, 110,*
  116, 210
Judaism *34, 36, 39, 47, 131,*
  135, 140-41, 146, 160, 170,
  174, 194, 210
Judge, William Q. *108, 172*
Jung, C. G. *184, 190, 253,*
  269, 309
Kabbalah. *See* Cabala
Kahil, Phez *252*
Kanter, Rosabeth Moss *73*
Kapleau, Philip *230*
Karma *112, 130-31, 133, 203-*
  4, 212, 296
Kelley, Dean M. *189, 329*
Kennedy, John F. *96, 183,*
  269-70
Kephart, William *77*
Kerouac, Jack *228-29*
Kerr, John *264*
Khan, Hazarat Inayat *238*
Kim, Young Oom *335*
Kipling, Rudyard *197*
Kirkland, Ohio *85*
Komeito, The (Clean Govern-
  ment Party) *233*
Koran. *See* Qur'an

Korr, Nathan Homer 157
Krishna 11, 25-26, 132, 146,
  184, 204, 209-17, 220, 248-50,
  296, 327
Krishnamarti 109
Ku Klux Klan 100, 347
Laredo, Texas 320
Latter-day Saints, Church
  of 89
LaVey, Anton 275-78
Leadbeater, C. W. 109
Leary, Timothy 224
Lebanon 77, 99, 143
Lee, Ann. See Stanley, Ann
  Lee
Levitations 272, 279
Liberal Catholic Church 115
Liberalism 95, 97, 104-6, 126,
  152, 188-90, 199, 262, 327
Lifespring 304
Lincoln, Eric 240, 242
Lindsey, Hal 263
Lippy, Charles 90
Lisbon, Portugal 56
London, England 91, 108,
  115, 217, 275, 364
London, Perry 300
Lord of the Second
  Advent 332, 337-39, 342
Lotus Sutra 232, 237
LSD 184, 224, 228
Luckmann, Thomas 19, 191,
  259
Lutherans 46, 95, 97, 352
Lyell, Charles 101
McAlister, R. E. 165
McBeth, Leon 265
McCollough, Walter 177
McKinney, William 189-90,
  194-95
MacLaine, Shirley 205, 285
McLoughlin, William 54, 97,
  190, 200
McNeill, William 127
Magic 20, 27-28, 34, 39-40,
  46-47, 84, 110-11, 122, 170,
  184, 258-59, 267, 271, 273,
  275, 278
Magna Mater 273
Mahaprabhu, Chaitanya 210
Maharaj, Upasni 246
Maharaj Ji, Sri Hans 217
Maharishi Heaven on Earth
  Development Corporation
  207
Maharishi, Mahesh Yogi 204-
  7, 209

Maharj Ji, Guru 199, 217-20
Mahayana Buddhism 136,
  138-39, 227, 232
Makiguchi, Tsunesaburo 233
Malcolm X (Malcolm Little)
  243
Manichaeanism 38-39
Manson, Charles 277, 344
Maranatha Christian
  Churches 326
Marin, Peter 300
Marks, William 89, 197
Marsden, George 154-55
Marty, Martin 19, 60, 187,
  193
Marxism 19, 342
Maslow, Abraham 292,
  301-2
Matchabelli, Norina 247
Meetings with Remarkable
  Men 251
Meher Baba 11, 203, 238,
  245-50, 303
Meher Baba, Lovers of 245
Meher Spiritual Center 245
Melton, Gordon 9, 23, 29, 90,
  109, 119, 129, 133, 137, 150,
  156, 161, 163, 171, 174, 184,
  186-87, 198-99, 207, 209, 222,
  224, 283, 287-88, 294, 296-97,
  303, 307-9, 335-36, 339, 345,
  362, 365-66, 370-71
Menninger Foundation 292
Mennonites 22, 73, 97, 100
Mental Cure, The 117
Mesmer, Franz Antoine 49,
  67, 288
Mesmerism 47, 49, 67, 103,
  112, 116, 123, 258
Mesopotamia 35
Methodism 98
Mexico 108, 320
Michelet, Jules 272
Middle Ages 15, 31, 37-41,
  43, 261
Millennium 1973 218
Miller, Elliot 294
Miller, William 83, 149
Millerism 149
Millerites 56, 91, 149
Mind Dynamics 304, 315
Mirandola, Pico della 287
Miscavige, David 312
Modalism 371
Mohan, Rajneesh
  Chandra 221
Monarchianism 371

Monarchianists 36
Montanists 58
Montgomery, John
  Warwick 44
Moody, Dwight L. 59
Moon, Sun Myung 199, 327,
  331-43
Moore, R. Laurence 23, 87,
  104, 281
Moorish-American Science
  Temple 145, 239
Mormon, Book of 84, 87,
  331
Mormonism 11, 30, 37, 51,
  59, 61, 82-87, 90, 160, 305,
  330-31
Mormons 25-26, 30, 56, 75-
  76, 82-88, 90-91, 95, 97, 329-
  30, 343, 373
Mosatche, Harriet 290
Moscow 251
Mother Ann. See Stanley, Ann
  Lee
Mt. Shasta 114-15
Muhammad 141-43, 145-46,
  249
Muhammad, Elijah 239, 242-
  45
Muhammad, Siyyid Ali 145
Muhammad, Wallace (Warith
  Dean Muhammad) 245
Muhammad Speaks 242
Murphy, Bridey 282
Murray, Margaret 271-72
Nation of Islam (Black
  Muslims) 11, 170-71, 239-
  45, 345
National Spiritualist
  Association 68
Nauvoo, Illinois 85, 89
Nazism 43, 190
Needleman, Jacob 201, 231,
  246-47, 249, 300
Neo-Rosicrucianism 109
Neoplatonism 31, 34, 41-42,
  66, 112, 127
New Age movement 11-12,
  30, 146, 192, 209, 236, 255,
  285-89, 293, 295-97, 321
New Day 173
New Harmony 57
New Thought 11, 62-63, 66,
  93, 98, 107, 115-20, 122-23,
  171, 174, 181, 261-62, 280,
  287-88, 303-4
Newport, John 141, 143, 211,
  214, 253, 310, 318-19, 334

Newton, Huey *42, 101, 295, 353*
Nichiren Shoshu of America (NSA) *11, 227, 231-37*
Niebuhr, H. Richard *359*
Nishi Hongwanji *138*
Nixon, Richard *186*
Northeast Kingdom Community Church *326*
Noyes, John Humphrey *75, 78-79, 83*
Numerology *47, 259, 266, 333*
Nye, Russel *57-59*
Nyland, W. A. *252*
O'Dea, Thomas *87*
Oberlin Theology *58*
Ofshe, Richard *321*
Olcott, Henry Steel *108-9, 137*
Omar, Sydney *265*
On the Road *229*
Oneida Community (Perfectionists) *11, 58, 72, 78*
Oneness Movement. *See* Jesus Only Movement
Order of the Golden Dawn *272*
Oriental Exclusion Act *186, 198*
Ouija boards *258-59*
Ouspensky, Peter D. *250-53, 261*
Outler, Albert *300*
Pak, Colonel Bo Hi *335*
Pakistan *99*
Palmistry *258-59, 265-67*
Paracelsus *42*
Parapsychology *28, 103, 184, 281, 320*
Parker, Theodore *65*
Patterson, Elizabeth *247*
Paul, Apostle *104, 134-35, 371-72*
Pauwels, Louis *258*
Pavlov, Ivan *102*
Peace Mission *170-75, 240-41*
Peale, Norman Vincent *118, 229, 290*
Pentecostal Assemblies of the World *166*
Pentecostalism *98, 148, 151-54, 164-65, 169, 176, 360, 373*
Pentecostals *22, 104, 153-54, 164-66, 170, 187, 333*
People's Temple *12, 325, 327, 344-54, 364*

Peters, Ted *286, 358, 360*
Petersen, William *245, 253*
Petrarch *42*
Pietism *46, 155, 292*
Pike, James A. *280*
Plain Truth *160-61*
Platonism *31, 36*
Plessy v. *Ferguson* *100*
Plotinus *34*
Plymouth Brethren *22, 372*
Point Loma, California *109*
Poland *99*
Poltergeists *67, 279, 281*
Poole, Robert *241-42*
Poona, India *222, 246*
Power for Abundant Living (PFAL) *369-71*
Power of Positive Thinking *118*
Prabhupada, A. C. Bhaktivedanta *199, 210-12, 217*
Presbyterians *46, 54, 83, 95-96, 375*
Primal therapy *291*
Princeton Theological Seminary *12, 368*
Process Church *275*
Prohibition *57, 96*
Psychic phenomena *111*
Psychosynthesis *185, 291*
Ptolemy, Claudius *35*
Pure Land Buddhism *138*
Puritanism *46*
Quakers *22, 75, 77*
Quebedeaux, Richard *357*
Quimby, Phineas P. *62, 115-18, 123*
Qur'an (Koran) *130, 141-43, 145*
Rader, Stanley *161*
Rajneesh, Bhagwan Shree *11, 204, 221-26, 303*
Rajneesh Foundation *11, 204, 221-22, 224, 226, 303*
Rajneeshpuram *222-23*
Rama, Swami *199, 212*
Ramakrisha, Sri *132*
Rasche, Carl *290*
Reagan, Ronald *193*
Reformation, The *15, 39-45, 48, 51, 86, 95, 185, 261, 366*
Reincarnation *40, 64, 68, 109-10, 112, 114, 119, 130, 199, 219, 241, 269-70, 273-74, 279, 281-82, 288, 296, 306, 349, 353*
Reisser, Paul *292*

Religion and the Decline of Magic *46*
Religious Science *63, 115, 118, 120-21*
Religious Science, Church of *115, 120-21*
Renaissance, The *15, 39-43, 45, 112*
Reorganized Church of Jesus Christ of Latter-day Saints *88-89*
Rettelmeyer, Friedrich *113*
Rhine, J. B. *103, 281*
Richardson, James *326, 345, 359*
Richardson, Sarah *80*
Righter, Carroll *265*
Rinzai Zen *139-40*
Robbins, Thomas *247-49, 326, 341*
Rockefeller, John D. *126*
Rogers, Carl *301*
Romanticism *51, 54, 56-57, 229, 271, 291*
Rome *33-34*
Roof, Wade *189-91, 194-95*
Rosemary's Baby *257, 275*
Rosenberg, John Paul *315*
Rosencreutz, Christian *44*
Rosicrucian Fellowship *113-14*
Rosicrucianism *43-44, 47-48, 60, 109, 113, 330*
Roszak, Theodore *26, 184*
Rousseau, Jean-Jacques *292*
Rowley, Peter *250-51*
Russell, Charles Taze *156-57*
Russell, George *112*
Russell, Jeffrey *39, 43, 261, 271-74, 276*
Russia *100, 107-8, 250-51, 270, 345*
Rutherford, Joseph Franklin *156-57*
Ryan, Leo *349, 351*
Sabellianism *371*
Sabellianists *36*
Sacred Gymnastics *251, 253*
Sadanaga, Masayasu *234*
Saint-Germain *114*
Salt Lake City *85*
Sant Mat *219*
Satan *32, 92, 158, 260, 275-78, 281, 333-34, 338, 342*
Satanic Church in America *277*

Satanism *11, 259, 270-71, 275-78*
Saugar, University of *221*
Scandal of Scientology, The 307
Scheppe, John C. *165*
Science and Health 118, 123-25
Science of Mind 121
Scientific Revolution *69*
Scientology *12, 192, 299, 301, 303-12, 315, 317, 320*
Scientology, Church of *303, 306-9*
Scientology: The Fundamentals of Thought 310
Second Great Awakening *55, 57, 75, 95, 98*
Secret Doctrine 109
Self-Realization Fellowship *132-34, 203-4*
Sequoia University *305*
Seventh-day Adventists *149-51, 159-60, 162, 329*
Seventh-day Adventist Church *149, 160*
Shakers *11, 51, 56, 58-59, 68, 72, 75-78, 80, 83, 95, 261, 352*
Shamanism *34*
Sheela, Ma Anand (Silverman) *223*
Shelley, Bruce *59, 104*
Shiite Muslim *142-43, 238*
Shupe, Anson *220, 306, 309-10, 349*
Siddhanta, Bhakti *210-11*
Siegelman, Jim *299*
Sikh *199, 203, 219*
Sikh Dharma *199*
Silva, Jose *320-21*
Silva Mind Control *12, 294, 299, 301, 303-4, 315-16, 320-21*
Smith, Alfred E. *96*
Smith, Joseph III *89*
Smith, Joseph *83-85, 87-90, 305, 331*
Social Gospel *98, 105*
Society of Avatar Meher Baba *245*
Sojourners 357
Soka Gakkai *231, 233-34*
Soto Zen *139-40, 227, 229-30*
Spencer, Herbert *102*
Spiritual Regeneration Foundation *205*

Spiritualism *11, 48, 51, 58-60, 62, 67-71, 103, 107-10, 112, 114-15, 122, 128, 169-70, 181, 192, 250, 258-59, 261, 265, 279-83, 287-88, 321, 330*
Spiritualistic phenomena *12, 108, 278*
Stalinism *43*
Stanley, Ann Lee *75, 161, 316*
Stark, Rodney *24, 37, 83, 188, 282, 311, 345*
Steiner, Rudolf *109, 113*
Stone, Barton *91*
Strang, James Jesse *88-89*
Strangites *88-89*
Subud *144-45, 239, 315*
Sufis and Sufism *139, 143-45, 238-39, 245-47, 249-51, 253, 296, 303*
Sufism Reoriented *238, 245*
Sunni Muslim *142-43, 238*
Sunset Corps *370*
Suzuki, Beatrice Lane *228*
Suzuki, D. T. *139, 228-30*
Suzuki, Shunryu *230*
Swedenborg, Emanuel *48-49, 60, 66-67, 103, 282, 287*
Swedenborgianism *47, 51, 112, 258*
Synanon *12, 253, 291, 301, 303, 320-22*
Synder, Gary *228-29*
Syria *99*
T-groups *253*
Tantric Buddhism *251*
Tarot *258, 266, 268, 273, 285*
The Exorcist 75
The Fourth Way 251-52
The Other Side 280
The Supreme Wisdom 242
Theosophy *11, 26, 43, 93, 98, 107-16, 128, 181, 185, 203, 258, 261, 265, 287-88, 294, 330*
Theravada Buddhism *136, 138-39*
Thirty Years' War *45*
Thomas, John *90-91*
Thomas, Keith *46*
Thoreau, Henry David *65, 128*
Tibet *108, 114, 136, 250*
Tighe, Virginia Burns *282*
Tingley, Katherine *109*
Tkack, Joseph *162*
Toda, Josei *233*
Toffler, Alvin *201*

Transactional Analysis *253, 291*
Transcendental meditation (TM) *204-9*
Transcendentalism *11, 51, 57, 60, 62, 64-66, 107, 112, 116, 181, 261, 287*
Trine, Ralph Waldo *115*
Troeltsch, Ernst *20-21*
Troward, Thomas *115*
Truzzi, Marcello *28, 265, 277-78*
Tucker, Ruth *84-85, 157, 162, 164, 303, 319, 326, 335, 337, 342, 364-66, 372*
Turtle Island *229*
UFOs *282-84*
Ukiah, California *348*
Ultradispensationalism *371-72*
Unification Church *12, 25, 30, 199, 236, 325, 327, 330-43, 346*
Unitarianism *46, 57, 128, 141*
United House of Prayer *175, 240*
United Pentecostal Church International *166*
Unity *115, 118-19, 303*
Unity School of Christianity *63, 118-19*
Universal Friend *11, 72, 80*
Universal Peace Mission Movement *170-76, 240-41, 345-46*
Universalists *60, 76*
University Bible Fellowship *326*
Upanishads *130*
Urim and Thummim *84*
Van Grosshoff, Carl Louis *114*
Vatican II *185*
Vedanta Society *132*
Vedas *130, 215*
Vineyard Christian Fellowship *357*
Vivekananda, Swami *132-33, 204*
Wali Farad Muhammad. *See* Fard, Wallace O.
Walker, Thane *252*
Wallis, Roy *21, 195, 290*
Warith Dean Muhammad. *See* Muhammad, Wallace
Washington, Joseph *168, 170*

Watchtower Bible and Tract Society 156-57
Watts, Alan 224, 228-30
Way, The 37, 327, 330, 356, 367-73
Way College of Emporia, The 369
Way Family Corps, The 370
Way of Zen, The 229
Wells, David 251, 328
Wesley, John 151-52
Whalen, William 158, 331
White, Ellen G. 151
Wierwille, Victor 327, 367-73
Wilkinson, Jemima 80, 83
Williams, Peter 173, 234,

240-41
Wilson, Bryan 21, 90
Witchcraft 11, 15, 39, 41, 43, 45, 47, 64, 255, 259, 270-76
Woods, Richard 114, 270, 289
Woodward, Kenneth 300-302, 313-14
World Parliament of Religions 128, 132, 139, 147
World Plan Executive Council 204, 207
Worldwide Church of God 11, 37, 93, 99, 148, 150, 159-63, 330, 343, 366, 371-72

Wuthnow, Robert 41, 182, 199, 281
Yamamoto, J. Isamu 337-38
Yamauchi, Edwin 36
Yankelovich, Daniel 190
Yasutani, Hakuun 230
Yeats, W. B. 112
Yinger, Milton 20
Yogananda, Paramahansa 133-34, 204
Young, Brigham 85, 88-90
Zen Buddhism 11, 64, 138-40, 192, 203, 227-31, 235, 290, 302-3, 313, 315, 317-18
Zenshuji Mission 140
Zoroastrianism 32, 376